Empire of the Senses

Empire of the Senses
The Sensual Culture Reader

Edited by

DAVID HOWES

Oxford • New York

First published in 2005 by
Berg
Editorial offices:
1st Floor, Angel Court, 81 St Clements Street, Oxford OX4 1AW, UK
175 Fifth Avenue, New York, NY 10010, USA

Berg is the imprint of Oxford International Publishers Ltd.

Library of Congress Cataloging-in-Publication data

Empire of the senses : the sensual culture reader / edited by David Howes.
     p. cm. — (Sensory formations)
   Includes bibliographical references and index.
   ISBN 1-85973-858-3 (cloth) — ISBN 1-85973-863-X (pbk.)
  1. Culture. 2. Senses and sensation. 3. Cognition and culture. I. Howes,
David, 1957- II. Series: Sensory formations series.

   HM621.E67 2005
   306—dc22

                                                        2004023159

British Library Cataloguing-in-Publication data

A catalogue record for this book is available from the British Library.

ISBN 1 85973 858 3 (Cloth)
      1 85973 863 X (Paper)

Typeset by JS Typesetting Ltd, Wellingborough, Northants.
Printed and bound by CPI Group (UK) Ltd, Croydon, CR0 4YY

www.bergpublishers.com

FSC
MIX
Paper from
responsible sources
FSC® C013604

Contents

Acknowledgments

This volume documents the growing body of knowledge concerning the multiple ways in which culture mediates sensation (and sensation mediates culture) in history, anthropology, geography, sociology, urban studies, literature, philosophy, and display culture, to name but a few of the disciplines represented by the contributors. I am indebted to all of the contributors, as well as my fellow editors in the *Sensory Formations* series, for their part in extending the bounds of sense and bringing on the sensuous revolution in scholarship. My deepest debt is to Constance Classen, who has played such a pivotal role in shaping how I think about and through the senses.

I wish to acknowledge the stimulation and support I have received from fellow members of the Concordia Sensoria Research Team. I also want to thank the many colleagues who have shared with me their own reflections on the senses: Wolfram Aichinger, Gilles Bibeau, Pennina Barnett, Fiona Candlin, Danièle Dubois, Chris Dunkley, Chris Gosden, Michael Herzfeld, Caro Howell, Annamma Joy, Nicholas Kasirer, David Le Breton, Annick Le Guérer, John Leavitt, Jean-Sébastien Marcoux, Sven Ouzman, Ruth Phillips, François Quiviger, Paul Stoller, David Sutton, Alison Sorbie, and Anthony Synnott.

I am grateful to the Chair of my department, Christine Jourdan; to Martin Singer, Vice-President; and to the President of Concordia University, Frederick Lowy, for their generous financial support for the *Sensory Formations* project. The research funding of the Social Sciences and Humanities Research Council of Canada and the Quebec Fonds pour la Formation de Chercheurs et l'Aide à la Recherche has also been vital to the realization of this project. I thank Karli Whitmore, Crystal Léger, and Elysée Nouvet for their research assistance, Lyle Robinson for his technical assistance, and George Classen for all of his editorial assistance.

Were it not for Kathryn Earle's keen sense for what comes next, and her enthusiastic support of the *Sensory Formations* project, this book and the series of which it is a part would never have materialized.

I thank my children, Jonathan and Emma, for having opened up many new worlds of sense for me, and all my other family members for their wonderful support and encouragement.

In closing, I would like to acknowledge my indebtedness to three former teachers at the University of Toronto: Roger McDonnell, who first piqued my interest in the subject of the senses in a course on the anthropology of religion; Marshall McLuhan, who clinched that interest with a talk given in the Senior Common Room of Trinity College one winter's eve in 1978 and, Northrop Frye, whose warm response to an essay called 'Echoes of Narcissus' written for his course on the Bible and Greek mythology continues to inspirit the direction of my thought.

The icon that appears at the start of each Part and Chapter derives from the frontispiece of a book about the senses as 'living inlets of learning', written by George Wilson and entitled *The Five Gateways of Knowledge* (second edition) published by Macmillan and Co. in 1857. The sketch is by the artist Noel Paton.

David Howes

Introduction
Empires of the Senses

Language games. Culture as discourse. World as text. Empire of signs. What has been called 'the linguistic turn' – which gained prominence in the 1960s – has dominated much of late twentieth century thought in the humanities and social sciences. According to this approach, all human thought and endeavor can be understood as structured by, and analogous to, language, so one may best look to linguistics for models of philosophical and social interpretation.

In the hyperliterate world of academia it is no surprise that writing and reading (or 'discourse') would have a particular appeal as paradigms for understanding social systems. Whereas formerly scholars might have felt that a shift from library to 'open-air' research required a corresponding shift in their investigative approach, the assurance from semioticians such as Barthes (1982) and Ricoeur (1970) that the world (and action in the world) was itself a 'text' has enabled legions of scholars to comfortably go right on 'reading' even when the book was replaced by a meal, a dance, or a whole way of life.

The Sensual Revolution

It has taken an ideological revolution to turn the tables and recover a full-bodied understanding of culture and experience. It has taken a sensual revolution. Once the encompassing grip of 'the science of signs' (modeled on linguistics) is broken, we are brought – perhaps with a gasp of surprise or a recoil of disgust – into the realm of the body and the senses. *Il y a du hors texte!* 'The limits of my language are *not* the limits of my world.'

From a sensory standpoint, the rhetorics of logocentricity do seem unbearably artificial and rigid. Philosopher Michel Serres notes that he wrote his book *Les cinq sens* (discussed in this volume by Steven Connor) in reaction to the sensorial poverty of contemporary theory.[1] Serres describes reading

1

the following line in Merleau-Ponty's classic *Phenomenology of Perception*: 'At the outset of the study of perception, we find in language the notion of sensation . . . ' Serres' immediate response – not a carefully worded critique, but a laugh! – a spontaneous, corporeal eruption into and disruption of the linguistic realm. Laughing breaks the spell of language and discursive reason. Similarly, Serres states 'My book *Les cinq sens* cries out at the empire of signs.' It apparently takes a visceral outburst to topple the tower of babble.

Serres derides the urban-dwelling scholars who sit huddled over their desks, basing their notions of perception on the bit of the world they glimpse through the window – and no doubt thereby overemphasizing the role of vision in their intercourse with the world. In *Les cinq sens* he describes the language-bound body as a desensualized robot, moving stiffly, unable to taste or smell, preferring to dine on a printed menu than eat an actual meal. In contrast to this disturbing scenario we have Serres' fantasy of a non-verbal paradise 'in which the body was free and could run and enjoy sensations at leisure.'

In another essay in this collection, Victor Carl Friesen describes the sensory life of the nineteenth century American naturalist Henry David Thoreau. Thoreau would seem to be a man after Serres' own heart: rejecting the alienation and artifice of urban life, seeking a wilderness paradise 'in which the body was free and could run and enjoy sensations at leisure.' Like Serres, Thoreau wished to go beyond the 'alluvion' of language and 'drench' himself in the sensuous world (Friesen 1984: 1). Indeed, Thoreau posits a fundamental opposition between writing – and perhaps speaking – and sensing: a 'sensuous man' finds it difficult to write about what interests him 'because to write is not what interests [him]' (Friesen 1984: 65). In joyful pursuit of sensorial immediacy, Thoreau wades in streams, perfumes himself with wild herbs and drinks the sap of trees.

Another hypothetical enactment of Serres' fantasy of sensual emancipation is carried out in 'Under the Jaguar Sun,' a story by Italo Calvino also presented in this volume. In *Les cinq sens* Serres opposes two images of the mouth: the speaking mouth, which is given primacy by the elevation of language, and the subordinate, tasting mouth. In Calvino's tale we are presented with a self-centered European couple whose speaking mouths have been shut by boredom and indifference, and who try to find a form of communication – or at least stimulation – through a 'gustatory exploration' of modern Mexico. If for Thoreau it is the wildness of nature that enables him to get in touch with his senses, for Calvino's couple it is the 'savagery' of a 'primitive' culture, namely pre-Columbian Mexico. First the savory Mexican cuisine draws the couple together in a ritual of shared flavor, and then revelations of pre-Columbian cannibalism stir them to imagine they are consuming each other as they eat. Too insipid to enjoy each other without this spice of exoticism, the couple thus attempt to fill the 'consuming void' of lovelessness they feel at the beginning of the story in a paroxysm of mutual mastication.[2]

'Under the Jaguar Sun' indicates how, from another perspective, Serres' sensual paradise might be what Marshall McLuhan (this volume) termed a sensorial 'heart of darkness' – a 'hypnotic' primitive state of simultaneous relations and sensory interanimation. The ultimate horror at the 'heart of darkness' is cannibalism, in which the human being is apparently de-differentiated from the natural world, and the feast of the senses includes the consumption of the human body itself. While Thoreau, in his gustatory communion with nature, believes that 'as the human race improves ... it will stop eating animals as surely as savage tribes in their improvement leave off cannibalism,' in Calvino's tale the aesthetized consumption of otherness leads to cannibalism.

These various visions of sensory immediacy are powerful. They are also markedly Western. It has been customary to associate the senses with nature, whether 'innocent' or 'savage.' The senses in this case symbolize the antithesis of culture and thereby provide Westerners weary of the sophistry of civilization with what seems like a welcome retreat into untutored sensation. The human sensorium, however, never exists in a natural state. Humans are social beings, and just as human nature itself is a product of culture, so is the human sensorium. In 'McLuhan in the Rainforest,' Constance Classen (this volume) demonstrates that even among supposedly primitive peoples, living in intimate contact with nature, sensory experience is permeated with social values. Tastes and sounds and touches are imbued with meaning and carefully hierarchized and regulated so as to express and enforce the social and cosmic order. This system of sensory values is never entirely articulated through language, but it is practised and experienced (and sometimes challenged), by humans as culture bearers. The sensory order, in fact, is not just something one sees or hears about; it is something one *lives*. Classen writes of the Tzotzil of Mexico, descendants of the Maya, who order their perception of society and cosmos through heat symbolism:

> In their daily lives, the Tzotzil constantly experience the thermal order of the universe: through the encompassing heat of the sun, through the change of temperature from day to night, summer to winter, highlands to lowlands, through the heat they expend in working, through the offering and consumption of 'heat' in ritual, through their positions around the household hearth, through the warmth of their very blood.

Even when the Tzotzil are speechless, cosmic meaning courses through their veins.

While McLuhan may have been misinformed about the nature of so-called primitive societies, however, his great insight into the senses still holds true: perception is not just a matter of biology, psychology or personal history but of cultural formation. Sensory channels may not be modeled after linguistic forms of communication – a perfume is not the same as a sentence – but they are still heavy with social significance. When Serres claims that the revolt against the domination of language will have to come from the senses, he is right. But it will not be a revolt which takes us outside the symbol systems of culture. From the empire of signs we enter the empire of the senses – and there are as many such empires as there are cultures.

The sensual revolution in the humanities and social sciences, hence, is not only a matter of playing up the body and the senses through evocative accounts of corporeal life, although these can be valuable, but of analysing the social ideologies conveyed through sensory values and practices and the process by which 'history [is] turned into nature' (Bourdieu cited in Geurts 2002: 195). The present book, with contributions from historians, anthropologists, geographers and literary scholars, among others, indicates the range of issues that an approach that involves 'sensing cultures' (in place of 'reading' them) may fruitfully address. The 'senses,' in fact, are not just one more potential field of study, alongside, say, gender, colonialism or material culture. The senses are the media through which we experience and make sense of gender, colonialism and material culture. And, in McLuhan's words, the medium is the message.

Now it is evident that, in writing about the senses, the contributors to this book are not escaping the confines of language. It would seem to be the fate of the senses that their astonishing power to reveal and engage should forever be judged and 'sentenced' in the court of language. When its powers of organization and interpretation are not inflated, however, language can be used creatively, critically, and sensitively, as the essays in this collection demonstrate. A certain paradox remains, a certain tugging of unstated sensibilities, a certain sense of alienation from lived experience. Steven Connor notes of Michel Serres that his 'own language denies in its use what his language maintains, namely the emptiness, abstraction and rigor mortis of language.' At the same time, it cannot help but affirm it. The limitations of language are unavoidable so long as language is the medium of communication. What it is possible to avoid, however, is the expansion of language into a structural model that dictates all cultural and personal experience and expression.

In addition to overturning linguistic paradigms of culture, one of the aims of the sensual revolution is to recover perception from the laboratory. Science and psychology typically understand perception to be private, internal, ahistorical and apolitical. Ignoring the role of culture makes it possible to universalize from experiments conducted on a limited sample of (usually) Western subjects. In 'Art as a Cultural System' Clifford Geertz (1983) speaks of meaning as socially constructed rather than springing 'from some grotto in the head.' The same is true of sensation. Just as meanings are shared, so are sensory experiences. This is why it is not enough to look at the senses as 'energy transducers,' 'information gatherers' or 'perceptual systems' (see Geary 2002; Gibson 1966, 1979; Goldstein 2002); they must also be understood as cultural systems. The work undertaken by the various contributors to this volume underscores the fact that perception is a shared social phenomenon – and as a social phenomenon it has a history and a politics that can only be comprehended within its cultural setting. It is true that significant individual variations may exist within society, and several of the essays in this volume examine such cases. However, such individual ways of sensing are always elaborated within the context of communal sensory orders.

Just as scientists usually fail to consider cultural factors in their study of perception, they usually fail to recognize that science itself is a product of culture. Scientific paradigms, in fact, are themselves heavily influenced by perceptual paradigms, as various contributions to this book attest. In 'The Witch's Senses,' Constance Classen describes some of the sensory and social machinations that enabled the rise of an eye-minded, rational world view. In 'The Death of the Sensuous Chemist,' Lissa Roberts documents how new scientific technologies and ideologies displaced the multisensory practices and mentality of eighteenth century chemistry. Today we are so accustomed to scientific visualism that we scarcely ever feel the desire for any other perceptual paradigms of the world. For example, we look at visual depictions of DNA without ever asking: What might it feel like? What might it taste like? How differently might DNA be understood through other sensory models? In fact, as an acid with a sugary 'backbone,' DNA seems well suited to certain flavor-based premodern cosmologies. For example, in the sixteenth century Jacob Boehme held that the 'flavour-forces' of sourness, sweetness and bitterness worked together to create life (Classen 1998: 21). Some scientists are now making the claim that perception is 'all in our DNA' – that is, that the way we perceive is genetically programmed (Hollingham 2004). It would be as true to say that our notions of DNA are all in our perception. Biology provides the clay, but culture is the potter.

Cultural studies of the senses should therefore be cautious in their use of scientific data. Science cannot provide a touchstone of truth or a higher authority for cultural analyses. This is not to say there is no 'truth' to science, but rather that it is a culturally bounded truth.[3] It would seem strange if an anthropologist studying the sensory symbolism of an African people were to use an interpretive model drawn from Asian medicine. Why then should it be fitting to use the findings of Western medicine in a similar case? In her discussion of neurobiologist Antonio Damasio's corporeal theory of consciousness, Kathryn Geurts points out that African peoples have their own theories about the embodied nature of consciousness. There are, in fact, many different theories regarding the nature of consciousness and the senses across cultures. In 'McLuhan in the Rainforest' Classen describes how the Amazonian Desana conceive of the brain as a beehive filled with honey of different colors, flavors, textures, and moral implications. The Peruvian Cashinahua hold that:

a wise man, *huni unaya*, has knowledge throughout his whole body. '*Hawen yuda dasibi unaia*, his whole body knows,' they say. When I asked them where specifically a wise man had knowledge, they listed his skin, his hands, his ears, his genitals, his liver, and his eyes. 'Does his brain have knowledge?' I asked. '*Hamaki* (it doesn't),' they responded. (Kensinger 1995: 280)

Cashinahua epistemology is grounded in an elaborate theory of the modularity of the body. There is no mind/body dichotomy for them, just skin knowledge, ear knowledge, eye knowledge and so forth.

The chief contemporary Western proponent of a theory of 'multiple intelligences' is the psychologist Howard Gardner. Limited by the sensory suppositions of his own culture, however, Gardner excludes taste and smell from his taxonomy of intelligences: 'when it comes to keen gustatory or olfactory senses, these abilities have little special value across cultures' (Gardner 1983: 61). This is non-sense. For many societies outside the West tasting and smelling *are ways of knowing* (see, for example, Stoller 1989; Pinard 1991; Schechner 2001). We also find indications of this in the premodern West, for example, in the etymology of words such as 'sapient,' which means both flavorful and knowledgeable, and the medieval 'nosewise' (Howes 2002). Interesting parallels may be drawn between scientific theories and cultural concepts and practices, but the former should generally not be employed as a basis for interpreting or 'validating' the latter. In fact, as regards the study of cultural phenomena, extraneous theories of all kinds are probably most useful insofar as they open us up to new ways of understanding. They are least helpful when they are taken as rigid frameworks into which all new material must be made to fit. The most elucidating cultural studies of the senses are those that bring out indigenous theories of perception.

Despite the increasing breadth and depth of the work being done on the senses in the humanities and social sciences, the cultural and historical study of the senses – or of 'sensual culture' as used here – is still suspect in the eyes of many scholars. Such scholars fear that an emphasis on sensation entails a loss of critical awareness and precipitates a slide into a morass of emotion and desire. (Indeed, accustomed as we are to associate sensuality with sexuality, for many the expression 'sensual revolution' may automatically evoke the notion of a 'sexual revolution,' rather than the encompassing interaction with the social and material world contemplated here.)[4] This is hardly a recent concern, but rather a contemporary expression of one of the crucial dichotomies of Western intellectual history: the divide between body and mind (often framed, as Classen points out, in terms of a conflict between female sensuality and male rationality). The classic opposition between sense and intellect has led to the notion that the expansion of sensory awareness (except in the case of sight, the most 'rational' of the senses) entails a diminution of intellectual activity. For example, in his essay on the 'confusion of the arts' Irving Babbitt stated that 'we can trace with special clearness in the romanticism of nineteenth century France this tendency toward a hypertrophy of sensation and an atrophy of ideas, toward a constantly expanding sensorium and a diminishing intellect' (cited in Classen 1998: 197). Is it indeed the case that the discipline that succumbs to feeling loses its mind?

Not, I would answer, if one eliminates the imaginary divide between thinking and feeling. If we hold, like the young Marx, that the senses are 'in their practice theoreticians' (Marx 1987: 107); that the mind is necessarily embodied and the senses mindful, then a focus on perceptual life is not a matter of losing our minds but of coming to our senses.

Intersensoriality

This book is divided into five sections. The first deals with the senses and cognition (or how 'culture tunes the neurons'). The next two sections explore the history and anthropology-geography of the senses. The last sections deal with two facets of sensory experience in modernity (and postmodernity): the everyday and the abnormal. Each of the sections has a brief introduction. While conceptually useful, this fivefold division is somewhat arbitrary as the different essays interrelate across boundaries of discipline, time and place. Certain basic themes, in fact, recur throughout the book. One of the most notable of these is emplacement. While the paradigm of 'embodiment' implies an integration of mind and body, the emergent paradigm of emplacement suggests the sensuous interrelationship of body-mind-environment. This environment is both physical and social, as is well illustrated by the bundle of sensory and social values contained in the feeling of 'home' (see Tuan 1995). The counterpart to emplacement is displacement, the feeling that one is homeless, disconnected from one's physical and social environment. A sense of displacement is often the plight of the socially marginal. It is also often the plight of the philosopher trying to imagine the nature of existence in an immaterial world of abstractions. In his novel *Repetition* Kierkegaard writes: 'Just as one discovers which land one is in by sticking a finger into the soil and smelling it: I stick my finger into life – it smells of nothing. Where am I? "The world." What does that mean?' (Kierkegaard 1972: 67 my translation).

What, indeed, can a disembodied existence or a desensualized world mean to us who only live through our bodies? Are we not better off sticking our fingers in the soil to determine our location by smell? Certainly the Andaman Islanders who consider odor to be the essence of life would think so (Classen this volume). Bringing the issue of emplacement to the fore allows us to reposition ourselves in relationship to the sensuous materiality of the world.

We usually think of emplacement in terms of our visible and tangible surroundings but we relate to and create environments through all of our senses. In his contribution to this volume, Oliver Sacks notes the particular richness of the non-visual world for the blind. He also offers a thought-provoking consideration of the role of mental visualization among both the blind and the sighted in creating a sense of place. Sacks' work reminds those of us who study sensation in cultural context of the interior dimensions of perception and of the potential for individual variations within society. Marshall McLuhan, in turn, takes us from the private sensory world of the individual to the shared sensory world of society. He claims that the spread of electronic media of communication has united society in a new kind of 'auditory space,' which, in turn, will lead to a new way of thinking about and interacting with the environment. In 'Places Sensed' Steven Feld explores the notion of acoustic space among the forest-dwelling Kaluli of Papua New Guinea, who know 'the time of day, season of year, and placement of physical space through the sensual wraparound of sound in the forest.' Our olfactory relationship to the environment as expressed through art and architecture is the subject of Jim Drobnick's 'Volatile Effects.' My chapter on 'hyperesthesia' examines how our sense of emplacement is increasingly dependent on sensory values produced and promoted by consumer capitalism – the trademark scents, the aesthetics of the mall, the car which 'caters to all of your senses. It also delves into how this commodification of sensation is being subverted in different ways in different places and from different subject positions.

A number of essays in this volume also consider the topic of displacement from the sensory and social environment. 'The Witch's Senses' brings out the perceived emplacement of the witch in the home and the attempts to displace her from the social and cosmic order. Lisa Law's 'Home Cooking' examines how displaced Filipino domestic workers in Hong Kong try to emplace themselves through reproducing the sensory comforts of home in the city core. (In turn, the citizens of Hong Kong feel displaced by this foreign sensory invasion of their city streets – 'as we all know, the streets are ... not designed for people to gather socially and eat together'.) In 'Movement, Stillness,' Bob Desjarlais explores the continuous sensory displacement of the homeless in Boston, from the threatening harshness of the streets to the intrusive regulations and commotion of the shelter, and often back again. For the homeless the concern is one of creating a safe space for oneself in a hostile world. This, in a different way, is also the concern of the sufferers from Environmental Sensitivities (ES) in Nova Scotia who are described by Chris Fletcher in 'Dystoposthesia.' Such sufferers find themselves displaced from their environment when they come to 'the realization that their bodily states are linked to a sensory incompatibility to the places they inhabit.' While Drobnick brings out the alienating effects of odorlessness in the architectural ideal of the 'white cube,' for those for whom the effluvia of the material environment have become poisons, emplacement is only fully possible within what might seem like the most alienating of architectural spaces: a rigorously monitored and purified clinic.

The most prominent theme of the essays collected here is what may be called intersensoriality, that is, the multi-directional interaction of the senses and of sensory ideologies, whether considered in relation to a society, an individual, or a work. Connor brings out how Serres describes the senses as interconnected in a knot.[5] This is a useful notion for enucleating both the complicated (imbricated or twisted) nature of everyday perception and the embodied 'compacity' of the senses. (Employing the metaphor of the knot takes us away from the model of the text, with its neatly separated, two-dimensional rows of characters, and suggests instead the multi-colored knotted symbol system of the Incas known as the *quipu* – see Classen and Howes [forthcoming].) Customarily Western scholars have tried to extract meanings from the sensory knots of culture. In a classic example, Hegel criticized Boehme's cosmology for being 'confined in the hard knotty oak of the senses... [and therefore] not able to arrive at a free presentation of the Idea' (cited in Classen 1998: 4). To dismiss Boehme's sensory imagery as unnecessary trappings for underlying ideas, however, is to miss the point: for Boehme sensations are themselves ideas, themselves creative forces. Rather than attempting to 'free' ideas from the knot of the senses, we should try to understand how meaning and sense are one (see further Rodaway 1994).

To imagine the senses as knotted does not mean that sensations must be conceptualized as simultaneous. Just as in making a weaving the strands are woven together in sequence, so in perception does one sensation often follow another to form different patterns of experience. One may see an apple before picking it up and eating it. One may smell a rose before seeing it. (In the days when America's forests were still in their primeval splendor, Englishmen sailing to Virginia could smell the fragrant coast many miles before it could be seen.) Dorinne Kondo's analysis of the sensory elements of the Japanese tea ceremony, or 'way of tea' (this volume), demonstrates how the process of sensory sequencing may be manipulated and invested with cultural significance. Kondo notes the emphasis on non-verbal symbolism in Japanese culture. The tea ceremony itself entails a cleansing and heightening of perception conducive to a state of silent contemplation. In the ceremony meanings are conveyed through sensory shifts, from garden to tearoom, from sound to silence, from the odor of incense to the taste of tea. Kondo describes the aesthetic order of the tea ceremony as an 'unfolding, a sequence of movement with tensions, climaxes and directionality.' Similarly Connor emphasizes that, in French, 'sens' means both sense and direction. The senses are 'ways' of perceiving.

As is well illustrated by the sensory sequencing of the tea ceremony, intersensoriality need not mean a synesthetic mingling of sensation. The strands of perception may be connected in many different ways. Sometimes the senses may seem to all be working together in harmony. Other times, sensations will be conflicted or confused. Either state may be employed as a social or aesthetic ideology. In *The Color of Angels*, for example, Classen (1998:

129) contrasts the different ideals of multisensoriality of the nineteenth century Symbolists and the twentieth century Futurists:

> While both Symbolists and Futurists advocated an integration of the senses and the arts, in the case of the former this union was to be harmonious, and in the latter it was rife with oppositions and disorder. The difference lay between a transcendent ideal of sensory harmony (whether 'natural,' as in the case of Baudelaire's 'Correspondences' or contrived, as in Huysmans' *Against Nature*) and the urban experience of sensory confusion.

Where the world-weary Symbolist retired to his den to dream up perfumed symphonies, the rough-and-ready Futurist felt vitalized by the discordant proletarian bustle of the street or factory.[6]

Intersensoriality, hence, does not necessarily imply a state of harmony, whether sensory or social. (In fact, warfare was an aesthetic ideal of early Futurism.) Nor does it necessarily mean a state of equality. The senses are typically ordered in hierarchies. In one society or social context sight will head the list of the senses, in another it may be hearing or touch. Such sensory rankings are always allied with social rankings and employed to order society. The dominant group in society will be linked to esteemed senses and sensations while subordinate groups will be associated with less-valued or denigrated senses. In the West the dominant group – whether it be conceptualized in terms of gender, class or race – has conventionally been associated with the supposedly 'higher' senses of sight and hearing, while subordinate groups (women, workers, non-Westerners) have been associated with the so-called lower senses of smell, taste and touch. Within each sensory field, as well, sensations deemed relatively unpleasant or dangerous will be linked to 'unpleasant,' 'dangerous' social groups. Within the field of smell, for example, the upper classes were customarily considered to be fragrant or inodorate, while the lower classes were held to be malodorous. George Orwell (1937: 159) described this olfactory division of society forcefully when he wrote that 'the real secret of class distinctions in the West' can be summed up in 'four frightful words... *The lower classes smell*.' This perception of malodor had less to do with practices of cleanliness than it had to do with social status: according to the sensory classification of society a low social status translated into a bad smell. Thus Orwell stated that a nasty smell seemed to emanate from 'even "lower class" people whom you knew to be quite clean – servants, for instance' (Orwell 1937: 160). Here we can see how sensations of disgust (as described by William Ian Miller in his contribution to this volume), are not just a matter of personal distaste but of social ordering. The transformation of class distinctions into physiological sensations is a powerful enforcer of social hierarchies (see Classen, Howes and Synnott 1994).

Such social and sensory hierarchies were supported in various ways by the 'scientific' theories of the day. Premodern (and often modern) medicine held women to be physiologically designed for domestic duties within the home (Classen 1998: 63–85). Natural philosophy considered non-Western peoples to be mired in the 'animalistic' world of the lower senses. In fact, in the nineteenth century the natural historian Lorenz Oken went so far as to postulate a racial hierarchy of the senses: at the bottom was the African 'skin-man' who emphasized tactility, followed by the Australian 'tongue-man,' the Native American 'nose-man,' the Asian 'ear-man,' and, at the top, the European 'eye-man' (Gould 1985: 204–5). Early science similarly found in the supposedly coarse physiology of the working class evidence of a 'coarse' nature (Corbin, this volume). Enlightenment theories of smell, for example, argued that the aristocracy's olfactory refinement derived from a greater cerebral refinement (Stafford 1994: 430). It is difficult to contest a sensory order that is backed up by science or religion. If sensory values are understood to be purely social constructions it is possible to imagine cultural alternatives. If, however, they are intrinsic to the immutable order of the universe, then to question the sensory model is to question the nature of reality.

Now that we have traced some of its distinctive features, the notion of a social ordering of the senses should be complexified. While for the sake of generalization one may speak of a society's 'sensory model' in the singular, in fact, more than one sensory model may be operating and interacting at a time. There may be groups within society with alternative ways of making sense. Such is the case, for example, of the Filipinas in Hong Kong discussed by Law or the homeless people Desjarlais studied in Boston. A new 'world view' may be rising as the former declines. We see this described in 'The Witch's Senses,' 'Death of the Sensuous Chemist' and 'Inside the Five Sense Sensorium.'

In situations of culture contact (whether colonial or postcolonial) indigenous sensory values will continue to circulate at the same time as a foreign sensory order is being impressed upon the local population. In 'Engaging the Spirits of Modernity' Marina Roseman notes how the Temiar of the Malaysian rainforest negotiate a dual sensory world of buzzing insects and ticking watches, river rafts and Land Rovers. From one perspective it seems the old culture is giving way to the new. Whereas the Temiar once used shining leaves as ceremonial decorations, now they may use shredded plastic bags. From another perspective, however, one sees that the new sensory experiences are being employed and understood according to traditional values and practices. In an increasingly denuded rainforest, shredded plastic makes a good substitute for the now hard-to-find traditional leaves, providing the shimmering, swaying motion requisite for Temiar ceremonial.

Any period of great cultural change will be a time of sensory confusion, for social revolutions are always sensory revolutions. This confusion may be experienced as an illness in the body of society or of the individual. It may also stimulate new social and creative projects. We can find both happening in the nineteenth century, when the increasing dominance of a rational, materialistic worldview, together with the introduction of powerful new technologies of communication and transportation, marginalized traditional religious and agrarian ways of life. Hans-Göran Ekman's essay on the late nineteenth century and early twentieth century writer August Strindberg offers a forceful example of how conflicts in a shared sensory order may be experienced in the bodies of individuals. In Ekman's account Strindberg tries to verify the nature of an uncertain world through the practice of a 'sensuous chemistry' (which, as we learned from Roberts' essay, had long been dismissed by the scientific establishment). Rather than arriving at sensory verities, however, Strindberg has an increasing sense of the 'falseness' of material sensations. He feels himself to be 'roughed-up' by the sensations of modernity. Riding in a train jolts his brain. Afterwards his legs seem to travel too slowly. Whereas buildings rushed past him in the train, now they appear to recede from his approaching body. There are no reliable proportions to life any more, no, in McLuhan's term, 'sense ratio,' or sensory reason. Strindberg's experience of 'deranged sensations' was at once deeply personal and an expression of the 'sensory derangement' of a society reacting to often scarcely comprehensible transformations. At the same time Strindberg's experience resonated with the contemporary program for an aesthetics of sensory derangement (proposed by Arthur Rimbaud and others) and resulted in extraordinary works of art. Strindberg's derangement enabled him to perceive new aesthetic arrangements.

The multidirectional character of intersensoriality means that no one sensory model can tell the whole story. This also applies to the senses themselves. No matter how culturally prominent a particular sensory field may be, it always operates interactively with other sensory domains and hence cannot reveal the whole story about the social sensorium. For example, that the sense of sight rose in importance in modernity is now generally accepted among scholars – indeed it would be difficult in our image-obsessed society to avoid the evidence of our eyes. However, the present glory of sight should not blind us to the continued cultural activity of the non-visual senses. While the impressive amount of contemporary work examining, critiquing or nuancing the prominence of vision may make sight seem like the only sensory show in town, the concept of intersensoriality reminds us that, no matter how prominent or engrossing one strand of perception may appear, it is still knotted into the fibers of our multisensory existence.

The Senses Collected

The painting on the front and back cover of this book is a remarkable depiction of a seventeenth century collection of valuables belonging to the Earl of Yarmouth. As well as being a record of material abundance and cultural refinement, however, *The Yarmouth Collection* (by an undetermined artist) is a portrait of a particular sensory order – or rather, of a number of sensory orders, which interact and challenge each other. That the painting is not just the record of the contents of a magnificent cabinet of curiosities or treasure chamber is indicated by the prominent presence of fruits and flowers. What one sees most immediately in this painting, in fact, is an empire of the senses constituted by the best the world has to offer. Fine fruits and a lobster are served up for the sense of taste. Roses and perfume bottles cater to the sense of smell. Musical instruments and a singing girl are ready to delight the ear. Intricately carved vessels and soft folds of cloth await a sensuous touch. The colorful assemblage with its glittering surfaces provides a feast for the eyes. In this microcosm earth, sea and sky are all symbolically present through representative objects and animals: minerals, plants, shells, birds. Space and time are themselves symbolized by the globe and the clock.

A closer look at the painting informs us that this 'empire of the senses' is very much a political empire. Rich and rare sensations have been brought together from all over the world (as is suggested by the presence of the globe). Not just artefacts and plants, but also animals and humans form part of this empire. The monkey, the parrot, and the enormous lobster all speak of wealth, exoticism and dominion. The African servant and the English girl (exemplars of the subordinate social groups of non-Westerners and women) are also valuable collectibles and docile subjects in this microcosm. We see here that everything has been displaced from its original setting and brought together to form a new world order.

The arrangement of the collection in the painting might appear to be haphazard or dictated only by aesthetic concerns, but the different objects and beings are in fact entwined through powerful bonds of sensuous and moral significance. The African and the monkey form a pair, mirror images, in fact, as they gaze at each other. The monkey is a customary emblem of the sense of taste and the African stands ready to serve the sense of taste with his ewer. Together they suggest the traditional trope of African lasciviousness and gluttony. The girl and the parrot form another pair. The parrot, as a symbol of chattering speech, duplicates the orality of the singing girl. This pair is suggestive of feminine loquacity. In her left hand the girl holds a bouquet of roses, making another symbolic allusion to the nature of women – attractive but insubstantial. That all the parts of the collection are at the disposal of the owner, that they are all, in a sense, dead to their own selves and living only as collectibles, is emphasized by the brilliant but lifeless lobster at the center of the painting.

This empire of the senses, however, is not without its own internal critique. Neither of the human members of the collection appears content with his or her lot. Neither appears interested in the collection itself. The African is turned away from the collection, distracted, disturbed. As he looks at his fellow captive, the monkey, is he trying to reconcile a confusion of sensory worlds or to remember a former way of life? The English girl gazes wistfully beyond the collection. What is she longing for that cannot be found in this hoard of riches? The drooping roses in her left hand indicate that she cannot be preserved indefinitely, like a marble statue. Among the words written in the songbook she holds in her right hand are 'death's black.' The parrot that stands on the book is poised to fly away. Other elements in the painting also suggest that all is not well within the empire. The clock, watch, hourglass and smoldering candle are all reminders of mortality. While earthly treasures might be plentiful, time is running out for storing up treasures in heaven. In fact, time was also running out for the Yarmouth collection. Deep in debt the Earl was obliged to sell much of his collection, perhaps shortly after its commemorative portrait was painted.[7]

The papers brought together here also represent a collection, as sensorially rich and variegated as the display depicted in *The Yarmouth Collection*, and as full of interpretative delights and challenges. Whereas *The Yarmouth Collection* is conventional in its use of sensory symbols, however, the essays here herald a revolution in the representation and analysis of culture.

Notes

1. *Les cinq sens* was first published in 1985. It is telling of the relative neglect in which the senses have languished until recently that the book is only now being translated into English. Also telling is the fact that it is passed over in silence by Martin Jay in his monumental analysis of 'the denigration of vision in contemporary French thought' (despite its obvious centrality to Jay's topic), although its author does flit across the last few pages of *Downcast Eyes* (see Jay 1993: 593–4) rather like the Owl of Minerva.

2. There is another dimension to this consumption of otherness which is brought out by Serres: that is the sacramental dimension in which food embodies the divine and provides the means for uniting with God. One of the fullest expressions of this association of eating with transcendent love and divine union can be found in the work of the medieval mystic Hadewijch of Brabant (cited in Rudy 2002: 97):

> [Love's] bonds bind all seams
> In one enjoyment, in one satisfaction.
> This is the bond that totally binds,
> so that each thoroughly knows the other
> in pain, in rest, in madness,
> and eats his flesh and drinks his blood,
> the heart of the one thoroughly devours the other's heart with storms,
> as he who is himself love showed us;
> he who gave himself to us to eat

gives that beyond human mind.
Thereby he gave us to know
that *that* was the nearest to [love]:
to thoroughly eat, thoroughly taste [and] thoroughly see from within

Calvino's couple may experience the desire to thoroughly eat and thereby thoroughly love each other, yet they lack the necessary integrity of heart. Despite the narrator's descriptions of gustatory revelations one suspects that the disaffected couple in this case are still only picking at their food.

3. Sometimes a change in sensory order helps. For example, Luca Turin's much-publicized vibrational theory of olfaction has provoked considerable controversy within the Western scientific community (Burr 2002) but would probably find ready acceptance among the Dogon of Mali, for whom 'sound and odour [have] vibration as their common origin' (Calame-Griaule cited in Howes and Classen 1991: 269). Similarly, Freud's old friend, Wilhem Fliess, would have found a far more receptive audience for his theory of a 'nasal-genital reflex' in Papua New Guinea than he ever did in Vienna (see Howes 2003: 202–3).

4. The title of the present book may remind some readers of the film by Japanese cinematographer Nagisa Oshima entitled 'L'Empire des sens' in French and 'In the Realm of the Senses' in English (but *Ai no corrida* or 'Corrida of Love' in Japanese). This film, which was censored in Japan, was intended as a retort to Barthes' (1982) representation of Japan as an empire of empty signs, whence perhaps its graphic portrayal of Japanese sexuality. The conflation of sensuality and sexuality implied by the film's French and English titles is a prime example of the Western tendency to contain the senses within the concept of carnality, which is not the case with the Japanese (see Kondo, this volume). For an alternative take on the senses through cinema see Canadian cinematographer Jeremy Podeswa's 1999 film *The Five Senses* and Laura Marks' *The Skin of the Film* (2000).

5. This idea of knots and knotted perceptions is also explored in 'On Listening to a Dream: The Sensory Dimensions' in Alfred Margulies' (1989) *The Empathic Imagination*.

6. See further the discussion of consensus versus conflict models of the sensorium in Howes (2003: xix–xxiii).

7. A complementary analysis of the symbolic elements of *The Yarmouth Collection*, along with a historical background, is offered by Robert Wenley (1991). See further Pamela Smith's 'Science and Taste' (1999) for an account of the life of the senses in seventeenth century Dutch society (the probable birthplace of the artist).

Bibliography

Barthes, R. (1982), *Empire of Signs*, trans. R. Howard, New York: Hill & Wang.

Burr, C. (2002), *The Emperor of Scent*, New York: Random House.

Classen, C. (1998), *The Color of Angels: Cosmology, Gender and the Aesthetic Imagination*, London and New York: Routledge.

—— and Howes, D. (forthcoming), 'The Sensescape of the Museum,' in E. Edwards, C. Gosden and R. Phillips (eds), *Sensible Objects*, Oxford: Berg.

——, Howes, D. and Synnott, A. (1994), *Aroma: The Cultural History of Smell*, London and New York: Routledge.

Freiberg, F. (2001), 'The Unkindest Cut of All?' *Senses of Cinema*, (12 January). See http://www.sensesofcinema.com/contests/01/12/senses.html

Friesen, V.C. (1984), *The Spirit of the Huckleberry: Sensuousness in Henry David Thoreau*, Edmonton: University of Alberta Press.

Gardner, H. (1983), *Frames of Mind: The Theory of Multiple Intelligences*, New York: Basic Books.

Geary, J. (2002), *The Body Electric: An Anatomy of the New Bionic Senses*, London: Weidenfeld and Nicholson.

Geertz, C. (1983), *Local Knowledge*, New York: Basic.

Geurts, K.L. (2002), *Culture and the Senses: Bodily Ways of Knowing in an African Community*, Berkeley: University of California Press.

Gibson, J.J. (1966), *The Senses Considered as Perceptual Systems*, Boston: Houghton Mifflin.

—— (1979), *The Ecological Approach to Visual Perception*, Boston: Houghton Mifflin.

Goldstein, E.B. (2002), *Sensation and Perception*, 6 edn, Pacific Grove CA: Wadsworth.

Gould, S.J. (1985), *The Flamingo's Smile*, New York: Norton.

Hollingham, R. (2004), 'In the Realm of Your Senses,' *New Scientist*, 181 (31 January): 40–3.

Howes, D. (2002), 'Nose-wise: Olfactory Metaphors in Mind,' in C. Rouby, B. Schaal, D. Dubois, R. Gervais and A. Holley (eds), *Olfaction, Taste and Cognition*, Cambridge: Cambridge University Press, pp. 67–81.

—— and Classen, C. (1991), 'Sounding Sensory Profiles,' in D. Howes (ed.), *The Varieties of Sensory Experience*, Toronto: University of Toronto Press, pp. 257–88.

Jay, M. (1993). *Downcast Eyes: The Denigration of Vision in Twentieth century French Thought*, Berkeley: University of California Press.

Kensinger, K. (1995), *How Real People Ought to Live: The Cashinahua of Eastern Peru*, Prospect Heights, IL: Waveland Press.

Kierkegaard, S. (1972), *La répétition*. In *Oeuvres complètes*, trans. P-H. Tisseau and E-M. Jacquet-Tisseau, Paris: Editions de l'Orante.

Marx, K. (1987), *Economic and Philosophic Manuscripts of 1844*, trans. M. Milligan, Buffalo: Prometheus Books.

Marx, L. (2000), *The Skin of the Film: Intercultural Cinema, Embodiment and the Senses*, Durham: Duke University Press.

Merleau-Ponty, M. (1962), *Phenomenology of Perception*, trans. C. Smith. London: Routledge.

Orwell, G. (1937), *The Road to Wigan Pier*, London: Victor Gollancz.

Pinard. S. (1991), 'A Taste of India,' in D. Howes (ed.), *The Varieties of Sensory Experience*, Toronto: University of Toronto Press, pp. 221–30.

Ricoeur, P. (1970), 'The Model of the Text: Meaningful Action Considered as a Text,' *Social Research*, 38: 529–62.

Rudy, G. (2002), *Mystical Language of Sensation in the Later Middle Ages*, London: Routledge.

Schechner, R. (2001), 'Rasaesthetics,' *The Drama Review*, 45(3): 27–50.

Smith, P.H. (1999), 'Science and Taste: Painting, Passions, and the New Philosophy in Seventeenth century Leiden,' *Isis*, 90: 421–61.

Stafford, B.M. (1994). *Body Criticism: Imaging the Unseen in Enlightenment Art and Medicine*, Cambridge MA: MIT Press.

Stoller, P. (1989), *The Taste of Ethnographic Things: The Senses in Anthropology*, Philadelphia: University of Pennsylvania Press.

Tuan, Y.-F. (1995), *Passing Strange and Wonderful: Aesthetics, Nature and Culture*, Tokyo and New York: Kodansha International.

Wenley, R. (1991), 'Robert Paston and the Yarmouth Collection,' *Norfolk Archaeology*, 41(2): 113–44.

Part I

The Prescience of
the Senses

'Culture Tunes
Our Neurons'

The lead chapter in this volume, by the neurologist Oliver Sacks, takes as its object the paradox of describing 'what the blind see.' In this chapter, Sacks does for blindness and visual thinking what he had earlier done for deafness (Sacks 1989), and a wide range of neurological disorders, from autism to Tourette's Syndrome (Sacks 1985, 1995). Unlike the dry 'case histories reported in conventional medical textbooks, the 'clinical tales' Sacks recounts teem with anecdotes and personal reflections. He describes the symptomatic worlds his patients inhabit in vivid, palpable detail, such that his 'case histories' read more like ethnographies (and he, in fact, characterizes his unique genre of medical writing as 'neuroanthropology'). In addition to exemplifying the skills of a 'sensuous ethnographer' (Stoller 1997) in his feelingful and profoundly reflexive accounts of the far borderlands of the mind where his neurological patients dwell, Sacks has been responsible for advancing a highly cultured critique of the cognitive sciences. He has been particularly concerned to expose the flaws in the two most basic tenets of classical (computational) neuropsychology – namely, the notion of the mind as a computer, and the notion of the specialization and localization of brain functions.

Consider the case of 'Dr. P.,' 'the man who mistook his wife for a hat.' Dr. P., who suffered from profound visual agnosia, was unable to recognize persons or everyday objects. He could not grasp particulars, only abstractions. Sacks' interactions with Dr. P. led him to conclude that 'our mental processes...involve not just classifying and categorising,' of which Dr. P. was still capable, 'but continual judging and feeling also' (Sacks 1985: 20), two capacities he lacked. In Sacks' estimation, the cognitive sciences are also lacking in attention to matters of feeling and judging, and he goes on to hold up Dr. P.'s case as 'a warning and parable – of what happens to a science which eschews the judgmental, the particular, the personal, and becomes entirely abstract and computational' (Sacks 1985: 20). We are not just calculators. 'We need the concrete and real,' Sacks insists.

According to the cognitive sciences, the mind makes the object. This proposition needs to be balanced by the recognition that the object makes the mind, and that both such makings are always mediated by the 'ways of sensing' or 'techniques of the senses' unique to a given culture and, within each culture, to each individual. This is what is meant by the phrase 'the prescience of the senses' as used here.

Sacks draws another, equally profound, conclusion from his study of Dr. P. He noticed that Dr. P. compensated for his inability to organize the world visually by, among other things, 'fac[ing] me with his ears' and 'do[ing] everything singing to himself' (Sacks 1985: 9, 17). In other words, Dr. P. cultivated a series of sensory techniques that enabled him to cope with the 'disaster' that had befallen his brain. This finding points to the extraordinary plasticity of our neural wiring, in addition to standing as a tribute to Dr. P.'s indomitable spirit.

In the piece included here, Sacks delves into the intricacies of the visual sensorium in both sighted and non-sighted individuals. It is literally fascinating to follow him as he draws out the implications of each of the seven cases he discusses, and goes on revising his conclusions concerning the multiple forms of human visuality to the very end of his essay.

Culture has a marginal place at best in conventional neuropsychology. But in Sacks' view, culture completes physiology, as appears from the following exchange with an interviewer from *Psychology Today*:

OS: Our culture beats on us constantly, and we see this most clearly in the occasional wild child, the wolf boy, who has been lost in the woods. Our nervous systems need culture as much as they need chemicals. Without language and culture, we are like headless monsters.

PT: The culture tunes our neurons...

OS: Right, and so the biological and the cultural are woven in us together from the very start, from the first days of life. This is why a pure view of physiology is not sufficient. It has to take in the whole world. (Anon 1995: 32)

The suggestion that 'culture tunes our neurons' provides an apt segue from Sacks' neurological investigations to the work of the man who took electronic communications technologies to be extensions of our nervous systems: Marshall McLuhan. It bears noting, as well, that McLuhan was no less fascinated than Sacks by the possibilities of perception and cognition opened up by the privation of vision. (For example, both Sacks and McLuhan's views on visual perception were shaped by reading Jacques Lusseyran's memoir of blindness.)

McLuhan started out in literature but graduated to cultural studies – *avant la lettre*, of course.[1] Even this capacious disciplinary label cannot do justice to the multiple strands of his thinking, particularly as regards the senses. For McLuhan both brought a multidisciplinary perspective to bear upon the study of the senses, and pursued the implications of his model of the 'kaleidoscopic sensorium' for the reconstruction of knowledges across a wide array of fields. 'Inside the Five Sense Sensorium,' the essay selected for this volume, weaves together architecture and urban planning, communications and psychology, history and anthropology, sociology and cultural studies (in both its high and popular varieties). In short, this essay is a 'knot' – in Michel Serres' sense – and untying as well as retying the diverse strands of McLuhan's argument constitutes one of the unifying threads of this volume.

It was McLuhan who gave us the notion of the *ratio of the senses.* Following Harold Innis' lead in *The Bias of Communication*, he traced the (allegedly) distorting impact of successive technologies of communication (oral, chirographic, typographic, and electronic – or, return of the oral) on the 'sense-*ratio*.' The term 'sense-*ratio*' as used by McLuhan means sensuous reason; that is, it refers to the proportional elaboration of the senses within a particular cultural logic. According to McLuhan (1962), it is only in consequence of the invention of writing and later print, which involved 'an exchange of an ear for an eye,' that 'reason' was reduced to classification, lineal (cause-effect) thinking and quantification – in short, calculation. But we are not simply calculators, as the electronic revolution in communication has brought home with a vengeance, plunging us, in McLuhan's words, into a dynamic universe of 'simultaneous relations' akin to the 'oral world' of 'tribal' societies.

Appreciating the impact and insight of McLuhan's theories does not mean overlooking their shortcomings. There are problems with the technological determinism and implicit evolutionism of McLuhan's theoretical position, and aspects of these will be addressed by the essays in this volume. These problems, however, do not detract from the fundamental soundness of his claim that our senses – and our sensibilities – are fashioned by culture and technology and not just given by biology.

Note

1. See, for example, *Culture Is Our Business* (McLuhan 1970). McLuhan's media image – as *the* 1960s guru – backfired on him: he became a victim of his own soundbites. Only recently have we begun to appreciate in any depth just how *prescient* were his takes (or 'probes,' as he called them) on virtually every topic of discussion in today's human sciences. See Cavell (2002) and Feld (this volume), as well as Mitchell (1992).

Bibliography

Anon. (1995), 'The Man Who Mistook His Wife for a What?', *Psychology Today*, 28(3): 28–33.

Cavell, R. (2002), *McLuhan in Space: A Cultural Geography*, Toronto: University of Toronto Press.

Innis, H.A. (1951), *The Bias of Communication*, Toronto: University of Toronto Press.

McLuhan, M. (1962), *The Gutenberg Galaxy*, Toronto: University of Toronto Press.

—— (1970), *Culture Is Our Business*, New York: McGraw-Hill.

Mitchell, W.J.T. (1992), 'The Pictorial Turn,' *Artforum* (March): 89–94.

Sacks. O. (1985), *The Man Who Mistook His Wife for a Hat and Other Clinical Tales*, New York: Harper and Row.

—— (1989), *Seeing Voices: A Journey into the World of the Deaf*, Berkeley: University of California Press.

—— (1995), *An Anthropologist on Mars*, Toronto: Knopf.

Stoller, P. (1997), *Sensuos Scholarship*, Philadelphia: University of Pennsylvania Press.

1

The Mind's Eye
What the Blind See

Oliver Sacks

In his last letter, Goethe wrote, 'The Ancients said that the animals are taught through their organs; let me add to this, so are men, but they have the advantage of teaching their organs in return.' He wrote this in 1832, a time when phrenology was at its height, and the brain was seen as a mosaic of 'little organs' subserving everything from language to drawing ability to shyness. Each individual, it was believed, was given a fixed measure of this faculty or that, according to the luck of his birth. Though we no longer pay attention, as the phrenologists did, to the 'bumps' on the head (each of which, supposedly, indicated a brain-mind organ beneath), neurology and neuroscience have stayed close to the idea of brain fixity and localization – the notion, in particular, that the highest part of the brain, the cerebral cortex, is effectively programed from birth: this part to vision and visual processing, that part to hearing, that to touch, and so on.

This would seem to allow individuals little power of choice, of self-determination, let alone of adaptation, in the event of a neurological or perceptual mishap.

But to what extent are we – our experiences, our reactions – shaped, predetermined, by our brains, and to what extent do we shape our own brains? Does the mind run the brain or the brain the mind – or, rather, to what extent does one run the other? To what extent are we the authors, the creators, of our own experiences? The effects of a profound perceptual deprivation such as blindness can cast an unexpected light on this. To become blind, especially later in life, presents one with a huge, potentially overwhelming challenge: to find a new way of living, of ordering one's world, when the old way has been destroyed.

In 1991, I was sent an extraordinary book called *Touching the Rock: An Experience of Blindness*. The author, John Hull, was a professor of religious education who had grown up in Australia and then moved to England. Hull had developed cataracts at the age of thirteen, and became completely blind in his left eye four years later. Vision in his right eye remained reasonable until he was thirty-five or so, and then started to deteriorate. There followed a decade of steadily failing vision, in which Hull needed stronger and stronger magnifying glasses, and had to write with thicker and thicker pens, until, in 1983, at the age of forty-eight, he became completely blind.

Touching the Rock is the journal he dictated in the three years that followed. It is full of piercing insights relating to Hull's life as a blind person, but most striking for me is Hull's description of how, in the years after his loss of sight, he experienced a gradual attenuation of visual imagery and memory, and finally a virtual extinction of them (except in dreams) – a state that he calls 'deep blindness.'

By this, Hull meant not only the loss of visual images and memories but a loss of the very idea of seeing, so that concepts like 'here,' 'there,' and 'facing' seemed to lose meaning for him, and even the sense of objects having 'appearances,' visible characteristics, vanished. At this point, for example, he could no longer imagine how the numeral '3' looked, unless he traced it in the air with his hand. He could construct a 'motor' image of a '3,' but not a visual one.

Hull, though at first greatly distressed about the fading of visual memories and images – the fact that he could no longer conjure up the faces of his wife or children, or of familiar and loved landscapes and places – then came to accept it with remarkable equanimity; indeed, to regard it as a natural response to a non-visual world. He seemed to regard this loss of visual imagery as a prerequisite for the full development, the heightening, of his other senses.

Two years after becoming completely blind, Hull had apparently become so non-visual as to resemble someone who had been blind from birth. Hull's loss of visuality also reminded me of the sort of 'cortical blindness' that can happen if the primary visual cortex is damaged, through a stroke or traumatic brain damage – although in Hull's case there was no direct damage to the visual cortex but, rather, a cutting off from any visual stimulation or input.

In a profoundly religious way, and in language sometimes reminiscent of that of St. John of the Cross, Hull enters into this state, surrenders himself, with a sort of acquiescence and joy. And such 'deep' blindness he conceives as 'an authentic and autonomous world, a place of its own ... Being a whole-body seer is to be in one of the concentrated human conditions.'

Being a 'whole-body seer,' for Hull, means shifting his attention, his center of gravity, to the other senses, and he writes again and again of how these have assumed a new richness and power. Thus he speaks of how the sound of rain, never before accorded much attention, can now delineate a whole landscape for him, for its sound on the garden path is different from its sound as it drums on the lawn, or on the bushes in his garden, or on the fence dividing it from the road. 'Rain,' he writes, 'has a way of bringing out the contours of everything; it throws a coloured blanket over previously invisible things; instead of an intermittent and thus fragmented world, the steadily falling rain creates continuity of acoustic experience... presents the fullness of an entire situation all at once... gives a sense of perspective and of the actual relationships of one part of the world to another.'

With his new intensity of auditory experience (or attention), along with the sharpening of his other senses, Hull comes to feel a sense of intimacy with nature, an intensity of being-in-the-world, beyond anything he knew when he was sighted. Blindness now becomes for him 'a dark, paradoxical gift.' This is not just 'compensation,' he emphasizes, but a whole new order, a new mode of human being. With this he extricates himself from visual nostalgia, from the strain, or falsity, of trying to pass as 'normal,' and finds a new focus, a new freedom. His teaching at the university expands, becomes more fluent, his writing becomes stronger and deeper; he becomes intellectually and spiritually bolder, more confident. He feels he is on solid ground at last.

What Hull described seemed to me an astounding example of how an individual deprived of one form of perception could totally reshape himself to a new center, a new identity.

It is said that those who see normally as infants but then become blind within the first two years of life retain no memories of seeing, have no visual imagery and no visual elements in their dreams (and, in this way, are comparable to those born blind). It is similar with those who lose hearing before the age of two: they have no sense of having 'lost' the world of sound, nor any sense of 'silence,' as hearing people sometimes imagine. For those who lose sight so early, the very concepts of 'sight' or 'blindness' soon cease to have meaning, and there is no sense of losing the world of vision, only of living fully in a world constructed by the other senses.

But it seemed extraordinary to me that such an annihilation of visual memory as Hull describes could happen equally to an adult, with decades, an entire lifetime, of rich and richly categorized visual experience to call upon. And yet I could not doubt the authenticity of Hull's account, which he relates with the most scrupulous care and lucidity.

Important studies of adaptation in the brain were begun in the 1970s by, among others, Helen Neville, a cognitive neuroscientist now working in Oregon. She showed that in prelingually deaf people (that is, those who had been born deaf or become deaf before the age of two or so) the auditory parts of the brain had not degenerated or atrophied. These had remained active and functional, but with an activity and a function that were new: they had been transformed, 'reallocated,' in Neville's term, for processing visual language. Comparable studies in those born blind, or early blinded, show that the visual areas of the cortex, similarly, may be reallocated in function, and used to process sound and touch.

With the reallocation of the visual cortex to touch and other senses, these can take on a hyperacuity that perhaps no sighted person can imagine. Bernard Morin, the blind mathematician who in the 1960s had shown how a sphere could be turned inside out, felt that his achievement required a special sort of spatial perception and imagination. And a similar sort of spatial giftedness has been central to the work of Geerat Vermeij, a blind biologist who has been able to delineate many new species of mollusk, based on tiny variations in the shapes and contours of their shells.

Faced with such findings and reports, neurologists began to concede that there might be a certain flexibility or plasticity in the brain, at least in the early years of life. But when this critical period was over, it was assumed, the brain became inflexible and no further changes of a radical type could occur. The experiences that Hull so carefully recounts give the lie to this. It is clear that his perceptions, his brain, did finally change, in a fundamental way. Indeed, Alvaro Pascual-Leone and his colleagues in Boston have recently shown that, even in adult sighted volunteers, as little as five days of being blindfolded produces marked shifts to non-visual forms of behavior and cognition, and they have demonstrated the physiological changes in the brain that go along with this. And in June 2003, Italian researchers published a study showing that sighted volunteers kept in the dark for as little as ninety *minutes* may show a striking enhancement of tactile-spatial sensitivity.

The brain, clearly, is capable of changing even in adulthood, and I assumed that Hull's experience was typical of acquired blindness – the response, sooner or later, of everyone who becomes blind, even in adult life.

So when I came to publish an essay on Hull's book, in 1991, I was taken aback to receive a number of letters from blind people, letters that were often somewhat puzzled, and occasionally indignant, in tone. Many of my correspondents, it seemed, could not identify with Hull's experience and said that they themselves, even decades after losing their sight, had never lost their visual images or memories. One correspondent, who had lost her sight at fifteen, wrote, 'Even though I am totally blind... I consider myself a very visual person. I still "see" objects in front of me. As I am typing now I can see my hands on the keyboard... I don't feel comfortable in a new environment until I have a mental picture of its appearance. I need a mental map for my independent moving, too.'

Had I been wrong, or at least one-sided, in accepting Hull's experience as a typical response to blindness? Had I been guilty of emphasizing one mode of response too strongly, oblivious to the possibilities of radically different responses?

This feeling came to a head in 1996, when I received a letter from an Australian psychologist named Zoltan Torey. Torey wrote to me not about blindness but about a book he had written on the brain-mind problem and the nature of consciousness. (The book was published by Oxford University Press as *The Crucible of Consciousness*, in 1999.) In his letter Torey also spoke of how he had been blinded in an accident at the age of twenty-one, while working at a chemical factory, and how, although 'advised to switch from a visual to an auditory mode of adjustment,' he had moved in the opposite direction, and resolved to develop instead his 'inner eye,' his powers of visual imagery, to their greatest possible extent.

In this, it seemed, he had been extremely successful, developing a re-markable power of generating, holding, and manipulating images in his mind, so much so that he had been able to construct an imagined visual world that seemed almost as real and intense to him as the perceptual one he had lost – and, indeed, sometimes more real, more intense, a sort of controlled dream or hallucination. This imagery, moreover, enabled him to do things that might have seemed scarcely possible for a blind man. 'I replaced the entire roof guttering of my multi-gabled home single-handed,' he wrote, 'and solely on the strength of the accurate and well-focused manipulation of my now totally pliable and responsive mental space.' (Torey later expanded on this episode, mentioning the great alarm of his neighbors at seeing a blind man, alone, on the roof of his house and, even more terrifying to them, at night, in pitch darkness.)

And it enabled him to think in ways that had not been available to him before, to envisage solutions, models, designs, to project himself to the inside of machines and other systems, and, finally, to grasp by visual thought and simulation (complemented by all the data of neuroscience) the complexities of that ultimate system, the human brain-mind.

When I wrote back to Torey, I suggested that he consider writing another book, a more personal one, exploring how his life had been affected by blindness and how he had responded to this in the most improbable and seemingly paradoxical of ways. *Out of Darkness* is the memoir he has now written, and in it Torey describes his early memories with great visual intensity and humor. Scenes are remembered or reconstructed in brief, poetic glimpses of his childhood and youth in Hungary before the Second World War: the sky-blue buses of Budapest, the egg-yellow trams, the lighting of gas lamps, the funicular on the Buda side. He describes a carefree and privileged youth, roaming with his father in the wooded mountains above the Danube, playing games and pranks at school, growing up in a highly intellectual environment of writers, actors, professionals of every sort. Torey's father was the head of a large motion-picture studio and would often give his son scripts to read. 'This,' Torey writes, 'gave me the opportunity to visualize stories, plots and characters, to work my imagination – a skill that was to become a lifeline and source of strength in the years ahead.'

All of this came to a brutal end with the Nazi occupation, the siege of Buda, and then the Soviet occupation. Torey, now an adolescent, found himself passionately drawn to the big questions – the mystery of the universe, of life, and above all the mystery of consciousness, of the mind. In 1948, nineteen years old, and feeling that he needed to immerse himself in biology, engineering, neuroscience, and psychology, but knowing that there was no chance of study, of an intellectual life, in Soviet Hungary, Torey made his escape and eventually found his way to Australia, where, penniless and without connections, he did various manual jobs. In June of 1951, loosening the plug in a vat of acid at the chemical factory where he worked, he had the accident that bisected his life. 'The last thing I saw with complete clarity was a glint of light in the flood of acid that was to engulf my face and change my life. It was a nano-second of sparkle, framed by the black circle of the drumface, less than a foot away. This was the final scene, the slender thread that ties me to my visual past.'

When it became clear that his corneas had been hopelessly damaged and that he would have to live his life as a blind man he was advised to rebuild his representation of the world on the basis of hearing and touch and to 'forget about sight and visualizing altogether.' But this was something that Torey could not or would not do. He had emphasized, in his first letter to me, the importance of a most critical choice at this juncture: 'I immediately resolved to find out how far a partially sense-deprived brain could go to rebuild a life.' Put this way, it sounds abstract, like an experiment. But in his book one senses the tremendous feelings underlying his resolution – the horror of darkness, 'the empty darkness,' as Torey often calls it, 'the grey fog that was engulfing me,' and the passionate desire to hold on to light and sight, to maintain, if only in memory and imagination, a vivid and living visual world. The very title of his book says all this, and the note of defiance is sounded from the start.

Hull, who did not use his potential for imagery in a deliberate way, lost it in two or three years, and became unable to remember which way round a '3' went; Torey, on the other hand, soon became able to multiply four-figure numbers by each other, as on a blackboard, visualizing the whole operation in his mind, 'painting' the suboperations in different colors.

Well aware that the imagination (or the brain), unrestrained by the usual perceptual input, may run away with itself in a wildly associative or self-serving way – as may happen in deliria, hallucinations, or dreams – Torey maintained a cautious and 'scientific' attitude to his own visual imagery, taking pains to check the accuracy of his images by every means available. 'I learned,' he writes, 'to hold the image in a tentative way, conferring credibility and status on it only when some information would tip the balance in its favor.' Indeed, he soon gained enough confidence in the reliability of his visual imagery to stake his life upon it, as when he undertook roof repairs by himself. And this confidence extended to other, purely mental projects. He became able to imagine, to visualize, for example, the inside of a differential gearbox in action as if from inside its casing. I was able to watch the cogs bite, lock and revolve, distributing the spin as required. I began to play around with this internal view in connection with mechanical and technical problems, visualizing how subcomponents relate in the atom, or in the living cell.

This power of imagery was crucial, Torey thought, in enabling him to arrive at a solution of the brain-mind problem by visualizing the brain 'as a perpetual juggling act of interacting routines.'

In a famous study of creativity, the French mathematician Jacques Hadamard asked many scientists and mathematicians, including Einstein, about their thought processes. Einstein replied, 'The physical entities which seem to serve as elements in thought are... more or less clear images which can be "voluntarily" reproduced and combined. [Some are] of visual and some of muscular type. Conventional words or other signs have to be sought for laboriously only in a secondary stage.' Torey cites this, and adds, 'Nor was Einstein unique in this respect. Hadamard found that almost all scientists work this way, and this was also the way my project evolved.'

Soon after receiving Torey's manuscript, I received the proofs of yet another memoir by a blind person: Sabriye Tenberken's *My Path Leads to Tibet*. While Hull and Torey are thinkers, preoccupied in their different ways by inwardness, states of brain and mind, Tenberken is a doer; she has travelled, often alone, all over Tibet, where for centuries blind people have been treated as less than human and denied education, work, respect, or a role in the community. Virtually singlehanded, Tenberken has transformed their situation over the past half dozen years, devising a form of Tibetan Braille, establishing schools for the blind, and integrating the graduates of these schools into their communities.

Tenberken herself had impaired vision almost from birth but was able to make out faces and landscapes until she was twelve. As a child in Germany she had a particular predilection for colors, and loved painting, and when she was no longer able to decipher shapes and forms she could still use colors to identify objects. Tenberken has, indeed, an intense synesthesia. 'As far back as I can remember,' she writes,

> numbers and words have instantly triggered colors in me... The number 4, for example, [is] gold. Five is light green. Nine is vermillion... Days of the week as well as months have their colors, too. I have them arranged in geometrical formations, in circular sectors, a little like a pie. When I need to recall on which day a particular event happened, the first thing that pops up on my inner screen is the day's color, then its position in the pie.

Her synesthesia has persisted and been intensified, it seems, by her blindness.

Though she has been totally blind for twenty years, Tenberken continues to use all her other senses, along with verbal descriptions, visual memories, and a strong pictorial and synesthetic sensibility, to construct 'pictures' of landscapes and rooms, of environments and scenes – pictures so lively and detailed as to astonish her listeners. These images may sometimes be wildly or comically different from reality, as she relates in one incident when she and a companion drove to Nam Co, the great salt lake in Tibet. Turning eagerly toward the lake, Tenberken saw, in her mind's eye, 'a beach of crystallized salt shimmering like snow under an evening sun, at the edge of a vast body of turquoise water... And down below, on the deep green mountain flanks, a few nomads were watching their yaks grazing.' But it then turns out that she has been facing in the wrong direction, not 'looking' at the lake at all, and that she has been 'staring' at rocks and a gray landscape. These disparities don't faze her in the least – she is happy to have so vivid a visual imagination. Hers is essentially an artistic imagination, which can be impressionistic, romantic, not veridical at all, where Torey's imagination is that of an engineer, and has to be factual, accurate down to the last detail.

I had now read three memoirs, strikingly different in their depictions of the visual experience of blinded people: Hull with his acquiescent descent into imageless 'deep blindness,' Torey with his 'compulsive visualization' and meticulous construction of an internal visual world, and Tenberken with her impulsive, almost novelistic, visual freedom, along with her remarkable and specific gift of synesthesia. Was there any such thing, I now wondered, as a 'typical' blind experience?

I recently met two other people blinded in adult life who shared their experiences with me.

Dennis Shulman, a clinical psychologist and psychoanalyst who lectures on Biblical topics, is an affable, stocky, bearded man in his fifties who gradually lost his sight in his teens, becoming completely blind by the time he entered college. He immediately confirmed that his experience was unlike Hull's:

> I still live in a visual world after thirty-five years of blindness. I have very vivid visual memories and images. My wife, whom I have never seen – I think of her visually. My kids, too. I see myself visually – but it is as I last saw myself, when I was thirteen, though I try hard to update the image. I often give public lectures, and my notes are in Braille; but when I go over them in my mind, I see the Braille notes visually – they are visual images, not tactile.

Arlene Gordon, a charming woman in her seventies, a former social worker, said that things were very similar for her: 'If I move my arms back and forth in front of my eyes, I see them, even though I have been blind for more than thirty years.' It seemed that moving her arms was immediately translated for her into a visual image. Listening to talking books, she added, made her eyes tire if she listened too long; she seemed to herself to be reading at such times, the sound of the spoken words being transformed to lines of print on a vividly visualized book in front of her. This involved a sort of cognitive exertion (similar perhaps to translating one language into another), and sooner or later this would give her an eye ache.

I was reminded of Amy, a colleague who had been deafened by scarlet fever at the age of nine but was so adept a lipreader that I often forgot she was deaf. Once, when I absent-mindedly turned away from her as I was speaking, she said sharply, 'I can no longer hear you.'

'You mean you can no longer see me,' I said.

'*You* may call it seeing,' she answered, 'but I experience it as hearing.'

Amy, though totally deaf, still constructed the sound of speech in her mind. Both Dennis and Arlene, similarly, spoke not only of a heightening of visual imagery and imagination since losing their eyesight but also of what seemed to be a much readier transference of information from verbal description – or from their own sense of touch, movement, hearing, or smell – into a visual form. On the whole, their experiences seemed quite similar to Torey's, even though they had not systematically exercised their powers of visual imagery in the way that he had, or consciously tried to make an entire virtual world of sight.

There is increasing evidence from neuroscience for the extraordinarily rich interconnectedness and interactions of the sensory areas of the brain, and the difficulty, therefore, of saying that anything is purely visual or purely auditory, or purely anything. This is evident in the very titles of some recent papers – Pascual-Leone and his colleagues at Harvard now write of 'The Metamodal Organization of the Brain,' and Shinsuke Shimojo and his group at Caltech, who are also exploring intersensory perceptual phenomena, recently published a paper called 'What You See Is What You Hear,' and stress that sensory modalities can never be considered in isolation. The world of the blind, of the blinded, it seems, can be especially rich in such in-between states – the intersensory, the metamodal – states for which we have no common language.

Arlene, like Dennis, still identifies herself in many ways as a visual person. 'I have a very strong sense of color,' she said. 'I pick out my own clothes. I think, Oh, that will go with this or that, once I have been told the colors.' Indeed, she was dressed very smartly, and took obvious pride in her appearance. 'I love travelling,' she continued. 'I "saw" Venice when I was there.' She explained how her travelling companions would describe places, and she would then construct a visual image from these details, her reading, and her own visual memories. 'Sighted people enjoy travelling with me,' she said. 'I ask them questions, then they look, and see things they wouldn't otherwise. Too often people with sight don't see anything! It's a reciprocal process – we enrich each other's worlds.'

If we are sighted, we build our own images, using our eyes, our visual information, so instantly and seamlessly that it seems to us we are experiencing 'reality' itself. One may need to see people who are color-blind, or motion-blind, who have lost certain visual capacities from cerebral injury, to realize the enormous act of analysis and synthesis, the dozens of subsystems involved in the subjectively simple act of seeing. But can a visual image be built using nonvisual information – information conveyed by the other senses, by memory, or by verbal description?

There have, of course, been many blind poets and writers, from Homer on. Most of these were born with normal vision and lost their sight in boyhood or adulthood (like Milton). I loved reading Prescott's *Conquest of Mexico* and *Conquest of Peru* as a boy, and feel that I first saw these lands through his intensely visual, almost hallucinogenic descriptions, and I was amazed to discover, years later, that Prescott not only had never visited Mexico or Peru but had been virtually blind since the age of eighteen. Did he, like Torey, compensate for his blindness by developing such powers of visual imagery that he could experience a 'virtual reality' of sight? Or were his brilliant visual descriptions in a sense simulated, made possible by the evocative and pictorial powers of language? To what extent can language, a picturing in words, provide a substitute for actual seeing, and for the visual, pictorial imagination? Blind children, it has often been noted, tend to be precocious verbally, and may develop such fluency in the verbal description of faces and places as to leave others (and perhaps themselves) uncertain as to whether they are actually blind. Helen Keller's writing, to give a famous example, startles one with its brilliantly visual quality.

When I asked Dennis and Arlene whether they had read John Hull's book, Arlene said, 'I was stunned when I read it. His experiences are so unlike mine.' Perhaps, she added, Hull had 'renounced' his inner vision. Dennis agreed, but said, 'We are only two individuals. You are going to have to talk to dozens of people... But in the meanwhile you should read Jacques Lusseyran's memoir.'

Lusseyran was a French Resistance fighter whose memoir, *And There Was Light*, deals mostly with his experiences fighting the Nazis and later in Buchenwald but includes many beautiful descriptions of his early adaptations to blindness. He was blinded in an accident when he was not quite eight years old, an age that he came to feel was 'ideal' for such an eventuality, for, while he already had a rich visual experience to call on, 'the habits of a boy of eight are not yet formed, either in body or in mind. His body is infinitely supple.' And suppleness, agility, indeed came to characterize his response to blindness.

Many of his initial responses were of loss, both of imagery and of interests:

A very short time after I went blind I forgot the faces of my mother and father and the faces of most of the people I loved... I stopped caring whether people were dark or fair, with blue eyes or green. I felt that sighted people spent too much time observing these empty things... I no longer even thought about them. People no longer seemed to possess them. Sometimes in my mind men and women appeared without heads or fingers.

This is similar to Hull, who writes, 'Increasingly, I am no longer even trying to imagine what people look like... I am finding it more and more difficult to realize that people look like anything, to put any meaning into the idea that they have an appearance.'

But then, while relinquishing the actual visual world and many of its values and categories, Lusseyran starts to construct and to use an imaginary visual world more like Torey's.

This started as a sensation of light, a formless, flooding, streaming radiance. Neurological terms are bound to sound reductive in this almost mystical context. Yet one might venture to interpret this as a 'release' phenomenon, a spontaneous, almost eruptive arousal of the visual cortex, now deprived of its normal visual input. This is a phenomenon analogous, perhaps, to tinnitus; or phantom limbs, though endowed here, by a devout and precociously imaginative little boy, with some element of the supernal. But then, it becomes clear, he does find himself in possession of great powers of visual imagery, and not just a formless luminosity.

The visual cortex, the inner eye, having now been activated, Lusseyran's mind constructed a 'screen' upon which whatever he thought or desired was projected and, if need be, manipulated, as on a computer screen. 'This screen was not like a blackboard, rectangular or square, which so quickly reaches the edge of its frame,' he writes.

My screen was always as big as I needed it to be. Because it was nowhere in space it was everywhere at the same time... Names, figures and objects in general did not appear on my screen without shape, nor just in black and white, but in all the colors of the rainbow. Nothing entered my mind without being bathed in a certain amount of light... In a few months my personal world had turned into a painter's studio.

Great powers of visualization were crucial to the young Lusseyran, even in something as non-visual (one would think) as learning Braille (he visualizes the Braille dots, as Dennis does), and in his brilliant successes at school. They were no less crucial in the real, outside world. He describes walks with his sighted friend Jean, and how, as they were climbing together up the side of a hill above the Seine Valley, he could say: '"Just look! This time we're on top... You'll see the whole bend of the river, unless the sun gets in your eyes!" Jean was startled, opened his eyes wide and cried: "You're right." This little scene was often repeated between us, in a thousand forms.'

'Every time someone mentioned an event,' Lusseyran relates, 'the event immediately projected itself in its place on the screen, which was a kind of inner canvas... Comparing my world with his, [Jean] found that his held fewer pictures and not nearly as many colors. This made him almost angry. "When it comes to that," he used to say, "which one of us two is blind?"'

It was his supernormal powers of visualization and visual manipulation – visualizing people's position and movement, the topography of any space, visualizing strategies for defense and attack – coupled with his charismatic personality (and seemingly infallible 'nose' or 'ear' for detecting falsehood, possible traitors), which later made Lusseyran an icon in the French Resistance.

Dennis, earlier, had spoken of how the heightening of his other senses had increased his sensitivity to moods in other people, and to the most delicate nuances in their speech and self-presentation. He could now recognize many of his patients by smell, he said, and he could often pick up states of tension or anxiety which they might not even be aware of. He felt that he had become far more sensitive to others' emotional states since losing his sight, for he was no longer taken in by visual appearances, which most people learn to camouflage. Voices and smells, by contrast, he felt, could reveal people's depths. He had come to think of most sighted people, he joked, as 'visually dependent.'

In a subsequent essay, Lusseyran inveighs against the 'despotism,' the 'Idol worship' of sight, and sees the 'task' of blindness as reminding us of our other, deeper modes of perception and their mutuality. 'A blind person has a better sense of feeling, of taste, of touch,' he writes, and speaks of these as 'the gifts of the blind.' And all of these, Lusseyran feels, blend into a single fundamental sense, a deep attentiveness, a slow, almost prehensile attention, a sensuous, intimate being at one with the world which sight, with its quick, flicking, facile quality, continually distracts us from. This is very close to Hull's concept of 'deep blindness' as infinitely more than mere compensation but a unique form of perception, a precious and special mode of being.

What happens when the visual cortex is no longer limited, or constrained, by any visual input? The simple answer is that, isolated from the outside, the visual cortex becomes hypersensitive to internal stimuli of all sorts: its own autonomous activity; signals from other brain areas – auditory, tactile, and verbal areas; and the thoughts and emotions of the blinded individual. Sometimes, as sight deteriorates, hallucinations occur – of geometrical patterns, or occasionally of silent, moving figures or scenes that appear and disappear spontaneously, without any relation to the contents of consciousness, or intention, or context.

Something perhaps akin to this is described by Hull as occurring almost convulsively as he was losing the last of his sight. 'About a year after I was registered blind,' he writes, 'I began to have such strong images of what people's faces looked like that they were almost like hallucinations.'

These imperious images were so engrossing as to preempt consciousness: 'Sometimes,' Hull adds, 'I would become so absorbed in gazing upon these images, which seemed to come and go without any intention on my part, that I would entirely lose the thread of what was being said to me. I would come back with a shock... and I would feel as if I had dropped off to sleep for a few minutes in front of the wireless.' Though related to the context of speaking with people, these visions came and went in their own way, without any reference to his intentions, conjured up not by him but by his brain.

The fact that Hull is the only one of the four authors to describe this sort of release phenomenon is perhaps an indication that his visual cortex was starting to escape from his control. One has to wonder whether this signalled its impending demise, at least as an organ of useful visual imagery and memory. Why this should have occurred with him, and how common such a course is, is something one can only speculate on.

Torey, unlike Hull, clearly played a very active role in building up his visual imagery, took control of it the moment the bandages were taken off, and never apparently experienced, or allowed, the sort of involuntary imagery Hull describes. Perhaps this was because he was already very at home with visual imagery, and used to manipulating it in his own way. We know that Torey was very visually inclined before his accident, and skilled from boyhood in creating visual narratives based on the film scripts his father gave him. We have no such information about Hull, for his journal entries start only when he has become blind.

For Lusseyran and Tenberken, there is an added physiological factor: both were attracted to painting, in love with colors, and strongly synesthetic – prone to visualizing numbers, letters, words, music, and so forth, as shapes and colors – before becoming blind. They already had an overconnectedness, a 'cross talk' between the visual cortex and other parts of the brain primarily concerned with language, sound, and music. Given such a neurological situation (synesthesia is congenital, often familial), the persistence of visual imagery and synesthesia, or its heightening, might be almost inevitable in the event of blindness.

Torey required months of intense cognitive discipline dedicated to improving his visual imagery, making it more tenacious, more stable, more malleable, whereas Lusseyran seemed to do this almost effortlessly from the start. Perhaps this was aided by the fact that Lusseyran was not yet eight when blinded (while Torey was twenty-one), and his brain was, accordingly, more plastic, more able to adapt to a new and drastic contingency.

But adaptability does not end with youth. It is clear that Arlene, becoming blind in her forties, was able to adapt in quite radical ways, too, developing not exactly synesthesia but something more flexible and useful: the ability to 'see' her hands moving before her, to 'see' the words of books read to her, to construct detailed visual images from verbal descriptions. Did she adapt, or did her brain do so? One has a sense that Torey's adaptation was largely shaped by conscious motive, will, and purpose; that Lusseyran's was shaped by overwhelming physiological disposition; and that Arlene's lies somewhere in between. Hull's, meanwhile, remains enigmatic.

There has been much recent work on the neural bases of visual imagery – this can be investigated by brain imaging of various types (PET scanning, functional MRIs, and so forth) – and it is now generally accepted that visual imagery activates the cortex in a similar way, and with almost the same intensity, as visual perception itself. However, studies on the effects of blindness on the human cortex have shown that functional changes may start to occur in a few days, and can become profound as the days stretch into months or years.

Torey, who is well aware of all this research, attributes Hull's loss of visual imagery and memory to the fact that he did not struggle to maintain it, to heighten and systematize and use it, as Torey himself did. (Indeed, Torey expresses horror at what he regards as Hull's passivity, at his letting himself slide into deep blindness.) Perhaps Torey was able to stave off an otherwise inevitable loss of neuronal function in the visual cortex, but perhaps, again, such neural degeneration is quite variable, irrespective of whether or not there is conscious visualization. And, of course, Hull had been losing vision gradually for many years, whereas for Torey blindness was instantaneous and total. It would be of great interest to know the results of brain imaging in the two men, and indeed to look at a large number of people with acquired blindness, to see what correlations, what predictions could be made.

But what if their differences reflect an underlying predisposition independent of blindness? What of visual imagery in the sighted? I first became conscious that there could be huge variations in visual imagery and visual memory when I was fourteen or so. My mother was a surgeon and comparative anatomist and I had brought her a lizard's skeleton from school. She gazed at this intently for a minute, turning it round in her hands, then put it down and without looking at it again did a number of drawings of it, rotating it mentally by thirty degrees each time, so that she produced a series, the last drawing exactly the same as the first. I could not imagine how she had done this, and when she said that she could 'see' the skeleton in her mind just as clearly and vividly as if she were looking at it, and that she simply rotated the image through a twelfth of a circle each time, I felt bewildered, and very stupid. I could hardly see anything with my mind's eye – at most, faint, evanescent images over which I had no control.

I did have vivid images as I was falling asleep, and in dreams, and once when I had a high fever – but otherwise I saw nothing, or almost nothing, when I tried to visualize, and had great difficulty picturing anybody or anything. Coincidentally or not, I could not draw for toffee.

My mother had hoped I would follow in her footsteps and become a surgeon, but when she realized how lacking in visual powers I was (and how clumsy, lacking in mechanical skill, too) she resigned herself to the idea that I would have to specialize in something else.

I was, however, to get a vivid idea of what mental imagery could be like when, during the 1960s, I had a period of experimenting with large doses of amphetamines. These can produce striking perceptual changes, including dramatic enhancements of visual imagery and memory (as well as heightenings of the other senses, as I describe in 'The Dog Beneath the Skin,' a story in *The Man Who Mistook His Wife for a Hat*). For a period of two weeks or so, I found that I could do the most accurate anatomical drawings. I had only to look at a picture or an anatomical specimen, and its image would remain both vivid and stable, and I could easily hold it in my mind for hours. I could mentally project the image onto the paper before me – it was as clear and distinct as if projected by a camera lucida – and trace its outlines with a pencil. My drawings were not elegant, but they were, everyone agreed, very detailed and accurate, and could bear comparison with some of the drawings in our neuroanatomy textbook. This heightening of imagery attached to everything – I had only to think of a face, a place, a picture, a paragraph in a book to see it vividly in my mind. But when the amphetamine-induced state faded, after a couple of weeks, I could no longer visualize, no longer project images, no longer draw – nor have I been able to do so in the decades since.

At a recent medical conference in Boston, I spoke of Torey's and Hull's experiences of blindness, and of how 'enabled' Torey seemed to be by the powers of visualization he had developed, and how 'disabled' Hull was – in some ways, at least – by the loss of his powers of visual imagery and memory. After my talk a man in the audience came up to me and asked how well, in my estimation, sighted people could function if they had no visual imagery. He went on to say that he had no visual imagery whatever, at least none that he could deliberately evoke, and that no one in his family had any, either. Indeed, he had assumed this was the case with everyone, until he came to participate in some psychological tests at Harvard and realized that he apparently lacked a mental power that all the other students, in varying degrees, had.

'And what do you do?' I asked him, wondering what this poor man *could* do.

'I am a surgeon,' he replied. 'A vascular surgeon. An anatomist, too. And I design solar panels.'

But how, I asked him, did he recognize what he was seeing?

'It's not a problem,' he answered. 'I guess there must be representations or models in the brain that get matched up with what I am seeing and doing. But they are not conscious. I cannot evoke them.'

This seemed to be at odds with my mother's experience – she, clearly, did have extremely vivid and readily manipulable visual imagery, although (it now seemed) this may have been a bonus, a luxury, and not a prerequisite for her career as a surgeon.

Is this also the case with Torey? Is his greatly developed visual imagery, though clearly a source of much pleasure, not as indispensable as he takes it to be? Might he, in fact, have done everything he did, from carpentry to roof repair to making a model of the mind, without any conscious imagery at all? He himself raises this question.

The role of mental imagery in thinking was explored by Francis Galton, Darwin's irrepressible cousin, who wrote on subjects as various as fingerprints, eugenics, dog whistles, criminality, twins, visionaries, psychometric measures, and hereditary genius. His inquiry into visual imagery took the form of a questionnaire, with such questions as 'Can you recall with distinctness the features of all near relations and many other persons? Can you at will cause your mental image to sit, stand, or turn slowly around? Can you ... see it with enough distinctness to enable you to sketch it leisurely (supposing yourself able to draw)?' The vascular surgeon would have been hopeless on such tests – indeed, it was questions such as these that had floored him when he was a student at Harvard. And yet, finally, how much had it mattered?

As to the significance of such imagery, Galton is ambiguous and guarded. He suggests, in one breath, that 'Scientific men, as a class, have feeble powers of visual representation' and, in another, that 'a vivid visualizing faculty is of much importance in connection with the higher processes of generalized thoughts.' He feels that 'it is undoubtedly the fact that mechanicians, engineers and architects usually possess the faculty of seeing mental images with remarkable clearness and precision,' but goes on to say, 'I am, however, bound to say, that the missing faculty seems to be replaced so serviceably by other modes of conception ... that men who declare themselves entirely deficient in the power of seeing mental pictures can nevertheless give lifelike descriptions of what they have seen, and can otherwise express themselves as if they were gifted with a vivid visual imagination. They can also become painters of the rank of Royal Academicians.' I have a cousin, a professional architect, who maintains that he cannot visualize anything whatever. 'How do you think?' I once asked him. He shook his head and said, 'I don't know.' Do any of us, finally, know how we think?

When I talk to people, blind or sighted, or when I try to think of my own internal representations, I find myself uncertain whether words, symbols, and images of various types are the primary tools of thought or whether there are forms of thought antecedent to all of these – forms of thought that are essentially amodal. Psychologists have sometimes spoken of 'interlingua' or 'mentalese,' which they conceive to be the brain's own language, and Lev Vygotsky, the great Russian psychologist, used to speak of 'thinking in pure meanings.' I cannot decide whether this is nonsense or profound truth – it is the soft of reef I end up on when I think about thinking.

Galton's seemingly contradictory statements about imagery – is it antithetical to abstract thinking, or integral to it? – may stem from his failure to distinguish between fundamentally different levels of imagery. Simple visual imagery such as he describes may suffice for the design of a screw, an engine, or a surgical operation, and it may be relatively easy to model these essentially reproductive forms of imagery or to simulate them by constructing video games or virtual realities of various sorts. Such powers may be invaluable but there is something passive and mechanical and impersonal about them, which makes them utterly different from the higher and more personal powers of the imagination, where there is a continual struggle for concepts and form and meaning, a calling upon all the powers of the self. Imagination dissolves and transforms, unifies and creates, while drawing upon the 'lower' powers of memory and association. It is by such imagination, such 'vision,' that we create or construct our individual worlds.

At this level, one can no longer say of one's mental landscapes what is visual, what is auditory, what is image, what is language, what is intellectual, what is emotional – they are all fused together and imbued with our own individual perspectives and values. Such a unified vision shines out from Hull's memoir no less than from Torey's, despite the fact that one has become 'non-visual' and the other 'hypervisual.' What seems at first to be so decisive a difference between the two men is not, finally, a radical one, so far as personal development and sensibility go. Even though the paths they have followed might seem irreconcilable, both men have 'used' blindness (if one can employ such a term for processes which are deeply mysterious, and far below, or above, the level of consciousness and voluntary control) to release their own creative capacities and emotional selves, and both have achieved a rich and full realization of their own individual worlds.

Bibliography

Galton, F. (1970), *English Men of Science: Their Nature and Nurture*, London: Cass.

Goethe, J.W. (1882), *Goethe's Letters from Switzerland and Travels in Italy*, trans. A.J.W. Morrison, New York: J.D. Williams.

Hull, J. (1990), *Touching the Rock: An Experience of Blindness*, New York: Pantheon Books.

Lusseyran, J. (1987), *And There was Light*, New York: Parabola Books.

Pascual-Leone, A and Hamilton, R. (2001), 'The Metamodal Organization of the Brain,' *Progress in Brain Research*, 134: 427–45.

Prescott, W. (1893), *Conquest of Peru*, London: Routledge.

—— (1900), *Conquest of Mexico*, London: George Routledge and Sons.

Sacks, O. (1985), *The Man Who Mistook His Wife for a Hat*, New York: Harper & Row.

Shams, L., Kamitani, Y. and Shimojo, S. (2000), 'What You See Is What You Hear,' *Nature*, 408: 788.

Tenberken, S. (2003), *My Path Leads to Tibet*, New York: Arcade Books.

Torey. Z. (1999), *The Crucible of Consciousness*, Melbourne: Oxford University Press.

—— (2003), *Out of Darkness*, Sydney: Picador Australia.

2

Inside the Five Sense Sensorium

Marshall McLuhan

In his *Landmarks of Tomorrow* Peter F. Drucker considers many of the new forms in modern production, management, and decision making. For example, owing to the new ways of moving and coding information, it has become difficult to exercise delegated authority. Instead, staff and line procedures in management and production are increasingly abandoned for small team patterns. When several people of diversified competences can tackle problems together, jobs get done. He stresses that the assembly line is obsolete. Exactly synchronized information on electric tapes makes one-thing-at-a-time unnecessarily slow and needlessly sequential.

We have all noticed how lineality has faded from the current scene. The chorus line, the stag line, the assembly line, all have gone the way of the clothes line. Even the seam has faded in whispers from nylons, and the party line is also in trouble. But have all these cruxes for lineality the same cause?

Just at the end of the nineteenth century Bernard Berenson had begun a crusade 'to endow the retinal impression with tactile values.' There was wide awareness that photography and other technological change had abstracted the retinal impression, as it were, from the rest of the sensorium. Thus, in 1893 Adolf Hildebrand the sculptor published a small book called *The Problem of Form*. He insisted that true vision must be much imbued with tangibility, and that creative, aesthetic awareness was touching and making. Such was the timeliness of his insistence that the theme of artistic vision as tangible, tactile, and based on the interplay of the senses began to enjoy acceptance in poetry and painting alike. The art historian Heinrich Wolfflin taught the Hildebrand stress on visual forms as haptic or tangible-tactile – and his pupil

Sigfried Giedion embodied it in his *Space, Time and Architecture*. How little these men foresaw television as the fulfillment of their program! Photography gave separate and, as it were, abstract intensity to the visual, a development which called for and received swift compensating strategy in the arts. Movies and photo-engraving created a further revolution in Western sensibilities, tending to high stress on pictorial quality in all aspects of human association. And I am bold to say that there has been no respite from this growing pictorial stress till the advent of television.

Many people have drawn attention to the television image as a mosaic mesh of luminous points comparable to a Seurat painting. And, as in Seurat, the effect of the TV mesh is to give strong stress to contour and sculptural quality. André Girard, the French painter who has done visual experiments for CBS and NBC, has said that it was his master Rouault, who made him interested in television. For Rouault made his effects as if by light *through*, rather than by light *on*, as occurs in stained glass. In fact, says Girard, Rouault was the painter of television before television. And, as in medieval glass, or in Seurat or Rouault, the retinal image is of low intensity or 'low definition,' as broadcasters say. Yet this 'low definition' elicits high empathy or participation on the part of the viewer. Perhaps it is just because of the low definition of the retinal image that there is such high participation and interplay of all the senses in television. In this respect the television viewer is a sort of skin diver, for all the senses are in play, but some of them in rather diminished intensity. This would seem to be a condition of synesthesia, that no one sense be allowed high intensity. It was a favorite observation of Le Corbusier that architectural form is most effective at night.

Let us consider the hypothesis that television offers a massive Bauhaus program of the re-education for North American sense life. That is to query whether the television image is, in effect, a haptic, tactile, or synesthetic mode of interplay among the senses, a fulfillment on a popular plane of the aesthetic program of Hildebrand, Berenson, Wolfflin, Paul Klee, and Giedion. Are the popular effects of TV in the cult of skin diving, of the small car, and of do-it-yourself similar to the ideals of synesthesia proposed by the avant garde painters of the late nineteenth century? Do the Beats and the teenagers with their amalgam of art, Zen, and repudiation of consumer values conform to the effects hoped for by the older schools of synesthesia?

In his 'Culture, Psychiatry, and the Written Word' (1959) J.C. Carothers explains the strange effects of a small degree of literacy on African native sensory life. The African lives typically in the hyperesthetic mode of the ear in which everything is related to everything else, as in a field of simultaneous relations. The European and North American, in contrast, tend to live in the cool visual mode in which people and things have a good deal of separate existence:

Whereas the Western child is early introduced to building blocks, keys in locks, water taps, and a multiplicity of items and events which constrain him to think in terms of spatio-temporal relations and mechanical causation, the African child receives instead an education which depends much more exclusively on the spoken word which is relatively highly charged with drama and emotion... rural Africans live largely in a world of sound – a world loaded with direct personal significance for the hearer – whereas the Western European lives much more in a visual world which is on the whole indifferent to him.

Carothers wants very much to make the point that people who live in an oral-aural world know none of the impersonal or detached attitudes of a visual-literate people. But it is not easy to explain this matter to literate societies. They tend to imagine that the numerous conventions of seeing and organizing their world are quite 'natural.' Such cases among students at Ohio State University are sent on a tour of the Ames Perception Laboratory for shock treatment.

That a non-literate man has no perspective experience, and that natives cannot see photos or follow movies, comes as a shock at least to the provincial Westerner. Just as difficult for the Westerner to understand is why the introduction of the phonetic alphabet among natives should be a traumatic experience. For the translation of the magical oral world into the neutral visual symbols of the phonetic alphabet is a total metamorphosis for native societies. As Carothers puts it: 'Both in regard to children generally and to members of non-literate societies at all ages, it is well known that thinking and behavior are partly governed by the supposed "power" of the word.' That is, native societies really live the Madison Avenue dream of a world controllable by the mere sound of words. Carothers observes: 'Indeed, one is constrained to believe that the eye is regarded by many Africans less as a receiving organ than as an instrument of the will, the ear being the main receiving organ.' In contrast, Carothers points out: 'For living effectively in the modern Western world, a well-developed sense of spatio-temporal relations and of causal relationship on mechanistic lines is required, and this is highly dependent on a habit of visual as opposed to auditory synthesis.'

Of course, Carothers is talking of the Cartesian and Newtonian world that has so little in common with that of Marconi and Heisenberg. It needs no very sharp observation to note that the moving radar antennae, which feed radar screens, are as dynamic and spherical in their coverage as any auditory 'field of relations' can be. And this is equally true of the television image. It is a two-dimensional mosaic mesh, a simultaneous field of luminous vibration that ends the older dichotomy of sight and sound. The Carothers point is still well taken. The native can still be translated out of his resonating, magical, oral world by the phonetic alphabet, which conveys him into a world of visual sequences. But it is hard to convey to the literate man the simple fact that there are no visual sequences in an oral, non-literate society.

What we must grasp is that television has the power of imposing its own conventions and assumptions on the sensibilities of the viewer. It has the power of translating the Western literate back into the world of non-literate synesthesia, just as effectively as the phonetic alphabet can hoick the native out of his haptic matrix into a world of mechanistic individualism, and sequential cause-and-effect relations.

Far from regarding these developments with any feeling of euphoria, I would suggest that when Hildebrand conducted his campaign for tactility against mere retinal pictorial impression, he was in the centre of a great cultural current which, from Cézanne in painting to Conrad in literature, swept up all into the 'Heart of Darkness' or 'the Africa within.' This drive towards 'spontaneity of consciousness' fostered the child cult, as well as primitivism of many varieties, but it represented a rebellion against merely visual culture – a rebellion that had begun in the eighteenth century with Rousseau and others. This Romantic rebellion against abstract and fragmented man reached great intensity with the attacks on industrialism and robotism in the nineteenth century. Everywhere among these enemies of abstract, visual, and mechanical order is stress on synesthesia and wholeness and tactility. For, in practice, tactility is less a separate sense than it is the interplay among the senses. When, therefore, I speak of the tactility of the television image, I mean this stepped-up interplay of the senses which the nineteenth century artists and polemicists struggled to foster in an aesthetically starved milieu. That nineteenth century program makes no sense to anybody who fails to understand the peculiar monopoly and separation of visual experience, at the expense of the other senses, which is imposed by print and its industrial, organizational extensions.

Television, then, is not part of the nineteenth century art program for the reconquest of synesthesia. Television is rather the overwhelming and technological success of that program after its artistic exponents have retired.

A cartoon or an abstract painting offers sparse data and demands much of the viewer by way of 'closure' or completion and fill-in. The television image, then, demands much participation from the audience compared to movie, radio, or photo. Its two-dimensional, contoured character fosters the tactile interplay of the senses which painters since Cézanne had stressed as needful. And this sculptural, contoured image with its tactile stress is, in the case of the television medium, given a scope and extent of vulgarization unknown even to movie, photo or newspaper.

What are some of the discernible dispositions with which television has imbued its publics since the mid-1950s? I am working from the observation that our technical media, since writing and printing, are extensions of our senses. The latest such extension, television, I am suggesting, is an extension, not just of sight and sound, but of that very synesthesia which the artists of the past centuries have stressed as accessible via the tangible-tactile values of the new vision. Television is not just sight and sound, but tangibility in its visual, contoured, sculptural mode. What have been the social effects of this sudden extension of our sight-touch powers? What have been the specific changes in our attitudes to public space, to privacy, and to the nature of environmental materials resulting from television? I am assuming that enough has been said to suggest why any new medium alters the existing sense ratios and proportions just as over-all colors are modified by any local shift of pigment or component.

Writing on 'The Shape of Theatre to Come' in the Toronto *Globe and Mail* (May 20, 1961), Herbert Whittaker begins: 'Never before in its history has the theatre been so conscious of its living quarters. The battle of proscenium vs. platform is not new, but it is attracting new armies of defenders on either side, and a major battle seems inevitable.'

The proscenium arch, new in the sixteenth century, offers the same approach to space as easel-painting, which also was new in the sixteenth century. It is a pictorial space to be filled in, not a space to be filled out, as it were. As Etienne Gilson explained it in *Painting and Reality*, until Giotto a painting was a thing. From Giotto to Cézanne a painting was the representation of something else. That is to say, a painting in modern times was expected to be *of* something, to have content. It constituted a space that had to contain something. This space was created by fixed point of view, lineal perspective and vanishing point. E.H. Gombrich in *Art and Illusion* has recently analysed 'the anguish of the third dimension' and explained its demise in the electric age. As Gyorgy Kepes put it in *The Language of Vision*: 'Literary imitation of nature tied to a fixed point of observation had killed the image as a plastic organism.' The fixed position of the man habituated to eye-on-the-page was favorable to a segmental and sectional sense of space, the use of the eye as a geometrical rather than as a tactile organ. This attitude was explained and deplored by Bishop Berkeley in his *New Theory of Vision* in 1709. But the real crisis for the third dimension came with electricity and telegraph, what de Chardin calls, in *The Phenomenon of Man*, 'a prodigious biological event.'

Herbert Whittaker is also describing the anguish of the proscenium arch and the triumph of the new 'wrap-around space': 'The platform stage, blatantly wrapping its audience around it, can keep control of a large audience with ease, and a little circling about. Its farthest customer is less than half as far away, because the stage projects out to meet him.' The platform stage, like the 'arena theatre,' offers, that is, maximal audience participation.

Similar to the battle between the picture-frame and the platform stage spaces is the much larger struggle between the large and the small car. The French have long said: 'In an American car you are not on the road, you are in the car.' Françoise Sagan's driving her car in her bare feet in order to have the full sense of being 'with it' is not a new European attitude to spatial participation. Now that the same attitude has come to North Americans it jeopardizes our automotive industry, if only because industrial leaders are unable to understand the new feeling for space. I say this new feeling is *directly* attributable to the highly empathic and haptic television image that evokes the immersion of *deep* participation, not just retinal experience, in the viewer. But it matters not whether the cause is television or the climate. The new attitude to space is here. And the preference for the wrap-around space of the small plane, the small boat, or the small car, is for a space that we don't get *into* but which, as it were, we *put on*. The small car is worn like shoes or pants. It transforms the motorist into a super pedestrian, and renders him odious and nauseating to all occupants of real cars. Noise is a necessary feature of small cars. Noise is part of the haptic, participational quality, a manifest flutter in the bottom.

Another way of getting at this new shift to the empathic, participational experience of spatial forms is to consider the changes in problems afflicting centers and margins today in many areas of organization, public and private, because at any period of media change there is a sort of galaxy of related forms that are precipitated into new prominence and new relevance amidst older forms.

Town planners are familiar with the new lines of force exerted upon already existing urban spaces by faster vehicles and by air travel. At a more personal level, the already existing habits of visual perception are today being radically modified by electric information movement, for the instantaneous creates an entire field of relations where before had been only a segment or a fragment or a single point of view. In an electric environment of global information flow, the interchangeability of out-of-doors and indoors is inevitable. The imminence of satellite broadcasting need not blind us to the fact that the world became a global village with the telegraph more than a hundred years ago. The effects of the telegraph on newspaper design, on verbal layout and story composition are familiar to us all, but we still imagine that politics can follow the pre-telegraph patterns of center-margin interplay. With electric media any place is a center. No place is a margin. And that we should need Cuba to remind us of this is no credit to human awareness of new situations.

As we move into a world of multiple centers without margins, every facet of space awareness is altered both in private and public existence. The very concept of privacy, which originated with print culture in the sixteenth century, can no longer be sustained by the traditional means of partitioning space. The teenager has solved the problem as best he can by using radio to create an auditory private space for his homework. The awareness and definition of 'auditory space' became prevalent through Helmholtz over a century ago. Today no architect can afford to be ignorant of auditory space, which now interpenetrates every phase of our visual world in public and in private. It is the act of hearing that itself creates 'auditory space,' because we hear from every direction at once. It is plain that this unique auditory quality now belongs to radar and television, as well as to the global telegraph. Yet even intelligent and, especially, literate people flee from the very idea of 'auditory space,' because, naturally, it cannot be visualized. Auditory space, so crucial to architectural problems today, is usually defined as 'a field of simultaneous relations without center or periphery.' That is, auditory space contains nothing and is contained in nothing. It is quite unvisualizable, and, therefore, to the merely print-oriented man, it is 'unintelligible.'

Today the entire human community is being translated into 'auditory space,' or into that 'field of simultaneous relations,' by electric broadcasting. It behooves the architect and town planner, above all, to know what this means. And the way to know the meaning of this rather drastic and unpleasant change is to watch how various advanced groups in our community have tackled it already.

In his book, *A Composer's World*, Paul Hindemith indicates how different spatial forms of the concert hall naturally alter the auditory space of the musical composition:

> A composer writing for a larger hall loses a good deal of the freedom afforded by the smaller one. Melodies, in order to be understood, must be written so that the physical and mental distance between the performers and listeners cannot distort them. In rhythm, metrical structures will push themselves into the foreground, due to their greater intelligibility. Thus rhythmic patterns which, in order to be grasped intelligently, require a keen analytic mind on the part of the listener ought to be avoided. Rapidly moving harmonies or harmonies of too great complexity are not advisable, for the same reason.

He points to the incongruity of classical music nowadays performed in Hollywood Bowls:

> So far no music has been written that would fit our gigantic stadiums and bowls. We are using them for the performance of classical music, music that depends on the closest physical and mental proximity of not more than a few hundred listeners, and now this music is blown up to fill spaces in which the listener in the last row of the third balcony hears the fiddles' tones about a second after he has seen the players' bows executing them (a second equaling one half measure in 4/4 time at ordinary walking tempo!).

However, when the cathedrals were white, in Corbusier's phrase, their new spaces evoked the new music of Perotinus. Hindemith comments on

> Perotin, for instance, who about 1200 wrote his Organa for the then overwhelmingly new spatial conception of the Gothic cathedrals. These pieces, by no means primitive, provided in their technical planning even for the echo

within those columned and vaulted halls, so that retarded echoing harmonies, intermingling with the straight progress of the normal harmonies, could not disturb the over-all impression.

In a sense, the architect has always been close to the musician in his concern with sculptural contour and resonance, but today the architect or planner of corporation structures has become very conscious of the pressure of new media in creating new structural forms. One of the foremost of these is Dr. B.J. Muller-Thym of Columbia and MIT, who explains how conventional, centralized structures are now ineffective:

> ...pyramidal organization structures, with many layers of supervision, and with functional division by specialty, simply did not work... But in these research organizations where work actually got done, when one studied them he found that whatever the organization chart prescribed, groups of researchers with different competences as required by the problem in hand were working together, cutting across organizational lines; that they were establishing most of their own design criteria for the work as well as their intended patterns of association... The older, many-layered, highly functionalized organizations were characterized by the separation of thinking from doing; thinking was generally allocated to the top rather than the bottom of the pyramid and to 'staff' as against 'line' components. Whatever the wishes of the company about the decentralized exercise of authority, authority inexorably gravitated toward the top of the structure.

Yet the sort of structures that Muller-Thym here designates as irrelevant today easily dominate our educational and political establishments. Are not the same kinds of confusion occurring in our confronting of spatial organization, of architecture and town planning? As the volume and speed of vehicle traffic increases, the older patterns of town and city undergo unbearable strains. The road ceases to be a link between different social spaces, town and country, city and suburb. The road tries to become the city. But as road tries to become city, the further speed-up of vehicle traffic occurs not on the road but in the air, and the logic of the jet plane would seem to render even the wheel itself obsolete.

So far as the dwellers in cities are concerned, an even greater revolution has already occurred in their daily lives. Some years ago I took a cue from Malraux's 'museum without walls' and began to write about 'classrooms without walls,' pointing to the fact that the space of the modern classroom is based on the printed book. The kind of uniform, repeatable enclosure of data from the press made it possible for the first time in history to have the same book in front of teacher and students alike. Before that, teaching had been mostly oral, and with small benefit of repeatable text or classroom spaces as we have long known them. Modern classroom seating plans persist in the spatial layout of the moveable types that gave us the printed page.

It seems quite obvious that the lineality that invaded every kind of spatial organization from the sixteenth century onward had as its archetype and matrix the metal lines of Gutenberg's uniform and repeatable types. Today when David Riesman in *The Lonely Crowd* writes of the decline of inner goals and inner direction, he testifies to the overlaying of lineal forms of reading experience by the new electric fields of multilevelled global awareness. The book thrives as never before, but its form is no longer constitutive or dominant. Surely this is why architectural design is entrusted now with a major task of sustaining traditional values achieved by print culture. How to breathe new life into the lineal forms of the past five centuries while admitting the relevance of the new organic forms of spatial organization (what I have explained as 'auditory space' above) – is not this the task of the architect at present? But what chance has he of tackling this task at all if he has no understanding of the media forms that informed the architecture of recent centuries or of the new media forms that inspire the Bauhaus fashions of the present? Is it not time that we began to think seriously about a consensus for our media, as we already try to think of some social relevance for structure and design in our buildings? If our massive new electric media are direct extensions of sight and sound and touch and kinesthesia, is there not urgent need to consider a possibility of a consensus or ratio and balance among these for our collective sanity? Even a slight disturbance of the balance among our private senses can drive us to wits' end. We live in a time when whole peoples have gone out of their wits when impelled by new massive forms such as radio. Psychologists explain that when the field of attention has a center without a margin we are hypnotized. Such is the condition of tribal man, past or present. The problem of design is to understand the media forces in such wise that we need never sink into the zombie tribal state where we can meet that Africa within which Conrad immortalized in his *Heart of Darkness*.

Bibliography

Carothers, J.C. (1959), 'Culture, Psychiatry, and the Written Word,' *Psychiatry*, 22: 307–20.

Chardin, P.T. de. (1959), *The Phenomenon of Man*, trans. B. Wall, New York: Harper.

Drucker, P.F. (1959), *Landmarks of Tomorrow*, New York: Harper.

Giedion, S. (1941), *Space, Time and Architecture*, Cambridge: Harvard University Press.

Gilson, E. (1957), *Painting and Reality*, New York: Pantheon.

Gombrich, E.H. (1960), *Art and Illusion*, New York: Pantheon.

Hildebrand, A. von. (1932), *The Problem of Form in Painting and Sculpture*, New York: G.E. Stechert & Co.

Hindemith, P. (1961), *A Composer's World: Horizons and Limitations*, New York: Doubleday.

Kepes, G. (1939), *The Language of Vision*, Chicago: Paul Theobald.

Muller-Thym, B.J. (1961), 'New Directions for Organization Practice,' in *Ten Years Progress in Management, 1950–1960*. New York: American Society of Mechanical Engineers.

Riesman, D. (1950), *The Lonely Crowd*, New Haven: Yale University Press.

Part II

The Shifting Sensorium

Historicizing Perception

The forming of the five senses is a labour of the entire history of the world down to the present.

Karl Marx, *Economic and Philosophic Manuscripts*

The first chapter in this section, 'Remembering the Senses' by Susan Stewart, was originally presented at the 'Material Memories' conference organized by the Victoria and Albert Museum and the Royal College of Art in 1998. Growing out of Stewart's influential study of material culture, *On Longing* (Stewart 1984), this paper examines the relations between sensation, memory and the production of art. Stewart presents a synopsis of the senses in Western philosophy and literature, noting how philosophers have been preoccupied with determining the status of the senses in relation to reality, and how the motif of 'the five senses' has figured as a central *topos* of Western literary production. Taking her cue from the young Marx, she brings out ways in which the senses are an historical, human formation. At the same time, the poet in her rebels against confining the history of the senses to an account of their 'regulation' and 'taxonomy,' and she seeks to portray their role in human creativity (and in the creation of the human) through pursuing various intimations of sublimity in the works of Marcel Proust. 'Remembering the Senses' sketches the contours of the argument which would crystallize in *Poetry and the Fate of the Senses*, where Stewart expounds 'a general theory of poetic forms – forms arising out of sense experience and producing, as they make sense experience intelligible to others, intersubjective meaning' (Stewart 2002: ix).

The next chapter is 'The Witch's Senses' by cultural historian Constance Classen. This is based on Classen's groundbreaking work on the gendering of perception in *The Colour of Angels* (1998). In contrast to Irigaray's (1985) centering of female perceptual difference in physiology, Classen brings out the cultural history behind such concepts as the dominating male gaze and the nurturing feminine touch. 'The Witch's Senses' examines how in pre- and early modern Europe feminine sensibilities were held to provide a basis for both domesticity and witchcraft. It was only by demonizing and exorcizing the suspect 'feminine' sensorium that the 'masculine' experimental philosophy propounded by the likes of Bacon and Harvey was able to contain the potentially supernatural and disruptive dimensions of 'women's work' and achieve an ocular mastery of (feminine) Nature. This debasing construction of female sensuality did not, however, go unchallenged. Classen relates how various women, such as Marinelli and Cavendish, creatively contested the biases of the dominant sensory order by attributing positive values to traditional feminine sensory traits and practices, and insisting that there remain 'some aspects of existence that cannot be forced into visibility.'

The theme of the conflict of the faculties in the early modern period is pursued further in the following chapter by literary scholar Carla Mazzio. Her essay centers on the 1607 comedy *Lingua, or The Combat of the Tongue and the Five Senses for Superiority*, which begins with Ladie Lingua (the tongue and language) sowing dissension within the pentarchy by planting a robe and crown for the five to discover and dispute. The sensorium quickly breaks down into warring sense organs, each proclaiming its own importance as the most representative of the senses. Lowly Tactus (touch) emerges as the most challenging and challenged of the combatants on account of his 'resistance to representation' and 'polymorphous diversity' in Mazzio's delightful phrase. For touch is dispersed throughout the body (hence impossible to pin down), its operations are 'immediate' (there is no medium between the body and the touchable world), and, if the truth be known, Tactus proclaims, every sense is a kind of touch. Such a conflation of distinctions, if allowed to stand, would undermine all categorization, all calculation, and all the Arts as well: for whither music to the ear or painting to the eye if touch is all there is? This truth is accordingly banished, and the hierarchy of the senses restored in the final act. But the play suggests that the troublesome questions about sensory boundaries – the issue of overlapping dominions – raised by upstart Tactus can never be finally resolved. The Renaissance understanding of the senses, while fundamentally hierarchical, was thus remarkably ex-centric or centrifugal in character. The agency of the non-visual senses had yet to be subdued by the 'hegemony of vision' (Levin 1993) or that of quantification – though that would come, as we see in the following chapter by science historian Lissa Roberts.

Roberts' 'The Death of the Sensuous Chemist' describes the late eighteenth century transition of chemistry from a field of human technique and sensuous analysis to a domain of laboratory technology and mathematical analysis. While in the old chemistry the body of the scientist verified the nature of the chemical world through his highly trained senses, in the new chemistry the scientist's body became only an accessory to the precision instruments of the laboratory. Roberts' introduces the notion of 'sensuous technology' to refer to the complex bodily techniques for sensibly investigating the qualitative characteristics of natural phenomena used by experimenters before the 'chemical revolution' and advent of precision scientific instrumentation.

Particularly striking, from a contemporary perspective, is Roberts' description of the extensive use of the non-visual senses in early chemistry. We are familiar with the 'eye-mindedness' of science, with its reliance on optical instruments and visual calculations and diagrams, we can hardly believe that any branch of science could ever have been 'nose-minded.' Yet Roberts describes how prominent eighteenth century chemists judged the progress of their experiments and the nature of their results by smell and even, at times, by taste. (Smell and taste are, after all, the 'chemical' senses.) The relative tardiness of chemistry to give up on the non-visual senses as media of knowledge was due in part to its direct involvement with the sensuous stuff of the cosmos and to its rich alchemical heritage of sensory symbolism. Thus eighteenth century chemists attempted both to classify air by smell and sniff out the nature of the soul (Stafford 1994: 423–428). Once chemistry adhered to the quantitative values that were already dominating in other sciences, much of this subjective, sensuous interpretation of existence was discarded. The result helped to transform the cosmos into what many would consider 'a dull affair, soundless, scentless, colourless; merely the hurrying of material, endlessly, meaninglessly' (Alfred North Whitehead, cited in Classen 1998: 5).

The final chapter in this section, 'Charting the Cultural History of the Senses,' is by a French historian who knows a great deal about the olfactory life of the eighteenth century: Alain Corbin. It was originally commissioned for a special issue of *Anthropologie et Sociétés* on 'Les cinq sens,' which I edited in 1990. Written between Corbin's *The Foul and the Fragrant* (1986) and *Village Bells* (1994) this piece gives the most complete rendition of Corbin's methodology as a historian of sensibility and perception. It describes the difficulties faced by the historian of the senses who, 'a prisoner of language' is obliged to rely on written texts, and the necessity of constantly sifting and evaluating sources of diverse provenance in an effort to discover 'the configuration of what is experienced and what cannot be experienced within a culture at a given moment.' A particular concern is the social hierarchy of perception: the sensory refinement of the aristocratic sphere does not comprehend the harsh tactile world of the manual labourer. Corbin's 'history of the senses' is distinguished from his countryman Michel Foucault's 'archaeology of perception' by its careful attention to recuperating the social and cultural life of those senses which have been sidelined by modernity, and by an emphasis on exploring the interplay of the senses, rather than simply tracing the genealogy of visuality. In this respect, Corbin's work is well matched with the other contributions to this section, for they all exemplify in their own way how there is more to history than meets the eye.

Bibliography

Classen, C. (1998), *The Color of Angels: Cosmology, Gender and the Aesthetic Imagination*, London and New York: Routledge.

Corbin, A. (1986), *The Foul and the Fragrant*, trans. M.L. Kochan, R. Porter and C. Prendergast, Leamington Spa: Berg.

—— (1990), 'Histoire et anthropologie sensorielle,' *Anthropologie et Sociétés*, 14(2): 13–24.

—— (1994), *Village Bells. Sound and Meaning in the Nineteenth Century French Countryside*, New York: Columbia University Press.

Irigaray, L. (1985), *This Sex Which Is Not One*, trans. C. Porter and C. Burke, Ithaca NY: Cornell University Press.

Levin, D.M. (1993), *Modernity and the Hegemony of Vision*, Berkeley: University of California Press.

Stafford, B.M. (1994), *Body Criticism: Imaging the Unseen in Enlightenment Art and Medicine*, Cambridge MA: MIT Press.

Stewart, S. (1984), *On Longing*, Baltimore MD: Johns Hopkins University Press.

—— (2002), *Poetry and the Fate of the Senses*, Chicago: University of Chicago Press.

3

Remembering the Senses

Susan Stewart

In a famous aphorism amid the discussion of alienation in the *Economic and Philosophic Manuscripts of 1844*, Marx (1964: 141) claimed that 'the forming of the five senses is a labour of the entire history of the world down to the present.' In suggesting that the senses are an historical, that is a human, accomplishment, Marx argued that the senses are not merely organs used in responding to, and apprehending, the world, but that the senses are also a powerful source of material memories. Such memories are material in that the body carries them somatically – that is, they are registered in our consciousness, or in the case of repression, the unconscious knowledge, of our physical experiences. And as sense experiences are registered and continued from generation to generation, the specific forms of their articulation and expression in works of art give us an historical account of how such experiences change and are transformed. Bergson (1988: 3) was to rephrase this idea in his 1908 *Matter and Memory*: 'there is no perception which is not full of memories. With the immediate and present data of our senses, we mingle a thousand details out of our past experience.'[1] This view of the senses as cumulative and accomplished, rather than given, brings forward the relations between sense activity, representation and expression. As Marx contended that the senses help us to overcome conditions of alienation that arise as we sell our labor and strive to possess private property, he brought forward the creative and cultural work of sense activity and leads us to think about the ways in which aesthetic forms both produce sense experience and result from it.

The senses have often been considered as a philosophical problem appearing on a boundary between what we refer to, perhaps for lack of better terms, as internal and external phenomena. Here the relation between external objects – that is, material forms and living organisms – and the phenomena of our immediate awareness of the world – color, shape, sound, smell, tactile feelings – is both distinguished and blurred. Visual and auditory senses depend upon relations to external objects and their properties; sounds and smells are public and external; tastes are private, yet external to the skin and membranes in that they require stimulation; feelings of heat or cold or warmth are partly internal and partly dependent on contact with external forms.

Philosophers have offered various descriptions of sense experience: John Locke in his *Essay Concerning Human Understanding* (1690) spoke of 'ideas of sense.' In the eighteenth century Bishop George Berkeley wrote in *A Treatise Concerning the Principles of Human Knowledge* (1710, Part I) and *Three Dialogues Between Hylas and Philonous* (1713) of 'sensible qualities' that are not independent of the mind, and David Hume wrote in his 1739 *Treatise of Human Nature* of 'impressions' inferred from empirical experience out of which all ideas are derived. Gilbert Ryle in *The Concept of Mind* (1949) and J. L. Austin in *Sense and Sensibilia* (1962) claimed that speaking of sense data as phenomena reified the perceived qualities of things. Such philosophical theories constantly return to a set of questions regarding the relations between sense experience and the expression of sense experience. What is the relation between sense experience and ideas? When do sense impressions require external stimulants? What is the status of a memory or hallucination or dream of sense experience? Are our sense impressions private or more or less public? In talking of an object's qualities do we form an object's qualities? Perhaps in searching for the relation between external and internal experiences of sense impression and in studying the historical manifestations of sense experience evident in works of art, we might find a way of approaching these questions that is more engaged with the dynamic between sense experience and thought than with their division.

Through work, play, sex, grooming and other activities the body engages the natural world with an ongoing mutuality. And yet even in what Maurice Merleau-Ponty called in his classic study, *The Phenomenology of Perception* (1962), a 'tacit' stance, the body is necessarily articulated as separate from the world. As the medieval tradition puts it, the drawbridges of the senses are opened and closed: here the human senses in their refinement and specialization serve as sentinels against the excesses the external world presents to interiority. Something of this notion survives in Freud's writings. In *Instincts and their Vicissitudes* (1915), for example, Freud (1953, xv: 120) described the nervous system as an apparatus that has the function of getting rid of the stimuli that reach it, or at least reducing them to the lowest possible level. The senses cluster and work at the openings of the body: through their operation, we engage in an epistemology of process. Orifices subdivide our experience, yet they are at the same time components of the body's general and synthesizing openness to the world. Consciousness is part of the ego's work of modulating and resisting such openness. Thus the opening and modulation of the senses takes part in a dynamic that is at the core of subjectivity itself. We might think here of the biological role of tactile communication in the establishment of homeostasis in the infant.[2] The senses blur the boundary between need and desire, biology and culture.

Thus the philosophical problem of the senses, in that it has emphasized the status of sensory experiences in relation to varying historical models of the real, has from the beginning appeared as well as a moral problem – a problem of the status of human experience and human conduct, with experience and conduct forming contrasting poles of passive and active agency. We may apprehend the world by means of our senses, but the senses themselves are shaped and modified by experience and the body bears a somatic memory of its encounters with what is outside of it.

The notion of 'five senses' is usually attributed to Aristotle, although we find that, in *De Anima*, taste and seeing are described as forms of touch.[3] Here the senses are connected to the elements in a system of correspondences. The eye is associated with water, which can absorb light; hearing is associated with air; smell with fire; and touch with earth. Aristotle made special mention of objects that are perceptible by single senses: color as the special object of sight, sound of hearing, flavor of taste. This specialization and heightening of the senses later played in complex ways into the historical development of the discourse on the senses.[4] Notions of sensibility and sensitivity are associated with the refining of the higher philosophical senses of seeing and hearing. The complexity of taste is often presented as a distinction ranging from coarseness to fineness: a set of terms so textural in its range that reaches back to the Aristotelian merger of taste and touch. Correlatively the problems of over-refined sensibilities of touch and smell become a concern which by the time of Freud was linked to regression, neuroses and even perversion.[5]

Yet accompanying this concern with specialized functions, Aristotle also put forward some initial observations of synesthesia. 'There seems to be a sort of parallelism,' he noted, 'between what is acute or grave to hearing and what is sharp or blunt to touch; what is sharp as it were stabs, while what is blunt pushes, the one producing its effort in a short, the other in a long time, so that one is quick, the other slow' (Aristotle 1941: 572). In Aristotle's doctrine the information provided by the external senses reached the internal senses by means of a common sense of touch.[6]

Louise Vinge has traced, in her literary history of the motif of the five senses, the notion of their hierarchy. For Aristotle touch (and thereby taste) was found in all animals and so became the lowliest sense. He contended that touch was the sense needed for being, whereas the other senses were necessary for wellbeing. He therefore posed a hierarchical order of the senses, from most to least valuable: vision-hearing-smell-taste-touch. From Aristotle, too, in the *Nicomachean Ethics*, came the opposition between Heroic Virtue (tending toward God and therefore abstraction) and pleasure (tending toward the animal and therefore the sensual). This theme, the dialogue or struggle between reason and sensuality appeared as well in, among other works,

Xenophon's retelling of the temptation of Hercules by Circe; the passage on the Eucharist in 2 Corinthians 10 where Paul taught that the backslidings of the Israelites in the desert show how spiritual meat and drink are corrupted into the unspiritual; through Augustine's account of his conversion in the *Confessions*, a number of bawdy French fifteenth century moralités; Chapman's 'Ovid's Banquet of Sense;' and Marvell's *Dialogue between the Resolved Soul and Created Pleasure.*[7]

Pliny contended in his *Natural History* that touch and taste were superior in man to the senses of animals, but that in all the other senses man is surpassed: eagles see more clearly; vultures smell more sharply; moles hear more distinctly (Vinge 1975: 38–9). Yet despite this position that valorizes the animal senses (a tradition extending to Suzanne Langer's essays on *Mind*, for example) the senses have been ranked in relation to their degree of immediacy – taste and touch, in direct contact with the world, are lowest, followed by smell, which forms a kind of mean distance to sight and hearing, which operate across distance and yet can be remembered at will (Langer 1972: i; see also Janson 1952). Hearing and sight, because of their link with philosophical contemplation and abstraction, hold the leading place. My own disability insurance policy, for example, pays far more for the loss of an eye than for the loss of a limb or hearing, and a lost sense of taste or smell goes unmentioned. Insurance policies are documents oriented toward the future; they never pay, even in madeleines, for lost memories.

The subject invented by disinterested desire, Hercules the scholar as opposed to Hercules tempted, is a kind of ideal picture of evolved, upright, man – vision and hearing directed toward the horizon and hence a spatialization of progress and self-consciousness. Taxonomy here is inextricably bound up with hierarchy: the partitioning of classes and cultures and the partitioning of the body itself. Such taxonomies assume that man's relation to the animal is analogous rather than contiguous.

In Medieval, Renaissance, and Enlightenment topoi, the domain of smell, taste, and touch is properly a domain of beasts. From the Jewish Hellenistic philosopher Philo's contention that, in exercising his will, man can act in opposition to the forces of his own nature (see Philo 1929, VI: 74–85) to Kant's arguments for the suspension of appetite in aesthetic judgments; this rhetoric of the animal and servile senses, aside from its obvious legitimizing force for philosophy, established a subjectivity separated from nature, protected by mediation, and propelled by a desire born out of the very estranged relation thus created. Of all the monuments of the cities on the plain, only the citadel of sight was left standing. In excess and deprivation, in taboo and manners, the economy of the senses is created and put into action.

It is clear that we could construct a history of the senses out of these discourses. That is, we could consider the history of the senses as the history of an economy that ranks the senses and regulates the body's relation to the social world in a transformed and transforming way. But this concern with regulation of the senses, although of paramount importance in constructing their history, seems to reify our alienation from the senses and takes us farther and farther away from an understanding of their broader place in aesthetic activity. Aesthetic activity bent to ideological ends is no longer aesthetic; it erases the free activity of pleasure and knowledge that the aesthetic brings to human life. When Marx wrote that 'the forming of the five senses is a labour of the entire history of the world down to the present,' he was not beginning with an assumption of the senses as natural or given processes to be restricted and formed by civilizing forces. Rather, he considered the senses as both influenced by and influencing historical developments in the species beyond the agency of individual subjects. Writing of vision he said: 'The eye has become a *human* eye, just as its object has become a social, *human* object – an object made by man for man. The senses have therefore become directly in their practice theoreticians.' He went on to propose that: 'Not only the five senses,' but what he called the 'mental' or 'practical' senses – will, love, etc. – come to be by virtue of their object, by virtue of humanized nature. The relation of a person to his or her senses is imagined by Marx as of increasing importance. The ongoing formation, even cultivation, of the senses was for Marx a recovery of that power of the body lost to the alienating effects of private property.

In line with Kant's account of aesthetic judgment as undertaken with a sense of purpose in the absence of any particular teleology, Marx argued that the emergence of the senses in their full power would occur once consciousness is freed from the material imperatives of need and having. 'The transcendence of private property,' he wrote, 'is therefore the complete *emancipation* of all human senses and quantities, but it is this emancipation precisely because these senses and attributes have become, subjectively and objectively *human*' (Marx 1964: 139). Humanized nature is contrasted to elemental need: 'for the starving man it is not the human form of food that exists, but only its abstract being as food ... the dealer in minerals sees only the commercial values, but not the beauty and unique nature of the mineral: he has no *minerological* sense' (Marx 1964: 141).

There is, therefore, a useful analog between what Marx called universal sense experience, projected and created by an ongoing human accomplishment of transcending the immediacy of use and need, and Kant's aesthetic with its similar refusal of determination by practical and even cognitive utility. Marx imagined the history of sense impression as a labor of emancipation that would only be finished in a moment of Hegelian fulfillment, a replete consciousness, where the senses, free of the contingency of nature and the political economy, were wholly determined and determining in accordance with human ends. Marx's version of the history of the senses might be seen as compensatory to the ways of looking at the senses I have emphasized thus far: the history of taxonomies, hierarchies and other models of the senses. And although his theory is characterized by a humanist emphasis, its humanism is not dependent upon a separation of the human and the animal. Taxonomies and hierarchies of the senses tend both to overestimate the role of human will and to overgeneralize the senses. Following Marx's notion of a history of the senses, an analysis of aesthetic acts and their consequences will be of more consequence than an account of the history of the sense's regulation.

When we consider the senses in relation to the arts, we often look to the senses as a thematic: the representation of the senses in the history of painting, drawings, engraving, sculpture and porcelain, characters in plays and novels typified or allegorized by means of their relation to sense impressions. As an example, one might take Caravaggio's *Doubting Thomas* (1602 or 1603), a painting in the Sans Souci Gallery in Potsdam. Caravaggio, the great practitioner of painting as immediate touch and gesture, here plays with the dynamic between the surface of the skin and the surface of the canvas. Through touch, he represents a touch that penetrates the reality of the representation itself. We could in fact only discover that this wound, like all painted wounds, is a trompe l'oeil effect on the skin of the painting by placing our finger where Thomas has placed his.

To the extent that works of art also make possible particular sense experiences, such thematic uses of the senses call forth an originary and complex kind of synesthesia – not just in the mixture of sense impressions as in 'a bright noise,' a 'cold color,' or a 'sharp aroma,' but as well in a synthesis of imagined and material experiences. The cold, dead, silent, smooth, or variegated surface of sculpture or porcelain evokes sensations of touch, warmth, smell, taste and hearing; the inanimate musical box pours forth its mechanical notes at our touch as if a responding living thing; Wagner's Tristan, says he, 'hears the light' and the audience hears it as well; conversely, the many scenes of figures crying out and hearing in Caravaggio's paintings make us feel we are in a world where we can hear painted images; and the illusions of moving pictures make us confuse our own rapid eye movements with the movements of a world.

There are few works of art that offer as many insights regarding the experiential relations between sense impressions, memory and artistic making so much as Proust's rigorous *Recherche* into time, and the loss of time. I want to consider two passages in this regard. The first is from Part 2, Chapter 3, of *Sodom and Gomorrah*:

> I had gone on horseback to call on the Verdurins and had taken an unfrequented path through the woods the beauty of which they had extolled to me. Hugging the contours of the cliff, it alternately climbed and then, hemmed in by dense woods on either side, dived into wild gorges. For a moment the barren rocks by which I was surrounded, and the sea that was visible through their jagged gaps, swam before my eyes like fragments of another universe: I had recognised the mountainous and marine landscape which Elstir had made the scene of those

two admirable water-colours, 'Poet meeting a muse,' and 'Young Man meeting a Centaur,' which I had seen at the Duchesse de Guermantes's. The memory of them transported the place in which I now found myself so far outside the world of today that I should not have been surprised if, like the young man of the prehistoric age, that Elstir had painted, I had come upon a mythological personage in the course of my ride. Suddenly, my horse reared; he had heard a strange sound; it was all I could do to hold him and remain in the saddle; then I raised my tear-filled eyes in the direction from which the sound seemed to come and saw, not two hundred feet above my head, against the sun, between two great wings of flashing metal which were bearing him aloft, a creature whose indistinct face appeared to me to resemble that of a man. I was as deeply moved as an ancient Greek on seeing for the first time a demi-god. I wept – for I had been ready to weep the moment I realised that the sound came from above my head (aeroplanes were still rare in those days), at the thought that what I was going to see for the first time was an aeroplane. Then, just as when in a newspaper one senses that one is coming to a moving passage, the mere sight of the machine was enough to make me burst into tears. Meanwhile the airman seemed to be uncertain of his course; I felt that there lay open before him – before me, had not habit made me a prisoner – all the routes in space, in life itself; he flew on, let himself glide for a few moments over the sea, then quickly making up his mind, seeming to yield to some attraction that was the reverse of gravity, as though returning to his native element, with a slight adjustment of his golden wings he headed straight up into the sky. (Proust 1996, IV: 581–2)

There may seem to be no more perfect textbook case of the experience of sublimity than this passage – the unfamiliar path, the dense wood on one side and the formidable gorge on the other, the sea glimpsed through jagged rocks, the sensation of the 'fragments of another universe' floating before the narrator's eyes. But what is the textbook? Proust, with typical attention, does not stop with the Burkean vista – rather, he has the narrator realign the unfamiliar in terms of the past, and, even more specifically, in terms of the mythological past represented in Elstir's paintings. As the narrator recalls these titles and frames, he rearranges the landscape before him as a scene known both to his imagination and his memory – a scene known, as it is experienced, as in fact completely unavailable to lived experience. All of nature is vestigial to this moment the narrator now knows by means of Elstir's works. However, the account is not yet finished; in fact this initial resolution is a kind of mistaken turn and only now will the narrator approach his subject, a subject that cannot be focused upon because he cannot yet know what it is. In this mistaken turn we find the distinction between voluntary and involuntary memory that Proust, throughout his art, is so constantly at pains to set before us, a distinction between conscious will and desire that for Proust enables the very possibility of art. As the narrator's conventional reverie on myth comes to a close, the horse senses an unknown sound and rears in fright. Proust describes the narrator's struggle to control the horse and his simultaneous weeping. We have left the world of Elstir's titles where poet is separate from muse and man is separate from centaur; here the man and the horse are fused in their physical response to a sound in the heavens: a specific sound proleptically connoting a specific source that nevertheless is unattributable until the great wings appear. But unlike the painting, which can be framed by habit, the aeroplane until this point has been only a name and not a being. In this sense, the encounter is not like the conventional representation of an encounter with a god; it is, as the realization of an unrealizable experience, an actual encounter with a god. Proust emphasizes the anticipatory reversal of emotion here – emotion comes first and knowledge arrives only by means of retrospection. The pilot seems to be travelling along a path as unfrequented as the narrator's own earthly path had been moments before. But this ready identification, this anthropomorphizing of the pilot, is abruptly broken by the pilot's quick ascent into the blue. In the remainder of his great novel, as Proust brings back the theme of the aeroplane, and particularly its place in war's technology of death, he emphasizes that it is not the aeroplane that is the point, but rather the encounter with what is beyond habit, what has been intuited by sense experience: the encounter of authentic sublimity.

The gods, of course, are immortal and in the moment when they are manifested in form, the form is both radiantly without clarity in space and ephemeral, ungraspable, in time. We remember Christ's interdiction to Mary Magdalene (John 20: 14–18) in their encounter after the resurrection: 'Noli me tangere.' This experience of sublimity, as Kant so acutely wrote, results in the self-congratulation of the human mind that for a moment has gone beyond the possibilities of what it can know about its own form.[8] Beyond a threshold of fear, and on the edge of a threshold of pain, the mind's anticipatory joy accelerates – closure comes with the recognition of intuition, not in comprehension.

Proust is well aware that our sensual apprehension of objects can result in a breakdown in intelligibility to others. It is not just that the fetishist, obsessed with the magical power of objects, wants to keep things to himself, but that the involuntary dimension of intuition and the carrying over of impressions into memory is something private to us; something that in fact forms us through an arbitrary but over-determined contingency. It is this issue that Proust addresses in this second passage, from *The Captive*:

> in a drawing room as in everything else, the actual, external aspect, verifiable by everyone, is but the prolongation, the aspect which has detached itself from the outer world to take refuge in our soul, to which it gives as it were a surplus-value, in which it is absorbed into its habitual substance, transforming itself – houses that have been pulled down, people long dead, bowls of fruit at suppers which we recall – into that translucent alabaster of our memories of which we are incapable of conveying the colour which we alone can see,

so that we can truthfully say to other people, when speaking of these things of the past, that they can have no conception of them, that they are unlike anything they have seen, and that we ourselves cannot inwardly contemplate without a certain emotion, reflecting that it is on the existence of our thoughts that their survival for a little longer depends, the gleam of lamps that have been extinguished and the fragrance of arbours that will never bloom again. (Proust 1996 V: 379).

In Proust's study, houses, the image of a face, bowls of fruit at suppers, the letters of Madame de Sévigné, any objects or referents from sense experience, have the capacity to be totems of the dead, totems by which we carry forward a memory of the dead that can never be total.

In concert with Proust's project, it seems that the place to begin in thinking about the relations between sense experience and memory is not only in the philosophical debates on the status of the senses in relation to reality, or in the history of courtesy books and other documentary records of first-person experience, but also in the history of art as the history of human making in accordance with human ends of expression. Art in this sense gives us an insight into the intersubjective aspects of sense experience.

Notes

1. Chris Frith's paper at the 'Material Memories' conference, 'Varieties of Memory: Insights from Cognitive Neuroscience,' gives a neurological perspective that is very much in concert with Bergson's. Frith argues that 'immediate experience is always structured by memory' and contends that memory is 'a mechanism by which experience in the past affects behavior in the future.'

2. 'It seems probable that the newborn infant, with its undeveloped, inadequate capacity for homeostasis, requires these experiences for maintenance of his internal equilibrium' (Frank 1960: 7).

3. Aristotle, *De Anima*: 'Hence it is that taste also must be a sort of touch, because it is the sense for what is tangible and nutritious' (Aristotle 1941: 601). 'I call by the name of special object of this or that sense that which cannot be perceived by any other sense than that one and in respect of which no error is possible; in this sense colour is the special object of sight, sound of hearing, flavour of taste. Touch, indeed, discriminates more than one set of different qualities' (Aristotle 1941: 567).

4. See David Summers (1987) for a survey of the relations between classical and Renaissance ideas regarding the senses.

5. See Freud's 1909 essay, 'Notes Upon a Case of Obsessional Neurosis,' in the *Standard Edition* (Freud 1953). For a discussion of the relation of smell to this case, see Norman Kiell (1976: 158).

6. Aristotle emphasizes through the argument in Books II and III of *De Anima* (see Aristotle 1941: 577–83) that 'Whatever can be said of what is tangible, can be said of touch, and vice versa; if touch is not a single sense but a group of senses, there must be several kinds of what is tangible' (Aristotle 1941: 577). See the discussion of this point in Jean Starobinski (1989).

7. See generally Louise Vinge, *The Five Senses: Studies in a Literary Tradition* (1975). For an example of such a 'moralité,' see Morawski (1927: 71–85). A brief survey of the topos of the five senses is given as well in Chew (1962: 192–5). For a more detailed discussion of the motif of 'the banquet of sense,' see Kermode (1971).

8. Immanuel Kant, 'Analytic of the Sublime,' Book II of *The Critique of Judgment*: 'But when in intuiting nature we expand our empirical power of presentation (mathematically or dynamically), then reason, the ability to [think] an independent and absolute totality, never fails to step in and arouse the mind to an effort, although a futile one, to make the presentation of the senses adequate to this [idea of] totality. This effort, as well as the feeling that the imagination [as it synthesizes empirical nature] is unable to attain to that idea is itself an exhibition of the subjective purposiveness of our mind, in the use of our imagination, for the mind's supersensible vocation' (Kant 1987: 128).

Bibliography

Aristotle (1941), 'De Anima,' in R. McKeon (ed.), *The Basic Works of Aristotle*, New York: Random House.

Bergson, H. (1988), *Matter and Memory*, New York: Zone.

Chew, S. (1962), *The Pilgrimage of the Life of Man*, New Haven: Yale University Press.

Frank, L.K. (1960), 'Tactile Communication,' in E. Carpenter and M. McLuhan (eds), *Explorations in Communication: An Anthology*, Boston: Beacon Press, pp. 4–11.

Freud, S. (1953), *The Standard Edition of the Complete Psychological Works of Sigmund Freud*, trans. and ed. J. Strachey, 24 vols, London: Hogarth Press.

Janson, H.W. (1952), *Apes and Ape Lore in the Middle Ages and the Renaissance*, London: Warburg Institute.

Kant, I. (1987), 'Analytic of the Sublime,' Book II of *The Critique of Judgment*, ed. W.S. Pluhar, Indianapolis: Hackett.

Kermode, J.F. (1971), 'The Banquet of Sense,' in *Shakespeare, Spenser, Donne*, New York: Viking Press.

Kiell, N. (1976), *Varieties of Sexual Experience: Psychosexuality in Literature*, New York: International Universities Press.

Langer, S.K. (1972), *Mind: An Essay on Human Feeling*, 3 vols, Baltimore: Johns Hopkins University Press.

Marx, K. (1964), *Economic and Philosophic Manuscripts of 1844*, ed. D.J. Struick, trans. M. Milligan, New York: International Publishers.

Morawski, J. (1927), La 'Moralité' du Coeur et des Cinq Sens, *Revue des Langues Romanes*, 65: 71–85.

Philo (1929), *Philo*, trans. F.H. Colson and G.H. Whittaker, 10 vols, London: Heinemann.

Proust, M. (1996), *In Search of Lost Time*, trans. C.K. Scott Moncrieff and T. Kilmartin, rev. D.J. Enright, 6 vols, London: Vintage.

Starobinski, J. (1989), 'The Natural and Literary History of Bodily Sensation,' in M. Feher, R. Naddaff and N. Tazi (eds), *Fragments for a History of the Human Body, Part Two*, New York: Zone, pp. 350–405.

Summers, D. (1987), *The Judgment of Sense: Renaissance Naturalism and the Rise of Aesthetics*, Cambridge: Cambridge University Press.

Vinge, L. (1975), *The Five Senses: Studies in a Literary Tradition*, Lund: Royal Society of Letters at Lund.

4

The Witch's Senses

Sensory Ideologies and Transgressive Femininities from the Renaissance to Modernity

Constance Classen

In the European hierarchy of the senses, the sensibilities of women traditionally ranked low. While men had mastery of the 'higher' senses of sight and hearing, women were linked with the 'lower' senses of touch, taste and smell. Both men and women were understood to make practical use of all of their senses: men could touch, women could see. Nonetheless, touch, along with taste and smell, was imagined to be essentially feminine in nature: nurturing, seductive, dissolute in its merging of self and other. Sight, and to a lesser extent hearing, was essentially masculine: dominating, rational, orderly in its discrete categorization of the world.

The symbolic division of perception into masculine and feminine territories carried immense social weight. Men were believed to be empowered by God and nature to see and oversee the world. Women were required by the same forces to stay at home, stitching the clothes, stirring the stew, and rocking the cradle. According to the seventeenth century *English Housewife* the list of skills deemed necessary for a 'complete woman' included: 'skill in physic [healing], cookery, banqueting-stuff, distillation, perfumes, wool, hemp, flax, dairies, brewing, baking, and all other things belonging to a household' (Markham 1986). No need to read or write, to participate in public discourses, nor even to set foot in the great world outside. The feminine sensory sphere consisted of labors associated with the intimately corporeal senses of touch, taste and smell.

The fact that feminine sensibilities were considered to be inferior and subservient to the masculine gaze did not, however, necessarily indicate a lack of potency. The so-called lower senses had powers of their own, powers that emanated from their presumed primal, irrational nature. Properly, women used their senses to care for their families: cooking, cleaning, sewing and nurturing. Improperly they dedicated their senses to fulfilling the coarse cravings considered innate to women: greed, lust, and a perverse desire for social dominion. Most improperly, women imbued their animal sensuality with supernatural force and became witches.

When the witch hunters undertook their great purge of the devil in human form in the fifteenth, sixteenth and seventeenth centuries one of their goals was to constrain the transgressive power of feminine sensuality. The witch was described as having a diabolic sensorium in which each of the senses was perverted from its proper use and endowed with satanic powers. The witch hunters took to heart St. Augustine's warning that the devil 'places himself in figures, he adapts himself to colors, he attaches himself to sounds, he lurks in angry and wrongful conversation, he abides in smells, he impregnates with flavors and fills with certain exhalations all the channels of the understanding' (Kramer and Sprenger 1948: 32). The threat posed by the witch's sensory powers was considered so grave it was suggested in Germany that accused witches be conveyed to prison blindfolded, gagged, and wheeled in a barrow (Lea 1957, I: 257).

The basis of the witch's powers was the suspect female sensorium. While men could be accused of witchcraft as well as women, the witch was typically represented as female and most of the witches brought to trial were women (Merchant 1980: 138). (Even male witches were symbolically female in their alliance with 'feminine' forces of corruption.) In the case of the witch all the faults customarily attributed to women were magnified and demonized. To begin with, witches defied sensory and social norms by using the feminine senses of touch, taste and smell as media for self-gratification, rather than self-sacrifice, and as avenues for empowerment, rather than instruments of service.

The most dangerous of the feminine senses was touch. A woman's touch was believed capable of debilitating and destabilizing men's bodies and minds. The biblical story of Samson provided an archetypal example of this effect, for Samson was robbed of his incredible strength when he lay his head in the lap of the seductive, deceitful Delilah (Judges: 13–16). The debilitating effect of feminine tactility was not only a matter of folklore, it was grounded in contemporary physiological theories. Such theories held that an excessive loss of semen led to physical and mental degeneration – as well as to blindness – in men. (As an added sign of his emasculation through the agency of female sensuality, Samson was blinded, deprived of his masculine visual power, by his captors.)

From a moral perspective, the gravest danger to masculine integrity posed by feminine tactility lay in its enticement to sin. So fearful were some of the early Christian monks of the corrupting powers of female sensuality that they fled even the touch of their mothers. If women gave life through their bodies, they were also imagined to deal death. Each carnal act was believed to sap a little more of the masculine life force so that a woman's touch ultimately ended in a man's death. John Donne described this notion in verse form in *The Anatomy of the World* (cited in Merchant 1980: 133).

> For [Adam and Eve's] marriage was our funerall:
> One woman at one blow, then killed us all.
> And singly, one by one, they kill us now.
> We doe delightfully our selves allow
> To that consumption; and profusely blinde,
> Wee kill our selves to propagate our kinde.

The constructive/destructive nature of feminine touch was dramatically illustrated by the spider – the zoological emblem of the sense of touch. Industriously spinning its web, the spider stood for the good housewife. Trapping and killing its prey, the spider signified the evil seductress.

While women's touch was generally suspect, it was the witch in whom touch reached its zenith of malevolent power. The 'touch of a witch is noxious and fatal,' wrote Nicholas Rémy in *Demonolatry* (Rémy 1930: 244). Witch hunting manuals anxiously warned that judges 'must not allow themselves to be touched physically by the witch' (Kramer and Sprenger 1948: 228). Witches, however, were also able to make their touch felt at a distance by, for example, piercing wax effigies of their victims. (When witches themselves were tortured, the Devil was believed to render them impervious to pain.)

The witch, who essentially represented a sinister image of woman freed of all moral constraints, was also the seductress par excellence. 'All witchcraft comes from carnal lust,' declared the fifteenth century witch hunting guide, *Malleus Maleficarum*. The witch continually sought out victims for her lust because, as the guide knowledgeably informed its readers, the 'mouth of the womb' is insatiable (Kramer and Sprenger 1948: 47). The witch had all the desires considered natural to women along with the supernatural powers with which to fulfill them. This combination was deemed so threatening to male supremacy that accounts circulated of men losing their genitals as a result of an encounter with a witch (Kramer and Spreager 1948: 119).

While the touch of a witch might set men aflame with desire, in thermal terms witches were cold. Ancient Greek humoral theory, which remained influential into modernity, characterized women as cold and wet in nature, and men as hot and dry. The distinct forms of male and female bodies were held to be due to these sensory traits. 'Cold, moist' women had soft, plump bodies. 'Hot, dry' men had firm, lean bodies. While heat caused male organs of generation to externalize, coldness kept female organs of generation nestled within the body. Heat and dryness supposedly made men vigorous, steadfast and forthright; cold and wetness made women inactive, unstable and deceitful (Maclean 1980: 31–5). The reputed coldness of the witch, and her association with dark, dank caves, confirmed her essential femininity and her destabilizing influence on society. When witches were burnt at the stake, their cold, wet feminine subversiveness was vanquished by hot, dry masculine righteousness.

What of the witch's other sensory attributes? When it came to taste, witches were notoriously gluttonous, for it was not just the 'mouth of the womb' which was deemed to be insatiable in women. André le Chapelain wrote in his *Art of Courtly Love* (1941: 207) that 'Woman is... such a slave to her belly that there is nothing she would be ashamed to assent to if she were assured of a fine meal, and no matter how much she has she never has any hope that she can satisfy her appetite when she is hungry.'

This feminine failing was traced back to the first woman, Eve, who brought sin into the world by craving the forbidden fruit in the Garden of Eden. In order to subdue their appetites, virtuous women were expected to lead lives of gustatory restraint. A sixteenth century behavioral guide for women, for example, counsels women to eat little and to remember that 'our first mother was thrown out of Paradise for a bite of food, and that many maidens... who went out of their homes in search of tasty delicacies lost their chastity' (Vives 1947: 1011). The most virtuous of women scarcely ate at all, as we learn from the biographies of fasting female saints (Bynum 1987).

While holy women had visions in which they spurned offers of food from demons (Bynum 1987: 147), witches were quite ready to satisfy their appetites through diabolic means. One Italian woman accused of witchcraft in 1432 confessed that she had 'begged [the Devil] for food [and] when he spread a quantity of food on the grass... she ate some... ' (Lea 1957, I: 232–33). Witches compounded Eve's sinful gluttony by eating the forbidden fruit of human flesh (as in the old fairy tales in which the witch eats the children she lures with treats). The witch's consumption of human beings was another sign of uncontrolled feminine fluidity transgressing the boundaries between self and other.

Also within the domain of taste, the witch perverted the traditional womanly role of food-giver by serving up poisons and potions. Poisoning, like witchcraft, was imagined to be a peculiarly feminine vice: 'As women in all ages have beene counted most apt to conceive witchcraft... so also it appeareth, that they have been the first inventers, and principal practisers of poisoning' declared the sixteenth century *Discoverie of Witchcraft* (Scot 1964: 112). The creation of magical potions, in turn, was a supernatural elaboration of the feminine art of cookery. The witch's brew had its basis in mother's stew.

Evil odors were another typical product of witchcraft. Witches manifested their potency through their olfactory emanations. When disguised as a beautiful temptress, the witch emitted a heavy, sweet scent which acted like a drug on her victims. When appearing as her own evil self, she emitted a malefic stink: '[Witches] exhale a stench from the mouth, the whole body, which is communicated to their garments and fills their houses and the vicinity and infects those who approach' (Lea 1957, III: 1489). Either way, the scent of a witch was a force of corruption and death.

The poisonous reek of the witch was an intensified form of the foul odor attributed to women in general. The cold wetness of the female body was imagined to predispose it to putridity. Not only did women corrupt others through their sensuality, therefore – they were themselves in a continuous state of decay. This putridity was particularly manifested in the production of odorous menstrual fluids. Even aside from any sorcerous intent, the odor of menstruation was believed to have malevolent influence (Martensen 1991: 107–9; Jacquart and Thomasset 1988: 73–5, 173–7). 'Women are... monthly filled full of superfluous humours,' the *Discoverie of Witchcraft* stated, 'whereof spring vapours, and are carried up, and conveyed through the nostrils and mouth, etc., to the bewitching of whatsoever it meet' (Scot 1964: 236). The noxious emissions natural to women were intensified in the case of the witch, whose physical putridity matched her moral corruption. The only women who were free from the malodors of decay were the fasting holy women who reputedly stopped menstruating and instead emitted a hot, dry, preservative 'odor of sanctity.'

The brews and potions of the witch were likewise powerfully aromatic. Odors were attributed a range of effects in premodern medicine, from transmitting and preventing illness to easing headaches and stomachaches (Classen, Howes and Synnott 1994: 40–2, 58–62). The odors, and flavors, of medicaments were hence believed to play a vital role in their curative power (Coulter 1975). As women were responsible for their families' health, every housewife was expected to know how to concoct a variety of remedies at home, often on the basis of aromatic herbs. Just as the witch's brew was based on mother's stew, the scented enchantments of the witch were an elaboration of the housewife's aromatic remedies. (In medieval Switzerland, for instance, peasant women were said to cause storms by boiling foul herbs in a pot and then exposing the pot to the sun – Lea 1957, I: 144.)

Touch, taste and smell. The sensory bases of both domesticity and witchcraft. One of the horrors of witchcraft, in fact, was that it made use of the domestic instruments and practices that were intended to keep women safely at home to transgress the social and cosmic order. A pot might be used for cooking dinner or for brewing a spell, a needle might be used for sewing clothes or for piercing an effigy, a broom might be used for sweeping the floor or for flying out the window. The tactile, gustatory and olfactory practices which were expected to keep women confined to close quarters, were transformed by witchcraft into media for mastering the world.

Witchcraft not only demonized the feminine sensorium by subverting the 'lower' 'feminine' senses, however. It also insidiously appropriated the 'higher' 'masculine' senses of sight and hearing, as well as the faculty of speech – sometimes characterized as a sixth 'sense.' Women's hearing was supposed to be guarded, both because discourses of state and erudition were above women's mental capacities and because women were easily misled. The Church father Tertullian wrote in this regard that 'evil angels were ever lurking about ready to assail even married women, much more virgins, through their ears' (Conybeare 1910: 233). The witch, however, was always listening in, eager for forbidden knowledge, and harkening to the words of the Devil.

Women's speech was similarly restricted. Ideally, men spoke and women were silent. In practice, women were imagined to speak non-stop (Vives 1947: 1042–44). In *The Art of Courtly Love* André le Chapelain advised men that all women are 'loud-mouthed' and will 'keep up a clamor all day like a barking dog' (le Chapelain 1941: 207). Women's compulsive orality was considered another product of their feminine fluidity: they gushed with speech as they gushed with body fluids. This connection was not merely symbolic for feminine volubility was held by some to result from uterine vapors irritating the brain (Maclean 1980: 41).

In relation to men, women were accused of two kinds of speech: seductive and nagging. The first employed feminine allurements, the second appropriated masculine authority. Often women were represented as becoming over-bearing nags after marriage. Thus the title character of *Epicoene or The Silent Woman* by Ben Jonson is a quiet-spoken woman who turns into a mannish loud-mouth after marriage, whereupon she is revealed to actually be a man in disguise (Jonson 1966). In the seventeenth century play *Lingua*, Speech, personified as a woman, is accused of being a witch and a whore, of criticizing men in authority, and of lending wives 'weapons to fight against their husbands' (Tomkis 1964: 331–463).

The witch's speech had all the factious, deceitful, seductive characteristics of women's speech endowed with supernatural influence. The authors of the *Malleus Maleficarum* wrote of the witch: 'For as she is a liar by nature, so in her speech she stings while she delights us. Wherefore her voice is like the song of the Sirens, who with their sweet melody entice the passers-by and kill them' (Kramer and Sprenger 1948: 46). Whether it wooed or cursed, sorcerous speech joined the other noxious effluvia of the witch's body.

Traditionally the highest sense in the sensorium was sight. It was the most noble, rational and masculine of the senses. As fundamentally irrational beings, women could scarcely be capable of manifesting clearsightedness. John Knox wrote in 1558: 'For who can deny but it repugneth nature that the blind shall be appointed to lead and conduct such as do see... And such be all women compared unto man in bearing of authority. For their sight in civil regiment is but blindness' (Knox 1985: 42–3).

As the free exercise of vision was considered presumptuous and dangerous in women, they were encouraged to keep their eyes downcast and to limit their visual scope to their home (Vives 1947: 1001, 1021, 1036). 'Put out their eyes if they wyll looke or gase undecentyle' urged 'A Rule for Women to Brynge Up Their Daughters' in 1566 (Hull 1982: 76).

When the witch defied convention and made herself mistress of the sense of sight, vision could no longer retain its association with reason. The demonic and feminine form of vision employed by the witch, therefore, became a medium of derangement. Hence Reginald Scot wrote in the *Discoverie of Witchcraft* that witches 'have such an unbridled force of furie and concupiscence naturallie that... upon everie trifling occasion, they (like brute beasts) fix their furious eies upon the partie whom they bewitch' (Scot 1964: 236). The witch's evil eye might injure a victim's body or gain mastery of his mind. 'We know from some experience,' the witch hunters inform us, 'that some witches... have importunately begged their gaolers... that they should be allowed to look at the Judge before he looks at them; and by so getting the first sight of the Judge they have been able so to alter the minds of the Judge or his assessors that they have lost all their anger against them' (Scot 1964: 236). Here sight is functioning more like a seductive/destructive smell or touch than the august medium of reason and order it ideally represented.

Once brought within the irrational, feminine domain of the witch, in fact, sight was degraded until it resembled one of the lower senses. The gaze of the witch was said to actually transmit a form of venom through the eyes, which then poisoned its victims. In this it was likened to the supposedly turbid, harmful sight of the menstruous woman. According to Aristotle, for example, the glance of a menstruating woman could tarnish a mirror (Thomas 1971: 438). The fact that it was often older, menopausal, women who were accused of witchcraft was not thought to disprove this association. It was rather explained that, as older women no longer had the natural outlet of menstruation for their corrupt internal fluids, the amount of venom issuing from their eyes was even greater than in young women (Jacquart and Thomasset 1988: 75). At times it is unclear in the treatises on witchcraft whether sorcery is a deviation from, or an outcome of, the feminine condition. The crucial issue was often that of women's moral responsibility for their evil actions (Merchant 1980: 140–3).

The malevolent gaze of the witch put the finishing touch, so to speak, on her sensory sorcery. George Sinclair wrote in *Satan's Invisible World Discovered* that 'Men and Women have been wronged by the touch of a Witches hand, by the breath and kiss of their mouth... [and] by their looks... as when a Witch sendeth forth from her heart thorow her eyes venemous and poysonful Spirits as Rayes' (cited in Lea 1957, III: 1326). In *The Discoverie of Witchcraft*, Scot (1964: 399) declared that though the witch's enchantments might 'begin by touching or breathing, it is alwaies accomplished and finished by the eie.'

The opposition between the eye of sorcery and the eye of reason, can, in retrospect, be seen as an opposition between mythological and rational understandings of the world, as well as between feminine and masculine typologies (Bordo 1987). The era of the witch hunts was a crucial period of development for the scientific world view that would come to dominate European thought. The scientist and the witch worked side by side, so to speak, for a century or more. During this period, indeed, dedication to the new experimental philosophy often coexisted with a belief in witchcraft (Easlea 1980: 201–7). For the scientist confidently to take charge of the cosmos, however, the witch had to be expelled. The 'old wives' tales' of the past needed to be replaced by, as the secretary of the Royal Society in England put it in 1664, the 'accurate observations and experiments... [of] a masculine philosophy' (Oldenburg 1965: 667). This involved not simply burning witches (because new witches could always take their place), but discrediting witchcraft itself, so that no witch could ever gain power again.

A revealing account of this ideological shift is recorded in the encounter of the prominent seventeenth century physician and 'experimental philosopher' William Harvey with a reputed witch. Harvey visited the witch in order to establish for himself the existence or non-existence of sorcery. Once in her home, the doctor sent the witch away on a pretext and then proceeded to dissect her familiar, a toad. Harvey's examination of the toad's entrails convinced him that this 'witch's familiar' was just like any other toad, and that the 'witch' was therefore just a deluded woman (Keynes 1966: 214).

Discovering that a presumed witch's familiar in the form of a toad was identical in its inner workings to all the other toads he had dissected was proof enough for Harvey of the non-existence of witchcraft. This discovery had a wider importance as well, for the experimental model required a world that was regular and consistent in nature in order to work. The results of experiments would not be reliable if supernatural forces, such as witchcraft, could transgress natural laws.

Ideally, Harvey would no doubt have liked to dissect the witch herself and establish *her* 'true nature' by peering into *her* insides. The toad stood as a substitute for the witch, an alter ego, and an appropriate representative of cold, wet, degenerate femininity. When Harvey dissected the witch's toad, he symbolically exposed the dark secrets of feminine nature to the rational masculine gaze.

Contemporary science, in fact, tended to view all of Nature either as a recalcitrant witch who had to be tortured into a confession, or as a coy female who must be obliged to reveal herself by the experimental method (Merchant 1980: 164–91; Jordanova 1989). In his program for the development of science, Francis Bacon insisted that 'nature exhibits herself more clearly under the *trials* and *vexations* of [experimentation] than when left to herself' (cited in Merchant 1980: 169). Thomas Sprat wrote in his seventeenth century *History of the Royal Society* that through the application of the new experimental philosophy 'the Beautiful Bosom of Nature will be Expos'd to our view' (Spratt 1966: 327). J.T. Desaguliers (cited by Nicolson 1966: 136) would later claim of Newton:

> Nature compell'd his piercing Mind obeys
> And gladly shows him all her secret Ways;
> 'Gainst Mathematics she has no Defence,
> And yields t'experimental Consequence.

In the new world order, unruly femininity was expected to be regulated and contained. The witch hunts had warned women that, just as they should not strive for mastery through the masculine domains of sight, hearing or speech, so they should not seek to empower themselves through traditional feminine pursuits associated with touch, taste and smell. Once the Age of Reason purportedly vanquished the specter of witchcraft, the potentially supernatural dimensions of women's work disappeared. Cooking, cleaning, and other housewifely chores were no longer paths to cosmic power and they duly contracted into their 'proper' domestic sphere.

Yet the supposed dangers of the feminine temperament were hardly eliminated. When, in the account of Harvey's meeting with a 'witch,' the woman returned home, she reputedly 'flew like a Tigris at [Harvey's] face' on finding her toad dissected. The report of the incident tells us that 'twas well his eyes were out of reach, well guarded with prominent bones, otherways it had gone ill with him' (Keynes 1966: 214–5). Significantly, the very moment when Harvey's witch is apparently revealed as a fraud is when she is described as most witch-like in her behavior. She is said to 'fly' at Harvey like a wild beast and to attack his eyes – the sensory seat of masculine rationality. The account informs us that the 'Good Doctor' was only able to escape by threatening to turn the woman over to the authorities. Even when they are divested of supernatural potential, therefore, female sensibilities still require strong social control to keep them in check.

Influential as they were, these cultural constructions of female sensuality did not go unchallenged. In the fifteenth century, for example, the French writer Christine de Pizan refuted many of the commonplaces concerning the nature of women. In *The Book of the City of Ladies* she lamented the number of 'famous men... so clear-sighted in all things, as it seemed' who had attacked woman's character: 'I could hardly find a book on morals where... I did not find several chapters or certain sections attacking women' (Pizan 1982: 4). In *The City of Ladies*, Reason, personified as a woman, defends the feminine reputation. To the contention that 'woman are naturally lecherous and gluttonous,' 'Lady Reason' responds that women are naturally sober and restrained. The notion that women are garrulous is countered with examples of women's wise speech. The physical weakness of women, in turn, is said to be compensated for by their 'freer and sharper' minds (Pizan 1982: 23, 25–6, 29–30).

In 1600 the Italian Humanist Lucrezia Marinelli published an essay on 'The Nobility and Excellence of Women.' In this work Marinelli assigned positive values to many traditional female sensory traits. For example, Marinelli argued that the coldness of women is more conducive to rational judgment than the heat of men, which overexcites the brain. It is only when men cool down with age that they become reasonable: 'In middle aged man the intensity of the warmth becomes more tepid than in youth, and coming closer to the feminine nature, he acts more wisely and maturely' (Allen and Salvatore 1992: 22).

Feminine fluidity, according to Marinelli, has similar advantages to coldness, acting to dampen excessive passion. As to women's purported foul odor, Marinelli argued that this characteristic more properly belongs to men, who are careless with their hygiene, than to women, who 'hate messiness which renders their pretty bodies ugly, and all those things that emanate stinky odor' (Allen and Salvatore 1992: 28). Speaking from experience, Marinellli notes that in some cases 'such a stench comes forth from [men] that women who stand by them are obliged to plug their nose' (Allen and Salvatore 1992: 28). Marinelli also clears women of the charge of deceitful speech and reattributes it to men, who slander women with their lies. All in all, according to Marinelli, '[women's] senses are ruled by reason' and not by corrupt passions (Allen and Salvatore 1992: 21).

Masculine domination of the rising field of science was also challenged by a number of women. In the seventeenth century one of these was Margaret Cavendish (a writer whose outpouring of texts on all subjects suggested to many a literary transcription of feminine fluidity).[1] Cavendish considered that women's experience in the kitchen gave them a sound basis for conducting experimental inquiries into Nature: 'Our Female-sex... would prove good experimental Philosophers, and inform the world how to make Artificial Snow, by their Creams, or Possets beaten in froth; and Ice, by their clear, candied, or crusted Quiddities or Conserves of fruits; and Frost, by their candied herbs and flowers... ' (Cavendish 1668: 105). Nature herself, acccording to Cavendish, was a housewife, employing her time 'in Brewing, Baking, Churning, Spinning, Sowing' (Cavendish 1668: 102). Women, therefore, with their domestic skills, were more likely to comprehend Nature's ways than men.

Likewise, Cavendish's husband responded to the question of Cavendish's qualifications for writing on matters of medicine, by saying such knowledge was common to any 'good Farmer's wife in the Country' (Cavendish 1655a: 'An Epistle'). If experimental philosophy was a new territory for women, medicine, at least, was not. Although the 'wise woman,' with her stock of remedies and charms, was often considered sister to the witch (Scot wrote that 'witch' and 'wise woman' were interchangeable terms – Thomas 1971: 436), the practices of healing generally fell within the feminine sphere. A prominent medieval female healer in Paris, for example, was described as 'touching, feeling and holding [patients'] pulses, body, and limbs'; inspecting urine samples, administering 'syrups to drink, comforting, laxative, digestive... ,' preparing 'baths and bandages,' and employing aromatic herbs – 'camomile leaves, meliot, and very many others' (Ross and McLaughlin 1949: 635–40). The healer in question was denounced for operating in the community at large and thereby usurping the role of the male physician, nonetheless, the techniques she employed (and which were common to the medical practice of the time) were themselves not far removed from customary housewifely activities. Indeed, as late as 1684, an English book of culinary and medicinal recipes exhorted women to be their 'own Chirugiens and Physicians, unless the case be desperate' (Wooley 1684: 8).

In the seventeenth and eighteenth centuries, however, medicine gradually distanced itself from the domestic realm, and from the feminine senses of touch, taste and smell. (The medical efficacy of odors and flavors, for example, was increasingly disavowed by physicians.) In general, while sensuous forms of healing continued to enjoy a certain popularity, by the eighteenth century they were often typed as quackery by the medical academy (Williams 1975). With the development of sight-based practices and technologies, such as anatomical dissection, clinical observation and microscopic analysis, medicine was transformed into a primarily *visual* science, suitable only for men (see Hillman 1997; Foucault 1975).[2]

Healing was further taken out of female hands by the increased pro-fessionalization of the field, for women were forbidden to follow men into university. Thus Gervase Markham, the author of another seventeenth century guide for housewives, decisively stated: '[The] most excellent art of physic is far beyond the capacity of the most skilful woman,... lodging only in the breast of the learned professors'; in his attack on 'Lady Doctors' the eighteenth century physician James M. Adair announced: 'it is time for the ladies to retire' (cited in Schiebinger 1989: 116).[3]

Even though scientific investigation might be firmly established as masculine territory, many women were still eager to try their hand at it. This feminine invasion of alien ground gave rise to many pointed jibes about women who forsake their proper sensory field to master masculine domains of sight. The 1726 play *The Humours of Oxford*, for example, commented that 'a Woman makes as ridiculous a Figure, poring over Globes, or thro' a Telescope, as a Man would... mending Lace' (Miller 1963: 79). In Molière's satire of scholarly women, *Les femmes savantes*, a husband complains that his wife has deserted the kitchen for the observatory: 'No science is too profound for [women]... They know about the movements of the moon, the North Star, Venus, Saturn, and Mars... but they don't know how my dinner, which I need, is coming along' (Molière 1896: Act 2, Scene 7). In *The Humours of Oxford*, 'Lady Science' confesses: 'I am justly made a Fool of for aiming to...

move into a Sphere that did not belong to me... I will destroy all my Globes, Quadrants, Spheres, Prisms, Microscopes... ' (Miller 1963: 79).

Yet not all women were convinced of the validity of scientific visualism, whether or not they were excluded from it. In her story *New Blazing World*, Cavendish positioned herself as Empress of a land inhabited by 'bear-men' experimental philosophers, 'bird-men' astronomers and 'ape-men' chemists, among others. The bear-men scientists try to understand nature by examining it through telescopes and microscopes. It soon becomes evident, however, that such magnifying lenses have a series of defects which lead them to present a grossly distorted image of the world. Lenses can produce a magnified image of a louse, but not of a whale; they can operate in light but not in darkness; they can enhance one sense but are no use to any of the others (Cavendish 1992: 140–5, 150–1). Their very reliance on light, in fact, makes it impossible for 'optick glasses' to perceive 'the obscure actions of Nature' (Cavendish 1668: Preface). The bear-men scientists themselves confess that 'their glasses would do them but little service in the bowels of the earth' (Cavendish 1992: 150). The inhabitants of the inner earth then enter the story to explain that they employ alternative modes of perception in their world. Optic devices can be of no use in discerning the non-visual lives of these beings unless scientists can provide 'glasses as are proper for their perception' (Cavendish 1992: 151).

The Empress tells the bear-men that: 'Your glasses are false informers, and instead of discovering the truth, delude your senses, wherefore I command you to break them' (Cavendish 1992: 141). The eye-minded bear-men, however, cannot do without their optical aids: '[They] kneeled down, and in the humblest manner petitioned that they might not be broken; for, said they, we take more delight in artificial delusions than in natural truths' (Cavendish 1992: 142). The experimenters are allowed to keep their lenses on condition that they not cause any public disturbance. While in Cavendish's own country experimental philosophers were shaping a new understanding of the world, in her fictional kingdom she makes them sources of irrationality and social disorder. Cavendish indicates the ultimate futility of trying to comprehend all mysteries through the power of sight by leaving her deluded bear-men hard at work on a magnifying glass by means of which 'they could spy out a vacuum' (Cavendish 1992: 145).

In another story by Cavendish, 'The Travelling Spirits,' a man asks a witch to help him travel to the moon. The witch responds that she is unable to do so, as 'the Natural Philosophers are the only men for that Journey' (Cavendish 1656: 249). ('It was not a Woman that invented Perspective-Glasses to pierce into the Moon' – Cavendish (1655b): 'To the Reader.') After other requests for journeys are turned down by the witch, the man finally asks her to take him to the center of the earth. 'That I can do (said she), and so obscurely, that the Natural Philosophers shall never spye us' (Cavendish 1656: 251).

The center of the earth in this story can be understood to represent the dark, inner, feminine world of sensibility, a world readily accessible to the witch, but inaccessible to the eye of reason or the instruments of modern technology. If one accepts Cavendish's subversive cosmology, it would seem that Harvey's eye-opening dissection failed to establish the unreality of witchcraft, that experimental philosophies cannot altogether fathom the secrets of Nature, and that there are some aspects of existence that cannot be forced into visibility.

Notes

1. For an analysis of Margaret Cavendish's struggles with and challenges to the gendered sensory order see Classen (1998: 98–106).

2. Botany was among the last of the new scientific fields to be removed from the feminine domain. The study of plants was thought to be a harmless and suitable hobby for women (who were themselves often compared to flowers), and as late as 1827 it was lamented that 'serious' male scholars of botany had to rely on the expertise of a 'garrulous old woman or pedantic spinster' (Schteir 1996: 111).

3. An eighteenth century verse warned male physicians of the threat to their income and status posed by female folk healers (Williams 1975: 184):

Dame Nature has giv'n her a Doctor's Degree,
She gets all the Patients and pockets the Fee;
So if you don't instantly prove her a Cheat,
She'll loll in her Chariot while you walk the street.

Bibliography

Allen, P. and Salvatore, F. (1992), 'Lucrezia Marinelli and Woman's Identity in Late Italian Renaissance,' *Renaissance and Reformation*, 28(4): 5–39.

Bordo, S. (1987), *The Flight to Objectivity: Essays on Cartesianism and Culture*, Albany NY: State University of New York Press.

Bynum, C.W. (1987), *Holy Feast and Holy Fast: The Religious Significance of Food to Medieval Women*, Berkeley: University of California Press.

Cavendish, M. (1655a), *The Philosophical and Physical Opinions*, London: J. Martin & J. Allestrye.

—— (1655b), *The World's Olio*, London: J. Martin & J. Allestrye.

—— (1656), *Nature's Pictures Drawn by Fancies Pencil to the Life*, London: J. Martin & J. Allestrye.

—— (1668), *Observations Upon Experimental Philosophy*, London: A. Maxwell.

—— (1992), *The Description of A New World Called The Blazing World*, ed. K. Lilley, London: William Pickering.

Chapelain, A. le. (1941), *The Art of Courtly Love*, trans. J.J. Parry, New York: Frederick Ungar.

Classen, C. (1998), *The Color of Angels: Cosmology, Gender and the Aesthetic Imagination*, London: Routledge.

——, Howes, D. and Synnott, A. (1994), *Aroma: The Cultural History of Smell*, London: Routledge.

Conybeare, F.C. (1910), *Myth, Magic and Morals: A Study of Christian Origins*, London: Watts.

Coulter, H.L. (1975), *Divided Legacy: A History of the Schism in Medical Thought*, vol. 1, Washington: Wehawken.

Easlea, B. (1980), *Witch Hunting, Magic and the New Philosophy: An Introduction to Debates of the Scientific Revolution 1450–1750*, Brighton: The Harvester Press.

Foucault, M. (1975), *The Birth of the Clinic: An Archaeology of Medical Perception*, trans. S. Smith, New York: Random House.

Hillman, D. (1997), 'Visceral Knowledge,' in D. Hillman and C. Mazzio (eds), *The Body in Parts: Fantasies of Corporeality in Early Modern Europe*, London: Routledge.

Hull, S.W. (1982), *Chaste, Silent and Obedient: English Books for Women, 1475–1640*, San Francisco CA: Huntingdon Library.

Jacquart, D. and Thomasset, C. (1988), *Sexuality and Medicine in the Middle Ages*, Princeton: Princeton University Press.

Jonson, B. (1966). *Epicoene or The Silent Woman*, ed. L.A. Beaurline, Lincoln: University of Nebraska Press.

Jordanova, L. (1989), *Sexual Visions: Images of Gender in Science and Medicine between the Eighteenth and Twentieth Centuries*, New York: Harvester Wheatsheaf.

Keynes, G. (1966), *The Life of William Harvey*, Oxford: Clarendon Press.

Knox, J. (1985), 'The First Blast of the Trumpet Against the Monstruous Regiment of Women,' in M.A. Breslow (ed.), *The Political Writings of John Knox*, Washington: Folger Books.

Lea, H.C. (1957), *Materials Toward a History of Witchcraft*, 3 vols, New York: Thomas Yoseloff.

Maclean, I. (1980), *The Renaissance Notion of Women: A Study in the Fortunes of Scholasticism and Medical Science in European Intellectual Life*, Cambridge: Cambridge University Press.

Markham, G. (1986), *The English Housewife*, ed. M.R. Best, Montreal: McGill-Queens University Press.

Martensen, R. (1994), 'The Transformation of Eve: Women's Bodies, Medicine and Culture in Early Modern Europe,' in R. Porter and M. Teich (eds), *Sexual Knowledge, Sexual Science: The History of Attitudes to Sexuality*, Cambridge: Cambridge University Press, pp. 107–33.

Merchant, C. (1980), *The Death of Nature: Women, Ecology and the Scientific Revolution*, New York: Harper & Row.

Miller, J. (1963), 'The Humours of Oxford,' in H.W. Wells (ed.), *Three Centuries of English and American Plays: England, 1500–1800*, vol. 3, New York: Redex Microprint Corporation.

Molière, J.-B. (1896). *Les Femmes savantes*, Boston: D.C. Heath.

Nicolson, M.H. (1966), *Newton Demands the Muse: Newton's Opticks and the Eighteenth Century Poets*, Princeton: Princeton University Press.

Oldenburg, H. (1965), 'The Publisher to the Reader,' in R. Boyle, *Experiments and Considerations Touching Colours*, in R. Boyle, *The Works*, ed. T. Birch, Hildesheim Germany: Georg Olms.

Pizan, C. de. (1982), *The Book of the City of Ladies*, trans. E.J. Richards, New York: Persea Books.

Rémy, N. (1930), *Demonolatry*, trans. E.A. Ashwin, London: John Rodker.

Ross, J.B. and McLaughlin, M.M. (eds) (1949), *The Portable Medieval Reader*, New York: Viking.

Schiebinger, L. (1989), *The Mind Has No Sex? Women in the Origins of Modern Science*, Cambridge MA: Harvard University Press.

Schteir, A.B. (1996), *Cultivating Women, Cultivating Science: Flora's Daughters and Botany in England, 1760 to 1860*, Baltimore: The Johns Hopkins University Press.

Scot, R. (1964), *The Discoverie of Witchcraft*, London: Centaur Press.

Spratt, T. (1966), *History of the Royal Society*, ed. J.I. Cope and H.W. Jones, St. Louis MI: Washington University Press.

Thomas, K. (1971), *Religion and the Decline of Magic: Studies in Popular Beliefs in Sixteenth and Seventeenth Century England*, London: Weidenfeld and Nicolson.

Tomkis, T. (1964), 'Lingua,' in W. Carew Hazlitt, *A Select Collection of Old English Plays*, New York: Benjamin Bloom.

Vives, J.L. (1947), 'Formación de la mujer cristiana,' in J.L. Vives, *Obras completas*, vol 1, ed.. L. Riber, Madrid: M. Aguilar.

Williams, G. (1975), *The Age of Agony: The Art of Healing 1700–1800*, London: Constable.

Wooley, H. (1684), *The Queen-like Closet or Rich Cabinet*, London: R. Chiswel.

5

The Senses Divided
Organs, Objects, and Media in
Early Modern England

Carla Mazzio

It is precisely because [physical pain] takes no object that it, more than any
other phenomenon, resists objectification in language.

Elaine Scarry, *The Body in Pain*

The history of the senses has been, essentially, the history of their objectification. Elaine Scarry (expanding on Marx's account of commodification),
writes that the 'socialization of sentience,' marks a process in which
'freestanding objects,' such as the telephone or tape recorder, 'remake the live
body' and 'make sentience itself an artifact' (Scarry 1985: 255). In a similar
vein, Raymond Williams (1990: 158) opens his essay on the reification of
'the medium' in aesthetic theory with an example drawn from a Renaissance
definition of sight:

'To the Sight three things are required, the Object, the Organ and the Medium.'
Here a description of the practical activity of seeing, which is a whole and
complex process of relationship between the developed organs of sight and
the accessible properties of things seen, is characteristically interrupted by
the invention of a third term ('medium') which is given its own properties, in
abstraction from the practical relationship. This general notion of intervening
and in effect causal substances, on which various practical operations were
believed to depend, had a long course in scientific thought.

This example marks, for Williams, an early history of the objectification of
'process' by a focus on mediation, in which 'a constitutive human activity
is... abstracted and objectified' (Williams 1990: 158). The question I wish

to address in this essay is whether such mediation extends in equal measure to all of the senses, particularly touch. For in contrast to vision and hearing (or optics and acoustics), which are, arguably, made legible by abstract logics of mediation and objectification (see Mitchell 1986: 118–19), the sense of touch proves interesting and complex to consider on account of its alleged 'immediacy.'

The history of touch is, essentially, a history of resisting objectification. In this essay, I will show how the peculiar status of touch in relationship to representation proved problematic in the context of early modern medical and philosophical writing about the senses, but by the same token figured productively in the context of specifically literary and affective representations, as exemplified in an early seventeenth century university drama entitled *Lingua, or the Combat of the Tongue and the Five Senses for Superiority* (Tomkis 1607).

Sensory Classification and the Object of Touch

The French theorist and psychoanalyst Didier Anzieu has pointed out the centrality of touch and its cognates in the English language, noting that the tactile substrate of linguistic and psychological development is exemplified by the fact that 'touch' is one of 'the longest [entries] in the *Oxford English Dictionary'* (Anzieu 1989: 13). While Anzieu's point is to underscore the ubiquity of touch subtending language acquisition, it is precisely the resistance of touch to definitive linguistic and conceptual categories that make it such an elusive subject of history.

The difficulty of 'pinning down' this sense in language is, for the historian of the senses, similarly operative in the realm of iconography. Whereas recent historical attention to the human hand as an icon of agency (see, for example, Goldberg 1990; Stallybrass n.d.; Richter-Sherman 2001) may seem to offer much to the historian of touch, it is notable that those parts of the hand considered most sensitive to touch (the palm and fingertips) cannot be fully understood within a logic of instrumentality and social agency.[1] To touch with the hand informs metaphors of interaction that are quite different from other manually inflected forms of engagement such as 'manipulation,' 'grasping,' and 'clutching.' 'Wind and water press against us and move us,' writes Susan Stewart (2002: 165), 'but they cannot be grasped ... we cannot contain them in our hands for more than a moment.' The reciprocal, fleeting, and 'non-teleological' aspect of touch that Stewart foregrounds might be understood to call into question the ways in which scholars and theorists attempt to grasp this particular dimension of sensation. For when humans touch there is a reciprocity of sensation at once physical and psychological that may be felt but not fully grasped. The cost of a touch that 'grasps' in a non-reciprocal manner is embodied in the myth of Midas, whose touch, in Anne Carson's (1998: 136) words, 'permit[s] him to freeze his own emotional life at the high point of desire.' For Midas, as for any theorist of touch, to get a 'handle' on touch, to reify it, may be to eclipse its power.

Elaine Scarry's work in *The Body in Pain* suggests why this might be so. According to Scarry (1985: 19, 5): 'Physical pain is language-destroying,' or more specifically, pain 'resists objectification in language.' To generalize from this principle, it is the sense of touch as much as the specific example of pain that poses problems for representation. For how might one write about a sensory mode that itself resists 'objectification in language'?

The resistance of touch to representation poses a challenge for the historian of the senses. For example, in Renaissance studies of the senses, vision and hearing have been most fully explored as dominant, and historically contingent, structures of cognition. Histories of drama, following Andrew Gurr (1996), regularly explore the sensory dimensions of what it meant to be 'audience' and 'spectator,' and studies ranging from Bruce Smith's *The Acoustical World of Early Modern England* (1999) to Michael O'Connell's *The Idolatrous Eye*: *Iconoclasm and Theater in Early Modern England* (2000), map out the historical contours of these particular sense perceptions.[2] Since Aristotle, touch has been aligned with both human and animal capacities, and contrasted with vision and hearing as senses integral to the ethical and intellectual contours of what it means to be human.[3] As such, it is no surprise that sensory modes traditionally linked with the work of the mind are frequently privileged in discourses of historical phenomenology and even audience response. But what of touch as a cultural phenomenon? A word used as often as 'spectator' and 'audience' to describe playgoers in the Renaissance was the 'assembly,' a word worth reintegrating into the sensory dimensions of theatrical experience, because it implied not only a coming together of persons, but a physical touching of bodies in space. This fact alone underscores the need for a more full-bodied approach to the understanding of Renaissance representations of the senses. Furthermore, given that touch is integral to humoral physiology (as touch detects temperatures and textures), to literary allegories of the senses and to social rhetorics of persuasion, sexuality, affect, disease and public health, this need may be considered acute.[4]

So, too, with the recent focus on the material object (as textual artifact, stage property, object of exchange, cultural spectacle, sumptuary habit), we might consider what happens to the tangible object in the domain of sensory perception. We might ask with the editors of *Subject and Object in Renaissance Culture*, not only 'where is the object?' in histories of Renaissance subjectivity, but where is the object that is touched, caressed, taken in hand? It is the hand that enables production, but it also touches – and is touched by – products. In early modern representations of touch, however, I want to suggest, the question becomes less 'where is the object?' than 'why *isn't* the object there?' Putting touch into a mix of material cultures seems to gesture toward a kind of materialism without an object, or more precisely, without specific objects. It is the resistance of touch to specificity, conceptual stasis, and rational models that is arguably at the heart of Renaissance representations of touch.

The relative marginality of touch as a subject of Renaissance history is arguably rooted in the conceptual history of touch itself. The five senses were classically defined by specific organs, mediums, and objects (for example, eye, air, and celestial objects, respectively). As Helkiah Crooke put it in *Mikrokosmographia: A Description of the Body of Man* (1615), 'Sense is a knowledge or discerning of the Object receyued formally in the Organ,' and 'in euery Sense there be three things especially to be stood vpon, the Object, the Medium and the Organ' (Crooke 1615: 653, 722). Touch, however, consistently eluded the specifics of all three categories, disrupting basic systems of classification that the senses 'stood vpon.' In terms of organs, for example, from classical to Renaissance treatises on anatomy, the entire body, the nerves, skin, fingertips, tongue, palms, the region about the heart, were alternatively imagined as the locus of touch.[5] 'This sense is exquisite in men,' writes Robert Burton in *The Anatomy of Melancholy*, 'and by his nerves dispersed all over the body' (Burton 1631: 139). Or as Crooke put it, 'al other Senses are restrayned within some small Organ about the brayne, but the Touching is diffused through the whole body' (Crooke 1615: 648). Whereas eyes, ears, nose, and tongue symbolize the modes of sensory perception they enable, touch is more difficult to represent, localize, and demonstrate. As such, as a facet of bodily, cognitive, and psychological experience, touch tends to resist the two operations of representation so integral to early modern somatic symbolism: synecdoche and metonymy.

This is not simply a theoretical point, but one integral to the representation of touch in the visual and verbal arts of the Renaissance. Although one might think the human hand an easy metonymy for touch, this was not always or even usually the case. One early allegorical drama of the five senses features characters named 'Eye' for vision, 'Ear' for hearing, and 'Tongue' for taste, but simply 'Touch' for touch; so that, in terms of basic forms of personification, here touch remains a sense without a synecdoche, a mode without a metonymy.[6] This sense without a metonymy itself becomes metonymic in much Renaissance drama for the psyche's approach to what the psyche cannot precisely locate or measure.

Conflict of the Faculties

The limitations of touch to be clearly represented become a source of comedy in Thomas Tomkis's 1607 *Lingua, or the Combat of the Tongue and the Five Senses for Superiority,* an academic drama about the social sensorium that was performed at Cambridge, reprinted five times by 1657, and featured a young Oliver Cromwell as Tactus in an early production. In this play, whereas Olfactus is represented by Odor (bearing Tobacco) and Auditus by Comedy and Tragedy (bearing music, poetry and other acoustical artifacts), Tactus is represented by Mendacio (the lie), aligned from the first with qualities of elusiveness and representational dispersion. Following Aristotle, touch is positioned here as the one sense most threatening to intellectual and ethical systems. But more precisely, as we will see, touch challenges the logic of synecdoche and metonymy upon which analogies between macrocosm and microcosm depend.

Tomkis' play is part of a tradition of academic dramas of the period, where students would inhabit theatrical parts that were *also* systemic parts (for example, the senses in 'Microcosmvs,' the affections in 'Pathopolis,' grammar in 'Grammarland,' or parts of rhetoric and mathematics).[7] Given the frameworks of knowledge these plays staged, it is no surprise that they were particularly attentive to the operations of *pars pro toto*, of the capacities and limitations of parts to represent wholes, or indeed anything at all. *Pars pro toto* is, of course, at the core of dramas of persons, props, and personifications on stage. But when the whole is elusive, mythical, or hopelessly fragmented, the representative 'part' can become an embarrassment. In *Lingua*, with the five senses at war, each sense vies for superiority by asserting his individual powers: Odor, a quality of Olfactus, claims to command such intoxicating fragrances that 'You in your heart would wish as I suppose, / That all your Body were transformed to Nose' (Sig. H3). The idea that man might be represented by such an undignified part sends up strategies of representation and dramatic conflict in allegorical drama. But it is Tactus in this drama who most powerfully represents the failure of *pars pro toto*. Of course, the body simply couldn't be all 'Nose,' but it *is* in many ways 'all touch,' and the question of how to represent that through organs and objects (and indeed, mediums) creates high points of comedy in *Lingua*.

What academic plays such as *Lingua* clearly demonstrate is that disintegration in the epistemological realm means dramatic potential in the literary and theatrical realm. This is particularly pointed in the domain of touch in Tomkis's play, which converts conceptual disintegration into comic tension. At the outset of the play, Lingua (the tongue) and Mendacio (the lie) conspire to undermine the pentarchy by setting the senses at odds. They plant a crown and robe for the senses to discover and fight over. Tactus is the first to discover these items, he covets them and mayhem ensues. In a formal competition for the crown, judged by Common Sense, each sense puts on a show featuring the 'objects' they bring into this little world of man. Tactus, when asked to signify his 'dignity by relation' (Sig. I2), first locates himself in that Galenic 'instrument of instruments, the hand,' but quickly dislocates himself both rhetorically and conceptually: 'I am the roote of life, spreading my virtue / By sinewes that extend from head to foot / To euery liuing part.' His narrative disperses as he proceeds to speak about every known medical and scientific commonplace about the necessity of touch, from protecting the body from danger to enabling it to feel a kiss, until Common Sense abruptly says, '*Tactus*, stand aside,' and proceeds to judge on behalf of those senses nearer to the brain. While Tactus fails to represent himself 'by relation' to a particular organ, perhaps more importantly, his actual 'show' highlights his failure to represent himself with specific 'objects.'

Whereas particular smells, sounds, sights, and tastes in Renaissance iconography quickly signify the power of discreet senses in relationship to the outside world, touch – by virtue of it's sheer diversity – is not easily demonstrated by any particular object. Tactus's 'show' in fact fails miserably because his cast of objects never 'shows': 'My lord, I had thought as other Senses did, / By sight of obiects to haue proued my worth,' staging 'a Gentleman enamored, / With his sweete touching of his Mistresse lippes, / And gentle griping of her tender hands, /And diuers pleasant relishes of touch,' but his mistress has such a complex costume that after five hours 'shee is scarse drest to the girdle':

> Thus 'tis, fiue houres agoe I set a douzen maides to attire a boy like a nize Gentlewoman: but there is such doing with their looking-glasses, pinning, vnpinning, setting, vnsetting, formings and conformings, painting blew vaines, and cheekes, such stirre with Stickes and Combes, Cascanets, Dressings, Purses, Falles, Squares, Buskes, Bodies, Scarffes, Neck-laces... Borders, Tires, Fannes, Palizadoes, Puffes, Ruffes, Cuffes, Muffes, Pussles, Fussles, Partlets, Frislets, Bandlets, Fillets, Croslets, Pendulets, Amulets, Annulets, Bracelets, and so many lets, that yet shee is scarse drest to the girdle: and now there's such calling for Fardingales, Kirtlets, Busk-points, shootyes &c. that seauen Pedlers shops, nay all Sturbridge Faire will scarce furnish her: a Ship is sooner rigd by farre, then a Gentlewoman made ready. (Sig I2)

The heap of absent objects clearly displaces the representational problems of touch onto the female sex. The character Fantasy responds: 'Tis strange, that women being so mutable, / Will neuer change in changing their apparell,' a comment that informs Patricia Parker's (1989) suggestion that the play stages male anxieties about the effeminizing potential of representation. But there is another realm of signification at work, for this lavish insult backfires in a particularly effective way. Like the logic of the excessive insult, where terms of abuse pile up, become detached from specific contexts, and ultimately refer to insultor rather than insultee, so here imagined objects accumulate to the point of being detached from both the specifically gendered world and, more importantly, the specifically material world. Although Tactus should be undermined by so many absent objects, in fact this works as a brilliant form of self-reference, a demonstration of the infinite diversity of touch, which subtends (and yet is not limited to) the entire world of drama. Through the absent materialization of a kiss and a couple gently touching, and the infinite world of props and objects that touch the actor's body, Tactus at once suggests his lack of dependence on any specific domain of 'objects' and asserts the dependence of the other senses at play in the theater on *him*.

That is, through their absence, the missing lovers and the missing objects work to evoke conceptions of touch subtending the domain of 'show.'

It may well be said that it is precisely the failure of a body to 'touch' the world, persons, and objects around it that underpin its ultimate power as a symbolic mode. For touch can seem all the more alluring and powerful when objects are held at a distance. Perhaps more interestingly in terms of *pars pro toto*, the failure of synecdoche is in fact the only way in which the polymorphous diversity of touch can be signified. For locating the many possibilities and powers of touch *simultaneously* is in and of itself a seemingly impossible task. If one dimension of touch is located in one part of the body, the other sensitive parts, functions, and capacities would be necessarily neglected or eclipsed: the touch of a blind man understanding depth and visual space with his hands could not also represent the force of a puncture or the unexpected touch of another; the feel of coins in a hand could not signify the place of touch in detecting temperature in and out of the body; the light sensation of a fingertip (or the fantasy of God *almost* touching Adam's finger) could not signify the rough, soft or liquid textures of food in the mouth. This is simply to emphasize that Renaissance allegories of the senses, depending as they did on synecdoche and metonymy, worked according to a logic that could not accommodate the diversity of touch.

It is important to note in this respect the recurrence of one motif in many allegories of the senses. It was a particular kind of touch (that which Tactus longs to represent): the erotic pleasures of lovers touching. The realm of the erotic, with desire always in some sense linked to what is not there, is perhaps the most powerful vehicle for representing the infinite potential and the elusiveness of touch. Lovers can touch heatedly, softly, blindly, roughly, they can touch each other's clothes, gloves, and jewels, they can devour each other, wound each other, and break each other's hearts, so the recurrence of erotic interaction as a 'specific' kind of touch implies the very antithesis of specificity and categorical distinction: the real power and danger of this sense in the early modern world.

The representational resistance of touch in terms of specific organs and objects was also operative in the theoretical realm of 'media.' Indeed, touch is hard to theorize because it is (in the most classical sense) 'unmediated,' or, to quote Aristotle, 'immediate' (Aristotle 1995: 435a, 16–20). 'Immediately,' a term that currently signifies a lack of distance between coordinates in time (simply meaning *now*), at an earlier period meant a lack of distance between objects in space. Of the five senses, touch was the most 'immediate,' at once resisting temporal stasis and having no spatial "medium" between the body and the touchable world (be it in the form of objects, bodies, textures, or temperatures). The other senses, writes Aristotle in *De Anima*, 'produce sensation by means of something else, that is, through media. But touch occurs by direct contact with its objects and that is why it has its name. The other sense organs perceive by contact too, but through a medium; touch alone seems to perceive immediately' (Aristotle 1995: 435a, 16–20). How does one account for a sense without a medium? What happens to this 'unmediated' sense in early medical and contemporary theoretical accounts of representation that look to the 'medium' as the message (McLuhan 1962)? Not surprisingly, the messages become difficult to decipher and even detect. In the context of studies of communications that have focused so heavily on 'media' and 'sense ratios,' technologies of touch often go relatively unnoticed. This is true even in the most practical sense: as Malcolm McCullough writes about contemporary computing: 'Touch technology is underdeveloped, and few interaction devices provide force or tactile feedback. Without touch, currently the most common complaint about computers is not about overload but deprivation. It is about the inability to touch one's work. Being *out of touch* is considered an occupational hazard: regular sensory deprivation turns you into a nerd' (McCullough 1996: 130).

Like so many other physiological metaphors now wandering ghostlike through the lexicon of computer interaction, 'digital' technology seems to have left those fleshly little digits in the dust. It is precisely to the question of digits (meaning both fingers and numbers) and sensory deprivation that I would now like to turn. For when the body in the Renaissance was imagined in quantitative terms, as it so often was, touch was either neglected or conspicuously disruptive. For 'touch' not only complicated categorization in medical thinking (organs, objects, and media), but the possibility of categorization as such. This sense is not only difficult to account for, but difficult to count.

Calculating Minds: From Synesthesia to the Sixth Sense

> The height of Heaven is taken by the staffe: the bottom of the sea sounded with lead: the farthest coast discovered by the compasse: the secrets of nature searched by wit: the anatomy of man set out by experience, but the abuses of Plaies cannot be showen, because they passe the degrees of the instrument, reach of the plummet, sight of the mind, and for tryall are never brought to the touchstone.
>
> Stephen Gosson, *The School of Abuse* (1579)

Quantitatively speaking, a 'touch' is a relatively insubstantial unit: not even a piece, or a part, but rather a point so small as to almost resist quantification. If touch resists quantification, how could it possibly measure up to the standards of 'rational' inquiry that emerged during the Renaissance? The latter period is commonly thought to have been characterized by a transformation in the '*ratio* of the senses,' marked by a heightened emphasis on 'visualization' and a new 'passion for measurement' – or *ratio*cination as quantification (Ong 1982;

Howes 1991). However, 'touch,' despite its minimal quantitative content, *did* mean in the Renaissance, 'to test' (hence 'touchstone' as a commonplace for locus of meaning or truth). What I want to do, therefore, is to put touch back into the test, and see what happens when touch is factored into the 'ratio of sense', particularly in the domain of theater. Tomkis' play is an apt site for such a test, for in *Lingua* the 'passion for measurement' and the 'visual bias' of sensory perception (Howes 1991) are turned inside-out and upside-down. This academic drama is preoccupied with the question of 'sense-ratios' (what sense is valued most being the central question of the play) and, perhaps most significantly, with the limits of quantitative models in representation of affect and tactile experience.

Tomkis makes light of the quantitative disruptions at once threatening and subtending the 'five senses,' which were among the many numerically conceptualized systems of the period ('the four seasons,' 'the four elements,' 'the four temperaments,' 'the seven arts,' 'the seven deadly sins,' 'the seven ages of man,' 'the twelve months,' and so forth).[8] This is rendered explicit from the first, as Ladie Lingua (the tongue and language) craves to be the 'sixth sense,' hoping to make just a slight alteration to the order of things (Sig. A3). Despite Auditus's discouragement ('what Sense hast thou to be a Sense / Since from the first foundation of the world, / We neuer were accounted more than fiue' [Sig. A3]), this 'vp-start' organ forges on, determined to 'increase the number' and be reclassified with the best. This urge to recalculate systems of knowledge is mirrored in the subplot by Lingua's culinary counterpart, Appetitus (a representative of Gustus) who hopes to expand the seven liberal arts to eight, including 'the honorable art of Cookerie' (Sig. D2). 'As for the *Academie* it is beholding to mee, for adding the eight prouince vnto noble *Heptarchie* of the liberall sciences' (Sig. D1). The link between Lingua and Appetitus recalls Plato's *Gorgias*, where cookery (as opposed to medicine) is established as an art of deception, and explicitly aligned with the deceptive powers of rhetoric. As such, Tomkis here emphasizes the moral as well as epistemological stakes of sensory unaccountability as it relates to rhetoric. But while it may be easy to discount a wagging organ and an appetitive chef as viable contenders in the 'Academie,' the numerical unaccountability in *Lingua* expands to the work of the five senses and, beyond, to the status of memory and history to boot. While Mendatio alludes to 'Master Register [i.e. recorded history] trudging hether, as fast as his three feete will carry vp his foure Ages' (Sig. F1), Memory himself complains about the chaos of contemporary 'history': 'A dog cannot pisse in a Noblemans shoe, but it must be sprinkled into the Chronicles' (Sig. D3). Memory is so overwhelmed that he loses track of time and things: he forgets himself, but remembers where he left his spectacles: 'I left them in the 349 Page of *Halls* Chronicles' (Sig. F3). It is the hopelessly particular realm of number that now preoccupies even the mnemonic function in this body of man. This play stages the perils of sense perception where mis-measuring compromises historical representation and rational modeling, but at the same time, it foregrounds the interrelationship between problems of calculative integrity and possibilities of drama.

The concept of a world that is whole or 'intact' is itself a world detached from the complexities of touch. The word 'intact' derives from *in* (not) and *tactus* (touched). The distinctly numerical failure of 'integrity' in Tomkis's allegory is part of the comedy of *Lingua's* 'irrationality,' but it is also integral to the synesthetic ordering and disordering of experience. As the senses become divided against each other, they seem capable not only of 'duplicity' but of infinite divisibility,[9] and importantly, it is the sense of touch that operates most conspicuously according to a logic of physiological and representational self-difference. Tactus is capable of taking many different forms: he lies, shape-shifts rhetorically, psychologically, and theatrically, dupes Olfactus, and 'schemes' against the others. It is not only Ladie Lingua (a would-be sense) but Tactus who explicitly challenges the foundation of ethical, social, and cosmic forms of 'integrity.' In the sensory domain of the play, the concept of a quantitatively challenged 'sense' is perfectly embodied in Tactus, whose power extends to 'euery particle of the body' (Sig I3), providing a conceptual double to the problem of memory awash in historical particulars. If 'allegories generated by the analogy of macrocosm to microcosm,' as Marshall Grossman (1998: 154) notes, 'reach synecdochic closure when the analogy assures that each and every perceived object, if viewed correctly, will produce a cosmic totality,' then *Lingua* explores the perils of synecdoche in a microcosm 'in touch' with itself.

But importantly, this drama of irrationality is less a clear inversion of the classical hierarchy of the senses than a logical extension of classical thought, where touch was impossible to accommodate within categorical systems.[10] Ladie Lingua's inaugural challenge to the order of five senses reflects a quantitative disorder already implicit within the 'pentarchy'. Of course in the allegorical system of the senses, the tongue can only signify *one* sense, not two. In the allegory and iconography of the period, the tongue (for example in Fletcher's 1633 allegorical poem *The Purple Island* – see Fletcher 1869) was a stand-in for all things gustatory (see Mazzio 1997). So the very idea that Lingua might signify another sense seems absurd. And yet, if we consider debates in the period about the fact that the tongue itself might represent not one, but two senses, and that the sense of taste and touch were difficult to distinguish, the premise becomes a little less absurd. As Aristotle put it in *De Anima*, 'The tongue perceives all tangible objects with the same part with which it perceives flavor' (Aristotle 1995: 423a, 19–20) and suggests that 'taste must be some kind of touch' (Aristotle 1995: 434b, 22).

Renaissance medical texts endlessly cited Aristotle on the debate about whether taste and touch were one and the same. Crooke, for example, argues vigorously for an affinity rather than an equivalence between the two senses: 'if hee [Aristotle] had meant that the Tast and the Touch did not differ in *Specie*, hee would neuer haue sayd that *Gustus* was *Tactus quidam*, but simply and plainly *Gustus* is *Tactus*, hee would not have sayd that Tast is a kinde of Touch, but that Tast is a Touch' (Crooke 1615: 716). Aristotle's distinction is crucial here for Crooke as a way of maintaining that these two must be 'esteemed distinct Senses':

> It may be also objected, that because both the Taste and the Touch are together in one & the same Tongue, that therefore they should be one and the same Sense. But the consequence is not good, for there is no organe of Sense, which beside his proper Facultie of Sensation is not also furnished with the Sense of Touching. But because the Sense of Tasting is not alwaies found where Touching is, and where it is found there is no other Faculty of Sensation: I conclude that not onely all the other Senses but the Taste also is a distinct and different Sense from the Touch. (Crooke 1615: 717–18)

Practically speaking, it does seem somewhat of a shame that the entire body cannot, as Crooke (following Aristotle 1995: 423a, 21) notes, experience taste. Such a conflation of senses for Crooke is 'not good,' however, not only because it marks a misreading of Aristotle and poses a problem of anatomical categorization, but because the conflation of touch and 'all the other Senses' would challenge the hierarchy of the senses that helps distinguish man from animal (Aristotle 1976: 137).

But the ideas and the vocabularies of taste and touch were deeply entwined in anatomical theories of this period, and this partnership extended into the domain of metaphor in the realms of music, rhetoric, and theology (where, for example, Eve's palm became as important as her tongue in the representation of original sin – O'Rourke Boyle 1998: 90–171). In the rhetoric of love it is the sweet touch that lingers in the memory, the beloved one devours with kisses, the gentle brush of a hand one might relish or savor. But the metaphorics of synesthesia (or better, sensory interanimation) become flattened by Crooke, who invokes commonplace tropes of synesthetic disorder in the political body to warn against sensory indiscretion: 'The Foote would see, and the Elbow would heare, and the sides would smell, and the crowne would taste, if in these parts there wer[e] a disposition to receiue the objects of these Senses' (Crooke 1615: 725). While Crooke hopes to restore the analytic order of thought through sensory discrimination, what is suggestive here is that debates about touch in relation to the other senses provide a kind of physiological basis for the interanimation of sensory modes (synesthesia) that surfaces so frequently in literary texts of the period. This is to say that whereas Tomkis's Ladie Lingua, for example, upsets the sensory system by her gender and linguistic non-sense, what is also at work is a broader question of anatomical categorization, sensory discrimination, and the distinct status of human perception itself.

The tactile substrate of sensory perception is integral to a number of early theories of sense. Despite the 'distance between organ and object' required by visual apprehension, for example, the debate about whether eyes emanated rays or received particles through the air when visualizing objects speaks to a material process of visualization at the most basic physiological level. So too, despite the privilege given to auditory consciousness in much religious writing of the period, the force of sound and air waves was generally understood to have the power to damage the brain, hence the labyrinthine structure of the auditory canal to protect the brain from direct acoustical contact: as John Davies puts it, 'So in th'Eares' labyrinth the voice doth stray / And doth with easie motion touch the braine' (Davies 1876: 67). Given the proximity to the material world necessary for the functioning of taste and smell, these senses were more explicitly aligned with the touchable world. But the logical conclusion of the necessity of touch for the functioning of all of the other senses is, for Crooke, no less than the decay of all intellectual knowledge: 'Furthermore,' he writes,

> if we will stand to *Aristotles* determination, that there can no other Sense subsist without Touching, then will it follow that this being taken away no sense can remaine. Now if the Senses be taken away, the whole family of Arts (which we said before did depend vpon their credit) must needs decay, nay you shall remooue the Sunne it selfe out of the World. If any Man doubt of this, let him seriously suruey all the Artes both Liberall and Mechanicall. (Crooke 1615: 649)

It is no surprise in this respect that Tomkis's Tactus aligns himself with Aristotle: 'Tell me what sense is not beholding to mee? / The nose is hot or cold, the eies do weepe / The eares do feele, the tast's a kind of touching, / That when I please, I can command them all, / And make them tremble when I threaten them' (Sig. I3). A bit like Shakespeare's Bottom fearing he might frighten the ladies with a roar, Tactus takes himself just a touch too seriously. Or does he? For without him, as we have seen above, no show could possibly go on. In the synesthetic dimensions of theater, it may be that only touch can really pull things together. For Crooke, if Aristotle is correct that no sense can 'subsist without Touching,' then the absence of touch would extinguish all possibilities of sense, at once conceptual and cultural, including 'all the Artes both Liberall and Mechanicall' (Crooke 1615: 649). This threat materializes in *Lingua*, but in a slightly different way, where the presence of touch potentially *expands* the number of the arts and sciences (as Appetitus would have it, from seven to eight) and the senses themselves.

Indeed, what I now want to consider is the extent to which touch was not only imagined to disable ways of calculating knowledge, but to open up new possibilities for articulating and understanding the sense of things. While direct contact was integral to medical explanations of touch, such as Crooke's, the idea of touch in literature often stretched the domain of the tactile beyond the bounds of the body itself, implying conditions of hyper

awareness and cognitive sensitivity. The commonplace iconography of the
spider as a representative of touch, for example, is worth exploring in this
respect because it expands the realm of sensitivity from body to environment.
As Davies writes, 'Much like a subtill spider, which doth sit / In the middle
of her web, which spreadeth wide; / If ought doe touch the vtmost thred of
it, / Shee feeles it instantly on euery side.' This passage has often been read
as alluding to the spread of nerves throughout the body. But the simile also
relocates touch from the physically proximate to the relatively distant space
of environment, perhaps providing the closest Renaissance analogy to the
contemporary notion of the 'sixth sense,' that eerily inexplicable receptivity
to seemingly undetectable environmental stimuli. Francis Bacon would liken
excess emotional receptivity to a whole environment of cobwebs, a 'Cob-web
Lawn... so tender as to feel everything' (Bacon 1737, I: 397).

Spiders make webs to protect themselves and entrap others, but what
makes them a powerful paradigm of 'sensing' in this period is that they can
feel without direct contact. The arachnid, or 'extrasensory,' powers of touch
as an alternative mode of receiving information are in fact highlighted by
Tomkis's Tactus, where the spider works less as a simile of tactile sensitivity
than a condition of knowing. 'For as a suttle Spider closely sitting, / In the
center of her web that spreddeth round, / If the least Flie but touch the
smallest thred, / She feels it instantly; so doth my self' (Sig. I3). The analogy
between nerves and the webbed texture of the spider is expanded out in this
play from the domain of the physical body and into the untouchable realms
of the cosmos. In one passage, Tactus is portrayed as 'scal[ing] the heavens'
on the 'cordage fine' spun from a spider's gut:

> The maskes are made so strong,
> That I my selfe vpon them scal'd the heauens,
> And bouldly walkt about the middle region,
> Where in the prouince of the Meteors,
> I saw the clowdie shops of Haile and Raine,
> Garners of Snow, and Christals full of dew,
> Riuers of burning Arrowes, Dens of Dragons,
> Huge beames of flames, and Speares like fire-brands.
> Where I beheld hotte Mars and Mercurie,
> With Rackets made of Spheares, and Balls of Starres,
> Playing at Tennis for a Tunne of Nectar. (Sig. E2)[11]

What is articulated here is a vivid form of 'gut' knowledge, or what David
Hillman (1997) has called 'visceral knowledge,' at odds with emergent forms
of scientific inquiry in the Renaissance. The spiders 'Of their owne gutts to
spinne a cordage fine' ('cordage,' invoking the Latin for 'heart') joins the
nerves and sinews in an unaccountable way of perceiving the world. This
way of sensing is unaccountable, or in other words, suspect, because many
of the objects in this ekphrastic whirlwind traditionally belong to Visus

(such as the planets, the heavens, the stars, all visible from a distance). This contrasts with Visus's use of Terra in his own performance: for while the earth is visible, it was elementally linked with the properties of touch. Visus only 'shows' Terra, noting 't'were an *indecorum Terra* should speak' (Sig. G1). The implication in this elemental allegory is that the articulation of touch is necessarily indecorous; that is, whereas touch may be fundamental (linked with the 'firmament'), the fact that it may also enable a kind of extrasensory (or suprasensory) mode of knowing is at once asserted and undermined in the passage above: not the least because it is Mendacio who is Tactus's spokesman in this instance.

Maddening Fantasies of Optical Self-knowledge

The inflated and deflated powers of touch are worked into *Lingua*'s plot in psychological as well as physical terms as Tactus first feigns madness and then becomes mad in fact. For to be 'touched' in this period involved a psychophysiology of temperament, where one could be physically affected and imbalanced by humoral and environmental forces. This concept was so common that Tactus takes full advantage of it. To deflect attention from the coveted crown and robe he sits upon to hide, Tactus performs his own cultural signification: he pretends that he is 'touched,' melancholy, and so 'out of touch' with his rational faculties that he thinks himself a glass urinal. He says to Olfactus, 'when I had ariu'd and set me downe, / Viewing my selfe, my selfe ay me was changed. / And thou now seest [me] to be a perfect vrinall.' 'I am an vrinal I dare not stirre. / For fear of cracking in the Bottom' (Sig. B3). More telling than this fragile firmament *extraordinaire* are associations that Tactus makes in imagining himself a man of glass: a fantasy with roots in medical and classical lore that is re-imagined in scatological terms. Tactus narrates his apparent transformation to glass by alluding to the Greek god of satire Momus's well-known fantasy that all men should have been made with a glass window, so that one might be able see into the innermost 'core.'

> No sooner had I parted out of doores,
> But vp I held my hands before my face:
> To sheild mine eyes from th'lights percing beames,
> When I protest I saw the Sunne as cleer,
> Through these my palms as through a prospectiue.
> No marueil, for when I beheld my fingers:
> I sawe my fingers neere transform'd to glass,
> Opening my breast, my Breast was like a window,
> Through which I plainely did perceiue my heart:
> In whose two Concaues I discernd my thoughts,
> Confus'dly lodged in great multitutes. (Sig. B3)

'[W]hy this is excellent,' responds Olfactus, '*Momus* himself can find no fault with thee / Thou'st make a passing liue *Anatomie*. / And decide the Question much disputed: / Betwixt the *Galenists* and *Aristotle*' (Sig. B3). What begins as a vivid account of touch being able to detect his own interior (while still a 'liue Anatomie'), accessing that 'confus'd' realm of thought within the body, ends in a parodic transformation of the self to a urinal, an object that most would not care to see inside. Hillman (1997) convincingly argues that the anatomical fantasy of accessing and seeing one's own and another's insides in the Renaissance always encodes a powerful disavowal of knowledge, a non-recognition of the quintessential otherness of both others and selves. In *Lingua*, that very fantasy is made as fragile as glass: self-recognition here hinges on conspicuous disavowal, since Tactus deploys a largely *visual* model of self-investigation. But the largely academic audience of the play well knows that this is a joke, since Tactus *fabricates* this elaborate disavowal as a way *not* to be seen by others, and to assert his agency.

Given the complexities of touch as a mode of perception in the play, Tomkis' parody of Momus's fantasy at the very least evokes the non-visual correlative of what it might actually mean to know things, in a physiological and affective sense, by heart. Much like Mendacio's dream of touching an untouchable universe, Tactus at least gestures toward the possibility of an alternative way of 'plainely' perceiving one's 'heart': not just seeing it but understanding the confused multitude of 'thoughts' within. Indeed, this Tactus is less dead than the 'liue Anatomies' that people so many Renaissance medical texts, who delicately point to their own grotesque insides without apparent concern, who might dangle their skin over a shoulder like a warm coat on a sunny day, flex their skinless muscles like so many classical bodies, or pose for a guide to the anatomy of the brain with a conspicuously halved cranium.[12] Unlike the living corpses of what Jonathan Sawday has called the Renaissance 'culture of dissection,' where 'the body had become subject to the gaze' (Sawday 1995: 18) Tactus is less a numb body pointing at itself than a 'liue Anatomie' trying to speak from inside out.

As tradition would have it, however, Tactus is ultimately 'found out.' Visus gets the crown, Auditus is next best, and though Tactus is deemed a mere 'necessity,' he gets the robe as a door prize. Common Sense attempts to restore proper numerical and conceptual order:

> The number of the *Senses* in this little world, is answerable to the first bodies in the great world: now since there bee but fiue in the Vniuerse, the foure elements and the pure substance of the heauens, therefore there can bee but fiue senses in our *Microcosme*, correspondent to those, as the sight to the heauens, hearing to the aire, touching to the earth, smelling to the fire, and tasting to the water, by which fiue meanes only the vnderstanding is able to apprehend the knowledge of all Corporeall substances. (Sig. I3)

Even at the end of the play, there is a dramatic dispute over the robe that Tactus has but Lingua wants. Much is made at the beginning of the play that 'there is but one [robe]' (Sig. BI), but Tactus and Lingua (and implicitly Gustus) continue to battle it out for the same sign, recalling the tension implicit in differentiating the senses of taste and touch, and implicity, all of the senses from each other, in the domain of language and theater. But it also implicates Tactus with the tongue as an instrument of speech, what many in the period considered to be the 'sixth sense' itself: Burton (1931: 137) writes of the five senses, 'you may add Scaliger's sixth sense of *titillation*, if you please; or that of speech, which is the sixth external sense according to Lullius.' In *Lingua*, 'speech' becomes entwined with sensory activity, for it is Lingua who first tempts Tactus into thinking he might rule the pentarchy, working to 'Clad my selfe in Silken Eloquence / To allure the nicer touch of Tactus hand' (Sig. A3). While Lingua ultimately fails 'to make the senses sixe' (Sig. A3), what is on display here is the power of theatrical language not only to 'allure' and 'move' but to activate the mobility and instability of the senses.

Interestingly, it is when Tactus loses his power to infiltrate and complicate the world of knowledge that the single 'object,' the robe, finally comes to signify touch. But more importantly, this single sumptuary habit has a somatic analogue in the play in the reduction of sensory complexity to a localized and vulnerable bodily object. Tactus's ability to disrupt or alter the order of things fully diminishes as he becomes vulnerable to physical (as opposed to cognitive and linguistic) forces stronger than he: his perceptual sensitivity is realized in the body as he is tickled: 'Ha, ha, ha, fie, I pray you leaue, you tickle me so, oh, ah, ha, ha, take away your hands I cannot indure, ah you tickle me, ah, ha, ha, ha, ah' (Sig. M2). 'We see no Man can tickle himselfe,' wrote Bacon (1627: 198) in *Sylva Sylvarum*, 'Tickling is euer Painfull, and not well endured. Indeed, tickles quickly become unbearable and the tactual takes a turn for the worse, as Tactus is touched with a 'pinch,' 'pinne,' and a 'stab' (Sig. M3), wracked with cramps, 'O the crampe, the crampe, the crampe, my legge, my legg' (Sig M.2), and his powers are diminished to sheer reactivity to the physical force of the world he now inhabits. He is actually disabled from wearing the robe (once again resisting the object) because he is overwhelmed by a kind of burning heat: 'Oh what a wild-fire creepes among my bowells: / Aetna's within my breast, my marrrowe fries, / And runnes about my bones, oh my sides: / My sides, my raines, my head, my raines, my head; / My heart, my heart, my liuer, my liuer, oh / I burne, I burne, I burne, oh how I burne' (Sig. K3). In this heartburn *par excellence*, Tactus becomes a kind of grotesque version of the self-demonstrating anatomy, reduced to locating his vulnerabilities in a series of individuated and hurt body parts: 'heart,' 'brains,' 'breast,' 'marrowe,' 'bones,' 'sides,' 'raines.' 'My heart, my heart, my liuer, my liuer.' Such a quick descent from a richly textured realm of plotting, perception, and knowing to a self defined by a series of single hurt organs, subject to anatomical investigation! What might have been a kind of tremulous public body becomes a spectacle of individually marked symptoms and vulnerabilities of physical touch. In a trajectory that, I argue elsewhere (Mazzio 2003), we can see at work in *Hamlet* and a number of tragic dramas and antitheatrical texts of the Renaissance, the epistemological complexity of touch in *Lingua* is ultimately contained by its materialization in the domain of hurt. The unbearable lightness of touch, the surprise of a tickle, a hint, or an unexpected twist, in rhetoric and logic as on stage, are extremely difficult – in Tactus's words – to 'indure.'

In this Early Modern world, while we see the 'body in pain' emerge as a model that resists 'objectification in language,' the dissolution works, paradoxically, to reify touch *as* pain, substituting the aliveness of touch as an aspect of affect and knowledge with the conspicuous rupture of an otherwise intact body. The physical concretization of sensory-emotional experience that transforms the body itself into its own object foregrounds the profound difficulty of sustaining concepts of touch as complex modes of mediation. If (to re-appropriate McLuhan's phrase) the medium is the message, then when the distance of objects and organs afforded by interanimation of tactile, acoustical, and visual metaphors collapses or, rather, becomes subject to a logic of proximity and material 'immediacy,' touch loses its power to signify. This is all the more reason to take seriously the elusiveness of touch to objects – for what is at stake is less the 'socialization of sentience' in the Marxian sense, than the sensitization of the social in the dramatically literary sense.

Acknowledgments

I am deeply grateful for the thoughtful responses of Bradin Cormack, William Ingram, Steven Mullaney, Joshua Scodel and Richard Strier. Members of the English faculty at the University of Chicago and the Renaissance Colloquium at Northwestern University also provided helpful comments on an early draft. My thanks also to the Huntington Library, where I researched the topic of touch.

Notes

1. Even for early materialists such as Lucretius, who claim that 'touch and nothing but touch... is the essence of all our bodily sensations,' touch has a peculiar ability to 'upset' sensory organization: 'It is touch... that is felt when the atoms are jarred by a knock so that they are disordered and upset the senses: strike any part of your

own body with your hand, and you will experience this for yourself' (Lucretius 1987: 72–3).

2. Much recent scholarship on the symbolics of the hand in Renaissance literature has emphasized the hand as an instrument of reading (Stallybrass, in progress), writing (Goldberg 1990), gesture (Bevington 1984), memory (Richter Sherman 2001), of labor, political agency, and contractual negotiation (Rowe 1999). But the hand as an instrument often looks quite different when it is represented as a receptor of touch.

3. See further Gozza 2000; Burnett 1991; Elkins 1996; Sawday 1995; and Freedman 1991. On the interanimation (as opposed to the isolation) of vision and hearing in this period, see Eisenstein (1979). For an earlier approach to the senses in Shakespeare, see Spurgeon (1935: 57–78, 82–83) which devotes twenty two pages to vision and hearing, compared to one and a half to touch.

4. Touch and taste, writes Aristotle, are 'are concerned with such pleasures as are shared by animals too (which makes them regarded as low and brutish)' (Aristotle 1976: 137). Touch is worthy of 'reproach... because it attaches to us not as men but as animals. So to enjoy such sensations and find the greatest satisfaction in them is brutish' (Aristotle 1976: 137). For a recapitulation of vision as the 'most precious, and the best... by it we learn and discern all things' and touch as the 'most ignoble' see Burton (1931: 138–39).

5. Much recent work on the body in contemporary literature and thought has integrated 'touch' as a technology of body, mind, and culture: while Anzieu (1989) maps out a kind of thermal and tactual unconscious, other theorists of the body such as Nancy (1994), Grosz (1994), Stewart (2002) and earlier, Irigaray (1980), have turned to 'touch' as a rich and largely neglected technology of perception.

6. This issue is still fully alive when Alexander Ross responds to ancient and contemporary medical writing in the mid-seventeenth century: 'The sense of tact either hath no medium, or else we must make the skin the medium; and the flesh, membranes and nerves the organ' (Ross 1651: 66). The singular use of 'organ' to encapsulate such complex and individuated parts of the body speaks to the extent to which the triad of organ, object and medium, though insufficient, was nonetheless continually invoked to organize the sensory modes.

7. For details on this morality drama, attributed to Jean Gerson and written between 1377 and 1384, see Vinge (1975: 60 n.27).

8. On the structure of the senses in relation to these basic analogical systems, see Vinge (1975: 11). Interestingly, the disequilibrium between the elements of sense (five) and the elements of the natural world (four) is of some concern to Aristotle in De Sensu, but as Vinge (1975: 17) notes, he quickly reconciles this by simply conflating taste and touch, which are both aligned with the earth.

9. This infinite divisibility of the senses dramatizes a classical paradox whereby indivisible properties of thinking and judging are inextricably linked with infinitely divisible sensory perceptions. See Aristotle, De Anima (esp. 427a–7b).

10. As Aristotle writes:

> For if touch is not one sense, but several, there must be several kinds of tangibles. It is difficult to say whether touch is one sense or more than one, and also what the organ is which is perceptive of the object of touch... For every sensation appears to be concerned with one pair of contraries, e.g., vision is of white and black, hearing of high and low pitch, and taste of bitter and sweet; but in the tangible there are many pairs of contraries, hot and cold, wet and dry, hard and soft, and all other like qualities. (Aristotle 1995: 422b, 18–28)

This, the touch that is not one, clearly complicates matters of classification. As such, despite Aristotle's analytical attempts to find the necessary 'solution' for this problematic sense, he finds more and more 'problems' posed by the protean and mysterious tactual realm. Ultimately, the sense of touch for Aristotle is the one sense necessary for all of the others to function.

11. The passage continues: 'And that vast gaping of the Firmament, / Vnder the Southerne pole, is nothing else, / But the great hazzard of their Tennis Court; / The Zodiack is the line; The shooting Starres, / Which in an eye-bright euening seem'd to fall, /Are nothing but the Balls they loose at Bandy' (Sig. E2).

12. On fantasies of optical self-knowledge, and for a series of 'self-figuring' anatomical figures, see Sawday (1995: 1–5, 38–39).

Bibliography

Anon. (1613), *Pathomachia: or, The Battel of Affections*, London: n.p.

Anon. ([1613] 1983), *Blame Not Our Author*, ed. Suzanne Gossett, New York: Malone Society.

Anzieu, D. (1989), *The Skin Ego: A Psychoanalytic Approach to the Self*, trans. C. Turner, New Haven CT: Yale University Press.

Aristotle (1976), *Nicomachean Ethics*, trans. J.A.K. Thomson, ed. Jonathan Barnes, London: Penguin.

—— (1995), *De Anima,* trans. W.S. Hett, Cambridge MA: Harvard University Press.

Bacon, F. (1627), *Sylva Sylvarum*, London: n.p.

—— (1737), 'Against Duelling,' in Peter Shaw (ed.), *The Philosophical Works of Francis Bacon, Baron of Verulam, &c. Methodized and made English from the Originals*, second edition, London: n.p.

Bevington, D. (1984), *Action is Eloquence: Shakespeare's Language of Gesture*, Cambridge MA: Harvard University Press.

Boas, F.S. (1914), *University Drama in the Tudor Age*, Oxford: Clarendon.

Burnett, C. (ed.) (1991), *The Second Sense. Studies in Hearing and Musical Judgement from Antiquity to the Seventeenth Century*. London: The Warburg Institute.

Burton, R. (1931), *The Anatomy of Melancholy*, ed. F. Dell and P. Jordan-Smith, London: Routledge.

Carson, A. (1998), *Eros the Bittersweet*, Normal IL: Dalkey Archive Press.

Crooke, H. (1615), *Mikrokosmographia: A Description of the Body of Man*, London: n.p.

Davies, J. (1876), '*Nosce Teipsum*,' in A.B. Grosart (ed.), *The Complete Poems of Sir John Davies*, London: n.p.

De Grazia, M., Quilligan, M. and Stallybrass, P. (eds) (1996), *Subject and Object in Renaissance Culture*, Cambridge: Cambridge University Press.

Elkins, J. (1996), *The Poetics of Perspective*, Ithaca: Cornell University Press.

Fletcher, P. (1869), 'The Purple Island,' in A.B. Grosart (ed.), *The Poems of Phineas Fletcher*, London: n.p.

Freedman, B. (1991), *Staging the Gaze: Postmodernism, Psychoanalysis, and Shakespearean Comedy*, Ithaca: Cornell University Press.

Goldberg, J. (1990), *Writing Matter: From the Hands of the English Renaissance*, Stanford: Stanford University Press.

Gosson, S. (1579), *The School of Abuse*, London: n.p.

Gozza, P. (ed.) (2000). *From Number to Sound. The Musical Way to the Scientific Revolution*, Dordrecht: Kluwer Academic Publishers.

Grossman, M. (1998), *The Story of All Things: Writing the Self in English Renaissance Narrative Poetry*, Durham: Duke University Press.

Grosz, E. (1994), *Volatile Bodies: Toward a Corporeal Feminism*, Bloomington: Indiana University Press.

Guarna, A. (1511), *Bellum Grammaticale*, Cremona: n.p.

Gurr, A. (1996), *Playgoing in Shakespeare's London*, Cambridge: Cambridge University Press.

Hayward, W. (1576), *Bellum Grammaticale: A Discourse of Gret War and Dissention betweene Two Worthy Princes, the Noune and the Verbe*, London: n.p.

Hillman, D. (1997), 'Visceral Knowledge,' in D. Hillman and C. Mazzio (eds), *The Body in Parts: Fantasies of Corporeality in Early Modern Europe*, New York: Routledge, pp. 81–105.

Howes, D. (1991), 'Sensorial Anthropology,' in D. Howes (ed.), *The Varieties of Sensory Experience: A Sourcebook in the Anthropology of the Senses*, Toronto: University of Toronto Press, pp. 167–91.

Hutton, L. (1583), *Bellum Grammaticale*, Oxford: n.p.

Irigaray, L. (1980), 'This Sex Which is not One,' in E. Marks and I. De Courtivron (eds), *New French Feminisms*, Amherst: University of Massachusetts Press, pp. 99–106.

Langdale, A.B. (1937), *Phineas Fletcher, Man of Letters, Science and Divinity*, New York: Columbia University Press.

Ling, N. (1598), *Politeuphia. Wits Common wealth*, London: n.p.

Lucretius (1987), *On the Nature of the Universe*, trans. R.E. Latham, Middlesex: Penguin.

Mazzio, C. (1997), 'Sins of the Tongue,' in D. Hillman and C. Mazzio (eds), *The Body in Parts: Fantasies of Corporeality in Early Modern Europe*, New York: Routledge, pp. 52–79.

—— (2003), 'Acting with Tact: Touch and Theater in the Renaissance,' in E. Harvey (ed.), *Sensible Flesh: On Touch in Early Modern Culture*, Philadelphia: University of Pennsylvania Press, pp. 159–86.

McCullough, M. (1996), *Abstracting Craft: The Practiced Digital Hand*, Cambridge MA: MIT Press.

McLuhan, M. (1962), *The Gutenburg Galaxy*, Toronto: University of Toronto Press.

Mitchell, W.J.T. (1986), *Iconology: Image, Text, Ideology*, Chicago: University of Chicago Press.

Nancy, J.-L. (1994), 'Corpus,' in J. Flower MacCannell and L. Zakarin (eds), *Thinking Bodies*, Stanford: Stanford University Press.

O'Connell, M. (2000), *The Idolatrous Eye: Iconoclasm and Theater in Early Modern England*, New York: Oxford University Press.

Ong, W.J. (1988), *Orality and Literacy: The Technologizing of the Word*, New York: Methuen.

O'Rourke Boyle, M. (1998), 'Eve's Palm,' in *Senses of Touch: Human Dignity and Deformity from Michelangelo to Calvin*, Leiden: Brill, pp. 90–171.

Parker, P. (1989), 'On the Tongue: Cross Gendering, Effeminacy, and the Art of Words,' *Style*, 23: 445–63.

Richter Sherman, C. (2001), *Writing on Hands: Memory and Knowledge in Early Modern Europe*, exhibition catalogue, Washington DC: Folger Shakespeare Library.

Ross, A. (1651). *Arcana microcosmi: or, The hid secrets of man's body discovered; in an anatomical duel between Aristotle and Galen*, London: n.p.

Rowe, K. (1999), *Dead Hands: Fictions of Agency, Renaissance to Modern*, Stanford CA: Stanford University Press.

Russell, M. (1829), *The Life of Oliver Cromwell*, Edinburgh: Constable.

Sawday, J. (1995), *The Body Emblazoned*, London: Routledge.

Scarry, E. (1985), *The Body in Pain: The Making and Unmaking of the World*, Oxford: Oxford University Press.

Shakespeare, W. (1963). *The Winter's Tale*, ed. J.H.P. Pafford, London: Methuen.

—— (1964). *King Lear*, ed. K. Muir, London: Methuen.

Smith, B. (1999), *The Acoustical World of Early Modern England*, Cambridge: Cambridge University Press.

Spurgeon, C. (1935), *Shakespeare's Imagery*, Cambridge: Cambridge University Press.

Stallybrass, P. (in press), How Many Hands Does it Take to Read (or Write) a Book.

Stewart, S. (2002), *Poetry and the Fate of the Senses*, Chicago: University of Chicago Press.

Tomkis, T. ([1607] 1913), *Lingua, or the Combat of the Tongue and the Five Senses for Superiority*, ed. J. Farmer, Amersham: Tudor Facsimile Reprints.

Vinge, L. (1975), *The Five Senses: Studies in a Literary Tradition*, Lund: Berlingska Boktryckeriert.

Williams, R. (1990), 'From Medium to Social Practice,' in *Marxism and Literature*, Oxford: Oxford University Press.

Zouch, R. (1610), *Fallacy; or, The Troubles of Great Hermenia*, Oxford: n.p.

6

The Death of the Sensuous Chemist

The 'New' Chemistry and the
Transformation of Sensuous
Technology

Lissa Roberts

If there is a single constant in human history, it is that we engage the world through the agency of our senses. This is not to say, however, that the manner of that engagement and the use to which it is put has not changed over time. Quite the contrary. Tracing these changes is crucial to understanding both the history of human identity – who do we experience ourselves to be? – and the history of science – how do we investigate and interpret the world in which we live? A common understanding is that the historical development of precision scientific instruments has extended our senses, allowing us to 'see' nature more precisely and therefore to understand it better. Exploring the history of chemistry demonstrates that the situation is far more complicated than this. A major component of the late eighteenth century chemical revolution entailed the introduction of investigative procedures that subordinated human sense to the calibrated readings of highly complex experimental apparatus. This not only made chemistry a more 'exact' science, it transformed the world of its investigation from one of qualitative distinctions that could only be apprehended by the senses to a standardized world of quantities that could be measured and manipulated in keeping with the 'objectivity' of laboratory hardware. Where human sense had once been valorized as a sensitive source of natural knowledge, its 'subjective' character came to be seen as an impediment. Sensuous traffic with nature was henceforth made to retreat to the privacy of the laboratory, hidden beneath layers of precision measurement, mathematical calculation and the public rhetoric of scientific objectivity.

As late as the mid eighteenth century, chemical reformers hoped to rely on the disciplined use of the five senses to unveil natural knowledge. Both Denis Diderot in his *Interprétation de la nature* ([1754] 1981) and Gabriel-François Venel in his *Encyclopédie* article 'chymie' (1754) opposed the quantitative superficiality of mathematical physics to their scientific aspirations for chemistry. They argued that mathematical physics obliterated knowledge of nature's heterogeneous richness as it ignored first-hand experience of natural processes in favor of mathematical calculation. Because common artisans manipulated nature on a daily basis, they knew more about its workings than did mathematical physicists. But, proceeding without metered reflection, artisans could not systematize and teach the wisdom that lay behind their skills. Contemporary chemistry, however, held out the promise of uniting the work of the hand and mind, of bringing reality to Bacon's dream of a House of Solomon in which cooperative, experimentally based ventures gave rise to an inductive fund of natural knowledge. The science of chemistry would satisfy human needs, both intellectual and material.

It was a seductive promise, but their vision left open what the precise outcome of this projected transformation would be. As was the case with so many other French reform programs, revolution replaced reform by the last decade of the eighteenth century. In the political realm, Enlightenment ideals gave way to Robespierre's bloody dream of a republic of virtue and its Napoleonic aftermath. In chemistry, the views espoused by Diderot, Venel and a community of like-minded chemists gave way to the revolution engineered by Antoine Laurent Lavoisier and a group of close associates.[1]

There are many ways to analyse this transition. One important approach that has not yet been applied has to do with examining how chemists investigatively deployed their senses in relation to the changing constellation of technologies on which they depended and what sort of knowledge they thereby produced. In other words, what part did the human body play in the changing network of eighteenth century chemistry?[2]

Popular accounts of the history of chemistry describe eighteenth century chemistry as 'advancing' through the introduction of new laboratory apparatus and procedures that afforded increased precision in analytical investigations. The growing dependence on complicated measuring devices in chemistry was simply a means of 'seeing' nature more clearly. In fact, this was not the case. The hard-won reliance on 'instruments of precision' and the transformation of chemical knowledge at this time from fundamentally qualitative to increasingly quantitative was part of a broader transformation in how chemists conceived of the world and their position in it. In place of a world once considered inhabited by sensibly rich and malleable substances, the 'new' chemists proffered a system of primary elements that combined in measurable proportions and strictly categorical ways to compose the entire world. Chemical practice was to be disciplined in keeping with this view.

Lavoisier has long been famous for championing instruments such as the balance. Recent studies disagree over whether his reliance on the balance should be seen as largely rhetorical or as manifesting a more profound element of his practice (Lundgren 1990; Bensaude-Vincent 1992). But, whatever his intentions, the ever-increasing deployment of instruments whereby quantitatively based assertions might be made signaled a fundamental shift in the discipline of chemistry (Roberts 1992). The language and practice of chemical measurement that Lavoisier and his colleagues promoted served simultaneously to discipline the chemical analyst, the subject, objects, and audience of his analyses.

Analysts had to master new experimental techniques that required them to subordinate and discipline their own bodies in the service of machines. The subject of their analysis – what counted as the discipline's fundamental questions and determinative data – had to be stabilized. As chemistry gained increasing status, its long-standing preoccupation with practical application was displaced by a more theoretically oriented perspective. Chemical knowledge was still geared toward application, but its productivity was enshrined in generalized laws and theories whereby nature itself was cast in productive terms.

In place of the particular signs of sensible evidence that had previously guided chemists through individual aspects of their art, the 'new' chemists sought determinative evidence that was transportable across qualitative and spatial borders alike. To attain generalizable measurements, the objects of chemical inquiry had to be made suitable through instrumental intervention and the post-facto application of mathematical 'corrections.' Finally, chemistry's audience had increasingly to voice their criticisms in terms dictated by measurement and its technologies. In this way, chemistry's literary, social, and material instruments joined with chemists' own bodies to direct their attention along a productive path in which the claims of individual sense no longer gave rise to scientific consensus.

What resulted was a shift in the pedagogical literature of chemistry and in what publicly constituted chemical evidence and knowledge.[3] As exemplified by Gabriel-François Rouelle's popular and influential chemistry course, which he taught at the Jardin du roi between 1742–68, aspiring chemists were trained at mid century to monitor the progress of chemical processes and make chemical determinations by sensibly examining qualitative characteristics. This meant that they had to be sensitized to the point that they could use their bodies to detect all the subtle qualitative distinctions necessary to pursue chemistry with success.

This contrasts with the approach enshrined in Lavoisier's *Traité élémentaire de chimie* (1789), the 'new' chemistry's hallmark of systematic practice and pedagogy. Here, the deployment of chemists' bodily senses was subordinately tied, almost to the point of invisibility,[4] to laboratory apparatus that yielded evidence in the form of quantitative measurements. Nowhere in the *Traité* were chemists advised to sharpen their sense of smell or taste so as to gain mastery over the world of their investigations. Rather, it proposed they learn to handle a number of instruments with sufficient dexterity to produce data that could then be manipulated either to corroborate or challenge the systematic assertions of their discipline.

As the century drew to a close, chemists increasingly subordinated their bodies to the material technology of their laboratories and began erasing the presence of direct sensory evidence from the public records of their discipline's literary and social technologies. This is not to say that chemists stopped smelling, tasting, touching, or listening in the service of their analytical activities. Rather, unmediated sense evidence played less and less of a public role in the scientific determination of knowledge, thanks to the 'new' chemists' efforts.

This essay introduces the term 'sensuous technology' to help make sense of this process. Building on Steven Shapin's seminal depiction of science as a web of material, social, and literary technologies in which 'the working of each depends upon and incorporates the others' (Shapin 1984: 507), 'sensuous technology' enables us to consider the way natural investigators used their bodies as part of this dynamically interactive network. The term 'sensuous technology' manifests a tension which is especially fruitful for investigating the process of 'modernization' in eighteenth century chemistry. It is informed by a phenomenological perspective in which humans are always engaged with the world through the directive agency of their bodies. This fact is so constant as to be practically invisible so it is important to remind ourselves that knowledge (and the way it changes over time) is a consequence of the particular form that our sensuous engagement with the world takes and to render that relationship explicit.

The term also has more historically specific resonance. Between the influence of the mechanical philosophy and the industrial revolution, machine metaphors gained increasing currency in the eighteenth century. The body itself came to be viewed as a machine in any number of ways: physiologically, psychologically, economically, even amorously. So too was it in fact enmeshed in an increasingly complicated web of man-made technologies as humans sought to increase their productive (and destructive) capacities. This was the context in which chemists transformed their discipline by the end of the eighteenth century.

Educating the Senses

In keeping with their advocacy of natural philosophical reform, Diderot and Venel held up the chemist Gabriel-François Rouelle for particular praise. As professeur-démonstrateur at the Jardin du roi, Rouelle instructed an entire generation of French chemists and chemical amateurs, training them to see, hear, smell, taste, and judge the world as he did. An examination of his course reveals both the dramatic nature of his pedagogy and how he used that drama to induce his students to participate in a world where it seemed nature could be known through the proper deployment of the senses. His props were immediately visible upon entry to the hall where he taught. Above and behind his podium stood a banner that announced the master's credo: 'Nihil est in intellectu quod non prius in sensu' – nothing is in the intellect that is not first in the senses. (Lavoisier would later quote Rouelle's motto in his *Traité élémentaire de chimie*, by which time the phrase took on a very different meaning.) Then Rouelle would enter, launching immediately into spell-binding demonstration-lectures that attracted large crowds of serious and fashionable students alike.

Historians have generally focused on the theoretical content of Rouelle's lecture course, teasing out a description of 'French Stahlianism' against which Lavoisier might later be seen as having rebelled (Secretan 1943; Rappaport 1960, 1961). But the lecture notes left by students such as Diderot and in particular A.-L. de Jussieu (from whose 1767 work the following citations are drawn)[5] reveal another tradition worthy of analysis: a practical tradition in which chemists relied on the disciplined use of their bodies in a simultaneous drive to reveal natural knowledge and productively manipulate chemical substances for utilitarian benefit. Virtually no lesson passed without Rouelle's explicit or implicit reliance on the measured use of his senses. Pedagogical success was then determined by whether he (and lecturers like him) was able to train others to deploy their bodies in similarly disciplined ways.

Rouelle began his course by defining chemistry and distinguishing it from physics. Physics treated bodies superficially in terms of their external measurements while chemistry was concerned with their particularities. Rather than seek general laws, the chemist's task was to analyse these peculiarities and generate individual facts (Jussieu 1767: 2). Training the senses was crucial to the process and purpose of chemistry. Rouelle's discussion of water offers a paradigmatic example. Prior chemists had treated water as a natural instrument – as a passive holding vessel or means of washing other chemical substances under investigation – and analysed it physically in terms of its mechanical relations with other bodies. As recounted by Jussieu (1767: 44), Rouelle argued that water could act on bodies chemically as well, drawing his evidence from the changing flavor he detected in water after performing an experiment in a *machine de Papin*.

Of paramount importance in this example is the subordinate relation of Rouelle's other laboratory instruments to the workings of his own sensuous technology. The purpose of laboratory furniture such as Papin's machine was to help expose phenomena to the determinative scrutiny of chemists' sensuous experience. This helps explain why Rouelle's introductory remarks on chemical instruments dealt almost exclusively with 'natural' instruments (water, air, fire, earth, and menstrua). Virtually the only pieces of equipment he discussed in this portion of his course, other than standard laboratory vessels and a variety of furnaces whereby instrumental fire might be regulated, were thermometers and his modified version of Hales' ([1727] 1969: 56) pedestal apparatus.

At first glance, Rouelle introduced his lectures with a comment that seems to belie the interpretation offered here: he referred to thermometers as 'necessary in physics and chemistry to justly discern the smallest degree of heat produced in bodies at the moment of their mixing and combination' (Hales 1969: 13). But, if we examine the records left of his practice, this objection literally dissolves. In keeping with Venel's description of a chemical 'artiste,' Rouelle's practical conduct was exemplary.

> The artist of whom we speak will never be so audacious [ne s'avisera de] as to estimate degrees of heat... with a thermometer or the succession of drops in a distillation process by a pendulum; he has, as workers very sensibly say, his thermometer at the tip of his fingers and his clock in his head. (Secretan 1943: 503)

When Rouelle referred to thermometers, he generally presented their use as analogous to human sense rather than as exact measuring devices. 'If one pours cold water on very pure fixed alkali, it excites sufficient heat to be very sensible to a thermometer' (Jussieu 1767: 116). The 'degrees of fire' he took them to record were not just numerically calibrated, but spanned ranges of observable phenomena. The 'first degree of fire,' for example, extended from the formation of ice to the medium point of boiling water (Jussieu 1767: 25).

To obtain more particular readings, students were advised to rely on themselves. In some cases, the correct temperature of a body might be judged by its color (Jussieu 1767: 112).[6] In other cases, sensuous states provided a scale of calibration.

> We have said that the figure of crystals varied according to the degrees of evaporation and cooling. Following Mr. Rouelle, we will establish the different degrees of evaporation relative to the heat that one employs. He establishes three degrees for evaporation, the first extends from the point of ice up to the heat of a fine summer day; this is called insensible evaporation. The second begins where the first ends, and extends up to the degree of heat at which one can no longer stand to place one's hand in water; this is mean evaporation. Finally, his third degree, which he calls either strong or rapid evaporation, extends from the second up to the point that the solution boils. (Jussieu 1767: 283)

As Rouelle's lectures made clear, it was not enough to say that chemists must rely on their senses and then set them loose in the laboratory. Individual odors, colors, and tastes signified specific compositions and could only be learned through experience, under the watchful tutelage of a recognized expert. Chemistry students had to learn what sense evidence was significant and how to use their bodies both to expose such evidence to critical scrutiny and to analyse it. To establish his authority in such matters, Rouelle often prefaced his remarks with criticisms of other, 'less critical,' chemists.

> The majority of chemists previously defined acids and alkalis by the effervescence they exhibited when mixed together. But this effervescence does not distinguish which is the acid and which is the alkali. Mr. Rouelle characterizes them by their taste and by the changes they effect in the blue tint of vegetable flowers. Acid has a severely bitter taste and changes the blue color of vegetable flowers to red. Alkalis change them to green and have the taste of spoiled urine. (Jussieu 1767: 11)

Once trained, the eyes, nose, ears, hands, and tongue of the chemist would guide him through the richly heterogeneous world of nature, delineating substances by their sensibly observable characteristics and effects (see, for example, Jussieu 1767: 131, 144, 148, 160, 167, and 184–91).

But isolating and identifying substances was far from chemists' only pursuit. They had also to gain mastery over a variety of chemical processes. Rouelle trained his students to employ their bodies as sensuous instruments in the service of this goal as well. He taught them to consider specific sensible states as evidence that a process or experiment was proceeding as desired. In some cases, such as the production of alcohol (both for consumption and for use in the laboratory), color and taste were prime indicators that all was going according to plan. In other cases, it was smell that indicated success: 'One puts the mixture in a cauldron and places it over the fire until it no longer fumes and begins emitting the odor of *fleur de pecher*, which indicates that all the volatile alkali has dissipated' (Jussieu 1767: 340). In all cases, chemists were guided by the vigilant and practiced use of their sensuous technology.

What part did the senses play when it came time to move from specifics to generalization? They simultaneously served a constraining and liberating role. On one hand, reliance on sense evidence grounded the chemist in a world of complex heterogeneity, not amenable to the construction of (quantitative) laws. Individual phenomena had to be linked in a never-ending chain of sensuous comparison, out of which general categories and relations only slowly emerged. As previously stated, this situation was reflected in the growing popularity and reliance on synoptic tables during the second half of the eighteenth century. On the other hand, sense evidence could be quite suggestive, providing a fruitful basis for analogical hypotheses. It allowed chemists to move back and forth between their mundane experiences and what they produced in their laboratories. Rouelle conjectured, for example, 'that the substance of electricity that emanates from electrified animals is analogous to phosphorous; what is certain is that the smell is the same' (Jussieu 1767: 343).[7] It was through the carefully reflective deployment of their sensuous technology that chemists had hopes of bridging the gap between laboratory production and knowledge of nature, creating thereby a full bodied system of chemistry.

Sense and Sensibility

Rouelle occasionally enlisted the senses of others to make his point. He relied on an animal's yelping response to contact with fixed alkalis, for example, to establish their caustic nature.[8] But if Rouelle and his contemporaries demonstrated little sensitivity to the 'feelings' of animals, neither did they demonstrate the compunction that we might today in exposing themselves to a variety of potentially discomforting situations. This included not only tasting and touching caustic substances but also smelling and ingesting substances that we have since come to find repugnant.[9]

On more than one occasion Rouelle made reference to the odor and taste of spoiled urine. So too did he regularly handle fecal matter. As recorded in notes from his lectures, this was all a matter of course. Such insouciance regarding situations that would offend current standards of delicacy was part of an investigative world in which sensuous technology was the dominant source of determinative evidence. Indeed, chemists' sensibilities provide a sort of indexical mirror image of the investigative processes they pursued. The more in direct touch they were with the world of their investigation, the less inhibited they seem in comparison to current standards of hygiene and gentility. It is thus worth noting that some of Rouelle's own students manifested revulsion at the thought of having to employ substances such as urine and feces. Precisely at a time when chemistry was coming increasingly to depend on intervention by technologies other than human sense, its practitioners began exhibiting sensitivity about their immediate contacts with nature.

A telling – and surprisingly early – example of this is a 1756 edition of Nicolas Lémery's *Cours de chymie* (originally published in 1675), annotated by a student of Rouelle's named Theodore Baron (cited and discussed by Secretan 1943: 359–77).[10] One of the most widely used chemistry textbooks of the first half of the eighteenth century, the *Cours de chimie*, placed empirical findings within a mechanistic framework, attempting a marriage between chemical practice and corpuscular philosophy. Baron registered revulsion throughout his edition for various products and processes whose employment Lémery recommended. Two examples illustrate this. Lémery had advised the internal application of urine to combat gout and the vapors. Baron took him and his followers to task for relying on urine's pretended medical virtues, which, he claimed, were not so well established. Neither did he consider it necessary to use urine when other remedies existed that were both more sure and less disgusting. 'It is only the absolute physical certainty of curing or alleviating that should guide the doctor in prescribing remedies... so contrary to the tastes of his patients' (Secretan 1943: 370).

Lémery used a variety of animals in the cures he prescribed. The scent of oil drawn from distilled snake cadavers treated female hysteria. Further distillation produced a salt to cure malignant fevers, apoplexy, epilepsy, paralysis, and venomous bites. Lémery prescribed an especially odorous liquid distilled from living snakes to combat the most severe cases. Also part of his curative menagerie were toads, woodlice, and crawfish, whose blood and excrement were used against epilepsy, apoplexy, paralysis, and hysteria. Baron did not understand why one needed recourse to the sort of alkali they yielded, 'especially that furnished by an animal as disgusting as the toad whose name alone frightens the imagination, when fixed alkalis drawn from the vegetable kingdom can furnish the same cure without causing us such repugnance' (Secretan 1943: 370).[11]

Baron is an interesting transitional figure precisely because his attitude surfaced so early in the half century of reforms that ultimately yielded the chemical revolution. In most other ways, his chemistry reads like a product of its time. For example, he cautioned against reliance on overly complicated laboratory equipment that obscured direct contact with nature and made clear their employers' pretensions (Secretan 1943: 363). Like his contemporaries, Baron continued to view laboratory instruments as adjuncts in the process of uncovering sensibly determined evidence (Secretan 1943: 360–1).

This is not to say that chemists did not care to improve the material technology they employed; only that they still subordinated its employment to human sense in the process of knowledgeable determination. If we return to Rouelle, for example, we find him looking forward to the day when chemists would have a complete enough understanding of solvents and their applications to fulfil their discipline's promise of mastery over nature's secrets. But first, he advised, chemists needed to overcome their own impatience, which drove them to continue using gross solvents simply because their sensible effects were more blatant. The action of more delicate solvents might be harder to detect, but their gentler nature would afford more sensitive dissolutions and yield a greater number of component substances. If chemists could be trained to apply their sensuous technology more assiduously, so too might they be trained to employ increasingly delicate material aids (Jussieu 1767: 11). It was through this sort of concerted escalation of technological deployment that Rouelle proposed advancing the discipline of chemistry. What he did not count on was a reversal in the determinative relation among the categories of technology at chemists' disposal.

Measure for Measure

In February 1786, Lavoisier and Jean-Baptiste Meusnier published an account of their demonstrations of water's de- and recomposition. They ended their memoir with a brief commentary on the need for greater precision in chemical experiments, the gist of which completely inverted the investigative relation between sensuous technology and the other instruments chemists used in their laboratories. Chemists, they wrote, had long believed they could live without the weights and measures to which general physics was indebted for its most brilliant discoveries. Instead, they relied on the relations between substances' sensibly revealed characteristics. But such an approach afforded only vague, qualitative notions that could never be made exact. Further, it limited chemists to the sensible realm, allowing a whole world of phenomena to pass unnoticed and unmeasured.

To remedy what they portrayed as chemistry's methodological short-comings and stimulate 'progress,' the authors recommended recourse to:

> the determination of volumes and weights of every constituent part of bodies under investigation, and the comparison of those weights and volumes among themselves and with other bodies. As these are the only means capable of revealing the principles of natural substances, chemists cannot be pushed with too much vigor to use them in their experiments. It is true that requiring everything be measured and calculated makes chemical operations more difficult and long, but one is well compensated for this added work by the immense advantage of never having to return over the same path. (Lavoisier and Meusnier 1786: 243–4)

Not only was sense evidence inexact and incomplete, then. Because it involved individual experience not subject to standardization, it could not stand for all time and space as objective, generalized knowledge. Future generations would have always to tread over the same ground, Lavoisier and Meusnier argued, experiencing anew the sensations of their predecessors.

Quantitative measurements, on the other hand, were universally transportable, provided they were calculated according to a standardized scale and corrected for local variation of temperature and pressure. But how might they be gathered with acceptable precision? To establish their system, the 'new' chemists had not only to develop new theories and a new nomenclature. They had also to promote the acceptance of complex and costly instruments that produced the measurements that warranted their theories and nomenclature.

From the 1770s onward, Lavoisier took pains to identify his work as modern, adding that the modernity to which he referred was traceable to recent work on aeriform fluids. The realization that a number of distinct airs existed opened an entirely new field of research. Given their largely insensible nature when not in an active state, their investigation mandated new and sensitive instruments to facilitate their manipulation and identification. In the march to systematize their examination and understanding, the network of instrumentation that gained acceptance helped direct and institutionalize the very way they were explained.

Many pneumatic investigators continued to rely on their senses, even after the turn of the century, identifying airs in terms of smells, tastes, sounds, and colors. Joseph Priestley, a pioneer in the field and opponent of 'premature' systematizing, used a veritable panoply of approaches to distinguish the airs he examined.[12] Color change or turbidity, crackling sounds, and smells all served his investigative purpose. Priestley, however, never systematized his research as a program for others to follow. He counseled only patient and exhaustive scrutiny of as many relevant phenomena as possible with whatever investigative means came to hand. His only caveats were that investigative techniques remain simple so as not to interfere with the workings of nature, and inexpensive so that others were not prohibited from using them. Natural investigators should engage in a communal drive aimed at exposing as many facts as they could (Priestley 1767: 579–80).

In contrast, Lavoisier and his colleagues not only systematized their views to form a general disciplinary program – they constructed a language that rhetorically organized the world in keeping with those views, and set out to convert others to their program. A central part of their 'missionary' work involved teaching the next generation of chemists to see, describe, and investigate the world as they did. Toward this end they sought to fill as many crucial teaching posts as possible. Additionally, Lavoisier published the *Traité élémentaire de chimie* to serve as a primer for the 'new' chemistry (Perrin 1981).

The book's third part, which describes 'the instruments and operations of chemistry,' fills almost forty percent of the entire book. Clearly Lavoisier viewed it as crucial to his task of systematically treating the elements of chemistry. Indeed, the instruments and procedures he described provided the very instrumental space within which his conceptions took the particularly systematic and apparently evident shape that they did. More specifically, his presentation of them as a coherent set of instruments and procedures points to the sort of evidence on which the 'new' chemistry rested. Henceforth, the officially acknowledged process of chemical investigation would subordinate sensuous technology to a variety of complex measuring devices.

Had more people been familiar with the experimental ways of 'modern' chemistry, Lavoisier (1789: xxxv) wrote, the views he presented to the Académie des Sciences would have been more readily understood and the science of chemistry generally would have made more progress. But people lacked a full account of the instrumentation upon which the 'new' chemistry relied; especially one written in chemistry's new language. By now using the new language to acquaint his readers with the instruments he employed and by placing this discussion at the end of his book, after his theoretical views and experimental findings were laid out, Lavoisier rhetorically linked theory, experiment, and instrument into an indissoluble whole. Acceptance of his instruments implied acceptance of how he structured chemical investigation generally (Roberts 1991b).

After digesting his book – but only after – aspiring chemists were advised to experience the practice of chemistry firsthand, either by attending demonstration-lectures or by directly familiarizing themselves with chemistry's instruments and methods in a laboratory. Lavoisier went so far as to quote Rouelle toward this end: 'Nihil est in intellectu... ' But what he trained them to observe was quite different from the training Rouelle had provided. Where Rouelle engaged the senses in a search for qualitative distinctions, Lavoisier looked largely to measurement for experimental determinations that supported his theoretical claims. This is not to say that chemists would no longer employ their senses; only that their use was constrained in the laboratory by the instruments with which they were engaged and dismissed in experimental reports and debates as inconclusive.

There were cases where the presence of chemists' bodies was deemed a downright nuisance. Lavoisier, for example, made repeated reference to temperature in his work, insisting that constancy was imperative to ensure precision. To secure stable temperatures, he advised his readers to keep their hands off the vessels that held test-substances, lest their body heat alter experimental circumstances (Lavoisier 1789: 322).

Finally, there were occasions in which chemists were advised literally to transform their bodies into appendages of a machine. For this purpose, they had to train certain portions of their bodies to function as an integral part of some instrumental set-up. One such example occurs in the midst of Lavoisier's discussion of the decomposition of atmospheric air by iron. For his instrumental set-up to yield a significant reading, Lavoisier had to raise the mercury in its vessel to a certain level. Relying on a specially rigged siphon, he attached his mouth and sucked out a portion of air from the vessel until the mercury was at the desired level. 'It is an art to raise the mercury in this way,' he commented. While difficult to master, however, it was superior to the unaided body which could never achieve measured precision (Lavoisier 1805, II: 65).

Making Water

There were times when Lavoisier could not attain the precision he thought requisite to determine an experiment's outcome. One such case involved his early attempts to produce water from what he came to call oxygen and hydrogen gas. Rather than turn to qualitative evidence derived from sense in subsequent trials, Lavoisier and his colleagues followed the adage that 'bigger is better.' To demonstrate that water is a compound of fixed quantities of oxygen and hydrogen, they deployed larger and more complex apparatus (Lavoisier register VII: 86; Lavoisier 1783). When others questioned their demonstrations and theory, they found themselves increasingly brought into the investigative world that the 'new' chemists were constructing. Not only did charges of Lavoisier's neglect of qualitative sense evidence give way to debates over instrumental precision. By raising new questions that could only be investigated under its auspices, the imposing and dramatic presence of the 'new' chemistry's sophisticated instrumentation made it increasingly difficult to return to the determinative deployment of sensuous technology.

Movement away from direct sensory determination is evident at all levels of Lavoisier's recorded practice, from the activities described in his private laboratory registers to his published reports. While Lavoisier and his colleagues still noted sensibly detected characteristics and consequences in the laboratory, their attention to such details was consistently subordinated to their concern over achieving measurements that corroborated their theory. For example, once Lavoisier and Meusnier settled upon the structure and size of their experimental setup, they measured component gases, the amount of water produced or lost, and any weight gain in the gun barrel they employed, and then compared these figures to what was mandated by their theory. Not once did they see discrepancies as reflecting on the validity of their theoretical position. Rather, they explained inconsistencies in terms of instrumental failure. Either luting was inadequate, air escaped through leather tubes, water adhered to the inside of flasks, vessels broke, or the gases used were insufficiently pure. Their challenge was to perfect their experimental set-up to the point that they got the measurements they expected (Lavoisier register VII: 75–105 and X: 21–380).[13] Their perspective is made clear by a comment recorded in the register: 'It therefore seems that the decomposition of water will be increasingly confirmed as greater care is taken in performing experiments, since in the midst of all the sources of uncertainty that accompanied past experiments, only the theory of water's decomposition into constant proportions and weight of dephlogisticated and inflammable airs could erase the contradictions and absurdities' (Lavoisier register VII: 102). Erasure meant not only discounting sensibly gauged problems such as the acidic nature of the 'water' produced in every trial before 1790 and 'explaining' quantitative discrepancies in terms of instrumental malfunction. It meant also subjecting quantitative findings to mathematical analysis for 'correction.'

Mathematical analysis thus replaced sensory analysis as the final step of chemical determination. Lavoisier justified this approach by arguing that mathematical analysis of inexact data drawn from various experiments compensated for the lack of precision in each. He claimed that it was only through this process of standardization that the essential elements of a general theory could be deduced (Lavoisier 1783: 371).

The first principle that stood behind this approach, was that 'the whole is always equal to the sum of its parts' (Lavoisier 1783: 339). While certainly a fruitful axiom, its application to experimental situations invariably required a level of idealization. As demonstrated by the actual course of investigations into the composition of water, there was constant ambiguity regarding what was meant by 'the whole.' Heat and light eluded measured detection. Oxygen and hydrogen gas, the parts deemed most relevant and measurable, were never completely contained.

Where other chemists began with the sentient particularities of their world, the 'new' chemists substituted an ideal limiting case. Where other chemists concluded their findings with qualitative determination, they transmuted the results of chemical processes into decontextualized quantities, but they did not work in a socio-cultural vacuum. Attempts to institutionalize the process of decontextualization through standardized measures were being made in a variety of sectors throughout France. The transformation that was taking place in chemistry was, in fact, a mutually reinforcing part of the broader transformation of French polity. While changes in attitude, policies, and practice in the macro-sphere resonated down to the level of chemistry, changes in chemistry circulated back to inform the larger context in which it was situated. Each realm exerted a constructive impact on the other.[14]

The introduction of the metric system and standardized weights and measures was one of the monumental achievements of the French Revolution. Under the *ancien régime*, weights and measures were a local affair, determined by tradition, specific use, and application to qualitatively different objects. (Different scales were used for different qualities of grain, for example.) As was their customary privilege, local lords controlled the standards employed in their area, often distorting them for their own benefit. The vast majority of *cahiers de doleances* drawn up by the Third Estate on the eve of the French Revolution addressed this abuse. They called on the king to establish 'un roi, une loi, un poids et une mesure.'

While the Third Estate called for an end to privilege and its abuses, a small coterie of reformers – including Lavoisier – turned the popular plea for equality into a positive plan of 'enlightened' action. In the name of the people, they lobbied for a system of weights and measures based completely on convention. No longer rooted in tradition and local usage, the metric system was intended to transcend boundaries of place and utilization, allowing for universal application and translation. In fact, it replaced time-bound custom and local networks of knowledge and exchange with the asserted authority of science and the state.

By calling for adoption of the metric and decimal systems, Lavoisier and his colleagues compounded the extent to which individual chemists' determinative control over their research was diminished. Not only was the autonomous application of sensuous technology increasingly eclipsed by 'modern' methods and instruments, traditional standards of measurement that related directly to local customs and applications had to be translated into a conventionally abstract, numerical scheme. When these new methods and measurements were then articulated in chemistry's new language and employed as warrants for the theoretical assertions made by Lavoisier and his colleagues, the process of standardization actually served to bolster the 'new' chemistry's asserted authority.[15]

Published reports on water's de- and recomposition show how this asserted authority functioned. During experimental trials, a number of mishaps occurred and the amount of oxygen obtained varied from 81 to 86 percent of the water lost, but, as Lavoisier and his colleagues publicized their findings, they rewrote history. Lavoisier idealized his demonstrations by referring to the gases he employed as pure and discounting the acidic nature of the water he obtained (see Lavoisier 1783: 335). The mishaps that took place were either read out of the public record or explained away as inconsequential.[16] Measured amounts were stabilized in the public record. The water produced in the 1783 demonstrations of composition was fixed at approximately five grams – 'which accords with the weights of the two united airs' – while experimental results had been closer to three. The percentages of oxygen and hydrogen obtained in the 1785 demonstrations of water's decomposition stabilized at 85 and 15 percent respectively of the water initially employed. These figures were publicly cited in journals, lectures and dictionaries, and were thereby etched in the minds of natural philosophy's literate audience (see, for example, *Encyclopédie Méthodique* 1792, II: 461).

Measured Responses

The 'new' chemistry's instrumentally informed and quantitatively oriented approach was promoted by such vehicles as the *Encyclopédie Méthodique*. In the article on the balance, for example, the fundamental importance of such devices was explained in the following terms:

> The balance is indispensable in a chemistry laboratory. This science owes all the progress it has made for the last few years to it. It is by precisely determining the weights of substances that one combines and the products of their combinations that one arrives at exact knowledge of the principles of many bodies and the proportions of those same principles. (*Encyclopédie Méthodique* 1792, II: 503–4)

But, not everyone was convinced by Lavoisier and his colleagues' claims of precisely measured determination. This section addresses responses to the 'new' chemists' claims.

Among the most vocal opponents of Lavoisier and his allies were the English chemists William Nicholson and Richard Kirwan. Nicholson began by attacking the issue of quantitative precision. He reasoned that because chemists were accustomed to analysing the objects of their inquiry in sensible terms, they often took it for granted that the reported quantities they read were accurate. But, as there were those who increasingly supported their theoretical claims with quantitative evidence, Nicholson felt duty-bound to publicize the limits of accuracy to which measurements were subject (Kirwan 1789: vii–x). He then zeroed in on the most blatant case of pretended precision:

> As reference to weights in the experiments of Mr. Lavoisier is made to constitute a great part of the arguments adduced to prove the composition of water, and its decomposition, I think it proper... to take notice that his writings abound with specific gravities of elastic fluids, carried to five places of figures, which are so far from being given as estimate numbers, that they are used as elements in results, carried to six, seven, and even eight places of figures... these long rows of figures, which in some instances extend to a thousand times the nicety of experiment, serve only to exhibit a parade which true science has no need of. (Kirwan 1789: x–xi)

Nicholson and Kirwan were not opposed to chemists using instrumentally derived measurements. Indeed, Nicholson viewed the determination of weights as 'half the business of a chemist' (Kirwan 1789: viii). What they did oppose was researchers using claims of accuracy to promote their measurements and theories as definitive.

In his own analysis of inflammable air, for example, Kirwan relied on a host of instrumentally obtained figures including the air's specific gravity, barometer and temperature readings, and the ratio of inflammable air's and atmospheric air's weights, but he based his final determination on evidence obtained directly by his senses. Relying on his knowledge of inflammable air's distinct smell he concluded that it bore no compositional relation to water because, though it lost its smell when extracted from iron filings over water, it retained its inflammability (Kirwan 1789: 27).

In 1785 Kirwan wrote to Lorenz Friedrich Crell, the influential editor of the *Chemische Annalen,* hoping to spur an internationally orchestrated reaction to the 'new' chemists' strong-arm assertions (*Chemische Annalen* 1785, II: 335). But the organized opposition he hoped for never materialized and Kirwan found himself increasingly isolated in his opposition to the 'new' chemistry. While men such as he were often quite good at pointing out isolated cases of the 'new' chemists' experimental errors or theoretical overstatements, they never marshaled a tightly constructed and systematically extensive network with which to maintain control over the field of chemistry. The 'new' chemists increasingly dominated their discipline through the imposition of dramatically persuasive instruments, the publication of books and journal articles that heralded chemistry's new system and nomenclature, and chemistry courses that did the same. Without an equally potent, competitive system the 'new' chemistry's opponents were bound for eventual defeat (Roberts, unpublished).

Finally, if reluctantly, Kirwan accepted the 'new' chemistry's dominion over his discipline. In 1791 he wrote a letter of resignation to Berthollet which was subsequently published in the *Encyclopédie Méthodique*. A similar letter from Joseph Black was excerpted on the same page. Attributing Lavoisier's success to his experimental ingenuity and prowess, Black wrote, 'The numerous experiments that you have done on a grand scale... were pursued with such care and scrupulous attention for detail that nothing could be more satisfying than the proofs at which you arrived' (*Encyclopédie Méthodique* 1796, III: 560).[17]

Joseph Priestley was not so impressed and never swayed from the opposition expressed in his *Reflexions on the Doctrine of Phlogiston and the Composition of Water* (1786/1798). A perusal of his critique shows he was not motivated by slavish devotion to phlogiston. As did Kirwan, he recognized the systematic nature of his opponents' work and the strength that each of their claims gained when buttressed by the other elements of their system. He therefore challenged the 'new' chemistry by exposing its self-reinforcing structure whereby individual claims gained strength from the act of systematization rather than on their own merit.

Priestley began by raising qualitative considerations that his opponents had brushed aside. The iron 'oxide' found in the gun barrel after the purported decomposition of water differed in color from that usually produced when iron absorbed dephlogisticated air and the water produced when dephlogisticated and inflammable airs were burned was virtually always acidic. His major focus, however, was on the inappropriateness and inadequacy of his opponents' experimental apparatus. The only time that even a small amount of relatively acid-free water was produced was when Lavoisier and his collaborators performed their experiment on a grand scale, but such a set-up was prohibitively expensive and difficult to handle. Not only did it yield data that required extensive mathematical tinkering, but almost no one else was in a position to repeat their work and substantiate their results. Their experimental data and the theoretical claims had to be taken as articles of faith. 'In such circumstances,' Priestley averred, 'one can not help but suspect the exactitude of this experiment's results and the truth of the conclusions drawn from it' (Priestly 1786/1798: 33; see also 19, 23, 32).

Advocates of the 'new' chemistry were undeterred by Priestley's reasoning. They set out instead to gain as many converts as possible, relying on education and the increasing availability of new instrumentation that was often simplified to accommodate amateur participation. Introducing chemists to the 'new' chemistry through the seemingly objective path of its precision instruments and analytic processes was an effective route to take. As chemists were disciplined to deploy their bodies in the service of an orchestrated network of apparatus, they would be brought into an even larger network that was interdependently composed of all of chemistry's technologies.

Conclusion

In 1789, Fourcroy was asked by the Société Royale de Médecine to review Lavoisier's *Traité élémentaire de chimie* (De Horne and Fourcroy 1789). Not surprisingly, he was enthusiastic about both the book and the new system of chemistry it presented. He praised Lavoisier for having disciplined an increasingly complex field of investigation through the establishment of a small number of fundamental principles and experimental procedures. Chemistry was henceforth to be organized and understood by examining the formative powers of a set of primary elements within the exacting context of quantitative precision.

The art of doing truly useful experiments and contributing to the progress of analytical science, Fourcroy wrote, consists in letting nothing escape, in collecting everything and subjecting it to measurement. Since 1772, he continued, Lavoisier had distinguished himself by following this exact method. It was through the aid of his experimental procedures – 'that new sense, added, so to speak, to those already possessed by the [scientist]' – that chemistry's new doctrines were founded (De Horne and Fourcroy 1789: 2).

Such was the positive assessment of the 'new' chemistry made by one of its foremost proponents. But should we content ourselves with this account? More specifically, should we view chemists' increasingly dominant reliance on complicated measuring devices simply as an historical extension of their senses? This chapter indicates that the matter is much more complex. For one thing, not all of the senses were equally 'extended' through the new methods and technologies. In the 'new' chemistry taste and smell virtually disappeared as formal media of chemical analysis. Touch and hearing were likewise largely sidelined. The importance of the sense of sight increased as regards the visual reading of the results produced by laboratory instruments (such as thermometers) but decreased with respect to the role of direct visual evidence (such as changes in color). The shift in sensory usage and the emphasis on quantitative over qualitative analysis served to bring chemistry more in line with the theories and practices of cognate sciences, and, more generally, moved chemistry away from the suspect, subjective, sensory realm to the idealized realm of objective rationality. While the rhetoric of modernity may have collapsed such shifts in scientific theory and practice into the trope of 'seeing nature more clearly' therefore, the vision of nature thereby promoted was in fact a careful construction. The use of precision instruments, mathematical calculation and a public discourse of scientific rationality yielded (and was dependent on) a world of standardized, measurable quantities.

In this chapter I have argued that the acquisition of scientific knowledge derives from a constantly changing network of interdependent instrumental practices, which include the deployment of the senses. As our encounter with the natural world is always mediated by perceptual, technological and cultural practices, the history of science cannot simply be accounted for in terms of our increased familiarity with nature. Both the structure and content of what we take to be science depend on a particular ideological orientation and on a particular selection and development of technological aids, including the sensuous technologies of the human body.

Notes

1. The reader should note that I refer to Lavoisier throughout this chapter, not as a lone hero who masterminded a revolution single-handedly but both as a central figure and symbol of an entire network of changes embodied in the successful introduction of innovative laboratory equipment, techniques, pedagogy and language.

2. Given the constant fact of scientific researchers' sensuous engagement with the world of their investigation, considering the body's changing role in the history of science should both offer significant insight into the development of scientific practice and reflect back on the history of the body in general. While this chapter does not explicitly relate its subject to the more general field of inquiry, connections should nonetheless be considered. See, for example Feher (1989), Outram (1989) and Stafford (1992).

3. For the importance of didactic literature in chemistry see Hannaway (1975) and Christie and Golinski (1982).

4. We might see this as a bodily analogue to what Steven Shapin (1989) has identified as 'invisible technicians.'

5. That is, all citations to Rouelle's lectures in what follows are drawn from Jussieu (1767). All translations are mine.

6. Josiah Wedgwood attempted to operationalize this approach by constructing a pyrometer that measured heat in terms of the changing colors of clay beads. See Roberts (1991b: 210).

7. For an example of the fruitful use of analogies based on Rouelle's chemistry, see Diderot ([1754] 1981).

8. 'Pure fixed alkalis applied to an animal's skin makes the same impression as a hot iron' (Jussieu 1767: 228). Compare Rouelle's experimental use of animals to his predecessor Stephen Hales ([1733] 1964) who seemed to think nothing of skinning animals alive and his contemporary Albrecht von Haller ([1755] 1936) who regularly poured vitriolic acid onto the skin of dogs. See also Thomas (1983).

9. Similar evidence can be drawn from contemporary electrical experimentation.

10. This work is cited and discussed by Secretan (1943: 359–77). Secretan notes that Lavoisier filled Baron's place in the Académie des Sciences in 1768. For an indication

that Baron's sense of delicacy was perhaps 'ahead of its time,' contrast the date of his utterances to the general views recorded in Corbin (1986).

11. For a related analysis of the changing role of sense evidence in medical diagnosis see Nicholson (1992).

12. In addition to the celebrated case of Priestley, it is worth considering the 'pneumatic medicine' pioneered by Thomas Beddoes and his colleagues in the 1790s. See Golinski (1992: chapter 6) and Schaffer (1990).

13. On the relation between measurement and theory in scientific practice see Kuhn (1977: 193): 'Quantitative facts... must be fought for, and in this fight the theory with which they are to be compared proves the most potent weapon. Often scientists cannot get numbers that compare well with theory until they know what numbers they should be making nature yield.'

14. On the need to develop symmetrical explanations regarding the constructive constitution of scientific knowledge and society see Latour (1990). The discussion that follows draws heavily on Kula (1984).

15. It should be noted that Lavoisier hoped his standard would be adopted not only in France but internationally. See Lavoisier folder 1260, Archives de l'Académie des Sciences.

16. To aid this process only some experiments were described. Lavoisier and Meusnier explained their selectivity in terms of thinking it wise only to report those cases in which their 'apparatus acquired the necessary degree of perfection.' See Lavoisier and Meusnier (1784: 363).

17. Note that Black based his judgment on published reports of Lavoisier's experiments.

Bibliography

Bensaude-Vincent, B. (1992), 'The Balance: Between Chemistry and Politics,' in L. Roberts (ed.), *The Chemical Revolution: Context and Practices* (special volume of *The Eighteenth Century: Theory and Interpretation*), trans. M.K. Kochan, R. Porter and C. Prendergast, Leamington Spa: Berg.

Berthelot, M. (1890), *La Revolution chimique*, Paris: Alcan.

Christie, J.R.R. and Golinski, J.V. (1982), 'The Spreading of the Word: New Directions in the Historiography of Chemistry 1600–1800,' *History of Science*, 20: 235–66.

Corbin, A. (1986), *The Foul and the Fragrant: Odor and the French Social Imagination*, Cambridge MA: Harvard University Press.

Diderot, D. ([1754] 1981), *Interprétation de la nature*, ed. J. Varloot and P. Casini, Paris: Hermann.

Feher, M. Naddaff, R. and Tazi, N. (eds) (1989), *Fragments for a History of the Human Body*, 3 vols, New York: Zone.

Golinski, J. (1992), *Science as Public Culture: Chemistry and Enlightenment in Britain, 1760–1820*, Cambridge: Cambridge University Press.

Guerlac, H. (1976), 'Chemistry as a Branch of Physics: Laplace's Collaboration with Lavoisier,' *Historical Studies in the Physical Sciences*, 7: 193–276.

Hales, S. ([1727] 1969), *Vegetable Staticks: or an Account of some Statical Experiments on the Sap of Vegetables*, London: MacDonald and Co.

von Haller, A. ([1755] 1936), *A Dissertation on the Sensible and Irritable Parts of Animals*, Baltimore: Johns Hopkins University Press.

Hannaway, O. (1975), *The Chemists and the Word: The Didactic Origins of Chemistry*, Baltimore: Johns Hopkins University Press.

Horne, M.M. de and Fourcroy, A.F. (1789), *Rapport sur le Traité élémentaire de chimie de M. Lavoisier, Fait a la Société Royale de Médecine, dans sa séance du 6 février 1789. Extrait des Registres de cette Compagnie*, Paris: Société Royale de Médecine.

Jussieu, A.-L. de (1767), *Cours de Chymie, Recueilli des leçons de M. Rouelle Apothicaire, Démonstrateur en Chymie au Jardin du Roi, de l'Académie Royale des Sciences de Paris*, Paris: Bibliothéque Musée de l'Histoire Naturelle, Ms. 1202.

Kirwan, R. ([1789] 1968), *An Essay on Phlogiston and the Constitution of Acids, to which are added notes exhibiting and defending the Antiphlogistic Theory, with additional remarks and replies by the author*, trans. W. Nicholson, London: Frank Cass & Co.

Kuhn, T. (1977), 'The Function of Measurement in Modern Physical Science,' in *The Essential Tension*, Chicago: University of Chicago Press.

Kula, W. (1984), *Les Mesures et les hommes*, Paris: Fondation de la Maison des sciences de l'homme.

Latour, B. (1990), 'Post-modern? No, Simply Amodern! Steps Towards an Anthropology of Science,' *Studies in the History and Philosophy of Science*, 21(1): 145–71.

Lavoisier, A.L. ([1783] 1862), 'Mémoire dans lequel on a pour objet de prouver que l'eau n'est point une substance simple,' reprinted in *Oeuvres de Lavoisier*, II, Paris: n.p., pp. 334–59.

—— (1786), 'Développement des dernières expériences sur la decomposition et la recomposition de l'eau,' Reprinted in *Memoires de chimie*, II: 219–44.

—— ([1789] 1965), *Elements of Chemistry*, trans. R. Kerr, New York: Dover.

—— (1805), *Mémoires de chimie*, ed. Mme. Lavoisier, 2 vols, Paris: n.p.

—— (n.d.), *Cahiers de laboratoire*, Archives de l'Académie des Sciences, Paris: n.p.

—— (1862), *Oeuvres de Lavoisier*, Paris: Imprimerie Impériale.

—— and Meusnier, J.-B. (1784), 'Mémoire ou l'on prouve, par la décomposition de l'eau, que ce fluide n'est point une substance simple,' in *Oeuvres de Lavoisier*, II: 360–73.

Lundgren, A. (1990), 'The Changing Role of Numbers in Eighteenth century Chemistry,' in T. Fransmyr, J.L. Heilbron and R.E. Rider (eds), *The Quantifying Spirit*, Berkeley: University of California Press, pp. 245–66.

Nicholson, M. (1993), 'The Art of Diagnosis: Medicine and the Five Senses,' in W.F. Bynum and R. Porter (eds), *Companion Encyclopedia of the History of Medicine*, London: Routledge.

Outram, D. (1989), *The Body and the French Revolution*, New Haven CT: Yale University Press.

Perrin, C. (1981), 'The Triumph of the Antiphlogistians,' in H. Wolfe (ed.), *The Analytic Spirit: Essays in the History of Science in Honor of Henry Guerlac*, Ithaca: Cornell University Press, pp. 40–63.

Priestley, J. (1767), *The History and Present State of Electricity with Original Experiments*. London: n.p.

—— (1774–1777), *Experiments and Observations of Different Kinds of Air*, 3 vols, London: n.p.

—— ([1786] 1798), *Reflexions sur la doctrine du Phlogistique et de la composition de l'eau, par Joseph Priestley*, trans. P.A. Adet, Paris: n.p.

Rappaport, R. (1960), 'G.F. Rouelle: Eighteenth century Chemist and Teacher,' *Chymia*, 6: 68–99.

—— (1961), 'Rouelle and Stahl, the Phlogistic Revolution in France,' *Chymia*, 7: 73–102.

Roberts, L. (1991a), 'Setting the Table: The Disciplinary Development of Eighteenth century Chemistry as Read Through the Changing Structure of its Tables,' in P. Dear (ed.), *The Literary Structure of Scientific Argument: Historical Studies*, Philadelphia: University of Pennsylvania Press.

—— (1991b), 'A Word and the World: The Significance of Naming the Calorimeter,' *Isis*, 82: 198–222.

—— (1992), 'Condillac, Lavoisier and the Instrumentalization of Science,' in L. Roberts (ed.), *The Chemical Revolution: Context and Practices* (special issue of *The Eighteenth Century: Theory and Interpretation*), trans. M.K. Kochan, R. Porter and C. Prendergast, Leamington Spa: Berg.

—— (1993), 'Filling the Space of Possibilities: Eighteenth century Chemistry's Transition from Art to Science,' *Science in Context*, 6: 511–33.

—— (n.d.), 'Communities in the Crucible: Toward a New Political History of the Chemical Revolution,' unpublished manuscript.

Schaffer, S. (1990), 'Measuring Virtue: Eudiometry, Enlightenment and Pneumatic Medicine,' in A. Cunningham and R. French (eds), *The Medical Enlightenment of the Eighteenth Century*, Cambridge: Cambridge University Press, pp. 281–318.

Secretan, C. (1943), 'Un Aspect de la chimie preLavoisienne,' *Mémoires de la Société Vaudoise des Sciences Naturelles*, 50(7): 220–444.

Shapin, S. (1984), 'Pump and Circumstance: Robert Boyle's Literary Technology,' *Social Studies of Science*, 14: 481–520.

—— (1989), 'The Invisible Technician,' *American Scientist*, 77: 554–63.

Stafford, B.M. (1992), *Body Criticism: Imaging the Unseen in Enlightenment Art and Medicine*, Cambridge MA: MIT Press.

Thomas, K. (1983), *Man and the Natural World: A History of the Modern Sensibility*, New York: Pantheon Press.

Venel, G.F. (1754), *Chymie Encyclopédie*, 8: 12–62.

7

Charting the Cultural History of the Senses

Alain Corbin

It is now more than half a century since Lucien Febvre called for a history of the sensibilities.[1] This would, he believed, be integrated into the study of the collective psychology that has been christened, rather hastily, the history of *mentalités* (Febvre 1938, 1941).[2] This vast project, expounded in many works by the author of *Combats pour l'histoire,* implied, above all, the analysis of the modalities of perception, the identification of the sensory hierarchy, and the reconstitution of systems of emotions. The study of the use of the senses was thus incorporated into what Lucien Febvre saw as the 'mental equipment,' a rigid concept that revealed the excessive reification for which the founder of *Annales* is today justifiably reproached. While Norbert Elias ([1939] 1975) was refining his analysis of the 'civilizing process,' and attempting to trace the progress of autocontention and the internalization of norms within Western society, Lucien Febvre proposed the study of the slow repression of emotional activity and greater rationality of behavior.

This project was subject to the intellectual influences and fashions of the day, suggested by a reading of J. Huizinga ([1919] 1955) and Georges Lefebvre ([1932] 1988), spurred on by the later vogue for the psychology of crowds (Nye 1975; Barrows 1981; Moscovici 1981), and stimulated by the works of Lucien Levy-Bruhl ([1922] 1923) and Charles Blondel (1928); today it appears obsolete.[3] It is useful, nevertheless, to recall its existence. It produced works which might profitably be re-read from the perspective of a historical anthropology of the senses (Mandrou [1961] 1976).

The attention paid to the regime of sensory values and to the hierarchy of the representations and uses of the senses within a culture owes something to the intuitions of Lucien Febvre, imprecise though these may have been.

At all events, it represents for the historian a project – or rather a gamble – which is risky but fascinating. Is it possible to discern retrospectively the nature of the presence in the world of people in the past through an analysis of the hierarchy of the senses and the balance established between them at a particular moment in history and within a given society? Is it possible to detect the functions of these hierarchies, and so identify the purposes which presided over this organization of the relations between the senses? Can we envisage submitting this research to diachrony, observing permanences, and detecting open ruptures or subtle differences? Is it helpful to connect modifications to the systems of emotions, which are more easily discernable, to those which operate in the hierarchy and balance of the senses? To respond to such questions is to accept the existence and validity of a history of sensibility, since it implies discovering the configuration of what is experienced and what cannot be experienced within a culture at a given moment.

By way of example, David Howes (1987) has offered a highly stimulating reading of the century 1750–1850 (see also Howes and Lalonde 1991), though one which needs to be backed up by long and patient research. According to Howes, the senses of proximity, of touch, taste and smell, which govern in depth the affective mechanisms, experienced an increase in their relative power from the end of the eighteenth to the middle of the nineteenth centuries, just when the outlines of the social order were becoming blurred. Smell, in particular, the sense of transitions (Howes 1987), of thresholds and margins, which reveals the processes by which beings and things are transformed, fascinated at this period of confusion, whilst the sense of sight was no longer able to read the hierarchies with the same assurance. This is convincing and, when all is said and done, perfectly logical. Specialists in literary history have now for some time emphasized the invasion of darkness, the obsessive fear of opaqueness and the hard battle then being fought by social observers and municipal authorities in their struggle to shed the purifying light of knowledge and power on the 'masses down below,' described by Victor Hugo. That said, the historian working in this field faces many problems; rigorous precautions are also essential, and it is this which forms my theme.

The first and simplest approach suggested to the researcher by the historical tradition known as positivist is to try to trace the evolution of the sensory environment; or, to put it another way, to draw up an inventory of the sensations that were present at a given moment in history in each social milieu. From this perspective, Guy Thuillier (1977: 230–44) has attempted to compile a catalogue and measure the relative intensity of the noises that might reach the ear of a villager in the Nivernais in the middle of the nineteenth century; and you can almost hear, as you read his book, the ringing of the hammer on the anvil, the heavy thud of the wooden mallet wielded by the cartwright, the insistent presence of bells and the whinny of horses in an aural environment where the noise of the engine or the amplifier was unknown. This approach, also found in J. Léonard (1986) is by no means negligible. It aids immersion in the village of the past; it encourages the adoption of a comprehensive viewpoint; it helps to reduce the risk of anachronism. But, quite clearly, it is based on a questionable postulate, it implies the non-historicity of the modalities of attention, thresholds of perception, significance of noises, and configuration of the tolerable and the intolerable. In the last analysis, it ends up by denying the historicity of that balance of the senses which is here my theme. It is as if, in the eyes of the author, the habitus of the Nivernais villager of the nineteenth century did not condition his hearing, and so his listening.[4]

Guy Thuillier's project deserves, nevertheless, to be refined. It can happen that, in a particular situation, noise assumes enormous importance. Let us take as an example an episode in the life of Lonlay-l'Abbaye, a tiny commune in the hills of Normandy. Here, the local peasants were in the habit of ordering their work according to the bells of the church, an *abbatiale* dating from the eleventh to the fourteenth centuries. In 1944 the destruction of the church tower by German troops meant that the traditional ringing had to be replaced by the noise of the powerful fire brigade siren installed in the center of the *bourg*, on the roof of the *mairie*. The farmers soon grew accustomed to the new sound, which symbolized modernity. In 1958 the church got back its tower. At the request of the inhabitants of the *bourg*, irritated by the daily howling of the siren, the municipal council decided to return to the old ringing. For more than a year the commune was rent by a war of noises.[5] The peasants clung to the new sound of the siren, which was clearer and, above all, louder; their adversaries declared their preference for the aesthetic quality and emotional power of vibrant bronze, proclaiming their rejection of the deafening noise of modernity. The peasants, en masse, invaded the *bourg*, threw stones at the *mairie*, and booed – almost subjected to 'rough music' – the leaders of the 'anti-siren party.' As feelings ran high, old divisions were revived: the former 'Gaullists' laid into the former 'Pétainists'; adulterous affairs and private vengeances surfaced. The media began to take an interest, and the conflict appeared on the front page of *France-Soir* and made the news bulletin of the radio station Europe No. 1. The curé saw his authority, hitherto never challenged, called seriously into question, and it was necessary for the archpriest of the deanery to visit the commune and appeal for calm. The harassed mayor soon succumbed to a coronary. Only recourse to a neutral political figure – a former deputy who was a native of the commune, to whom the municipal council offered the post of mayor – succeeded in restoring peace, if not harmony. Henceforward, everyday at noon, the siren blared whilst the bells rang.

Such an episode, a true analysis of which requires an analysis of anthro-pological structures, was in large part a matter of symbols; the traditional hostility between town – the *bourg* – and country was also a factor. But it reveals another division, a social dichotomy in the use of the senses, in the perception of thresholds of tolerance, and in the significance of noises; it calls for a different analysis of the presence of sounds.

Let us return to the difficulties that await the historian who wishes to study the organization and balance of the senses. The most obvious obstacle lies in the transience of the evidence. It is true that knowledge of techniques and tools, of the structure of the landscape and of dietary habits or hygienic practices makes it possible to reconstitute the sensory environment, at least approximately. The transience of the evidence concerns rather the use of the senses, their lived hierarchy and their perceived significance. However, historians know very little about the evolution of systems of appreciation;[6] they are ill-informed about the respective configurations of the agreeable and the disagreeable, the fascinating and the repulsive, the sought-after and the rejected, the tolerable and the intolerable, within the culture they study. Usually they are unaware of the relative role of each of the senses in practices of exchange, or in modes of communication. But information of this sort is indispensable to the perception of social cleavages; without it, there can be no true history of the representations of the self and the other within each of the groups studied.

There is, however, no shortage of sources that tell us about all these historical subjects. Let us take first the writings that reveal the system of norms, and that make it possible to identify the techniques of sensory restriction operating within the society under consideration. If we confine ourselves to France in the first two-thirds of the nineteenth century, there are many educational books and manuals of hygiene that reveal the normative. The authors of these works were expected to devote a chapter to the *percepta* (see, for example, Levy 1844). They were required to lay down precepts of hygiene or of education with regard to the sensory organs. In so doing, they decreed, and helped to impose, a hierarchy of the senses.

The literature in which people wrote about themselves constitutes an abundant source for anyone embarking on the sort of anthropological enquiry under consideration here. Unfortunately, this was a socially restricted practice. Alain Girard (1963), Béatrice Didier (1976), Michelle Perrot and Georges Ribeill (1985; see also Corbin 1987, 1990), among others, have shown that keeping a private journal was at this period more common in the provinces than in Paris, that it was predominantly a petty bourgeois practice, and that it frequently attracted people who felt frustrated, suffocated by their family, and lacking other means of self-expression than private writing. This explains the over representation of women and homosexuals within the ranks of the diarists. The acuity with which the self was heard, and the distribution between the felt and the unremarked, varied considerably according to the group to which the diarist belonged. Also, this meticulous self-accounting, and preoccupation with decline, which no editorial design as yet toned down, was in practice short lived. It was during the course of the eighteenth century that the private journal, especially the 'therapeutic journal' kept by British invalids (Corbin [1988] 1994), came gradually to replace family record books and spiritual journals. For a few decades self-scrutiny, gradually being laicized, offers the historian analyses of fascinating precision.

There is no better source for tracing those processes of increasing delicacy, of withdrawal into oneself, of a new vulnerability to the wounds suffered in the social fray, which have been described by Emile Durkheim ([1897] 1966) and Norbert Elias. There is no better source for anyone who seeks to understand the historicity of the affective mechanisms, to discover the configuration and functioning of the systems of emotions, or discern the ways in which the senses were educated and employed. The diarists also constantly record their cenesthetic impressions or, to put it another way, those perceptions of the inner sense about which Montaigne had spoken, that murmuring of the viscera to which the elites of the nineteenth century were so attentive before the emergence of psychoanalysis (Starobinski 1981; Azouvi 1984).

This writing about oneself tells us in detail, to take just one example, about the measurement of sexual pleasure, and about the employment of the caress. Men kept count of their sensual pleasures; so, which is less common, did Loomis Todd, whose detailed record of her intimate practices has been described by Peter Gay (1984). Of course, such documents tend to overestimate the representations and uses of the senses, as well as the modes of sensibility peculiar to those who dared and knew how to listen to and express their perceptions, their impressions and their emotions. Further, these sources provide only scattered and fragmentary evidence, which it is obviously difficult to quantify. The authors, it is hardly necessary to say, were not setting out to reveal the organization of the balance of the senses. But the historian is today only too well aware of facing an eternal dilemma; 'to accept a weak scientific status in order to achieve striking results, or accept a strong scientific status in order to achieve negligible results' (Ginzburg [1986] 1990).

It is, by the same token, difficult to perceive the coherence of the material collected, unless, that is, paroxysmal situations expose contrasts. When there are abrupt confrontations of systems of perception and emotions, antagonistic configurations sometimes emerge with valuable precision. The scenes of massacre at the end of the eighteenth century, and the far rarer instances in the first decades of the nineteenth century, provide precious information about the habitus of the protagonists. The clarity of the division between the jubilation of the murderous mob and the horror felt by the sensitive soul makes it easier to read sensory behavior. The delicate spectator gazes at the scene as if from a distance; he adopts a 'spectatorial' attitude; the visual analysis creates in him that revolt of the being that constitutes horror.

The member of the mob, right at the heart of the confusion, who participates in the killing, in its acts and its cries, and who receives its sounds and smells in the liberation of the Dionysiac impulses of the crowd, does not visually analyse the picture; unlike the spectator, he experiences the events through the senses 'of proximity' – touch and smell – but he could not describe the spoliation of bodies and scenes of horror, which he does not experience in this way (Corbin [1990] 1992). The pathetic, so common at the end of the eighteenth century, like the picturesque, implies a mechanics of the gaze and the use of a socially restricted sensory hierarchy.

But here, surreptitiously, we are falling into the trap that consists, for the historian, of confusing the reality of the employment of the senses and the picture of this employment decreed by observers. Let us take as an example what was written by naval hygienic specialists on the subject of the sensibility of the sailor (Corbin [1982] 1986: 147–8).[7] In this inferior being, taste and smell were corrupted by the use of tobacco, delicacy of touch was destroyed by the handling of ropes, that of hearing by the proximity of the artillery, that of sight by the salinity of the environment. In a word, the sailor had essentially lost the sharpness of his senses; he had become an insensitive being.

Portraits of this sort – and they exist for every social category – impress by their coherence; but they were clearly subject to the situation in which whoever drew, not to say decreed them, wrote. In this particular example, the author, usually a naval doctor, had to mark the distance that separated him from his subject and, even more, include his reader, to whom he was linked by a subtle connivance, in this desire to distinguish. The deprecatory picture also helped to justify the conditions which the unfortunate sailor was compelled to endure. Louis Chevalier (1958), though elsewhere a remarkable analyst of the social imagination of the bourgeoisie, has to some extent forgotten this legitimizing purpose.

Above and beyond this desire to distinguish, the author naturally painted his picture in the colors of the then prevailing scientific knowledge. At a time when neo-Hippocratism was extremely powerful, it was customary to deduce the appearance and sensibility of individuals from the qualities of the earth, air and waters which surrounded them (*circumfusa*), the food they ingested (*ingesta*), the clothes they wore (*applicata*), and the activities in which they engaged (*gesta*). Like the grain of their skin, the use they made of their senses reflected this coherence.[8] Accordingly, it was at this period commonplace to proclaim the insensitivity of touch of the peasantry;[9] the skin of the tiller of the soil was hardened by labor, when, that is, it was not covered with 'as it were a sort of scale.'[10] The coarseness of this creature enslaved to the soil was in keeping with the portrayal of the whole social scene, though this is not to say that I wish systematically to deny the reality of the individual features that composed it.

This description of the other, authoritatively presented, was equally subject to the prevailing ethical code; this required a value judgement to be passed on the respective usage of each of the senses. Modern historians have skillfully analysed the way in which 'penitentials' – and so, probably, the injunctions of confessors – detailed the types of sin induced by these five gates of the devil (Delumeau 1983; Arnold 1984). We know also that the emphasis on the dangers of sight inclined people either to lower their eyes, so as to avoid temptation, or raise them in the direction of heaven; as a result, the pious soul feared a horizontal gaze directed at the world and its perils, unless it was with the intention of proceeding to a charitable inventory of its piteous miseries.[11]

In the same way, description of the use of the senses – and probably the use of the senses itself, though to what degree? – obeyed, images of health and sickness, and therefore the divisions laid down by doctors. Accordingly, the importance of hysteria in representations of the healthy and the unhealthy led, at the end of the nineteenth century, to a discrediting of the use of smell in order to avoid any suspicion of a too highly developed olfactory sensibility, then perceived as a symptom of hysterical hyperesthesia.

All these logics are to be found, usually with a slight time lag, at the heart of fiction. In the prestigious Rougon-Macquart novels, Zola reproduced the social cleavages described by scholars and social observers a few decades earlier. Among the populace, according to Zola, touch was all, a sign of their closeness to the animal; men and women fought and came together brutally. Among the bourgeoisie and the aristocracy, seduction required distance, a visual caress, a trail of perfume, in sum, an assumed delicacy in the use of the senses.

The precautions that historians need to adopt follow from these all-too-brief considerations. Before embarking on an enquiry, they must know the representations of the sensory system and the ways in which it functioned. In short, they must be capable of deciphering all the references and of detecting the logic of the evidence ordered by the dominant scientific convictions at the period under consideration. Clearly, a document subject to belief in the theory of animal spirits cannot be analysed using the same key as a text that refers to the cerebral topography outlined by Brocq. The way in which authors see the localization and configuration of the central seat of sensibility, the circulation of messages by the circuit of nerves, is essential to an understanding of their writings. It implicitly orders their perception of the hierarchy of the senses. Over the centuries the theoretical exaltation or disqualification of smell is thus conditioned by images of the nervous system. The importance accorded to the diaphragm by certain eighteenth century physiologists greatly influenced representations of the relative role of sensory messages in the release of emotions. All this constitutes a jumble of facts; it is still wise to recall them. This type of precaution demands all the more rigor and subtlety in that, as a general rule, the traces of several scientific systems mingle confusedly together under the eye of the analyst of a single document.

For a retrospective enquiry it is necessary to take account of the habitus that determines the frontier between the perceived and the unperceived, and, even more, of the norms which decree what is spoken and what left unspoken. We need, in fact, to be careful not to confuse what is not said with what is not experienced. The historian can never be absolutely sure whether the emergence of an innovation, observed by reading documents, indicates a transformation of the way in which the senses were used and of the emotional system or, more simply, the crystallization of new rhetorical forms. It is still the case that the latter, as they spread, helped to shape behavior.

Unlike the anthropologist, who, by enquiry and interrogation, can circumvent these dangers and avoid the traps set by the inertia of language, the historian, in his perilous quest for the sign, can call on no true procedure for verification. Like the hunter crouched in the mud, searching for the trace of some invisible game, he has to deduce the behavior of the other from minute and subtle indicators (Ginzburg 1990).

History, it is clear, is here not so much a matter of scientific knowledge as of conjectural skill. The researcher may, at the very most, claim to identify objectively the moment of emergence of a discourse, or of a type of evidence. The historian can never know exactly what, in the great vogue for the picturesque at the end of the eighteenth century, derived from the proliferation of a rhetorical genre or a pictorial technique, and what indicates the elaboration and social diffusion of a way of seeing. Nothing can prove that a mode of appreciation does not exist before it is spoken or, with even greater reason, before it is theorized. Only one thing is certain: the prolixity of the discourse and the system of norms that it propagates help to determine its later uses.

A prisoner of language even more than the anthropologist, the historian must strive, at the very least, to identify what it is that conditions the frontier between the spoken and the unspoken. The historian needs to know that the banal is frequently silent, like the perception of a new emotion, awareness of which is not yet very clear, or a means of expression not yet fully worked out. The noise of traffic is today tending to disappear from the evocation or description of big cities, although it is not clear whether it is no longer noticed because of its omnipresence and the fact that no one heeds it, or whether its extreme banality leads insidiously to its being passed over.

In contrast, the inertia of language practices encourages people to continue to say what they no longer perceive or experience. The use of metaphor sets traps for the careless analyst; and the fine book by Anne Vincent-Buffault (1986), devoted to the history of tears, to some extent suffers from the fact that the author sometimes takes literally metaphorical, or simply conventional, formulas that in no way prove the reality of the practices.

To work on the documents of the past also requires prior knowledge of the injunctions of modesty, of the configuration of the obscene and of the contours of the inexpressible, which themselves have their history. The interdict that weighed, in the nineteenth century, on description of the embrace and the pleasure of the body, and of the taste, smells and sounds of sensual pleasure, can easily lead to an overestimation of the primacy of the visual, which is less subject to this injunction to silence.

At a disadvantage compared with the anthropologist, the historian, let us repeat, has access to hardly any other sources than those that involve language. It is, nevertheless, useful to explore whatever, in social rituals and techniques of communication, shows how the senses were used. There is a field of research, extending from the handshake to ways of transmitting information, which is as yet untilled. How, for example, can one claim to study the peasantry of the mid-nineteenth century without a detailed analysis of the mechanisms for the spreading of rumor?[12] On the afternoon of a fair, a social theater unfurled, consisting of exchanges of words, looks, gestures and smells, taking place within the warm, deafening, overcrowded inns located close to the market meeting place.

It is important, in conclusion, to guard against pessimism, while being well aware that all that concerns the history of sensorial behavior and the affective mechanisms forms simply a program of research. Such analyses, inexact though they may be, reveal cleavages of an anthropological nature. The Westerners of the nineteenth century – and this is just one example suggested by our temporal and geographical field of study – attached such importance to analysis of the sensory environment and to description of the ways in which the senses were used when they engaged in social observation, that it is essential to tackle this difficult subject. We will never fully understand this period if we stop at the study of statuses, positions, degrees of wealth or signs of condition. The most important cleavages were then to do, if not with biology,[13] at least with the habitus. The organization of the sensory regime constitutes one of the major elements in the formation of the social imagination. This is not to say that the latter is simple; far from it. It resulted from a permanent tension between the conviction that the senses then called 'social' – sight and hearing – were the most noble, but that touch was certainly the fundamental sense which gave experience of objects, whilst taste and smell, senses of survival, revealed the true nature of things.

Social cleavages echoed this dichotomy. The decreed hierarchy of the senses both ordered and reflected the hierarchy that functioned within society. The way in which individuals made use of touch, smell, hearing and sight made it possible to distinguish two groups: the first were in constant contact with the inertia of matter, were accustomed to exhausting toil, and were spontaneously capable of feeling with their flesh an animal pleasure, produced by contact; the second, thanks to their education in and habit of social commerce, and their freedom from manual labour, were able to enjoy the beauty of an object, demonstrate delicacy, subdue the instinct of the affective senses, and allow the brain to establish a temporal gap between desire and its gratification. The balance that was decreed in the use of the senses justified the logic of social cleavages, and both delineated in depth and legitimized the decisive hierarchies.

In a century too hastily defined as that of money, the major cleavages were ordered round the distinction between immediacy and the imposition of delays, submission to direct contact and the capacity to keep a distance. In the last analysis, what was decisive was the degree of delicacy of the hand, the greater or lesser aptitude to silence and detachment, the level of the thresholds of tolerance, the unequal vulnerability to disgust and enthusiasm suggested by refinement. In all this, the regime of the sensory values was closely involved.

Notes

1. For a critique of this notion, see the proceedings of the conference on 'Histoire des sciences et mentalités' held at the University of Paris-1 on 19 March 1983 and published in *Revue de synthèse* (1983): 111–12.

2. Both articles reprinted in Febvre (1953).

3. For a critique of this notion, see in particular Chartier (1983).

4. It should be said that Guy Thuillier has much refined his analysis since 1977; his excellent section on the gaze in his *L'imaginaire quotidien au XIXe siècle* (1985) takes account of some of these reservations.

5. I quote this conflict because I lived through it. Guy Thuillier (1977: 242) has stressed that 'village chronicles are extremely rich in the history of bells' in the nineteenth century.

6. Paradoxically, specialists in ancient history, long accustomed to reading anthropology, are here better informed than historians of the nineteenth century. I refer, in particular, to the fine book by Marcel Detienne ([1972] 1977).

7. A number of nineteenth century authors relate occupation and the ways in which the senses were employed. Without wishing to deny the influence of occupation, it must be remembered that nineteenth century social observers' taste for professional taxonomy risks exaggerating this type of criterion. Nevertheless, the flair required of the policeman, given the poverty of methods of identification, and the gaze of the medical practitioner in this golden age of clinical medicine, are good examples of the influence of profession on the use of the senses; though we should not forget professional expertise.

8. For the coherence between the description of space and the social scene, see M.-N. Bourget (1988).

9. Whilst at the same time emphasising how much the people relied on this inferior sense.

10. The marquis de Mallet, in 1866, discussing the peasants of the northern part of the department of Dordogne, quoted in Corbin (1992).

11. Guy Thuillier (1985: 6–12) emphasizes the persistence of the ancient 'policing of the gaze' right up to the mid nineteenth century in convents and in girls' boarding schools; after which there was a 'liberation of the gaze,' in particular at oneself, before watching television imposed new forms of captivity.'

12. See the special number of *Genre humain*, 5 (1982), 'La Rumeur.'

13. For the growth of biological depreciation in the discourse hostile to the nobility, see de Baecque (1989).

Bibliography

Arnold, O. (1984), *Le Corps et l'Ame. La Vie des religieuses au XIXe siècle*, Paris: Le Seuil.

Azouvi, F. (1984), 'Quelques jalons dans la préhistoire des sensations internes,' *Revue de synthèse*, CV: 113–33.

Baecque, A. de (1989), 'Le discours anti-noble (1787–1792). Aux origines d'un slogan: "Le peuple contre les gros",' *Revue d'histoire moderne et contemporaine*, 36: 3–28.

Barrows, S. (1981), *Distorting Mirrors: Visions of the Crowd in Late Nineteenth Century France*, New Haven and London: Yale University Press.

Blondel, C. (1928), *Introduction à la psychologie collective*, Paris: Armand Colin.

Bourget, M.-N. (1988), *Déchiffrer la France. La Statiatique départementale à l'époque napoléonienne*, Paris: EAC.

Chartier, R. (1983), 'Histoire intellectuelle et histoire des mentalités, trajectoires et questions,' *Revue de synthèse*, 111–12: 277–307.

Chevalier, L. (1958), *Classes laborieuses et classes dangereuses à Paris pendant la première moitié du XIXe siècle*, Paris: Plon

Corbin, A. ([1982] 1986), *The Foul and the Fragrant*, trans. A. Sheridan, Leamington Spa: Berg.

—— ([1987] 1990), 'Backstage,' trans. A. Goldhammer, in *A History of Private Life*, vol. 14, *From the Fires of Revolution to the Great War*, Cambridge MA: Belknap Press, pp. 451–667.

—— ([1988] 1994), *The Lure of the Sea: The Discovery of the Seaside in the Western World 1750–1840*, trans. J. Phelps, Cambridge: Polity.

—— ([1990] 1992), *The Village of Cannibals: Rage and Murder in France, 1870*, trans. A. Goldhammer, Cambridge: Polity.

Delumeau, J. (1983), *Le Péché et la peur. La Culpabilisation en Occident, XIIIe–XVIIIe siècle*, Paris: Fayard.

Detienne, M. ([1972] 1977). *The Gardens of Adonis: Spices in Greek Mythology*, Atlantic Highlands NJ: Humanities Press.

Didier, B. (1976), *Le journal intime*, Paris: Presses Universitaires de France.

Durkheim, E. ([1897] 1966), *Suicide*, trans. J.A. Spaulding and G. Simpson, New York: Free Press.

Elias, N. ([1939] 2000). *The Civilizing Process: Sociogenetic and Psychogenetic Investigations*, trans. E. Jephcott, Oxford: Blackwell.

Febvre, L. (1938), 'Psychologie et histoire,' *Encyclopédie francaise*, vol. 8, *La Vie mentale*, Paris: Société de gestion de l'Encyclopédie francaise.

—— (1941), 'Comment reconstituer la vie affective d'autrefois? La sensibilité et l'histoire,' *Annales d'histoire sociale*, 3.

—— (1953), *Combats pour l'histoire*, Paris: Armand Colin.

Gay, P. (1984), *The Bourgeois Experience. Victoria to Freud*, Oxford: Oxford University Press.

Ginzburg, C. ([1986] 1990), *Myths, Emblems, Clues*, trans. J. and C. Tedeschi, London: Hutchinson Radius.

Girard, A. (1963), *Le journal intime et la notion de personne*, Paris: Presses Universitaires de France.

Howes, D. (1987), 'Olfaction and Transition: An Essay on the Ritual Use of Smell,' *Canadian Review of Sociology and Anthropology*, 24(3): 398–416.

—— and Lalonde, M. (1991), 'The History of Sensibilities: Of the Standard of Taste in Mid-Eighteenth Century England and the Circulation of Smells in Post-Revolutionary France,' *Dialectical Anthropology*, 16: 125–35.

Huizinga, J. ([1919] 1955), *The Waning of the Middle Ages*, London: Penguin.

Lefebvre, G. ([1932] 1988). *La Grande Peur de 1789*, Paris: Armand Colin.

Léonard, J. (1986), *Archives du corps. La Santé au XIXe siècle*, Rennes: Ouest-France.

Levy, M. (1844), *Traité d'hygiène publique et privée*, Paris: Jean-Baptiste Baillière.

Levy-Bruhl, L. ([1922] 1923), *Primitive Mentality*, trans. L.A. Clare, London: George Allen & Unwin.

Mandrou, R. ([1961] 1976), *Introduction to Modern France, 1500–1640: An Essay in Historical Psychology*, trans. R.E. Hallmark, New York: Holmes & Meier.

Moscovici, S. (1981), *L'Age des foules. Un traité historique de psychologie des masses*, Paris: Flammarion.

Nye, R.A. (1975), *The Origins of Crowd Psychology: Gustav le Bon and the Crisis of Mass Democracy in the Third Republic*, London: Sage Publications.

Perrot, M. and Ribeill, G. (1985), *Le journal intime de Caroline B*, Paris: Montalba.

Starobinski, J. (1981), 'Brève histoire de la conscience du corps,' *Revue française de psychanalyse*, 45(2): 261–79.

Thuillier, G. (1977), *Pour une histoire du quotidien au XIXe siècle en Nivernais*, Paris and The Hague: Mouton.

—— (1985), *L'imaginaire quotidien au XIXe siècle*, Paris: Economica.

Vincent-Buffault, A. (1986), *Histoire des larmes*, Marseilles: Rivages.

Part III

Sensescapes

Sensation in Cultural Context

The challenge of the anthropology and geography of the senses is to apprehend the world anew by attending to local 'ways of sensing.' The idea of 'sensescape' may prove useful here. It is the idea that the experience of the environment, and of the other persons and things which inhabit that environment, is produced by the particular mode of distinguishing, valuing and combining the senses in the culture under study.

The first chapter derives from one of Constance Classen's early works on the senses titled *Worlds of Sense* (1993). In it she takes up Marshall McLuhan's notion of cultures as consisting of contrasting 'sense ratios' but questions both his essentialization of the senses of sight and hearing and his treatment of 'oral societies' as a homogeneous class. She insists on the importance of attending to how the senses are constructed and lived in specific social milieu. Citing the examples of the sensory orders of the Ongee, Tztotzil and Desana, she shows how there is as much sensory diversity within the category of 'oral societies' as there is between 'oral' and 'literate societies,' such as the West. Of particular interest is her account of how different cultures understand the same senses differently, privileging some characteristics over others, such as color over line in the visual field, or temperature over texture in the field of touch. The implication is that the meaning of the senses is in their use, and that perception is always mediated by the prevailing order of sensory values.

Kathryn Linn Geurts also explores this notion of sensory order. She found that the Anlo-Ewe of Ghana are particularly attuned to the internal sense of balance, and construct the external senses as different modalities of 'feeling in the body.' Theirs is an audile-tactile or kinesthetic sensory universe in which proprioception is key. This orientation is manifest in the Anlo-Ewe image of the foetus sitting on a stool in the womb; in the custom of women and children balancing huge loads on their heads; and in how different ways of walking are interpreted as indexing a person's moral compass. Critical to her understanding of the Anlo-Ewe sensory order was the experience of 'rolling up' into herself in response to a climatic moment in the telling of the Anlo-Ewe migration myth. Empathizing with this disposition, feeling along with her research subjects, Geurts is able to add an important new dimension to 'embodiment' as a paradigm for anthropology (Csordas 1990). She does so through her careful attention to describing the differential priority and relations between the senses, rather than concentrating on 'the body' *per se*. Also of note is her radical critique of the neurobiologist Antonio Damasio's account of consciousness from the standpoint of an Anlo-Ewe epistemology of the senses. She makes an eloquent plea for situating Western academic psychology in cross-cultural perspective.

Steven Feld's essay represents a sustained reflection on the transformation of space into place among the Kaluli of Papua New Guinea. It is a key contribution to the growing literature on 'emplacement' as a paradigm for anthropology and geography (Rodman 1992). Feld gives concrete expression to the idea of sensescape by asking 'What of place as heard and felt?'[1] Taking his cue from McLuhan's notion of 'acoustic space,' he introduces the concept of 'acoustemology,' and goes on to describe how the Kaluli make sense of their environment in predominantly sonic terms. By showing 'that as place is sensed, senses are placed,' Feld articulates a dynamic, culturally sensitive alternative to the view of the environment as a set of 'affordances' which comes out of ecological psychology (Gibson 1966, 1979), as championed by Ingold (2000) in anthropology and Rodaway (1994) in geography. Without some sense of how the senses are 'culturally attuned,' in Feld's terms, there is no telling what information the environment might afford.

Dorinne Kondo's essay on the Japanese tea ceremony dates from the early 1980s, and is in some ways a classic of symbolic anthropology. It is analogous, for example, to Clifford Geertz's celebrated essay on the Balinese cockfight (1973), where the notion of cultures 'as texts' was first introduced and where a single ceremony was shown to condense all the propositions of a given culture's 'world view.' However, Kondo's ethnography is not filtered by 'the model of the text' *à la* Geertz. She keeps her senses about her throughout her exposition of the ritual. By so doing she gives the lie to the suggestion that 'textualization' is the beginning and end of anthropology, or in the words of Stephen Tyler: 'Perception has nothing to do with it' (cited and discussed in Howes 2003: 22–26, 40). Perception – in multiple, carefully-sequenced modalities – has *everything* to do with the experience of the tea ceremony, and Kondo's eminently sensible interpretation of it. How could it be otherwise given that the tea ceremony is ultimately concerned with instilling a state (*mushin* or 'emptiness') that surpasses all verbalization? Indeed, Kondo lucidly demonstrates the extent to which Japanese civilization is an 'empire of the senses,' not merely one 'of signs' as interpreted by Barthes (1982).[2]

The last two chapters of this section have to do with displacement. Marina Roseman's essay, 'Engaging the Spirits of Modernity,' is about the multiple senses of objects that traverse cultural boundaries. She relates how the forest-dwelling Temiars of Malaysia dream of Western products and technologies, such as wristwatches and Land Rovers, and elaborate songs about their sensory properties in order to capture their spirits. The dream songs, which have the effect of socializing these alien objects, are in turn used to channel healing energies in the context of Temiar trance dances. Incidentally, the flow of modernization is not all one-way. The indigenous peoples of Malaysia have also figured on the sending end of globalization. For example, the dream principles of the neighbouring Senoi (or Semai) were picked up on by psychologist Kilton Stewart (not altogether accurately) during a sojourn in the 1930s, and subsequently popularized in the United States, leading to the foundation of a whole school of dream practice and interpretation: Senoi Dream Theory (Domhoff 1985).

The final chapter, by the cultural geographer Lisa Law, has to do with the multiple senses of persons who traverse cultural frontiers – specifically, Filipino domestic workers in Hong Kong. Law's account of the senses in diaspora is keyed to the way these migrant workers actively create places that emulate a 'sense' of home through sights, sounds, tastes, aromas they produce themselves, and for which there is no 'affordance' whatsoever in the actual construction of the city – namely, Hong Kong's empty business district on a Sunday. The flocking of Filipinas to the city core is denounced on aesthetic and hygienic grounds by members of the dominant society. This conflict over the sensuous (re)construction of space by the migrant workers during their leisure hours is a powerful testimony to the politics of differing sensory strategies for making sense of the city. With her notion of the senses as 'situated practice' Law opens up a dynamic new terrain for geographical investigation.

Notes

1. Feld's essay may also be understood as framing a 'participatory aesthetics' of environment, centered on the sentient subject, as distinct from the 'embodied subject' of phenomenology and the 'detached observer' of the classical Western imaginary, landscape painting and cartography (see Berleant 1985).

2. See further the discussion in note 3 of the introduction to this volume. For an account of the textual revolution, and its relationship to the sensual revolution in anthropological understanding see Howes (2003: chapter 2).

Bibliography

Barthes, R. (1982), *Empire of Signs*, trans. R. Howard, New York: Hill & Wang.

Berleant, A. (1985), 'Toward a Phenomenological Aesthetics of Environment,' in D. Ihde and H. Silverman (eds), *Descriptions*, Albany: State University of New York Press, pp. 112–28.

Classen, C. (1993), *Worlds of Sense: Exploring the Senses in History and Across Cultures*, London and New York: Routledge.

Csordas, T. (1990), 'Embodiment as a Paradigm for Anthropology,' *Ethos*, 18: 5–47.

Domhoff, G.W. (1985), *The Mystique of Dreams: A Search for Utopia Through Senoi Dream Theory*, Berkeley: University of California Press.

Geertz, C. (1973), *The Interpretation of Cultures*, New York: Basic Books.

Gibson, J.J. (1966), *The Senses Considered as Perceptual Systems*, Boston: Houghton Mifflin.

—— (1979), *The Ecological Approach to Visual Perception*, Boston: Houghton Mifflin.

Howes, D. (2003), *Sensual Relations: Engaging the Senses in Culture and Social Theory*, Ann Arbor: University of Michigan Press.

Ingold, T. (2000), *The Perception of the Environment: Essays on Livelihood, Dwelling and Skill*, London and New York: Routledge

Rodaway, P. (1994), *Sensuous Geographies*, London: Routledge.

Rodman, M. (1992), 'Empowering Place: Multilocality and Multivocality,' *American Anthropologist*, 94(1): 640–55.

8

McLuhan in the Rainforest

The Sensory Worlds of Oral Cultures

Constance Classen

The proliferation of visual imagery in modernity promotes the notion that the world is, above all, something to *see*. This is conveyed, for example, by the expression 'world view,' which implies that cosmologies, or systems of belief, can be visually mapped by anyone with an adequate overview. Scholars who argue that this model is the cultural result of the visualism produced by literacy and therefore not applicable to non-literate societies, offer another sensory paradigm for understanding the cosmologies of such societies: that of aurality, expressed in the term 'oral/aural culture.' Rather than being structured by sight, oral cultures are said to be animated by sound.

The most prominent proponent of this divide between visual/literate and aural/oral societies was Marshall McLuhan. McLuhan held that non-literate societies were governed by the power of the word and hence by the power of sound. With regard to the use of sight-based paradigms for understanding the world, McLuhan's colleague Walter Ong, made the further point that:

> As a concept and term, 'world view'... reflects the marked tendency of technologized man to think of actuality as something essentially picturable and to think of knowledge itself by analogy with visual activity to the exclusion, more or less, of the other senses. Oral or nonwriting cultures tend much more to cast up actuality in comprehensive auditory terms, such as voice and harmony. Their 'world' is not so markedly something spread out before the eyes as a 'view' but rather something dynamic and relatively unpredictable, an event-world rather than an object world... (Ong 1969: 634)

Following this approach, many anthropologists have presented ear-minded interpretations of non-literate societies, in works with titles such as *A Musical View of the Universe* (Basso 1965).

Aurality is indeed a driving force in many cultures around the world. In *Inca Cosmology and the Human Body*, for example, I explored how the indigenous inhabitants of the Andes lived in a world created, animated and integrated through sound (Classen 1993). Following McLuhan's literate/oral theory of culture to the letter, however, leads to *all* non-literate cultures being typed as auditory. Yet there is no compelling reason why the simple absence of the visual medium of writing should automatically make a society ear-minded. Often the sensory qualities emphasized by a society, in fact, are not so much linked to the dominant medium of communication as they are to the perceived medium of creation and life.

McLuhan did not himself attempt to sound out his theories in a variety of oral societies. In fact, the highly literate McLuhan could not help but see what he called tribal cultures as realms of mental obscurity, epitomized for him by the view of Africa portrayed in Conrad's *Heart of Darkness* (McLuhan 1961: 54). If we take McLuhan – or rather his theories – out of the city and into the rainforest, into the heart of oral cultures, we begin to see things in a rather different light. It becomes clear that there is considerable sensory diversity among non-literate peoples and that no one sensory model will hold true for all. In order to uncover the sensory diversity of cultural life it is not enough to extrapolate a perceptual model from the dominant mode of communication. One must rather follow the approach proposed by David Howes in *The Varieties of Sensory Experience* and examine 'how the patterning of sense experience varies from one culture to the next in accordance with the meaning and emphasis attached to each of the modalities of perception' (Howes 1991: 3).

In what follows the sensory models of three non-literate societies will be presented as described in the work of their respective ethnographers. These societies are the Tzotzil of Mexico, the Ongee of Little Andaman Island, and the Desana of Colombia. All three are traditional oral cultures and should therefore, according to McLuhan, emphasize aurality. Yet each has a very distinct way of making sense of the world: the Tzotzil accord primacy to heat in their cosmology, the Ongee to odor, and the Desana to color. The rich diversity of sensory symbolism in these different societies reveals the inadequacy of grouping and interpreting all traditional societies as oral/aural, and the importance of expanding our perceptual field to appreciate other systems of sensory and symbolic organization.

A Modern Maya Cosmology: Thermal Dynamics

Thermal symbolism is widespread among the indigenous cultures of Latin America. Classificatory schemes based on concepts of heat and cold can be found from the Southern Andes to Northern Mexico. This diffusion might be due in part to the impact of the Spanish Conquest, for the Spanish brought to the New World ancient theories of humoral medicine, according to which health is based on an equilibrium of hot, cold, wet and dry elements. The thermal symbolism employed by many of the cultures of Latin America, however, is more encompassing than that expressed by Western humoral theory, and indeed can vary significantly from place to place. While the Tzotzil of Mexico, examined here, classify men as hot and women as cold, for example, the Barasana of Colombia hold that men are 'cold' and women are 'hot' (Hugh-Jones 1979: 111).

Nowhere in Latin America is thermal symbolism more elaborated than among the descendants of the Maya in Central America and Mexico. A particularly striking example of such symbolism can be found in the cosmology of the Tzotzil of the Chiapas highlands of Mexico. The Tzotzil, an agricultural people whose religion blends indigenous and Catholic practices, believe that heat is the basic force of the universe. The Tzotzil call the cool highlands where they live *sikil? osil*, 'Cold Country,' while the warm Pacific lowlands are called *k'isin?_osil*, 'Hot Country.' The cardinal directions of east and west are respectively known as *lok'eb k'ak'al* 'emergent heat,' and *maleb k'ak'al* 'waning heat.' (North and south are called the 'sides of the sky.') Consequently morning is called 'heat is rising now,' noon is called 'half-heat,' and afternoon, 'in the waning heat' (Gossen 1974: 10–19, 31).

The annual passage of time in the Chiapas highlands is marked by the cycle of indigenous and Catholic festivals. The close associations between the Tzotzil words for day and festival and the Tzotzil word for heat, means that these festival cycles can also be understood as heat cycles. Thus the sentence 'It is three days before the festival of Saint John,' for instance, has the underlying meaning of 'It is three daily cycles of heat before a major (religious) cycle of heat' (Gossen 1974: 32).

Everything in the universe is thought to contain a different quantity of heat, or dynamic power. As regards humans, men are believed to possess more heat than women, making women symbolically cold by contrast. At birth, however, both men and women are deemed to be cold, possessing little innate heat. Newborns, consequently, are bathed in warm water, censed, wrapped in blankets and ritually presented with 'hot' chili peppers, in order to keep them warm until they have acquired enough heat to survive on their own (Gossen 1974: 37; Vogt 1976: 20, 23, 207).

Humans continue to accumulate heat throughout their lives, according to Tzotzil cosmology, reaching a thermal peak just before death. Events deemed to increase an individual's heat, and therefore power, include being baptized, marrying, becoming a shaman, and officiating in communal rites. Thus, 'the man who is very old, a high-ranking shaman and a veteran of all levels of the [ceremonial] system, possesses the greatest heat possible for a human being' (Vogt 1976: 24).

Illness, in turn can seriously deplete a person's supply of heat, or else, in the case of a fever, produce a dangerous overheating. In the case of the latter, the patient is cooled down through the administering of cool baths and symbolically cold medicines and foods. In the case of the former, the patient is treated with 'hot' medicines and foods and undergoes a series of sweat baths (taken in the morning in order to benefit from the heat-force of the rising sun) (Vogt 1976: 82–90). In this way, Tzotzil healers try to establish a healthy temperature level in their patients.

The Tzotzil believe that when a human is born the sun lights a candle in the sky. The word for this candle, ?ora, also means time, for the length of one's candle determines the length of one's time on earth. When the candle burns out, one dies. At death, a person is said to grow completely cold. A certain amount of heat-force is necessary for the deceased to make the journey to *Vinahel*, the afterworld, however, and this is supplied through the burning of candles and incense and the drinking of 'hot' alcohol by the participants in the funeral rites (Gossen 1974: 15; Vogt 1976: 24).

Thermal symbolism is omnipresent in Tzotzil ritual. 'All the "culturalizing" agents in the ceremonies are involved with "heat": the heat of the fire to cook tortillas; the heat of the burning incense over the candles; the heat needed to produce cane liquor; the heat needed to grow flowers for the shrines' (Vogt 1976: 115). At the same time as Tzotzil rituals emphasize heat, the participants have their senses of smell and taste engaged by fragrance and food, their sense of hearing by music and speech, and their sense of sight by colorful and symbolically significant decorations. Thermal symbolism is thus integrated into a multi-sensory symbolic system.

As might be expected from the close association of heat with light, visual symbolism is of particular importance to the Tzotzil. Like their forbears, the Mayas, the Tzotzil color code the cosmos, assigning different colors to the four quarters and center of the world. The colors used by the Tzotzil in ritual are aligned with this cosmic color scheme. Shamans are also thought to have visionary sight, and often use sight as a medium of divination (Vogt 1976: 32, 90, 132, 205).

Interestingly, much of the visual and other sensory symbolism employed by the Tzotzil contains thermal references; colors, food, and even speech are classified as hot or cold. Red, for example, is used to signify heat, and black, to signify coldness. Corn, one of the staples of the Tzotzil diet, is believed to possess a high degree of heat, while the potato, another staple, is classified as cold. Ordinary language is said to be cold because it is disorderly and unbounded. Ritual language, on the other hand, is classified as hot because it is fixed, stylized and repetitious. The 'ancient words' used in sacred songs and prayers are the hottest language of all. Believed to have been created at the beginning of time, ancient words have the accumulated heat of all the ages (Gossen 1974: 40, 48–9). This system of correspondences enables the basic thermal schema of Tzotzil cosmology to be reinforced through all of the senses.

The fundamental organizing symbol of Tzotzil cosmology and the ultimate source of heat-force is the sun, called 'Our Father Heat.' In Tzotzil ritual, the sun is evoked in a multitude of ways. The table on which the ritual meal is served in Tzotzil ceremonies, for example, represents the trajectory of 'Our Father Heat' across the sky. The red stripes running along the table cloth signify the east-west passage of the sun. At the head of the table stands the 'hot' cane liquor, representing the rising sun. At the foot is placed the 'cold' salt, symbolizing the setting sun. The 'hottest' part of the table, the head, is reserved for the gods; senior members of the community sit on either side of the head, while low-status 'cold' participants sit around the foot (Vogt 1976: 40–41).

The social order of the Tzotzil community is structured according to the thermal order of the cosmos, with the most important members associated with the hot rising sun, and the least important with the cold setting sun. Through their placement in communal rituals, individuals know their degree of importance in the 'thermometer' of social status. At the same time, such rituals serve to establish an exchange of heat-force between humans and deities. Burning candles, called 'tortillas for the gods,' are offered to the deities, while corn tortillas and cane liquor, the 'heat of the sun' are consumed by the human participants (Vogt 1976: 50). In this way the circulation of heat force through the cosmos is assured.

The same principle of thermal social order found in Tzotzil ritual can be seen in the organization of the Tzotzil household. Gary Gossen writes of the Tzotzil community of Chamula:

> The importance of heat is ever present in Chamula life... The daily round of Chamula domestic life centers on the hearth, which lies near the center of the dirt floor of nearly all Chamula houses. The working day usually begins and ends around the fire, men and boys sitting and eating to the right of the hearth..., women and girls to the left of the hearth. Furthermore, men in this patrifocal society always sit on tiny chairs, which raise them above the cold, feminine ground, and wear sandals... Women, in contrast, customarily sit on the ground and always go barefooted. (Gossen 1974: 36–37)

The relationship between male and female, hot and cold, is expressed in mythological terms by the Tzotzil by the relationship between the sun and the moon. The Tzotzil say that the moon gave birth to the sun and that the sun then blinded his mother with hot water during a sweat bath. This act established the superiority of the sun's heat-force over that of the moon, and made the female moon dependent on the male sun (Gossen 1974: 328).

Similarly, in the Catholicism practiced by the Tzotzil, female saints take second place to male saints. The feast days of female saints are given less importance than those of male saints, while during the period between the winter and summer solstices, a time of increasing atmospheric heat and, by analogy, of male power, no major female saints are honored.

In Tzotzil cosmology the hot solar male principle is associated with moral order whereas the cold lunar female principle is associated with disorder. During the period of ascending heat from midnight to noon, therefore, the sun is believed to control female disorder. The period of declining heat, from noon to midnight, by contrast, is potentially a time of female disorder and immorality (Gossen 1974: 41–42).

The use of heat as a force of domination is characteristic of Tzotzil mythology. Indeed cosmic conflicts are often conceptualized as heat battles. The people of the first mythological age of the world, for instance, are said to have cooked their children in hot water and eaten them, a use of heat-force to transgress the moral order. The sun then destroyed the first people, either through fever, boiling rain, or a hot flood according to different versions of the myth, defeating heat through heat (Gossen 1974: 331, 336, 346).

Perhaps the best example of the dominance of thermal symbolism in Tzotzil mythology is the Tzotzil version of the crucifixion of Jesus.

> A long time ago, the Jews decided that they were going to kill 'Our Father' (the Sun). They caught him in a tree and tried to hang him, but he would not die. He went to hide in a sweat-bath house... They decided to try to burn him, again without success, for he came out of the fire younger than he was before. They decided that it would rejuvenate them also, so all the Jews jumped into the fire and died... This is why they always burn the Judas on Holy Saturday. (Gossen 1974: 156)

Here the Tzotzil have transformed the central myth of Christianity into a thermal allegory, with the heat-force of 'Our Father,' the arbitrator of cosmic order, triumphing over that of the 'Jews,' the representatives of cosmic disorder. Taking the analogy further, the Tzotzil interpret the Ressurection as the rising of the sun in the east (Gossen 1974: 337).

From the individual to society to the cosmos, thermal symbolism pervades Tzotzil thought, expressing the primal concepts of both energy and structure. The Tzotzil not only express their cosmology in thermal terms, however – they *feel* it throughout their bodies. Heat, indeed, can envelop a person's body more completely than any other sensory stimulus, from head to toe, inside and out. It can travel from as far away as the sun, and yet affect one as intimately as a touch. Heat is essential for life, without it one dies; and when one dies, one loses one's heat. In their daily lives, the Tzotzil thus constantly experience the thermal order of the universe: through the encompassing heat of the sun, through the change of temperature from day to night, summer to winter, highlands to lowlands, through the heat they expend in working, through the offering and consumption of 'heat' in ritual, through their positions around the household hearth, and through the warmth of their very blood.

A South East Asian Cosmology: Odor Control

In Little Andaman Island in the Bay of Bengal live the Ongee, a hunting and gathering people who have limited contact with the outside world. For the Ongee smell is the fundamental cosmic principle. Odor is the source of personal identity and the reason for communal life, a system of medicine and a system of communication, it determines temporal and spatial movements, it produces life and causes death. By controlling odor, the Ongee control their cosmos (Pandya 1987; 1993).

When an Ongee wishes to refer to himself as 'me,' he puts a finger to the tip of his nose, the organ of smell. This is not only because of the centrality of olfaction in Ongee thought, but also because living beings are thought to be composed of smell. The most concentrated form of odor, according to the Ongees are bones, believed to be solid smell. The Ongee thus say that 'smells are contained in everybody like tubers are contained in the ground' (Pandya 1987: 17). An inner spirit is said to reside within the bones of living beings. While one is sleeping, this internal spirit gathers all the odors one has scattered during the day and returns it to the body, making continued life possible (Pandya 1987: 100, 167).

The Ongee hold illness to result from either an excess or a loss of odor. The former is caused by cold, which 'solidifies' the liquid odor in a person's body producing a sensation of heaviness. The latter can result from injury, which causes a 'flow of odor,' or from an elevated body temperature, which liquefies the hard smell of the skeleton and causes it to be released by the body. In this case, the sensation is one of lightness.

The basic treatment for an excess of odor consists of warming up the patient in order to 'melt' the solidified smell. A loss of odor, in turn, is treated by painting the patient with white clay to induce a sensation of coolness and restrict the flow of odor from the body. Curing illness in the Ongee system of medicine thus deals mainly with inducing or restricting the release of odor. Men are believed to be more susceptible to olfactory imbalances than women, as menstruation is thought to provide women with a natural means of regulating their odor-weight (Pandya 1987: 107, 145, 211).

The concern of the Ongees to maintain a healthy state of olfactory equilibrium is expressed in their forms of greeting. The Ongee equivalent of 'how are you?' is '*Konyune? onorange-tanka?,*' 'how is your nose?' or literally 'when/why/where is the nose to be?' If one responds that one is heavy, one sits down on the lap of the inquirer and rubs one's nose on that person's cheek. This ceremonial act is supposed to remove some of the excess odor that is causing the sensation of heaviness. If the response is that one feels light, the inquirer blows on one's hand as a way of 'infusing' odor and weight. These two acts of rubbing the nose and blowing on the hand are described by the Ongees as *e?geie kwayabe*, shifting smells, from one to the other (Pandya 1987: 114–15).

Death is explained by the Ongee as the loss of one's personal odor. They believe that they kill the animals they hunt by letting out all of their smell and that they themselves are hunted by spirits, called *tomya*, who kill them by absorbing *their* odors. Birth, in turn, is caused by a woman's consuming food in which a hungry spirit is feeding.

Growth is conceptualized in terms of olfactory development. The Ongee word for growth, *genekula*, means a process of smell. A newborn has soft bones and no teeth, hence possesses little odor. On growing up, a child develops the condensed odor contained in hard bones and teeth. In old age a person loses odor through illness and the loss of teeth, until death reduces the person to a boneless, odorless spirit – which will eventually be born again as a human (Pandya 1987: xii, 19, 111–12, 312).

Life for the Ongee is a constant game of olfactory hide-and-seek. They seek out animals in order to kill them by releasing their odors, and at the same time try to hide their own odors both from the animals they hunt and from the spirits who hunt them. 'To hunt' in the Ongee language is expressed by *gitekwabe*, meaning 'to release smell causing a flow of death.' The word for hunter, in turn, is *gayekwabe*, 'one who has his smell tied tightly' (Pandya 1987: 102).

The Ongee employ different techniques to keep their smell 'tied tightly.' Living in community is believed to unite the odor of individuals and lessen their chances of being smelled out by hungry spirits. When moving as a group from place to place, the Ongee are careful to step in the tracks of the person in front, as this is thought to confuse personal odors and make it difficult for a spirit to track down an individual. The Ongee also screen their odor through the use of smoke. When travelling in single file, the person at the head of the group carries burning wood so that the trail of smoke will cover the odor of all those walking behind. For the same reason, the Ongee keep fires burning at all times in their villages and have smoke-filled, unventilated homes. Indeed, for the Ongee a true fire is characterized not by the heat or light it produces but by its smoke. The Ongee even attribute an olfactory dimension to the sun as they believe it to produce an invisible smoke (Pandya 1987: 126–7, 133–6).

The Ongee limit their smell emission by painting themselves with clay. Clay paints are believed to help bind smells to the body and the different designs used in painting alter the ways in which the body releases smell. Thus an Ongee whose body has been painted will declare 'The clay paint has been good! I feel that my smell is going slowly and in a zig-zag manner like the snake on the ground!' (Pandya 1987: 137). The Ongee also dab clay paint on their skins after a meal of meat in order to prevent the smell of the consumed meat from warning living animals that one of their kind has been killed and eaten.

While the Ongee generally try to avoid encounters with spirits, there are occasions on which they deliberately summon them. The Ongee retain the bones of their ancestors, for instance, both to keep their potentially harmful spirits under control and to be able to invoke their aid by means of the smell released by the bones. Another way of communicating with one's ancestral spirits consists of painting a specific design on one's skin with clay paint. The pattern of painted and unpainted skin is believed to determine the nature of the odor released by the body, making it possible to send one's ancestors a message in olfactory code. Indeed, the Ongees believe that, by altering their body odors through the application of clay paint, they can communicate with all other beings. This communication through smell is called *minyelange.* which literally means to remember (Pandya 1987: 111, 139–40, 147–9).

The most important occasion on which spirits are summoned by the Ongees is when a man wishes to undertake a visit to the spirit world. Every Ongee man is expected to undertake this dangerous journey once during the male initiation rite. At this time, contrary to ordinary practice, the Ongee make every effort to attract spirits by odor: men refrain from the use of odor-restricting clay paints; women and children disperse their body odors to the winds by swinging on swings, and baskets of rotten pigs' meat are hung on the trees.

This olfactory exhibition takes place so that the spirits will come and take the male initiate away with them to their world, where he can learn of their ways and appease them by making offerings. Only married men can undergo this rite, as it is their wives who ensure that the initiates have a safe journey to and from the spirit world. The initiates' wives help their husbands become light enough to travel with the spirits by inhaling their odor. They also undertake to shift the initiates' body odor/weight from their upper to their lower bodies through massage. This shift in odor/weight distribution is thought to enable the initiates to float up to the spirit world. When the initiates return from the spirit world, the women massage their odor/weight back into their upper bodies so that the returned initiate 'can remain safely and heavily with us' (Pandya 1987: 226, 231, 259, 286).

The initiation rite is called *tanageru,* which literally means blue-red but in fact has an olfactory basis. The blue referred to, *tana,* is ash blue and is associated with the lightness of ash, a quality which in turn is associated with an absence of odors. Ashes also have the characteristic of causing temporary blindness when blown in the eyes, and thus are associated with the spirits, who cannot see, but only smell. The red referred to, *ougeru,* is hot red, and is associated with red clay paint, used to make one sweat and release smell when one is heavy with odor. The initiation rite is therefore called *tanageru,* blue-red, because first one becomes light or empty of odor, like blue ash, in order to travel with the spirits, and then one grows heavy with odor, like one who uses red clay to release an excess of personal odor, in order to return to the world of the living. In the words of an Ongee, 'The young man has to be made into *tana,* light and spirit-like... [T]he light body... has to come back and become *oegeru,* heavy and human' (Pandya 1987: 235).

While most Ongee men only travel to the spirit world during their initiation, the shaman, called *torale*, visits with spirits regularly. When a *torale* is ready to undertake such a journey, he absents himself from the community and allows the spirits to absorb his smell and carry him away with them. This situation would result in death for the ordinary person, however the *torale*, through his skillful negotiations with the spirits, is able to return safely with knowledge of benefit for the community.

From the vantage point of the spirits, above the forest, the *torale* learns of the movement of the winds, spirits, and smells, the elements that order Ongee time and space. The Ongee seasonal cycle is based on the winds that blow in from different directions throughout the year, dispersing odor and bringing scent-hungry spirits. The Ongee conduct their own migrations from the coast to the forest according to this cycle: during the seasons when the spirits are believed to be hunting at sea, the Ongee hunt in the forest, and during the seasons when the spirits are believed to be hunting in the forest, the Ongee hunt along the coast. The information the *torale* brings from the spirit world helps the Ongees plan their movements so as to continue to successfully play their game of olfactory hide and seek with the spirits (Pandya 1987: 98–9, 168–78, 330–3).

In terms of the Ongee sensory model as a whole, the senses of smell, taste and touch are said to be shared by spirits and humans, while sight and hearing are believed to be particular to humans. The Ongee associate these latter senses with the two principal groups into which their society is divided: turtle hunters and pig hunters. Turtle hunters are said to have a keen sense of sight, and pig hunters a keen sense of hearing. Marriage is supposed to take place between individuals of opposite moieties 'so that hearing and seeing is completed.' This union of hearing and sight is expressed in the term *gawakobe*, which means to speak so that the hearer 'sees' what one means and is able to show it to others (Pandya 1987: 58, 247–8).

Complementing the coupling of sight and hearing in the Ongee sensory model, is the union of olfaction and touch: heaviness, hardness and coldness are associated with the retention of odor; lightness, softness and heat, with its emission. Olfaction, indeed, underlies all sensory processes, as the ultimate reason for sensory knowledge of any kind is to be better able to maintain the cosmos in a dynamic olfactory balance.

Odor is thus what literally makes the Ongee world go round. The very alternation of life and death between the Ongees and the spirits that lies at the heart of Ongee cosmology is ordered by an olfactory model: the inhaling and exhaling of breath. The spirits inhale the exhaled odor of a human causing the death of the human and the birth of a spirit. Conversely, a spirit dies and a human is born when a woman consumes a spirit in her food. The Ongee explain the alternating nature of their cosmos by saying that 'it is never possible to inhale and exhale at the same time' (Pandya 1987: 165). Without this continuous process of exchange, the Ongee cosmos would be still and lifeless. As the Ongee say, 'We have to give and take... otherwise all the game of "hide and seek" will come to an end' (Pandya 1987: 278).

An Amazonian Cosmology: Coloring the World

For the Tzotzil the vital force of the cosmos is heat, and for the Ongee it is smell, but the Desana of the Amazonian rainforest believe the cosmos to be animated by color. In Desana cosmology, the sun creates life through mixing and matching color energies. Each color is associated with a different cultural value: yellow, for example, is associated with male procreative power; red with female fertility; blue with transition and communication; and green with growth. The cosmos itself is composed of layers of colors; on top is the creative yellow light of the sun, then the blue transitional region of the Milky Way, followed by the red, fertile earth, and underneath the fresh green of *Ahpikiondia*, Paradise (Reichel-Dolmatoff 1971: 24–5, 47).

All people are said to receive an equal amount of color energies at birth, and at death these colors return to the Sun. Animals and plants also contain chromatic energies in differing proportions according to their distinct natures. Indeed, the whole process of the distribution, procreation and growth of people, animals and plants is seen by the Desana as a chromatic energy flow that has to be carefully watched over and controlled by shamans.

The Desana shaman, called *paye*, observes the world at large by looking within a rock crystal which functions as a microcosm. His task is to blend and balance the different colors of the spectrum within the crystal to maintain an equilibrium of forces without (Reichel-Dolmatoff 1978a: 246–71; 1979: 117–28).

Color symbolism pervades Desana life. Apart from the colors attributed to the natural and supernatural worlds, there are the colors the Desana use in their homes and artefacts. The *maloca*, communal house, is painted male yellow in front and female red at the back. In feather crowns, yellow feathers signify the procreative power of the sun and blue feathers contact and communication. The shield used in rituals is imagined to reflect a red light on the exterior and a pink light in the interior – colors of uterine protection. Other forms of color symbolism apply to benches, mats, pottery, baskets and musical instruments (Reichel-Dolmatoff 1971: 110–18).

Activities, as well as objects, are color coded by the Desana. Procreation, for example, is thought of as a pattern of red female dots against a bright yellow male background. This image is called *nomeri*, which means 'to paint with fine dots.' Cooking is also conceived of as a color process. Smoking meat is believed to transform the potentially dangerous yellow component of the meat into a safe red. After the meat is smoked it is cooked in a pot to render it an edible brown. The tripod structure used for smoking meat symbolizes this color transformation: the lower part is said to be yellow, the grid in the center is said to be red, and the upper part, from which the processed food is removed, is brown, the color of edible food. Fire itself is said to contain the yellow of the sun and the red of the earth in its flames, and the blue of the Milky Way in its smoke, making it a symbol of cosmic energy (Reichel-Dolmatoff 1978b: 278–9, 282–3; 1971: 108).

Illness is another type of color process, for the Desana define most diseases as an imbalance of color energies. By passing his crystal over a patient's body and carefully observing the changes in color reflections within it, the Desana shaman is able to detect such an imbalance. Once the shaman has pinpointed the color flaw, he invokes the chromatic energies contained within the crystal to 'touch up' the patient's color chart, adding certain hues, blending others, dimming an overly bright color or brightening a dull one. Once the proper balance of colors is restored the patient is cured (Reichel-Dolmatoff 1978b: 265–8; 1979: 120).

Extensive as the color symbolism of the Desana is, it forms but one part of the sensory symbolism elaborated by the Desana. Colors constitute a primary set of energies in Desana cosmology; a secondary set is formed by odor, temperature and flavor. Odor is thought to be the result of the combination of color and temperature and is used by the Desana to classify people, animals and plants. Flavor, thought to arise from odor, is less important than the latter but still culturally elaborated. For example, different flavors are associated with different kin groups and used to regulate marriage (Reichel-Dolmatoff 1978b: 271–5).

This secondary set of sensory energies supplements the primary color energies in Desana cosmology and ritual. Thus in cooking, for example, it is not only the colors of different foods that are manipulated but also their odors and flavors. In healing rituals, shamans may invoke a variety of sensory forces, along with color energies, to aid the recovery of their patients. Desana artefacts also manifest a multisensory significance. A basket, for instance, has meaning associated not only with its color and function, but also with the design of its weave, its texture, and the odor and taste of the vines of which it is made (Reichel-Dolmatoff 1985: 24; 1971: 175–87).

Even a specific sensory phenomenon can evoke a train of multisensory associations for the Desana. A certain pattern of color, for example, will bring to mind related odors and flavors and their symbolic role in Desana social life and cosmology. Similarly, a particular sound will be associated with a color, temperature and odor, and thought to convey a specific message to the brain by its vibrations. For example, the drawn-out sounds of a certain large flute played by Desana men are said to have strong yellow color, a very hot temperature, and a male odor. 'The melody is said to be of a merry kind and is associated with the image of a multitude of fish running upriver to the spawning beds. The vibrations produced by the sounds are said to trigger a message which refers to child-rearing' (Reichel-Dolmatoff 1981: 91).

The importance the Desana assign to light and color, and the ways in which they interrelate the senses, undoubtedly derive in large part from their experience with hallucinogenic drugs. The narcotic used by the Desana, *banisteriopsis caapi*, produces hallucinations that are characterized by colorful imagery and a synesthetic mingling of sensory perceptions. According to the Desana, the narcotic vine was born when the Sun impregnated a woman through the eye with his light. The child – the narcotic – was made of light and overwhelmed men with its brilliance. 'Everything happened through the eye,' the myth proclaims (Reichel-Dolmatoff 1978b: 4).

Narcotics are taken by Desana men on almost all ritual occasions. The visions produced by the narcotics are believed to provide glimpses of the creation of the cosmos and the iconic images that embody original ideals. At the same time they are thought to induce states of consciousness which will lead an individual to act in accordance with social norms. The senses primarily involved in this process are sight, hearing and smell. Through the use of hallucinogens and a controlled sensory environment shamans attempt to induce the following four processes: 'to make one see, and act accordingly,' 'to make one hear, and act accordingly,' 'to make one smell, and act accordingly,' and 'to make one dream, and act accordingly.' Indeed, Desana shamans state that their main task as spiritual leaders is to direct the brain functions of the members of their communities through sensory manipulation (Reichel-Dolmatoff 1981: 76–7, 90–5):

The Desana conceptualize the brain itself in terms of complex sensory imagery:

> In [one] image the brain is formed by a bundle of pencil-shaped hexagonal tourmaline crystals standing closely packed side by side; each crystal contains a sequence of colors which, from bottom to top, express a range of sensibilities. In another image a brain consists of layers of innumerable hexagonal honeycombs; the entire brain is one huge humming beehive... Each tiny hexagonal container holds honey of a different color, flavor, odor, or texture, or it houses a different stage of insect larval development... A brain can be seen as a bouquet of flowers, a fluttering cluster of butterflies, a glistening swarm of tiny tropical fish, or a quivering mass of multicolored frogs. (Reichel-Dolmatoff 1981: 82–83)

All of these different sensory characteristics are associated with cultural values. These values primarily concern marriage, procreation, and food, but also deal with other aspects of Desana life. Thus, after drawing an outline of a brain for the ethnographer Gerardo Reichel-Dolmatoff, one Desana man 'pointed rapidly to different areas... and said: "*Here it is prohibited to eat fish; here it is allowed; here one learns to dance; here one has to show respectful behaviour*"' (Reichel-Dolmatoff 1981: 84).

The Desana believe that the universe consists of two parts, the material world of the senses, *maria turi* (our dimension), and the divine world of pure, abstract ideals, *gahi turi* (other dimension). The two halves of the brain are conceived of in a similar fashion, the right hemisphere, called 'existential-first,' is concerned with practical affairs and biological processes, while the left hemisphere, called 'abstract-first,' is the seat of moral law. The function of the right hemisphere is basically to put the ideals of the left hemisphere into practice. The Desana help the right hemisphere do this by coding virtually all sensory impressions to serve as reminders of the original ideals (Reichel-Dolmatoff 1981: 86–93).

For the Desana, existence in this world is a dream, a mere reflection of the reality which exists in the 'other dimension.' After death, those Desana who have lived according to the dictates of moral law awake into the reality of the other dimension. Therefore, while on the one hand the Desana appear to be the most sensualist of peoples, dwelling on and assigning meaning to each and every sensory stimuli, they are, on the other hand, the most idealist. The value of sensory perception lies not in itself, but in its ability, when culturally coded, to lead one away from the material world of the senses to the timeless, abstract world of ideals.

Conclusion

The Tzotzil, the Ongee and the Desana each conceptualize the vital force of the cosmos in terms of a different sensory energy. These sensory energies order space and time, determine health and illness, life and death, and govern social and personal identity. In each of these cultures putting the cosmos in order, and putting one's house in order, involves putting the senses in order.

A number of interrelated points can be made from this cross-cultural exploration of sensory orders. The first is that the dominant sensory medium of symbolic orientation can vary widely from culture to culture and can only be understood within the context of a particular culture and not through generalized external sensory paradigms. It would be impossible to adequately encompass the cosmologies of the Tzotzil, the Ongee, or the Desana by either the visual or auditory models proffered by Western scholars. These cosmologies are so powerful in their differing sensory symbolism that they shatter conventional Western perceptual models and open us up to completely new sensory universes.

The second point is that the sense most symbolically elaborated by a culture is not necessarily the sense of most practical importance, as a medium of communication or otherwise. The three cultures examined here can all be classified as oral cultures with regards to their dominant medium of communication, yet they are not all aural cultures. The Tzotzil symbolically orient themselves by temperature, the Ongee by smell. The color-minded Desana, appear, at first sight, to be as visualist as the West.

This leads us to the next point. Not only do Western sensory paradigms force all cultures into a visual or oral/aural model, they also recognize only one kind of visuality – that of the West – and one kind of aurality – that of the generic non-literate 'tribal' culture. Yet the visualism of the Desana, with its emphasis on integrating and animating color energies is surely very different from the visualism of the West, with its emphasis on linearity, detached observation and surface appearance. In fact, the 'world view' of the Desana is rather a sensory kaleidoscope, with color shifting into smell and then into flavor and so on. Similarly, aurality is not an unchanging concept across cultures but is 'colored' by the sensory and symbolic associations given to it by a particular people.

McLuhan (1962: 28) has written that 'non-literate cultures experience such an overwhelming tyranny of the ear over the eye that any balanced interplay among the senses is unknown at the auditory extreme.' However, to understand a culture's sensory model, it is not only the dominant sense of symbolic elaboration that must be considered, but the interplay of all the senses. Though McLuhan might imagine that in the 'hyperesthetic mode of the ear' a hypnotic confusion of sensory values prevails (see McLuhan 1961: 50, 54), in fact, as we find with the Desana, a synesthetic awareness does not necessarily involve a heightened sense of aurality nor does it necessarily signify a loss of differentiated sensory meaning. No culture could be more careful in its manner of classifying and interrelating (or keeping apart) different sensory qualities than the Desana.

In each of the cultures examined here it is not only the hierarchy of the senses that is significant but also the ways in which the senses are related. Thus in a Tzotzil ritual meal, eating results in an increase in personal temperature, while in an Ongee initiation rite massage leads to a loss of one's personal odor. Among the Desana, who assign cultural values to almost all sensory stimuli, maintaining the proper relationships among sensory categories – or establishing a 'balanced interplay of the senses' – is essential to maintaining social and cosmic order.

Sensory models are conceptual models, and sensory values are cultural values. The way a society senses is the way it understands. For example, the ethnographer A.R. Radcliffe-Brown, coming from a visual culture that emphasizes clear-cut distinctions, found the ideas of the Andaman Islanders concerning spirits to be 'floating and lacking in precision' (cited in Pandya 1987: 13). Yet in the intermingling, olfactory culture of the islanders (who include the Ongee) 'floating and lacking in precision' is precisely how spirits are characterized. Spirits, like odors, travel on the winds, coming and going, sharing the same world inhabited by humans. They are not confined to any one place, they '[do] not have a distinct shape yet can be experienced everywhere (Pandya 1987: 234). The 'imprecision' that a visual culture may find disturbing, therefore, can be normative for an olfactory culture and, whereas a visual culture may emphasize location, an olfactory culture will emphasize movement.

It is not simply that a society's mode of thinking and acting is ordered by the cultural consequences of the sensory properties it prioritizes, however. Sensory values not only frame a society's experience, they express its ideals, its hopes and its fears. Justice and life are conceptualized in terms of temperature or smell. Death is a loss of heat or a loss of odor. Fertility and procreation are colors.

As sensory values are social values, sensory relations are also social relations. The relationship between hot and cold in Tzotzil cosmology structures the relationship between men and women. The relationship between sight and hearing in Ongee cosmology structures the relationship between pig hunters and turtle hunters. Among the Desana, marriage takes place between kin groups classified with different odors and flavors.

These sensory relations are, at the same time, moral relations. By classifying men as hot and women as cold the Tzotzil are not merely conveying the idea of different sexes through different thermal sensations, they are making a statement about the different status and roles of men and women in their society. Heat is associated with order and power, coldness with disorder and impotence. The classification of men as hot, therefore, makes them dominant instruments of order in Tzotzil society, wheareas women's classification as cold makes them subordinate instruments of disorder. The penalty of defying this moral system is made clear by myth: women, and all other elements of disorder, who attempt to possess the power of heat are destroyed by heat. Thus in one Tzotzil story the female moon is scalded by the male sun in order to ensure that her radiance is less than his. In another, a disapproving husband uses hot chile pepper to kill his overly lustful, and therefore unacceptably hot, wife (Gossen 1974: 312, 328).

Structures of power within a society can also receive sensory expression in the differential allocation of sensory powers. For example, among the Ongee, only men are allowed to undertake the journey to the spirit world and thereby gain an 'overscent' of the olfactory processes that govern the cosmos. Likewise, among the Desana, only men are allowed access to the hallucinogens that provide a transcendent insight into cosmic reality. Those groups marginalized by the dominant sensory/social order, however, may develop alternative orders, or ways of making sense of the world.

By imbuing sensory values with social values, cultures attempt to ensure that their members will perceive the world aright. When sensory orders express cosmic orders, cosmologies are not only learnt through hearing or reading, but lived through the body. Every time a Tzotzil woman walks on the cool earth with her bare feet she is reminded of her symbolic coldness. The Tzotzil feel their cosmology through the temperature of their bodies, the Ongee breathe in theirs with every breath. The Desana see their cosmology in colors, hear it in music, taste it in their food. These sensory cosmologies make us aware of the many different ways in which cultures shape perception, and the inability of standard Western models to comprehend such sensory and symbolic diversity. When cultures are approached on their own sensory terms rather than through the paradigms dictated for them by outsiders, what we discover are not world views or oral/aural societies, but worlds of sense.

Bibliography

Basso, E. (1985), *A Musical View of the Universe: Kalapalo Myth and Ritual Performance*, Philadelphia: University of Pennsylvania Press.

Classen, C. (1993), *Inca Cosmology and the Human Body*, Salt Lake City: University of Utah Press.

Gossen, G.H. (1974), *Chamulas in the World of the Sun: Time and Space in a Maya Oral Tradition*, Cambridge MA: Harvard University Press.

Howes, D. (ed.) (1991), *The Varieties of Sensory Experience: A Sourcebook in the Anthropology of the Senses*, Toronto: University of Toronto Press.

Hugh-Jones, S. (1979), *The Palm and the Pleiades*, Cambridge: Cambridge University Press.

McLuhan, M. (1961), 'Inside the Five Sense Sensorium,' *The Canadian Architect*, 6: 49–54.

—— (1962), *The Gutenberg Galaxy: The Making of Typographic Man*, Toronto: University of Toronto Press.

Ong, W.J. (1969), 'World as View and World as Event,' *American Anthropologist*, 71(4): 634–47.

Pandya, V. (1987), 'Above the Forest: A Study of Andamanese Ethnoamenology, Cosmology and the Power of Ritual,' Ph.D. dissertation, University of Chicago.

—— (1993), *Above the Forest: A Study of Andamanese Ethnoanemology, Cosmology and the Power of Ritual*, Bombay: Oxford University Press.

Reichel-Dolmatoff, G. (1971), *Amazonian Cosmos: The Sexual and Religious Symbolism of the Tukano Indians*, Chicago: University of Chicago Press.

—— (1978a), *Beyond the Milky Way: Hallucinatory Images of the Tukano Indians*, Los Angeles: UCLA Latin American Center Publications.

—— (1978b). 'Desana Animal Categories, Food Restrictions, and the Concept of Color Energies,' *Journal of Latin American Lore*, 4(2): 243–91.

—— (1979), 'Desana Shamans' Rock Crystals and the Hexagonal Universe,' *Journal of Latin American Lore*, 5(1): 117–28.

—— (1981), 'Brain and Mind in Desana Shamanism,' *Journal of Latin American Lore*, 7(1): 73–98.

—— (1985) *Basketry as Metaphor: Arts and Crafts of the Desana Indians of the Northwest Amazon*, Los Angeles: Occasional Papers of the Museum of Cultural History, University of California.

Vogt, E.Z. (1976), *Tortillas for the Gods: A Symbolic Analysis of Zinacanteco Rituals*, Cambridge MA: Harvard University Press.

9

Consciousness as 'Feeling in the Body'
A West African Theory of Embodiment, Emotion and the Making of Mind

Kathryn Linn Geurts

[The] neurobiology of consciousness faces two problems: the problem of how
the movie-in-the-brain is generated, and the problem of how the brain also
generates the sense that there is an owner and observer for that movie.

Antonio Damasio, *The Feeling of What Happens:*
Body and Emotion in the Making of Consciousness

In *The Feeling of What Happens*, neurobiologist Antonio Damasio suggests
that central to human consciousness, and to the problem of how we
know what we know, is the experience of bodily feeling. He posits that
consciousness involves two things: the brain engendering mental patterns
that we call images of objects, and the brain engendering a 'sense of self
in the act of knowing' (Damasio 1999: 9). In arguing that the two are
intimately linked through bodily feeling, Damasio puts forth an innovative
theory of consciousness, which, in effect, holds 'I feel, therefore I know.'
His incorporation of emotion and bodily feeling – or 'the interior milieu'
– into studies of the brain and cognition is to be applauded. But from the
standpoint of anthropology, as I want to show, the culture-bound quality of
many of his claims seriously weakens his position.

In West Africa, ideas about how we know what we know have been
articulated by Anlo-Ewe people through their concept of *seselelame* – a
concept that embraces a panoply of inner states. While many Anlo-Ewe
speakers translate the term into English as feeling in the body, the flesh

64

or the skin, the phoneme *se* can be considered a basic perception verb, rendering *seselelame* as perceive-perceive-at-flesh-inside. Ewe linguist Felix Ameka has confirmed that the phrase *se-se-le-la-me* can be used to translate both emotion and sense perception, and that 'lower level terms for various experiences in Ewe, like the superordinate label *seselelame*, do not distinguish between emotion, sensation, perception, cognition, etc. Instead, there are components that link to a bundle of these things at one and the same time' (Ameka 2002: 44–5).

Damasio suggests that perhaps the most novel idea in his book is that 'consciousness begins as a feeling, a special kind of feeling, to be sure, but a feeling nonetheless... a feeling of knowing' (Damasio 1999: 312). This is an important theoretical move for neuroscience, since it overcomes the conventional Cartesian split between mind and organism or body (see further Damasio 1994). Damasio's ideas are all the more interesting because of close parallels they have with Anlo-Ewe theories of the relations between embodiment and consciousness. For example, one Anlo colleague explained to me: 'You can feel happiness in your body, you can feel sorrow in your body, and you can feel other things, like cold. *Seselelame* describes all of these things because it is hearing or feeling in the body.' At another point in our conversation, he referred to the experience of going to the theater: 'You go and watch it, and you feel something inside. You hear music, see the actors act very well, and you feel something inside. You applaud, get up and dance, or shout something. That is a feeling and it comes through *seselelame*.'

Western academic psychologists rarely bother to consider what insights might be gained from the study of other psychologies than their own – that is, from so-called ethno-psychologies. This neglect has been criticized from within psychology itself by Markus, Kitayama and Heiman (1996: 859), who argue that 'psychological processes are not just "influenced" but are thoroughly culturally constituted, and as a consequence, psychological processes will vary with sociocultural context.' Furthermore, while still acknowledging the potential for certain psychic universals within the human species, Markus et al. propose that the discipline of psychology is guilty of 'prematurely settling on one psychology, that is, on one set of assumptions about what are the relevant or most important psychological states and processes, and on one set of generalizations about their nature and function' (Markus et al. 1996: 858). Here we will consider how a number of Damasio's assumptions and generalizations – including his restricted focus on individual rather than intersubjective consciousness and his penchant for cinematic metaphors (for example, consciousness as 'movie-in-the-brain') – are challenged by Anlo-Ewe perspectives on feeling and consciousness.

Ewe-speaking people have traditionally inhabited the land that is now southeastern Ghana as well as southern Togo, and Ewes are close in ethno-linguistic terms to Fon-speaking people in Benin. Anlo-Ewe refers to a group of primarily Ghanaian Ewes whose homeland is considered the coastal area of the Volta region and the terrain immediately around the Keta Lagoon. In the twenty-first century, however, many Anlo people live in diaspora, in Accra and other parts of Ghana, as well as in Europe and the United States. During the early and mid-1990s, I carried out ethnographic research with Anlo people to learn how we might better understand Anlo ways of being-in-the-world through a study of their sensory order. In our discussions and research, Anlo individuals and I found that their sensory order did not map well onto a five-senses model of touch, taste, hearing, sight and smell. Instead, they pointed to *seselelame* as a more generalized feeling in the body that includes both internal senses (such as balance and proprioception) and external senses, as well as other perceptual, emotional, and intuitive dimensions of experience.

When comparing Anlo ideas about bodily feeling with Antonio Damasio's theories about consciousness and the self, we find that certain weaknesses of a disciplinary and culture-bound nature surface in his claims. For example, Damasio's theory of consciousness, being informed by the discipline of neurobiology, is centered upon the individual subject, structural and neurological in orientation while an Anlo theory of consciousness is intersubjective, phenomenological and processual in character. Secondly, Damasio's theory is imbued with the values of 'technological individualism' (a fundamentally Western bourgeois ideology) as evidenced both by his focus on the individual subject and by his reliance on certain metaphors – consciousness as 'stepping into the light' and as a 'movie-in-the-brain' – rooted in sensorial biases that are taken for granted in the West but are not universally salient. Anlo ideas about sensory experience and consciousness, summed up in their phrase *seselelame*, help us to explore the ways in which Damasio's perspective is gounded in 'one set of generalizations' and needs to be supplemented with others in the interests of making psychology more properly cross-cultural.

Cultural Categories and Culturally Elaborated Modes of Attention to the Body

Seselelame is best understood in reference to what anthropologist Thomas Csordas (1993) has called 'somatic modes of attention.' By this phrase Csordas is referring to 'culturally elaborated ways of attending to and with one's body in surroundings that include the embodied presence of others' or 'culturally elaborated attention to and with the body in the immediacy of an intersubjective milieu' (Csordas 1993: 138–9). According to Csordas:

> Because we are not isolated subjectivities trapped within our bodies, but share an intersubjective milieu with others, we must also specify that a somatic mode of attention means not only attention to and with one's own body, but includes attention to the bodies of others. Our concern is the cultural elaboration of

sensory engagement, not preoccupation with one's own body as an isolated phenomenon. (Csordas 1993: 139)

Seselelame is an ideal illustration of a culturally elaborated form in which many Anlo people attend to and interpret their own bodies while simultaneously orienting themselves to the bodies of those around them. In one of its uses, it seems to refer to a specific sense or kind of physical sensation that we might call tingling in the skin (sometimes a symptom of impending illness), but in other uses it refers to sexual arousal, heartache, passion, and even pain. In yet other uses, it refers to a kind of inspiration (to dance or to speak), but it can also be used to describe something akin to intuition (when there is uncertainty as to the source of a given feeling). Finally, it is also presented as a generalized (almost synesthetic) feeling in or through the body.

One Anlo colleague whom I call Raphael made reference to the close links in Anlo psychology among sensation, perception, emotion, cognition, and moral reasoning, and stressed how *seselelame* needed to be understood in relation to the Anlo concepts of *sidzedze* (to recognize) and *gomesese* (to understand). He offered a hypothetical situation as an example. Say he heard someone talking about a woman who had been hit by a car (a common occurrence in Accra), he would experience certain negative or sad feelings about what this person had just undergone. Supposing he also came to the realization that the injured woman was married to one of his good friends, Raphael suggested, 'Your sense will tell you that you have to visit them and express sympathy. Your brain has quickly worked and actually told you your sympathy is called for at that point in time.'

Sidzedzenu meant that you had 'taken the thing to mind' or you had actually 'observed the situation, analysed it and realized' something about it. He suggested that the English word 'recognize' could be used as a translation for *sidzedze* and *sidzedzenu* meant 'thing recognized.' But beyond simple translation, Raphael wanted to focus our attention on some aspects of the process captured by the intersection of these terms. A coalesence had occurred of *seselelame* (feeling in the body) with certain memories and thoughts, and out of that process sprang a recognition – a sense of or perspective on what the dialogue really meant to him. *Gomesese*, or 'understanding,' came into play, and Raphael summarized his point by suggesting that 'when you have a sensation – some source of *seselelame* – you must analyse and understand what that thing can create within you or within the other inmates of the house. So it is a message, an external message, that you get and you have to – in a way – analyse it properly.' The process of 'analysing properly' consisted of *seselelame* (feeling in the body) and *sidzedzenu* (thing recognized) and *gomesese* (understanding or standing underneath it).

In relation to Damasio's ideas about consciousness, it is noteworthy that Raphael stressed how you have to analyse and imagine what the 'messages' create within you *and* within 'the other inmates of the house.' This draws our attention to the inter-subjective character of *seselelame* or how it is a way of 'attending to and with one's body in surroundings that include the embodied presence of others' (Csordas 1993: 138–9). Furthermore, Raphael's account of consciousness was deeply imbued with sensibilities about movement (kinesthesia) and inter-subjectivity – namely, going to visit the couple and expressing sympathy. Thus, the 'messages' noted by Raphael were not interpreted as cinematic images, but rather the messages catapulted him into a consciousness premised on movement and emotion.

A second example will further illustrate this point. An Anlo woman named Beauty Banini wanted to explain to me and my research assistant what *seselelame* meant to her, and so (like Raphael) she constructed a hypothetical situation. Beauty painted a picture of herself incapacitated by a swollen foot, but attempting to attend a public event while suffering from this condition. She reflected on the fact that because of her inability to walk, she would have to stay put in a chair – even while a buffet of deliciously scented food was laid out nearby. Beauty explained that *seselelame* would come into play in the following manner. While up at the buffet table, a close sister-colleague of hers might collect two plates of food – one for herself, and one for Beauty (left behind by the swollen foot). After eating the food, Beauty indicated she might express: *Ne enyona fieku la eyae wonya na adzikula* ('if it goes on well with the tigernut harvester, then it will be well with the groundnut harvester'). This proverb captured how she would share a feeling of union, oneness, or harmony with her sister-colleague. An unspoken need or desire (for the food) would be met with an unspoken response (presentation of the plate), and so, Beauty explained, because it was well with that sister, it also sat well with her – creating a profound sense of satisfaction (*dzidzeme* or *nudzedze*). Through the capacities of *seselelame* – a kind of mingling of sensibilities – a feeling arose inter-subjectively, on the part of both women, that this transaction should occur. The one took action, and it resulted in a deep sense of harmony and satisfaction for both.

For Anlo people, these are the ways in which *seselelame* (feeling in the body, flesh, or skin), *gomesese* (understanding), and *sidzedzenu* (recognition) are implicated in the making of consciousness. Consciousness implicitly involves bodily feeling and inter-subjectivity. In addition, accounts of consciousness often involve complex references to movement and sensorimotor activities. I would suggest that this emphasis on inner senses in Anlo reflections relates to a heightened valuation of kinesthesia and balance (which I will discuss momentarily).

The other bodily experiences and inner states typically associated with *seselelame* include: *nusese* – aurality, or hearing; *agbagbadodo* – balance, equilibrium; *azolizozo* or *azolinu* – walking, or kinesthesia; *nulele* – tactility, contact, touch; *nukpokpo* – visuality, or seeing; *nudodo* and *nudodokpo* – tasting; *nuvevese* – smelling; and, finally *nufofo* – vocality or talking. I have discussed this terminology in detail elsewhere (Geurts 2002a: 37–69). Here I just want to make two points. The first is that many Anlo people believed that loss of hearing was the most grave impairment of sense perception, not only because deafness cuts you off from people, but because with this loss would come a disruption to your sense of balance. This brings out how 'hearing' (*nusese*) and 'feeling' (*seselelame*) in the body are linked in Anlo experience. 'Hearing' and 'smelling' (*nuvevese*) are also intimately linked, such that Anlo people are wont to say *Mese detsi la fe veve*, which could be translated as 'I hear the soup's aroma.' Thus, hearing and smelling are not strictly affairs of the ear or nose; they are affairs of the whole body, or interplay of the senses (*seselelame*).

To summarize, *seselelame* was provided as a specific sense by some people, in addition to serving as a descriptor for sentience in general. With referents ranging from proprioception, and balance, to a more generalized feeling throughout the body, *seselelame* may be said to serve as a foundational schema in Anlo society from which specific sensory and emotional fields arise. In the next section I will focus on specific examples of *seselelame* and an Anlo theory of inner states as a way to flesh out some of the implications of Anlo epistemology for Damasio's theory of consciousness.

Kinesthesia and the Making of Consciousness

In the history of psychology, speculations about how the brain works have often been influenced by the technology of the day (such as aqueducts in the ancient world, the machine in Descartes' time, and so forth). They have also been influenced by changing notions of the person (see Mauss 1979). Damasio's theory is a prime example of such cultural and historical influence. As I will show, his account of consciousness is pervaded by certain 'thematized aspects of the world' (Csordas 1994: 5) revolving around (a) individual ownership and (b) living in a media-dominated environment. This is the state of 'technological individualism.' It is the state that undergirds Damasio's notion of consciousness as private and cinematic, among other things.

As will be recalled, for Damasio, the 'neurobiology of consciousness faces two problems: the problem of how the *movie-in-the-brain* is generated, and the problem of how the brain also generates the sense that there is an *owner and observer* for that movie' (Damasio 1999: 11, emphasis mine). To elaborate, the main problem is one of 'understanding how the brain inside the human organism engenders the mental patterns we call... the images of an object' (Damasio 1999: 9). By object, Damasio means anything from 'a person, a place, a melody, a toothache, a state of bliss,' and by image he means 'a mental pattern in any of the sensory modalities, e.g. a sound image, a tactile image, the image of a state of well-being' (Damasio 1999: 9). A further problem has to do with how the brain succeeds at 'generating the appearance of an owner and observer for the movie within the movie' (Damasio 1999: 11).

In the course of expounding his theory, Damasio suggests that in this rough metaphor the movie has as many sensory tracks as our nervous system has sensory portals – sight, sound, taste, and olfaction, touch, inner senses, and so on (Damasio 1999: 9). However, a moment's reflection reveals that movies do not have multiple sensory tracks. They have but two. There is an overpowering audio-visualism in our cinematic encounters, and such encounters are undeniably devoid of aromatic, kinesthetic, and tactile experiences (notwithstanding some generally unsuccessful efforts at screening films in 'sensuround' or in 'smellorama'). This fact is, however, elided by Damasio's unreflective appropriation and use of the 'movie-in-the-brain' motif as a metaphor for consciousness.

Damasio's account of consciousness is further weakened, from a cross-cultural standpoint, by his invocation of the theatrical experience of 'stepping into the light.' He suggests that 'when self first comes to mind and forevermore after that, two-thirds of each living day without a pause, we step into the light and we become known to ourselves. And now that the memory of so many becomings has created the persons we are, we can even imagine ourselves walking across the stage under the light' (Damasio 1999: 315). Evidently these individualistic and performance-based notions of consciousness have a great deal of personal significance for Damasio, and it is probable that they would also have salience for most of his readers – given the visualism and cinematic obsession of many people in modern, industrialized societies. In what follows, however, we shall see how Anlo people would be more likely to emphasize stepping and balance than illumination, adaptability instead of stability, and walking in place of movie-going in their accounting for consciousness.

A word about stability. 'In all the kinds of self we can consider,' writes Damasio (1999: 134), 'one notion always commands center stage: the notion of a bounded, single individual that changes ever so gently across time but, somehow, seems to stay the same.' Damasio goes on to discuss the physiological mechanisms which allow for this 'structural invariance,' or what it is that 'provides the mind with a spine, is single, and is same' (Damasio 1999: 135). Thus 'the roots of individual perspective, ownership and agency' can all be traced to brain structures. Damasio betrays no consciousness whatsoever that the emergence of a sense of self as owner dates only from the seventeenth century (on the origins of the ideology of 'possessive individualism' see Macpherson 1962). Nor does his 'one body one self' model (see Damasio 1999: 142–3) allow any room for other 'kinds of self,' such as multiple selves, to be considered. But the idea of multiple consciousnesses (or selves) inhabiting the same body is in fact quite common, as the widespread cultural phenomenon of spirit possession attests (Lambek 1981). The (alleged) stability of Damasio's 'interior milieu' thus bears the traces of a particular cultural and historical process, and not simply a biological one. Anlo ideas about the mutability of bodies and minds contrast with Damasio's single-minded views of self.

During my fieldwork, I observed that Anlo caregivers engaged in a variety of socialization routines with the stated intention of creating flexible, supple, and balanced persons. Newborn babies often received a ritualized first bath aimed at beginning the process of making flexible bodies and inculcating 'adaptability' as a character trait. A common Ewe proverb was, *Ne neyi akpokplowo fe dume eye wotsyo ako la, wo ha natsyo ako* – meaning, 'If you visit the village of the toads and you find them squatting, you must squat too.' Altering one's body posture symbolized adaptability, rendering the saying emblematic of the local sensory valuation of kinesthetic suppleness as well as flexibility in social behaviors and attitudes toward others.

Why did Anlo-Ewe people feel a need to raise children with an orientation towards adaptability? Several factors account for this habit, but primarily a lack of industry and commercial opportunities in the Anlo homeland has meant that people have often had to migrate out for work, and as an ethnic minority in Ghana (less than 10 percent of the population), even in the capital city (Accra), many Anlo people found themselves living in circumstances in which other languages and social customs often dominated. Caretakers reflected on how experiencing and knowing flexibility in an embodied dimension and at an early age (for example, through manipulated and massaged joints during the bath), helped to produce flexibility in character and psychological outlook. Convergence of the somatic and psychological was also evident in how a sense of kinesthesia (movement and the way you walk, sometimes referred to as *azolizozo*) was directly linked to your character and way of life – *azolime*. In other words, to most Anlo, an agile body was to a flexible mind as comportment was to character.

This bodily poetics was not lost on midwives who often spoke of the baby in the womb as sitting on a little stool (the placenta). For centuries stools have held profound spiritual significance in Anlo-land and throughout West Africa, so I found this metaphorical connection between the placenta and a stool highly suggestive. It seemed to link the not-yet-born child to a concern with posture and balance: an imagined baby was composing or arranging her body into a still and balanced form, poised on an African stool, even in the womb.

For centuries West African craftsmen have been carving these symmetrical and sleek wooden stools (*zikpui*). It is instructive to consider the physical experience of resting on an Anlo *zikpui* as a means of thinking through the pre-eminence of *seselelame* (feeling in the body) in Anlo-Ewe approaches to making meaning. The absence of a plank against which to lean your back, along with the presence of a sculpted seat, invites you to balance your body in such a way that it stills proprioceptive and kinesthetic sensations. A projection of the baby resting atop a placental-ancestral stool, therefore, has the power to invoke a strong feeling. It is from the placenta that a baby derives its sustenance (nutrients, oxygen, and blood), and it is in relation to the ancestral stool that members of the lineage sustain themselves – by knowing who they are and to what group they belong. A wedding of the somatic and the psychological is achieved by drawing on cultural orientations toward balancing and kinesthesia, as well as rich symbolic references to an element of material culture that signifies the lineage.

Kinesthesia is beyond question a highly valued sensory modality in many Anlo contexts. What makes it pertinent here is that many Anlo socialization routines indicate parental awareness of (or vigilance concerning) how a child's comportment or style of walk both instantiates and reflects his (or her) temperament or disposition. The Anlo-Ewe language helps us to consider these claims, as it contains an extensive repertoire of terms to describe the ways in which people move and walk (see Geurts 2002a: 73–84; and 2002b). For example, *zo kadzakadza* is used to indicate a person moving, behaving, feeling like a lion: assertive, forceful, and majestic, exhibiting an air of challenge as if ready for a fight. *Zo dziadzia* refers to moving with intent and purpose, feeling like you have a mission; whereas, *zo gbozoe* indicates coming and going, aimlessness, not having any sense of direction. Other terms – from *zo lumolumo* and *zo bafobafo*, to *zo bulabula* and *zo kodzokodzo* – are also used to comment on mannerisms, comportment, a person's disposition and feelings, and to sum up an individual's moral compass.

Take the word *zo lugulugu* (referring to bodily motions such as swaying, tarrying, dawdling, or moving as if drunk) and the way it can be used to refer to a person's character. In the rural area where I lived during 1994 and 1995, two young boys in our compound often played about in the process of fetching water. They ran in circles, darted from one side of the compound to the other, walked backwards, and generally engaged in ludic behavior in the process of carrying out this chore. Their parents and other caregivers inevitably scolded them for this behavior and frequently complained that they never went straight to the well but were always 'going this way and that,' fooling around, distracting each other from the task, and consistently stirring up trouble. As an outsider I initially perceived this behavior as harmless playing, but gradually came to appreciate the distress it produced for caregivers because their fear was about how the orientations expressed in these displays would begin to dominate the boys' characters.

This anecdote reveals a local perspective that if you move in a *lugulugu* fashion you experience sensations of *lugulugu*-ness and begin thinking in a *lugulugu* way and become a *lugulugu* person which is then evident to others from the way your *lugulugu* character is embodied in your *lugulugu* walk. Or, if you consistently think in a *lugulugu* way you will also move in a *lugulugu* fashion and basically develop into a *lugulugu* person, which will then be embodied in a *lugulugu* kind of walk.

Thus, for Anlo people, there is a clear connection between bodily habits and who you are or who you become: your character, your moral compass is embodied in the way you move, and the way you move embodies an essence of your nature. The logic or consciousness that I have just described is not merely about people seeing the child walking *lugulugu* and thinking that he was wayward, but about the sensations the child would experience in the body, and then the imaginative structures that would develop in the mind – structures that would then be perceived (by all involved) as a culturally constituted and objectified phenomenon called *lugulugu*. In the context of this cultural logic, no real distinction exists between the development of bodily habits and psychological outlook. Instead, they are deeply intertwined.

Interoception and 'Folding into Oneself'

We are now in a position to appreciate how kinesthesia, balance and flexibility contribute to Anlo sensibilities and to the ways in which they think about feeling and consciousness. The etymology of their name, in fact, provides the next clue to how significant the 'inner senses' are for so many Anlo people.

'Anlo' has a variety of meanings, the most common being a designation for an ethno-linguistic group (dialect of Ewe) with which they are associated. A less well known meaning of Anlo is revealed by their migration myth, an account of their sojourn 300 years ago to settle the area now designated their homeland.

In the middle of the seventeenth century, the Dogboawo Ewes were a subjugated class living in the walled city of Notsie (the ruins of which are located in current day central Togo). Deplorable conditions led to their eventual escape, and as the Dogboawo fled they fanned out west and south of Notsie. Those who followed an elder named Togbui Wenya, their migration story goes, traveled all the way to the coast and halted on the littoral that is now the southeastern portion of Ghana. This was an arduous journey, and it is said that that when they arrived at the coast Togbui Wenya collapsed from exhaustion or folded into himself and declared: *Nyeamea menlo afiadeke yiyi megale nunye o* ('I am rolled up, coiled up from exhaustion, and I can travel no further'). Under Togbui Wenya's leadership, the migrants settled right there on the coast, and established communities later known as Keta and Anloga.

When people related this story to me, and they reached the moment when Togbui Wenya declared *nyeamea menlo*, they often folded their own bodies inward in the way that they imagined their ancestor had done more than 300 years before. They described him curling up or folding into himself – a gesture reminiscent of the fetal position – and in the Ewe language, the term for this bodily gesture is *nlo*. This is the same *nlo* that we find in their appellation – Anlo-Ewe – and so encoded in their very name is this memory of Togbui Wenya's sorrow, grief, and fatigue.

For quite a while during fieldwork I was unable to make connections between my interest in sensory experiences and the interests of many Anlo individuals in telling me stories such as these. Eventually, however, this 'folding into oneself' – as a bodily gesture brimming with symbolism and iconicity – served as a link to *seselelame* (Geurts 2003). Figuring out an Anlo sensorium included more than just mapping or translating sounds, touches, tastes, sights, and smells. A reflective, introspective, or even interoceptive flavor permeates Anlo accounts of feeling in the body (*seselelame*), and this inwardness seemed connected to their cultural memory of 'folding into oneself.' That is to say, expressed in this migration myth about their freedom from slavery was a nostalgic feeling for Togbui Wenya and an emotional connection to the long walk their ancestors pursued, and to the exhaustion they felt upon arriving at the coast. The act of 'folding into oneself' indexes introspection, and at the same time positions the body to engage internal senses such as balance and proprioception, so that *seselelame* can be understood as a 'somatic mode of attention' (Csordas 1993) particularly attuned to interoceptively oriented bodily feeling.

Feeling in the Mouth

Damasio goes to considerable lengths to discredit the idea that consciousness depends on the presence of language. He argues that 'core consciousness' is generated by 'brain devices' or 'neural structures' that operate automatically, and that the 'proto-self' of core consciousness differs from the second-order 'autobiographical self' of extended consciousness. Language is deemed to play a role in the construction of the latter self. In a radical (and nowhere justified) about-face, however, Damasio projects language – or 'storytelling' – *back* into the constitution of the proto-self: 'Wordless storytelling is natural,' Damasio (1999: 188) tells us, and goes on all the time in the brain's 'representations' of what happens. These 'representations' (or sequential images) in turn make possible the verbal translation of experience at higher-order levels of consciousness.

Damasio expands upon what he means by 'wordless storytelling – or 'the nonverbal nature of core consciousness' – as follows:

> I do not mean narrative or story in the sense of putting together words or signs in phrases and sentences. I do mean telling a narrative or story in the sense of creating a nonlanguaged map of logically related events. Better to think of film (although the film medium does not give the perfect idea, either) or of mime – Jean-Louis Barrault miming the story of the watch theft in *Les Enfants du Paradis*. (Damasio 1999: 184–5)

Note Damasio's lapse into cinematic imagery when words fail him.

Limitations of space prevent me from commenting further on the contradictions that plague the motif of 'wordless storytelling' in Damasio's work. In any event, those contradictions are for him to resolve. Let me turn instead to a consideration of an Anlo philosophy of speech and embodied consciousness.

I experienced the telling of the Notsie migration myth (discussed above) numerous times while I sojourned in Anlo-land. I even began folding my body inward during the climax of the story when we reached the moment of Togbui Wenya's exhaustion and fatigue. Myths by design are meant to arouse such feelings and sensory imagery (Kracke 1992), so this came as little surprise. But some of the links between language and bodily feelings were not as easy to comprehend. I found myself reflecting on the feeling of the tonally inflected utterance *nyeamea menlo*, and considering the reverberations in the body when one makes that open *o* sound inside the mouth. (It has qualities similar to that of the syllable 'om' or 'aum' used as a mantra in Eastern meditative arts.) These experiences and reflections helped me to begin crossing over into an understanding of why speech is considered a sense by many Anlo people and by many West Africans.

Speaking and sensing belong in different categories for many Westerners in part because we tend to conceptualize speaking as an 'active externalization of data' and we think of sensing as a passive reception of stimulus from something outside our body (Classen 1993). But Anlo speakers emphasize similarities and relationships in the experiences of speaking, eating, drinking, breathing, kissing, regulating saliva, and so forth. Just as sensing in their language is rooted in a more generalized notion of *seselelame* (feel-feel-at-flesh-inside), speaking too falls within a broader category of experience they call *sesetonume* (feeling in the mouth). An example of the links between speaking and a certain kind of illness may help to demonstrate further the sensorial aspects of speech.

While I lived in rural Ghana I attended about fifteen births, and in this connection I often witnessed the effects of something Anlo-speakers referred to by using the term *enu*, which translates as 'mouth.' In cases where labor pains were severe, when there was a delay in labor, or in the face of various complications during birth, the attending midwife usually sprayed the woman's abdomen with saliva, and brushed it with a 12 inch whisk, in an effort to discard the causes of *enu*.

Enu is the term for a category of 'spiritual sicknesses' that includes a host of afflictions to pregnant women, and illnesses that can kill children or render them deaf and unable to speak. The cause is deemed bad will or enmity among household members or kin. But contrary to what we might expect, it is not the meaning of the words expressing malice or malevolence that causes someone to fall ill, but rather the sensory power contained in the sounds themselves.

The most common meaning of the word *enu* is simply 'mouth,' but it also refers to opening, entrance, edge; contents, quantity; effect (Westermann 1973: 177). Pregnant women and other vulnerable adults can be seized with *enu* because of disrespectful, wicked, or evil things that pass through the mouths of people in the household. In fact, through *sesetonume* (feeling in the mouth) you can absorb your own bad speech, and so speaking is believed to be one of the primary forces involved in the etiology of *enu*. Children, on the other hand, are not believed to contract *enu* from their own *sesetonume*, or feelings in the mouth, but rather through bodily absorption of the physical power of the words of others.

Much has been written about speech in African contexts containing a power or energy independent of its referential quality (see Stoller 1989; Peek 1994). Words are not only information or knowledge but also sound, so in addition to their meaning, words have a physical force which operates not only at the site of the ear and mind but throughout the entire body. In fact, the Anlo term for speech and talking (*nufofo*) contains the morpheme *fo*, which means to strike, beat, blow. This symbolizes the dynamic power ascribed to the words themselves. As a scholar of the neighboring Fon people has stated: 'Critical to the activation potential of speech is both its transferential nature and its potent social and psychodynamic grounding' (Blier 1995: 77). The 'transferential nature' of *nufofo* (speaking) includes more than imparting meaning or 'mental ideas,' for in *enu*, speaking is one of the culprits in the transference of emotional and physiological disturbance, especially to children. In the presence of an acrimonious verbal exchange, it is not simply the meaning of the dialogue which causes children and pregnant women to fall sick, but rather it is perceived as a manifestation of *seselelame* and the animosity and rancor is transferred to their bodies in part through the striking action of the sound of speech itself. This reinforces a local phenomenology in which 'Speech is irreversible; that is its fatality. What has been said cannot be unsaid, except by adding to it' (Blier 1995: 76–7). So it is not simply the hearing of an argument and the consequent psychological effect that is at issue here, but rather the notion that once speech containing animus is externalized, adults can absorb their own anger through *sesetonume* (feeling in the mouth) and children absorb the rancor through *seselelame* (feeling in the body, flesh, or skin).

Concluding Remarks

In his emphasis on the interior milieu and on the 'idea of consciousness as a feeling of knowing,' Damasio's position comes close to an Anlo model of how we know what we know. However, Damasio is hampered by the constraints of his own culture. He seeks to bring psychology and philosophy together under the aegis of biology (Damasio 1999: 13), but Damasio's biology, untempered by anthropology, results in a skewed (culturally naive) understanding of human capacities. That is, the absence of an anthropological sensibility from his thinking about consciousness results in a failure of reflexivity – and, in particular a failure to recognize the cultural biases that remain embedded in his theory. There are other ways of being-in-the-world than that of technological individualism – the mindset of so many people in contemporary Western bourgeois societies. This essay presents one such alternative – thereby challenging psychology to become more cross-cultural and to explore and respect the psychologies of other societies as sources of often profound theoretical and practical insight.

As a neurobiologist, we might expect Damasio to stress individual consciousness, for neurobiology is pre-eminently the science of the individuated human being. However, his theory is seriously weakened, from an anthropological standpoint (see Csordas 1994), by his attachment to the notion of 'one body, one self' (Damasio 1999: 143). With its echoing of 'one person, one vote,' this approach reveals how Damasio implicitly subscribes to a philosophy of 'possessive individualism' (Macpherson 1962). Unlike an Anlo view of self as inherently intersubjective and rooted in shared feelings, Damasio's theory is a very bourgeois view of self – as exemplified by his repeated references to 'ownership' and being the 'proprietor' of images and of experiences (see Damasio 1999: 183). Interpreting Damasio's thought in light of a non-Western tradition (Anlo-Ewe epistemology) has allowed us to throw many of his unthought assumptions into relief. In this way we can see that an Anlo-Ewe theory of consciousness, implicit in their language and their whole way of life, deserves equal consideration as a theory of how consciousness works.

Acknowledgments

The research on which this chapter is based has been ongoing since 1992, with fieldwork carried out during 1993–95 supported primarily by a Fulbright-Hays Doctoral Dissertation Research Abroad Grant (#P022A30073). More recent fieldwork in Ghana was made possible by funds from Hamline University's College of Liberal Arts, and by expert research assistance from Elvis Gershon Adikah. I am deeply grateful for the endless generosity of a network of Anlo-Ewe people who have been hosting my family and me for years and encouraging me to persist with this challenging project. I would like to give special thanks to David Howes for his invitation to contribute to this volume, and for his brilliant insight and guidance in the development of this piece.

Bibliography

Ameka, F.K. (2002), 'Cultural Scripting of Body Parts for Emotions: On "Jealousy" and Related Emotions in Ewe,' *Pragmatics and Cognition*, 10(1 and 2): 27–55.

Blier, S.P. (1995), *African Vodun: Art, Psychology, and Power*, Chicago: University of Chicago Press.

Classen, C. (1993), *Worlds of Sense: Exploring the Senses in History and Across Cultures*, London and New York: Routledge.

Csordas, T.J. (1993), 'Somatic Modes of Attention,' *Cultural Anthropology*, 8(2): 135–156.

—— (1994). *The Sacred Self: A Cultural Phenomenology of Charismatic Healing*, Berkeley: University of California Press.

Damasio, A.R. (1994), *Descartes' Error: Emotion, Reason, and the Human Brain*, New York: Avon Books, Inc.

—— (1999), *The Feeling of What Happens: Body and Emotion in the Making of Consciousness*, San Diego and New York: Harcourt, Inc.

Geurts, K.L. (2002a), *Culture and the Senses: Bodily Ways of Knowing in an African Community*, Berkeley: University of California Press.

—— (2002b), 'On Rocks, Walks and Talks in West Africa: Cultural Categories and an Anthropology of the Senses,' *Ethos*, 30(3): 178–98.

—— (2003), 'On Embodied Consciousness in Anlo-Ewe Worlds: A Cultural Phenomenology of the Fetal Position,' *Ethnography*, 4(3): 363–95.

Kracke, W. (1992), 'Myths in Dreams, Thought in Images: An Amazonian Contribution to the Psychoanalytic Theory of Primary Process,' in B. Tedlock (ed.), *Dreaming: Anthropological and Psychological Interpretations*, Santa Fe NM: School of American Research Press, pp. 31–54.

Lambek, M.J. (1981), *Human Spirits: A Cultural Account of Trance in Mayotte*, New York: Cambridge University Press.

Markus, H.R., Kitayama, S., and Heiman, R.J. (1996), 'Culture and "Basic" Psychological Principles,' in E.T. Higgens and A.W. Kruglanski (eds), *Social Psychology: Handbook of Basic Principles*, New York: Guilford Press, pp. 857–913.

McPherson, C.B. (1962), *The Political Theory of Possessive Individualism*, Oxford: Clarendon Press.

Peek, P. (1994), 'The Sounds of Silence: Cross-World Communication and the Auditory Arts in African Societies,' *American Ethnologist*, 21(3): 474–94.

Stoller, P.M. (1989), *The Taste of Ethnographic Things: The Senses in Anthropology*, Philadelphia: University of Pennsylvania Press.

Westermann, D. ([1928] 1973), *Ewefiala or Ewe-English Dictionary*, Nendeln/ Liechtenstein: Kraus-Thompson Organization Ltd., Kraus Reprint. Original edition, Berlin: Dietrich Riemer/Ernst Vohsen.

10

Places Sensed, Senses Placed

Toward a Sensuous Epistemology of Environments

Steven Feld

The sense of place: the idiom is so pervasive that the word 'sense' is almost completely transparent. But how is place actually sensed? How are the perceptual engagements we call sensing critical to conceptual constructions of place? And how does this feelingful sensuality participate in naturalizing one's sense of place? These questions guide my inquiry into the sensing and sensuality underlying how places are named and poetically evoked by Kaluli people of Bosavi, Papua New Guinea. My desire is to illuminate a doubly reciprocal motion: that as place is sensed, senses are placed; as places make sense, senses make place. Because sound and an ear- and voice-centered sensorium are central to Kaluli experience and expression in the tropical rainforest, the goal of this exploration is to interpret what I call an acoustemology, by which I mean local conditions of acoustic sensation, knowledge and imagination, embodied in the culturally particular sense of place resounding in Bosavi.

The chapter opens with brief notes on sensation, sound, synesthesia, and soundscapes that provide context for the general framework of my inquiry, that of a social phenomenology and hermeneutics of senses of place. I outline ways in which research on acoustic experience and expression of place has remained relatively underdeveloped and then introduce the sound world of the Kaluli.

Sense, Embodiment, Synesthesia

'Perception does not give me truth like geometry but presences' (Merleau-Ponty 1962: 14). What are these 'presences' that are given in perception? Merleau-Ponty insisted that they were first the presences of feeling and perceiving bodies, bodies whose sensory experience was never fully sublimated to abstract cognition. Sensations, he urged, were always experienced presences, presences of what later cognitive psychologists and philosophers called an 'embodied mind' (Varela, Thompson, and Rosch 1991), or a 'body in the mind' (Johnson 1987).

But the senses, the body's 'sensorimotor surfaces,' are not limited to embodied presences, and they constitute more than experiential sites for establishing points and places of physical and social contact (Straus 1963). Drew Leder's *The Absent Body* (1990), develops this line of critique to ask why, if the body is so central to sensory experience, if it so actively situates the subject, might it also be so experientially absent or out-of-focus. Why is the body not the direct thematic object of one's attention and experience, and why does it recede from direct experience? Leder develops these questions by addressing Merleau-Ponty's (1963) observation, made in *The Structure of Behavior* that 'to be situated within a certain point of view necessarily involves not seeing that point of view' (Leder 1990: 12). He elaborates: 'This constitutes the necessary supplement to the Gestaltist figure-background description of perception.' As Merleau-Ponty (1962: 13) writes [in *The Phenomenology of Perception*]: 'one's own body is always the third term, always tacitly understood in the figure-background structure, and every figure stands out against the double horizon of external and bodily space' (Leder 1990: 13).

Leder's conjecture as to why some bodily dimensions are always experientially foregrounded while others are backgrounded relies on the same 'figure-ground gestalt to characterize not only the body's field of experience but the structure of the experiencing body itself' (Leder 1990: 24). He claims that 'these modes of absence arise directly out of the fundamental structure of embodiment,' further characterizing 'the lived body as an ecstatic/recessive being, engaged both in a leaping out and a falling back. Through its sensorimotor surface it projects outward to the world. At the same time it recedes from its own apprehension into anonymous visceral depths. The body is never a simple presence, but that which is away from itself, a being of difference and absence' (Leder 1990: 103; see also Schilder 1950; Levin 1985).

Establishing this complex and multiple presence and absence of the body clearly implicates another interactive figure- and background, that of the senses. Lived experience involves constant shifts in sensory figures and grounds, constant potentials for multisensory or cross-sensory interactions or correspondences. Figure-ground interplays, in which one sense surfaces in the midst of another that recedes, in which positions of dominance and subordination switch or co-mingle, blur into synesthesia, 'the transposition of sensory images or sensory attributes from one modality to another' (Marks 1978: 8). Synesthesia points to the complexity of sensory ratios, the rich connections inherent in multiple sensation sources, the tingling resonances and bodily reverberations that emerge from simultaneous joint perceptions (Cytowic 1989). This 'medley of the senses bleeding into each other's zone of expectations' (Taussig 1993: 57) reveals how 'the synesthetic, like the metaphoric in general, expands the horizon of knowledge by making actual what were before only potential meanings' (Marks 1978: 254). Taussig's *Mimesis and Alterity* argues that this metaphoric and synesthetic potential recalls mimesis, 'the magical power of replication... wherein the representation shares in or takes power from the represented' (Taussig 1993: 2). This same metaphoric and synesthetic potential also recalls iconicity, the ways in which perceiver and perceived blur and merge through sensuous contact, experiencing inner resemblances that echo, vibrate, and linger as traces from one sensory modality to another, present at one level while absent at others, continually linking bodily experience to thought and to action (Feld 1988; Jackson 1989: 119–55; Ohnuki-Tierney 1991).

But sensation, sensual presence, is still more, more than embodiment, more than perceptual figure-grounds, more than the potential for synesthesia. It was Henri Bergson's insight, long ago, in *Matter and Memory*, that 'there is no perception which is not full of memories. With the immediate and present data of our senses, we mingle a thousand details out of our past experience' (Bergson [1908] 1988: 33). Hence, 'what you have to explain... is not how perception arises, but how it is limited, since it should be the image of the whole, and is in fact reduced to the image of that which interests you' (Bergson [1908] 1988: 40). Bergson's problem – linking the active body as a place of passage to processes of making memory – is developed in Edward Casey's (1987) *Remembering*. He writes:

> Moving in or through a given place, the body imports its own emplaced past into its present experience: its local history is literally a history of locales. This very importation of past places occurs simultaneously with the body's ongoing establishment of directionality, level and distance, and indeed influences these latter in myriad ways. Orientation in place (which is what is established by these three factors) cannot be continually effected *de novo* but arises within the ever-lengthening shadow of our bodily past. (Casey 1987: 194)

Because motion can draw upon the kinesthetic interplay of tactile, sonic, and visual senses, emplacement always implicates the intertwined nature of sensual bodily presence and perceptual engagement.

Landscape, Acoustic Space, Soundscape

The overwhelmingly multisensory character of perceptual experience should lead to some expectation for a multisensory conceptualization of place. But by and large, ethnographic and cultural geographic work on senses of place has been dominated by the visualism deeply rooted in the European concept of landscape. Denis Cosgrove has analysed how two distinct notions of landscape, both sharing a pervasive visualism, have merged in the West. In the first instance, over some 400 years,

> the idea of landscape came to denote the artistic and literary representation of the visible world, the scenery (literally that which is seen) which is viewed by a spectator. It implied a particular sensibility... closely connected to a growing dependency on the faculty of sight as the medium through which truth was to be attained: 'seeing is believing.' Significant technical innovations for representing this truth included single-point perspective and the invention of aids to sight like the microscope, telescope, and camera... (Cosgrove 1984: 9)

In the second case, that of landscape as a notion incorporated into the analytical concerns of academic geography, the concept 'denotes the integration of natural and human phenomena which can be empirically verified and analysed by the methods of scientific enquiry over a delimited portion of the earth's surface... ' (Cosgrove 1984: 9). Cosgrove argues that these two senses of landscape 'are intimately connected both historically and in terms of a common way of appropriating the world through the objectivity accorded to the faculty of sight and its related technique of pictorial representation' (Cosgrove 1984: 9).

But what of place as heard and felt? Place as sounding or resounding? In contrast to the long history of the landscape idea in both artistic and scientific inquiry and representation, approaches to ways in which worlds are sonically apprehended have shallower histories. Arguing this point, that the 'hearsay' of aural-oral experience was never accorded the same evidential or representational primacy as visual 'insight,' Edmund Carpenter and Marshall McLuhan introduced the notion of 'acoustic space' in their journal *Explorations* (1953–9). The term derived from their projects at the University of Toronto Center for Culture and Technology concerning media transformations, specifically the ways the history of orality and literacy could be reinterpreted from the vantage point of electronic communications in the twentieth century. In this context, Carpenter's article on acoustic space was the first statement describing the cultural implications of directionally simultaneous and diffuse ear-point (Carpenter 1960). His later studies went on to relate acoustic space to visual-auditory interplays, as in the way the Inuit experience of spherical dynamic space in the Arctic relates to local artistic imagination and process, especially visual puns, and depiction of motion, depth, and non-containment (see Carpenter 1971, 1973, 1980).

The notion of 'auditory space' also emerged in the mid-1950s in an entirely different context. The music philosopher Victor Zuckerkandl, drawing substantially on the philosophy of Henri Bergson and Martin Heidegger, and on the psychophysics, and the Gestalt and perceptual psychology of William James, Géza Révész and Erwin Straus, argued vigorously against the notion that music is purely an experience of tone as time. He did so by detailing ways that space is audibly fused with time in the progression and motion of tones (Zuckerkandl 1956: 267–348). While this interpenetration of auditory space and time has not had a general impact on theorizations of space and place, *Music and the External World,* the first volume of Zuckerkandl's *Sound and Symbol* (1956), has certainly had a particularly critical impact elsewhere, as in Kathleen Higgins's vigorous philosophical critique of musical Platonism (Higgins 1991), in anthropological explorations of ritual, music and sound symbolism in the work of Ellen Basso (1985) and Paul Stoller (1989: 101–22), and in Roy Wagner's (1986) theoretical essays on symbol and metaphor.

Just as Zuckerkandl the musician influenced anthropologists, Carpenter the anthropologist principally influenced musicians. When composer Murray Schafer organized the World Soundscape Project at Simon Fraser University in 1970, the Carpenter and McLuhan ideas, marginal both in the anthropology of the arts and in cultural geography in the 1950s and 1960s, were introduced to composers and acousticians in a new framework, the study of the sound environment and acoustic communication. Schafer's group began recording, observing, and acoustically analysing the sonic experience of space and place, especially in Canada and Europe, and developed an analytical vocabulary, a notation system, and a comparative framework for the study of acoustic space and its human interpretation and feedback. This work went under the general rubrics of two terms coined by Schafer, 'acoustic ecology' and 'soundscape design.'

Schafer and his colleagues disseminated their ideas in media ranging from music compositions to radio collages, and from technical reports to print and cassette travel journals, all of which led to a general synthesis, Schafer's (1977) *The Tuning of the World.* This book has drawn substantial attention to the acoustic complexities of environments, especially northern ones, but its impact has largely been felt among musicians, acousticians, architectural designers, and audio and radio artist-composer-recordists (for example, see Truax 1984; Schafer 1993; Werner 1992). Acoustic ecology and soundscape studies have had rather less impact on ethnographers who might study how people hear, respond to, and imagine place as sensually sonic. On the other hand, humanistic geography, deeply impacted by perspectives from phenomenology in the 1970s and 1980s, began to notice the acoustic dimensions of place somewhat less cautiously (for example, Buttimer and Seamon 1980; Seamon 1979; Seamon and Mugerauer 1985; Tuan 1977), but rarely explored them, and never in the fully grounded way that would draw anthropological attention.

The work of the Carpenter-McLuhan-Schafer lineage was not taken up seriously by anthropopologists; indeed, it was criticized by those most interested in its consequences for analysing both the senses and orality-literacy issues (Feld 1986; Finnegan 1988: 139–74). Despite its stated concern with sensory ratios, this line of thinking often reified a visual-auditory great divide, one that reproduced some variant of the notion that: 'Seeing is analytical and reflective. Sound is active and generative' (Schafer 1985: 96). Such oversimplified rhetoric led most ethnographers to turn their ears, and sparked the critical tack taken by Don Idhe, whose phenomeno-logical essay *Listening and Voice* pointed out the futility of countering the historical centrality of visualism in Western analytic discourses by simply erecting an anti-visualism (1976: 21). What Idhe called for instead, – a call recently echoed by anthropologist David Howes in *The Varieties of Sensory Experience* (1991: 3–21, 167–91) – was a reevaluation of all the senses from the standpoint of their interplay. Only then, Idhe and Howes both claimed, could a serious analysis of sound emerge in an adequately experiential or ethnographic way. Given recurring tendencies to essentialize vision as a characteristic of the West (for example, Ong 1982), in polar opposition to a presumed centrality of sound, smell, and taste that is essentialized to non-Western cultural 'others,' a reevaluation of sensory ratios must scrutinize how tendencies for sensory dominance always change contextually with bodily emplacement. That perspective informs my position on sound in sensory experience, specifically its implications for interpreting life worlds of Kaluli people in Papua New Guinea.

Towards an Acoustemology

If, '… in perceiving, our whole body vibrates in unison with the stimulus… [then] hearing is, like all sense perception, a way of seizing reality with all our body, including our bones and viscera' (Gonzalez-Crussi 1989: 45; compare Idhe 1976: 81, also Ackerman 1990: 186–90, on ways sound penetrates the body). Sound, hearing, and voice mark a special bodily nexus for sensation and emotion due to their complex coordination of brain, nervous system, head, ear, chest, muscles, respiration, and breathing. 'The vocal mechanism involves the coordinated action of many muscles, organs and other structures in the abdomen, chest, throat and head. Indeed, virtually the entire body influences the sound of the voice either directly or indirectly' (Sataloff 1992: 108). Moreover, hearing and voice are connected by auditory feedback and by physical resonance, the immediate experience of one's presence through the echo-chamber of the chest and head, the reverberant sensation of sound, principally one's own voice. By bringing a durative, motional world of time and space simultaneously to front and back, top and bottom, and left and right, an alignment suffuses the entire fixed or moving body. This is why hearing and voicing link the felt sensations of sound and balance to those of physical and emotional presence.

This position problematizes Abu-Lughod and Lutz's argument that 'emotion can be studied as embodied only after its social and cultural – its discursive – character has been fully accepted' (Abu-Lughod and Lutz 1990: 13). Although they assert that 'as cultural products [emotions] are reproduced in individuals in the form of embodied experience' (Abu-Lughod and Lutz 1990: 12), it seems unwise to abstract discourse, or the production and circulation of topics through speech styles and genres, from the embodied voice, the site of verbal articulation, the resounding place of discourse as fully feelingful habits. Emotions may be created in discourse, but this social creation is contingent on performance, which is always emergent through embodied voices (see Urban 1991: 148–71).

Acoustemology, acousteme: I'm adding to the vocabulary of sensorial-sonic studies to argue the potential of acoustic knowing, of sounding as a condition of and for knowing, of sonic presence and awareness as potent shaping forces in how people make sense of experiences. Acoustemology means an exploration of sonic sensibilities, specifically of ways in which sound is central to making sense, to knowing, to experiential truth. This seems particularly relevant to understanding the interplay of sound and felt balance in the sense and sensuality of emplacement, of making place. For places are as potentially reverberant as they are reflective, and one's embodied experiences and memories of them may draw significantly on the interplay of that resounding-ness and reflectiveness.

Acoustemology means that as a sensual space-time, the experience of place potentially can always be grounded in an acoustic dimension. This is so because space indexes the distribution of sounds and time indexes the motion of sounds. Yet acoustic time is always spatialized; sounds are sensed as connecting points up and down, in and out, echo and reverb, point-source and diffuse. And acoustic space is likewise temporalized; sounds are heard moving, locating, placing points in time. The placing of auditory time is the sonic envelope created from the layered attack, sustain, decay, and resonance of sounds. The placing of auditory space is the dispersion of sonic height, depth, and directionality. Space-time inevitably sounds in and as figure and ground, as comingness and goingness. It's presence is forward, backward, side to side, heard in trajectories of ascent, descent, arch, level, or undulation. What these rather abstract formulations suggest, in simple terms, is that experiencing and knowing place – the idea of place as sensed, place as sensation – can proceed through a complex interplay of the auditory and the visual, as well as through other intersensory perceptual processes.

Bosavi Acoustemology: Bodily Unity of Environment, Senses and Arts

In common with their rainforest neighbors on the Great Papuan Plateau and in the surrounding rainforest region of Papua New Guinea, Kaluli people hear much that they don't see. The diffuseness of sound is significant in the tropical forest environment, and the bodily orientation of its inhabitants through hearing, listening and voicing has strongly impressed itself on ethnographers who have worked in the area (for example, Feld 1990; E.L. Schieffelin 1976; Sørum 1989; Weiner 1991). Kaluli commonly develop acute hearing for locational orientation. Whether it is used in marked forest activities such as hunting by sound, or in mundane ones, such as walking along forest trails or attending to the details of the surrounding bush from inside a village longhouse, the locational information available from sound in this environment often greatly exceeds that available from vision, in both variety and salience. Even though one quickly realizes that hearing is the most culturally attuned sense in Bosavi, audition is always in an interplay with other senses, particularly in a tense dialectic with vision. This is because much of the forest is visually hidden, whereas sound cannot be hidden. A Kaluli man named Jubi once impressed this on me by analogy. He said that just as the identities of costumed ceremonial dancers, or those of spirit mediums performing in total darkness, are revealed only by the presence of a singing or speaking voice, the presences of forest places are sonically announced even when visually hidden away.

Acoustic revelatory presence is thus always in tension with visual hidden presence in primal experiences of the forest. Linking experience and expression, this same tension adheres in Kaluli poetic concepts, for example the intersensory desire to interpret songs, conversations, arguments, or stories by 'turning over' (*balema*) their surfaces to reveal their *heg* 'underneath' or *sa*, 'inside.' 'Turned over' 'insides' and 'underneaths' reveal resonant depths, meanings, subtleties, and implications of sounds, song poetics, stories, allegorical speeches, or dance costumes just as they reveal the hidden presences of forest locales – the significance of the way places are physically shaped, such as the way rocks, waterfalls, mountains, or creeks emerge as presences with meaningful 'inside' and 'underneath' pasts. Thus the commonplace notion, that objects and events are always more than they appear to be, takes on a particularly sensual and poetic character when it comes to Kaluli modes of interpreting the depths and dimensions of local experience.

Another way the Kaluli dialectic between what is hidden and what is revealed emerges is powerfully signaled by the intersensory iconic *mama*, 'reflection' or 'reverberation.' *Mama* is one's image in water, or in the mirror; it is the close-up reflection of oneself in the eyeball of another, the visual presence of the self apart from the self. It is also the lingering audio fragment of a decaying sound, its projection outward as it resounds by vanishing upward in the forest. Like the fading sharpness of a mirror image, mama is the trace of audio memory, fragmentary sonic remembrances as they reverberate. An *ane mama*, a 'gone reflection-reverberation,' is a spirit, a human absence returning in imagined (often avian) presence. Announced by flashes of sight, or, more typically, by conspicuous sounds experienced without the accompaniment of a corresponding visual image, an *ane mama* presence instantly stimulates feelingful memories.

These Kaluli vision-sound interplays are also locationally intersensual to smell. Any number of everyday examples could be cited. It is hard to imagine the trickling of a shallow creek at a stand of sago palms without smelling the aromas of fresh or rotting sago pith; the experience and memory of sago place presence is deeply multisensory. Similarly, the dense sensuality of evening darkness, with voices overlapping the misting light rains and insects and frogs of the nearby bush, is sensually continuous with smoky aromas that fires or resin torches release into the longhouse and diffuse out into the ever-moist night air. Evoking the diffuseness of this motional sensorium, the processes of sound and smell are incorporated into the same Bosavi verb, *dabuma*, or absorption by ear and nose. Hearing is the unmarked form, the major kind of sensory absorption or taking in; smelling requires marking the odor's name before the verb, such that the action of smell carries the linguistic feel of 'hearing the odor.' The metaphoric potential here inversely plays on the familiar Western synesthetic notion that the pleasures of music have long been absorbed as the 'perfume of hearing' (Ackerman 1990: 202).

At its broadest, the multisensory character of Bosavi acoustemology is suggested by the complexities of everyday practices linking sensory experience of the rainforest to artistic processes in visual, verbal, musical, and choreographic media. These practices are encompassed in discourse by two synesthetic metaphors; 'lift-up-over sounding,' *dulugu ganalan*, and 'flow,' *a:ba:lan*. Both of these are important to Kaluli experience and expression of emplacement. Because I have discussed *dulugu ganalan* in some detail before (Feld 1988), I here review its importance to the interplay of the senses only briefly, and then concentrate on 'flow.' 'Flow' concerns the interrelated sense and sensuality of water flowing through and connecting land forms, as well as the voice flowing through and connecting the thinking, moving, feeling, body. It also concerns the hold, the lingering grip, of sound and poetic song, the resoundingness of voice in silent memory. These notions of flow all merge in the performance of the path maps that are a central feature of poetic song texts.

'Lift-up-over sounding' is the metaphoric construct that prescribes and describes natural sonic form for Kaluli people. Calling attention to both the spatial ('lift-up-over') and temporal ('sounding') axes of experience, the term evokes the way all sounds necessarily co-exist in fields of prior and contiguous sounds. When applied to the sound world of the rainforest, 'lift-up-over sounding' highlights the observation there are no single discrete sounds to be heard. Everything is mixed into an interlocking soundscape. Forest sounds constantly shift figure and ground to create staggered alternations and overlaps, a sense of sound that is completely interlocked and seamless. One hears no unison in nature. Presence and absence of sound or changes in its direction and dimension coordinate space as intersecting upward and outward. Sounds constantly interact to produce the sensation that one sound is momentarily about to stand out from the others, while at the same time conveying the sense that any primacy is fluid, as quickly lost as it is gained.

In the tropical rainforest height and depth of sound are easily confused. Lack of visual depth cues couple with the ambiguities of different vegetation densities and with ever-present sounds, such as the hiss of water, to make depth often sensed as the diffuseness of height moving outward, dissipating as it moves. 'Lift-up-over sounding' precisely yet suggestively codes the ambiguous sensation that auditorially, kinesthetically, and sensually projects a space-time: upward *feels* like outward. This placing of sound is at once a sounding of place. One knows the time of day, season of year, and placement in physical space through the sensual wraparound of sound in the forest. This way of hearing and sensing the world is internalized as bodily knowledge, part of the everyday 'body hexis' (Bourdieu 1977: 87), the naturalized regime of 'body techniques' (Mauss [1935] 1979) basic to routine Kaluli encounters in their world.

Kaluli transform these everyday encounters with acoustic figure-grounds, extending their naturalness from the experience of the rainforest soundscape to their own vocal and instrumental music. Voices and rattles are made to 'lift-up-over' like the trees of the forest canopy; sounds of drums and work tools are made to 'lift-up-over' like tumbling waterfalls into swirling waterpools. These ideas are elaborated by Kaluli in musical practices favoring dense and layered cooperative singing or sounding that always avoids unison. To create a 'lift-up-over sounding,' voices or instruments or both must be in-synchrony while out-of-phase. To be 'in-synchrony' means that the overall feeling is one of togetherness, of consistently cohesive part coordination in sonic motion and participatory experience. Yet the parts are also 'out-of-phase,' that is, at distinctly different and shifting points of the same cycle or phrase structure at any moment, with each of the parts continually changing, even competing, in degree of displacement from a hypothetical unison. Additionally, 'lift-up-over sounding' is created in timbre, by textural densification, through a layering of attacks, decays, and fades, of playful accelerations, lengthenings and shortenings, of the fission and fusion of sound shapes and phrases. Musical parts that interlock, alternate, or overlap create a form of participation that blurs competition and cooperation, mirroring the larger Kaluli tendency toward tense egalitarianism in social activities ranging from speech and work to negotiation, transaction, and exchange.

In concert with these dimensions of musical creativity, face-painting styles visually mirror sonic 'lift-up-over sounding' through a parallel figure and ground principle in the texture contrast between shiny and dull and the color contrast between black and red. Ceremonial costumes further exploit textural densification by mixing many types of materials, blending and layering fur, bird feathers, red, black, and white paints, shells, woven bands, bamboo, rattles, palm streamers, and colorful leaves. As the ceremonial dancer bobs up and down in this paraphernalia, layers of 'in synchrony and out-of-phase' sound emanate from his shells and streamers in motion, 'lifted-up-over' by his drum, rattle, or voice.

Taking in nature, music, body painting, costume, and choreography, 'lift-up over sounding' metaphorically unites Kaluli environment, senses, and arts.

Bibliography

Abu-Lughod, L. and Lutz, C. (1990), 'Introduction: Emotion, Discourse, and the Politics of Everyday Life,' in C. Lutz and L. Abu-Lughod (eds), *Language and the Politics of Emotion*, New York: Cambridge University Press, pp. 1–23.

Ackerman, D. (1990), *A Natural History of the Senses*, New York: Random House.

Basso, E.B. (1985), *A Musical View of the Universe: Kalapalo Myth and Ritual Performances*, Philadelphia: University of Pennsylvania Press.

Basso, K. (1988), '"Speaking with Names": Language and Landscape among the Western Apache,' *Cultural Anthropology*, 3(2): 99–130.

Bergson, H. ([1908] 1988), *Matter and Memory*, New York: Zone Books.

Bourdieu, P. (1977), *Outline of a Theory of Practice*, trans. R. Nice, New York and Cambridge: Cambridge University Press.

Buttimer, A. and Seamon, D. (eds) (1980), *The Human Experience of Space and Place*, New York: St. Martin's.

Carpenter, E. (1960), 'Acoustic Space,' in E. Carpenter and M. McLuhan (eds), *Explorations in Communications*, Boston: Beacon Press, pp. 65–70.

—— (1971), 'The Eskimo Artist,' in C. Otten (ed.), *Anthropology and Art: Readings in Cross-Cultural Aesthetics*, Garden City: Natural History Press, pp. 163–70.

—— (1973), *Eskimo Realities*, New York: Holt Rinehart & Winston.

—— (1980), 'If Wittgenstein Had Been An Eskimo,' *Natural History*, 89 (2): 72–7.

Casey, E.S. (1987), *Remembering: A Phenomenological Study*, Bloomington: Indiana University Press.

—— (1993), *Getting Back into Place: Toward a Renewed Understanding of the Place-World*, Bloomington: Indiana University Press.

Cosgrove, D.E. (1984), *Social Formation and Symbolic Landscape*, London and Sydney: Croon Helm.

Cytowic, R. (1989), *Synesthesia: A Union of the Senses*, Berlin and New York: Springer-Verlag.

Feld, S. (1988), 'Aesthetics as Iconicity of Style, or, "Lift-up-over Sounding": Getting into the Kaluli Groove,' *Yearbook for Traditional Music*, 20: 74–113.

—— ([1982] 1990), *Sound and Sentiment: Birds, Weeping, Poetics and Song in Kaluli Expression*, second edition, Philadelphia: University of Pennsylvania Press.

—— (1991), *Voices of the Rainforest*, CD/cassette, Salem MA: Rykodisc.

Finnegan, R. (1988), *Literacy and Orality*, Oxford: Basil Blackwell.

Gonzalez-Crussi, F. (1989), *The Five Senses*, New York: Vintage.

Higgins, K.M. (1991), *The Music of Our Lives*, Philadelphia: Temple University Press.

Howes, D. (ed.) (1991), *The Varieties of Sensory Experience: A Sourcebook in the Anthropology of the Senses*, Toronto: University of Toronto Press.

Idhe, D. (1976), *Listening and Voice: A Phenomenology of Sound*, Athens: Ohio University Press.

Jackson, M. (1989), *Paths Toward a Clearing*, Bloomington: Indiana University Press.

Johnson, M. (1987), *The Body in the Mind: The Bodily Basis of Meaning, Imagination, and Reason*, Chicago: University of Chicago Press.

Leder, D. (1990), *The Absent Body*, Chicago: University of Chicago Press.

Levin, D.M. (1985), *The Body's Recollection of Being*, London: Routledge Kegan Paul.

Marks, L. (1978), *The Unity of the Senses: Interrelations among the Modalities*, New York: Academic Press.

Mauss, M. ([1935] 1979), 'Body Techniques,' in *Sociology and Psychology: Essays by Marcel Mauss*, London: Routledge & Kegan Paul, pp. 97–123.

Merleau-Ponty, M. (1962), *The Phenomenology of Perception*, trans. C. Smith, New York: Humanities Press.

—— (1963), *The Structure of Behavior*, Boston: Beacon Press.

Ohnuki-Tierney, E. (1991), 'Embedding and Transforming Polytrope: The Monkey as Self in Japanese Culture,' in J.W. Fernandez (ed.), *Beyond Metaphor: The Theory of Tropes in Anthropology*, Stanford: Stanford University Press, pp. 158–89.

Ong, W.J. (1982), *Orality and Literacy*, New York: Methuen.

Sataloff, R. (1992), 'The Human Voice,' *Scientific American*, 267(6): 108–15.

Schafer, R.M. (1977), *The Tuning of the World*, New York: Knopf.

—— (1985), 'Acoustic Space,' in D. Seamon and R. Mugerauer (eds), *Dwelling, Place and Environment*, Dordrecht: M. Nijhoff, pp. 87–98.

—— (1993), *Voices of Tyranny, Temples of Silence*, Indian River, Ontario: Arcana Editions.

Schieffelin, E.L. (1976), *The Sorrow of the Lonely and the Burning of the Dancers*, New York: St. Martin's Press.

Schilder, P. (1950), *The Image and Appearance of the Human Body*, New York: International Universities Press.

Seamon, D. (1979), *A Geography of the Lifeworld: Movement, Rest and Encounter*, New York: St. Martin's.

Seamon, D. and Mugerauer, R. (eds) (1985), *Dwelling, Place and Environment*, Dordrecht: M. Nijhoff.

Sørum, A. (1989), 'The Aesthetics of Spacetime: Temporality and Perception in New Guinea,' paper read at the Annual Meeting of the American Ethnological Society.

Stoller, P. (1989), *The Taste of Ethnographic Things: The Senses in Anthropology*, Philadelphia: University of Pennsylvania Press.

Straus, E. (1963), *The Primary World of Senses: A Vindication of Sensory Experience*, Glencoe: Free Press.

Taussig, M. (1993), *Mimesis and Alterity: A Particular History of the Senses*, New York: Routledge.

Truax, B. (1984), *Acoustic Communication*, Norwood NJ: Ablex.

Tuan, Y-F. (1977), *Space and Place: The Perspective of Experience*, Minneapolis: University of Minnesota Press.

Urban, G. (1991), *A Discourse-Centered Approach to Culture*, Austin: University of Texas Press.

Varela, F., Thompson, E. and Rosch, E. (1991), *The Embodied Mind: Cognitive Science and Human Experience*, Cambridge MA: MIT Press.

Wagner, R. (1986), *Symbols That Stand for Themselves*, Chicago: University of Chicago Press.

Weiner, J. (1991), *The Empty Place: Poetry, Space, and Being among the Foi of Papua New Guinea*, Bloomington: University of Indiana Press.

Werner, H. (1992), *Soundscapes Akustische Landschaften: Eine Klangökologische Spurensuche* (TSNE Volume 1), Basel: The Soundscape Newsletter Europe Edition.

Zuckerkandl, V. (1956), *Sound and Symbol: Music and the External World* (Bollingen Series, 44), Princeton: Princeton University Press.

11
The Way of Tea
A Symbolic Analysis

Dorinne Kondo

I

The tea ceremony presents a unique challenge to the anthropologist, for the essence of tea and of Zen is said to elude logical, discursive analysis. Zen favors experience and intuition over intellection, and although the tea ceremony has given rise to a long tradition of scholarly exegesis, the Zen arts[1] continue to emphasize the primacy of transcendence through alogical, non-verbal means.[2] This dialectic of experience and native exegesis is at one level unassailable and must play a key role in any attempt to understand the meaning and symbolism of the ceremony.

Tea ceremonies may be held on a variety of occasions, depending on the season, the time of day, the school of tea, and so forth. The following description is of the full-length, formal, midday rite (*shogo chaji*) lasting from three to five hours. Because of its length, the years of expertise required to host such a gathering, and the expense and preparation involved, it is not the most commonly practised variant – forms of the *usucha*, or thin tea, ceremony are – but I have selected this *chaji* for analysis because it is considered the 'standard *chaji* by which all others are created' (Palmer 1976: 71). Moreover, training in tea is designed to make the student capable of hosting such a ceremony.

Focusing on a single 'ideal typical' ceremony seemed desirable for two reasons. First, since my concern is to explore the implications of an internal, semantic analysis, this 'standard *chaj'* as described in tea manuals and as taught to pupils, casts into relief the structure, form and sequence of the rite, providing a text to penetrate from within. Secondly, although precise details of the ceremony may vary according to type and to context, this form constitutes a basic orchestral 'score,' realized in slightly different ways in each performance. In my experience as a student of tea and according to informants' statements, both culturally constructed meaning (especially Zen aesthetics) and the symbolic orchestration of the ceremony do appear to shape the attitudes of participants in highly significant ways. Accordingly, for the purposes of this article, questions of indexical or pragmatic meaning (tea as conspicuous consumption, a domestic art, and so forth) are left in abeyance. An exhaustive analysis would, of course, include these various levels of semantic and pragmatic meaning, both at a particular point in time and as they change over time (see, for example, Tambiah 1979). The intent, then, is to focus on a single variant, as an illustrative object for the methods used to deconstruct the ritual, and as a potential point of entry into other such 'texts' (cf., for example, Barthes 1974). The particular version described is a *shôgo chaji* in the style of the Ura Senke school, performed with the *ro*, or sunken hearth, used between November and April.

II

Zenrei

Guests are generally invited to the ceremony a week in advance, and ideally the principal guest pays a call on the host (*zenrei*) to accept the invitation (Sen 1979: 62).

Arrival

In classic tea gardens, the guests arrive at the gate, where the paving stones have been sprinkled with water, a signal for them to enter. They proceed to a room called the *yoritsuki*, in the outer garden, where they change clothes and put on clean split-toed socks. From there they advance to the waiting room or *machiai*, and await the rest of their number. If it has not already been determined, they select a principal guest (*shokyaku*) who is first in order, and a final guest (*tsume*) who brings up the rear. In each instance a special knowledge of the ceremony is desirable. If there is an assistant to the host, the guests may be served *osayu*, hot water, to which a delicate flavoring may be added (Ishikawa 1976: 67). The guests view the scroll, flowers and implements displayed in the *machiai*, waiting area, and then proceed to the *koshikake machiai*, or waiting arbor. The host returns to the tea room, leaving the gate to the inner garden slightly ajar, and the guests follow in single file, setting out on the garden path of stones. This is glossed explicitly in some works as the path into enlightenment. When the last guest reaches the inner *roji*, he or she shuts the middle gate. In the inner garden, the guests advance to the stone basin, or *tsukubai*, to purify their mouths and hands with water.

Seki-iri

The next phase of the ceremony is called *seki-iri*, literally, entering into one's seat. Leaving the sandals propped against the wall of the tea room, the principal guest crawls through the *nijiri-guchi* (literally, the crawling-in entrance) with a crouch and slide motion. The extremely small size of the entrance is said to inculcate humility.

The principal guest then proceeds to the *tokonoma*, or alcove, kneeling before it to view the scroll hung there. This work of art and the tea flowers that appear there later, set the mood for the occasion. The principal guest then proceeds to his or her seat, as each guest examines the scroll. The last guest shuts the door of the *nijiri-guchi* with a click, a signal for the host to appear.

Shozumi (Arranging of Charcoal)

The host waits in the *mizuya* (small preparation area adjacent to the tea room) until the guests are in place and then appears at the host entrance to exchange formal greetings with the guests. The host then returns to the *mizuya* and brings out charcoal, tongs, and incense burner, and begins to smooth the ashes in the brazier into a pattern. After the fire is started, the contents of the incense burner are emptied into the brazier. The guests admire the fire, then the principal guest asks to see the incense holder, which they all examine in sequence as the host retires to the service area. He or she returns to retrieve the incense holder and to announce that 'a frugal meal' will be served.[3]

Kaiseki

Kaiseki is food for the tea ceremony. Each guest is given a small individual tray with a bowl of rice, one of soup, and perhaps a dish of vegetables and/or fish, though other foods may be offered in addition. *Sake* is also served. *Kaiseki* should be fresh, natural, and appropriate to the season, and portions should be small. The host does not partake, but may stay to serve the guests *sake*. He or she retires again to the *mizuya* until they finish eating. The guests eat, wipe their bowls and chopsticks with small squares of paper they have brought along and, when finished, sharply click their chopsticks on the tray, a signal for the host to remove their utensils. *Omogashi*, moist sweets, are then carried out in lacquer boxes, one sweet per box, and after the guests partake they retire to the waiting arbor.

Nakadachi

The interlude here is called *nakadachi* – middle standing – a chance for the guests to stretch their legs. They may talk quietly and enjoy the beauty of

the garden. A gong calls them back to the tea hut, and they enter exactly
as they did before.

Koicha

The next segment is the real height of the tea ceremony: the preparation and
drinking of *koicha*, thick tea. The scroll in the alcove has now been replaced
by a *chabana* (tea flower) arrangement. The guests admire the arrangement,
take their proper places, principal guest in the seat of honor near the alcove,
and sit quietly as the host brings in separately: (a) water jar (*mizusashi*); (b)
tea bowl, tea scoop, tea caddy; (c) receptacle for waste water (*kensui*), lid
stand, and bamboo dipper. The host purifies the caddy and scoop by wiping
them with the tea napkin, rinses and wipes the bowl, and prepares tea. These
minutely prescribed acts are performed with a graceful economy of motion.
The guests watch in complete silence. This is considered the climax of the
ceremony.

The guests then partake of the thick tea, drinking in sequence from a single
bowl, the principal guest first, the *tsume*, or final guest, draining the bowl,
wiping it, and returning it to the host. The *haiken* or examination follows, a
question-answer session between the principal guest and the host, centering
on the names and historical associations of the various tea implements. With
the completion of the *haiken* and the removal of the utensils, the *koicha*
segment concludes.

Gozumi

At this point there may be a rebuilding of the charcoal fire, a process called
gozumi, paralleling the first lighting of the fire, *shozumi*. Replacing the incense
is a small tray or *tabako-bon*, bearing a piece of charcoal in a cup, and a
bamboo 'ashtray,' as well as a pipe and a tiny amount of tobacco.

Usucha

The *usucha* segment follows. The sequence of actions parallels that in the
koicha ceremony, with the following key differences: (a) *usucha* itself is a
less concentrated form of the same tea; it is thinner and lighter and can be
whipped into a froth, wheareas *koicha* must be kneaded and then stirred;
(b) the specific tea utensils for *usucha* are defined as more informal, though
not necessarily less replete with historical associations; (c) *higashi* – light,
dry sweets eaten with the fingers – are served, and one eats them while one's
tea is being made, which contrasts with the formal presentation of *omogashi*
in lacquer boxes. *Omogashi* are eaten with a special pick before partaking of
koicha; (d) more conversation is allowed during *usucha*; (e) instead of sharing
a single bowl of tea, each guest drains the bowl and then examines it. If

desired, the guest may request additional servings of tea. In brief, *usucha* is more informal, lighter and freer in tone.

When all guests have partaken, the principal guest asks the host to end the ceremony. At this point the guests examine the tea container and the tea scoop, as the host removes the other utensils in the reverse order from which they were initially carried into the room. The examination completed, the host returns to answer questions about the utensils. The ceremony closes with formal greetings (*aisatsu*), with both sides expressing their appreciation. The guests leave the room, principal guest last, and close the door of the *nijiri-guchi*. They then turn to face the tea house, as the host opens the *nijiri-guchi* and silent bows are exchanged. This is the *okurirei*, or farewell. The host remains waiting until the guests are no longer in sight, and then closes the door. On the following day the chief guest should call informally upon the host to express the group's appreciation (Palmer 1976: 77).

III

The aesthetic sensibility informing the way of tea traces its roots through Zen Buddhism, to Chinese Ch'an Buddhism and Taoism. Tea ceremony, like other Zen arts, is a religious/aesthetic/philosophical 'way' (in Japanese, *michi* or *dō*; in Chinese, *tao*). This *dō*, an elusive concept to define, could be glossed as 'the inner essence of reality' (Bellah 1957: 61). Accordingly, the 'way' of tea, like the other Zen master arts, is more than mere artistic or technical proficiency: it is a path to Enlightenment.

According to Zen doctrine, Enlightenment is *mu* – emptiness or nothingness. Zen ideals include qualities such as *mushin*, selflessness or detachment, and *munen*, *musō*, freedom from all ideas and thoughts. Efforts to master the intricate discipline of tea or another Zen art constitute a process of self-realization, whereby one so thoroughly incorporates the form that it – or other worldly concerns, such as the desire to perform well – no longer requires one's conscious attention. This is the state of 'emptiness.' Through tea or another Zen art, a person may be said to attain the states of *yūgen* or *kotan* (*yūgen no kyōchi*, *kotan no kyōchi o tassuru*). *Yūgen* is a term associated closely with No drama. It bespeaks the evanescence and pathos of life, hinting at the eternal and infinite. It is subtle elegance and profundity. *Kotan* is defined as seasoned simplicity, when everything unnecessary (for example, worldly thoughts and cares) has fallen away, leaving only the essential core.

The pathway to this state lies in action and intuition; logic and elaborate verbal exegesis are correspondingly downplayed. For example, in tea, as in all the master arts, instruction has little in common with Western didactic methods; instead, one learns through observation, imitation, illustration, and performance – that is, through non-verbal means. This form of learning is thought to be exceedingly difficult, a hardship, for unless one undergoes hardship (*kurō*) one cannot become a mature practitioner of the art. Hardship polishes the soul as well as one's technique. To attain the state of *kotan* therefore requires years of practice, discipline, even mental and physical suffering (cf. Kondo 1982). Mastery may take an entire lifetime but consciousness of technique and painstaking years of practice dissolve in the pure action of creation.[4]

But perhaps the Zen doctrine bearing most directly on the tea aesthetic is the emphasis on the *mundane* as a sphere of action and a source of beauty. The Buddha nature, hence the path to Enlightenment, is to be found in every sentient being and in the most everyday activities.[5] Extending this exaltation of the mundane to the aesthetic realm, Zen describes a fusion of opposites in which the beautiful and the ordinary are no longer distinct. This leads to the aesthetic appreciation of imperfection and poverty, of *sabi* and *wabi*. Inasmuch as the qualities can be defined, *sabi* is the beauty of the imperfect, the old, the lonely, while *wabi* is the beauty of simplicity and poverty (Hasumi 1964: 51; Ludwig 1974: 47). So closely are these qualities associated with the tea ceremony that the ceremony of the great master Sen no Rikyu was called *wabi cha*, or *wabi* tea.[6]

Typically, both Japanese and Western scholars analyse the tea ceremony as a method of self-realization (for example, Suzuki 1970; Herrigel 1953) and/or in terms of the Zen aesthetic (for example, Okakura 1964; Suzuki 1970). These explanations are compelling – even unassailable. Zen philosophy and aesthetics form the consciously held attitudes of the tea adept, and enactment of the ceremony gives life to these beliefs. Yet, there are key questions traditional philosophical and aesthetic approaches do not explore. Are there 'rules' that would enable us to account for the sequencing of the ceremony? Why is there a seemingly inordinate amount of repetition? How do the various media – auditory, visual, gestural, olfactory, gustatory – interact, and do they do so in some intelligible way? What dictates the pre-eminence of *koicha* as the most formal segment of the ceremony? A formal semantic analysis that addresses such questions must be based on a thorough grounding in ethnographic detail, while going beyond native exegesis to illuminate more precisely the structure and sequence of the ritual and how these in turn act persuasively to generate a feeling of exceptional experience.

IV

Like narrative, ritual is an unfolding, a sequence of movement with tensions, climaxes and directionality. The ritual process must create a ritual domain, 'by seducing participants into involvement with its form and... [by] propelling the now-transformed participants out into life' (Peacock 1969: 172).

I will argue that, in the tea ceremony, the principal symbolic devices accounting for the movements of the rite are: (a) a constant contrast between the ritual and the mundane and degrees thereof; (b) the use of boundaries to maintain these differences; (c) the sensible qualities of objects and substances used in the ceremony and the transposition of these qualities into various sensory media; (d) perhaps most important, the repetition of sequences and the occurrence of homologous structures, objects, actions, as the principal means of signifying the progression of the ritual.

A logical point of departure for analysis is the physical, spatial arrangement of the tea garden and hut. The garden is an especially salient feature, for it is the first apprehensible signal that one is entering the ritual world. Consequently, it must prepare the participant, beginning to restructure his attitude appropriately.

A diagram of the garden follows. It should be noted that, like the many variants of the tea ceremony itself, tea gardens also differ from one another. The choice of a particular arrangement ultimately lies with the host. However, though certain details may vary, the basic structure of the inner and outer *roji* does not change; moreover, the impression imparted by each section of the garden must differ, with the outer garden more normal and ordinary, the inner more set apart from the everyday world.

First, the garden itself is demarcated from the outside world by the gate. Upon entering, guests find the garden in turn is divided into the inner and outer *roji*, or dewy path. The outer *roji* comprises two principal structures, the *machiai* or waiting room, and the *koshikake machiai*, the waiting bench or waiting arbor. The former is enclosed and floored with tatami mats, the latter is roofed but open. Near the *koshikake machiai* is the privy or *setchin*, used primarily for display; it may be inspected if the guests so desire, as it, too, has been purified and prepared for the guests' aesthetic enjoyment. The path in the outer garden is direct, generally a paved stone walkway, and is thus primarily functional or utilitarian. The only real criterion for the outer *roji* is that it be scrupulously clean. The garden is pleasant, with a free, light atmosphere, and flowering trees may be allowed there (Allan Palmer, personal communication). The outer *roji* is a preliminary step into ritual time.

As one moves into the inner garden, the atmosphere shifts to one of serene tranquility and harmony with nature. Everything in the inner garden reflects an induction into the ritual domain. Guests may no longer speak loudly, nor may they touch upon frivolous topics of conversation, for presumably they have left their earthly concerns behind. The path is irregular and divided, to provoke aesthetic interest and leisurely contemplation. Ferns, small plants and trees and especially moss, are in evidence; no flowering plants are allowed. Everything must be simple and artless, 'things such as grow wild in the hills' (Kuck 1940: 198–9). The feeling of the inner garden is one of *wabi* and *sabi*.

The principal feature of the inner garden is the water basin, or *tsukubai*. Water is the purificatory agent par excellence in Japanese culture and it is represented in the inner garden by the water in the basin that the guests use to purify themselves.[7] Thus the presence of water, and the wetness of

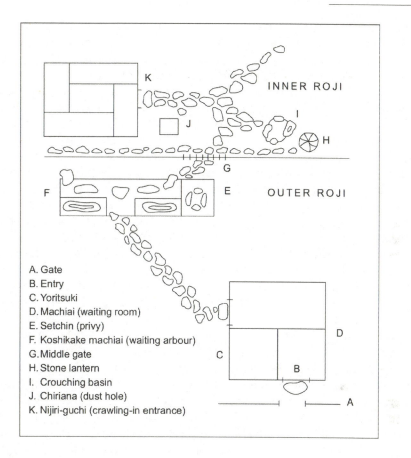

Figure 11.1 The spatial arrangement of a typical tea garden.

A. Gate
B. Entry
C. Yoritsuki
D. Machiai (waiting room)
E. Setchin (privy)
F. Koshikake machiai (waiting arbour)
G. Middle gate
H. Stone lantern
I. Crouching basin
J. Chiriana (dust hole)
K. Nijiri-guchi (crawling-in entrance)

the garden and its structures, is a metaphor for freshness, naturalness and purity.

Just before entering the tea room, the guests pass a hole in the earth, called *chiriana* or 'dust hole.' This is filled with clippings of trees and plants, and symbolizes the 'receptacle for the dust of the world' (Ishikawa 1976: 61).

Clearly, the passage from the outer to the inner garden is a journey through physical *and* symbolic space, advancing from the mundane to the ritual.[8] Boundaries and mediating structures contribute to the evocation of a 'world apart.' Before the participants set foot on the *roji*, they must enter through the gate and advance to the *yoritsuki*. Unlike everyday life, where one would announce one's entrance into the foyer with an 'excuse me,' during the tea ceremony the gate is left open and water sprinkled on the paving stones signals that the guests may enter (Ishikawa 1976: 56; Sen 1979: 10). This is recapitulated at the middle gate and at the entrance to the tea room; in each case the door or gate is left slightly open, again a signal to the guests that they may proceed into the next part of the tea gardens. The middle gate is a boundary marker directly mediating between outer and inner gardens. At the outset it is left half closed, to maintain a relation of contiguity between the outer and the inner gardens, to symbolize that they share the same qualities. Yet the gate cannot be flung wide open lest this leave the inner garden too vulnerable to the relative worldliness of the outer. When the final guest passes through the gate, he or she shuts it firmly. This symbolically closes off ritual space from the mundane. Again, once the final guest enters the tea room, the door is firmly shut with a click to seal off all reminders of the outside.

Mediation also takes place on the level of the buildings of the garden. The *machiai* and the tea room itself form a homologous pair; each is small, enclosed, tatami lined, and a scroll hangs in each. Again, meaning arises through contrast. The *machiai* is informal, lighter and airier than the tea room. A smoking tray, a sign of informality, is displayed there, whereas no smoking is allowed in the tea room. In the tea hut, the symbolic connotations of tea served there contrast with the purificatory but still comparatively mundane *osayu*, or hot water. Near the gate, however, deep in the outer garden and almost in the inner one, is the *koshikake machiai* (waiting arbor), another mediating structure. Physically, it is placed almost between gardens, although it is considered part of the outer *roji*. And unlike the *machiai* itself, it has no precise analogue in the ceremony. It is open and thus differs from either the tea hut or the *machiai,* to allow the guests to enjoy the beauties of nature. In the space between the *machiai* and the tea room, the beauties of the garden must prepare the participant for entry into the ritual world proper. The *koshikake machiai* is thus a midpoint in the symbolic continuum from the mundane to the ritual: not quite a building, not quite the garden, but something of both.

The following table summarizes the differences between the various parts of the garden:

Table 11.1   Differences between the parts of the garden

Outside	Mediator	Outer garden	Mediator	Inner world
	Gate	Waiting room	Waiting arbor	Tea room
	Yoritsuki	Hot water	Gate	Tea
		Flowers		Moss
		Trees		Ferns
		Direct path		Indirect
		Fire		Water
		Utilitarian		Aesthetic
		Physical		Spiritual
		Mundane		Ritual

Movement from the outside world into the tea garden is thus a step into the ritual world; movement from one part of the garden to the other is a further progression into the domain of ritual time and space. This both strips the guests of their worldliness and envelops them in a ritual atmosphere of *sabi/wabi*.

The meaning of any single element is opaque when viewed in isolation, but acquires significance when contrasted to its analogues in other parts of the ceremony and to the mundane world outside. Relative formality/informality is symbolized through the exploitation of differences and similarities among features. The tea garden stands in contrast to the world outside; in the garden itself, the outer garden was this-worldly and informal, the inner formal. The same principles apply not only to the induction of the participant into ritual time but in the easing of symbolic intensity and the return into the mundane world. One example would be the building of the first fire (*shozumi*) and the building of the second fire (*gozumi*). *Shozumi* is a prelude to the *koicha* segment, the formal climax of the ceremony; thus there is a logical imperative to render this part of the ceremony relatively formal. The mood is set with the slow patterning of the ashes in the brazier and the burning of incense to fill the air with the fragrance of spirituality. During the second building of the fire, no such careful patterning is necessary; indeed the segment can be omitted altogether. The host may bring out cushions to make the guests more comfortable and carries out the smoking tray. One recalls that this was last seen in the *machiai*. Thus, although the guests are forbidden to smoke in the tea room, the smoking tray signifies informality; it represents the act of smoking, an informal activity, and it is metonymically associated with the structures of the outer garden and the outer world. This recapitulation of elements creates formality and a spiritual, contemplative mood in *shozumi*, and an informal atmosphere in the *gozumi*, a quick descent from the intensely formal symbolism of *koicha*. Accordingly, in juxtaposing the two separated sequences of *shozumi* and *gozumi*, the significance of each, their relative formality or informality, is clarified. Moreover, examining the relationship of segments occurring in sequence also enables us to illuminate their respective meanings. The positioning of *gozumi* after the solemn *koicha* segment highlights the worldliness of the former and the formal mood of the latter. In short, the entire ritual moves along the axis of relative this-worldliness or other-worldliness, and systematically uses the devices of metaphor, metonym and contrast to communicate those differences.

V

Now that certain basic symbolic mechanisms informing the tea ceremony have been identified, what of the movement of the sequence as a whole? The progression is encoded in a seemingly chaotic concatenation of modes. Rather than focusing on all of them simultaneously, we will trace one thread throughout the entire sequence: the auditory channel and the role of silence, signals, and verbal versus non-verbal symbolism in conveying an impression of increasing and then decreasing symbolic intensity. The auditory mode is one that immediately presents itself for analysis, for two reasons. First, the pre-eminence of non-verbal over verbal expression is a general theme in Japanese culture.[9] Secondly, this general emphasis is carried over into the realm of Zen doctrine and aesthetics.[10]

In this cultural context, it is not surprising that in the tea ceremony the progressive induction into ritual time is reflected in an increasing emphasis on non-verbal modes of communication. The climax of each segment – the patterning of the ashes, the preparation of both *koicha* and *usucha* – is always performed in utter silence. And the *koicha* segment, in its entirety the symbolic apex of the ceremony, is the most silent and solemn of all the major sequences. But the situation is more complex than a simple equation between silence and the ritual world, noise and the mundane, might indicate.

Beginning from a sharp demarcation from the mundane (a non-verbal signal – the open door – at the entrance to the house) which signifies entry into an 'exceptional' domain, emphasis shifts from verbal channels to increasingly non-verbal modes. The initial emphasis is on human interaction; for example, conversation is permitted, and bows (albeit silent ones) are exchanged at the middle gate. This is reversed when the guests actually enter the tea room. They first bow, not to the person of the host, but to objects: the scroll, the brazier and so on. In Japan, objects in general are not considered atomistic entities, but extensions of people (cf. Bachnik 1978; Kondo 1982). These objects are symbolic extensions of the host, but that acknowledgement is first transmitted indirectly, heightening this connexion between person and object.

This reversal is perpetuated moreover, in other specific contexts throughout the ceremony. The host is always signalled through 'percussion' as opposed to speech (cf. Needham 1967). The noise of the tea room door as it shuts tells him or her that the guests have completed their entry. The click of the chopsticks on the tray indicates that the guests have finished their meal. After the interval the guests are summoned back to the tea room by a gong, and not by a personal greeting from the host (cf. Vogt 1977). Here, an initially social, and hence more informal, interaction between persons contrasts with the entry into the ritual domain of non-verbal sounds, and especially silence.

It is interesting to note that ritualized verbalizations – primarily questions and polite formulae – are uttered at certain junctures, generally to admire and comment upon the art objects used during the ceremony. This creates within each major segment (*shozumi*, *koicha*, *usucha*, and so forth) small increments in symbolic tension, climaxes and denouements. The first involves a combination of verbal exchanges and non-verbal acts; the climax occurs entirely in silence, with the sequence eventually shifting back to the verbal, and thus more informal, mode in the denouement. For example, after the intensely solemn preparation and drinking of *koicha*, the verbalizations involving the presentation of the tea bowl, the questions surrounding the tea utensils, in fact symbolically mark a winding down of the ritual. From the climax of *koicha* preparation to a less formal, more social question-and-answer session that is less bound and fixed, one moves to the even more informal *usucha* preparation and the still more informal questions and answers following that. Accordingly, the progression of the ceremony forms a steady decompression from the periods of heightened symbolic intensity. At this point, then, we can summarize the functions of auditory signs in the tea ceremony: *percussive* – signalling; *verbal* – social, relatively informal; *silence* – symbolic intensity, the height of ritual time.

The contrast between verbal and non-verbal modes as one pivot of the syntactic structure of the ritual begins to articulate the process of movement, but in order to understand more precisely the sequencing of the ceremony, one must focus upon the central opposition of ritual versus mundane, and its metaphorical representation in the sensible qualities of the substances and the objects used in the tea ceremony.

VI

In examining the role of substances in the ceremony, three features are highlighted: (a) setting apart the ritual from the mundane; (b) the similarities and differences in consecutively occurring sequences; (c) creating significant contrasts between similar but discontinuous parts of the ritual (first and second fires, *osayu-kaiseki-koicha-usucha*). This is a movement from the metaphorically mundane to the metaphorically ritual and back again.

First, many of the substances used are particular to the ceremony itself and are only infrequently found in other contexts. For example, among the foods, *kaiseki* is by definition a tea-ceremony meal. This type of refined cuisine can also be found in restaurants that specialize in such elegant delicacies but its primary association is with the way of tea. Ceremonial sweets form another specialized category. Both *omogashi* and *higashi* are ritual terms, and both are beautiful aesthetic creations, smaller and more elegant than the usual everyday confections. One could conceivably use regular sweets in the place of proper *omogashi* or *higashi* (when I was a student of tea, we did this to economize, as tea ceremony sweets, being specialties, are expensive); equally, one could buy tea ceremony sweets to eat at home. Yet the chief function of *omogashi* and *higashi* is ceremonial.

Similar arguments could be advanced for the non-food substances. The tea itself is associated chiefly with the ceremony, symbolized in the special ritual terms *koicha* and *usucha*. Both are forms of *matcha*, powdered green tea. *Usucha*, thin tea, might be served to guests informally, but to my knowledge, *koicha* – a thick, concentrated form of *matcha* – is rarely, perhaps never, encountered outside the context of the ceremony. Of the other non-food substances, both are in some way special. *Osayu*, hot water, is not commonly consumed in everyday life. *Sake* is one of the typical Shinto offerings to the gods and is found in many Shinto rituals; thus it has sacral connotations. Accordingly, both food and non-food substances create a symbolic cleavage between the ritual and the mundane.

Substances also symbolize the movement of the ceremony. On entering the tea room, for example, the sequence begins with fire, air and incense (rendered special by the connotations of incense as a substance) and moves toward increasing intensity with the eating of the fresh foods, drinking of the strong, alcoholic *sake*, eating the moist sweets, and performing another ablution with cool, fresh water.[11] The entire first half of the rite is a slow, elaborate preparation for the climax of *koicha*; it is thought that to drink this thick tea without proper fortification might be dangerous. After the climax, the ceremony moves again to the element of fire and of tobacco smoke, not incense, signaling a much more informal mood, and then to the eating of dry sweets (informal because they can be picked up and eaten with the hands) and the drinking of weak or thin tea.

Several points are important to note: (a) Purification with cold water always precedes entry into the tea room, and in each case presages a significant heightening of the ritual atmosphere. (b) The core of the ceremony could be said to correspond to metaphorical spirituality and the substances used have cultural significance: *sake*, moist sweets made especially for the tea ceremony, the purificatory cold water ablution, and then the thick tea. All these occur in sequence, together, and thus form a 'bundle of relations' with considerable symbolic impact. (c) The pre-eminence of *koicha* can be explained in terms of the metaphorical qualities of the substance itself.[12] Tea symbolizes the introspective qualities associated with Zen: an awakening of the senses and a contemplative atmosphere (Watts 1957: 190; Suzuki 1970: 298).

Although not perfectly symmetrical, it is as though the ritual begins from the core and works outward so that the sequences on either side of the climactic episodes recapitulate one another. There is a reversal from one half to the other as the sequence itself builds to a high point, bringing together elements in a certain order. In the process of re-entry into the mundane, the opposite sequence is followed. Not only is this demonstrated at the general level of major sequences – it occurs within each segment; for example, when the host takes utensils out of the room in the reverse order from which they were first brought in.

The ritual also makes full use of similar segments occurring in discontinuous parts of the sequence. Take, for example, the partaking of food and drink during the ceremony. Here, the similarities provide a contrastive ground for the salient *differences* among these segments. The relative formality of these sequences (*osayu*, *kaiseki* and *sake*, *omogashi* and *koicha*, *higashi* and *usucha*) is highlighted in juxtaposition, symbolizing the progressive induction and release of the participant. In *osayu*, no foods are served, and the drink itself is nothing but hot water, though some delicate flavoring agent can be added. This, then, is a 'weak' drink – different from everyday Japanese beverages and hence signalling an entry into ritual time, but not concentrated, hence not symbolically powerful. *Sake*, which follows, is powerful and strong, and thus symbolically more intense than *osayu*. It holds dual associations, with social, hence more mundane, activity on the one hand, and as a common feature in the Shinto (not Zen) religion. *Koicha* signifies its strength even in its heavy texture. It is a thick distillate of a natural product, powdered tea leaves, and thus is imbued with these qualities in highly concentrated form. It is a substance peculiar to the ceremony itself. *Usucha* partakes of these same qualities, but in less intense fashion. It is slightly less special as it is a less concentrated form of the same tea. It is not the most common beverage served to guests, but one could do so – or prepare a bowl for one's own consumption; thus, it is less purely ceremonial in its connotations. Again, the basic movements of the rite, from the more ordinary to the more extraordinary and back again, are encoded even in the sensible properties of the substances used in the various segments of the ritual. Schematically represented, the ritual is divisible as shown in Table 11.2.

The repetition, with variation, of similar sequences is thus a major mode of symbolizing the progression of the ritual. The similarities act as background for the differences in meaning among these segments.

In sum, in the tea ceremony one finds many symbolic devices: (a) metaphor (wetness as a metaphor for freshness and purity, tea as a metaphor for the ceremony itself); (b) metonym, part standing for whole, or relations of contiguity and proximity (to outer garden and outer world); (c) repetition of sequences in different parts of the ceremony, compelling the mind to explore the similarities and differences between these sequences; (d) position of elements in the sequence, for example, when the *kaiseki-sake-omogashi-koi cha* segment takes on heightened symbolic intensity because these elements occur in combination. Any taken alone would not have the same meaning; (e) an element of reversal, in which the return to the mundane is symbolized by reversing the original sequence; (f) contrast among segments and between ritual and non-ritual food and drink, serving as markers of entry into the ritual domain.

Table 11.2 Schematic representation of the ceremony

Informal	Formal	Formal	Informal
Osayu	Sake	Koicha	Usucha
Weak	Strong	Thick (strong)	Thin (weak)
No food	Kaiseki	Omogashi	Higashi

An internal analysis of ritual should not rest at a simple tripartite structuring of a sequence or constructing a matrix of binary oppositions. Rather, one can attempt to recapture with some precision the movements of the rite. Yet even this is far from complete. In what other ways might the participants be compelled to feel serenely at peace?

VII

Redundancy of message among the sensory modes and the repetition of sequences is a key rhetorical/symbolic device in the ceremony. Let us begin with the interaction of the graphic, gestural, gustatory, tactile and verbal sensory channels and the process of objectification, or the transposition of intangible qualities into various sensory modes. The performative creation of the ritual domain begins in the *yoritsuki* where the guests put on fresh *tabi*, brush the dust off their clothes and change their attire. Here, in leaving behind their everyday clothing, they physically divest themselves of reminders of the everyday world. This progressive shedding of worldly concerns continues during their procession in the garden and is powerfully symbolized in the passing of the *chiriana* (dust hole) near the tea room. Here is one's final opportunity to brush away the pollutions and contingencies of everyday life before entering the tea room. One last reminder of this entry into a ritual domain is the act of removing one's sandals and standing them up outside the hut. This transmutation of qualities – in this case, pollution or this-worldliness – into physical objects and tangible properties, is one of the most compelling of performative acts. It gives ritual a literalness that verbal communication rarely achieves. After ridding themselves of mundane objects and hence 'mundaneness' in general, the participants are ready to absorb 'ritualness' in its many forms.

Beginning with the purity, freshness and naturalness of the garden, the transfer of symbolic qualities intensifies. For example, the ritual ablution with water not only washes away the 'dust of the world,' it also metonymically transfers the qualities of water – freshness and purity – to the persons of the guests themselves. The crouching actions at the basin and at the entrance to the tea room signify humility. Once again it is important to note the representation of a mental state by an action, and the performative aspect involved: performing these actions is as good as having the right attitude, for it should induce the right attitude.

In the tea room the ritual atmosphere heightens. For example, incense is burned in the tea room, an act with religious connotations in Japanese culture.[13] The tone it sets is immediately sacral and contemplative. The scrolls and the flower arrangement set the mood and the theme for the particular ceremony, and by viewing these art objects, the sentiments expressed through the visual and graphic media are, ideally at least, transferred to the viewer in order to structure his or her mental attitude. Just as a Zen painting may leave an empty expanse of white, so the mind of the participant should achieve the same emptiness, *mushin*.

The drinking of tea itself is preceded by the climactic moments of its preparation, where the bounded movements, the graceful yet logical progression of actions, express the essence of peace and calm. In drinking the aesthetic infusion, one partakes not only of the tea and of the qualities it embodies, but of the care, the grace and the selflessness that went into its preparation. The viewing of the tea bowl, its asymmetry and coarseness to the touch, its imperfections, the tea implements and their associations, all contribute further to the symbolic intensity of the ceremony. Like the notes of a baroque score, different symbols in different modes occur in profusion, yet move smoothly forward in an intelligible sequence.

The interaction of various sensory media creates a multiple layering of meanings that 'all add up to just one "message"' (Leach 1976: 41). Though there may be qualitative and significant differences among the various sensory modes – and I believe there are, as Jakobson, (1960), Langer (1942) and Lévi-Strauss (1969) have pointed out – the gathering of these elements into a single ceremony tends to highlight the similarities among them. Moreover, though the referents of a single symbol may be myriad, the location of the symbol in the nexus of the tea ceremony narrows its meaning or accents a certain meaning to the partial exclusion of others. This homology of code among the sensory modes is one of the major sources of the tea ceremony's symbolic efficacy and power.

What, then, of the constant repetition of actions and sequences? I would argue that it provides a contrastive background for the subtle changes that take place from one segment of the ritual to another. The basic similarity in the sequence renders any changes all the more striking. In this case, redundancy is not 'superfluity.'[14] Rather, through the subtle variations in the message and in the media into which it is transposed, persuasive symbolic power is inevitably intensified.[15] In short, in the tea ceremony, redundancy creates an intensification of meaning in and of itself, and it is a vehicle of meaning for the minute but significant changes that may occur in the repetition of a sequence.

VIII

Finally, this allows something more general to be said about the nature of ritual itself. Should ritual be a mere communicative device designed to impart a simple, discursive message, there would be little apparent rationale for the existence of the ritual form. Ritual 'messages' can be repetitive, prodigally so, freely drawing upon all the sensory modes and all manner of symbolic devices. Folk belief may also encourage a view of ritual as rigid, convention-bound and inimical to real, spontaneous feeling. Why, say these pragmatists, make such a fuss over drinking a cup of tea?

Perhaps the answer to these riddles lies with the Zen masters. For at least in the tea ceremony, and perhaps in other rituals as well, it is by becoming one with the rules that the possibility of transcendence lies.[16] The formality of ritual also enables the participant to forget the contingencies of everyday life and frees the mind for 'greater thoughts.'[17] Ritual, then, need not be an ossified form interfering with 'true' feeling and spontaneity. In fact, form separates the ritual from the everyday and distinguishes the casual partaking of a cup of tea from *chanoyu*, the way of tea. By its precise orchestration of sequence and the interrelations among symbols in different sensory modes, the tea ceremony articulates feeling and thought, creating a distilled form of experience set apart from the mundane world.

Acknowledgments

Several people have read this manuscript in draft form. I should particularly like to thank S.J. Tambiah, John C. Pelzel, Matthews Hamabata and Vincent Crapanzano for their perceptive comments. Of course, final responsibility lies solely with the author.

Notes

1. Among them *gadō* (the way of poetry), *kyūdō* (the way of archery), *kendō* (the way of the sword) and *bushidō* (the way of the warrior).

2. Scholars have long been sensitive to the differences and similarities among various sensory modes (for example, Jakobson's visual and auditory signs, Langer's discursive and presentational symbols). As a method of representation and symbolization, discursive language, like any mode of communication – the plastic arts, music, gesture and so on – excels at certain tasks and is less suited for others. Roland Barthes, the structuralist literary critic, dares to imply that an art closely related to tea – *haiku* – is refractory to Western schemes of analysis: 'it resists us, finally loses the adjectives that a moment before we had bestowed upon it, and enters into that suspension of meaning that to us is the strangest thing of all, since it makes impossible the most ordinary exercise of our language, which is commentary (Barthes 1992: 110).

3. The practice of ritual modesty is a common part of Japanese etiquette. Here, unlike the polite understatement of everyday life, *kaiseki* is in fact a frugal meal, at least in terms of the amount of food served – though often the dishes are expensive seasonal delicacies.

4. Suzuki (1970: 31) relates a classic admonition about Zen ink painting, but the principle applies to all the Zen arts: 'Draw bamboos for ten years, become a bamboo, then forget all about bamboos when you are drawing.'

5. Ludwig cites a famous Taoist aphorism to that effect: 'In bearing water and chopping wood, there lies the wonderful Tao' (Ludwig 1974: 39). In the tea ceremony, then, Enlightenment lies in the preparing and drinking of a cup of tea.

6. The tea room itself, for example, embodies pure *sabi-wabi*:

> The tea hut is extremely bare and almost devoid of color. If a flower is arranged in a vase, it is usually a single, small blossom of some quiet hue or white. The tea utensils are not of exquisite porcelain but of coarse pottery, often a dull brown or black and imperfectly formed. The kettle may be a little rusty. Yet from these objects we receive an impression not of gloominess or shabbiness but one of quiet harmony and peace...
> (Tsunoda et al. 1958: 281)

The aesthetic of *sabi* and *wabi* is central to an understanding of the ceremony, not only for the sense of what constitutes 'tea style' in the performance of the ceremony (grace, calm, silence, economy of movement), but in its related arts: flower arranging, pottery, scrolls, cooking, gardens and so on. Briefly, the same values of simplicity, asymmetry, age, roughness, austerity and monochrome color are observed in the ancillary arts. The tea garden is, like all Japanese gardens, simple, peaceful and tranquil, but it should have these qualities to a heightened degree, imparting an impression of being shut away from the outside world. Tea gardens are usually bare of flowers, using instead less showy plants to create a harmonious aesthetic quality. The tea room is small, bare and dimly lit. Tea style in flowers is known for its simplicity and naturalness. Usually a *chabana* arrangement consists of a single flower and a few leaves. Its distinctiveness is reflected in the verb used to describe the process of arranging: whereas for most other styles of flower arranging one applies the term *ikeru* (to arrange), with *chabana* one must *ireru* – put or place into. '*Chabana* is a delightful anomaly in the sphere of *ikebana*. It has no rules; its charm lies in its exquisite simplicity. It cannot be taught, it can only be felt' (Davidson 1970: 10–11).

The tea bowls are of rough pottery, often uneven and lopsided; the most famous types of tea ware (such as, Raku and Oribe) tend to be black, dullish red, dull brown, or a combination of black and dark green. These are purest *sabi-wabi*. The scrolls or paintings hung in the alcove are usually of Zen origin; a scroll might be a laconic Zen epigram, or an ink painting. In either case, it is generally simple black on white.

7. It is also represented indexically through the presence of moss, which requires a moist environment in order to survive. Moreover, one recalls that the name of the garden itself, the Dewy Path, restates this association with wetness, purity, and freshness, and that the path itself is in fact sprinkled with water just prior to the arrival of the guests.

8. Architect Fumihiko Maki argues that the concept of *oku*, the depths, characterizes Japanese architecture (for example, shrines, streets, arrangement of rooms in a house). The division of the garden into inner and outer *roji*, for instance, is also characteristic of shrine precincts where the outer path is relatively straight wheareas the inner path indirect and winding. This 'create(s) a sense of drama and ritual in the process of approaching' the *oku* (Maki 1979: 59). Here the dimensions of space and time are both implied.

9. There are countless examples, but I shall cite only a few. Perhaps the ideal form of communication in Japan is *ishin denshin*, a highly developed empathy in which mutual sensitivity obviates the need for words. Lebra (1976: 115) describes this as follows: 'Words are paltry against the significance of reading subtle signs and signals and the intuitive grasp of each other's feelings.' Studies of childhood socialization practices in Japan and the United States consistently point to the greater emphasis in Japan on non-verbal interaction between mother and infant. (See, for example,

Caudill and Weinstein 1969.) An ideal for masculine behavior (indeed, for anyone) is *fugen jikkō*, silent action. That is, one should prove one's worth through action, not through empty words.

10. The term *ma* – interval, pause, space, room – is crucial here, for it is used both in everyday social interaction and as an aesthetic concept. *Ma* exists in Zen paintings and in flower arrangements, where the brush strokes or lines of the flowers and branches describe a space. It corresponds, in this context, to the emptiness of *mu* in Zen doctrine. But *ma* is not simply spatial; it can also signify a pause, a silence. A conversation should have *ma*, appropriate spacing or intervals, to punctuate the rhythms of speech. One is not obligated to fill the silence with words. The spacing in this case contributes to a sense of repose. *Ku*, emptiness – as in the empty space of air – is an important related concept.

11. The five elements (wood, water, fire, earth, metal) from Chinese cosmology, undoubtedly play a part here, and to some extent feature in exegeses of the symbolism of tea. Indeed, one could say that preparing and drinking tea unites the five elements: wood (charcoal); water (for tea); fire; earth (tea bowl); metal (brazier).

12. Tea embodies the naturalness of *sabi* and *wabi*: a powder made of ground-up leaves, it unites these natural elements with the natural element of water, to create a representation, in palpable form, of the Japanese aesthetic. And finally, its thick texture and concentrated state are metaphorical expressions of the intensity of the ritual experience, here distilled into its very essence, a single bowl of tea. The tea is, in a sense, the ritual experience itself. In Fernandez's (1977) terms, the tea is a metaphor that is particularly 'apt'; it embodies the ideas informing the ceremony, as well as making logical sense in terms of the progression of the sequence.

13. It is what one offers to the ancestors, and is sometimes thought to have curative powers; it is also closely associated with Buddhism.

14. Leach (1976) argues that patterning or redundancy helps the receiver understand the message being communicated.

15. Through capitalizing on the qualities of the particular modes involved (for example, the discursive nature of language, the simultaneity of visual stimuli, the palpability of objects).

16. This is a profound theme in Japanese culture, underlying pedagogy, definitions of person, maturity, role fulfillment, and so forth. See for example, Kondo (1982).

17. Lest the reader fear that I am spinning webs of fantasy, it does seem that this feeling of tranquility and of losing oneself in the rules is in fact conveyed to the participants, however implicitly or imperfectly. One informant told me of her experience. Taking tea solely as a wifely art, she kept a diary of her feelings about the ceremony. Even at a young age, she felt that, once learned, the rules allowed her to think of greater things. In daily life minor matters and small decisions absorb one's conscious attention and energy. Ritual liberates one from the necessity of diverting energy to these trivialities, to learn the rules so completely that one's actions no longer occupy one's attention. Thus the powers of thought and feeling can be directed toward that which is truly meaningful.

Bibliography

Bachnik, J. (1978), 'Inside and Outside the Japanese Household,' thesis, Harvard University.

Barthes, R. (1992), *Empire of Signs*, trans. R. Howard, New York: Hill & Wang.

—— (1974), *S/Z*, New York: Hill & Wang.

Bellah, R. (1957), *Tokugawa Religion*, Boston: Beacon Press.

Caudill, W. and Weinstein, H. (1969), 'Maternal Care and Infant Behavior in Japan and America,' *Psychiatry*, 32: 12–43.

Davidson, G. (1970), *Classical Ikebana*, New York: A.S. Barnes.

Edwards, W. (1982), 'Something Borrowed: Wedding Cakes as Symbols in Modern Japan,' *American Ethnologist*, 9: 699–711.

Fernandez, J.W. (1977), 'The Performance of Ritual Metaphors,' in D. Sapir and C. Crocker (eds), *The Social Use of Metaphor*, Philadelphia: University of Pennsylvania Press.

Hasumi, T. (1962), *Zen in Japanese Art*, London: Routledge & Kegan Paul.

Herrigel, E. (1953), *Zen in the Art of Archery*, New York: Pantheon.

Ishikawa, S. (1976), 'An Invitation to Tea,' *Chanoyu Quarterly*, 16: 65–70.

Jakobson, R. (1960), 'Linguistics and Poetics,' in T. Sebeok (ed.), *Style in Language*, Cambridge MA: MIT Press.

Kondo, D. (1982), 'Work, Family and the Self: A Cultural Analysis of Japanese Family Enterprise,' thesis, Harvard University.

Kuck, L. (1940), *The Art of Japanese Gardens*, New York: John Day.

Langer, S.K. (1942), *Philosophy in a New Key*, Cambridge MA: Harvard University Press.

Leach, E. (1976), *Culture and Communication*, Cambridge: Cambridge University Press.

Lebra, T.S. (1976), *Japanese Patterns of Behavior*, Honolulu: University Press of Hawaii.

Lévi-Strauss, C. (1969), *The Raw and the Cooked*, New York: Harper & Row.

Ludwig, T.M. (1974), 'The Way of Tea: A Religio-aesthetic Mode of Life,' *History of Religions*, 14: 28–50.

Maki, F. (1979), 'Japanese City Spaces and the Concept of Oku,' *Japan Architect*, 264: 50–62.

Needham, R. (1967), 'Percussion and Transition,' *Man*, (N.S.), 2: 606–14.

Okakura, K. (1964), *The Book of Tea*, New York: Dover.

Palmer, A. (1976), '*Temae: chaji*: Conclusion and Variation,' *Chanoyu Quarterly*, 16.

Peacock, J.L. (1969), 'Society as Narrative,' in *American Ethnological Society Proceedings*, Seattle: University of Washington Press.

Sen, S. (1979), *Chado: The Japanese Way of Tea*, Tokyo: Weatherhill.

Tambiah, S.J. (1973), 'The Form and Meaning of Magical Acts,' in R. Horton and R. Finnegan (eds), *Modes of Thought*, London: Faber & Faber.

—— (1979), 'A Performative Approach to Ritual,' in *Proceedings of the British Academy* 65, London: Oxford University Press.

Tsunoda, R., DeBary, W.T. and Keene, D. (eds) (1958), *Sources of Japanese Tradition*, New York: Columbia University Press.

Vogt, E.Z. (1977), 'On the Symbolic Meaning of Percussion in Zinacanteco Ritual,' *Journal of Anthropological Research*, 33: 231–44.

Watts, A. (1957), *The Way of Zen*, New York: Vintage.

12

Engaging the Spirits of Modernity

Temiar Songs for a Changing World

Marina Roseman

In a Chinese logging camp at the edge of the forest in Kelantan, Malaysia, piles of logs await pickup for their final journey out of the jungle and into the global economy. The camp complex, constructed out of wood and covered with the zinc roofing common to hastily built, commercial forest enterprises, includes dormitories for predominantly Chinese timber workers and truck drivers, kitchen, cafe, and grocery store. Forest-dwelling Temiars drop in periodically to buy food and sundries, or eat in the cafe. Logging trucks roll in, emptying their loads, and the jungle's spoils accumulate like jewels in a dragon's lair. Back behind the living quarters, the run-off from bathing structures and latrines fouls a small rivulet emerging from a limestone outcropping about 10 feet upstream. The limestone cliff is pocketed with caves worn by falling water, so soon to be polluted by the effluvia just downstream.

From the spirit of this waterfall, Temiar shaman and headman Ading Kerah received a song during his dreams. The spirit emerged in the shape of a young Chinese woman, who stepped out of the cab of a passing logging truck, stylishly dressed in a miniskirt. The stench, filth, and – from the viewpoint of a Temiar forest dweller rather than a timber company executive – devastation of the logging industry are concentrated in the camp's gathering of workers and products. Yet from this site, arising like a phoenix out of dung, came the Logging Camp Cave's spirit. Her song will be used in ceremonies for help in healing – or for the many other uses to which dream song ceremonies are directed: to mark important moments in the agricultural cycle; to welcome

212

or send off travelers; to mark a mourning period's end; or to celebrate the experience of dancing, trancing, and singing with the spirits.

The miniskirted Chinese Lumber-camp Cave Spirit, with her gift of song for use in healing, comprises one of many instances in which Temiars engage the spirits of modernity for their own purposes. Spirit practices – these imaginative realms of dream and song – are critical sites for the engagment of local peoples with global processes. Spirit songs sung to effect individual healings address, as well, the health of a social group traumatized by loss of land and resources.

Over the last 20 years I've charted the effects of rainforest deforestation, land alienation, and Islamic evangelism upon Temiar self and society. Ading Kerah's dreamsong is a striking instance of ways I've seen Temiars draw the spirits into history through the power of expressive culture. Animated signs absorb the crash of disjunctured pasts and presents in Temiar ceremonial performance. Community members exploit the ability of motions and odors, musical sounds and glimmering colors to cross temporal and ontological boundaries, transcend geographic and cosmological space, polyphonically signal multiply layered identities, and phenomenologically resituate experience.[1]

On the one hand, I am impressed by the resilience of Temiar ethno-psychology and cosmology, which is able to engage the spirits of foreign things and people – whom they call 'outforesters' (gɔb), 'those who come from beyond the forest' – within an indigenous discursive system of power and knowledge, thereby retaining agency. On the other, I am concerned that such shamanistic incorporation of the Outforest Other might presage an ideological acceptance of material disenfranchisement, as Temiars focus upon the flash of a spiritguide's beauty, rather than mobilizing to resist their material losses. Yet I have come to see this ability to grasp a spirit's healing song from those people, things, and technologies that have so thoroughly assaulted their material resource base as an act of social suturing, an art of survival, a technology for maintaining personal and social integrity in the face of nearly overwhelming odds.

Dream songs have long provided Temiars a site for mediating encounters with their forest environment (Roseman 1991). The realm of songs, dreams, and spiritmediumship provides a space for Temiars to incorporate the knowledge and power of 'out-forester' peoples and commodities, as well. Temiar dream song receipt is based in an ethnopsychology that posits multiple soul-components that may become detached and animated as 'spirit'; these include the head soul (rəwaay), locus of expression and vocalization; the heart/breath soul (hup), locus of stored thoughts, feelings and memory; the shadow soul (wɔg), a reflective emanation; and odor soul (ŋɔɔy), a composite of things eaten and transported by a person.

During dreams, usually the head- and sometimes the heart-soul component of both dreamer and the beings he or she might encounter become temporarily detached. Taking imaginal form as miniature human beings, dreamer and spirit proceed to communicate. A song taught to the dreamer, as soul-component vocalized, becomes a channel for re-establishing contact with that spirit during night time, housebound ceremonies. The spirit may also designate certain fragrant leaves (implicating odor souls), dance steps, and other performance parameters that will be recreated ceremonially to activate its presence in the human realm. The spirit, Temiars say, is able to see far above the forest canopy; made present in the shaman's song, it brings its extensive knowledge and perspective to bear upon human illnesses.

Activated spirit, when temporally and contextually bounded in dream and ceremony, infuses power and knowledge into a medium, who is thereby empowered to heal. But when spirit is excessively animated outside the bounds of dream and ceremony, illnesses of spirit intrusion or soul loss may result. In such cases, mediums call upon their spiritguides to seek out the source of the illness. Through singing and trance dancing, mediums move ceremonially into the realm of detached spirit to extract, replace, or resituate spirit-components in the patient and the cosmos. Some mediums specify particular spiritguides for assistance with specific illness complexes; others say that whatever spiritguide arrives can deal with an illness by virtue of its paramount status as animated spirit.

Spiritguides make themselves known primarily through their songs and dance movements. Indeed, music packs its boundary-crossing power via its detachability, as sound resonates from its source through space, whether crossing social boundaries of natal and affinal affiliation as in Suyà shout songs (Seeger 1988), through temporal zones of generational kin as in Mapuche tayil (Robertson 1979), or across cosmological categories of bound soul and unbound spirit in Temiar dream songs. If, as Attali ([1977] 1985: 4) suggests, music is prophetic, a herald of times to come, then the increased potential for detachability and reproducibility initiated by recording technologies in the late 1800s, heralding what has come to be called the schizophonic realm of separable and reassemblable sounds, are the audible sign of the transnational era. 'Music,' Attali continues, 'makes mutations audible. It obliges us to invent categories and new dynamics to regenerate social theory... ' (Attali [1977] 1985: 4). Temiar ontology and epistemology suggest a level of comfort with multiplicity and detachability, which they call upon, in dream songs and healing ceremonies, as they respond to disjunctures between the local and the global that increasingly impinge on forest life.

The Politics of Space

The dense jungle constitutes both refuge and sustenance for Temiars, and holds within it powers both benevolent and malevolent. Temiars tap into this circuit of power, rendering the unknown known, in their dream songs, received from the sprits of the landscape, its flora, and fauna. Temiars negotiate their geopolitical terrain with a double vision that responds simultaneously to spiritual and material presences. The forest's edge, porous boundary between forest and out-forest, and the river, flowing between the domains of deeper upstream forest and downriver marketplace, link forest and non-forest domains. The space above the forest canopy, and the long distance vision it affords, constitutes another realm of fantasy and fear. Home in its highest reaches to the thunder and lightning diety ʔɛŋkuuʔ, feared for the floods and storms he unleashes, it is also home in its lower reaches to things of the 'above ground,' like birds.

Temiar hunter-horticulturalists refer to themselves as sɛnʔɔɔy sɛŋrɔk, 'people of the forest,' in their Austroasiatic Mon-Khmer language. They are one among a number of peninsular Malaysia's aboriginal peoples, termed 'Orang Asli' or 'Original Peoples' in contemporary Malay and the anthropological literature. Temiars have long engaged with peoples and things from beyond the forest, whom they call gɔb. The term is qualified according to the perceived ethnicity of the out-forester person or item: gɔb məlayu for the Austronesian-speaking Malays who now constitute the nation's mainstream Islamic population; gɔb putih or 'white foreigners' for the British colonials and other Euro-Americans who preceded and followed them; gɔb cina and gɔb ʔindiyah for the Chinese and Tamil workers brought to work British tin mines and rubber plantations; gɔb jəpun, for the Japanese occupiers during World War II. Songs sung during Temiar healing rituals now include those received from the spirits of the tunnels built by the Japanese, as well as those from market goods arriving from downriver Malay settlements.

Rivers and footpaths, red dirt military and logging roads that came later, and the asphalt roads that followed them, wind their way out of, into, and through the jungle, connecting Temiars with 'upstream' (teh) and 'downstream' (rɛh). In an indigenous musical terminology rich with metaphors of movement through the landscape, Temiar songs are conceived of as 'paths' bestowed during dreams by spiritguides, who have the knowledge and vision to see through and soar above the density of the jungle scene and forest canopy. 'Upstream' is traditionally associated with things of the deeper jungle, including both benevolent spiritguides and malevolent illness agents. 'Downstream' – the direction of the marketplace, big towns, and non-aboriginal Others penetrating into forest territory – is also a realm of things, people, and experiences both positively and negatively charged.

The dense forest once provided a refuge for Temiars from intercultural interactions.[2] These included symbiotic economic and cultural exchanges among forest peoples with peasants and petty entrepreneurs linked to transoceanic trade routes. Jungle products such as sandalwood, resin, rattan, medicinal herbs, and fruit were exchanged for 'out-forester' items such as salt, iron, and cotton cloth in earlier times – batteries, gym shorts and T-shirts, or cash nowadays.[3] The interpenetrable distinctions offered by forest's edge – while always porous – have become increasingly jumbled in the transnational era. Temiars currently face their cosmology gone wild: 'market' (kədey 'town, shop') illnesses now come from Chinese and Malay logging camps upstream, from whence only forest illnesses once emerged. Temiar healing ceremonies draw on songs received from Malay, Chinese, and forest spiritguides to grapple with the diversity of illness sources.

The Sensory Experience of Modernity: The Airplane Song

To soar like a bird is a spirit's privilege: to see long distances, returning visions and knowledge through the conduit of song. From that airspace above the rainforest canopy, the spiritspace of cool winds and liquid mists, of entranced head-souls flying and spirits' long-range vision, Temiars now receive dream songs from airplanes and parachute drops as they do from birds, from wristwatches as well as pulsing insects. Foreign peoples and things are socialized in dreams, brought into kinship relations as spirit familiar 'child' to the Temiar dreamer as 'parent.' Strange people, things, and technologies become humanized, even Temiar-ized, their potentially disruptive foreign presence now tapped for use as a spirit familiar in Temiar ceremonies.

Hi-tech phenomena arriving with colonialism and postcolonialism, such as airplanes, bring mixed blessings: parachute drops of food during the rainy season, when subsistence travels can be harder to perform, were dropped from the sky by British colonials, and later by the Malay Department of Aboriginal Affairs. But planes, which in Temiar memory date to the Japanese Occupation of 1941 to 1945, also brought bombs that strafed communists hiding in the jungle during the Malaysian 'Emergency' (1948–65). Desire and destruction coalesce in the airplane as it brings foodstuffs on the one hand, and death on the other.

While I was recording a nighttime housebound singing ceremony in the settlement of Lambok, in the area of Kuala Betis, Ulu Kelantan in 1981, Busu Puteh (or, Taaʔ Busuuʔ, Old Man Busu), sang a song received from the Airplane Spirit. Old Man Busu had strong kinship ties to the Betis and to the Perolak River valleys, an area in the heart of the Kelantan known for the origination and continuation of songs in the Taŋgəəy genre. His father was from Perias, near the origination point of another important Kelantan Temiar genre, səlombaŋ. He sang various songs received by spirits, some from his own dreams and others given to him through ceremonializing together with song-receiving relatives. Amidst the songs of the Taŋgəəy genre, received from things 'above ground' like birds, mammals, and flowers, and his Selombaŋ repertoire, received from the waterserpent səlombaŋ of the 'underground,' he sang the song his grandfather had received from an airplane spirit during the 1940s and 1950s.

Busu Puteh's grandfather received the Airplane Song in the Taŋgəəy genre, characterized by melodies that begin with a relatively flat melodic contour opening out slightly into a narrow range of tones constituting the melodic core that, compared with other Temiar vocal genres, remains relatively restricted. This constraint is particularly noticeable in Taŋgəəy from the Perolak and Betis River Valleys, where Lambok is situated. The Taŋgəəy tone row may be expanded by the periodic insertion of a jɛnhook phrase, which begins on a pitch higher than those forming the melodic core, and descends, often reaching the tonal center.

Temiar dream songs are constructed of verses formed from two or three song phrases, alternated in variable patterns, with the periodic insertion of a jɛnhook phrase. The song phrase melodies are repeated while song text is varied extemporaneously. Each phrase sung by the initial singer is repeated heterophonically or, using Feld's term (Keil and Feld 1994: 118), in 'echo polyphony' by a female chorus. As is characteristic of Taŋgəəy, the Airplane Song's first song phrase begins with a flat melodic contour, rhythmically elaborating the tonal center of E. Through most of the song, the first song phrase is repeated twice, then followed by a second song phrase, which expands the melody to include a whole tone above the tonal center (F#).

In addition to its relatively flat melodic contour and restricted melodic range, songs of the Taŋgəəy genre exhibit a characteristic use of repeated one-syllable vocables such as 'doh ʔoh doh' , 'nah nah.' In the Airplane Song, the vocables 'bom bom bom' render Japanese Occupation and British Air Force bombs cognate with the deathly shocking rumbles and pops of the ferocious Temiar Thunder diety, ʔɛŋkuuʔ. This period, and the 'Emergency' that followed, were a horrifying time for Temiars as the jungle became contested territory, while conflicting parties threatened their lives as they vied for their allegiance. The song text describes the actions and visions of the Airplane Spirit from the nəgəriʔ Jəpun, the country of Japan:

1-1	I alight
1-2	Bomb, bomb, bomb [trailing behind] me
2-1a	I sing in [entranced] forgetfulness
2-1b	A person from long ago
2-2	Here, me here, for all time
3-1a	Flying across from the country of Japan
3-1b	Many types
3-2	I throw out here
4-1a	I arrive with wooden planks, see young women not yet having born children
4-1b	In which house shall I descend?
4-2	Bomb, bomb, bomb, here with the childless young women
5-1a	I am a Siamese boss
5-1b	I am a Japanese boss
5-1c	We ask your blessings
5-2	Bomb, bomb, bomb, to me here.

The song weaves a narrative of disconnected images reflecting upon the destructive power of this flying being, embodying the experience of a forest people caught in the whirl of global forces. The flat melodic contour, restricted tonal range, and jɛnhook-phrase vocables of the Airplane Song exhibit stylistic markers of the Taŋgəəy genre, the ur-genre of Kelantan, received from 'things above ground' (like the birds), but not quite as high as the 'top of the sky' where thunder lives. Busu Puteh's grandfather musically charts his experience of the other, placing the Airplane Spirit with other things from above ground. In musical genres, then, Temiars map their experiential universe, locating that which is Other within reach of the self. This musical rendering is comparable to cartographic acts whereby European explorers and emerging nation-states traced the changing surfaces of their experience of the world in geopolitical maps (Mignolo 1991; Winichakul 1994). Temiar genres link parameters of musical structure with particular compositional sources or 'spirit guides' from which those genres are received, thereby constructing a musical map of the universe.[4]

Temiar mediums engage the tiger's ferocious power in the musico-ceremonial genre Panooh (Mamuug), and that of Lightning in the genre ʔɛŋkuuʔ, tapping these energies for their own devices as a 'technology of healing.' So too, Taaʔ Busu engages the dangerous power of deathly Japanese bombers with his 'Airplane Song.' Busu Puteh's grandfather may not be able to affect the global forces impinging upon his forest refuge, but by incorporating the tumultous events of history into musical structure, and then performing it, he situates himself as an active agent rather than passive participant.

How is modernity experienced at the site of the body? And how do Temiars deploy spirit practices to mediate that experience? Temiars often discuss modern things and experiences as shocking, startling, shaking you up, precipitating pathological detachment of the head soul. Instead of a raft on the river, now you're in a Land Rover bumping over logging roads and getting shaken up. The assault upon the senses is not necessarily experienced in terms of a primitivist to modern linear progression – from soothing to startling times, for example. Rather, the sensory assault of loud engines, sudden noises, jerky rides is grafted onto previous categories of startling phenomena.

Temiars recognize sensory experiences that can be harmful to health in their autochthonous forest environment: the sudden flash of lightning followed by a clap of thunder can startle a person's head soul into sudden detachment, leading to the illness of soul loss (rɛywaay). Preventive treatment, whether addressing indigenous or modern precipitating events, is drawn from therapeutic resources long brought into play to avoid the debilitating consequences of startle. Children, whose souls are less firmly attached, are more vulnerable to soul loss; following the warning flash of lightning, adults and older children hurriedly place their hands over younger children's ears to guard them from the potential startle of the thunderclap. During trance, another time when head souls are more labile, participants will call out from the sidelines 'Kɛg, cəwok! Be aware of the dogs!' reminding trancers to maintain some level of awareness to guard against startle from a sudden dog bark. The continual duple rhythm of the bamboo tubes, rhythmic ostinato to changing melodies throughout a healing and trancing ceremony, provides the ongoing familiarity of sound to cushion against startle. The urban-bound traveler might present himself to a medium or an elder who will blow into, shape, and strengthen head and heart soul, making sure they are firmly situated to withstand the assaults to come.

The guns and bombs of the Second World War and the Emergency are an extreme example of the assaulting sensory experiences Temiars were to experience. Busu Puteh's grandfather dreamed the Airplane Spirit, taming the strange and the horrific by transforming its essential being into a spirit guide. The words and melody given by the enspirited airplane are nested within the rhythm of the bamboo tubes, symbolically embedded within the familiar pulsation of the rainforest soundscape and the human heart (Roseman 1991: 168ff). The Temiar world was dramatically transformed during Japanese Occupation and Emergency, yet subsequent musical 'change' is not necessarily found in the transformation of formal musical parameters of healing songs, in this case. Rather, it is found in the intentional use of traditional discursive structures to encompass altered circumstances. Temiars cushion the shock of the 'uncanny' by embedding new phenomena in a familar dynamic process of dream song composition, performance practice, instrumentation, and musical structure. The strangeness is in the familiarity.

Shimmer, Shudder, and Swirl

Shamanistic discourse entangles the empirically observable with the magically real, a world of multiple realities in which even 'things' of out-forester others, airplanes and canned sardines, participate. During healing ceremonies, the moment when the interpenetration of self and alter, human and spirit occurs is aesthetically marked by 'shimmering' in the visual, kinetic, tactile, and auditory channels. The glimmer of hearthfire lights on shredded leaves of ritual ornaments, in its simultaneous presence and absence, disassembles the visual field. Shimmering things, combining movement and light, exist at the fuzzy boundary between the visual and the kinetic. Among Temiars, flashing and glittering items like mirrors, trees with white trunks, or the anthropologist's glossy paper are handled carefully during potentially dangerous moments such as illness, the time prior to ceremonies, or when working in clearings where refracting light might attract the attention of the thunder deities.

Temiars say they don't just 'see' the shimmer of the leaves, they experience a sympathetic shivering – in their hearts, they say, the Temiar locus for emotion and memory. When a night-time, house-bound singing and trance-dancing ceremony is in progress beneath the shimmering leaves, the movements of the dancers lead from a gentle sway into periodic shudders (kɛnrooʔ), which replicate the shimmer in the kinetic realm. These moments of quickening and destablization mark the onset of the transformative experience of trance. The female chorus accompanying the dancers with bamboo-tube percussion watch for the dancer's shudders, speeding up their tempo and subdividing the beat. The starker clarity of their oscillating duple rhythms high-low, high-low, becomes densified (bə-ʔasil, 'crowded'), fuzzing the boundaries between sound and silence high-high low-low, high-high low-low, in acoustic sympathy with the visual shimmer, kinetic shudder, and experiential shiver.

In performance, then, Temiars employ a variety of tools that 'beg the difference' between sound and silence (densification of the bamboo tube percussion, crowded = bə-ʔasil), one tone and another (vibrato, melisma, melodies that wind and tug like a river = bar-wɛ̃jwɛ̃j), light and darkness (shimmer, sparkle = bɛ̃yug), one bodily position and another (shudder = kɛnrooʔ). Dancing on the edge of the gap, they encounter and embody the people, things, and places that surround them. In a paradox of adaptation and resistance, they expropriate power and knowledge from the commodities that simultaneously link them ever more securely into the lowest social classes of mercantile and post-industrial capitalism.

Healing is performed by shamans themselves and surrounded by dancers involved in the performative transformation of trance. Entranced, Temiars move from a position of the relatively distinct subject in relation to the Other, through the visual glimmer, acoustic densification, and kinetic shudder that 'begs the difference,' to an experience they describe as a sensation of internal (and sometimes external) 'swirling.' In the swirl of trance, trancers momentarily move beyond difference, then slowly reawaken to the world of distinctions. In this space of difference stated and undermined, patients are moved from illness to health.

One of the central ornaments transforming a house into a ceremonial space is the tənamuuʔ. In its simplest form, the tənamuuʔ is a leaf whisk, suspended from the rafters by vine or rope, to hang just above the heads of standing participants. This is the place where spirits first alight on their arrival into the ceremonial space. From here, their healing songs and fluids are dispersed through medium and chorus into patients and other participants. This, too, is the most potent place for healing ministrations to occur; patients, if they are well enough to be moved, are often seated below the tənamuuʔ.

Spirits, when giving their songs during dreams to Temiar mediums, elaborate upon the shape and types of leaves to be incorporated into the tənamuuʔ, the simplest being a rattan hoop strung with leaves, the more elaborate including multitiered hoops. Often, leaves are strung at head height from ropes or vines to produce a square shape demarcating the outer perimeter of the ceremonial space. One of the commonest leaves to find in the tənamuuʔ are the long, slender, light-colored leaves of shredded palm known as kəwar (in Malay, *palas*; Licuala species). The fragrance of fresh forest leaves and flowers adds to the ritual sensorium, and their sap literally and metaphorically brings the presence of visiting spiritguides flowing into the bodies of ceremonial participants.

In the Temiar community of Bihay, I came across an astounding sight. This Temiar settlement was once surounded by the dense green growth of the forest; now, in 1992, the forest was denuded. In the headman's house, ceremonial paraphenalia hung from the rafters, a sign of recent healing and singing sessions. The elaborate tənamuuʔ was formed of multitiered hoops, decreasing in size as they ascended – like a layered cake. Additional ornaments included the square shape demarcating the outer perimeter of the ceremonial space. But this tənamuuʔ was not strewn with long, wavy strands of shredded kəwar leaves. Instead, the tənamuuʔ was made from shredded plastic bags. These bags, in which Temiars carry home market-bought produce to replace the forest foods no longer there to hunt or gather, had become a replacement for ceremonial leaves now too far or scarce to find.

Wondering what type of spirit would feel at home among the shredded plastic, I asked: 'What kind of spiritguide requested these leaves?'

'As long as they shimmer,' answered the headman's wife, implying that these plastic 'leaves' retained a quality essential for attracting and activating the spirits. Her answer led me to rethink what, in a pared-down world, was absolutely necessary to make a Temiar ceremonial performance happen, and what the need for these shining shreds implied about ceremonial intent.

'Is it still possible to heal, can the cool liquid kahyɛk still flow through these "leaves"?'

The headman's wife pointed to the few cəbaay leaves mixed in with the shredded plastic bags, pointing out that forest leaves still maintained their presence within these new-fangled ornaments. 'Yes,' she replied, 'we can still suck out the illness, and replace it with the healing liquids of the spirits. We can still dance, swaying gracefully, shuddering into trance, swirling in our hearts, as the bamboo tubes beat. As long as they shimmer.'

Acknowledgments

Field research with Temiars of Kelantan and Perak in 1981–2, 1991, 1992, and 1995, has been conducted under the auspices of the Social Science Research Foundation, Asian Cultural Council, Wenner Gren Foundation for Anthropological Research (Grant No. 4064), National Science Foundation (BNS81-02784), Research Foundation of the University of Pennsylvania, with additional travel funds provided by Universiti Sains Malaysia and Malaysian

Air Lines (1991). Analysis and writing were furthered by a Guggenheim Foundation Fellowship (1996–7), Professional in Residence Fellowship from the Annenberg School for Communications at University of Pennsylvania (1996–7), and National Endowment of Humanities Fellowship (2000).

Notes

1. A growing literature addresses the ways in which expressive culture expands to encompass the often disconcerting experiences of modernity; see, for example, Comaroff and Comaroff (1993); Ferzacca (2001); Roseman (1996).

2. Dentan (1992) discusses the historical significance of an intact forest refuge for the development of unique Senoi cultural characteristics such as non-violence.

3. Gianno (1990), for example, charts the history of the resin trade among the Semelai, another Orang Asli group.

4. Recordings of a number of Temiar spirit song genres, as well as intrumental music, can be found on the compact disc *Dream Songs and Healing Sounds: In the Rainforests of Malaysia*. Smithsonian/Folkways Recordings SF CD 40417 (Roseman 1995).

Bibliography

Attali, J. ([1977] 1985), *Noise: The Political Economy of Music*, Minneapolis: University of Minnesota Press.

Comaroff, J. and Comaroff, J. (eds) (1993), *Modernity and its Malcontents: Ritual and Power in Postcolonial Africa*, Chicago: University of Chicago.

Dentan, R.K. (1992), 'The Rise, Maintenance, and Destruction of a Peaceable Polity: A Preliminary Essay in Political Ecology,' in J. Silverberg and J.P. Gray (eds), *Aggression and Peacefulness in Humans and Other Primates*, New York: Oxford University Press.

Ferzacca, S. (2001), *Healing the Modern in a Central Javanese City*, Durham NC: Academic Press.

Gianno, R. (1990), *Semelai Culture and Resin Technology*, New Haven CT: The Connecticut Academy of Arts and Sciences.

Mignolo, W.D. (1994), 'The Moveable Center: Geographical Discourses and Territoriality During the Expansion of the Spanish Empire,' in F.J. Cevalios-Candau, J. Cole, N.M. Scott and N. Suárez-Araúz (eds), *Coded Encounters*, Amherst: University of Massachusetts.

Robertson, C. (1979), '"Pulling the Ancestors": Performance Practice and Praxis in Mapuche Ordering,' *Ethnomusicology*, 23(3): 395–416.

Roseman, M. (1991), *Healing Sounds from the Malaysian Rainforest: Temiar Music and Medicine*, Los Angeles: University of California Press.

—— (1995), *Dream Songs and Healing Sounds: In the Rainforests of Malaysia*, Washington DC: Smithsonian/Folkways Recordings SF CD 40417 (compact disc and descriptive notes).

—— (1996), '"Pure Products go Crazy": Rainforest Healing in a Nation-state,' in C. Laderman and M. Roseman (eds), *The Performance of Healing*, New York: Routledge, pp. 233–69.

Seeger, A. (1988), *Why Suyà Sing: A Musical Ethnography of an Amazonian People*, Cambridge: Cambridge University Press.

Winichakul, T. (1994), *Siam Mapped: A History of the Geo-Body of a Nation*, Honolulu: University of Hawaii Press.

13

Home Cooking

Filipino Women and Geographies of the Senses in Hong Kong

Lisa Law

Architecture, because it is always assumed to be *somewhere*, is the first visual evidence of a city's putative identity. In this regard, the symbolic landscape of Central exerts a particular fascination not only for filmmakers and photographers, but also for the domestic workers from the Philippines who take it over on Sundays when it is closed to traffic.

A. Abbas, *Hong Kong: Culture and the Politics of Disappearance*

My first visit to Hong Kong was in 1994. Like every dutiful tourist, topping my agenda was a *Star Ferry* ride from Kowloon to Hong Kong Island. The *Star Ferry* affords spectacular views of urban hyperdensity and provides ample photo opportunities to capture the symbolic landscape that has come to represent the Hong Kong experience. One Sunday I boarded the ferry at Tsim Sha Tsui, took a few photographs as we crossed the channel, then disembarked at the Central terminal. As I wandered through the tunnels and streets leading up to the space-age architecture of the Hong Kong and Shanghai Bank, my focus shifted from monuments to people as it became evident I was among an exclusively Filipino community. While stories of the gathering at Central are common in the Philippines, I was not prepared for the intensity of the crowd.

My first and most profound memory of this experience was awakening to the phenomenon. In the distance a woman was bellowing 'peso, peso, pesooooo!' in the melodic tone used by street vendors to solicit business in the Philippines. The peso is the Philippine national currency, but this locution is difficult to express literally. In musical terms it is generally

224

patterned in three measures of two beats, with the first beat of each measure somewhat staccatoed. The first five notes are the same but are followed by a final prolonged note that ascends a full octave (this explanation, without doubt, will not do it justice). For me that voice, that particular rhythm and intonation, recalled the Philippines I had known from 1991 to 1993. My pace quickened as I was irresistibly lured towards it. A few moments later I found myself at one corner of Statue Square, where an entrepreneurial woman was trading Filipino pesos for Hong Kong dollars at rates slightly higher than local banks. It was the convenience of trading currency at this busy spot, she explained, and there were always domestic workers needing to buy pesos for travelling to the Philippines or to include a little cash for financially worse-off relatives in their regular letters home.

Ask any Filipino domestic worker what they do in Hong Kong on a Sunday, and you will be told about the spectacular gathering dubbed 'Little Manila.' In and around Central Hong Kong more than 100,000 Filipino women cast off the cultural conventions of their Chinese employers for one day a week, and eat Filipino food, read Filipino newspapers/magazines and consume products from an abundant number of Filipino specialty shops. It is not unusual to see women procuring manicures or haircuts on the pavement, or having group photographs taken in the street. The queues for the phone booths and at the post office are a sight in themselves, and when domestic workers are not posting letters or chatting long distance they are writing and reading letters to and from distant loved ones. This ritual gathering has taken place since the early 1980s and is now a spectacle of modern life in Hong Kong.

My fleeting but intense encounter is relevant to geographical discussions about space, place and culture. Moving from the *visual* consumption of Central Hong Kong to the *aural* recognition of Little Manila, it signifies the everyday experience of cultural difference and suggests that the senses might play a vital role in mediating the spaces of multicultural cities. This vignette also imagines the possibility of appreciating cultural difference as an embodied encounter, and how space/place might help constitute embodied subjects. While this approach may not appear particularly novel, relatively little attention has been paid to processes of embodiment that consider the interrelationships between bodies and senses in the city. Despite feminist critiques of vision, or research into the politics of music and soundscapes, the senses are often assumed to be an intrinsic property of the body – a natural and unmediated aspect of human *being*. Here I argue that the senses are far from innocent; they are a situated practice that can shed light on the way bodies experience different spaces of culture.

To address these issues I introduce Little Manila, a place that could at once appear a cliché, an ethnic enclave, a site of resistance. Each week it disrupts the hegemonic space of Central Hong Kong, and local perceptions of this gathering as a disorderly crowd of unruly foreign women call attention to multicultural tensions in the city's urban fabric. When experienced from the inside, however, Statue Square and its environs become a home away from home for migrant women, a place of remembering and forgetting, and a lively place full of laughter, songs and home cooking. Rather than reduce Little Manila to a site of resistance, where domestic workers merely repudiate their servant status in the metropolis, here I unravel some of the relationships between personal, urban and transnational space these women negotiate on a weekly basis.

Although the politics of more quotidian forms of sensory knowledge and feeling are not easily decipherable, Seremetakis (1994: 4) has argued that 'a politics of sensory creation and reception [is] a politics of everyday life.' Taking this assertion seriously, I argue that the senses tell us something different about the politics of diasporic experience and suffuse diverse spaces in the city with new meaning. Little Manila is where domestic workers recover from more subtle forms of sensory reculturation that occur in Chinese homes, and in the process they create new ways of engaging with city life. It is also a place where Filipino women express a creative subjective capacity with the potential to displace the hegemonic images that describe their lives and work – if only for one day a week.

One way to imagine how bodies and spaces are produced in Central is to consider different 'senses' of the city. Recasting the senses as a situated practice allows the gathering in Little Manila to be a form of embodied experience that both 'takes place' and is 'produced.' Mapping 'sensuous geographies' (Rodaway 1994) through an 'anthropology of the senses' (Stoller 1989; Classen et al. 1994; Seremetakis 1994) provides new ways of connecting the cultural spaces of Hong Kong and the Philippines, revealing more subtle forms of power that are experienced across aesthetic practices. Eating Filipino food in Little Manila is a particularly good example. Food is significant for its ability to evoke a multifaceted experience of place, for by cooking and eating Filipino food on Sundays, domestic workers consume different experiences of Hong Kong, home and nation.

This chapter moves through three parts. In the first part Little Manila is contrasted with women's experiences in the domestic sphere during the six-day working week. Although the stories told represent extreme forms of maltreatment reported to non-government organizations, they also suggest a cultural context that gives Little Manila its tactical meaning. I engage with Foucauldian perspectives of power, which privilege the visual to theorize the relationship between these private/public spaces, but argue that accounts that stress discourse or vision tend to reduce Central to an uncomplicated site of power/resistance. In considering Little Manila less as a spectacle of modern life and more as a contested site of aesthetic/sensorial culture, I aim to provide a more complex account of its significance. In the second part, Central is portrayed as a landscape transformed through sensory experience each week. I take the example of Filipino food that is ceremonially eaten at Sunday gatherings, and how its taste, texture and aroma help embody these women as national subjects. I contrast the conviviality of eating Filipino fare with the cultural politics of food consumption in the city, elaborating how food is enmeshed with Chinese-Filipino corporeal and material relations. Finally, in the third part of the chapter, I bring these geographies of vision, sound, taste, texture and aroma together to consider how diasporic populations might be understood as producing different sensorial landscapes.

Although a methodology for researching sensory landscapes is far from apparent, and the practice and meaning of the several senses is difficult to capture in words, the importance of ethnographic research cannot be denied. I have therefore chosen a narrative strategy that begins with my own encounter with Little Manila, moves through domestic workers' experiences of Hong Kong domestic space, and then recounts the ritual phenomenon of gathering. I stress the importance of ethnographic fieldwork in perceiving these geographies and suggest that insights about sensorial culture provide new maps of people and places in the city.

Sensing the City

During 1997/98 I completed a series of interviews with non-government organizations (NGOs) working on behalf of domestic workers in Hong Kong. These interviews explored extreme forms of domestic worker experience and the role activists play in mediating negative images of overseas Filipino women (see Law 2002).

In NGO offices domestic work is a serious political issue. Individual cases of maltreatment and abuse are integrated into larger advocacy programs addressing the politics of labor migration. Witness the entrance to one NGO office where an exhibit of newspaper articles reporting suspicious domestic worker deaths calls attention to discrimination against Filipinos in Hong Kong. Inside, women are seeking paralegal assistance to fight cases against abusive employers or wrongful dismissal, in order to be permitted to seek further employment. These stories and cases paint a grim picture of life and work in the big city.

In addition to offering crisis counseling and assistance with legal documents, NGOs ensure these cases are brought to the attention of the popular press, where they form part of a narrative of domestic work. Within this narrative, Filipino women are encoded as victims – as poor domestic workers enduring slave-like conditions. When supplemented by accounts of Hong Kong's history of bonded servants and the uneven nature of capitalist development, a naturalized representation of Hong Kong/Philippines social and economic geographies is transposed onto the social relations of domestic work (for example, employer/employee, dominant/subordinate). The domestic sphere is thus a key site where such relations are seen to be playing out.

Some studies of domestic work have conceptualized Filipino women as corporeal subjects, often utilizing Foucauldian frameworks to discuss the 'disciplining' of these bodies through their employment and ethnic status. Constable (1997) focuses on domestic workers in Hong Kong and examines how Filipino women learn ways of disciplining themselves to avoid being recognized through negative ethnic stereotypes (for example as being lazy and/or sexually dangerous). Domestic workers wear simple clothing at work, cut their long hair short and, in an effort to come across as better servants, timetable their days into rigorous routines. Domestic workers thus become 'docile bodies,' and unwittingly participate in their own oppression (see also Pratt 1998).

Foucauldian analyses that rely on the panoptic gaze have the tendency to coalesce and condense the gaze with hegemonic power. But this gaze has come under scrutiny by both feminist and postcolonial critics (see for example, Hartsock 1990; Bhabha 1994). Through these lenses domestic workers are recognized, at best, as resisting the power of ethnic stereotypes, rather than pursuing different ways to experience their social world. Although it is important to connect domestic work to the social and economic realities of labor migration and ethnic politics, and to interrogate the discrimination Filipino women experience overseas, these analyses imply that Filipino women have little room to negotiate their lives outside a domestic worker identity. Within this grid of identity and meaning, regrouping in NGO offices or congregating in Central merely become cathartic experiences and expressions of resistance where women identify themselves as exploited workers. In this way Little Manila is deprived of a broader political significance and being Filipina is always about being a domestic worker. In Hong Kong, however, the majority of domestic workers do not tend to visit NGO offices unless they are in negative or abusive situations. Most women spend their week in a cramped apartment taking care of the needs of employers, and their time off in Little Manila. The six-day working week undoubtedly shapes women's lives on Sunday, but the relationship between these times and places escapes direct correspondence. Below I examine how women become embodied subjects that exceed – rather than merely resist – their denigrated role as 'maid.'

This is not to imply that Little Manila is somehow removed from power. It is the rather different assertion that Filipino women, like other diasporic communities, are weaving together aspects of culture and power that are difficult to unravel without new theoretical tools. In Little Manila domestic workers temporarily disrupt their position within a hierarchy of employer/ employee social relations, and in the process define new networks and links across a range of spaces that redefine their Hong Kong identity. Put another way, Little Manila is a 'social space' (Lefebvre 1991), a space saturated with Hong Kong/Philippines social and economic geographies that reflect the political economy of labor migration and domestic work. Filipino women

– by virtue of their status as live-in domestic workers – have few places in their everyday lives to feel 'at home,' and gathering in Central provides relief from working in a foreign culture. At the same time, the city itself is always active and fluid – filled with signs and meanings that connect different places, people and relationships at different junctures. Gathering in Central is certainly about a day away from a difficult working week but it is also about the freedom of the streets where new vantage points on life and work abroad are possible. It is this transformation that disrupts binaries of employer/employee, as Filipino women connect the Philippines to Hong Kong in new ways, to different cultures and spaces, and their relationship to the city is transformed. I now turn to the visual space of Central to explore these ideas further.

Hong Kong Vistas

The symbolic vista that has come to represent Hong Kong's urban culture helps to shape this visual sense of the city. Whether experienced through direct architectural encounters, photographs from the *Star Ferry* or through Jackie Chan action films, the visual experience of Hong Kong is bound up with issues of culture and cultural identity. Abbas has critically analysed this cultural space of (post)colonial Hong Kong, suggesting that it is architecture that upholds the colonial space of the metropolis. Architecture, he contends, 'has the dangerous potential of turning all of us, locals and visitors alike, into *tourists* gazing at a stable and monumental image' (Abbas 1997: 65).

In visual terms, Little Manila could be understood as a *part of* Central's symbolic landscape: one that functions as both spectacle and subversion. If a spectacle is a social relationship mediated by images (Debord 1977), then Sunday crowds expose the transformations occurring in the privacy of modern homes; that is, transforming employment opportunities for Chinese women. As Hong Kong joined the ranks of Asia's 'miracle' economies in the 1970s, the number of women prepared to work as domestics on a live-in basis dwindled. They were drawn to more autonomous and financially lucrative service and industry jobs, and a shortage of women willing to work as domestics become apparent. In 1975, 1,000 Filipino women arrived in Hong Kong on government-approved domestic worker contracts. By 1998 they numbered 140,500, and now form a vibrant foreign community (AMC 1999). Little Manila brings these new social relations of households into public view, in a symbolic space that usually evokes economic prowess.

But Little Manila simultaneously critiques the disparities and disloca-tions of this global city. As poorer women migrate to wealthier countries to enhance their opportunities for social mobility, and as they congregate in central business districts to exchange news and hawk goods from home, confident narratives of economic progress are called into question. Filipino women gather by the hundreds in the open ground floor of the Hong Kong and Shanghai Bank, juxtaposing global capital with transnational labor migration. The inequalities of global capital, and the dislocation of Filipino women, are inscribed in a spatial relation. Much like Wilson's (1997: 129) likening of the city to a 'palimpsest' or 'a writing block on which words are written, erased or partly erased and written over, time and again,' this assemblage re-inscribes the meaning of global capital at this site. On Sundays at least, Hong Kong's success as a 'miracle' economy is written over with migrant remittances and the petty trading of pesos for dollars, exposing the centrality of cheap migrant labor in building Asia's 'economic tigers.'

Few residents would be enthusiastic about incorporating Little Manila into Central's predominant meaning. In Hong Kong, as in Singapore, there are tensions between those who acknowledge the need for foreign women without a private residence to engage in leisure activities and those who would prefer domestic workers gather in less conspicuous places (see Yeoh and Huang 1998, 1999). Nevertheless, negative views of Sunday gathering have prompted the government and businesses to erect temporary barriers along cement ledges and in corners that might encourage sitting. Stringent regulations prohibiting hawking have also seen an increased police presence in the area. Witness, for example, Yang's letter of 26 June 1998 to the *South China Morning Post* titled 'Congestion eyesore for tourists' (p. 20):

> The heavy gatherings of Filipino domestic helpers in the streets (especially in Causeway Bay near Victoria Park) on Sundays has become a problem for pedestrians. As we all know, the streets are... not designed for people to gather socially and eat together... They must also be an eyesore for tourists. Surely the Government could do something to... prevent an important amenity in the city from being spoiled.

Or Chulani's letter of 8 July 1998, also in the *South China Morning Post*, 'Must clean up Central' (14), proposing that government: 'prohibit squatting, hawking and eating in public areas; open normal traffic on all roads in Central so that the Filipino maids have no place to sit, squat and sleep... The Hong Kong and Shanghai Bank should erect barriers round its headquarters, to prevent crowds of Filipinos from gathering.'

These letters are a regular feature in local newspapers and are reminiscent of the 1992 proposal to encourage Filipino women to congregate in underground car parks (Lowe 1997; Constable 1997). They also suggest a preference for domestic workers to be 'out of sight.' Unlike their earlier Chinese counterparts, foreign domestic workers are a visible presence in public spaces. Although they are regularly seen during the working week – when they transport children to and from school, or shop for groceries in the markets – their presence in Little Manila is beyond such duties. Here they congregate collectively for pleasure and leisure rather than individual duty.

Each week a space that usually signifies a vibrant business culture turns into a festive Filipino gathering. From the early hours each Sunday, Central bustles with women attending church, remitting money home, sending packages through express parcel services, buying Filipino delicacies to share with friends and so on. But what does this disruption, or turning, mean? Consider the point of view of Abbas (1997: 87):

> Is Statue Square on Sundays an example then of the *détournement* or diversion of a space of power into a space of pleasure? This is unfortunately not entirely the case because the weekly congregations take place only by permission, and come Monday everything returns to 'normal.' No contestation has taken place. Perhaps the takeover of Central is more clearly an example of the fascination that the symbolic spaces of power exert on those excluded from them. The powerless are allowed to see Central – like looking at so many goods through a shop window – but not to touch it.

What this suggests is an aestheticization of space that relates more to images of postmodernity (cf. Harvey 1989; Jameson 1984) than debates about power, identity and struggles for equity or respect. Filipino women are left gazing at the monumental images of Hong Kong, merely embodying their (unfulfilled) desire. But the assumed depoliticizing force of aestheticization is a situated knowledge and is more relevant to phenomena such as shopping malls, theme parks and other spaces geared towards mass consumption (Jacobs 1998). Central Hong Kong may typify postmodern visual consumption if viewed from the *Star Ferry*, one could argue, but Little Manila does not. To neglect the significance of this gathering as a negotiated space of ethnic and cultural identity, and as a place of 'the uncommodified activity of dreaming' (Tadiar 1997), is to deny Filipino women subjectivity. The aesthetics of Little Manila remain trapped within a binary view of power – of the powerful versus the powerless.

Let us detour, for a moment, to a different sense of the city – one saturated with aromas – to explore these issues of power further. After reading Yang's letter (quoted above) I felt impelled to revisit Victoria Park (the site of his complaint), because my own impression had not been the presence of 'heavy gatherings' of Filipino women in that part of the city. One Sunday I entered the park, and rather than being surrounded by great gatherings of Filipino women was overwhelmed by that marvelous aroma of Indonesian clove cigarettes. Wandering around Victoria Park, for me at least, confirmed statistics of the growing number of Indonesian domestic workers in Hong Kong. Although women from the Philippines have dominated this labor market since the 1970s, there were 31,800 domestic workers from Indonesia in 1998 (AMC 1999). In Victoria Park they too were enjoying their day off. The fact that the aroma of cloves and chatter in Indonesian dialects could elude Yang, or indeed that signs prohibiting hawking and littering had been posted in Tagalog and not Bahasa Indonesia, merely demonstrates the powerful associations between 'Filipino' and 'domestic worker' in Hong Kong. More generally, different odors and aromas can create the effect of 'olfactory maps' of cities, which enable people to 'conceptualize their environment by way of smell' (Classen et al. 1994: 18). Olfactory geographies 'evoke place' as well as 'memories of place' (Rodaway 1994). For some, cloves might create aromas with positive associations that signify inclusion, for others they can signify distance and cultural difference. Consider, for example, a letter to a Hong Kong newspaper which laments the 'filthy stench in the air late on Sunday evenings' (cited in Constable 1997: 36). The use of 'filthy stench,' with its implications of refuse and contamination, articulates with ongoing discussions about how to 'clean up' Central and indeed Hong Kong more generally. Why the city might need cleaning up is a matter of interpretation, and there looms a possibility that some residents desire the odorless experience of the city as it appears on film.[1] 'Filth' and 'stench' are words usually associated with civic (un)cleanliness, but the perceived olfactory differences between social classes or ethnic communities produce, and are themselves produced by, classification systems that relate more to cultural ideologies than to odors or aromas themselves (Classen et al. 1994). Therefore, the 'filthy stench' of Central is not only disagreeable: it reaffirms unfavorable images of Filipino women as backward and unruly. Their apparent refusal to comply with modern sensibilities produces images of Filipino domestic workers as disorderly and undisciplined – in seeming contradiction to their employment as organizers of domestic space.

These contested sights and aromas suggest that aesthetics are not autonomous from their political, economic and social milieu. More importantly, they point to how differing aesthetic politics may be articulated through differing urban senses. The optical lens that situates Filipino women gazing at Hong Kong monuments almost colludes in excluding them from the dynamism of city life. The olfactory aesthetics and politics of Little Manila can, in contrast, be seen to disrupt the colonial space of Hong Kong architecture by dislocating its dominant visual meaning. On Sundays, at least, Central's morphology and monuments are unable to construct Filipino women as colonial subjects, servants or voyeuristic consumers. Paying attention to the olfactory politics of Little Manila opens up the political possibilities of its aesthetics and recognizes how the senses help to create a place like 'home.' If we connect the senses to questions of power and the cultural economy of labor migration, then we may better understand the diverse ways migrants cope with living in global cities.

Home Cooking

On Sunday, 31 August 1997, a date many will remember as the day of Princess Diana's car crash, I had been invited to a party for a domestic worker named

Deenah who was fortunate to have her thirtieth birthday fall on her day off.[2] Arlene, also a domestic worker and my part-time research assistant, arrived at 10.30 a.m. to accompany me to the meeting place. Arlene is from Ifugao Province in the Philippines but her friends are from various parts of Luzon (the Philippines' main northern island). There are some general rules of thumb for locating friends from different provinces in the Philippines: Cebuanos congregate around City Hall, Nueva Vizcayans in the northeastern part of Statue Square and Illocanos near the statue of Sir Thomas Jackson (popularly known as 'the black statue'). When Arlene became exhausted with conveying the details of Little Manila's regions she exclaimed: 'it's just like a map of the Philippines!' Regional networks are strong in Hong Kong, partly for reasons of language/dialect but also because of networks of families and friends. New acquaintances are often introduced as sisters, cousins or aunts, or friends from high school, college or university.

We wandered around Statue Square and the congested streets leading up to World Wide Plaza, where we stopped to buy a cold drink. The crowds were unusually thick at this time of day and it took a full 20 minutes to cross the mall and find a shop that sold Coke. Unable to find a seat amongst the hundreds of Filipino women, we went out to the streets and began looking for the party troupe. A few had congregated on a shop step near Giorgio Armani, and we sat to drink and wait. Arlene introduced me to Mary and Cha, who were comparing cosmetics they had purchased that morning. Cha decided to paint her fingernails for the party, lamenting that polish was 'too difficult' during the working week: 'My employer doesn't like it and anyway it just comes off when I wash the floor.' The step we sat on was watched over by a Chinese security guard employed to ensure no one crossed his plastic tape barrier, although everyone laughed as he scolded us for placing our shopping bags beyond the magic line. What he was guarding – apart from a small horizontal piece of concrete – completely eluded me. Mary, who noticed my disdain, offered the explanation that he was 'just following orders.'

When a critical mass had assembled we fought the crowds to the Hong Kong and Shanghai Bank, where we took a tram to the party site. From the tram stop we wandered to a small green square where the party was to be held, arriving just after midday. About twenty close friends had been invited, most of whom Deenah knew from the Philippines but including others she had met in Singapore. More than half of the women were married, and had brought along letters – complete with photos of husbands and children – to read. As I glanced through snapshots and heard stories of children in school, and of new family homes and businesses financed by overseas work, Arlene commented: 'It's too sad that these families are not together.' She quickly flashed a mischievous grin, however, and claimed Mary's husband was so terribly ugly that she was desperate to work abroad. Everyone squealed with laughter. Mary retorted: 'I'm taking care of my family, experiencing life and seeing the world.'

We spent the next hour waiting for the last guests, who had to travel long distances from the New Territories. To pass the time we assembled into various poses for photos to be sent back to the Philippines. Some women read letters, Arlene switched on the portable CD player and a few women sang along with the music. Deenah modelled a wig she had recently purchased while on holiday in Thailand, while others chatted about Giordano's latest bargains on T-shirts. The festivities really began when Deenah opened several Tupperware dishes that contained food she had prepared for the party, and the air became filled with aromas of rice, ginger and vinegar. Deenah is permitted to cook Filipino food in her employers' home, and had prepared a series of Filipino delicacies including chicken *adobo*, *pinakbet* (vegetables) and *bangus* (fish). We were all provided with a paper plate and chopsticks and helped ourselves to the food. About half-way into the meal, however, I noticed that chopsticks were quickly being replaced by thin plastic gloves that Deenah had also brought along. Deenah looked at me and queried: 'You like?' Asserting my own cultural capital, I abandoned my clumsy attempt at chopstick etiquette and opted for these more pliable eating utensils. Peals of laughter were soon replaced by endless conversations about what our favorite foods were, the availability of ingredients to make regional dishes and how much everyone missed eating rice with *every* meal. Filipinos often enjoy eating with their hands, but because there are few places in Hong Kong's parks and squares to wash up before or after eating, many women opt for disposable gloves. It was a moment of casting off Chinese customs to enjoy the *taste*, *aroma* and *texture* of home. 'We are,' as Bell and Valentine (1997) have suggested, 'where we eat.'

Birthday parties are a particularly good reason to celebrate, but they are not the only reason to enjoy the conviviality of Central. The simple pleasure of sharing a meal with family and friends is a welcome respite from the weekly routine of preparing meals for employers and eating alone in maids' quarters. Women can also relish an assortment of familiar tastes – some prepared personally for the day, others made by friends, hawkers or fast food outlets. 'We are where we eat' is more than an ironic aphorism, however, where food acquires its meaning through the place it is assembled and eaten. In Hong Kong it is the Philippines (home) that has to be prepared (cooked) for food to take on its homely significance.

The Philippines is experienced each Sunday through a conscious invention of home – an imagining of place through food and other sensory practices that embody Filipino women as national subjects. 'Home cooking' thus becomes an active creation: a dislocation of place, a transformation of Central, a sense of home. In savoring Filipino food, for example, senses of taste, touch, vision and smell all become active. Eating thus becomes a productive and self-conscious pursuit, not merely an organic, innate or derivative activity. Putting aside chopsticks not only disrupts the routine of everyday eating, it is about enjoying eating with the hands. It is less about a refusal to use chopsticks than about enhancing flavor – a practice well known at home. The senses thus connect Hong Kong to the Philippines not through binary forms of power but through alternative geographies of employment, work, travel and life experience.

There is a growing academic interest in food and 'foodways' (the routes through which food travels) that relate to two interrelated issues. On the one hand, there is growing recognition that the centralization of food production and consumption policies tends to eliminate regional varieties of food products in local, regional and global markets. On the other hand, an emphasis on the importance of material culture to contemporary cosmopolitan experience has increased awareness that food might be a pertinent example of an 'entangled' object (cf. Thomas 1991; Crang 1996). Bringing these perspectives together to consider the meaning of food in Hong Kong provides insights about the importance of 'home cooking' to migrant populations around the world (see also Seremetakis 1994). For it is the entangling of foodways in webs of culture, economics and politics that enables the presence of some foods and not others in shops, restaurants or households. The absence of familiar material culture, and its subtle evocations of home, is surely one of the most profound dislocations of transnational migration.

It is common knowledge that the preparation and consumption of food in Hong Kong is important in defining its vibrant culinary culture, but it is less well known that these practices also help define the awkward relationships that arise when a foreign worker enters the space of the family. Deenah, for example, is not representative of the domestic worker population in that many women claim they are either not permitted to cook or simply do not feel comfortable preparing Filipino foods in Chinese homes. I gleaned this knowledge from a number of women who were eating snacks in the Filipino dry goods shops that are common in Central, and have more recently opened doors in neighborhoods such as Mei Foo, Sai Kung and Tuen Mun. Indeed, food consumption practices in Chinese homes – as everywhere – are 'crossed by complex webs of power relations between household members' (Bell and Valentine 1997: 59; see also Pratt 1998 on Philippine food in Vancouver).

Filipino women are employed to organize domestic spaces, but this may or may not include the kitchen, depending on the disposition of the employer. In some instances Filipino women are perceived as inept in operating household appliances – a stereotype generated in the 1970s, when domestic workers were recruited from rural Philippines. In other households women claim their employers deem Filipino food to have a 'bad smell,' and prefer to eat these foods outside the workplace. Equally important might be a desire for employers to maintain control over the visceral substances that influence Cantonese health, vitality and longevity. It would be a great responsibility for foreign women to purchase and prepare the hundreds of herbs and tonics used in everyday cooking. These power relations of food preparation are constituted at least partly through Chinese vulnerabilities, notions of 'cultural pollution' (Douglas 1966) and stereotypes of Filipino women as poor and uneducated.

A growing number of Filipino dry goods shops and fast food outlets cater to weekday shoppers and Sunday picnics. This food is clearly packaged for migrant workers, however, rather than constituting part of a cosmopolitan food culture in the city. In the two outlets of Jollibee (the Philippines' equivalent of McDonalds), for example, the clientele is almost exclusively Filipino. This contrasts starkly with the dozens of franchises of McDonalds dominated by Chinese patrons. Jollibee serves classic Filipino snack foods such as fried chicken with rice and uniquely seasoned hamburgers – foods that do not seem to appeal to the Chinese palate. Furthermore, there are simply too few places for more than 100,000 women to buy Filipino fare, helping to galvanize a vibrant food-hawking culture in Statue Square. Entrepreneurial domestic workers with sympathetic employers earn extra money through this 'side business' each week and, if they evade temporary raids by the police, fill the gap in certified eating establishments. Filipino food, in Cantonese homes or in its 'fast' forms, does not appear to represent the processes of 'acculturation and hybridization' that have come to characterize popular ethnic cuisine in Hong Kong (Indian, Japanese, Thai, Western) or in the West (Bell and Valentine 1997: 16). Although this disconnection between food cultures might suggest that Filipino cuisine lacks exotic appeal for the discriminating Chinese palate, it also signifies the social and cultural distance between employers and domestic workers. It is through the process of ingesting Filipino food, however, that domestic workers create new associations between Hong Kong and the Philippines. Ethnic cuisine 'only becomes a self-conscious, subjective reality when ethnic boundaries are crossed' (cited in Bell and Valentine 1997: 114). Whether at a birthday party on the street or in a fast food outlet in Central, eating chicken *adobo* becomes a way in which nation and ethnicity are resignified. These foods become national dishes through their appearance in Hong Kong, and their consumption is suffused with cultural politics.

In summary, Filipino food is entangled with three aspects of Chinese–Filipino material and corporeal relations. First, food becomes contested matter in Hong Kong homes. Claims about food odors are impossible to disentangle from ethnic stereotypes, and whether or not domestic workers are allowed to cook Filipino food is an issue of power within households. Second, and partly as a result, Filipino food undergoes a process of revision when it crosses ethnic boundaries. It articulates national identity in a way it could not in the Philippines, and on Sundays becomes a positive signification of cultural difference. Finally, Filipino food evokes familiar senses of taste-texture-aroma and, particularly when consumed in Central, evokes a sense of home: Little Manila. This latter process incorporates elements of history and memory, of past and present times and spaces, helping to create a familiar place where memories of life in the Philippines and migration to Hong Kong might be explored from another perspective.

Producing Sensory Landscapes

Sensory landscapes of cities suggest less conventional forms of ethnic politics, and reveal how diasporic populations find original ways of engaging with urban life. Little Manila is a hybrid site – one that creates new connections between Hong Kong and the Philippines and between being a domestic worker and a Filipina. Much like Appadurai's (1996) 'ethnoscapes,' this reproduction of culture and identity fails to be recuperated through notions of essential national identities or marginal ethnic groups. As Appadurai (1996: 48) argues:

> As groups migrate, regroup in new locations, reconstruct their histories, and reconfigure their ethnic projects, the *ethno* in ethnography takes on a slippery, nonlocalized quality, to which the descriptive practices of anthropology will have to respond. The landscapes of group identity – the ethnoscapes – around the world are no longer familiar anthropological objects, insofar as groups are no longer tightly territorialized, spatially bounded, historically unselfconscious, or culturally homogeneous.

Little Manila is such an ethnoscape, a frame of reference for life and work abroad. I now turn to the dynamic interactions between material culture, memory and the senses that help give Little Manila these original and hybrid meanings.

Perception and memory connect the body with material culture. As women sit on straw mats to eat *pinakbet* or *adobo*, or stand in enormous queues to buy familiar goods from the Philippine Products Store, there is constant chatter about home: 'How is your daughter's schooling?' 'Do you have photos of Alma's wedding?' 'Did you hear that Fe's husband is unfaithful?' But these conversations are also punctuated with ones about daily life in Hong Kong: 'When are you finish-contract?' 'How is your employer treating you?' 'Can you speak Cantonese yet?' Little Manila is not an 'authentic' but a simulated home (Baudrillard 1995). It is produced through a complex articulation of nostalgia and desire within a different and contemporary context. Central Hong Kong is, after all, *not* Manila.

In relation to current debates about the aesthetics of cities, nostalgia is usually understood as the inauthentic or depthless consumption of history. History is presented as decoration, and is intended for visual consumption. But the role of nostalgia in transforming Central into Little Manila does require a depth of emotion, and is rather like Seremetakis' sense of the word in that it evokes the desire or longing to journey in time and space. This journey is embarked on from and in Little Manila, a place which captures everyday experience from another 'oblique angle' and 'gives rise to a new or alternative perceptual landscape' (Seremetakis 1994: 14). In other words, the Sunday journey from Hong Kong to the Philippines constitutes, and is itself constituted through, a landscape that simulates home while enabling new perspectives on the past and the present.

Material cultures, and the senses they evoke, are integral to this journey. As discussed above, the touch and taste of food are important in embodying Filipino women as national subjects. But sensory landscapes are about the whole body – including sight/vision. Let me consider this point by drawing on the peculiar effect of photographs of distant loved ones placed on the walls of Philippine homes. While in some cultures photographs of overseas family members signify absence, in the Philippines these photos enhance presence in that they recreate moments of togetherness that have been shared between family and friends. Photographs from overseas may transform domestic spaces in the Philippines, but in Little Manila this process works in the other direction. Snapshots of loved ones viewed in Central remind women why they are in Hong Kong – to meet family responsibilities – and have the effect of bringing the Philippines into the foreground. On the other hand, snapshots taken in Central rarely include monumental architecture, and are more likely to include friends, Sunday picnics or photos that impart Hong Kong's wealth (such as poses in front of a Mercedes). Viewing photos of loved ones at Deenah's party inspired nostalgia, reflection and very Filipino jokes. Photos also serve to introduce lives at home to new friends met while overseas, and evoke a sense of family. Photographs reinforce these social relations and generate a transnational sense of communal life (see further Cannell 1997, 1999).

Other objects of material culture facilitate this journey. A similar case could be made for the letters that are read or written in Little Manila as they embellish photographic images with narratives. The letters of overseas Filipino women represent tremendous subjective power, and Tadiar (1997: 178) has argued that letters represent 'doses of human time, time with subjective value.' As with photos, letters play a role in constituting Little Manila's perceptual landscape, for not only do letters create human *time* – they create a *place* of contemplation and subjective meaning where Hong Kong is experienced from another perspective. Life and work is described/ written not merely from the stable identity of domestic worker but from the alternative perspectives of sisters, daughters, wives, cousins and friends. Moreover, these letters rewrite women's marginal economic status in Hong Kong with economic success stories of new homes and businesses in the Philippines. Like photographs, letters travel in both directions, and form a part of a self-reflexive experience of life abroad.

This dynamic interaction between food, photos, letters and other artifacts enables the production of an alternative sensorium called Little Manila. If sensory landscapes are constituted by emotional and historical layerings that evoke gestures and discourses that open up their stratigraphy (Seremetakis 1994: 7), then Little Manila can be understood through the multiple meanings of food, through the photographs and letters that enhance the presence of family and friends and through the melodic songs of street vendors. All of these are suffused with echoes of 'home.'

Conclusion

> The aesthetic awareness of the senses... plays a foundational role in experience, which, in turn, is the heart of ethnographic fieldwork.
>
> P. Stoller, *The Taste of Ethnographic Things*

The consumption of Filipino food in Hong Kong is a salient example of how everyday experience can become a performative politics of ethnic identity. Much like the global commodity that reshapes global cultural landscapes, Filipino food articulates both 'place and movement – and, through those, identity and identification' (Bell and Valentine 1997: 191). Along with music, letters and photographs, food helps to transform Central into Little Manila each week, and allow women to disrupt the social and economic geographies that attribute them with a stable (and marginal) domestic worker identity. The sounds, sights and aromas of Little Manila dislocate the authoritative visual space of Hong Kong culture, and create a place where Filipino women feel at home. In so doing, women find new ways of engaging with city life, and their relation to the city is transformed. These are the geographies of Hong Kong-based Filipino identities – ones that allow domestic workers to be involved in the production of cosmopolitan culture abroad.

The stories told here show how domestic workers are able to negotiate relations that are about more than globalization, gendered labor migration or ethnic discrimination. But these are still relations of power. Geographies of the senses articulate the cultural politics of difference and inequality, making new spatial connections between home/away and between dominant/subordinate and power/resistance. While Little Manila is always about the politics of labor migration and domestic work, it is also inhabited by unique signs and symbols that allow Filipino women to define their own social worlds and their own, situated resistances. In so doing, they transgress their circumscribed role as 'maid.' Geographies of these senses tell us something different about urban culture and diasporic experience, providing fresh insights to corporeal relations. Conceiving them as an embodied practice enables new maps of the city – maps integral to embodied cultural geographies.

Notes

1. Strate (1986), for example, discusses how the media create deodorized representations for their audiences. This might also be the case for cities such as Hong Kong, where visual culture dominates the senses (see also Classen et al. 1994)

2. I mention Diana's death here partly because of its situated representation in the Hong Kong press. Few countries, I expect, would have noted that Diana had a Filipino domestic worker.

Bibliography

Abbas, A. (1997), *Hong Kong: Culture and the Politics of Disappearance*, Hong Kong: Hong Kong University Press.

AMC (Asian Migrant Centre) (1999), *Asian Migrant Yearbook*, Hong Kong: AMC.

Appadurai, A. (1996), *Modernity at Large: Cultural Dimensions of Globalisation*, Minneapolis: University of Minnesota Press.

Baudrillard, J. (1995), *Simulacra and Simulation*, trans. S.F. Glaser, Ann Arbor: University of Michigan Press.

Bell, D. and Valentine, G. (eds) (1997), *Consuming Geographies: We Are Where We Eat*, London: Routledge.

Bhabha, H. (1994), *The Location of Culture*, New York: Routledge.

Cannell, F. (1997), 'Filipino Kinship, Phantom Houses and Fantasies of the Feminine,' paper presented at the Globalization and Ethnicity Conference, Faculty of Social Sciences, Research Centre Religion and Society, Amsterdam.

—— (1999), *Power and Intimacy in the Christian Philippines*, Cambridge: Cambridge University Press.

Classen, C., Howes, D. and Synnott, A. (1994), *Aroma: The Cultural History of Smell*, London: Routledge.

Constable, N. (1997), *Maid to Order in Hong Kong: Stories of Filipina Workers*, Ithaca NY: Cornell University Press.

Crang, P. (1996), 'Displacement, Consumption, and Identity,' *Environment and Planning*, 28: 47–67.

Debord, G. (1977), *Society of the Spectacle*, Detroit: Black & Red.

Douglas, M. (1966), *Purity and Danger: An Analysis of the Concepts of Pollution and Taboo*, London: Routledge.

Hartsock, N. (1990), 'Foucault on Power: A Theory for Women?' in L.J. Nicholson (ed.), *Feminism/Postmodernism*, New York: Routledge, pp. 157–75.

Harvey, D. (1989), *The Condition of Postmodernity*, Oxford: Blackwell.

Jacobs, J.M. (1998), 'Staging Difference: Aestheticization and the Politics of Difference in Contemporary Cities,' in R. Fincher and J.M. Jacobs (eds), *Cities of Difference*, New York: Guilford Press, pp. 252–78.

Jameson, F. (1984), 'Postmodernism or the Cultural Logic of Late Capitalism,' *New Left Review*, 146: 53–92.

Law, L. (2002), 'Sites of Transnational Activism: Filipino NGOs in Hong Kong,' in B. Yeoh, P. Teo and S. Huang (eds), *Gender Politics in the Asia Pacific Region*, London: Routledge, pp. 205–22.

Lefebvre, H. (1991), *The Production of Space*, trans. D. Nicolson-Smith, Oxford: Blackwell.

Lowe, C. (1997), 'The Outsiders Voice: Discourse and Identity among the Filipino Domestic Workers in Hong Kong,' paper presented at the International Conference on Gender and Development in Asia, Chinese University of Hong Kong, Hong Kong.

Pratt, G. (1998), 'Inscribing Domestic Work on Filipina Bodies,' in H. Nast and S. Pile (eds), *Places Through the Body*, London: Routledge, pp. 283–304.

Rodaway, P. (1994), *Sensuous Geographies: Body, Sense and Place*, London: Routledge.

Seremetakis, C.N. (ed.) (1994), *The Senses Still: Perception and Memory as Material Culture in Modernity*, Chicago: University of Chicago Press.

Stoller, P. (1989), *The Taste of Ethnographic Things: The Senses in Anthropology*, Philadelphia: University of Pennsylvania Press.

Strate, L. (1986), 'Media and the Sense of Smell,' in G. Grumpet and R. Cathcart (eds), *Inter/Media*, Oxford: Oxford University Press, pp. 400–11.

Tadiar, N. (1977), 'Domestic Bodies of the Philippines,' *Sojourn: Journal of Social Issues in Southeast Asia*, 12(2): 153–91.

Thomas, N. (1991), *Entangled Objects: Exchange, Material Culture and Capitalism in the Pacific*, Cambridge MA: Harvard University Press.

Wilson, E. (1997), 'Looking Backward: Nostalgia and the City,' in S. Westwood and J. Williams (eds), *Imagining Cities: Scripts, Signs, Memory*, London: Routledge.

Yeoh, B. and Huang, S. (1998), 'Negotiating Public Space: Strategies and Styles of Migrant Female Domestic Workers in Singapore,' *Urban Studies*, 35: 583–602.

—— (1999), 'Spaces at the Margins: Migrant Domestic Workers and the Development of Civil Society,' *Environment and Planning*, A 31: 1149–67.

Part IV

The Aestheticization of Everyday Life

Aestheticization Takes Command

> It is only after you have come to know the surface of things ... that you can venture
> to seek what is underneath. But the surface of things is inexhaustible.
>
> Italo Calvino, *Mr. Palomar*

According to Virginia Postrel, author of *The Substance of Style*, we live in 'a new age of aesthetics' – an age in which 'design is everywhere, and everywhere is now designed' (Postrel 2003: 24). Who has not noticed the growing emphasis on the 'sense appeal' of commodities, stores and human bodies? Attractive design is no longer a luxury: 'We, [as] customers, demand it' (Postrel 2003: 5).

What is driving this 'aestheticization of everyday life'? To gain a purchase on this process we need to trace the history of the concept of aesthetics. Derived from the Greek *aisthesis*, meaning sensation, the term was coined by the philosopher Alexander Baumgarten in the eighteenth century.

For Baumgarten aesthetics had to do with the perfection of perception and only secondarily with the 'perception of perfection,' or beauty. His new 'science of sense cognition' was to occupy an intermediary rung, as a 'science of the lower cognitive power' (sense perception) in contradistinction to 'the higher cognitive power' (reason). By limiting aesthetics to the perception of the 'unity-in-multiplicity of sensible qualities' Baumgarten hoped to insulate it from being reduced to 'arid' intellectual knowledge. He believed that the intellect was 'the poorer' for the fact that it traffics exclusively in 'distinct ideas,' as opposed to the 'confused and indistinct ideas' generated by the senses. For Baumgarten, therefore, the disposition to sense acutely meant attending to the nature of sensory experience in itself, rather than trying to rationalize perception (Gregor 1983: 364–5).

Baumgarten's new 'science' was quickly appropriated and just as quickly subverted by his contemporaries. They replaced his emphasis on the sensuous disposition of the artist with a taxonomy of 'the five arts' (architecture, sculpture, painting, music and poetry). The scope and criteria of the various arts were delimited in terms of the dualism of vision (epitomized by painting) and hearing (epitomized by either music or poetry). The 'dark' or 'lower' senses of smell, taste and touch were deemed too base to hold any significance for the fine arts. Theater and dance were also excluded on account of their hybrid character, since they played to both vision and hearing at once (see Rée 2000).

Baumgarten's worst fears concerning the rationalization of perception were realized in Immanuel Kant's *Critique of Judgment* (1790). Kant attempted to transcend the dualism of vision and hearing and replace it with a fundamental division between the 'arts of space' (for example, painting) and the 'arts of time' (for example, music), accessible to 'outer intuition' and 'inner intuition' respectively (Rée 2000: 58–60). It could be said that Kant rarefied aesthetics by divorcing it from perception and substituting intuition. After Kant, aesthetic judgment would be properly neutral, passionless and disinterested (see Eagleton 1990; Turner 1994). This definition of aesthetics guaranteed the autonomy of the enclave now known as 'art' but at the expense of sensory plenitude.

The first chapter in this section helps us to recuperate a sense of the aesthetic as Baumgarten imagined it – that is, of aesthetics as 'the perfection of sense perception as such.' In 'A Tonic of Wildness,' Victor Carl Friesen explores Henry David Thoreau's (1817–62) sensuous appreciation of the natural world. Friesen approaches Thoreau as a naturalist rather than a literary figure. This is an important move for it means that, instead of deflecting our attention to the intertextuality of Thoreau's position in Western or American literature, Friesen is able to focus on the intersensuality of Thoreau's relationship with his surroundings. Furthermore, whereas Thoreau has often been portrayed as 'a stoic and an ascetic' (Friesen 1984: xiii), he was, in fact, avid for sensory pleasure (though of such a 'simple' kind that it seemed like asceticism to jaded urbanites).

Thoreau's rather idiosyncratic aesthetics was not purely the fruit of his appreciation of nature, as he was influenced by the aesthetic theories of his day.[1] Furthermore, while Thoreau sought to immerse himself in nature he was still near enough to civilization for the encroachments of modern technology – telegraph wires and railways – to form part of his landscape. Friesen astutely points out, however, that Thoreau strove to subject these external theories and elements to his own empathetic 'sensuous approach to nature,' which demanded 'that all senses must ever perceive in a fresh manner' and that even technology be 'naturalized.'

Thoreau used his botanical strolls through the New England woods to, in his terms, 'feed his senses with the best that the land affords' and achieve a state in which his 'body [was] all sentient.' For Thoreau, 'the best that the land affords' did not mean rich or exotic fare, but such 'every-day phenomena' as leaves and berries, winds and waters, intensely appreciated and 'digested.' Thoreau thus achieved a state of heightened aesthetic awareness of the everyday. Contemporary aesthetic theory, however, has passed over Thoreau in favor of another nineteenth century poet-stroller, Baudelaire, apotheosized by Benjamin (1973). Baudelaire's relative popularity in this regard is due to his role as an observer of modern urban life, or as a 'botanist of the pavement' (Clarke 2003: 207). While Thoreau has more to say about the life of the woods than the dynamics of the street, however, his emphasis on sensory refreshment though immersion in nature can help to correct an overly artful – and, as it were, urbane – understanding of aesthetic expression and judgment.

The second chapter, by curator and critic Jim Drobnick, delves further into the excluded matter of (post-Kantian) aesthetic theory – in this case, the world of smell. Drobnick documents how 'museum atmospheres' have changed in recent years, from being ideally anosmic or smell-less 'white cubes' to being pervaded by 'wafting perceptions.' Indeed, scent has become 'one of *the* most fashionable additions to the museum's repertoire of effects,' especially in postmodern, entertainment-oriented display venues. This re-odorization of public spaces is complemented by what Drobnick calls the 'olfactory turn' in contemporary art, which has resulted in recent generations of artists producing ever more 'volatile artworks.' Drobnick classifies these artworks into olfactory types, employing such criteria as 'olfactocentrism' and 'dialectical odors.' His essay hence takes us beyond 'the aesthetic gaze' in a singularly pungent fashion.

The Drobnick chapter brings us to the subject of 'the aestheticization of everyday life' as theorized by sociologist Mike Featherstone in a seminal chapter of *Consumer Culture and Postmodernism*. 'If we examine definitions of postmodernism,' Featherstone (1991: 65) writes, 'we find an emphasis upon the effacement of the boundary between art and everyday life, the collapse of the distinction between high art and mass/popular culture, a general stylistic promiscuity and mixing of codes.' Featherstone proceeds to disclose 'the *genealogy* of *postmodernité*' (or what Postrel calls 'the aesthetic age') and bring out its linkages with modernity. In one of its senses 'the aestheticization of everyday life can refer to the project of turning life into a work of art' (Featherstone 1991: 66). Featherstone cites the example of the artistic countercultures that sprang up in mid- to late-nineteenth century European urban centers, such as Berlin and Paris – the preserve of Baudelaire and company. In its most salient sense for us now, however, 'the aestheticization of everyday life refers to the rapid flow of signs and images which saturates the fabric of everyday life in contemporary society' (Featherstone 1991: 67). As Postrel (2003: 4) suggests, 'Aesthetics has become too important to be left in the hands of the aesthetes,' whence the growth of the so-called culture industries, 'with painting moving into advertising, architecture into technical engineering, [and] handicrafts and sculpture into the industrial arts, to produce a mass culture' (Featherstone 1991: 73). The burgeoning importance and salience of 'design' spells both an extension of art into the everyday, and the end of art's autonomy, or perhaps even 'the end of art' and 'the end of reality' at once (following Baudrillard 1983), as images and reproductions proliferate endlessly, and 'culture' is everywhere and nowhere.

Featherstone might have added 'mixing of the senses' to his definitions of postmodernism. This is the message of Drobnick's chapter and also the theme of the following chapter, 'HYPERESTHESIA.' In this chapter I analyse the role played by the senses in the transition from the ascetic discipline of Calvinism to the aesthetic hedonism of Calvin Klein. My essay points to the instrumentalization of the senses as the driving force behind the transformation of industrial capitalism into the consumer capitalism of today. But the 'sensual logic' of 'late' capitalism is shown to be far more pervasive and invasive than many contemporary cultural critics (such as Jameson, Baudrillard) would think. Its 'logic' is not confined to the projection of dream worlds of consumer gratification (and ever receding prospects of satisfaction); rather it massages *all* the senses (including some you never even thought you possessed).[2] At the same time, the hyperestheticization of everyday life in the interests of moving merchandise is shown to come at a price – to capitalism itself.

The following chapter, by postmodern writer Italo Calvino, takes us on a 'true journey' to Mexico in the company of a tourist couple. Bent on 'ingesting' the local culture, the couple end up using Mexican cuisine as a medium for the metaphorical cannibalization of each other. This exquisitely flavored short story offers a literary evocation of 'the perfection of gustation.' In this story, as in the other two tales of hearing and smell that accompany it in 'Under the Jaguar Sun,' Calvino is concerned to enucleate the 'way of thinking' embedded in a given 'way of sensing.' He also demonstrates how everyday sensory experiences may be transfigured by extraordinary revelations.

The next chapter, by one of the foremost theorists of postmodernism, Steven Connor (1989), presents an exegesis of philosopher Michel Serres' *Les cinq sens* (soon to appear in English translation). As noted in the Introduction, *Les cinq sens* 'cries out against the Empire of Signs,' or what could be called the linguistic domination of perception. It does so by an imaginative exploration of the ways in which the senses mingle with, and entwine, each other and the world – that is, by plumbing the 'interficiality' (Cavell 2002) of our everyday experience of reality. While Serres may have succeeded in deranging conventional anatomies of the senses with his celebration of 'the ceaseless unravelling and reknitting of the body,'[3] Connor nevertheless finds a disturbing lacuna in Serrres' philosophy of sensory emancipation. According to Connor, Serres fails to come to grips with suffering, degradation, and death – or, in a word, entropy. This is a theme to which we shall return in the last part of this volume.

Studies of aestheticization customarily concentrate on that which appeals, to the exclusion of that which offends.[4] But every aesthetic judgement has an underside, and it is this which confronts us in William Ian Miller's social critique of the judgment of distaste in 'Darwin's Disgust.' There is something delightfully postmodern about the very notion of an 'anatomy of disgust' (Miller 1987) as opposed, for example, to the more serious (high modernist) notion of an 'anatomy of criticism' (Frye 1957). However, Miller does not just play with disgust. Miller exposes how in the case of disgust, we are 'in the grip of a sensation' that is both socially produced and fraught with social and moral consequences. Disgust polices. It undermines intimacy and precludes identification with others, thereby forcefully structuring our capacity for sociality.

Miller's constructionist and relational approach to the subject of 'disesthesia' explodes many of the essentialist notions we take for granted. He argues that disgust (despite its etymology) is not primarily about taste. It is more about touch and smell, and the divisions of inner and outer, self and other. In this regard, 'Darwin's Disgust' is particularly illuminating in its assessment of the sensory and social bases of the Freudian myth which holds that the rise of civilization produces a diminution in importance of olfactory stimuli. With respect to our topic of 'the aestheticization of everyday life' Miller's essay reminds us that we need not be pleased with everything we perceive. We may also, at times, be disgusted.

Notes

1. Thus, for example, Friesen documents Thoreau's indebtedness to the English landscape painter and writer Gilpin.

2. Put another way, 'late' capitalism is much more, than a 'civilization of the image,' and it cannot be theorized adequately without account being taken of its increasingly multisensory materiality. The difficulty here stems from the sensory bias intrinsic to the very notion of 'theorization': theory comes from the Greek *theorèin* meaning 'to gaze upon.' It is high time for all of the senses (not solely vision) to become 'directly in their practice theoreticians' (the young Marx cited and discussed in Howes 2003: 238n3, 239n6).

3. It is particularly instructive to read Serres' undoing of sensory boundaries in light of Carla Mazzio's account in Chapter 5 of early modern attempts to divide and hierarchize the sensorium.

4. For example, Stallybrass and White (1986) bring out how the exclusion of the grotesqueness of peasant sensibilities (as expressed in Carnival) helped to shore up bourgeois identity, but also (precisely on account of its exclusion) became an object or site of (sublimated) desire. To explore the modulation of desire is not the same as dealing squarely with the materiality of disgust as Miller does.

Bibliography

Baudrillard , J. (1983), *Simulations*, New York: Semiotext(e).

Benjamin, W. (1973), *Charles Baudelaire: A Lyric Poet in the Era of High Capitalism*, trans. H. Zohn, London: New Left Books.

Calvino, I. (1985), *Mr Palomar*, trans. W. Weaver, London: Secker & Warburg.

Cavell, R. (2002), *McLuhan in Space: A Cultural Geography*, Toronto: University of Toronto Press.

Clarke, D.B. (2003), *The Consumer Society and the Postmodern City*, London: Routledge.

Connor, S. ([1989] 1997), *Postmodernist Culture: An Introduction to Theories of the Contemporary*, Oxford: Blackwell.

Eagleton, T. (1990), *The Ideology of the Aesthetic*, Oxford: Blackwell.

Featherstone, M. (1991), *Consumer Culture and Postmodernism*, London: Sage.

Friesen, V.C. (1984), *The Spirit of the Huckleberry: Sensuousness in Henry David Thoreau*, Edmonton: University of Alberta Press.

Frye, N. (1957), *Anatomy of Criticism*, Princeton: Princeton University Press.

Gregor, M.J. (1983), 'Baumgarten's Aesthetica,' *Review of Metaphysics*, 37: 357–85.

Howes, D. (2003), *Sensual Relations*, Ann Arbor: University of Michigan Press.

Jameson, F. (1991), *Postmodernism, or, The Cultural Logic of Late Capitalism*, Durham: Duke University Press.

Kant, I. (1951), *Critique of Judgment*, trans. J.H. Bernard, New York: Hafner.

Miller, W.I. (1987), *The Anatomy of Disgust*, Cambridge MA: Harvard University Press.

Postrel, V. (2003), *The Substance of Style: How the Rise of Aesthetic Value is Remaking Commerce, Culture, and Consciousness*, New York: HarperCollins.

Rée, J. (2000), 'The Aesthetic Theory of the Arts,' in P. Osborne (ed.), *From an Aesthetic Point of View: Philosophy, Art and the Senses*, London: Serpent's Tail, pp. 57–70.

Stallybrass, P. and White, A. (1986), *The Politics and Poetics of Transgression*, London: Methuen.

Turner, B.S. (1994), 'Introduction,' in C. Buci-Glucksmann (ed.), *Baroque Reason: The Aesthetics of Modernity*, London: Sage.

14

A Tonic of Wildness

Sensuousness in Henry David Thoreau

Victor Carl Friesen

When I see the sulphur lichens on the rails..., I feel like studying them again as a relisher or tonic, to make life go down and digest well, as we use pepper and vinegar and salads.

Henry David Thoreau

The railway was often admired in the nineteenth century for its thrilling speed. It took the great American naturalist Henry David Thoreau, to find 'a relisher and tonic' in the humble lichens growing on the rails. Thoreau's life as a woodsman, in fact, is permeated by his desire to drink in and drench himself with the refreshing vitality of the natural world. In the fulfillment of this desire all sensory phenomena may act as food and drink for a parched spirit. Thoreau (1906, VIII: 496) writes that: 'A man should feed his senses with the best that the land affords.' The best, however, does not mean luxurious fare, but 'what his senses hourly perceive,' in the 'every-day phenomena' of a life in tune with nature. From these he derives his 'satisfaction' (Thoreau 1906, XIV: 204). The acuity of Thoreau's senses as they perceive such phenomena and his pervasive use of each sense shows just how satisfactory such a life can be.

This sensory acuity is manifest in Thoreau's description of the subtle blending of waning sunlight and evening moonlight as the latter, 'shedding the softest imaginable light,' gains prominence with the end of day. 'What an immeasurable interval there is,' he writes, 'between the first tinge of moonlight which we detect, lighting with mysterious, silvery, poetic light the western slopes, like a paler grass, and the last wave of sunlight on the eastern slopes! It is wonderful how our senses ever span so vast an interval,

251

how from being aware of one we become aware of the other' (Thoreau 1906, VIII: 284).

This last sentence hints at three factors which inform Thoreau's sensory awareness. First, we might ordinarily assume that the phenomenon of changing light is strictly a matter of vision. Thoreau, however, speaks of 'senses' spanning the interval and elsewhere tells how the non-visual senses 'serve, and escort, and defend [sight]' (Thoreau 1958: 165). Here he detects the changes in light not only through the eye but through the ear as well, for 'already the crickets chirp to the moon a different strain' (Thoreau 1906, VIII: 284). Secondly, his perception throughout the 'interval' seems attentive and continuous. He disciplines himself to sense all that he can. 'Objects are concealed from our view,' he writes elsewhere, 'not so much because they are out of the course of our visual ray... as because there is no intention of the mind and eye toward them' (Thoreau, XVII: 285). Thirdly, he says that awareness of one phenomenon prompts his awareness of another. He may mean that one phenomenon accentuates the other by contrast – however slight the difference may be in this instance of sunlight and moonlight. Or he may mean that his being aware of the first phenomenon causes him to anticipate the second. He is ready to perceive it. Both effects are important to his sensuous approach to nature.

Many times Thoreau refers to the acuteness of his senses in terms of his anticipation and/or training. Consider his visual sense first. While in the Maine woods, he notes that the river he is on is an inclined plane, for he observes the waterline against the shores. His companion does not perceive the slope, we are told, not having Thoreau's experience as a surveyor. The very last entry in the *Journal*, made when Thoreau was already dying of tuberculosis, continues in a similar vein. He notices furrows made by the rain, 'all... perfectly distinct to an observant eye, and yet could easily pass unnoticed by most' (Thoreau 1906, XX: 346). But he also has eyesight acute in itself. In the Maine woods he sees a dragonfly half a mile distant; at Walden Pond he sees a water bug dimple the surface a quarter mile away. Sensitive to color, he can detect sassafras from as great a distance as half a mile because of its peculiar orange-scarlet tint. And one winter day, in mid-afternoon, he discerns a star in the skies overhead. Truly he has said that his eyes are flocks, roaming about the far mountains and sky and feeding on them.

Thoreau's sense of hearing is no less acute than his sense of sight – and for similar reasons. He has trained his ears both to distinguish slight sounds – he hears not only the cluck after a whippoorwill's note, but as well a fly-like buzzing – and to be anticipatory of them. Thus he has no need to go to the world of fine arts for music but can hear music in the simplest sounds, from the humming of telegraph wires to the clicking of oarlocks. Even the silence of night is to him audible and 'something positive.' 'It is musical and thrills me,' he writes (Thoreau 1906, X: 471–2). (There is a suggestion here too of hearing celestial sounds; see further Friesen 1984: chapter 7.)

The acuity of Thoreau's other senses is also noteworthy. His sense of smell, by his own account, is a much perfected sense, akin to that of an animal. When, for instance, he lands on an island in the Sudbury River, he notices at once the scent of wilted leaves. That he chooses to record this one sensation shows how significant it must be to him. Similarly he *smells* the first appearance of muskrats in the spring and, on another occasion, detects a fox's scent from a trail that must have been at least 12 hours old.

While Thoreau (1906, II: 241) calls the sense of taste 'commonly gross,' it is central to his appreciation of nature. On his walks Thoreau is constantly nibbling from the plants about him and making comparisons. The sensitivity of his palate to the gustatory nuances of the forest is maintained by his customary diet of simple foods, which keep his taste unjaded. The sense of touch, in turn, is continually stimulated by Thoreau's interaction with the natural environment of woods, waters, and winds. When climbing a hill, he detects the different temperatures of the air strata he passes through, and on a hill itself he suggests that he feels even the 'atoms' (Thoreau 1906, VII: 13) of wind, that is, its minute constituents, touching his cheek. He writes elsewhere: 'My body is all sentient. As I go here or there, I am tickled by this or that I come in contact with, as if I touched the wires of a battery. I can generally recall – have fresh in my mind – several scratches last received. These I constantly recall to mind, reimpress, and harp upon' (Thoreau 1906, XIV: 44).

If his body is all sentient, Thoreau does attach some superiority to one of the senses – the sense of sight. He holds it foremost because with it he can detect color and form. It is color that stains the windows in the cathedral of his world (Thoreau 1906, IX: 442). He finds it the 'more glorious' to live in his native Concord because one of its birds, the common blue jay, is 'so splendidly painted' (Thoreau 1906, XVII: 319). His heart leaps up at the sight of a rainbow; he devotes a separate essay to the beauty of trees in autumn. In the *Journal* he is enchanted by the colors of the wood duck: 'What an ornament to a river to see that glowing gem floating in contact with the water! As if the hummingbird should recline its ruby throat and its breast on the water. Like dipping a glowing coal in water! It so affected me' (Thoreau 1906, XIV: 17). It is the contrast here which enhances the picture for him.

Thoreau's response to warm colors, such as red, is somewhat different from his response to cool tints, such as blue. The associations he makes with each of them go beyond the actual functioning of his sense of sight to tell us something that he considers important – the effect of this one sense on his total being. While his associations are for the most part conventional, they are nonetheless highly personal because of his emotional involvement. Warm colors for him are summery and speak of the earth, and he appropriately reacts warmly to them, whereas cool colors tend to be wintry and associated with things of the heavens, something to be reflective about.

Of the warm colors, red is Thoreau's favorite: he loves to see any redness in vegetation (Thoreau 1906, VIII: 489). It is the color of colors, he says in 'Autumnal Tints,' and speaks to our blood. Red foliage, he writes, shows nature as being 'full of blood and heat and luxuriance' (Thoreau 1906, VIII: 490). While Thoreau delights in the feast for the eyes provided by reds, oranges and yellows, he realizes that they cannot be the staple of his diet. Thus he writes of yet another warm color, but one sober in its aspect: 'Brown is the color for me, the color of our coats and our daily lives, the color of the poor man's loaf. The bright tints are pies and cakes, good only for October feasts' (Thoreau 1906, XVIII: 97–8).

Thoreau is also rapturous at times about cool blues and azures, but these tints, found predominantly in the sky above and in the waters which reflect it, are often wedded to meditation. These colors suggest a limitless space to Thoreau and serve as a stimulus for far-reaching thoughts. For example, the sight of his 'elysian blue' shadow on snow causes Thoreau to reflect about the nature of his own being: 'I am turned into a tall blue Prussian from my cap to my boots, such as no mortal dye can produce, with an amethystine hatchet in my hand. I am in raptures at my own shadow. What if the substance were of as ethereal a nature?' (Thoreau 1906, XIV: 115).

In recording the colors of his world, Thoreau notices what would be commonly overlooked by others. He sees the gem-like play of colors of fungi on a stump and notices too the irridescence left on a patch of water by a decaying sucker. To him the irridescence is like the 'fragments of a most wonderfully painted mirror' (Thoreau 1906, XIV: 343) and he leans over the edge of his boat, admiring it as much as he would a sunset sky or rainbow. Often he goes out of his way – indeed such going becomes his way of life – to notice particular colors in nature. He walks an extra half-mile to examine the changing colors of a tree; he wades through cold water in order to gaze at cranberries. But he seems to go out of his way most frequently in winter when the landscape is less vivid than in other seasons. One day, with a temperature of six below zero, finds him pacing up and down a road, waiting until the light is right: he wants to observe the pinkish cast on a snowy hill at sunset. After the moment has passed, he discerns as well a delicate violet tinge on the hill (Thoreau 1906, XVII: 395–6). Another evening he notices the rose color of the snow and '*at the same time*' (he italicizes this last phrase) notices a greenish hue in nearby ice, having, as he says, been looking out for such coincidence (Thoreau 1906, XIX: 61).

Thoreau's eye is as sensitive to forms and outlines in nature as to colors. He detects the earth's muscles in leafless tree limbs (Thoreau 1906, XVII: 260) and in firm, curving beaches (Thoreau 1906, XVIII: 75), while flowing waters and swaying foliage are the wrists and temple of the earth (Thoreau 1906, XIX: 138). He can feel their pulse with his eye. 'A man has not seen a thing who has not felt it,' he says (Thoreau 1906, XIX: 160). Seeing for him becomes something which is not distinct from either outward (tactile) feeling or from inward feelings. Both kinds of feeling are evident when he devotes three pages of 'Autumnal Tints' to the form of an oak leaf. 'What a wild and pleasing outline, a combination of graceful curves and angles!' (Thoreau 1906, V: 279) he exclaims over it. He first treats the leaf anatomically, referring to its broad sinuses or long lobes. But his enthusiasm over its form prompts him to find another descriptive image, this one geographical. The leaf is an island or a pond with rounded bays and pointed capes, and he becomes a mariner at sight of it. It is like a miniature Walden Pond, whose scalloped shoreline he also loves to follow with his eye (Thoreau 1906, II: 206).

When leaves are more distant, that is, still on a tree above him, Thoreau is pleased to see their shapes enhanced because of the bright sky behind them. The leaves then 'grasp... skyey influences' (Thoreau 1906, V: 278) or stamp their meaning 'in a thousand hieroglyphics on the heavens' (Thoreau 1906, I: 166). The outline of them gains in richness for him as the number of interstices increases through which the light straggles. More border is thus provided along which his eye can travel with what amounts really to a caress. Pines, he can say, make a 'graceful fringe to the earth' (Thoreau 1906, I: 167), while elsewhere he notes that his eyes 'nibble the piny sierra which makes the horizon's edge, as a hungry man nibbles a cracker' (Thoreau 1906, XVII: 450).

The features of a natural scene often seem to Thoreau like the components of a picture, and this awareness in turn affects how he will continue to see the scene. The atmosphere and trees present not a kind of screen to gaze at but the glass and frame of a painting. In *A Week* he says at one place that the 'air was so elastic and crystalline – that it had the same effect on the landscape that a glass has on – a picture, to give it an ideal remoteness and perfection' (Thoreau 1906, I: 45). And in 'Autumnal Tints' he refers to the sunset painted daily behind a frame of elms, making a picture worthier than any found in a gallery.

An eighteenth century landscape painter and writer, William Gilpin, whose works on Picturesque beauty Thoreau read, probably caused Thoreau to look for certain beauties in nature that he might not otherwise have noticed so soon (for a discussion of Gilpin's ideas on the Picturesque see Barbier 1963: 98–147). Thoreau, wishing to make his visual sense serve him to the fullest, was only too willing to learn from other observers. Thus he writes to a friend that Gilpin's books have been his thunder lately. After reading the artist's *Remarks on Forest Scenery* (1791) he writes in his *Journal*, 'The mist to-day makes those near distances which Gilpin tells of' (Thoreau 1906, IX: 444), or 'Thinking of the value of the gull to the scenery of our river in spring... , [I find that] Gilpin says something to the purpose' (Thoreau 1906, IX: 416). It is as if Thoreau were looking at the landscape afresh, through the eyes of a painter. In another journal entry Thoreau's description of an autumn scene (Thoreau 1906, XX: 89) is reminiscent of a Gilpin painting: a shining stream framed by shrubbery, the horizon blurred by smoke, clouds billowing upwards, man and his works seeming insignificant against a panorama of nature. All this is seen by him in a downward perspective from a railroad causeway.

It should not be thought that Thoreau is here permeated by aesthetic ideas of the late eighteenth century. For one thing, he, as sensuous man, generally wants to be central (and significant) in the richly satisfying world about him. He is unlike, then, another British artist of the period, Richard Wilson, whose style is similar to Gilpin's in depicting grand scenery, or the nature poet James Thomson, whose *The Seasons* (1730), portrays man as inconsequential before the forces of nature. If anything, Thoreau is akin to Jane Austen, who in *Sense and Sensibility* (1811), dramatizes the pros and cons of Picturesque ideas and clearly speaks for the gentle and the familiar in landscape rather than the 'sublime.' According to Edmund Burke's *The Sublime and the Beautiful* (1756), the sublime features of nature, those of great magnitude, produce sensations of pain and terror. Influential artists like Gilpin were preoccupied in experiencing such scenes and having viewers experience them in their paintings. But Thoreau's one excursion into sublime scenery, up Mount Katahdin, makes him prefer his own native Concord, although he does not regret the climb (see further Friesen 1984: chapter 3).

For another thing, Thoreau is not concerned primarily with a romantically Picturesque view but with a view of as much nature, in all its variety, as possible. At Walden he stands on tiptoe when looking at his horizons. Gilpin looks at nature with only the eye of an artist, and Thoreau criticizes him for doing so. Nature is more than near distances and side screens and backdrops to Thoreau. It is a living thing, like himself, which he wants to respond to with his whole being, not just with the sense of sight but with the other senses as well.

If Thoreau does not already see acutely enough, the hearing of a cricket, he tells us, whets his eyes. Sound to him can be as exhilarating as color and form. It is 'coincident with an ecstasy' (Thoreau, 1906, XII: 39), and he devotes a whole chapter to it in *Walden*. Thoreau himself is musical. He plays the flute and sometimes sings as he walks outdoors. He says in another context that which is still applicable here: 'Man's progress through nature should have an accompaniment of music. It relieves the scenery, which is seen through a subtler element, like a very clear morning air in autumn. Music wafts me through the clear, sultry valleys' (Thoreau 1906, VII: 316).

The dominant sound described in Chapter IV of *Walden* is that of the locomotive. It seems 'natural' in that its whistle sounds like the scream of a hawk. Yet the whistle's regularity – the farmers set their clocks by it – gives it away. The train is not natural, and Thoreau distrusts it. Its time is unlike the perfect time of the music box, the regular measure of which tells of 'its harmony with itself' (Thoreau 1906, VII: 316). The locomotive lacks this lofty harmony. Its sound does not come from God, and only its smoke *goes* to heaven – the cars are going to Boston. Thoreau therefore changes his image from that of a hawk to that of a horse, the usual iron horse in this case. The horse, we know, has been trained to harness in order to perform hard, routine work. Thoreau admires the purposefulness of his horse-locomotive, but he is ambivalent about the sounds it emits. Its 'snort like thunder' and its 'blowing off the superfluous energy' (Thoreau 1906, II: 129, 130) seem heroic, while its 'freight' of sounds – bleating of calves and hustling of oxen – give one the sensation of a pastoral valley going by. But he knows that this machine is whirling away the once prevalent pastoral life, and he does not want his ears spoiled by its hissing. Better to 'thrust an avenging lance between the ribs of the bloated pest' (Thoreau 1906, II: 214), he says later in *Walden*.

Alongside the railroad running past Walden Pond is the telegraph line. From this invention of man Thoreau hears sounds with which he is in sympathy, for nature plays the tune. The wires humming in the wind are his aeolian harp. 'Thus I make my own use of the telegraph,' he says, 'without consulting the directors' (Thoreau 1906, VIII: 498). He listens directly to the humming of the wires, analysing the sound, noting that the loudest volume occurs near a post, where the wires are tautest. Or he applies his ear to the post itself and hears the hum 'within the entrails of the wood' (Thoreau 1906, IX: 11). Then it seems as if every pore of the wood is seasoned with music. He compares the sound to that of an organ in a cathedral. As with sight, the auditory sensation is also something he can feel, but here he need not speak metaphorically. The ground at his feet does vibrate: the latent music of the earth, he says, has found vent in the telegraph harp.

Thoreau is often intoxicated with purely natural sounds, such as bird songs. He makes special trips to various parts of Concord township to hear them – for example, the singing of warblers in Holden Swamp. But it is the strain of the wood thrush that prompts this outburst: 'I would be drunk, drunk, drunk, dead drunk to this world for it forever' (Thoreau 1906, XII: 39). It is, he says, a fountain of youth to all his senses and his favorite among bird songs. This accolade is noteworthy when we realize that the journal entries for most Aprils tend to be largely a record of his listening to the many spring birds.

As with his sense of sight, Thoreau in his hearing responds eagerly to 'coarser' stimuli. A rooster's crowing, he thinks, is 'the most remarkable of any bird's.' He imagines hearing this bird in its wild state, its call 'clear and shrill for miles over the resounding earth, drowning the feebler notes of other birds, – think of it!' (Thoreau 1906, II: 141). The cawing of a crow to him is 'delicious' (Thoreau 1906, XIII: 112), while the calling of a loon is so thrilling that he could lie awake for hours listening to it when camping in the Maine Woods. He thinks that the call of this loon is superior to one heard back in Concord because here the call's wildness is enhanced by the surrounding scenery.

How Thoreau's other senses are fed, we see, affects his auditory response, for he is not only hearing the bird's voice but sensing the 'voice' of nature as well. Thus when he hears the doleful notes of owls in his own native

Concord, he thinks the sound 'admirably suited to swamps and twilight woods' (Thoreau 1906, II: 139), for it expresses the meaning of nature then and there. He loves to hear their wailing. Nature itself is but a musical instrument, and the birds and other creatures only touch the stops. Its sounds are the language spoken without metaphor (Thoreau 1906, II: 123), a language which speaks directly to his sense of hearing. The sounds are pleasing in themselves, but because of their involvement with the whole of nature, they also have pleasing associations. A nuthatch's nasal call becomes 'the handle by which [his] thoughts [take] firmly hold on spring' (Thoreau 1906, XVIII: 15), for instance.

Other pleasing sounds to Thoreau come from animals other than birds and even from inanimate nature. He is refreshed by the barking of a dog at night (he likes to bathe his being in those waves of sound), and by the trump of bullfrogs, which he celebrates in *Walden* (only here it is the frogs amidst their Stygian chorus who appear to be the ones intoxicated). Insects, too, come in for their round of praise. A mosquito's hum affects him like a trumpet; it speaks of the world's vigor and fertility. The creaking of crickets particularly pleases him because he refers to it continually. He describes it as the most earthy, the most eternal, 'the very foundation of all sound' (Thoreau 1906, VIII: 306) – reminding him once more that heaven is here on earth. All the earth is vibrant with music, and Thoreau has shown us indeed his 'appetite for sound' (Thoreau 1906, XVI: 227).

Thoreau holds that the sense of smell is the most reliable of the senses. And there are odors enough in nature to remind him of everything even if he had no other senses. In spring all nature is a bouquet held to his nose, in fall a spray of fragrant dried herbs. He smells what he calls the 'general fragrance of the year' (Thoreau 1906, XIII: 361) and is almost afraid that he will trace the fragrance to one plant. Occasionally when he perceives a singular scent that cannot identify, he walks about smelling each likely plant in an effort to find the source of the fragrance, while at the same time not neglecting the aroma of 'old acquaintances' (Thoreau 1906, XV: 5) which grow rankly nearby. Such a process leads him to the giant hyssop while in Minnesota. In Concord the process does fail once, with regard to a sweet new fragrance from a flooded grassland, but his satisfaction in trying to trace it to the wild grape, the eupatorium, and even the fresh grass is worthwhile in itself.

Thoreau is always on the trail of some scent, as his frequent hikes to Wheeler Meadow attest, and remembering all these fragrances is a balm to his mind. Whether he detects 'earthiness' (Thoreau 1906, X: 40) or a 'certain volatile and ethereal quality' (Thoreau 1906, V: 295), he feels refreshed and expanded. The scents that might be termed ethereal are those like the fragrance emitted by the wild apple blossom. Thoreau esteems this flower for its copious scent and notes that the resulting apples are 'worth more to scent your handkerchief with than any perfume which they sell in the shops' (Thoreau 1906, V: 295). He perceives that another fruit, the

wild grape, perfumes a river for a mile of its length, and he takes home
bunches to scent his room. But it is the more pungent odors of nature that
most intoxicate him. ('Intoxicate' is one of Thoreau's favorite words when
he is describing how natural phenomena affect his senses.) The fragrance
of evergreen woods he finds 'bracing' (Thoreau 1906, III: 17), and making
up his bed while camping in Maine he spreads spruce boughs particularly
thick about the shoulders the better to smell the scent. Another evergreen,
a club moss, becomes his smelling bottle. He is constantly bruising plants
to gratify his sense of smell: hickory buds for their spicy fragrance; sassafras
for its odor of lemon; black-cherry leaves for their rummy scent; pennyroyal
for its medicinal aroma. This last plant he stuffs into his pockets to scent
him thoroughly.

Even the vile odor of skunk cabbage invigorates Thoreau: 'It is a reminiscence of immortality borne on the gale'(Thoreau 1906, VIII: 5). This belief,
we find, is echoed in his eulogy to the dicksonia fern:

> To my senses [it] has the most wild and primitive fragrance, quite unalloyed
> and untamable, such as no human institutions give out, – the early morning
> fragrance of the world, antediluvian, strength and hope imparting. They who
> scent it can never faint. It is ever a new and untried field where it grows, and
> only when we think original thoughts can we perceive it. (Thoreau 1906, XVIII:
> 349–50)

His response here is similar to what his ear tells him about the telegraph
harp or what his eye says concerning the color red. All speak to the primal
man, to his blood and nerves, because what they say antedates time. These
sensations were already present when the world was a continuous morning
and man was youthful and heroic. So, Thoreau believes, man can be again – in
this case, if he smell the fern. His sense of smell will have proved 'oracular'
(Thoreau 1906, X: 40), and the world will be new to him.

If Thoreau smells every plant that he picks, he also tastes every berry that
he passes by. While Thoreau notes sensations of taste less often than those
of the other senses, his occasional walking companion, Ellery Channing
(1873), still concluded that Thoreau had an edible religion. What Channing
probably had in mind was Thoreau's *devotion* to sampling through taste
almost everything that grows, his *reverence* of this activity. When Thoreau is
in the Maine woods, for example, he finds that the stem of a round-leaved
orchis tastes like a cucumber. One gets the impression that he has already
tasted the other parts of the plant as well. While there too he engages in
digging up lily roots (which means a great deal of slow, grubbing work amidst
hordes of mosquitoes) and reports that the roots raw taste like green corn.
The white froth oozing from pitch pines, on the other hand, has no taste at
all, he says. On another occasion he taps an oak in late October to see why
this particular tree gets its autumn colors so late. He finds it full of sap and

immediately tastes it: 'It has a pleasantly astringent, acorn-like taste, this strong oak-wine' (Thoreau 1906, V: 282).

But Channing's statement is true in another way. Tasting (and eating and drinking) to Thoreau is religious if rightly conducted. By distinguishing the true savor of food and not being grossly concerned with the metabolic needs of the body (certainly Thoreau's position as he samples nature's variety), he is 'relate[d]... to Nature, ma[d]e... her guest and entitle[d]... to her regard and protection' (Thoreau 1906, XI: 331). Nature takes on divinity, and eating becomes 'a sacrament, a method of communion, and ecstatic exercise' (Thoreau 1906, VII: 372). For this reason he can, as he says in *Walden*, be inspired through the palate. His edible religion transmutes what might ordinarily be sensuality into an inspiriting sensuousness. He writes in the *Journal*: 'After I had been eating... simple, wholesome, ambrosial fruits on [a] hillside, I found my senses whetted, I was young again, and whether I stood or sat I was not the same creature' (Thoreau 1906, X: 219).

Most of what Thoreau drinks and eats may be termed simple and often ambrosial. For a drink, we discover in *Walden*, he prefers not a cup of coffee, which would dash the hopes of a morning, but rather water. Even of water that has not yet settled, the kind he is offered at John Field's shanty, he drinks a hearty draught, while 'excluding the motes with a skillfully directed undercurrent' (Thoreau 1906, II: 299). In *A Week* he tells of lying down flat in order to drink 'pure, cold springlike water' from horses' hoofprints (Thoreau 1906, I: 194). Again, as with his other senses, natural associations enhance his sensuous response. A more ambrosial drink for him is offered him while in the Maine woods, a 'beer' made from the sap of evergreens::

> It was as if we sucked at the very teats of Nature's pine-clad bosom in these parts, – the sap of all Millinocket botany commingled, – the topmost, most fantastic, and spiciest sprays of the primitive wood, and whatever invigorating and stringent gum or essence it afforded steeped and dissolved in it, – a lumberer's drink, which would acclimate and naturalize a man at once, – which would make him see green, and, if he slept, dream that he heard the wind sough among the pines. (Thoreau 1906, III: 30)

Here indeed is the tonic of wildness, spoken about in *Walden*.

With regard to food, Thoreau may be tempted to eat a wild animal (a woodchuck in *Walden*), but when he tries such tonic of wildness (some squirrels in *A Week*), he abandons it in disgust. He generally has a repugnance to the eating of meat because of what he calls its 'uncleanness' (Thoreau 1906, II: 237). Here it is not so much the actual taste he dislikes – when some strips of moose meat are wound on a stick and roasted over an open fire in the Maine woods, he pronounces the food 'very good' (Thoreau 1906, III: 317) – but the accompaniments of preparation, the skinning of the animal and cutting up of the meat. The soil and grease and gore are simply offensive to him. But there is another reason why he finds flesh distasteful. When he speaks of the 'small red bodies' of the squirrels (Thoreau 1906, I: 237) and of the 'naked red carcass' of a moose (Thoreau 1906, III: 128), he is sensing that these animals, stripped of their outward guise of fur, are fellow creatures to him. As the human race improves, he says in *Walden,* it will stop eating animals as surely as savage tribes in their improvement leave off cannibalism.

Thoreau's greatest taste, then, is for vegetable food. He can get his tonic of wildness by eating wild fruit, the food he writes most about. Although he finds chokecherries to be scarcely edible, he enjoys the acrid-sweet savor of acorns and tastes sand cherries 'out of compliment to nature' (Thoreau 1906, II: 126). The acidic flavor of cranberries he terms a sauce to life that no wealth can buy. It is 'refreshing, cheering, encouraging' and sets one 'on edge for this world's experiences' (Thoreau 1906, X: 36). His favorite among the wild fruits seems to be the wild apple, to which he devotes a separate essay, 'Wild Apples.' It is an 'ovation' (Thoreau 1906, XIII: 526) to taste one. He prefers to eat it out of doors, for not only does its savor seem to be increased then but the other senses are fed too: '[It] must be eaten in the fields, when your system is all aglow with exercise, when the frosty weather nips your fingers, the wind rattles the bare boughs or rustles the few remaining leaves, and the jay is heard screaming around... Some of these apples might be labeled, "To be eaten in the wind"' (Thoreau 1906, V: 312).

The wind to Thoreau is a velvet cushion he likes to lean against. His sense of touch, thermal or tactile sensations, can never be sated. If the frosty weather bites one cheek, he turns the other; when the sun shines upon him, he 'bathes' (Thoreau, XI: 38) in its warm presence. He prefers the warmth coming directly from the sun and not by way of radiation from the earth because it is direct contact for which he wishes. At night he wades through lakes of cold air that collect in a low pasture as one might wade in a lake of water. Wading through real water, he finds it 'delicious' to 'let [his] legs drink [the] air' (Thoreau 1906, XVI: 349). He responds joyously to the touch of water as well, complaining only that he cannot seem to get wet through as he wishes. To him bathing means sensuous luxury: 'To feel the wind blow on your body, the water flow on you and lave you, is a rare physical enjoyment' (Thoreau X: 207). The effect is heightened because he feels in touch with the rest of nature too: a muskrat uses the same 'tub,' and a leaping fish dimples the surface of his bath water.

Another satisfaction that stems from bathing is the sensation that must follow: Thoreau rejoices to be wet so that he might be dried. Thus when he comes to a river while out hiking, he walks through, is dried by the sun and wind on the other side, and continues on. He says he would like to take endwise the rivers in his walks. That way, apparently, he would prolong the sensation of being wet and his anticipation of becoming dry. 'Pray what were rivers made for?' (Thoreau 1906, X: 202) he asks with regard to bathing.

But he does find another use which gratifies his sense of touch – boating. He describes the sensation in his *Journal*: 'The waves seem to leap and roll like porpoises,... and I feel an agreeable sense that I am swiftly gliding over and through them. It is pleasant, exhilarating, to feel the boat tossed up a little by them from time to time. Perhaps a wine-drinker would say it was like the effect of wine' (Thoreau 1906, XIV, 317). In *A Week* he says that undulation is the most ideal motion – yet another phenomenon to become intoxicated about.

On land, the kinesthetic element of Thoreau's sense of touch is emphasized. Not only does he perceive a kind of muscular movement in the earth, but he seems to participate in it. When he describes the earth in March as a great leopard lying out at length, 'drying her lichen and moss spotted skin in the sun' (Thoreau 1906, XVIII: 97), he suggests his own sensuous ease with the returning warm days. He does in fact describe this 'skin' as a fur rug spread to be reclined on. He could stroke this mossy sward, he says; 'it is so fair' (Thoreau 1906, XVIII: 97). There are other times when he *has* to stroke the sward, as it were, in order to find his way back to his hut at night. Then his feet feel the faint track he can not see while his hands feel the pine trees. This activity he describes as 'pleasant' (Thoreau, II: 187).

With regard to the vegetation covering the earth, Thoreau, in gratifying his sense of touch, actively seeks out sensuous experiences. His position now is somewhat different from being more-or-less passive when the wind blows at him or water washes over him. Direct contact means the constant handling of the plants he sees, smells, or tastes. He picks up acorns because they feel so glossy and plump. With wet and freezing fingers he feels amid the snow for the green radical leaves of the shepherd's purse. Or he writes his name in the hoary bloom covering thimbleberry shoots. Such bloom, he observes elsewhere, like our finest qualities, can be preserved only with delicate handling.

Thoreau realizes that a sensuous approach to nature demands that all senses must ever perceive in a fresh manner. With regard to sight, he knows that the time of day and the season of the year in which he looks at a particular phenomenon affect his perception of it. By letting an interval pass before confronting again this same phenomenon, he perceives some slight change in it. He becomes intimately acquainted with it, discerns its uniqueness. Thus he examines some aspect of nature in fair weather and foul – or better yet, as be says in *The Maine Woods*, is there while the change in weather occurs. The terrestrial browns, he finds, become '*glowing*' (Thoreau 1906, XVIII: 45) when it rains. He observes phenomena too under various conditions of light, noting the change in appearance. When he sees the grayish andromeda against the sun, for example, he discovers the shrub to be the 'ripest, red imbrowned color' and makes this note in his *Journal*: 'Let me look again at a different hour of the day, and see if it is really so' (Thoreau 1906, IX: 431). The seasonal changes are more striking, and even though expected, can still be truly an eyeopener: he writes that Flint's Pond in winter, once it is covered with snow, is so wide and strange that he can think of nothing but Baffin's Bay.

A change in vantage point is another way of gaining a fresh perception. By elevating his view, Thoreau, in 'Autumnal Tints,' finds that the forest becomes a garden. When he notices that the Concord River appears dark looking upstream and silvery bright looking downstream, he writes another memorandum to himself: '*Mem*. Try this experiment again; i.e., look not toward nor from the sun but athwart this line' (Thoreau 1906, IX: 394–5). And at Walden he inverts his head and notices that the surface of the pond resembles the finest thread of gossamer. (Emerson previously wrote of this kind of experiment in the 'Idealism' section of his essay on *Nature* [1903, I: 4].) Often his changes in perspective border on the infinitesimal. He says: 'It is only necessary to behold thus the least fact or phenomenon, however familiar, from a point a hair's breadth aside from our habitual path or routine, to be overcome, enchanted by its beauty' (Thoreau 1906, XIV: 44). By turning his head 'slightly' (Thoreau 1906, V: 262), he sees the foliage of a maple appear to be flurries of snow, stratified by a driving wind.

Thoreau may also look narrowly through his eyelashes to see the landscape as an Impressionist painter might, or he may look above the object in question and see, as he says, with the under part of his eye. With this latter technique a stubble field in the light of a setting winter sun appears brighter than usual. He thus gains a fresh impression with what he elsewhere calls a sauntering of the eye rather than by a looking directly at an object. Similarly, a reflection in the water presents him with a new picture because he seems to see from all those many points on the surface of the water from which objects are reflected. A certain oak, for instance, looks greenish-yellow standing before some woods. Its reflection, however, is black and is seen not against woods but a clear whitish sky. The water permits him to see the tree from below and at the same time alters the coloring. He tells us in another instance that he gains 'myriad eyes' (Thoreau 1906, VIII: 253), while the contrast of the actual scene with its 'rhyme' (Thoreau 1906, IX: 403) in the water enhances both scenes for him.

Echoes are to the ear what reflections are to the eye and assist the sense of hearing to perceive in a fresh manner as well. An echo presents Thoreau with a new sound since the original sound has been transcribed through 'woodland lungs' (Thoreau 1906, VIII: 81). Again he notes the contrast, this time between the original sound and the accompanying echoes. At a lake in the Maine woods he notices that the echoes of a loon's laugh one morning are actually louder than the bird's call. The bird, he discovers, happens to be in an opposite bay under a mountain, and the sounds reflect like light from a concave mirror. Thoreau's position makes him the focus. Other contrasts in sound leading to a new perception can be obtained deliberately. For example, he submerges his head under water and then raises it to hear again the same sounds of nature but as if for the first time. Sometimes, he gains a fresh impression when he is not listening for any sound at all but has it break into his thoughts. This method may be termed a sauntering of his ear. As with sight, a fuller perception of a phenomenon occurs when he is outdoors to hear it at different times of day, at different times of year. At night, sounds seem amplified, because winds are usually calm; and in winter, sounds become clear and bell-like, having 'fewer impediments [in the landscape] to make them faint and ragged' (Thoreau 1906, V: 166).

As with sight and sound, so it is with Thoreau's other senses in trying to perceive in a fresh manner; he smells plants before and after a rain and in various stages of growth; he tastes wild apples in autumn and in winter after they have been frozen; he gauges the sun's warmth on his back during a winter walk and during a summer stroll. Each contrast amounts to a new sensation. He is always experimenting with his reception of sense data and thereby gratifying more richly each of his five senses.

Bibliography

Barbier, C.P. (1963), *William Gilpin: His Drawings, Teaching, and Theory of the Picturesque*, Oxford: Clarendon.

Channing, W.E. (1873), *Thoreau: The Poet Naturalist*, Boston: Roberts Brothers.

Emerson, R.W. ([1863] 1903), *The Complete Works of Ralph Waldo Emerson*, vols I–XII, Centenary Edition, Boston: Houghton Mifflin.

Thoreau, H.D. (1906), *The Writings of Henry David Thoreau*, vols. I–XX, Walden Edition, Boston: Houghton Mifflin.

—— (1958), *Consciousness in Concord: The Text of Thoreau's Hitherto "Lost Journal" (1840–41)*, ed. P. Miller, Boston: Houghton Mifflin.

15

Volatile Effects

Olfactory Dimensions of
Art and Architecture

Jim Drobnick

'Volatile effects' is a phrase utilized by Walter Pater in his dismissal of architecture from the realm of the aesthetic. He postulated that architecture, as the most concrete and utilitarian of arts, could not evoke the subtleties of the human spirit; rather, it could only present an artistic sensibility via oblique traces and ethereal suggestions: 'Architecture which begins in a practical need, can only express by vague hint or symbol the spirit or mind of the artist... [T]hese spiritualities, felt rather than seen, can but lurk about architectural form as volatile effects, to be gathered from it by reflection' (quoted in Vidler 1992: 60).

Contrary to Pater's denial of architecture's artistic potential, I would like to appropriate and rehabilitate such 'lurking' sensations, 'vague hints' and 'volatile effects' as precisely the terms that can be employed to describe an olfactory approach to architecture. For Pater, these effects were more metaphorical than real, gathered as it were by reminiscence and reflection. In contrast, the volatile architectures I will discuss below are vividly sensorial and experiential – they are literally fragrant, pungent or reeking. The aromatic dimension of buildings is one that has been for the most part neglected in architectural theory, yet the effects created by odoriferous materials, ventilated scents and other wafting perceptions can significantly influence one's experience of a structure. It would be simplistic to merely celebrate the inclusion of odors as some kind of corrective to the inodorate state of architectural thinking, I will instead outline a few of the issues and problematics of smell, art and architecture.

Across a diversity of sites – from galleries, museums and site-specific installations to office buildings, theme-park entertainments and the public space of the city – the presence of smell has multiple significations. In recent years, artistic practices have set up a series of charged relations between olfaction and architecture that force a rethinking of the sense of smell as well as of the paradigm of the white cube and a dynamic of display that is purely visual.[1] The anosmia of the white cube, and of architecture in general, have led artists to intervene and transform the pristine features of certain spaces through the use of aromatic substances to destabilize their geometric sanctity and diffuse fragrances into the transcendental air. I will first examine the inodorateness of the white cube and the ideology implicit in the processes of reduction (sanitization, streamlining, deodorization) that have contributed to its development as the paragon of exhibition display. The second section explores the use of smell as a self-conscious and strategic addition to the 'museum atmosphere,' especially in postmodern, entertainment-oriented museum venues. The phenomenology of architecture constitutes the third section, and here I consider how scents can be a central element in revitalizing an attention to materiality and the lived experience of buildings. The final section discusses volatile artworks that provoke olfactory reconceptions of architecture and space.

Anosmic Cubes

The 'white cube,' despite numerous challenges and critiques, remains the paradigmatic architectural form for experiencing contemporary art. Given the obviousness of the white cube's function as a 'visual machine' (Celant 1996), its inodorateness hardly requires mentioning. In contemporary art-conservation discourse, for example, smells are pathologized as a form of pollution or symptomatic of pests, a threat to both the collection and personnel, thus rendering olfactory artworks as immediately suspicious if not dangerous.

The link between the anosmia – or smell-lessness – of the white cube and discourses of hygiene has its roots in the deodorizing campaigns of the late eighteenth century, and this 'olfactory intolerance' has continued in earnest ever since, widening its scope from urban and public spaces to interior and domestic domains (see Corbin 1986). Despite the vigilant removal of smells, however, no place is truly inodorate. Brian O'Doherty's famous comparison of the white cube to other examples of ascetic architectures in the religious, legal and scientific realms is a telling one (O'Doherty 1986: 14). While the buildings that house churches, courtrooms and laboratories may share with the white cube a certain transcendence, formality or efficiency, they also flaunt extremely distinctive olfactory identities (at least in my experience: incense, leather, formaldehyde).

Deodorization is thus always incomplete and imperfectly realized – places still have characteristic smells. The hygienic impulse operative here, then, is one that exists at the level of discourse and ideology, but which is only partially enactable at the level of practical experience. The white cube often bears the vaporous exudations of newly finished paintings, varnished woodwork or latexed walls, as well as other odoriferous traces pertaining to building maintenance and use. Such smells even enjoy a 'marked' aspect, for they signify that the space is clean, refreshed and ready for the next exhibition.[2] White paint, smooth surfaces and geometric perfection point not only to an intolerance of the olfactory, but to a distrust of the organic, of the sensual, of anything alluding to the realities and controversies of the external world.

The white cube also functions as a disciplinary technology, a means to compartmentalize, isolate and train perception. It is, as Barbara Kirshenblatt-Gimblett (1991: 416) notes, an apparatus for 'single-sense epiphanies.' In many ways, viewing behavior at museums extends the 'civilizing process,' articulated by Norbert Elias (1994), since the arts have long been utilized as an arena for the development of manners. The result of this training is never simply to exercise or develop the body and its potential, but to produce what Tony Bennett (1995) calls 'prudential subjects.' Museums in the nineteenth century overtly acknowledged their goal of disciplining and disinfecting the subordinate classes. The imperative of sanitization was intended in both metaphorical and literal terms with regard to the bodies, minds and souls of the indigent, the working poor, recent immigrants and ethnically diverse populations. The rationale of hygiene as a tool for social engineering and/or exclusion is one that continues to this day; advocates for the homeless must continue to go to court to protect access to libraries and other public places.

Inodorateness is essential to the white cube's ability to assume a neutral status, and to its disassociation from the economic and social worlds. Being inodorate permits the white cube to define itself as a zero-degree status of display, the mythic fundament out of which art objects emerge *ex nihilo*. The olfactory nowhereness of the white cube justifies its authority and defends a pretense towards universality; for to express an identifiable odor would be to admit to particularized interests. As Christoph Grunenberg writes about the development of the Museum of Modern Art, the primary exemplar of this aesthetic: '[The white cube] liberated modern art from its common association with decadence, insanity, sensuality and feminine frivolity; simultaneously, it revealed the inherent masculinity and authoritarian character of formalist aesthetics' (1994: 205).

As much as the white cube is a haven from the chaos of the contemporary, industrial, cosmopolitan world and its hectic pace, a space isolated from social and political cares, protected from history, contingency and accountability, the inverse – i.e. the everyday – is positioned as pathological, dangerous, degenerate.

Museum Atmospheres

A curious development has been brewing recently regarding the inclusion of smell in the once sterilized realm of the museum. Articles in the popular press not only note olfactory absence, but make demands for its inclusion. Witness a reviewer's disappointment at the display of 1960s costumes and music memorabilia at the Rock and Roll Hall of Fame and Museum:

> Does this exhibit 'capture the spirit of the psychedelic era?' Hell no. This is a collection of historical objects in a museum. There's not a whiff of patchouli oil in the place. It smells like school. If you want to get an idea of what the psychedelic era was like, find a copy of Electric Music for the Mind and Body by Country Joe and The Fish, put *Section 43* on that dusty turntable in the corner, light some incense, turn out all the lights and set your mind to 'wander.' (Feniak 1997: A14)

And in a laudatory review of 'The American Lawn' at the Canadian Centre for Architecture, praises were heaped upon the innovative display technology, which engaged visitors by providing creative ways to see, touch, interact with and move around the exhibition – but mourned the absence of the smell of grass: 'Our suspicions that the museum experience can never truly simulate the real thing are confirmed, however: the fragrance that is so much a part of the "lawn experience" is missing' (Adams and Dyer 1998: J1–2).[3]

How should these comments be interpreted? Are they evidence of a nostalgia for times past so excessive that objects without the requisite immediacy frustrate more than satisfy? Does today's audience expect the museum to provide a sensorially complete experience – to counteract the anesthetized routine of everyday life? Is this the first intimation of a groundswell of support for something like a 'museum of smells' – as Andy Warhol (an enthusiastic perfume collector) envisioned 30 years ago?

Early in the twentieth century, Clive Bell derided the gloominess of a 'museum atmosphere' that enveloped works of art and asphyxiated visitors; 'Society,' he suggested, 'can do something for itself and for art by blowing out of the museums and galleries the dust of erudition and the stale incense of hero-worship' (Bell 1958: 173, 185). What Bell was advocating by means of olfactory reference was a revolution in museum philosophy, one that privileged the direct experience of emotion over that of scholarly sycophantism, that favored inclusivity and democratization over mediation and intimidation by experts, that permitted visitors to make their own decisions and judgments rather than accepting the dogma of tradition. How literally Bell meant his comments about ventilating and reodorizing the museum is a matter of debate, but in the 1980s, institutions as diverse as amusement parks, living history sites, heritage centers, science museums and other tourist attractions began to infuse their exhibitions with a wide variety of smells for reasons remarkably similar to the ones Bell articulated: to provide intense, immediate sensations, to make cultural experiences accessible to all, and to engage visitors in a personal, interactive manner.

Below are four perspectives on how postmodern museums utilize smell in their exhibitions: as heterogeneous stimulation, for sensory saturation, as an indicator of authenticity, and to engage with visitors on a more subtle perceptual level, one with implicit physiological or psychological effects.

Postmodern museums are defined against their modernist counterparts by virtue of their heterogeneity. That is, they participate in and exemplify the postmodern trend towards ambiguously defined spaces, ones that combine multiple functions and behaviors. The failure of the patrician class to preserve the museum as an elite, personal enclave has forced it to welcome a larger and more diverse public. Without abandoning the prestige of 'high' art, commercial, culinary and entertainment factors have been intertwined with what is traditionally deemed (or conceived of as) the 'aesthetic.' Museums have appropriated elements from theme parks, malls, boutiques, food courts and other types of cultural architectures. Given the indistinct boundaries and blurring of activities, aromas from in-house restaurants and cafés, perfumes from gift shops and other odors cross over the threshold and permeate the inner sanctum of artistic worship.

Heterosmia, a preponderance of smells from disparate sources, is my term to signify the condition of the postmodern museum. This is in contradistinction to the anosmic condition of the conventional museum. Heterosmia is not necessarily a condition sought out by postmodern art institutions; it is more an unintended result of the mixing and close juxtaposition of previously separated activities. Like the indoor mall, in which scents from a myriad of shops circulate and commingle, the heterosmic condition of the postmodern museum is one that has developed as a consequence of decisions about real estate, tourism, audience attendance and the desire to transform a specialized institution into a one-stop, multiple-interest entertainment package.

Advances in aroma diffusion technology and the chemistry of synthetic compounds have led to scent being one of *the* most fashionable additions to the museum's repertoire of effects. Synthetic scents imply a certain power over nature, over history, over the limitations of visual artifacts; they demonstrate an institution's hipness towards multimedia and sensory-saturated viewing environments; they prove a vivid marketing tool; and serve as a quick fix for the image of the museum so that, despite the multiple crises challenging its credibility, it can avert self-scrutiny and structural change.

The use of smell as part of the 'five senses experience' – or what I call *aromatopia* – gives the impression that an exhibition is a comprehensive, fully embodied encounter. Employed mostly by living museums and populist entertainments with a quasi-educational agenda, aromatopias draw upon the literary conception of the five senses (prevalent for the past two millennia) to convey the feeling of a complete, total, and all-encompassing nature. In some postmodern attractions, the rhetoric of total experience is nothing but a gimmick: a Madame Tussaud's exhibit supposedly featuring 'the smells of London' consists merely of theatrical smoke in the Chamber of Horrors. Other examples are better intentioned and more earnest. Living museums, for instance, seek to convey the full sensory experience of what it was like to live in a previous historical era: 'You can see and touch clothes as they were in the sixteenth century, you can eat Tudor food, you can listen to Tudor speech patterns, songs and music, use Tudor tools, walk around Tudor buildings, smell Tudor herbs' (Walsh 1992: 101). This multi-sensory strategy challenges the pedantry and dullness of the old-fashioned history museum, with its overreliance on text, images and decontextualized artifacts. Reliving the smells of a medieval town or pioneer homestead sets up expectations that require examination, as spectacle and myth collide with education and history. Like Foucault's 'heterotopia' (1986), aromatopias are sites of polyvalency where orthodox behaviors are shed and alternative possibilities temporarily inhabited. The intensity and diversity of smells demarcates the museum's experience as decidedly 'other' – one olfactorily coded to be outside the routine of the ordinary and everyday.

Perhaps the most problematic employment of smells is their use to artificially heighten the 'realism' of the viewing experience, affirm the 'authenticity' of objects, and secure the 'legitimacy' of the representations of other historical periods or cultures. Whether it is the Museum of the City of New York, where visitors experience facsimiles of historical documents, such as the Declaration of Independence, that are specially scented to smell 'old,' or the Smithsonian, where garbage and urine smells were diffused for an exhibit on the inner city, smells have been tactically employed to convey factuality, validity, the real (Eco 1986: 11; Smith 1989: 132). Alexander Wilson provides, for example, the following description of a Disney ride where synthesized odors reinforce the realism of virtual environments:

> [W]e sail past simulated examples of biotic communities, whole underground rooms like display cases in a natural history museum, only here when you cross the desert region a hot wind blows in your face, and the jungle smells of water and decaying plants. Around another bend in the river we reach the Family Farm, which in turn smells faintly of hay and cowshit. (Wilson 1993: 169)

Critiques of simulation and the hyperreal have proliferated in regards to audio and visual media, but little attention has been devoted to the synthetic, postmodern uses of smell (for a discussion of smell as a postmodern sense see Classen et al. 1994: 203–5). The discussion usually falls into two categories: the celebratory and the cynical. While glorifying rhetoric may be brought to task for its uncritical acceptance, negative readings of smell veer close to being backhanded apologies for visual dominance. For Kevin Walsh, the use of manufactured smells foregrounds a central problematic that, in essence, pertains to the use of smells to *represent* at all:

The decontextualizing of smells from an historical period and placement in a twentieth century tourist attraction seems highly dubious as each person visiting the centre will have a different perception or attitude towards a smell and it is quite likely that it will be very different from those held by the people who originally produced and lived with the smells. The problem is compounded by the fact that one begins to wonder if Victorian streets, Medieval universities and Viking villages were all steeped in the same, obviously-artificial, chemical-odor version of wet cats. (Walsh 1992: 112–13)

One can certainly fault profit-oriented museums for recycling the same olfactory sensations in dissimilar contexts, but at what point does this critique emerge from a latent bias against the olfactory? And to what degree is it a circuitous defense of ocularcentrism? It is inconsistent to single out smells just because they are artificially produced (that is, mediated), or variable in interpretation, and not also critique other museum information that is also mediated or variable; this would basically undermine the entire museological enterprise. The mutability of smell frustrates a quasi-authoritarian demand for the systematized deployment of 'correct' meanings and experiences. The distrust of the sensual has a long history in Western culture, a distrust that can be distilled into a contest between representational and presentational modes of information.

The argument against the use of synthesized rather than actual smells is stronger. Instead of confirming the authenticity of a certain experience, fake smells distort olfactory discrimination and sever the ability to connect odors to their natural sources (Damian and Damian 1995: 130). In the search for predictable, cost-effective exhibit aromas, the disciplining and training of the senses (presumably one of the museum's goals) is sacrificed.

Smells, however, can still serve as a strategic intervention. In contrast to the highly mediated, homogenized, simplified and commercialized use of artificial odors, the presentation of scent in a context-specific manner still holds a potential to reconfigure the museum experience. As museums shift away from basing their legitimation on master narratives and prescriptive interpretations, exhibits that include extra-visual sensory experiences grant heightened status to the subjective nature of knowledge production, and foreground experiences that are partial and uncertain. Authority and coherence are guaranteed not by collections and curatorial directives, but by each visitor's experience (MacDonald and Silverstone 1990). Physical engagement, argues Tracy Davis (1995), activates museumgoers to 'perform' rather than 'consume' the content; that is, visitors are inserted into that indeterminate domain where they must individually negotiate the tension between the museum's framing ideology and the immediacy of personal experience. Disparate sensory information may not easily coincide or harmonize, and indeed may foreground difference and contradiction – effecting a museum experience that is interrogative, temporal, pluralistic.

The featuring of smells and the full range of the senses in the museum undermines visual predominance not only on a perceptual level, but on a political one as well. Countering the primacy of the visual opens up the museum to behaviors, activities and identities that are not necessarily Western, privileged and masculine, and which fail to produce collectible artifacts. Marginalized, private or everyday experiences, such as those typically associated with women's domestic labor, can be given distinction and value (Porter 1996).

Other kinds of olfactory presences, such as those at the Holocaust Museum in Washington DC, provide compelling evidence that no text, image or audioguide is able to convey. As Davis (1995: 35–6) writes of the museum's pungent 'Shoe Exhibit': '[I]ntellectual horror at an already familiar narrative of recent genocide is compounded by olfactory confirmation in a gallery where the odor of decomposing shoe leather cannot be obliterated by even the most energetic air conditioner... [T]he shoes' odor invades visitors' bodies and in so doing cements concept to experience.'

This reinvigorated form of realism, whereby volatile particles of the exhibit literally bridge the gap between artifact and visitor, operates according to Davis (1995: 35–6) 'on a micro-sensory level in order to trigger a cognitive appreciation for ideas way beyond the reach of mere historical verisimilitude.' The fleshy smell of the shoe leather is a signifier in excess of language, one that is unexpected, unhyped. For exhibits to go beyond the visual presentation of objects, and engage with the other senses, is to venture into the dynamic realm of becoming rather than the static domain of being.

Mise-en-scents

Despite the best efforts of architects, urban planners and sanitary reformers over the last two centuries to evacuate all odors from the built environment, it is nevertheless a fact that every place bears an olfactory trace. Whether these mise-en-scents are the product of habitation and use (like cooking aromas or sweat), or result from the intentional use of fragrant materials (such as sandalwood in Indian temples), buildings exude a volatile identity that is impossible to capture in renderings or photography. Baudelaire called the smell of a room 'the soul of the apartment' (quoted in Corbin 1986: 169), and references to the olfactory nature of architecture are essential to defining the mood and emotional tenor of a place.

An interest in the phenomenology of the built environment arises when architecture is regarded not only as a representation of power or status, as a functionalist entity, as a rationalized project subservient to cost-effectiveness, or as a technological fetish – but as an intimate influence on the quality of lived experience. Phenomenological architects call for a pronounced intensification of presence – an embrace of buildings' potential to be mysterious, enlivening, contemplative. The sterility and lifelessness of modernist architecture, due in part to standardized methods of production, dulls or even negates the senses. A phenomenological focus seeks to reinvigorate architecture's ability to capture the poetry of existence, and hence re-establish its meaningfulness to everyday life, by cultivating diverse sensory experiences and a heightened sensitivity towards the immediate physicality of the world.[4]

It would be a mistake, however, to characterize the focus on the sensory as deriving from an anti-theoretical stance. Feminist, urban activist and non-Western critics all argue for a more enlightened engagement with affect and presence to, respectively, counteract masculinist ideals of spatial logic, ameliorate intimidating and alienating architecture, or provide alternatives to the Western predilection for artificial materials and ocularcentric experience. Deconstructive architecture, despite its reputation as a conceptual end-game, depends heavily on an enhanced phenomenological edge to achieve its transgressive effects. While the use of odors has yet to be a significant factor, the assault upon idealized geometries, the privileging of fragmented, heterogeneous construction, and the performative understanding of buildings as 'events' are principles consistent with an olfactory orientation. And architecture informed by the writings of Georges Bataille, Jacques Derrida and Gilles Deleuze and Félix Guattari – which is characterized by discourse on amorphousness, indeterminacy and states of becoming – implicitly lays the foundation for a theoretical understanding of volatile architecture.

The medium for olfaction, air, may seem an unlikely construction substance, yet such an impossibility has spurred a number of utopian, spiritual and artistic visionaries over the centuries to contemplate floating cities. Despite the impracticality of this perennial fantasy, immaterial buildings have gained a degree of actuality through technological advances in climate simulation. Fujiko Nakaya manifested a veil of fog around the Pepsi-Cola Pavilion at the 1970 Expo in Osaka, a project of the Experiments in Art and Technology group (Klüver et al. 1972). The white geodesic dome, outfitted with atomizers to create miniscule water droplets, appeared to be simultaneously decomposing into mist and condensing from the atmosphere. An even more ethereal edifice, *Blur Building*, designed by architects Elizabeth Diller and Ricardo Scofidio as a pavilion for the 2002 Swiss Expo, consisted merely of a lattice of walkways, platforms, piping and nozzles (Diller and Scofidio 2002). From afar, its elliptical cloudlike form hovered above Lake Neuchatel, drawing water from below and gradually evaporating into the ocean of air. Inside, visitors wandered through a hazy, humid realm with only occasional breaks to the open sky. Ephemeral, nebulous, shifting and intangible, these vaporous constructions point to some of the distinctive characteristics of olfactory architecture and its potential for unusual experiences.

Attention to olfaction and the phenomenology of architecture also brings forth ethical issues of personal and public accountability. Lest they be dismissed as merely a question of ornamentation, scents are a powerful and significant presence because of their potential health and psychological effects. On the one hand, 'sick' buildings – caused by inadequate ventilation and the build-up of low-level toxic emissions from construction materials – are an example of the health hazards resulting from the neglect of architecture's atmospheric dimension (Engen 1991: 43–9). On the other, there is an ethical quandary raised by the overly eager embrace of the practice known as 'environmental' or 'ambient fragrancing' – whereby scents are diffused through ventilation systems in order to optimize employee performance, subliminally influence consumers' buying behaviour, or effect a kind of mass medication in subways, schools and prisons. Ideas about 'scent slavery' and mind control perfumes may seem akin to paranoid obsessions or science fiction scenarios, but the ethics of olfactory manipulation – or 'sensory engineering' as the industry prefers to designate it – is a topic with implications that have been ominously unaddressed by its advocates (see, for example, McCarthy 1996). One might ask why an intervention by smell should be construed as any more coercive than other elements of the built environment, such as colored lights or piped-in music. The answer is precisely the chemical nature of olfaction. Because actual molecules are ingested into the body, critics of environmental fragrancing argue that affected individuals should be given the opportunity to provide voluntary, informed consent (Damian and Damian 1995: 108–40).

Scentworks

In working against the inodorate ideology of architecture in general and the white cube in particular, artists have engaged with aromatic materials to counter, confuse and corrupt assumptions of purely optical experience. The five categories of work that I'll speak about here – respectively, olfactocentrism, pungent loci, structural essences, olfactory affect and dialectical odors – set up a series of charged relations between olfaction and architecture that rethink the paradigm of the white cube as well as the significance of the sense of smell itself.

Olfactocentrism

The visual focus of the gallery depends upon architecture to isolate viewers from the outside world, protect them from the distractions and chaos of the city, and secure a contemplative calm in which to commune with works of art. Olfactocentric works, however, demonstrate how odors can obstruct and otherwise frustrate the gallery's visual hegemony. For Arman, the gallery is a container that can be filled with urban detritus just as easily as with artworks. *Le Plein* (or 'Full-Up') (1960) packed the gallery floor-to-ceiling with industrial waste, household cast-offs and organic garbage. Viewers were excluded from the gallery except for a three-foot area inside the door, and were left to view the installation from the very street where the garbage was collected. While the visual excess was tolerable, the putrefaction of the debris sealed the show's fate and caused it to be closed after only 13 days.

If Arman's work explores excess as an artistic strategy, Michael Asher's work, which foregrounds the subtleties of air flow and the ambient, contextual aspects of the art experience, explores the zero degree of artistic intervention. Removing the doors and windows of New York City's Clocktower gallery (1976) literally and figuratively aired out the stuffiness of an institutionally overdetermined environment and opened the space to the external, unpredictable elements of the weather and the olfactory irritations of the urban atmosphere. Both these works interrupt conventional viewing habits by allowing in precisely what the architecture of the gallery is designed to exclude: noise, pollution, weather, garbage, smells.

Pungent Loci

Defining places by physical, visual, kinesthetic or discursive means – by the use of fences, lookout stations, paths, signs – are commonplace practices, ones that have been effectively employed by artists interrogating the politics of looking and institutional appropriations of the landscape. This tradition of 'marked sites,' a genre of earthwork practice, involves drawing attention to specific locations, temporarily occupying them and transforming their experience via authorial presence. Contrary to the egoism so often associated with monumental earthworks, artworks engaging with *pungent loci* – an olfactory parallel to *genius loci* or 'spirit of the place' – emphasize subtlety. Pungent loci exist at the edge of sensory awareness even as they demarcate the physicality of a place.

Katharina Fritsch's *Perfume in Hallway* (1984) transformed a liminal architectural feature into one haunted with significance. Located in the stairway leading to the gallery, this olfactory ambush enveloped unsuspecting passersby with a fleeting vapor. The sensation that someone had left invisible, aromatic evidence of their passing animated the stairway with a sense of the uncanny. Like the stirring of a long-forgotten memory, or the scented visitations recorded in ghost stories and after-death communications, Fritsch's rendezvous with an odor recast the curving balustrade into a stage for confronting an ethereal otherness. Fritsch's pungent loci metamorphosed a functional aspect of institutional architecture into one resonating with allusions to passing strangers, absent bodies and mythical states of being.

Teresa from Madrid with Yellow Dress (1997), a domestic intervention by Thomas Zitzwitz, involved the application of seven smells to various portions of a New York City apartment. Spread amidst everyday, lived-in clutter, the aromas mark, divide up and concentrate visitors' attention upon details and nooks of the residence. Without prompting, it might be difficult to know which smells the artist applied and which ones were already ambient; in other words, all smells in the space become heightened. As a series of pungent loci, Zitzwitz frustrates reductive relationships, and instead offers up provocative olfactory clues that inspire contemplation of the narrative logic between smell and place.

Structural Essences

The sensory and emotional impact of olfactory artworks set up an encounter in which viewers experience a revitalized engagement with the materiality of the built environment. As often as architecture tends to recede into the background of perception, becoming merely a frame for activities and events, artists utilizing odorous elements foreground the experiential and phenomenological aspects of a building's walls, floors and other features. Unlikely construction substances invite multisensorial inspection and assert the veracity of matter by revealing the effects of time, transformational processes and human utilization.

Organic substances such as those featured in Olafur Eliasson's *The Moss Wall* (1995) or Anya Gallaccio's roomful of roses (*Red on Green*, 1992) and expanse of chocolate (*Stroke*, 1993) greet visitors with an overpowering scent long before actual viewing. Bringing the natural world into the neutral white cube forces a confrontation between the earthly and the industrial, the sensual and the sterilized – in which one must rethink the essence of architecture that is decomposing, edible or alive. If organic materials have a tendency to yield to romanticist or sentimental notions of nature, Per Barclay's room filled with motor oil (*Untitled*, 1989) strikes a more apocalyptic note. On the one hand, the dense, mirroring liquid challenges gallerygoers to tolerate its toxic fumes and appreciate its unusual aesthetic qualities; on the other, the uninhabitability of the room alludes to the costs of unbridled pollution and warns of a future submerged in oily waste.

Olfactory Affect

The contestation over definitions of 'place' have gained special emphasis in the postmodern era of global capitalism, tumultuous real-estate speculation, enhanced mobility and 'schizophrenic' spatialities. David Harvey, for instance, attributes the significance of place to the fact that it is a radically threatened entity which can no longer be taken for granted. If places are no longer precise or stable physical domains, they are still 'constructed in our memories and affections through repeated encounters and complex associations' (Harvey 1993: 4).

Given such instabilities, 'olfactory affect' is a key means by which identifications with place are enacted. Smell, an integral component of emotional investment, works implicitly to convey a 'structure of feeling' – that unrepresentable, inarticulable sense of lived experience (Williams 1977: 128–35). Artworks engaging with olfactory affect use smell as an active, affective presence to simultaneously express private interpretation and communal meaning. By isolating certain odors or mimicking a specific *mise-en-scent*, artists address not only the experience of olfactory affect but also its social and political dimensionality.

Oswaldo Maciá's *1 Woodchurch Road, London NW6 3PL* (1994–5) selects and highlights the odors of a small apartment complex in northwest London. The five garbage cans present a cross-section of the smells the artist found most characteristic of the building and its ethnically diverse occupants: mothballs, olive oil, Listerine, eucalyptus, baby powder. This polyodorous *tranche-de-vie* reveals the degree to which place and community are inherently plural and heterogeneous, in defiance of the reactionary rhetorics of a singular British identity.

Olfactory affect takes on a fetishistic twist in a work by Kate Ericson and Mel Ziegler that synthesizes and bottles the distinctive scent of the French National Archives in Paris (1992). The odor is a mixture of decaying leather and paper, mustiness and sweat, created in collaboration with a scent expert, a 'nose' from the perfume house of Nina Ricci. Evoking a sense of indulgent luxury, and conjuring up the aristocratic world of Proust or Huysmans, the archives' odor is given out like olfactory hors-d'œuvres at an exclusive cocktail party. As much as the archives aspire to inculcate a sense of certainty about the ideology of the nation, this decaying 'smell of history' is an insistent reminder of mortality and impermanence.

Dialectical Odors

Places, besides having physical and subjective dimensions, are also defined ideologically. My term *dialectical odors* describes the strategic use of smell as an intervention into – and means to critique – abstract or essentialist political conceptions of space. It draws from Walter Benjamin's concept of the 'dialectical image' – an image that 'interrupts the context into which it is inserted' (quoted in Buck-Morss 1989: 67). Dialectical odors contradict the conventional assumptions of place and space, render them more openly schizophrenic, introduce complexes of competing meanings and draw out the implicit political dynamics. Dialectical odors remain unreconciled to their location, unharmonized with the ambience of the architectural environment.

Janet Murray's pair of bathroom installations, *Expulsion from Paradise* (1988), intervenes into the antiseptic utopia of the restroom. Eden is partially recreated by the addition of bulrushes, water lettuce, wild ginger, lilies and birds of paradise, which exude a refreshing, verdant challenge to the acrid smell of urinal disinfectant. These miniature oases seek a reconciliation between the indoor and the outdoor, deodorized culture and the bounty of nature, the germ-free and the life-sustaining. The conflicting odors redolent in this restroom *ikebana* confounds the judgments dividing the damned and sterile from the innocent and fertile, redirecting the process of elimination into one of cultivation.

Architecture's role in regulating gender is the focus of Mark Lewis's (1989) *Une Odeur de luxe*. Lewis's dialectical odors work contrary to those that merely mask offensive odors, they attempt to expose and corrupt the ideology of sexual difference and what Lacan (1977: 151) terms 'urinary segregation.' By atomizing women's perfume in the men's bathroom and men's cologne in the women's, Lewis interrogates the politics of identity construction and its performative maintenance. These transgendered diffusions of odor, rendering each space (and each person within it) olfactorily hermaphroditic, forces a confrontation with architecture's role in naturalizing sexual difference as an unproblematic binary opposition.

My text begins with the white cube and ends with the bathroom – suggesting a tempting parallel between the two, especially given their similar formation by the civilizing process and the ideology of cleanliness. Both the bathroom and the white cube are products of modern technology, a disengagement from the body, the neutralization of certain sensations, not to mention deodorization. While the pleasure and refinement manufactured in the white cube is the inverse of the bathroom's negotiation with the body's base materiality, they nevertheless share a modus operandi. It is only a small step from 'ornament and crime' to 'ornament and grime,' for both partake of an 'aesthetics of elimination' (see Lupton and Miller 1992).[5]

It would be a mistake to conclude, however, that because the white cube privileges certain kinds of sensory awarenesses, it cannot function otherwise. The white cube is a paradoxical space – at once the paradigm of exclusion and visual hegemony and an enabler for sensory experiences of all modalities. If it has been a necessary precedent for the acceptance of modern art, it has also acted as a significant site for artists to launch critiques about issues – not only concerning the conventions of the artworld, but aso spatial and corporeal politics, identity and gender issues, tensions between the built and natural environments – that suffuse Western society as a whole.

Acknowledgments

Versions of this text were presented at the Universities Art Association Conference (1998) and the conference 'Uncommon Senses' (2000). I would like to thank these audiences and, in particular, Jennifer Fisher, David Howes, Constance Classen, Kim Sawchuk and Brian Foss for their constructive feedback. Research for this text was generously supported by a series of personal and team research grants from the Social Sciences and Humanities Research Council of Canada.

Notes

1. See my overview of the 'olfactory turn' in the visual arts in 'Reveries, Assaults and Evaporating Presences' (Drobnick 1998).

2. The irony of spreading an odor such as pine or lemon on clean surfaces, and thus in a sense 'dirtying' them in the process of cleaning, is mentioned by Trygg Engen (1991) and Kathleen McHugh (1997).

3. In fact, contrary to the reviewers' lament, the smell of grass was very much evident in a lawn sculpture by Mel Ziegler on the CCA's grounds.

4. See the special issue of *Architecture and Urbanism*, July 1994, with articles by Steven Holl, Juhani Pallasmaa and Alberto Pérez-Gómez.

5. 'Ornament and crime' refers to Adolph Loos' infamous but influential diatribe against the excesses of design that are a central tenet of modern architecture (see Miller and Ward 2002).

Bibliography

Adams, A. and Dyer, H. (1998), 'The Patch Where the Mower is King,' *The Montreal Gazette*, June 27: J1–2.

Bell, C. (1958), *Art*, New York: Capricorn Books.

Bennett, T. (1995), 'The Multiplication of Culture's Utility,' *Critical Inquiry*, 21(4): 861–89.

Buck-Morss, S. (1989), *The Dialectics of Seeing: Walter Benjamin and the Arcades Project*, Cambridge MA and London: Routledge.

Celant, G. (1996), 'A Visual Machine: Art Installation and its Modern Archetypes,' in R. Greenberg, B.W. Ferguson and S. Nairne (eds), *Thinking About Exhibitions*, London and New York: Routledge, pp. 371–86.

Classen, C., Howes, D. and Synnott, A. (1994), *Aroma: The Cultural History of Smell*, London and New York: Routledge.

Corbin, A. (1986), *The Foul and the Fragrant: Odor and the French Social Imagination*, trans. M.L. Kochan, R. Parker and C. Prendergast, Leaming Spa: Berg.

Damian, P. and Damian, K. (1995), *Aromatherapy: Scent and Psyche*, Rochester VT: Healing Arts Press.

Davis, T.C. (1995), 'Performing and the Real Thing in the Postmodern Museum,' *The Drama Review*, 39(3): 15–40.

Diller, E. and Scofidio, R. (2002), *Blur: The Making of Nothing*, New York: Abrams.

Drobnick, J. (1998), 'Reveries, Assaults and Evaporating Presences: Olfactory Dimensions in Contemporary Art,' *Parachute*, 89(Winter): 10–19.

Eco, U. (1986), *Travels in Hyperreality*, trans. W. Weaver, San Diego, New York, London: Harcourt Brace Jovanovich.

Elias, N. (1994), *The Civilizing Process*, Oxford: Blackwell.

Engen, T. (1991), *Odor Sensation and Memory*, New York: Praeger.

Feniak, P. (1997), 'What a Short, Odd Trip It Is,' *Globe and Mail*, May 10: A14.

Foucault, M. (1986), 'Of Other Spaces,' *Diacritics*, 16(1): 22–7.

Grunenberg, C. (1994), 'The Politics of Presentation: The Museum of Modern Art, New York,' in M. Pointon (ed.), *Art Apart: Art Institutions and Ideology Across England*

and North America, Manchester and New York: Manchester University Press, pp. 192–211.

Harvey, D. (1993), 'From Space to Place and Back Again: Reflections on the Condition of Postmodernity,' in J. Bird, B. Curtis, T. Putnam, G. Robertson and L. Tickner (eds), *Mapping the Futures: Local Cultures, Global Change*, New York and London: Routledge, pp. 3–29.

Kirshenblatt-Gimblett, B. (1991), 'Objects of Ethnography,' in I. Karp and S. Lavine (eds), *Exhibiting Cultures: The Poetics and Politics of Museum Display*, Washington: Smithsonian Institution Press, pp. 386–443.

Klüver, B., Martin, J. and Rose, B. (eds) (1972), *Pavilion*, New York: E.P. Dutton.

Lacan, J. (1977), 'The Agency of the Letter in the Unconscious or Reason since Freud,' in *Écrits: A Selection*, trans. A. Sheridan, New York: W.W. Norton.

Lupton, E. and Miller, J.A. (1992), *The Bathroom, the Kitchen and the Aesthetics of Waste: A Process of Elimination*, Cambridge MA: MIT List Visual Arts Center.

MacDonald, S. and Silverstone, R. (1990), 'Rewriting the Museums' Fictions: Taxonomies, Stories and Readers,' *Cultural Studies*, 4(2): 176–91.

McCarthy, B. (1996), 'Multi-Source Synthesis: An Architecture of Smell,' *Architectural Design #121*, 66(5/6): ii–v.

McHugh, K. (1997), 'One Cleans, the Other Doesn't,' *Cultural Studies*, 11(1): 17–39.

Miller, B. and Ward, M. (eds) (2002), *Crime and Ornament: The Arts and Popular Culture in the Shadow of Adolph Loos*, Toronto: YYZ Books.

O'Doherty, B. (1986), *Inside the White Cube: The Ideology of the Gallery Space*, Santa Monica: Lapis Press.

Porter, G. (1996), 'Seeing Through Solidity: A Feminist Perspective on Museums,' in S. MacDonald and G. Fyfe (eds), *Theorizing Museums*, Cambridge MA: Blackwell, pp. 105–26.

Smith, J. (1989), *Senses and Sensibilities*, New York: John Wiley & Sons.

Vidler, A. (1992), *The Architectural Uncanny: Essays in the Modern Unhomely*, Cambridge MA and London: MIT Press.

Walsh, K. (1992), *The Representation of the Past: Museums and Heritage in the Post Modern World*, London and New York: Routledge.

Williams, R. (1977), *Marxism and Literature*, Oxford: Oxford University Press.

Wilson, A. (1993), 'Technological Utopias,' *The South Atlantic Quarterly*, 92(1): 169.

16

HYPERESTHESIA, or, The Sensual Logic of Late Capitalism

David Howes

> One of the great unfinished tasks of twentieth century marxian theory has been to write a materialist history of the senses. How have the senses been organized by relations of production and exchange? How in particular have they been organized under capitalism? And how has this organization shaped capitalist society's cultural pursuits?
>
> Margaret Cohen, 'The Art of Profane Illumination'

In this chapter, I would like to take up the task of writing a materialist history of the senses. I will argue that one of the reasons this task remains 'unfinished' to date is due to Marxian theory's failure to 'acknowledge consumption' (Miller 1995a, 1995b).[1]

The chapter proceeds by first returning to Marx and examining the philosophical roots of his materialism; second, tracing the role of the senses in the transition from industrial to consumer capitalism; third, excavating what could be called 'the sensorial subconscious' of the state we are in now – namely, 'late capitalism' (Jameson 1990); and, finally, extending the practice of materialist analysis to encompass the social life of the senses on the margins of the global consumer society. There, as we shall see, capitalism's glitter is not all that it is imagined to be by those theorists whose senses have been 'massaged' (McLuhan and Fiore 1967) by living all their lives at the center.

Sensory Deprivation and Industrial Capitalism

There are few more dramatic ruptures in the history of Western thought than Marx's apparent break with the idealist tradition of German philosophy (Synnott 1991). '[M]an is affirmed in the objective world not only in the act of thinking, but with *all* his senses' proclaimed the young Marx in the *Economic and Philosophic Manuscripts of 1844* (Marx 1987: 108). Whereas Hegel had interpreted world history in terms of the progressive unfolding of Spirit, Marx held that 'the *forming of the five senses* is a labor of the entire history of the world down to the present' (Marx 1987: 109). He was inspired to accord such primacy to the senses by the writings of the materialist philosopher Ludwig Feuerbach. In his doctrine of sense perception, Feuerbach argued that it is not only nature or external objects that are experienced by the senses but '*Man, too, is given to himself only through the senses*; he is an object for himself only as an object of the senses' (Feuerbach 1966: 58).

Marx's portrayal of the state of the senses in nineteenth century bourgeois society was in turn influenced by the writings of the utopianist Charles Fourier. Fourier (1851) believed that societies could be judged according to how well they gratified and developed the senses of their members. He argued that the senses were debased by the civilization of his day, in which most people were unable to afford any sensory refinements and in which all people, no matter their rank, were continually confronted with disagreeable sensory impressions, such as the stench and din of the streets. Furthermore, even if sensory pleasures were to be made more available, most people would be unable to appreciate them as their senses remained brutish and undeveloped. These sensory ills, according to Fourier, were the result of a society obsessed with the accumulation of private possessions to the detriment of the general wellbeing.

There are numerous echoes of Fourier in Marx's discussion of the condition of the proletariat in the *Economic and Philosophic Manuscripts*. For example, Marx describes how the senses of the worker, living amidst 'the *sewage* of civilization,' are deformed until he loses all notion of sensory refinement and 'no longer knows any need... but the need to *eat*' (Marx 1987: 117). Marx returned to this theme of the stripping of the senses in *Capital*, where he described the conditions of factory work:

> Every organ of sense is injured in an equal degree by artificial elevation of temperature, by the dust-laden atmosphere, by the deafening noise, not to mention danger to life and limb among the thickly crowded machinery, which, with the regularity of the seasons, issues its list of the killed and the wounded in the industrial battle... Is Fourier wrong when he calls factories 'tempered bagnios'? (Marx 1954, I: 401–2)

The sensory deprivation of the proletariat was to be expected, given the grueling conditions of factory work and so-called living conditions in the industrial slums. But Marx insisted that not even among the bourgeoisie are the senses fulfilled. All of the capitalist's senses are ultimately fixed on one object – capital; and, while the enjoyment of wealth is one of the objects of capitalism; even better is sacrificing pleasure in order to accumulate more wealth. 'The less you eat, drink and read books; the less you go to the theater, the dance hall, the public-house; the less you ... sing, paint, fence, etc., the more you *save* – the *greater* becomes your treasure which neither moths nor dust will devour – your *capital*' (Marx 1987: 118–19).

Developing Fourier's diagnosis, Marx laid the blame for the alienation of the senses in capitalist society on the dehumanizing regime of private property, and envisioned a world in which 'the transcendence of private property [would entail] the complete *emancipation* of all human senses and qualities' (Marx 1987: 139). 'Only through the negation of the demeaning and oppressive tyranny of capitalist property relations could humankind's 'species being' come into its own. Only through the objectively unfolded richness of man's essential being is the richness of subjective *human* sensibility (a musical ear, an eye for beauty of form – in short *senses* capable of human gratifications, senses confirming themselves as essential powers of *man*) either cultivated or brought into being' (Marx 1987: 108).

In the *Communist Manifesto*, Marx and Engels heralded the collapse of the capitalist economic order. The portents of this dissolution included, among other things: the concentration of the proletariat in ever greater masses, the increasingly agitated character of all social relations due to the constant revolutionizing of the instruments of production, and the reduction of personal worth to commodity status. In short, all of the contradictions of bourgeois society had become manifest on its surface, and the illusion of society could no longer hold.

Reading the *Communist Manifesto* now, when the capitalist system seems more firmly entrenched than ever, what most stands out about this text is how brilliantly Marx and Engels foretold *the future of capitalism*, rather than its demise. For example, Marx and Engels wrote:

> The bourgeoisie has through its exploitation of the world market given a cosmopolitan character to production and consumption in every country... In place of the old wants, satisfied by the productions of the country, we find new wants, requiring for their satisfaction the products of distant lands and climes. In place of the old local and national seclusion and self-sufficiency we have intercourse in every direction, universal interdependence of nations. And as in material, so also in intellectual production. The intellectual creations of individual nations become common property... The bourgeoise, by the rapid improvement of all instruments of production, by the immensely facilitated means of communication, draws all, even the most barbarian, nations into civilization. (Marx and Engels 1967: 84)

This passage encapsulates a remarkably prescient description of the phenomenon that has in recent years come to be theorized as 'globalization'

(Featherstone 1990). The fine food halls and corner stores of Europe and America filled with produce 'from distant lands and climes' (see, for example, Cook and Crang 1996; James 1996), the global flow of capital (and people) that has resulted in the 'universal interdependence of nations' (see, for example, Robbins 1998), the Hollywood movies and other elements of American popular culture that have become the 'common property' (or transcultural patrimony) of everybody from Chile to Katmandhu (see, for example, Dorfman 1983; Iyer 1989; Appadurai 1996) all speak to the in-escapable truth of this passage. Summing up their vision of globalization as cultural homogenization, Marx and Engels (1967: 84) wrote: 'In one word, [the bourgeoisie] creates a world after its own image.'

Nevertheless, the apparent flash of insight that this passage contains must not be allowed to distract attention from the limitations of Marx's analysis of capitalism's laws of motion. Marx's gaze always remained centered on the factory and the stock market, and although he may have succeeded at exposing the secrets of the capitalist mode of production through his penetrating analysis of the manufacturing process and wage labor, he neglected an equally salient development – namely, the *presentation* of commodities in the department stores and world exhibitions that sprang up in the mid-nineteenth century (Bowlby 1985; Cummings and Lewandowska 2000). The birth of these 'palaces of consumption' heralded a transformation in the nature of capitalism with far-reaching implications – the transformation from industrial capitalism (as Marx knew it) to the consumer capitalism of today. For capitalism does not work by surveillance and the extraction of the labor power and value of the worker alone; it also works by generating spectacle and creating consumer desires of all sorts in all people, including the worker (Galbraith 1958, 1967; on surveillance see Foucault 1979, on spectacle Debord 1983).

Sensory Stimulation and Consumer Capitalism

The growing social importance of consumption in the nineteenth century was evident in the new venue for shopping, the department store. With its theatrical lighting, enticing window displays and its floor after floor of entrancing merchandise – 'each separate counter... a show place of dazzling interest and attraction' (Dreiser cited in Saisselin 1984: 35) – the department store presented a fabulous spectacle of consumer plenty and accessibility. Previously, goods had been kept behind counters and it was presumed that a customer would enter a shop with the purpose to buy. In the department store, by contrast, goods were largely out in the open and anyone could enter simply with the purpose of having a look. The expectation was that the display of goods in such abundance would prove so seductive that even those who were 'just looking' would be lured into buying, particularly given the atmosphere of pleasurable self-indulgence that prevailed. In his novel *Sister*

Carrie Theodore Dreiser described the bewitching effect of the department store displays on a potential customer: 'Fine clothes... spoke tenderly and Jesuitically for themselves. When she came within earshot of their pleading, desire in her bent a willing ear... "My dear," said the lace collar... "I fit you beautifully; don't give me up"' (cited in Saisselin 1984: 36).

The department store thus appeared on the scene as an enormous candy store with a cornucopia of goodies to satisfy the taste of the bourgeoisie for fashionable but affordable style. It was able to do so thanks to advances in mass production – specifically, the mechanical reproduction of styled or imitation goods. Mass production brought previously exclusive luxury items within the reach of the bourgeoisie, and even the working class (Miller 1987). As Walter Benjamin (1969) noted with regard to art, what such imitation goods lose in authenticity they gain in mobility: 'fine' art, 'fine' furniture, 'fine' clothes can now go anywhere and everywhere as mass production finds its match in mass consumption.

The counterpart to the (often female) shopper in the new consumer palaces was the (male) *flâneur*, the voyeuristic idler who treated the whole city as though it were a department store, a variegated spectacle of goods to be viewed and occasionally sampled (Benjamin 1973). 'The prime requisite of an expert *flâneur*,' according to the American novelist Henry James, was 'the simple, sensuous, confident relish of pleasure' (cited in Saisselin 1984: 19). Yet, as a suitable admirer of the new society of spectacle, the *flâneur* found his primary sensory pleasure simply in watching, the watching which in a visualist age would increasingly seem to offer a total sensory experience in itself. In his study of the aesthetics of nineteenth century consumption, Rémy Saisselin (1984: 25) writes: 'The *flâneur* [was] a conscious observer for whom the word *boredom* had become meaningless: he animated all he saw; admired all he perceived. He strolled, observed, watched, espied... '

As Saisselin goes on to point out in *The Bourgeois and the Bibelot*, the phenonemon of the *flâneur* went hand in hand with that of the photographer, both aesthetic observers, insiders and outsiders at once, both constantly skimming the surfaces of urban life for their rich bounty of visual impressions. The photographer, however, was equipped with the technological means to fix visual impressions on paper, turning the images themselves into objects of display and desire. The mass production of images, which occurred in the 1800s, thus complemented the mass production of styled goods or imitations. With this proliferation of images and imitations appearance increasingly came to overshadow – and even obliterate – substance (Boorstin 1962; Ewen 1988).

In an essay on photography published in 1859, Oliver Wendell Holmes wrote: 'Every conceivable object of Nature and Art will soon scale off its surface for us. Men will hunt all curious, beautiful, grand objects, as they hunt cattle in South America, for their skins and leave the carcasses as of little worth' (cited in Ewen 1988: 25). The analogy to hunting here is significant for it indicates that the photographic reproduction of the world is not a passive multiplication of images but an active appropriation of all 'curious, beautiful, grand objects.' The notion of the 'carcasses' of objects being left behind 'as of little worth' once their photograph was taken points to a state of affairs in which photographic (and shortly, cinematic) imagery would become more powerful and influential than objects themselves. In *All Consuming Images* Stuart Ewen (1988: 25) states that Holmes correctly 'laid out the contours by which the phenomenon of *style* operates in the world today.' Style deals exclusively in surface impressions, hence possessing the 'right look' becomes all important.

If the primary sensory mode of consumer culture was (and remains) that of visual display, the non-visual senses were not left to one side. As Ewen notes, the sense of touch was also appropriated by marketers as a crucial medium of sensory persuasion. Thus, in a 1930s book entitled *Consumer Engineering*, the business professors Sheldon and Arens write:

> Manufacturing an object that delights this [tactile] sense is something that you do but don't talk about. Almost everything which is bought is handled. After the eye, the hand is the first censor to pass on acceptance, and if the hand's judgment is unfavorable, the most attractive object will not gain the popularity it deserves. On the other hand, merchandise designed to be pleasing to the hand wins an approval that may never register in the mind, but which will determine additional purchases... *Make it snuggle in the palm.* (Sheldon and Arens cited in Ewen 1988: 49–50)

Raymond Loewy, commonly regarded as the father of industrial design in the United States, was alert to the significance of tactile stimulation. In a seminal chapter on 'Design and Psychology' in his 1951 autobiography *Never Leave Well Enough Alone*, he wrote: 'The sensory aspects of the normal human being should be taken into consideration in all forms of design. Let's take the Coca-Cola bottle, for instance. Even when wet and cold, its twin-sphered body offers a delightful valley for the friendly fold of one's hand, a feel that is cozy and luscious' (quoted in Fulton Suri 2002: 163).

Loewy's insight has been borne out by the rapid expansion of 'human factors' research within the field of industrial design. Initially concerned with solving problems of usability (such as efficiency, safety, learnability, adaptability), designers are now increasingly preoccupied with generating affectivity or 'pleasure with products' (Green and Jordan 2002). 'Pleasure is an emotional benefit that supplements product functionality' (Desmet and Hekkert 2002: 62), and has become a value in its own right. '*Don't think affordances, think temptation*'; and, '*Don't think beauty in appearance, think beauty in interaction*' has become the new design credo (Overbeeke 2002: 11). Indeed, tapping the subjective sensory preferences of the consumer and creating enticing 'interfaces' has come to take precedence over conventional design principles. Ornamentation has been decriminalized, and not just in the museum (Drobnick, this volume) but in all things, from personal computers to toilet brushes (Postrel 2003; Kälviäinen 2002). A new, aesthetically charged understanding has taken shape, according to Virginia Postrel in *The Substance of Style*, an understanding attentive to all the ways in which visual and tactile qualities (color and form) affect people's feelings and evaluations of products. In place of judgments like 'This is good design' (the preserve of the designer, or rational expertise), now the desired response is one of 'I *like* that' (the preserve of the consumer, or personal pleasure) (Postrel 2003: 10; Kälviäinen 2002: 88): 'People pet Armani clothes because the fabrics feel so good. Those clothes attract us as visual, tactile creatures, not because they are "rich in meaning" but because they are rich in pleasure. The garments' utility includes the way they look and feel' (Postrel 2003: 77).

The social logic of *flânerie*, summed up by Susan Buck-Morss (1989: 346) in the phrase 'look, but don't touch,' has been eclipsed, leading to a breakdown in the consumer's defenses. This breach has been compounded by the recognition that physical contact between server and shopper 'exerts influence on customer's behaviors by enhancing liking of the salesperson and by creating higher emotional involvement with the shopping situation,' as well as heightening the shopper's inclination to comply with a server's request (Hornik 1992: 451). The invisible hand of the market has been transformed into the knowing touch of the salesclerk.

Branding the Senses: The Progressive Privatization of Sensation

Factoring tactile stimulation into the design of products and strategies of salesmanship makes good business sense for two further reasons, according to the sensual logic of late capitalism. The first has to do with the problem of advertising clutter. The consumer landscape has been transformed into a visual jungle of logos, billboards and neon signs, such that 'advertising wear-out' through visual fatigue quickly sets in. *Touch revivifies.*

The second has to do with the progressive privatization of the visible spectrum of forms and colors as companies scramble to trademark and/or patent the aesthetic packaging or 'trade dress' of their products. For example, to protect their brand equity from would-be imitators, the Owens-Corning Fiberglass Corporation has trademarked the color pink for its residential insulation material, and Eastman Kodak has been granted exclusive rights to the use of the distinctive combination of yellow, black and red on its film products (Solomon et al. 1999: 49–51). This development raises the specter of the 'color depletion' or 'color scarcity' problem in trademark law – that is, the risk that the monopolization of all usable colors (and color combinations) by a few large competitors will place new entrants to the market at a significant competitive disadvantage because there won't be any colors left to exploit (Jones 2003). *Adding feel provides an additional dimension for product differentiation.*

Consumer capitalism has, in fact, increasingly made it its business to engage as many senses as possible in its drive for product differentiation and the distraction/seduction of the consumer. 'Multisensory marketing,' or the new 'technocracy of sensuality' as Wolfgang Haug (1986) dubbed it, reached its height in the late twentieth century with artifical scents added to a range of products from cars to crayons, with muzak modulating people's moods as they cruise the plushly carpeted or smoothly tiled aisles of department stores and boutiques, and with cafes and fast-food outlets always on hand for gustatory gratification. Everything seems designed to create a state of *hyperesthesia* in the shopper.

The sensual logic behind this makeover of the body of the commodity and the shopping environment is transparent enough: multiplying the sensory channels through which the 'buy me!' message is communicated enhances the likelihood of the message being registered and acted upon by the customer. For example, it has been found that 'when choosing between two similar food or beverage products, 81 percent of consumers would choose one they could both smell and see over one they could only see'; similarly, piping 'slow music' into grocery stores has been discovered to lead to shoppers paying longer visits and spending more money (Solomon et al. 1999: 53, 82). Marketers and designers now hold 'body-storming' focus groups (see Bonapace 2002: 191) in an effort to divine the most potent sensory channel, and within each channel the most potent sensory signal, through which to distinguish their products from those of their competitors and capture the attention of potential customers. 'Perceptual positioning' now means everything to moving merchandise.

Not surprisingly, there has been a drive to privatize the auditory and olfactory aspects of commodities as well as the visual in recent years. The first trademark of a scent was secured in 1990 by a California company, which used a floral fragrance reminiscent of Plumeria blossoms to odorize its sewing thread and embroidery yarn (Classen et al. 1994: 201). Likewise, Harley-Davidson recently sought to trademark the (allegedly) distinctive 'hog' sound of one of its motorcycle engines revving. These legal maneuvers to protect (and expand) market share – that is, to colonize by canalizing the 'mind-space' of the consumer – have not gone uncontested. All of the original concerns around 'color depletion' are now being trotted out again around sound and smell scarcity, as courts give in to demand after demand for the registration of this and that sensory aspect of trade dress (Edelstein and Leuders 2000; Jones 2003). The question arises: how long will it be before every aspect of sensation is brought under the thrall of intellectual property rights?

This hyperestheticization of everyday products may seem excessive from a strictly functional perspective. But it is, in fact, strongly motivated, commercially speaking. The aesthetic functionality of odorizing products, for example, has been confirmed by the results of a survey that involved asking a group of subjects to identify a range of odors. The researchers found that product scents such as crayons, baby powder and bubble gum proved to be more recognizable than such distinctive natural odors as lemon and coffee. Moreover, subjects consistently associated a brand name with a product scent: *Crayola* crayons, *Johnson & Johnson's* baby powder, *Bazooka* bubble gum (Classen et al. 1994: 203). This evidence of recession in the general population's consciousness of natural odors, and *precession* of branded scents, is of acute interest to marketers. To them, it confirms that 'the unique sensory quality of a product can play an important role in helping it to stand out from the competition, especially if the brand creates a unique association with the sensation' (Solomon et al. 1999: 49).

It is in the domain of taste that capitalist sensualism (forget realism) has enjoyed some of its greatest successes with respect to the commodification of 'subjective *human* sensibility' (Marx). No business is more shrouded in secrecy than that of the artificial flavor industry, where the great 'Flavor Houses' of the New Jersey industrial corridor, and elsewhere, compete with each other, and with Nature, to divine and develop new tastes to gratify the ever-changing palates of consumers. Many of the flavors consumers crave today have no natural prototype (for example, the cola in Coca-Cola), and even those that do have for the most part been turned into 'larger-than-life' savors in the process of being synthesized. It is in this connection that the society of the spectacle looks to have mutated into something much grander: the society of the simulacrum. As noted in *Aroma*:

> The widespread replacement of natural flavours with artificial imitations which we find in the contemporary food industry exemplifies how, in Jean Baudrillard's words, the world has come to be 'completely catalogued and analysed and then artificially revived as though real' [1983: 16]. Artificial flavours are created by the synthetic reproduction of individual flavour notes present in the original natural flavours [though never all of them, only those deemed 'essential']. The flavorist may thus be regarded as the arch-agent in the process of production outlined by Baudrillard where: 'the real is produced from miniaturized units... and with these it can be reproduced an indefinite number of times' [1983: 3]. (Classen et al. 1994: 204)

Welcome to the Experience Economy: Tapping the Sensorial Subconscious

Capitalism has evidently come a long way since the days when production was the keystone of the economy and the reproduction of capital seemingly depended on stripping the senses of the laborer and curbing those of the bourgeoisie. Now the focus appears to be on seducing the senses of the consumer in the interests of valorizing capital. This sea-change in the sensual logic of capitalism is what lies behind the transformation in 'values' whereby work discipline, thrift and moderation have been replaced by self-fulfillment, impulse buying and conspicuous consumption. It was the new modes of implanting the body and senses of the consumer in the world of goods that brought about this mutation in attitudes, not vice versa (see Bauman 1983; Clarke 2003: 133).

The hypersensuality of the contemporary marketplace has been theorized by a new generation of business professors. In an article entitled 'Welcome to the Experience Economy' published in the *Harvard Business Review*, Joseph Pine II and James Gilmore assert that forward-thinking companies no longer produce goods or supply services, but instead use services as the stage and goods as props for creating 'experiences' that are as stimulating for the consumer as they are memorable. The authors identify a series of 'experience-design principles' that include: *theme the experience* (for example, 'eatertainment' restaurants such as Planet Hollywood or the Rainforest Cafe); *mix in memorabilia* (for example, an official T-shirt for a rock concert); and, above all, *engage all five senses*:

> The more senses an experience engages, the more effective and memorable it can be. Smart shoeshine operators augment the smell of polish with crisp snaps of the cloth, scents and sounds that don't make the shoes any shinier but do make the experience more engaging… Similarly, grocery stores pipe bakery smells into the aisles, and some use light and sound to simulate thunderstorms when misting their produce.
> The mist at the Rainforest Cafe appeals serially to all five senses. It is first apparent as a sound: Sss-sss-zzz. Then you see the mist arising from the rocks and feel it soft and cool against your skin. Finally, you smell its tropical essence, and you taste (or imagine that you do) its freshness. What you can't be is unaffected by the mist. (Pine and Gilmore 1998: 104)

The examples cited by Pine and Gilmore could be multiplied. There has been a veritable explosion in the number of ads touting the sense appeal of commodities in recent years. Typical of this trend is the following advertising copy for a particular luxury automobile:

> *You Might Expect A Luxury Sedan To Cater To Your Senses. But All Six of Them?*
> The sixth sense is a keen, highly intuitive power – a power of perception – that goes far beyond the five senses. That's according to the dictionary.
> According to our engineers, it comes standard with every Lexus ES 300. Let us explain.
> Have you ever been in a new place and felt like you had been there before? Some call it déjà vu, but we call it ergonomics: the uncanny ability of our cabin to have everything in exactly the place you would most likely want it. So whether it's the knob for the climate control system or the switch for the power window or the buttons for the optional six-disc CD auto-changer, or

whatever – the first time you reach for it, the very first time, it will be there, as if you had placed it there yourself. Kind of spooky.

Of course, we also do a lot for your other senses: the look of a sleek, aerodynamic body, the feel of gentle lumbar support, the smell of available handcrafted leather upholstery, and the soothing sound of eight strategically placed speakers. As for taste, it's in everything we do. Figuratively speaking, of course.

As this copy brings out, thanks to advances in 'human factors' research, no sense is left unturned in the contemporary marketplace. In fact, they may even be multiplied in order to promise ever more consumer satisfaction.

The strategy of appealing to all five senses is a compelling one, to be sure. However, this strategy cannot of itself overcome 'advertising wear-out' when, as is increasingly the case, all of a given brand's competitors are doing the same. This has led to the emergence of an alternative technique, which involves tapping the sensorial subconscious, instead of simply blanketing all of the consumer's external receptors. This alternative stratagem is best exemplified by ZMET (Zaltman Metaphor Elicitation Technique) invented and patented by Gerald Zaltman of the 'Mind of the Market' Lab at Harvard University. Before examining this technique, however, it is instructive to consider some of its precursors, such as the 'art' of subliminal persuasion.

In a famous (if flawed) experiment carried out at a New Jersey drive-in movie theater in 1957, the Subliminal Projection Company flashed messages saying 'Drink Coca-Cola' and 'Eat Popcorn' during a screening of the film *Picnic*. The images went by at too fast a rate for viewers to be aware that they had seen them. This subliminal messaging nevertheless had the effect of augmenting popcorn sales by 20 percent and Coke sales by as much as 60 percent. A public outcry ensued when the experiment was reported in the press, for how could consumers make rational decisions about consumption choices if their minds were being 'broken and entered' in this way? These fears, however, only stoked the fad for marketers inserting and vigilant consumers trying to spot visual and aural 'embeds' everywhere (for example, suggestively shaped ice cubes or barely audible soundtracks) (Key 1974; Solomon et al. 1999: 60–2).

A similar furore erupted in the mid 1990s at the height of the olfactory revolution in the marketplace (when all manner of commodities came to be imbued with signature scents), this time sparked by media reports of the notorious case of the scented Las Vegas slot machines (Classen et al. 1994: 196). The concern here was that marketers were once again circumventing the consumer's conscious awareness, or 'rational faculties,' by targeting messages directly to the most primitive part of the brain, the limbic system, seat of the emotions and memory. In other words, consumers were being led by the nose instead of being addressed through the more legitimate (read: 'rational') channels of visual and verbal communication.

There is an undeniable thrill to the experience of the subliminal, which may explain the popularity of these subconscious perceptual techniques for purposes of moving merchandise, however damaging to 'rational choice' models of consumer behavior they may be. Another undeniable source of pleasure (and hence attention) is synesthesia. Synesthesia involves short-circuiting the conventional five sense model and experience of perception. It establishes cross-linkages between the modalities at a subconscious level, and so opens up a whole new terrain – the terrain of the inter-sensory – for marketers and designers to work their magic.

The genius of the Zaltman Metaphor Elicitation Technique consists in the way it maps – or better, excavates – these cross-linkages, and models them in 'actionable ways' (for example, to guide the development of ad copy or to divine the best product design and packaging). This ten-step research tool involves image-collecting, sorting, storytelling, digital imaging, and creating videos on the part of the research subjects. The videos are used because: 'People think differently when they think "in motion" than when they think in still images or pictures' (Zaltman and Coulter 1995: 42). ZMET also involves subjects being asked to say 'what is and is not the taste, touch, smell, color, sound and emotional feeling' related to the particular research topic (for example, a brand name or a product design) being investigated. For example, one subject's 'nonvisual sensory images' of a certain brand of intimate apparel included: 'the taste of medicine, but not dessert; the feel of sandpaper and silk, but not of cream; the sound of static, but not that of a waterfall; the smell of sulfur, but not of roses; the color brown, but not red; the feeling of anxiety, but not of peacefulness' (Zaltman and Coulter 1995: 42). By tapping the sensorial subconscious in this way, a wide range of synesthetic equations is uncovered. These equations are then worked (along with the visual and verbal material elicited by other means) into 'consensus maps' by ZMET researchers. Marketers and designers in turn use these 'consensus maps' to identify those sensory transfers that best 'focus our attention, capture our imagination, please us, and enhance persuasion' (Nelson and Hitchon 1999: 355).

The inter-sensual logic behind this latest revolution in marketing can be discerned behind such advertising headlines as 'Taste the Rainbow' for *Skittles* candy; 'the Loudest Taste on Earth' for *Spicy Doritos* corn chips; and, 'A Gentle Whisper of Color' for *Chanel* pastel eye color makeup. As for product design, synesthesia is the idea behind all the new computer programs that enable users to transform music into color graphics. But this is obvious. Other design applications of synesthesia (using other sensory combinations besides sight and sound) are being developed all the time (Kälviäinen 2002). For example, the cleaner *Vim Oxy-Gel* (with 'active oxygen') offers 'Pure cleanliness you can see and feel!'

Is synesthesia the ultimate weapon in the 'sign wars' (Goldman and Papson 1996) of contemporary advertising and product design? Not quite, for it is not uniformly persuasive across all categories of products (see Nelson and Hitchon 1999; Howes 2003b). But in its subliminality it comes close to being the perfect weapon.

The Social Life of the Senses on the Margins of the Global Consumer Society

We have glimpsed something of the sensual logic of late capitalism. We have examined its ingenious battery of sensory (and inter-sensory) techniques for overcoming the separation of subject and object or environment. But do these techniques work in practice? Do '[the] data we receive from our sensory systems *determine* how we respond to products' (Solomon et al. 1999: 49, emphasis mine)? Here it is instructive to shift focus from the center to the margins of the global consumer society.

The captains of global capitalism certainly assume that exposure to the representational machinery of capitalist sensualism will induce changes in the consumption behavior of those on the periphery. For example, the fact that Western-style public displays of affection are considered improper in India does not stop Star TV from beaming American movies and television shows with such content into India, nor Indians from watching them. Global marketers expect that this viewing will quickly turn to imitating, and, in turn, create a need for a whole new range of personal care products. As one global marketer explained: 'When you want to be physically closer to people a lot, then you tend to want to look better, smell better. So the [Indian] market will grow for cosmetics, perfumes, after-shaves, mouthwashes and so on' (Dyer 1994). This case (for further examples see Classen and Howes 1996) seems to confirm Marx's and Engels' point: 'In one word, [the bourgeoisie] creates a world after its own image' (Marx and Engels 1967: 84).

Marx's and Engels' vision of globalization as cultural homogenization finds further support in the way national élites in many African countries are called 'white men' by their less affluent countrymen, as among the Hausa of Nigeria. The traditional Hausa sensory or 'aesthetic order' may be seen as vulnerable to capitalist makeover as the trappings of social standing displayed by these (Westernized) role models 'trickle down.' What is more, the premium attached to 'brilliance' in the Hausa aesthetic order has made quartz watches attractive substitutes for silver bracelets, and enamelware for gourds. 'Brilliant!' says the global marketer, perceiving yet another niche opening up.

However, when we exchange the perspective of the global marketer for that of the ethnographer Eric Arnould (1989), we begin to appreciate the multiple respects in which Western products are, in fact, being *re-made* in Hausaland. According to Arnould, the emphasis in Hausa consumption practices remains on what is *done* with objects rather than having them, and the prime context for the encounter with novel Western goods is the bridal display, not the department store. The Hausa marriage ceremony provides an emotionally, aesthetically and socially charged atmosphere for the transfer of cultural meanings to novel objects, and significantly conditions personal choice. What is more, the most desirable products, from an islamized Hausa perspective, are 'Meccan goods,' which are infused with grace. Grace is one quality no Western designer or marketer has so far been able to simulate, or likely ever will.

The Hausa case is not unique. 'Preference formation' is always a cultural matter, not simply a personal one. When Temiars of Malaysia dream of Western consumer goods, or use strips of plastic (on account of their much prized 'glitter') in the construction of their spirit altars, it is not the American dream they are dreaming (Marchand 1985; Roseman, this vol.). When Papua New Guineans buy Johnson & Johnson's baby powder at their local tradestore, it is not for use on infants but for purifying corpses and mourners, asperging the heads of ritual performers, and for body decor (Howes 2003: 217–18). Zimbabweans use Lifebuoy Soap not to wash their bodies but to add a much-valued sheen to their skin, and for fish bait (Burke 1996). These striking examples of consumer-added values or 'meanings' and uses underscore the importance of factoring local 'modes of consumption' into any account of how the senses have been organized by the expansion of capitalist relations of production and exchange.[2]

The above examples also bring out how consumption cannot be grasped exclusively in terms of the reception or internalization of the 'messages' of some hypostatized 'code' (to use Baudrillard's terminology). As the growing body of research on cross-cultural consumption shows, there is no guarantee that 'the intentions of the producer will be recognized, much less respected, by the consumer from another culture' (Howes 1996: 6; von Gernet 1996; Foster 1996/97; Coote, Morton and Nicholson 2000; Stahl 2002). Consumption is an *active* (not a passive) process, where all sorts of meanings and uses for products are generated that the designers and marketers of those products never imagined.

Quite apart from the way in which consumers from the margins consistently override the 'directions for use' of globalized commodities in their practices of everyday life,[3] there is the growing phenomenon of local rejection of transnational commodities and resistance to Western-style consumer capitalism. Consider the rise of *Ostalgie* in the former German Democratic Republic – that is, the new demand for old GDR products (including lemonade, washing powder, coffee, transistor radios, TVs and cars, such as the *Trabant*) as a matter of conscious preference to (Western) brand name goods.

> [The] very otherness of GDR products, manifest in their physicality that can be seen, felt, tasted, smelled, and heard, serves as the starting point of these journeys into the past [i.e. East German people indulging in *Ostalgie*]. These

products, however, are not only the basis for individual acts of remembering, but they also signify a group identity for their former consumers: since all former citizens of the GDR were – by necessity – also consumers of its goods, they can find an exclusive identity as former consumers and purchasers of these products since they all have once shared the specific [un-branded] knowledge about these products. (Blum 2000: 231)

Suffice it to say that the handling, the rumble, the fumes, and especially the sight of a Trabant is unlike the sensory surround of a Lexus.

Even in those countries, like Japan, which have gravitated to the center of the capitalist world economic order, one finds pockets of people deploying their senses to resist the commodification of experience:

To some Japanese nativists, their people's best hope of liberating themselves from Western cultural domination and rediscovering their Japanese souls lies in the process of *jikkan* – 'retrospection through actual sensation.' Thus the smell of incense at a shrine or the tactile and kinesthetic sensations of sitting on tatami *(suwaru)* rather than sitting on a chair *(koshikakeru)* can produce a reconnection with the eternal, authentic Japanese culture and soul. (Tobin quoted in Classen and Howes 1996: 179)

The cases of domestication and resistance to the forces and products of global capitalism discussed above point to a significant lacuna in the marxian theory of the value of the commodity form. Let us shift our focus from the margins back to the center of the global consumer society to explore this lacuna.

Commodities do not only conceal the social relations of their production (as Marx showed); they are also used by consumers to *express* social relations by virtue of their materiality – that is to say, their sensory properties. Consider Table 16.1, a 'Table of tactile oppositions in fabrics' found in a North American textbook of consumer behavior. As Table 16.1 shows, the sensual relations between different sorts of fabrics serve to express gender relations, and thereby render sensible the categories of male and female, in addition to providing individual consumers with the means to articulate their 'identity' or social location.

Table 16.1 Table of tactile oppositions in fabrics (after Solomon et al. 1999: 55, Table 2-1)

Perception	Male	Female	
High class	Wool	Silk	Fine
Low class	Denim	Cotton	↑
	Heavy ⟷ Light		Coarse

The marxian theory of value notoriously occludes the sensuous or aesthetic characteristics of the commodity form. This is because the system of industrial capitalism that reigned during Marx's day, and which constituted the ground of his thought, foregrounded production and free-market exchange, just as it privileged a utilitarian attitude toward the value of commodities (for example, the use-value of a coat consists in the protection from the elements it affords, never mind its cut or quality of its cloth). Indeed, according to Marx, at the moment a commodity becomes an object of exchange (an exchange-value) 'all sensuous characteristics are extinguished' and it becomes 'supersensible,' which is to say 'interchangeable' with the exchange-value of any other commodity, or of money (quoted in Keenan 1993: 165, 181). As noted elsewhere, 'by analysing commodities exclusively in terms of their use- and exchange-value, Marx elided what could be called their ["sense"] – namely, the sensuous contrasts which set one commodity off from another and give expression to cultural categories as well as express differences in social location' (Howes 2003a: 205). It is tempting to call this 'sense' the 'sign-value' of the commodity, following Baudrillard (1970, 1981, 1996), but the matter is more complex than that. The notion of 'sign-value' ushers in the idea of the 'system of objects' as 'structured like a language.' Many voices now caution against such a 'simplistic equation between language and materiality, mainly due to the unordered and seemingly unstructured nature of consumption' (Blum 2000: 234; see further Miller 1998; Dant 1999; Stahl 2002).

In the 'aesthetic plenitude' of the current conjuncture, it is increasingly difficult to discern any evidence for a 'code of objects' (*pace* Baudrillard). Tweens use Kool-Aid – that gustatory icon of middle-class family life – as a flamboyant hair dye, and it is not only Rastafarians who sport dreadlocks. Table 16.1 only holds to a limited extent in the age of mix-and-mutate when no one wants to match. Code-scrambling has become the order of the day. Virginia Postel puts it well when she writes:

> A sort of chemical transformation through recombination is, in fact, where much of today's aesthetic plenitude comes from. Like atoms bouncing about in a boiling solution, aesthetic elements are bumping into each other, creating new style compounds. We are constantly exposed to new aesthetic material, ripe for recombination, borrowed from other people's traditional cultures or contemporary subcultures. Thanks to media, migration, and cultural pluralism, what once was exotic is now familiar (Postrel 2003:12)

While Postrel's point in *The Substance of Style* – namely, that there is more substance to style than was previously thought, and 'personalization' now rules the wardrobe – is well taken, the fact remains that there is something endearingly and dangerously naive about her privileging of hedonics over semantics and social status (see above on people petting Armani clothes). The sensory properties of commodities have been multiplied dramatically in 'the aesthetic age,' as we have seen, but the cultural (as opposed to personal) logic behind this development should not be lost from view. Postrel appears to be guilty of 'taking the ideology of consumption for consumption itself' (Clarke 2003). What she calls 'the aesthetic imperative' is but the velvet glove that fits 'the imperative to consume.' The latter imperative 'demands, above all, that the body "be *made fit* to absorb an ever-growing number of sensations the commodities offer or promise"' (Bauman cited in Clarke 2003: 146). Hence the growth of 'human factors' research and all of the ways designers now 'think beauty in interaction' (Overbeeke 2002) the better to make the fit between subject and product a seamless one. Hence too the growth of self-instruction manuals like *The Bluffer's Guide to Wine* which instill routines geared towards 'ensuring that the consumer might will and act to absorb *more* of the sensations on offer' (Clarke 2003:146; see further Joy and Venkatesh 1994). As the proliferation of such self-help treatises attests, the age of simulation has taken on a very personal meaning for its denizens. Don't think disappearance of reality in representation; think disappearance of the self! In postmodernity it seems that simulation has become the existential ground of personality itself.

Some cultural critics, most notably Frederic Jameson, author of *Postmodernism, or The Cultural Logic of Late Capitalism*, rail against the new 'depthlessness,' demise of affect (along with the subject), and cannibalization of styles in our postmodern times. Jameson points, for example, to the new urban ensembles around Paris where 'there is absolutely no perspective at all' with the result that 'one cannot position oneself' (Stephanson 1989: 47–8). His antidote to all this is something called 'cognitive-mapping' (Jameson 1991).

While one might agree with Jameson that the situation is critical, one must question the feasibility of his strategy of critique. How can cognitive-mapping possibly find the purchase – or generate the (transcendent) depth – necessary to cut through the sensory profusion of late capitalism? The best antidote, I suggest, is *sensitive-training* of the sort practised by Japanese nativists when they cultivate the capacity for *jikkan* (see above), or the gustatory curriculum introduced in French schools to counter the hegemony of *fast-foodisme* by instilling in pupils a (renewed) taste for *haute cuisine* (Puisais and Pierre 1987). The latter strategy may pale in comparison with the sensory reforms imagined by Charles Fourier in his designs for the utopian society of Harmony, where gastrosophers and amateurs would rule the world (see Fourier 1851; Classen 1998), but at least it offers the possibility of finding some sort of purchase within the system, rather than apart from it, like cognitive-mapping – for what if there is no apart?

Other theorists question whether our situation is as critical as Jameson maintains. Mike Featherstone, for example, points to evidence showing that the individual subject, affectivity, and reality have not really been eclipsed – at least, not to the extent claimed by Jameson and other postmodern critics (or aficionados like Baudrillard). Taking the example of Disneyland (which is treated as paradigmatic of postmodern hyperspace and simulation by Jameson), Featherstone notes:

> It has been argued that increasingly the contemporary tourist (or 'post-tourist') approaches holiday locations such as resorts, theme parks, and increasingly museums in the knowledge that the spectacles offered are simulations and accepts the montaged world and hyper-reality for what it is [Urry 1988]. That is, they do not quest after an authentic pre-simulational reality but have the necessary dispositions to engage in 'the play of the real' and capacity to open up to surface sensations, spectacular imagery, liminoid experiences and intensities without the nostalgia for the real. (Featherstone 1989: 130)

If Featherstone is correct,[4] then it appears that the age of simulation has collapsed into one of mere stimulation (not that one should underestimate how powerfully commercially *motivated* the stimuli on offer are). In other words, capitalist sensualism has fallen victim to its own success, its own hype, as far as '*determin[ing]* how we respond to products' (Solomon et al. 1999) is concerned. It doesn't (see Howes 2003b).

One of the precipitating factors of this collapse would seem to be the makeover of the body of the commodity. As noted above, massive resources are now being poured into getting the sense appeal of things 'just right.' It is understandable why this strategy backfired: multiplying the sensory stimuli emitted by the merchandise and designing for affectivity (i.e. pleasure with products) was bound to undermine the very instrumentality, the very rationality of the system whose ends it was supposed to serve. The hyperestheticization of the body of the commodity has deconstructed its utility. With utility now in recession, a space has opened up where people can 'make sense' of things in all sorts of non-commercial, 'non-rational,' but aesthetic ways, like using Lifebuoy soap to give a sheen to one's skin, or deploying Kool-Aid as a hair dye.

Could it be that in the sensory profusion of the contemporary marketplace, the consumer has been let out of the glove? Not likely. But this question leads to another equally perplexing one: what theory of value could possibly capture the 'aesthetic plenitude' of the current conjuncture? Certainly not a labor theory, unless consumption be considered a form of labor. But how would that work? Should the so-called productivity of the consumer be counted as part of the Gross National Product (GNP)? If so, how is it possible to measure the value of the endless innovation in the 'senses' (meanings and uses) of things worked by latter day consumers?[5] Consumer-added value undermines the valorization of capital even as it appears to confirm it insofar as money will have been exchanged for some item, which is then re-valorized by the consumer. This exchange-value expressed in the money equivalent is, however, nothing more than the 'ghost' of the commodity, whereas the 'senses' of the commodity are palpable, and subject to multiple appropriations (see Howes 2003a: 221–9). This points to a looming crisis in the circuits of capitalist production and exchange. Now that consumption, rather than production or exchange is the 'scene of action,' there is increased risk of those circuits short-circuiting.

Perhaps, in the final analysis, it is for the consumption of the senses themselves in late capitalism that our epoch will be remembered.

Acknowledgments

This chapter is a product of the conjuncture of two lines of research, 'Culture and Consumption' (1998–2001) and 'The Sense Lives of Things' (2002–5), both of which projects were generously supported by the Social Sciences and Humanities Research Council of Canada. I wish to thank the members of the Culture and Consumption Research Group and the Concordia Sensoria Research Team for the many stimulating discussions we have had around the subject of this chapter.

Notes

1. I would submit that Margaret Cohen fails to 'acknowledge consumption' when she asks only 'How have the senses been organized by relations of production and exchange?'

2. To take an historical example, the Algonquian Indians traded furs for glass beads with the French in seventeenth century Quebec and there was also quite a traffic in prayer beads. But the Algonquians did not admire the beads simply for their 'brilliance'; they also occasionally ground them up and smoked them because 'the respiratory route' was the standard route for the ingestion of power-laden substances (von Gernet 1996: 170–6).

3. It should not be overlooked that the creative misuses discussed here can have destructive as well as subversive consequences, as in the tragic case of the 'misuse' of infant formula in many Third World countries (see Classen and Howes 1996).

4. It is not clear to me from Featherstone's account how 'post-tourists' acquire 'the necessary dispositions.'

5. Of course, if Western consumers were all that ingenious or creative at 'using commodities otherwise,' recycling would be far more advanced than it is (but see Coote, Morton and Nicholson 2000; Gregson and Crewe 2003). Also, entrepreneurs are always seeking to 'recuperate for capitalism' the latest novel usage, whence the endless proliferation of 'labor-saving devices' on department store shelves.

Bibliography

Appadurai, A. (1996), *Modernity at Large: Cultural Dimensions of Globalization*, Minneapolis: University of Minnesota Press.

Arnould, E. (1989). 'Toward a Broadened Theory of Preference Formation and the Diffusion of Innovations: Cases from Zinder Province, Niger Republic,' *Journal of Consumer Research*, 16: 239–66.

Baudrillard, J. (1970), *La société de consommation*, Paris: Gallimard.

—— (1981), *For a Critique of the Political Economy of the Sign*, Minneapolis: University of Minnesota Press.

—— (1983), *Simulations*, trans. P. Foss et al., New York: Semiotext(e).

—— (1996), *The System of Objects*, trans. J. Benedict, London: Verso.

Bauman, Z. (1983), 'Industrialism, Consumerism and Power,' *Theory, Culture and Society*, 1(3): 32–43.

Benjamin, W. (1969), *Illuminations*, trans. H. Zohn, New York: Schocken.

—— (1973), *Charles Baudelaire: A Lyric Poet in the Era of High Capitalism*, trans. H. Zohn, London: New Left Books.

—— (1979), *One-Way Street and Other Writings*, trans. E. Jephcott and K. Shorter. London: New Left Books.

Blum, M. (2000), 'Remaking the East German Past: *Ostalgie*, Identity, and Material Culture,' *Journal of Popular Culture*, 34(3): 229–253.

Bonapace, L. (2002), 'Linking Product Properties to Pleasure: The Sensorial Quality Assessment Method' in W.S. Green and P.W. Jordan (eds), *Pleasure with Products: Beyond Usability*, London: Taylor & Francis, pp. 189–217.

Bowlby, R. (1985), *Just Looking: Consumer Culture in Dreiser, Gissing and Zola*, New York: Methuen.

Buck-Morss, S. (1989), *The Dialectics of Seeing: Walter Benjamin and the Arcades Project*, Cambridge MA: MIT Press.

Burke, T. (1996), *Lifebuoy Men, Lux Women: Commodification, Consumption, and Cleanliness in Modern Zimbabwe*, Durham: Duke Univerrsity Press.

Clarke, D.B. (2003), *The Consumer Society and the Postmodern City*, London: Routledge.

Classen, C. and Howes, D. (1996b), 'The Dynamics and Ethics of Cross-Cultural Consumption,' in Howes, D. (ed.), *Cross-Cultural Consumption*, London and New York: Routledge, pp. 178–94.

Classen, C., Howes, D. and Synnott, A. (1994), *Aroma: The Cultural History of Smell*, London and New York: Routledge.

Cohen, M. (1994), 'The Art of Profane Illumination,' *Visual Anthropology Review*, 10: 44–9.

Cook, I. and Crang, P. (1996), 'The World on a Plate: Culinary Culture, Displacement and Geographical Knowledges,' *Journal of Material Culture*, 1(2).

Coote, J., Morton, C. and Nicholson, J. (2000), *Transformations: The Art of Recycling*, Oxford: Pitt Rivers Museum.

Cummings, N. and Lewandoska, M. (2000), *The Value of Things*, Basel: Birkhauser.

Dant, T. (1999), *Material Culture in the Social World*, Buckingham: Open University Press.

Debord, G. (1977), *The Society of the Spectacle*, Detroit: Red and Black.

Desmet, P.M.A. and Hekkert, P.P.M. (2002), 'The Basis of Product Emotions,' in W.S. Green and P.W. Jordan (eds), *Pleasure with Products: Beyond Usability*, London: Taylor & Francis, pp. 61–8.

Dorfman, A. (1983), *The Empire's Old Clothes: What the Lone Ranger, Babar, and Other Innocent Heroes Do to Our Minds*, New York: Pantheon Books.

Dyer, G. (1994), 'How Star TV Can Sell Aftershave and Curb Totalitarianism At the Same Time,' *The Montreal Gazette*, 21 May.

Edelstein, J.S. and Leuders, C.L. (2000), 'Recent Developments in Trade Dress Infringement Law,' *Idea*, 40: 105–37.

Ewen, S. (1988), *All Consuming Images: The Politics of Style in Contemporary Culture*, New York: Basic Books.

Featherstone, M. (1989), 'Postmodernism, Cultural Change, and Social Practice,' in D. Kellner (ed.), *Postmodernism/Jameson/Critique*, Washington DC: Maisonneuve Press, pp. 117–38.

—— (ed.) (1990), *Global Culture*, London: Sage.

Foucault, M. (1979), *Discipline and Punish*, trans. A.M. Sheridan Smith, New York: Vintage Books.

Fourier, C. ([1851] 1968), *The Passions of the Human Soul and their Influence on Society and Civilization*, trans. J Morell, New York: A.M. Kelley.

Fulton Suri, J. (2002), 'Designing Experience: Whether to Measure Pleasure or Just Tune In?' in W.S. Green and P.W. Jordan (eds), *Pleasure with Products: Beyond Usability*, London: Taylor & Francis, pp 161–74.

Feuerbach, L. (1966), *Principles of the Philosophy of the Future*, trans. M. Vogel, Indianapolis: Bobbs-Merrill.

Foster, R. (1996/97), 'Commercial Mass Media in Papua New Guinea: Notes on Agency, Bodies, and Commodity Consumption,' *Visual Anthropology Review*, 12(2): 1–17.

Galbraith. J.K. (1958), *The Affluent Society*, Boston: Houghton Mifflin.

—— (1967), *The New Industrial State*, Boston: Houghton Mifflin.

Goldman, R. and Papson, S. (1996), *Sign Wars: The Cluttered Landscape of Advertising*, New York: The Guilford Press.

Green, W.S. and Jordan, P.W. (eds) (2002), *Pleasure with Products: Beyond Usability*, London: Taylor & Francis.

Gregson, N. and Crewe, L. (2003), *Second-Hand Cultures*, Oxford: Berg.

Haug, W. (1986), *Critique of Commodity Aesthetics: Appearance, Sexuality and Advertising in Capitalist Society*, trans. R. Bock, Minneapolis: University of Minnesota Press.

Hornik, J. (1992), 'Tactile Stimulation and Consumer Response,' *Journal of Consumer Research*, 19: 449–55.

Howes, D. (1996), 'Introduction: Commodities and Cultural Borders,' in D. Howes (ed.), *Cross-Cultural Consumption: Global Markets, Local Realities*, London: Routledge, pp. 1–16.

—— (2003a), *Sensual Relations: Engaging the Senses in Culture and Social Theory*, Ann Arbor: University of Michigan Press.

—— (2003b), 'Evaluation sensorielle et diversité culturelle,' *Psychologie françoise*, 48(4): 117–25.

James, A. (1996), 'Cooking the Books: Global or Local Identities in Contemporary British Food Cultures?' in D. Howes (ed.), *Cross-Cultural Consumption*, London and New York: Routledge, pp. 77–92.

Jameson, F. (1991), *Postmodernism, or, The Cultural Logic of Late Capitalism*, Durham: Duke University Press.

Jones, P. (2003), "'Tis a tale full of sound and colour – signifying nothing?' *The Lawyers Weekly*, 23(9).

Joy, A. and Venkatesh, A. (1994), 'Postmodernism, Feminism, and the Body: The Visible and the Invisible in Consumer Research,' *International Journal of Research in Marketing*, 11: 333–57.

Kälviäinen, M. (2002), 'Product Design for Consumer Taste,' in W.S. Green and P.W. Jordan (eds), *Pleasure with Products: Beyond Usability*, London: Taylor & Francis, pp. 77–96.

Keenan, T. (1993), 'The Point is to (Ex)Change It: *Reading* Capital *Rhetorically*,' in E. Apter and W. Pietz (eds), *Fetishism as Cultural Discourse*, Ithaca, NY: Cornell University Press, pp. 152–85.

Key, W.B. (1972), *Subliminal Seduction*, New York: Penguin.

Loewy, R. (1951), *Never Leave Well Enough Alone*, New York: Simon & Schuster.

Marchand, R. (1985), *Advertising the American Dream: Making Way for Modernity, 1920–1940*, Berkeley: University of California Press.

Marx, K. (1954), *Capital: A Critique of Political Economy*, volume 1, trans. S. Moore and E Aveling, London: Lawrence & Wishart.

—— (1987), *Economic and Philosophic Manuscripts of 1844*, trans. M. Milligan, Buffalo: Prometheus Books.

Marx, K. and Engels, F. (1947), *The German Ideology*, ed. R. Pascal, New York: International Publishers.

—— (1967), *The Communist Manifesto*, intro. A.J.P. Taylor, Harmondsworth: Penguin.

McLuhan, M. (1962), *The Gutenberg Galaxy*, Toronto: University of Toronto Press.

—— (1964), *Understanding Media*, New York: New American Library.

—— and Fiore, Q. (1967), *The Medium is the Massage*, New York: Bantam.

Miller, D. (1987), *Material Culture and Mass Consumption*, Oxford: Blackwell.

—— (ed.) (1995a), *Acknowledging Consumption*, London: Routledge.

—— (1995b), 'Consumption and Commodities,' *Annual Review of Anthropology*, 24: 141–61.

Nelson, M.R. and Hitchon, J.C. (1999), 'Loud Tastes, Colored Fragrances, and Scented Sounds: How and When to Mix the Senses in Persuasive Communication,' *Journal of Mass Communication Quarterly*, 76(2): 354–72.

Overbeeke, K., Djadjaliningrat, T., Hummels, C. and Wensveen, S. (2002), 'Beauty in Usability: Forget about Ease of Use!' in W.S. Green and P.W. Jordan (eds), *Pleasure with Products: Beyond Usability*, London: Taylor & Francis, pp. 9–17.

Pine II, B.J. and Gilmore, J.H. (1998), 'Welcome to the Experience Economy,' *Harvard Business Review*, 76(4): 97–105.

Postrel, V. (2003), *The Substance of Style*, New York: HarperCollins.

Puisais, J. and Pierre, C. (1987), *Le Goût et l'enfant*, Paris: Flammarion.

Rajagopal, A. (1998), 'Advertising, Politics and the Sentimemental Education of the Indian Consumer,' *Visual Anthropology Review*, 14(2): 14–31.

Robbins, R. (1998), *Global Problems and the Culture of Capitalism*, Boston: Allyn & Bacon.

Saisselin, R.G. (1984), *The Bourgeois and the Bibelot*, New Brunswick NJ: Rutgers University Press.

Sheldon, R. and Arens, E. (1976), *Consumer Engineering: A New Technique for Prosperity*, New York: Arno Press.

Solomon, M.R., Zaichkowsky, J. and Polegato, R. (1999), *Consumer Behaviour: Buying, Having and Being*, Scarborough ON: Prentice-Hall Canada.

Stahl, A. (2002), 'Colonial Entanglements and the Practices of Taste: An Alternative to Logocentric Approaches,' *American Anthropologist*, 104(3): 827–45.

Stephanson, A. (1989), 'Regarding Postmodernism: A Conversation with Frederic Jameson,' in D. Kellner (ed.), *Postmodernism/Jameson/Critique*, Washington DC: Maisonneuve Press, pp. 43–74.

Synnott, A. (1991), 'Puzzling Over the Senses: From Plato to Marx,' in D. Howes (ed.), *The Varieties of Sensory Experience*, Toronto: University of Toronto Press, pp. 61–76.

—— (1993), *The Body Social: Symbolism, Self and Society*, London and New York: Routledge.

Tester, K. (ed.) (1994), *The Flâneur*, London and New York: Routledge.

Urry, J. (1988), 'Cultural Change and Contemporary Holiday-Making,' *Theory, Culture and Society*, 5(1): 35–55.

von Gernet, A. (1996), 'Reactions to the Familiar and the Novel in Seventeenth century French-Amerindian Contact,' in L. Turgeon, D. Delâge and R. Ouellet (eds), *Cultural Transfer, America and Europe: 500 Years of Interculturation*, Québec: Les Presses de l'Université Laval, pp. 169–88.

Zaltman, G. (1996), 'Metaphorically Speaking,' *Marketing Research*, 8(2): 13–20.

Zaltman, G. and Coulter, R. (1995), 'Seeing the Voice of the Customer: Metaphor-based Advertising Research,' *Journal of Advertising Research*, (July/August): 35–51.

17

Under the Jaguar Sun

Italo Calvino

'Oaxaca' is pronounced 'Wa*ha*ka.' Originally, the hotel where we were staying had been the Convent of Santa Catalina. The first thing we noticed was a painting in a little room leading to the bar. The bar was called Las Novicias. The painting was a large, dark canvas that portrayed a young nun and an old priest standing side by side; their hands, slightly apart from their sides, almost touched. The figures were rather stiff for an eighteenth-century picture; the painting had the somewhat crude grace characteristic of colonial art, but it conveyed a distressing sensation, like an ache of contained suffering.

The lower part of the painting was filled by a long caption, written in cramped lines in an angular, italic hand, white on black. The words devoutly celebrated the life and death of the two characters, who had been chaplain and abbess of the convent (she, of noble birth, had entered it as a novice at the age of eighteen). The reason for their being painted together was the extraordinary love (this word, in the pious Spanish prose, appeared charged with ultra-terrestrial yearning) that had bound the abbess and her confessor for 30 years, a love so great (the word in its spiritual sense sublimated but did not erase the physical emotion) that when the priest came to die, the abbess, 20 years younger, in the space of a single day fell ill and literally expired of love (the word blazed with a truth in which all meanings converge), to join him in Heaven.

Olivia, whose Spanish is better than mine, helped me decipher the story, suggesting to me the translation of some obscure expressions, and these words proved to be the only ones we exchanged during and after the reading, as if we had found ourselves in the presence of a drama, or of a happiness, that made any comment out of place. Something intimidated us – or, rather, frightened us, or, more precisely, filled us with a kind of uneasiness. So I will try to describe what I felt: the sense of a lack, a consuming void. What Olivia was thinking, since she remained silent, I cannot guess.

Then Olivia spoke. She said, 'I would like to eat *chiles en nogada.*' And, walking like somnambulists, not quite sure we were touching the ground, we headed for the dining room.

In the best moments of a couple's life, it happens: I immediately reconstructed the train of Olivia's thought, with no need of further speech, because the same sequence of associations had unrolled in my mind, though in a more foggy, murky way. Without her, I would never have gained awareness of it.

Our trip through Mexico had already lasted over a week. A few days earlier, in Tepotzotlan, in a restaurant whose tables were set among the orange trees of another convent's cloister, we had savored dishes prepared (at least, so we were told) according to the traditional recipes of the nuns. We had eaten a *tamal de elote* – a fine semolina of sweet corn, that is, with ground pork and very hot pepper, all steamed in a bit of cornhusk – and then *chiles en nogada*, which were reddish brown, somewhat wrinkled little peppers, swimming in a walnut sauce whose harshness and bitter aftertaste were drowned in a creamy, sweetish surrender.

After that, for us, the thought of nuns called up the flavors of an elaborate and bold cuisine, bent on making the flavors' highest notes vibrate, juxtaposing them in modulations, in chords, and especially in dissonances that would assert themselves as an incomparable experience – a point of no return, an absolute possession exercised on the receptivity of all the senses.

The Mexican friend who had accompanied us on that excursion, Salustiano Velazco by name, in answering Olivia's inquiries about these recipes of conventual gastronomy, lowered his voice as if confiding indelicate secrets to us. It was his way of speaking – or, rather, one of his ways; the copious information Salustiano supplied (about the history and customs and nature of his country his erudition was inexhaustible) was either stated emphatically like a war proclamation or slyly insinuated as if it were charged with all sorts of implied meanings.

Olivia remarked that such dishes involved hours and hours of work and, even before that, a long series of experiments and adjustments. 'Did these nuns spend their whole day in the kitchen?' she asked, imagining entire lives devoted to the search for new blends of ingredients, new variations in the measurements, to alert and patient mixing, to the handing down of an intricate, precise lore.

'*Tenían sus criadas,*' Salustiano answered. ('They had their servants.') And he explained to us that when the daughters of noble families entered the convent, they brought their maids with them; thus, to satisfy the venial whims of gluttony, the only cravings allowed them, the nuns could rely on a swarm of eager, tireless helpers. And as far as they themselves were concerned, they had only to conceive and compare and correct the recipes that expressed their fantasies confined within those walls: the fantasies, after all, of sophisticated women, bright and introverted and complex women

who needed absolutes, whose reading told of ecstasies and transfigurations, martyrs and tortures, women with conflicting calls in their blood, genealogies in which the descendants of the conquistadores mingled with those of Indian princesses or slaves, women with childhood recollections of the fruits and fragrances of a succulent vegetation, thick with ferments, though growing from those sun-baked plateaus.

Nor should sacred architecture be overlooked, the background to the lives of those religious; it, too, was impelled by the same drive toward the extreme that led to the exacerbation of flavors amplified by the blaze of the most spicy *chiles*. Just as colonial baroque set no limits on the profusion of ornament and display, in which God's presence was identified in a closely calculated delirium of brimming, excessive sensations, so the curing of the hundred or more native varieties of hot peppers carefully selected for each dish opened vistas of a flaming ecstasy.

At Tepotzotlán, we visited the church the Jesuits had built in the eighteenth century for their seminary (and no sooner was it consecrated than they had to abandon it, as they were expelled from Mexico forever): a thea-ter-church, all gold and bright colors, in a dancing and acrobatic baroque, crammed with swirling angels, garlands, panoplies of flowers, shells. Surely the Jesuits meant to compete with the splendor of the Aztecs, whose ruined temples and palaces – the royal palace of Quetzalcóatl! – still stood, to recall a rule imposed through the impressive effects of a grandiose, transfiguring art. There was a challenge in the air, in this dry and thin air at an altitude of two thousand meters: the ancient rivalry between the civilizations of America and Spain in the art of bewitching the senses with dazzling seduc-tions. And from architecture this rivalry extended to cuisine, where the two civilizations had merged, or perhaps where the conquered had triumphed, strong in the condiments born from their very soil. Through the white hands of novices and the brown hands of lay sisters, the cuisine of the new Indo-Hispanic civilization had become also the field of battle between the aggressive ferocity of the ancient gods of the mesa and the sinuous excess of the baroque religion.

On the supper menu we didn't find *chiles en nogada*. From one locality to the next the gastronomic lexicon varied, always offering new terms to be recorded and new sensations to be defined. Instead, we found *guacamole*, to be scooped up with crisp tortillas that snap into many shards and dip like spoons into the thick cream (the fat softness of the *aguacate* – the Mexican national fruit, known to the rest of the world under the distorted name of 'avocado' – is accompanied and underlined by the angular dryness of the tortilla, which, for its part, can have many flavors, pretending to have none); then *guajolote con mole poblano* – that is, turkey with Puebla-style *mole* sauce, one of the noblest among the many *moles*, and most laborious (the prep-aration never takes less than two days), and most complicated, because it requires several different varieties of *chile*, as well as garlic, onion, cinnamon, cloves, pepper, cumin, coriander, and sesame, almonds, raisins, and peanuts,

with a touch of chocolate; and finally *quesadillas* (another kind of tortilla, really, for which cheese is incorporated in the dough, garnished with ground meat and refried beans).

Right in the midst of chewing, Olivia's lips paused, almost stopped, though without completely interrupting their continuity of movement, which slowed down, as if reluctant to allow an inner echo to fade, while her gaze became fixed, intent on no specific object, in apparent alarm. Her face had a special concentration that I had observed during meals ever since we began our trip to Mexico. I followed the tension as it moved from her lips to her nostrils, flaring one moment, contracting the next (the plasticity of the nose is quite limited – especially for a delicate, harmonious nose like Olivia's – and each barely perceptible attempt to expand the capacity of the nostrils in the longitudinal direction actually makes them thinner, while the corresponding reflex movement, accentuating their breadth, then seems a kind of withdrawal of the whole nose into the surface of the face).

What I have just said might suggest that, in eating, Olivia became closed into herself, absorbed with the inner course of her sensations; in reality, on the contrary, the desire her whole person expressed was that of communicating to me what she was tasting: communicating with me through flavors, or communicating with flavors through a double set of taste buds, hers and mine. 'Did you taste that? Are you tasting it?' she was asking me, with a kind of anxiety, as if at that same moment our incisors had pierced an identically composed morsel and the same drop of savor had been caught by the membranes of my tongue and of hers. 'Is it *cilantro*? Can't you taste *cilantro*?' she insisted, referring to an herb whose local name hadn't allowed us to identify it with certainty (was it coriander, perhaps?) and of which a little thread in the morsel we were chewing sufficed to transmit to the nostrils a sweetly pungent emotion, like an impalpable intoxication.

Olivia's need to involve me in her emotions pleased me greatly, because it showed that I was indispensable to her and that, for her, the pleasures of existence could be appreciated only if we shared them. Our subjective, individual selves, I was thinking, find their amplification and completion only in the unity of the couple. I needed confirmation of this conviction all the more since, from the beginning of our Mexican journey, the physical bond between Olivia and me was going through a phase of rarefaction, if not eclipse: a momentary phenomenon, surely, and not in itself disturbing – part of the normal ups and downs to which, over a long period, the life of every couple is subject. And I couldn't help remarking how certain manifestations of Olivia's vital energy, certain prompt reactions or delays on her part, yearnings or throbs, continued to take place before my eyes, losing none of their intensity, with only one significant difference: their stage was no longer the bed of our embraces but a dinner table.

During the first few days I expected the gradual kindling of the palate to spread quickly to all our senses. I was mistaken: aphrodisiac this cuisine surely was, but in itself and for itself (this is what I thought to understand,

and what I am saying applies only to us at that moment; I cannot speak for others or for us if we had been in a different humor). It stimulated desires, in other words, that sought their satisfaction only within the very sphere of sensation that had aroused them – in eating new dishes, therefore, that would generate and extend those same desires. We were thus in the ideal situation for imagining what the love between the abbess and the chaplain might have been like: a love that, in the eyes of the world and in their own eyes, could have been perfectly chaste and at the same time infinitely carnal in that experience of flavors gained through secret and subtle complicity.

'Complicity': the word, the moment it came into my mind – referring not only to the nun and the priest but also to Olivia and me – heartened me. Because if what Olivia sought was complicity in the almost obsessive passion that had seized her, then this suggested we were not losing – as I had feared – a parity between us. In fact, it had seemed to me during the last few days that Olivia, in her gustatory exploration, had wanted to keep me in a subordinate position: a presence necessary, indeed, but subaltern, obliging me to observe the relationship between her and food as a confidant or as a compliant pander. I dispelled this irksome notion that had somehow or other occurred to me. In reality, our complicity could not be more total, precisely because we experienced the same passion in different ways, in accord with our temperaments: Olivia more sensitive to perceptive nuances and endowed with a more analytical memory, where every recollection remained distinct and unmistakable; I tending more to define experiences verbally and conceptually, to mark the ideal line of journey within ourselves contemporaneously with our geographical journey. In fact, this was a conclusion of mine that Olivia had instantly adopted (or perhaps Olivia had been the one to prompt the idea and I had simply proposed it to her again in words of my own): the true journey, as the introjection of an 'outside' different from our normal one, implies a complete change of nutrition, a digesting of the visited country – its fauna and flora and its culture (not only the different culinary practices and condiments but the different implements used to grind the flour or stir the pot) – making it pass between the lips and down the esophagus. This is the only kind of travel that has a meaning nowadays, when everything visible you can see on television without rising from your easy chair. (And you mustn't rebut that the same result can be achieved by visiting the exotic restaurants of our big cities; they so counterfeit the reality of the cuisine they claim to follow that, as far as our deriving real knowledge is concerned, they are the equivalent not of an actual locality but of a scene reconstructed and shot in a studio.)

All the same, in the course of our trip Olivia and I saw everything there was to see (no small exploit, in quantity or quality). For the following morning we had planned a visit to the excavations at Monte Albán, and the guide came for us at the hotel promptly with a little bus. In the sunny, arid countryside grow the agaves used for mescal and tequila, and *nopales* (which we call prickly pears) and cereus – all thorns – and jacaranda, with its blue flowers. The road climbs up into the mountains. Monte Albán, among the heights surrounding a valley, is a complex of ruins: temples, reliefs, grand stairways, platforms for human sacrifice. Horror, sacredness, and mystery are consolidated by tourism, which dictates preordained forms of behavior, the modest surrogates of those rites. Contemplating these stairs, we try to imagine the hot blood spurting from the breast split by the stone axe of the priest.

Three civilizations succeeded one another at Monte Albán, each shifting the same blocks: the Zapotecs building over the works of the Olmecs, and the Mixtecs doing the same to those of the Zapotecs. The calendars of the ancient Mexican civilizations, carved on the reliefs, represent a cyclic, tragic concept of time: every fifty-two years the universe ended, the gods died, the temples were destroyed, every celestial and terrestrial thing changed its name. Perhaps the peoples that history defines as the successive occupants of these territories were merely a single people, whose continuity was never broken even through a series of massacres like those the reliefs depict. Here are the conquered villages, their names written in hieroglyphics, and the god of the village, his head hung upside down; here are the chained prisoners of war, the severed heads of the victims.

The guide to whom the travel agency entrusted us, a burly man named Alonso, with flattened features like an Olmec head (or Mixtec? Zapotec?), points out to us, with exuberant mime, the famous bas-reliefs called 'Los Danzantes.' Only some of the carved figures, he says, are portraits of dancers, with their legs in movement (Alonso performs a few steps); others might be astronomers, raising one hand to shield their eyes and study the stars (Alonso strikes an astronomer's pose). But for the most part, he says, they represent women giving birth (Alonso acts this out). We learn that this temple was meant to ward off difficult childbirths; the reliefs were perhaps votive images. Even the dance, for that matter, served to make births easier, through magic mimesis – especially when the baby came out feet first (Alonso performs the magic mimesis). One relief depicts a cesarean operation, complete with uterus and Fallopian tubes (Alonso, more brutal than ever, mimes the entire female anatomy, to demonstrate that a sole surgical torment linked births and deaths).

Everything in our guide's gesticulation takes on a truculent significance, as if the temples of the sacrifices cast their shadow on every act and every thought. When the most propitious date had been set, in accordance with the stars, the sacrifices were accompanied by the revelry of dances, and even births seemed to have no purpose beyond supplying new soldiers for the wars to capture victims. Though some figures are shown running or wrestling or playing football, according to Alonso these are not peaceful athletic competitions but, rather, the games of prisoners forced to compete in order to determine which of them would be the first to ascend the altar.

'And the loser in the games was chosen for the sacrifice?' I ask.

'No! The winner!' Alonso's face becomes radiant. 'To have your chest split open by the obsidian knife was an honor!' And in a crescendo of ancestral patriotism, just as he had boasted of the excellence of the scientific knowledge of the ancient peoples, so now this worthy descendant of the Olmecs feels called upon to exalt the offering of a throbbing human heart to the sun to assure that the dawn would return each morning and illuminate the world.

That was when Olivia asked, 'But what did they do with the victims' bodies afterward?'

Alonso stopped.

'Those limbs – I mean, those entrails,' Olivia insisted. 'They were offered to the gods, I realize that. But, practically speaking, what happened to them? Were they burned?'

No, they weren't burned.

'Well, what then? Surely a gift to the gods couldn't be buried, left to rot in the ground.'

'*Los zopilotes*,' Alonso said. 'The vultures. They were the ones who cleared the altars and carried the offerings to Heaven.'

The vultures. 'Always?' Olivia asked further, with an insistence I could not explain to myself.

Alonso was evasive, tried to change the subject; he was in a hurry to show us the passages that connected the priests' houses with the temples, where they made their appearance, their faces covered by terrifying masks. Our guide's pedagogical enthusiasm had something irritating about it, because it gave the impression he was imparting to us a lesson that was simplified so that it would enter our poor profane heads, though he actually knew far more, things he kept to himself and took care not to tell us. Perhaps this was what Olivia had sensed and what, after a certain point, made her maintain a closed, vexed silence through the rest of our visit to the excavations and on the jolting bus that brought us back to Oaxaca.

Along the road, all curves, I tried to catch Olivia's eye as she sat facing me. But thanks to the bouncing of the bus or the difference in the level of our seats, I realized my gaze was resting not on her eyes but on her teeth (she kept her lips parted in a pensive expression), which I happened to be seeing for the first time not as the radiant glow of a smile but as the instruments most suited to their purpose: to be dug into flesh, to sever it, tear it. And as you try to read a person's thoughts in the expression of his eyes, so now I looked at those strong, sharp teeth and sensed there a restrained desire, an expectation.

As we re-entered the hotel and headed for the large lobby (the former chapel of the convent), which we had to cross to reach the wing where our room was, we were struck by a sound like a cascade of water flowing and splashing and gurgling in a thousand rivulets and eddies and jets. The closer we got, the more this homogeneous noise was broken down into a complex of chirps, trills, caws, clucks, as of a flock of birds flapping their wings in an aviary. From the doorway (the room was a few steps lower than the corridor), we saw an expanse of little spring hats on the heads of ladies seated around tea tables. Throughout the country a campaign was in progress for the election of a new President of the Republic, and the wife of the favored candidate was giving a tea party of impressive proportions for the wives of the prominent men of Oaxaca. Under the broad, empty vaulted ceiling, 300 Mexican ladies were conversing all at once; the spectacular acoustical event that had immediately subdued us was produced by their voices mingled with the tinkling of cups and spoons and of knives cutting slices of cake. Looming over the assembly was a gigantic full-color picture of a round-faced lady with her black, smooth hair drawn straight back, wearing a blue dress of which only the buttoned collar could be seen; it was not unlike the official portraits of Chairman Mao Tse-tung, in other words.

To reach the patio and, from it, our stairs, we had to pick our way among the little tables of the reception. We were already close to the far exit when, from a table at the back of the hall, one of the few male guests rose and came toward us, arms extended. It was our friend Salustiano Velazco, a member of the would-be President's staff and, in that capacity, a participant in the more delicate stages of the electoral campaign. We hadn't seen him since leaving the capital, and to show us, with all his ebullience, his joy on seeing us again and to inquire about the latest stages of our journey (and perhaps to escape momentarily that atmosphere in which the triumphal female predominance compromised his chivalrous certitude of male supremacy) he left his place of honor at the symposium and accompanied us into the patio.

Instead of asking us about what we had seen, he began by pointing out the things we had surely failed to see in the places we had visited and could have seen only if he had been with us – a conversational formula that impassioned connoisseurs of a country feel obliged to adopt with visiting friends, always with the best intentions, though it successfully spoils the pleasure of those who have returned from a trip and are quite proud of their experiences, great or small. The convivial din of the distinguished gynaeceum followed us even into the patio and drowned at least half the words he and we spoke, so I was never sure he wasn't reproaching us for not having seen the very things we had just finished telling him we had seen.

'And today we went to Monte Albán,' I quickly informed him, raising my voice. 'The stairways, the reliefs, the sacrificial altars...'

Salustiano put his hand to his mouth, then waved it in midair – a gesture that, for him, meant an emotion too great to be expressed in words. He began by furnishing us archeological and ethnographical details I would have very much liked to hear sentence by sentence, but they were lost in the reverberations of the feast. From his gestures and the scattered words I managed to catch (*'Sangre... obsidiana... divinidad solar'*), I realized he was talking about the human sacrifices and was speaking with a mixture of awed participation and sacred horror – an attitude distinguished from that of our crude guide by a greater awareness of the cultural implications.

Quicker than I, Olivia managed to follow Salustiano's speech better, and now she spoke up, to ask him something. I realized she was repeating the question she had asked Alonso that afternoon: 'What the vultures didn't carry off – what happened to that, afterward?'

Salustiano's eyes flashed knowing sparks at Olivia, and I also grasped then the purpose behind her question, especially as Salustiano assumed his confidential, abettor's tone. It seemed that, precisely because they were softer, his words now overcame more easily the barrier of sound that separated us.

'Who knows? The priests... This was also a part of the rite – I mean among the Aztecs, the people we know better. But even about them, not much is known. These were secret ceremonies. Yes, the ritual meal... The priest assumed the functions of the god, and so the victim, divine food...'

Was this Olivia's aim? To make him admit this? She insisted further, 'But how did it take place? The meal...'

'As I say, there are only some suppositions. It seems that the princes, the warriors also joined in. The victim was already part of the god, transmitting divine strength.' At this point, Salustiano changed his tone and became proud, dramatic, carried away. 'Only the warrior who had captured the sacrificed prisoner could not touch his flesh. He remained apart, weeping.'

Olivia still didn't seem satisfied. 'But this flesh – in order to eat it... The way it was cooked, the sacred cuisine, the seasoning – is anything known about that?'

Salustiano became thoughtful. The banqueting ladies had redoubled their noise, and now Salustiano seemed to become hypersensitive to their sounds; he tapped his ear with one finger, signalling that he couldn't go on in all that racket. 'Yes, there must have been some rules. Of course, that food couldn't be consumed without a special ceremony... the due honor... the respect for the sacrificed, who were brave youths... respect for the gods... flesh that couldn't be eaten just for the sake of eating, like any ordinary food. And the flavor...'

'They say it isn't good to eat?'

'A strange flavor, they say.'

'It must have required seasoning – strong stuff.'

'Perhaps that flavor had to be hidden. All other flavors had to be brought together, to hide that flavor.'

And Olivia asked, 'But the priests... About the cooking of it – they didn't leave any instructions? Didn't hand down anything?'

Salustiano shook his head. 'A mystery. Their life was shrouded in mystery.'

And Olivia – Olivia now seemed to be prompting him. 'Perhaps that flavor emerged, all the same – even through the other flavors.'

Salustiano put his fingers to his lips, as if to filter what he was saying. 'It was a sacred cuisine. It had to celebrate the harmony of the elements achieved through sacrifice – a terrible harmony, flaming, incandescent... ' He fell suddenly silent, as if sensing he had gone too far, and as if the thought of the repast had called him to his duty, he hastily apologized for not being able to stay longer with us. He had to go back to his place at the table.

Waiting for evening to fall, we sat in one of the cafes under the arcades of the *zócalo*, the regular little square that is the heart of every old city of the colony – green, with short, carefully pruned trees called *almendros*, though they bear no resemblance to almond trees. The tiny paper flags and the banners that greeted the official candidate did their best to convey a festive air to the *zócalo*. The proper Oaxaca families strolled under the arcades. American hippies waited for the old woman who supplied them with *mescalina*. Ragged vendors unfurled colored fabrics on the ground. From another square nearby came the echo of the loudspeakers of a sparsely attended rally of the opposition. Crouched on the ground, heavy women were frying tortillas and greens.

In the kiosk in the middle of the square, an orchestra was playing, bringing back to me reassuring memories of evenings in a familiar, provincial Europe I was old enough to have known and forgotten. But the memory was like a *trompe-l'oeil*, and when I examined it a little, it gave me a sense of multiplied distance, in space and in time. Wearing black suits and neckties, the musicians, with their dark, impassive Indian faces, played for the varicolored, shirtsleeved tourists – inhabitants, it seemed, of a perpetual summer – for parties of old men and women, meretriciously young in all the gleam of their dentures, and for groups of the really young, hunched over and meditative, as if waiting for age to come and whiten their blond beards and flowing hair; bundled in rough clothes, weighed down by their knapsacks, they looked like the allegorical figures of winter in old calendars.

'Perhaps time has come to an end, the sun has grown weary of rising, Chronos dies of starvation for want of victims to devour, the ages and the seasons are turned upside down,' I said.

'Perhaps the death of time concerns only us,' Olivia answered. 'We who tear one another apart, pretending not to know it, pretending not to taste flavors anymore.'

'You mean that here – that they need stronger flavors here because they know, because here they ate... '

'The same as at home, even now. Only we no longer know it, no longer dare look, the way they did. For them there was no mystification: the horror was right there, in front of their eyes. They ate as long as there was a bone left to pick clean, and that's why the flavors... '

'To hide that flavor?' I said, again picking up Salustiano's chain of hypotheses.

'Perhaps it couldn't be hidden. *Shouldn't* be. Otherwise, it was like not eating what they were really eating. Perhaps the other flavors served to enhance that flavor, to give it a worthy background, to honor it.'

At these words I felt again the need to look her in the teeth, as I had done earlier, when we were coming down in the bus. But at that very moment her tongue, moist with saliva, emerged from between her teeth, then immediately drew back, as if she were mentally savoring something. I realized Olivia was already imagining the supper menu.

It began, this menu, offered us by a restaurant we found among low houses with curving grilles, with a rose-colored liquid in a hand-blown glass: *sopa de camarones* – shrimp soup, that is, immeasurably hot, thanks to some variety of *chiles* we had never come upon previously, perhaps the famous *chiles jalapeños*. Then *cabrito* – roast kid – every morsel of which provoked surprise, because the teeth would encounter first a crisp bit, then one that melted in the mouth.

'You're not eating?' Olivia asked me. She seemed to concentrate only on savoring her dish, though she was very alert, as usual, while I had remained lost in thought, looking at her. It was the sensation of her teeth in my flesh that I was imagining, and I could feel her tongue lift me against the roof of her mouth, enfold me in saliva, then thrust me under the tips of the canines. I sat there facing her, but at the same time it was as if a part of me, or all of me, were contained in her mouth, crunched, torn shred by shred. The situation was not entirely passive, since while I was being chewed by her I felt also that I was acting on her, transmitting sensations that spread from the taste buds through her whole body. I was the one who aroused her every vibration – it was a reciprocal and complete relationship, which involved us and overwhelmed us.

I regained my composure; so did she. We looked carefully at the salad of tender prickly pear leaves (*ensalada de nopalitos*) – boiled, seasoned with garlic, coriander, red pepper, and oil and vinegar – then the pink and creamy pudding of *maguey* (a variety of agave), all accompanied by a carafe of *sangrita* and followed by coffee with cinnamon.

But this relationship between us, established exclusively through food, so much so that it could be identified in no image other than that of a meal – this relationship which in my imaginings I thought corresponded to Olivia's deepest desires – didn't please her in the slightest, and her irritation was to find its release during that same supper.

'How boring you are! How monotonous!' she began by saying, repeating an old complaint about my uncommunicative nature and my habit of giving her full responsibility for keeping the conversation alive – an argument that flared up whenever we were alone together at a restaurant table, including a list of charges whose basis in truth I couldn't help admitting but in which I also discerned the fundamental reasons for our unity as a couple; namely, that Olivia saw and knew how to catch and isolate and rapidly define many more things than I, and therefore my relationship with the world was essentially via her. 'You're always sunk into yourself, unable to participate in what's going on around you, unable to put yourself out for another, never a flash of enthusiasm on your own, always ready to cast a pall on anybody else's, depressing, indifferent... ' And to the inventory of my faults she added this time a new adjective, or one that to my ears now took on a new meaning: 'Insipid!'

There: I was insipid, I thought, without flavor. And the Mexican cuisine, with all its boldness and imagination, was needed if Olivia was to feed on me with satisfaction. The spiciest flavors were the complement – indeed, the avenue of communication, indispensable as a loudspeaker that amplifies sounds – for Olivia to be nourished by my substance.

'I may seem insipid to you,' I protested, 'but there are ranges of flavor more discreet and restrained than that of red peppers. There are subtle tastes that one must know how to perceive!'

The next morning we left Oaxaca in Salustiano's car. Our friend had to visit other provinces on the candidate's tour, and offered to accompany us for part of our itinerary. At one point on the trip he showed us some recent excavations not yet overrun by tourists. A stone statue rose barely above the level of the ground, with the unmistakable form that we had learned to recognize on the very first days of our Mexican archeological wanderings: the *chacmool*, or half-reclining human figure, in an almost Etruscan pose, with a tray resting on his belly. He looks like a rough, good-natured puppet, but it was on that tray that the victims' hearts were offered to the gods.

'Messenger of the gods – what does that mean?' I asked. I had read that definition in a guidebook. 'Is he a demon sent to earth by the gods to collect the dish with the offering? Or an emissary from human beings who must go to the gods and offer them the food?'

'Who knows?' Salustiano answered, with the suspended attitude he took in the face of unanswerable questions, as if listening to the inner voices he had at his disposal, like reference books. 'It could be the victim himself, supine on the altar, offering his own entrails on the dish. Or the sacrificer, who assumes the pose of the victim because he is aware that tomorrow it will be his turn. Without this reciprocity, human sacrifice would be unthinkable. All were potentially both sacrificer and victim – the victim accepted his role as victim because he had fought to capture the others as victims.'

'They could be eaten because they themselves were eaters of men?' I added, but Salustiano was talking now about the serpent as symbol of the continuity of life and the cosmos.

Meanwhile I understood: my mistake with Olivia was to consider myself eaten by her, whereas I should be myself (I always had been) the one who ate her. The most appetizingly flavored human flesh belongs to the eater of human flesh. It was only by feeding ravenously on Olivia that I would cease being tasteless to her palate.

This was in my mind that evening when I sat down with her to supper. 'What's wrong with you? You're odd this evening,' Olivia said, since nothing ever escaped her. The dish they had served us was called *gorditas pellizcadas con manteca* – literally, 'plump girls pinched with butter.' I concentrated on devouring, with every meatball, the whole fragrance of Olivia – through voluptuous mastication, a vampire extraction of vital juices. But I realized that in a relationship that should have been among three terms – me, meatball, Olivia – a fourth term had intruded, assuming a dominant role: the name of the meatballs. It was the name *'gorditas pellizcadas con manteca'* that I was especially savoring and assimilating and possessing. And, in fact, the magic of that name continued affecting me even after the meal, when we retired together to our hotel room in the night. And for the first time during our Mexican journey the spell whose victims we had been was broken, and the inspiration that had blessed the finest moments of our joint life came to visit us again.

The next morning we found ourselves sitting up in our bed in the *chacmool* pose, with the dulled expression of stone statues on our faces and, on our laps, the tray with the anonymous hotel breakfast, to which we tried to add local flavors, ordering with it mangoes, papayas, cherimoyas, guayabas – fruits that conceal in the sweetness of their pulp subtle messages of asperity and sourness.

Our journey moved into the Maya territories. The temples of Palenque emerged from the tropical forest, dominated by thick, wooded mountains: enormous ficus trees with multiple trunks like roots, lilac-colored *macuilis*, *aguacates* – every tree wrapped in a cloak of lianas and climbing vines and hanging plants. As I was going down the steep stairway of the Temple of the Inscriptions, I had a dizzy spell. Olivia, who disliked stairs, had chosen not to follow me and had remained with the crowd of noisy groups, loud in sound and color, that the buses were disgorging and ingesting constantly in the open space among the temples. By myself, I had climbed to the Temple of the Sun, to the relief of the jaguar sun, to the Temple of the Foliated Cross, to the relief of the *quetzal* in profile, then to the Temple of the Inscriptions, which involves not only climbing up (and then down) a monumental stairway but also climbing down (and then up) the smaller, interior staircase that leads down to the underground crypt. In the crypt there is the tomb of the king-priest (which I had already been able to study far more comfortably a few days previously in a perfect facsimile at the Anthropological Museum in Mexico City), with the highly complicated carved stone slab on which you see the king operating a science-fiction apparatus that to our eyes resembles the sort of thing used to launch space rockets, though it represents, on the contrary, the descent of the body to the subterranean gods and its rebirth as vegetation.

I went down, I climbed back up into the light of the jaguar sun – into the sea of the green sap of the leaves. The world spun, I plunged down, my throat cut by the knife of the king-priest, down the high steps onto the forest of tourists with super-8s and usurped, broadbrimmed sombreros. The solar energy coursed along dense networks of blood and chlorophyll; I was living and dying in all the fibers of what is chewed and digested and in all the fibers that absorb the sun, consuming and digesting.

Under the thatched arbor of a restaurant on a riverbank, where Olivia had waited for me, our teeth began to move slowly, with equal rhythm, and our eyes stared into each other's with the intensity of serpents' – serpents concentrated in the ecstasy of swallowing each other in turn, as we were aware, in our turn, of being swallowed by the serpent that digests us all, assimilated ceaselessly in the process of ingestion and digestion, in the universal cannibalism that leaves its imprint on every amorous relationship and erases the lines between our bodies and *sopa de frijoles, huachinango a la vera cruzana*, and *enchiladas*.

18

Michel Serres'
Five Senses

Steven Connor

> Once words came to dominate flesh and matter, which were previously
> innocent, all we have left is to dream of the paradiasical times in which the
> body was free and could run and enjoy sensations at leisure. If a revolt is to
> come, it will have to come from the five senses!
>
> Michel Serres, *Angels: A Modern Myth*

Les cinq sens is a book in which Serres attempts to remake or redeem the body,
which is to say redeem it from the condition of addiction, or subordination
to the word-become-flesh. His is not a present but an evanescent body, a
body that builds itself anew through its senses. Even as the body depends
on its senses, they are the body's power of exceeding or being beside itself. I
will ask about the kind of temporality the senses comport, and suggest that
there is a monism of the manifold in Serres' exclusion of negativity, pain
and death.

Serres has spoken of his distaste both for the hermeneutics of critique and
suspicion, and for the phenomenology of Heidegger and Merleau-Ponty,
both of whom he finds risibly thin and bodiless. In his conversations with
Bruno Latour, he suggests that *Les cinq sens* actually had its origin in a kind
of laughing revulsion from the emaciated nature of phenomenology:

> When I was young, I laughed a lot at Merleau-Ponty's *Phenomenology of Perception*.
> He opens it with these words: 'At the outset of the study of perception, we find
> in language the notion of sensation...' Isn't this an exemplary introduction?
> A collection of examples in the same vein, so austere and meager, inspire the
> descriptions that follow. From his window the author sees some tree, always

in bloom; he huddles over his desk; now and again a red blotch appears – it's a quote. What you can decipher in this book is a nice ethnology of city dwellers, who are hypertechnicalized, intellectualized, chained to their library chairs, and tragically stripped of any tangible experience. Lots of phenomenology and no sensation – everything via language... My book *Les Cinq sens* cries out at the empire of signs. (Serres with Latour 1995: 131–2)

Les cinq sens is part of the turn that Serres' work undertook during the 1980s from a certain kind of philosophically respectable and recognizable commentary to the work of invention, a work characterized by lightness, freedom, associativeness, caprice. 'There is a time for abstract science and then another one for things... the works of my youth... I henceforth find old, precisely because they are very learned or strictly under surveillance. Luckily, the more one writes, the younger one becomes. Finally, no more surveillance; finally, I can play truant – no more school at all' (Serres with Latour 1995: 100). *Les cinq sens* insists on the gymnastic possibility and need of the mind. It is the book in which Serres begins to stretch his limbs, to burst into flames, the book in which he first makes his scandalous approach to things. In it he declares that the world exists.

So I will be saying that it is a book that marks a significant point in Serres' writing. But in marking a break, a break-out, an exit or an inclination, a rift in the fabric of Serres' work, it also folds itself back into that fabric, leading everywhere into it, a work that, as we have begun to become accustomed to recognizing, consists of little else but these saltations, these leaps of faith, intuition or inclination. After *Les cinq sens*, Serres' work would never be quite the same: 'never the same after that never quite the same but that was nothing new... never the same but the same as what for God's sake,' as we read in Beckett's *That Time* (Beckett 1986: 390). 'Everything that you do is "in the midst"', suggests Bruno Latour to Serres, and wins his simple consent, glad, as it may be, or weary, in the words: 'All right' (Serres with Latour 1995: 146).

Les cinq sens consists of five chapters, entitled 'Voiles' , 'Boîtes' , 'Tables,' 'Visite' and 'Joie.'

Voiles

No book on the senses can avoid evoking Condillac's famous, fabular statue, the thought-experiment at the beginning of the *Essay on the Faculties*, in which Condillac imagines a statue deprived, in turn, of every sense but one. But Condillac's statue, or the procedure that produces it, functions in Serres' text as a menace, or as a philosophical disgrace: it represents the threat of subtraction or abstraction, of analysis itself. Serres' aim is not to start with the statue and gradually to animate it, by draping it, one by one, in the separate senses, giving it interiority, movement. This action of clothing, one might imagine, is the exact equivalent of Descartes' sensory striptease, the action of systematic doubt in which he attempts to strip away from reason all the gorgeous, questionable habiliments of the senses, stripping away indeed the flesh itself, and then the bones, leaving finally, exposed to its own view, exposure itself, self-exposure itself.

In fact the book begins with a parody of the Cartesian question: where is the soul? Serres' answer is that the soul is not to be located in one solitary and invariant quasi-position in the body, the pineal gland, but rather in the contingencies of the body with itself, and with its environment. The soul of the pilot of a ship extends coenesthetically into the whole of his vessel, just as the driver parking a car feels his fingertips extending all the way to his front bumper, and the amputee continues to occupy the empty space of their severed limb.

The soul is to be found also in the way in which the self touches itself.

> I touch one lip with my middle finger. Consciousness dwells in this contact. I start to explore it. Often consciousness conceals itself in folds, lip resting on lip, palate closed on tongue, teeth against teeth, eyelids lowered, tightened sphincter, the hand closed into a fist, fingers pressed against each other, the rear surface of one thigh crossed on the front face of the other, or one foot resting on the other. I bet that the homunculus, tiny and monstrous, of which each part is proportional to the magnitude of sensation, swells in those automorphic places, when the skin tissue folds upon itself. By itself, the skin takes on consciousness... Without this folding-over, this contact of the self with itself, there would be no internal sense, no body of one's own, or even less coenesthesia, no body image, we would live without consciousness, featureless, on the point of vanishing. (Serres 1998: 20)

Commentators on the skin, such as Didier Anzieu, have frequently observed its duality, which allows us both to touch and be touched at once. But, for Serres, this self-touching is never merely symmetrical. At every touching of oneself, every contingence, soul or consciousness crowds disproportionately on one side or other of the transaction, and is relatively absent from the other. When I cut my fingernails, I am more in my right hand than in my left; but you cannot touch your hand with your shoulder, no matter which hand is in question (though another person's shoulder can touch your hand). Serres returns to this question in *Le Tiers-instruit* in 1991 (everything in Serres's writing crosses its own path sooner or later). There he argues that the world is sensible because it lists, because it has orientation or laterality; everything has a left hand or a right hand, it leans in certain directions, pulled into shape, gait or posture by gravity or conductivity or impulse, or lack or habit: 'There is no such thing as balanced indifference. There is no center or axis; it cannot be found, or is absent. Orientation can thus be said to be originary, invariable, irreducible, so constantly physical that it becomes metaphysical' (Serres 1997: 15).

This means that all of us are lop-sided, hemiplegic, carrying around with us a Siamese twin, an intimate stranger, who is and yet is not of our flesh. The condition of anosognosia, first described by Joseph Babinski in 1908, in which patients deny ownership of a paralysed limb or other portion of themselves is only the intensification of this split condition. Everything on our left is a not-self. But, in this sense, our sinister self, our gaucheness, is distributed unequally and intermittently across different portions of the body. Whether 'self' resides, or is touched off, is our right hand, that which actively touches, and is therefore white, or transparent; wherever 'not-self' or less-than-self, that which is touched, which cannot touch back (the shoulder, the foot) is found, it is black, alien.

But these relations, though formalizable as a black and white dichotomy, in fact are mobile. For one thing, we have more than two hands. To some degree, whenever we touch, we grow a temporary hand. V.S. Ramachandran reported a neurological correlative for this effect in patients whose hands had been amputated but who reported intense sensation in their missing hands when their faces and upper arms were stroked. The reason for this seems to be the proximity of hands and face on the sensory map draped over the surface of the cerebellum, which allows a vacated or inactive area of hand sensation in the brain to be colonized by neighboring areas (the proximity of genitals and feet on the map accounts for the orgasmic sensations in the feet experienced during sex by those with leg amputations) (Ramachandran and Blakeslee 1999: 25–38).

Just as the map on the cerebellum is being shown to be much more plastic and revisable than we ever thought, so we are continually rewriting the map of inner and outer, self and not-self, on the surface of our skins. In *Genesis*, published in 1982, Serres had evoked the gymnastic condition of the body-become-hand as the image of a kind of blankness, an indetermination, and thus readiness to be absorbed in thought, contemplation or experience; like the body of the dancer, like the thought of the inventive rather than merely critical thinker, the hand is a flight of forms from possible to possible:

The hand is no longer a hand when it has taken hold of the hammer, it is the hammer itself, it is no longer a hammer, it flies transparent, between the hammer and the nail, it disappears and dissolves, my own hand has long since taken flight in writing. The hand and thought, like one's tongue, disappear in their determinations...

Inventive thinking is unstable, it is undetermined, it is un-differentiated, it is as little singular in its function as is our hand. The latter can make itself into a pincer, it can be fist and hammer, cupped palm and goblet, tentacle and suction cup, claw and soft touch. So what is a hand? It is not an organ, it is a faculty, a capacity for doing, for becoming claw or paw, weapon or compendium. It is a naked faculty. A faculty is not special, it is never specific, it is the possibility of doing something in general. To talk about the faculties of the soul is a great misnomer, when we are differentiating between them: the soul is also a naked faculty. It is nakedness. We live by bare hands. Our hands are that nakedness I find in gymnastics, that pure faculty, cleared up by exercise, by the asceticism of un-differentiation. I think, un-differentiated. Thus I am anyone, animal, element, stone or wind, number, you and him, us. Nothing. Nobody. Blank. Bare. (Serres 1995b: 30, 34–5)

In *Les cinq sens*, the white or blank hand/body gives way to a more variegated form. Now, the soul is inscribed in the coming and going of subjectivity on the surface of the skin as the residue of its contingencies, the play of light and shadow, of the whiteness of subjectivity and the shade of objectivity.

It remains to draw or paint. Isolate if possible, the secret little zones where the soul is always in residence, the corners or folds of contingency, isolate too, if possible the unstable zones where the soul knows how to play with another as though with a ball, mark out the spheres and slabs which become subjects only when face to face with objects, the dense and compact regions which remain objects always, alone or facing those which objectify them, deserts lacking in soul, black; this drawing rarely marks off compact zones, for these explode, fuse and flee in narrow strips of colour, forming hills, chimneys, passages, corridors, flames, zigzags and labyrinths, look at the changeable, wavelike and fugitive soul on the skin, on the surface, streaked, crowded, tiger-striped, zebra-striped, barred, troubled, constellated, gorgeous, torrential, and turbulent, incendiary. (Serres 1998: 21)

Serres himself is what he calls a corrected, or completed left-hander, a natural left-hander who was compelled to write with his right hand. The result is the condition of the bicameral chimera or hermaphrodite, the one who can cross to the other side of himself, who can write two-handed (Serres 1997: 17–20.) But this chimera-like condition can belong to us all. The crossing of the left hand and the right hand in the individual body is the condition for the meeting of the body and the world.

Skin is central to the 'philosophy of mingled bodies' that Serres inaugurates here because of the principle of contingence:

in the skin, through the skin, the world and the body touch, defining their common border. Contingency means mutual touching: world and body meet and caress in the skin. I do not like to speak of the place where my body exists as a milieu, preferring rather to say that things mingle among themselves and that I am no exception to this, that I mingle with the world which mingles itself in me. The skin intervenes in the things of the world and brings about their mingling. (Serres 1998: 97)

The skin, and touch signify, finally, for Serres, a way of being amidst rather than standing before the world, that is necessary for knowledge. Knowledge, which has previously and traditionally thought of itself as an unveiling or stripping bare, is offered here as a kind of efflorescence, an exploration amid veils, a threading together of tissues. 'Tissue, textile and fabric provide excellent models of knowledge, excellent quasi-abstract objects, primal varieties: the world is a mass of laundry' (Serres 1998: 100–1) Serres dreams of a one-to-one map of the world, reproducing all its fractal singularity, that would be its skin, in what he calls a 'cosmic dream of an exquisite cosmetic on the skin of each thing' (Serres 1998: 36). For Serres, the cosmic and the cosmetic remain in intimate communication with each other: nothing is deeper than adornment.

We thus encounter what will be something like a principle of functioning of *Les cinq sens*; the effort to separate the senses out, displaying them adjacent to each other, like countries on a map, plan or table of correspondences, will be gently and repeatedly precluded by the requirement to knot them together. It will emerge that each sense is in fact a nodal cluster, a clump, confection or bouquet of all the other senses, a mingling of the modalities of mingling. Thus, in 'Voiles,' we hear of a sequence of six allegorical tapestries from the Château de Boussac in the Musée de Cluny known collectively as the *Lady with the Unicorn*. These tapestries depict the different senses in turn. There are six and not five of them since medieval philosophy decrees the existence of a sixth, unifying or common sense, the sense of selfhood, whereby the self apprehends itself as itself. This Serres identifies with the skin and the faculty of touch: the skin, he says, 'carries the message of Hermes.' Where topography is visual, 'topology is tactile' (Serres 1998: 99). The skin encompasses, implies, pockets up all the other sense organs: but, in doing so, it stands as a model for the way in which all the senses in their turn also invaginate all the others.

Boîtes

The second chapter, 'Boîtes,' concerns sound and hearing, sometimes thought of as the most libertine and promiscuously sociable of the senses. And yet in this chapter are to be found some of the most ill-tempered and unsociable things that Michel Serres has ever written. The setting or frame for the chapter is the ruined theatre of Epidaurus, in which Serres sits in the early morning, seeking in its gathered silence a cure from the racket, not only of human noise, the immense exchange of communications, but also the interior noise of the body, its incessant exchange of messages to itself.

Surprisingly, the theatre of Epidaurus, having the form of an immense ear or auditory pavilion marked out in the ground, visible from space, funneling sound to its center, comes to be a sinister image for Serres. He compares it to another remarkable theater at Pinara, in which an amphitheatre opens on to a cliff occupied by the dead, buried standing up.

Hearing is understood in this chapter, in which the duality promised in the French word *entendre* is powerfully at work, in terms of a work of transformation. Hearing takes what Serres calls the hard, *le dur*, and converts it into information, *le doux*, or the soft (Serres 1998: 141–9). This exchange is effected by the senses, or by the work of sensation, which, in turning raw stimulus into sensory information, also make sense of the senses, effecting a slight declination, or deflection within the word *sens* itself: sense becomes sense. These transformations are effected in every organism by a series of processes of transformation that Serres is wont to call 'black boxes.' He means by this processes whose initial conditions are known and whose outcomes are known, but whose actual processes of transformation remain inaccessible to view or understanding.

Performing the work of many black boxes, each receiving and reintegrating the output from other black boxes, we are all of us therefore in the condition of Orpheus, who takes the inchoate cries and howls of the natural world and turns them into music. But music, for Serres, is not the simple and once-and-for-all transformation of noise into information, of the natural into the cultural. Rather it is the looping, labyrinthine interchange of the hard and the soft. The labyrinth of the ear, with its complex invaginations of inner and outer, represents not a single diaphragm, or site of one-way transmission, but a complex, one might say fractal, landscape of transformations and recursions, which itself transmits as well as receives. Uncoil the cochlea, Serres suggests, and one finds a kind of piano, sounding out high and low frequencies: the ear receives vibrations, says Serres, but also broadcasts them, to a sensory apparatus, or third ear, which must in turn receive and integrate them (Serres 1998: 183). The ear is no more to be located in one place than the skin. For Serres, the body itself is caught up in a process of hearing, which implicates skin, bone, skull, feet and muscle. Just when we thought hearing was going to be put in its place, Serres evokes its own mingled or implicated nature. Just as the ear consists in part of a skin, so the skin itself is a kind of ear, which both excludes and transmits exterior vibrations:

> At the beginning, the whole body or organism raises up a sculpture or statue of tense skin, vibrating amid voluminous sound, open-closed like a box (or drum), capturing that by which it is captured. We hear by means of the skin and the feet. We hear with the cranial box, the abdomen and the thorax. We hear by means of the muscles, nerves and tendons. Our body-box, stretched with strings, veils itself within a global tympanum. We live amid sounds and cries, amid waves rather than spaces the organism moulds and indents itself... I am a house of sound, hearing and voice at once, black box and sounding-board, hammer and anvil, a grotto of echoes, a musicassette, the ear's pavilion, a question mark, wandering in the space of messages filled or stripped of sense... I am the resonance and the tone, I am altogether the mingling of the tone and its resonance. (Serres 1998: 180–1)

It is necessary for the body to form and retain itself in its complex and always transitory entirety, like the red spot on Jupiter, or the weather system formed out of pure movement, like the whorl of the ear itself, if it is not to be subjected to one of two fates: violent dissolution by and into pure materiality on the one hand, or rarefaction into the softness of information on the other. These two alternatives are embodied mythically for Serres in the persons of Orpheus and Eurydice. Orpheus, the originator of music, is finally torn apart, subjected to auditory extinction, in the *sparagmos* or dismembering effected by the howling Bacchantes. For Serres, analysis of this final moment of the Orpheus myth is supererogatory, since it represents the mutilating or dissective work of analysis itself, which leaves Orpheus a mere talking or singing head (Serres 1998: 173). Eurydice, on the other hand, is spectralized by the excess of information: for Serres, she is the body captured by language, and thereby rendered so soft and nebulous, as to be no more than a shade, or a name. Between the two, in the musical condition of transition, there is the body, not an object, but a work of sensation, neither shade nor dismembered corpse, but a complex knot, niche or enclave within flux. Orpheus, singing the name of Eurydice, attempts to harden or substantiate her form, bequeathing to death her numbness, redeeming her from the muteness of mere language into speaking embodiment.

The raising of Eurydice by Orpheus is precisely the work of cure and remaking that Serres sets out to effect in this work. Orpheus invokes: raises with the voice the body into speaking substance. It is important to distinguish Orpheus, who risks and eventually loses, from Ulysses, who is exposed to the disintegrative power of sound, but keeps himself immune from it, by binding himself to the mast, and thus wins. Orpheus visits the underworld, and loses: 'visit' is a word that will become important later in *Les cinq sens*.

There are three kinds of hearing offered in this chapter. There is first of all propriocentric hearing, the hearing of oneself, the gurgling of the viscera, the cracking of the bones, the thudding and pulsing of the blood, even the firing of the neurons, to which all of us are continuously exposed and that for most of the time, unless we are subjected to the rending tortures of tinnitus, we integrate unconsciously without effort. Then there is the hearing that constitutes the social contract: the blaring bedlam of the exchange of noise and signals, signals and noise. In fact, the first is the model for the second. In both of these cases, hearing attempts to close itself upon itself, in a circuit of self-hearing, tightening the coil of the ear. There is the hearing of oneself that forms the model increasingly for all communication: 'We can neither speak nor sing without the feedback loop that ensures that we hear our own voices' (Serres 1998: 140). This is autistic acoustics, a hearing deafened by itself.

But there is also the hearing that puts one apart from oneself, the hearing that doubles or remakes the body, just as the hand extends and exceeds itself and the body to which it belongs and which it is.

> The I thinks only when it is beside itself. It feels really only when it is beside itself. The linguistic I is shrunk down to the large memory of language, the indefinite integral of others, the closure of its open group, freezing itself in

habit... I only really live beside myself; beside myself I think, meditate, know, beside myself I receive the given, vivacious, I invent beside myself. I exist beside myself, like the world. I am on the side of the world beside my talkative flesh.

The ear knows this space. I can put the ear on the other side of the window, projecting it great distances, holding it at a great distance from the body.

Lost, dissolved in the transparent air, fluctuating with its nuances, sensible of its smallest comas, shivering at the least derision, set free, mingled with the shocks of the world, I exist. (Serres 1998: 119)

This kind of exposed hearing, which breaks the circuit of hearing-oneself, constitutes the third form of audibility:

In myriads, things cry out. Often deaf to alien emissions, hearing is astonished by that which cries out without a name in no language. The third cycle, initiated by the rarest of hearing, and which requires that one be deaf both to oneself and to the group, requires an interruption of the closed cycles of consciousness and the social contract, may already be called knowledge. (Serres 1998: 141)

There is no question of merely opening oneself to the inhuman, or the natural, of bypassing the black box, not least because the exposure to things in themselves is what forms the black box. (The senses are in things, are in the self-sensing of things.) Our house of experience, which includes not just each individual body, but also what Serres calls the 'orthopedic sensorium' (Serres 1998: 190) of our social structures, must remain sufficiently open, the social ear sufficiently labyrinthine to allow the capture of the unintegrated, or the disintegrative, and the rapture of the ear by what forms and deforms it.

Hearing is finally the unlocalizable mediation, or labyrinthine knotting together of these two kinds of process, or the two sides of the black box, exposure and integration.

Tables

Tables begins with a bottle of wine, a bottle of 1947 Yquem, shared with a friend. This wine will flow throughout the rest of the chapter that follows it, a chapter that is concerned to evoke and celebrate the most despised, the least aesthetic of the senses, taste and smell combined. It is perhaps unsurprising that Serres finds these senses the most refractory to language, and therefore the most despised by it. French, Serres observes, has no word, other than the specialised 'anosmia,' for the lack of taste. The absence of the very word for the absence of taste redoubles, redoubles the authority of the language that has no need even to mark this deficiency (Serres 1998: 254). Taste and smell open what Serres calls the 'second mouth,' the mouth displaced and overtaken by the first, golden mouth, the chrysostomos, of language. This second mouth is characterized by gift, grace, dispensation, opening, rather than accumulation. Smell and taste differentiate; though what they differentiate is always itself composite.

Odor is spirit, the work of transformation, or transubstantiation, which Serres prefers to read through the action of cooking rather than alchemy, therefore not as refinement or purification, but as the work of combination or alloying of substance.

Serres conjures up a grotesque primal scene, a mingling of different philosophical banquets, which include Plato's Symposium, the Last Supper and the banquet of Don Giovanni. In it, the petrified, linguistic body, reduced to the condition of a statue or robot or automaton, is no longer able to smell or taste. The statue, or mobile talking head, its limbs creaking, its tongue and nostrils parched with dialectic, dines off the menu: the women who do the cooking off-scene, also do the eating. But opposed to the statue is the body of Christ. The incarnational metaphor has two sides for Serres. Considered in its perfected form, the body of the Assumption, the raised or resurrected body, stands for the Word-Made-Flesh and the Flesh-Made-Word of the annunciation – in other words, the statue. 'When it is saturated by the word, the body loses its antique graces... [grace] flees the body when the word becomes flesh' (Serres 1998: 267).

Set against the body of the Assumption, the body raised up into language, is the body consumed at the Last Supper. This body, which circulates in the form of bread and wine, is not a fixed, but a mobile transubstantiation. It signifies the grace or gratuitousness or givenness of what Serres calls 'le donné.' The world abounds: 'le monde abonde.' How, Serres enquires, can the eye requite the sun for its light, how can the palate repay the vine? Set against the classical table of correspondences or equivalences, language as restricted economy, there is the table at which eating and drinking takes place, which exceeds this economy, Serres claims. Smell and taste are apt carriers of this transformative mobility, this metabolic circulation of elements which transform as they circulate. Smell and taste, themselves an irreducible composite, form the body as what Serres beautifully calls a 'bouquet of vicariances.'

Visite

It seems clear enough from the first three sections how the book is going to be structured. They deal, in turn, and in series, with skin and touch; with hearing; and with taste and smell conjoined. Between the third and fourth sections of the book, something happens, a kind of lurch, or swerve, an inclination, or clinamen, in Lucretius's term. In one sense, things seem to be going too fast: there are two chapters left, and only one sense remains to be dealt with, that of sight. But there is also a slowing down: for in fact we wait in vain for an exposition of sight in either of the two last chapters, or not in any daylit, head-on kind of way. Neither chapter completes the formation of the homunculus undertaken through the other chapters.

In fact, vision has appeared throughout *Les cinq sens* as a negative reference point for the other senses. Where the other senses give us the mingled body, vision appears on the side of detachment, separation. Vision is a kind of dead zone, as the petrifying sense, the non-sense, which it is the role of the other senses to make good or redeem. Thus, we hear of the work of vision undertaken by Pierre Bonnard in paintings such as the *Nude in the Mirror* and *The Garden* in the chapter 'Voîles': 'The eye loses its pre-eminence in the very domain of its dominance, painting. At its extremity, impressionism returns to its really originary sense, that of contact. The nude, ocellated like a peacock, recalls us to the weight and pressure of things, to the heaviness of the column of air above us and its variations' (Serres 1998: 35). However, vision itself is at length redeemed in the chapter entitled 'Visite.' This chapter is concerned, to all appearances, not with looking, but with voyaging. In other words, Serres seems in this chapter to be deflecting the French 'sens' – sense – into another direction, in fact, into direction, itself.

The sensible for Serres, means the changeable, that which is capable at any moment of a change of direction:

> Sensible has a sense comparable to that of adjectives with the same termination. It reveals the always-possible change of direction. The magnetised needle thus enacts sensibility. At the minute and ubiquitous solicitations of quality, dimension and intensity, sensibility trembles, fluctuates and scans with dancing excursions the spaces through which it is showered and summoned by things, by the world, and by others... Open like a star, or quasi-closed, like a knot to all directions, mobile in every dimension and scanning everywhere, sensibility gives itself, indefatigably, to this dancing excursion, a functional intersection until the very hour of its death. (Serres 1998: 404–5)

It is this that allows vision to make its appearance, or to speak its appearance, but obliquely, in the word 'visit.' 'The term "visit" and the verb "to visit" mean at first looking and seeing; they add to it the idea of itinerary – the one who visits, goes to see' (Serres 1998: 334). Visiting, is, so to speak, vectorial vision, itinerant or excursive vision, vision on the move.

> In general, the bearer of the look, in traditional philosophy, does not move: it sits down to look, through a window at the blossoming tree: a statue posed on affirmations and theses. But we see things rarely in a condition of arrest, our ecological niche incorporates innumerable movements... The earth turns, our global position of vigil lost its stability long ago, even the sun, the giver of light, is in motion, en route to some other part of the universe. (Serres 1998: 405)

Looking as visiting is therefore the sense that involves deflection, displacement, and gathers into itself the redirection or deflective nature of all sense experience:

Displacements for the purpose of seeing borrow pathways, crossings, intersections, in order that scrutiny may focus on the detail or pass into a global synthesis: changes of scale, sense and direction. The sensible, in general, holds together all senses, all directions, like a knot or general intersection... Visitation explores and details all the senses of the sensible implicated or compacted in its knot. How could one see the compacted capacity of the senses if one separates them? We have visited this capacity without dissociating the senses of the word visit. (Serres 1998: 406)

Visiting the senses, in the way that this book attempts to do, partakes of the action of the senses themselves, as they visit the world, in actions of excursion, or self-exceeding:

Spirit sees, language sees, the body visits. It always exceeds its site, by displacement. The subject sees, the body visits, surpasses its own position, goes out from its role or word... The body goes out from the body in all senses (*dans tous les sens*), the sensible knots up this knot, the sensible in which the body never persists in the same plane or content but plunges and lives in a perpetual exchange, turbulence, whirlwind, circumstance. The body exceeds the body, the I surpasses the I, identity delivers itself from belonging at every instant, I sense therefore I pass, chameleon, in a variegated multiplicity, become halfcaste, quarteroon, mulatto, octoroon, hybrid... We have visited the compacity of the given. (Serres 1998: 408–9)

Joie

The final chapter offers us yet another candidate for the sixth or common sense: this is the sense of bodily joy, or ecstasy. Here, Serres evokes astonishingly the seraphic pleasures of self-exceeding, to be found, for example, in the pleasures of swimming, of running, in the human fascination with the trampoline, or in the playing of rugby. Here, the body becomes itself in playing with, or transforming itself.

The body is the site of the non-site: a teeming plurality that overruns and overrules every vicious and narrow dichotomy; but this is guaranteed by the most implacably dichotomous way of arguing that is imaginable. On one side language, science and corporate rationality: on the other side the life of the body. On the one side the global, on the other, the play of locality. On the one side, the statue; on the other, the veil, the visit.

This book derives its demand and its joy from its refusal of language, its delirious flight beyond, or recoil backwards from language. Language, we hear time and again, makes one into a statue, identified variously with the statue of Don Giovanni, with Condillac's senseless statue. It petrifies one's skin, it empties one's mouth of taste, it occupies the body.

We have lost hopelessly the memory of a world heard, seen, perceived, experienced joyfully by a body naked of language. This forgotten, unknown animal has become speaking man, and the word has petrified his flesh, not merely his collective flesh of exchange, perception, custom and power, but also and above all his corporeal flesh: thighs, feet, chest and throat vibrate, dense with words. (Serres 1998: 455)

But Serres also comes bizarrely to depend upon a reified or statuary idea of language itself. Language abstracts, makes the things of the world insubstantial, it alienates us from sensation. Language, in the memorable metaphor that Serres supplies in the closing pages of the book, is like a vast sea in which the things of the world have been irretrievably drowned, like an Atlantis or Titanic. But this metaphor, which insists on language's inundation, on the deathliness or petrifaction of the living, joyful body effected by language, itself enforces such a petrifaction in its own monochromatic or reifying view of language. Language is here an essential, absolutely homogeneous principle: its nature and effects universal and unvarying. Like the ocean, language is all one thing as far as the eye can see and as deeper than did ever plummet sound. Discourse is deluge; it is itself deluged in homogeneity.

Serres's own language denies in its use what his language maintains, namely the emptiness, abstraction and rigor mortis of language. Language, for Serres, is nothing less, nor anything else, than *logos* (Technology, Serres says in *Angels* (1995: 71), is *techne* become *logos*, just as phenomenology signifies appearance that speaks itself, which becomes the speaking of itself.) But Serres's language is always more, and other, than this. It is a language full of device and address, brimming with undigested material, spiky with the kind of hardness that Serres finds in music. His is the effort to incarnate, with the very language that he insists is toxic or paralysing. 'Yes, I have lost my Eurydice: I want to create a body present here and now, but I have only pure abstraction, this vocal emission, soft: Eurydice, Eurydice, I wanted so much to give you life and all I could write was philosophy' (Serres 1998: 171). It is possible, it insists against the current of what Serres insists, pushing upstream against the flow that converts the hard into the soft, for language as music, to remain open to the unintegrated: language can be a kind of tympanum between the human world of linguistic addiction and the world of the given, the *donné*, which can take the impress of the hardness of things (the howling of animals, the breaking of stones), even as it transmits and translates them.

In the end, the body is not merely the body: not mere mass, which must be subjected to a work of transformation, or analysis, or understanding. Despite the insistence upon incarnation, and the recurrence of Christian images of resurrection in the book (the book begins with a passage describing Serres' escape from a burning vessel, which is a violent kind of parturition, and ends with the words 'resurrection, or renaissance'), the body does not rise again in Serres' work. This is because the body, or more particularly the senses, is never a mere object, but itself a kind of work. The body is the work of transforming mere sensitiveness into sense and sensibility both: the body is its work of transformation. There is no chance of getting back to the body, since it is the nature of the human body to be self-organizing and therefore self-surpassing. In the end, Serres' work is founded upon the unbreachable continuity of this work of self-transformation and self-organization, which the body conducts through sensation, and the work of organization undertaken by Serres' own writing about the body: the body forms itself, he writes, like a book. In folding sense over sense, translating flesh into word, Serres mimics and participates in the work of self-translation, self-complication, undertaken by sensation itself.

In the final section of the chapter entitled 'Joy,' Serres suddenly relaxes the severity of his denunciation of language. For our epoch, he says, is no longer the epoch of language. What dominates now are the code, the algorithm, information. Where language sought to fix and petrify its objects, distributing them in patterns of invariant conversion and exchange, information dissolves the object by operationalizing it. The body that has become a series of genetic codes is no longer a linguistic body, but a source of production; no longer locked in place, but rather disseminated and multiplied. Language loses its three dimensions of power: the referential (taken over by science), the seductive (taken over by media and advertising), and the performative (taken over by the power of technoscience).

The era of the linguistic animal has come to a close. It is this death, or supersession of language which Serres wants to claim has made this book, this way of seizing the body in language, repeatedly said to be impossible, suddenly, though perhaps only for the time being, possible. *Les cinq sens*, says Serres, 'celebrates the death of the word' (Serres 1998: 455). It is this death that makes possible, indeed imperative a new way of knowing. It seems to pardon language. Language has become redundant in the era of information and technoscience. This redundancy, this ragged spectrality, makes possible a return to the primal adventure of philosophy, faced with and able to start out once again from the bottomless mystery of the givenness of things, now, and perhaps just for now, apprehensible otherwise than as the mere task or antagonist of the linguistic subject-protagonist: 'Forgetful, detached, the subject plunges into the unforgettable world' (Serres 1998: 461). Language is subsumed in the body's powers of self-invention. 'Every time an organ – or a function – is freed from a previous obligation, it invents' (Serres 1998: 460), Serres observes: the hands, freed from the work of locomotion in homo erectus, occupy themselves in making tools; the mouth, freed from the need to grip and seize, invents speech. Freed from the function of naming, categorizing and distributing, language-memory becomes available for a similar self-reinvention.

Sans

It seems incongruous that *Les cinq sens* should end with such an account of epochal loss and inauguration. For the book *Les cinq sens*, perhaps like the five senses themselves, seems to have no memory, no sense of temporal progression. Like so many other Serres texts, the time of the text forms a kind of climate, or weather-system, shifting, recoiling, gathering, intensifying, diffusing: time, in French *temps*, as Serres frequently observes, is already available to be thought of as a kind of weather. Serres proposes no chronology of sense development, for example, as others working on these questions have sometimes been tempted to do. It is unclear whether or not the senses are merely before time – primordial, before reason, language and the categories of linguistic time – or multitemporal, belonging to the crumpled or folded time, the temporal complexion, that Serres evokes in his discussions with Bruno Latour.

Serres celebrates abundance, increase, invention: the body is, repeatedly and in the end, the principle of propagation. Serres will have it no other way. The senses are the body forming and reforming itself. As such the body is a miraculous nook in the flux, a negentropic eddy or swirl in the current that traverses it yet which it delays.

Les cinq sens moves: in moving through its material, the senses, it also moves through itself. It begins and ends with this auto-contingency, this self-touching, that faces outwards and inwards, backwards and forwards, at the same time. In doing so, it disobeys the fundamental law of time, the law of entropy or going out. Its vitalism refuses limit, suffering, degradation, exhaustion. In the celebration of grace, gratuity, giving, expenditure, abundance, over equivalence and conservation, and therefore also dying out or depletion, *Les cinq sens* denies the equivalence of the first and second laws of thermodynamics, the law of conservation and the law of decay. Serres ignores the mortality of the body, the fact that the body is the carrier or amplifier of entropy as well as its temporary remission.

In the 'Boîtes' chapter, Serres imagines with a kind of horrified amusement Socrates heroically speaking right up to the instant of his death. Serres cannot believe that the *imperium* of language should seek to abut so closely upon death, suffuse every last atom of existence, leaving open no chink of grace, no space of animal existence before death. It is for this reason that language, for Serres, is death. But Serres proposes here another kind of exceptionless plenitude, a plenitude that allows no exteriority, nothing that cannot be gathered up and redeemed in the self-renewing abundance of time. Where Socrates encroaches upon death, Serres incorporates it. In both cases, death is denied. Serres is bitterly opposed to the warlike Hegelian dialectic that, in its way of subduing time to a line, actually denies time, cancelling its contradictions. But Serres's own irenic testimony to abundance and redemption works as a kind of atemporal or multitemporal dialectic, and exhibits its own stalling effect. Despite his homage to the pleasures of company, literally the breaking of bread together, and of conversation, the world of Serres' senses is an unsociable world; where are the others in all of this contingency of self with self? The answer is, perhaps, that Serres refuses the anthropomorphism of alterity, refuses to close the system of relations off with the claustrophobic or finally autistic calamity or catastrophe of the self in its relations to the human other.

Something is omitted in Serres' abundant and all-inclusive celebration of the senses. That something is loss, depletion, mortality, omission. There is an abhorence in Serres' senses, a hole where negativity should be. If the sensitive body is excursive, if its nature is to list or lean into the wind, to go out from itself, this advance is into the condition of its own mortality, into its own slow going or going out, against a background of finally invariant and unremissable degradation. Serres makes us aware of the direction or itinerary of the senses, of the *sens* in the *sens*. But we may hear another variant in this transformation of the senses into themselves. The word *sens* is after all only the merest modulation of the mouth away from *sans*. The senses acquaint us and themselves with the condition of their own decay that will leave us sans eyes, sans ears, sans teeth, sans everything. French would allow us to say it in the following motto: *Les sens ont le sens du sans*. The senses have the sense of the less. The senses move towards lessness. They list to the leastmost. The senses take lessening's course. The lessons of the senses, like those of the Mock Turtle, are aptly enough so-called, for they get less and less.

Serres celebrates the ceaseless unravelling and reknitting of the body, in the principle of giving out, *dépense*, that is always itself renewed, that can never give out. There is no place, no time for this in Serres' five senses, which, in their ceaseless coming and going, are always, as we have seen, on the increase, rather than come and gone in no time. This intolerance of the exteriority represented by death and degradation, makes for a certain paradoxical claustration in Serres' work, makes it a monism of the manifold. There is nothing Serres can do with it, because there is nothing anyone can do with it, this slow going, this ungraspable, unknowable, unignorable squandering of energy that in the end is what we will have amounted to. There is nothing we can do with it, though it has everything to do with us.

Bibliography

Beckett, S. (1986), *Collected Dramatic Works*, London: Faber & Faber.
Ramachandran, V.S. and Blakeslee, S. (1999), *Phantoms of the Brain: Human Nature and the Architecture of the Mind*, London: Fourth Estate.
Serres, M. (1995a), *Angels: A Modern Myth*, trans. F. Cowper, Paris and New York: Flammarion.
—— (1995b), *Genesis*, trans. G. James and J. Nielson, Ann Arbor: University of Michigan Press.

—— (1997), *The Troubadour of Knowledge*, trans. S. Faria Ginser and W. Paulson, Ann Arbor: University of Michigan Press.

—— (1998), *Les cinq sens*, Paris: Hachette.

—— and Latour, B. (1995), *Conversations on Science, Culture and Time*, trans. R. Lapilus, Ann Arbor: University of Michigan Press.

19

Darwin's Disgust

William Ian Miller

Modern psychological interest in disgust starts with Darwin, who centers it in the rejection of food and the sense of taste. Consider his account:

> The term 'disgust,' in its simplest sense, means something offensive to the taste. It is curious how readily this feeling is excited by anything unusual in the appearance, odour, or nature of our food. In Tierra del Fuego a native touched with his finger some cold preserved meat which I was eating at our bivouac, and plainly showed utter disgust at its softness; whilst I felt utter disgust at my food being touched by a naked savage, though his hands did not appear dirty. A smear of soup on a man's beard looks disgusting, though there is of course nothing disgusting in the soup itself. I presume that this follows from the strong association in our minds between the sight of food, however circumstanced, and the idea of eating it. (Darwin 1965: 256–57)

Darwin is right about the etymology of disgust. It means unpleasant to the taste. But one wonders whether taste would figure so crucially in Darwin's account if the etymology hadn't suggested it. The German *Ekel*, for instance, bears no easily discernible connection to taste. Did that make it easier for Freud to link disgust as readily with the anal and genital as with the oral zone (see S. Miller 1986: 295; Freud 1953a, II: 177–78)? I suspect that the English word is in some unquantifiable way responsible for the narrow focus on taste, oral incorporation, and rejection of food in psychological treatments of disgust (see Tomkins 1963; Rozin 1982; Izard 1984, 1987). Before the word 'disgust' entered the English lexicon in the first quarter of the seventeenth century, taste figured distinctly less prominently than foul odors and loathsome sights. Disgust undoubtedly involves taste, but it also involves – not just by extension but at its core – smell, touch, even at times sight and hearing. Above all, it is a moral and social sentiment. It plays a motivating and confirming role in moral judgment in a particular way that has little if any connection with ideas of oral incorporation (see Freud 1953a: 177–8; Haidt, McCauley, and Rozin 1994; Haidt, Rozin et al. 1998). It ranks people and things in a kind of cosmic ordering.

I use the word 'disgust' to indicate a complex sentiment that can be lexically marked in English by expressions declaring things or actions to be repulsive, revolting, or giving rise to reactions described as revulsion and abhorrence as well as disgust (see Wierzbicka 1986). Disgust names a syndrome in which all these terms have their proper role. They all convey a strong sense of aversion to something perceived as dangerous because of its powers to contaminate, infect, or pollute by proximity, contact, or ingestion. All suggest the appropriateness, but not the necessity, of accompanying nausea or queasiness, or of an urge to recoil and shudder from creepiness.

Disgust, however, is not nausea. Not all disgust need produce symptoms of nausea, nor all nausea mark the presence of disgust. The nausea of the stomach flu is not a sign or consequence of disgust, although, should we vomit as a result, the vomiting and the vomit might themselves lead to sensations of disgust that would be distinguishable from the nausea that preceded it. The nausea of a hangover, however, is more complex, accompanied as it often is by feelings of contamination, poisoning, and self-disgust, as well as shame and embarrassment. On the other side, things or deeds we find disgusting put us in the world of disgust when we have the sense that we would not be surprised should we start feeling queasy or nauseated, whether or not we actually do so. Disgust surely has a feel to it; that feel, however, is not so much of nausea as of the uneasiness, the panic, of varying intensity, that attends the awareness of being defiled.

Let us put that aside for now and look more closely at the passage from Darwin. Is it food and taste that elicit disgust as a first-order matter? 'In Tierra del Fuego a native touched with his finger some cold preserved meat which I was eating at our bivouac, and plainly showed disgust at its softness; whilst I felt utter disgust at my food being touched by a naked savage, though his hands did not appear dirty.' In this passage, long before food ever reaches a mouth to raise the issue of its taste, we have suggestions of other categories that implicate disgust: categories of tactility as in cold (meat) versus hot, soft versus firm; overt categories of purity such as raw versus cooked, dirty versus clean; categories of bodily shame, naked versus clothed; and broader categories of group definition, Tierra del Fuego versus England, them versus us. For the native, it is not ultimately the softness of the preserved meat so much as what eating it means about the person eating it. For Darwin, it is not just that someone touched his food (with clean hands no less), but that the person doing the touching was a *naked savage* who had already offended him. In the first clause the savage is merely a curious native in the two senses of curious: curious because strange and curious subjectively as a dispositional trait that makes him poke at Darwin's food. But once he finds Darwin's food disgusting, Darwin redescribes him downward as a naked savage capable of polluting his food. Before this interaction Darwin could look at the native with the contempt of bemusement or indifference or with a kind of benign contempt that often is itself a component of curiosity. The native, however, gets too close and gives real offense, and the inkling of threat is enough to transform a complacent contempt into disgust.

Would Darwin have been as disgusted by the native touching his food if the native had not insulted it by registering his revulsion? Or had the native already discerned Darwin's disgust for him and decided to use it to toy with him by touching his food? Would Darwin have been less disgusted if the native had touched him rather than his food? Food plays a role here, to be sure, and both actors share a deep belief that you pretty much are what you eat. The native recoils at the idea of what manner of man could eat such stuff, whereas Darwin fears ingesting some essence of savagery that has been magically imparted to his food by the finger of the naked savage. But oral ingestion is put in play here only because food is acting as one of a number of possible media by which pollution could be transferred. The issue is the doubts and fears each man's presence, elicits in the other and the little battle for security and dominance by which they seek to resolve it; it is a battle of competing disgusts.

Less loaded with politics is the smear of soup on a man's beard, 'though there is of course nothing disgusting in the soup itself.' Again it is not food that is disgusting; Darwin's own explanation says it only becomes disgusting by the 'strong association... between the sight of food... and the idea of eating it.' But this can't be right. The sight of the man with his beard befouled is disgusting long before any idea of eating the soup on his beard ever would, if ever it could, occur to us. The association of ideas is not of seeing food in a beard and then imagining eating that food. If the soup is disgusting as food, it is so only because beard hair would be in it. Now that is disgusting. We could see this, in accordance with the structural theory of Mary Douglas (1966), as a manifestation of things becoming polluting by being out of place (discussed more fully in Miller 1997: chapter 3). That captures some of the problem but doesn't explain the sense that it is more the hair than the soup, more the man than the food, that elicits disgust. The soup on the beard reveals the man as already contaminated by a character defect, a moral failure in keeping himself presentable in accordance with the righteously presented demand that he maintain his public purity and cleanliness of person and not endanger us by his incompetence. It needn't have been soup or bread crumbs that incriminated him; it could just as well have been bits of lint or even soap residue. No doubt, however, the soup would be more disgusting than either lint or soap. The soup, after all, unlike lint or soap, might have fallen onto his beard from his mouth or from a spoon that had already been in his mouth. It is thus not our fear of oral incorporation that makes the soup disgusting to us but his failure to have properly orally incorporated it.

Yet suppose that it was not a naked savage who touched Darwin's meat but a cockroach that walked across it. Would the issue then be one primarily of ingesting food? Even here I think the matter is more complex. A roach walking across our arm would elicit disgust too and perhaps even more than if it walked across our food, and we are not about to eat our arm. The roach (and the naked savage) is disgusting before it touches our food; its contaminating powers come from some other source.

Since Darwin, as we have already observed, the non-Freudian literature on disgust has focused on disgust as an affect linked originally and functionally to the sense of taste. I have attributed this focus to the unintended effects of the etymology of the English word disgust. If we list those qualities that we tend to associate with disgust-eliciting things, however, we find that attributes of taste figure no more saliently than those of smell or touch.

Touch

The qualities of consistency and feel provide the bulk of our lexicon of disgust. Thus the oppositions squishy versus firm, moist versus dry, sticky versus non-adhering, scabby versus smooth, viscid versus free flowing, wriggling and slithering versus still. Add further certain qualities without easily paired opposites, for which the opposite is simply the absence of the trait: oily, filmy, curdly, gooey, slimy, mucky. All these qualities deserve some special comment. For one thing, it is easier to come up with words to describe disgusting sensations when these are moist, viscid, pliable, than when they are dry, free flowing, or hard. For every disgusting scabby or crusty thing there are tens of disgusting oozy, mucky, gooey, slimy, clammy, sticky, tacky, dank, squishy, or filmy things. And even the scabby and the crusty borrow their disgustingness from the fact that they are formed from the coagulation of viscous substances. Note how hard it is to find non-pejorative terms to describe some of these consistencies, primarily those which are characteristics of what I earlier called life soup. Just how is it possible to name slime or indicate something that slithers without the term taking on a heavy negative moral and aesthetic baggage?

Consider the case of oil, which shares with slime a slippery smoothness and similar viscosity. Oil is as good as the slimy can get; it has the capacity to lead a life of ritual purity, being transparent and having the capacity to make things shine. When from olives it anointed kings and Homeric heroes or when blessed it served in the sacrament of extreme unction. In this role it was not only pure but purifying. But oil came soon to have a less exalted life. Not initially disgusting in the material world, it came to be infected by the meaning it acquired in the moral world. The same capacities that made it useful as a lubricant, its slipperiness, smoothness, and adhering characteristics, when applied to moral traits served to describe a particularly vile character. Glib, oily, unctuous, greasy. It is in the moral world that oil sinks to the slimy; and once morally infected it loses its pristine quality in the world of matter (see Sartre 1992: 771). Oil also suffered from its religious pretensions. Unction was made unctuous and slimy by the human capacity for fawning and hypocrisy.

The diction governing tactile disgust reveals certain presumptions and tendencies about the way we conceptualize disgust; these are captured by the oppositions I noted at the beginning of this section. Even if we discount for the bad associations that come with the words themselves we are still left with the distinct sense that things that are slimy, sticky, slithery, wriggly, oily, or viscid are more likely to elicit disgust than those without such qualities. Again, I am not saying that the category of disgust cannot be constructed differently, only that it exhibits certain tendencies and probabilities. Presumably rice farmers have long been acclimated to muck, eel fisherman to slimy slitheriness, nurses and doctors to evil-smelling and decaying bodies. And because we are dealing with probabilities and presumptions, these presumptions can be overcome by context and the kinds of expectations context generates. That which should be moist can disgust by being dry, that which should be supple can disgust by being hard, that which should be thick or viscous can disgust by being watery, the very word 'watery' being a pejorative of concepts like clear, fluid, limpid, or pellucid.

But the presumptions are there and one wonders if they are themselves solely generated by culture or if they work to constrain cultural choices. I suspect that more cultural work is needed to make slitheriness non-disgusting than to make it disgusting. We might discern here two categories of tactile disgustingness. In the first are those things that disgust by failure to accord with expectations. Such would be the disgustingness of human skin that feels like a reptile's, or, for that matter, a reptile's that feels like a human's. In the second category expectations of disgust are met in full by disgust unless love or inurement prevents it. This is the realm of the slimy, oozy, sticky, squishy, wiggly, and slithery. What draws the disgusting to these qualities? Douglasian structuralism doesn't give a non-reductive answer;[1] with a little ingenuity it could provide an answer for each culture, but it would still not account for the tendencies of so many different cultures to converge in agreement that slime and ooze, feces and menstrual blood, are on the polluting side of the equation.

Might it be that disgust itself has a structure that it imposes on cultural orderings? This is hardly an outrageous proposition. Cultures surely vary in the degree to which they call on disgust to back their moral ordering, but to the extent that they look to disgust (or something like it) rather than, say, guilt or fear, certain things must follow. Even here culture can override the tendencies that come with the disgust affect, but it has to work harder to do so. Once a culture erects the classification pure/impure the clear and free-flowing will be valued as against the slimy and viscid. Another constraint imposed on the category of the disgusting may well come from certain broadly shared ideas of what purity means. Here the influences work in two directions. Disgust constrains the possible attributes of the pure, while the idea of the pure, in turn, supplies precise content to the disgusting. Purity seems necessarily to involve a certain sense of the discreteness of a thing, of its inviolability, and its disconnectedness with other things. If this is so things that stick will be presumptively contaminating. Then what of slippery, slithery things that are impossible to get a grip on? These surely don't stick but they leave filmy, clammy, or oily substances that do. Slime is slime because it doesn't flow away quickly (see Sartre 1992: 774–75). Clear free-running things will thus be presumptively pure. A culture could override these presumptions or even stand them on their head. But it would take more work, a longer story, to do so than to go, so to speak, with the flow.

Purity must be defined against the impure and the impure against it; purity cannot exist as a concept without creating its contrary. Culture is stuck here with the nature of certain mental concepts, which can exist only as oppositions and contrasts.[2] Black needs white, good needs evil, virtue needs vice, or the first term makes no sense. And in the strange way that qualities give rise to their contrary or are reducible to a common underlying concept, so the word cleanness itself may owe its origins to stickiness. In one of those uncanny etymologies (see Freud 1953b) that shows a word meaning itself and its opposite, the *Oxford English Dictionary* notes that some philologists believe *clean* to derive from an Indo-European stem meaning 'to stick,' 'with the suggested connexion of sense that sticky things, such as oil, give a clear surface, or "make the face to shine"'. I think it may be less the luminous shine than the sticking itself. Water and clear, free-flowing liquids clean by washing away, by rinsing. Oil, unlike water, must be understood to purify not by rinsing but by adhering and bonding. In this it behaves quite like a pollutant, which with its extraordinary powers of contagion has the ability to adhere to or mingle with anything it touches. In order to do battle with the impure the purifying agent must itself be able to stick to what it touches so as to shield it, as with oil, or mingle with the pollutant so as to wash it away, as in purification by ablution. Whether water or oil, the purifying agent must give itself up for the general cause of purity. The pure thus borrows from the impure its disgusting qualities to fight against it. The fear is, of course, that pollutants stick only too well whereas it takes a heady dose of wishful thinking to believe purity to be as contagious as pollution.

The skin is our chief organ of touch and, strangely, some of the things we least like to touch parody the form if not quite the function of skin. Take the skin on heated milk for instance. Some, like Julia Kristeva (1982: 2–3), find this the *pièce de resistance* of the disgusting. Part of its loathsomeness is the feel of it in the mouth, not unlike the disgust that a hair produces. It seems that crusts, skins, and films covering fluid interiors have a special ability to elicit disgust. The phenomenon of coagulation, of curdling, unites ideas of bubbling, seething, generative surfeit, with ideas of fermentation and rot. It is the green mantle on the standing pool again. The curd, the milk scum, thus reproduce the central themes of disgust elicitation: the eternal recurrence of viscous, teeming, swarming generation and the putrefaction and decay that attend it. It is as if the milk, when heated, spontaneously generates a loathsome image of gestation itself: a membrane appearing to cover warmish fluids. Life must be packaged just right not to make us cringe when it touches us.

A subsystem of the sense of touch processes temperature. Coldness couples with clamminess to mimic death, heat couples with hellfire to produce sulfurous stenches. Yet, as a general rule, extreme temperatures do not elicit disgust. (Pain, not disgust, is the specie of the extremes.) The cold clamminess of death is no less than 60°F; once we get below 32°F we are in the world of crystalline purity. And well before we get above 212°F we enter a world purified by fire. Fire does not disgust unless accompanied by foul odors, but lukewarmness, or body temperature, might well do so. We will sit on a public toilet seat with less upset when it is cold than when we discern that it is warm from the warmth of a prior user. Body heat is in some way as polluting as more material pollutants in that setting. Temperature, it seems, disgusts precisely in those ranges in which life teems – that is, from the dank of the fen to the mugginess of the jungle; this is the range in which sliminess exists, for slime ceases to be when frozen solid or burnt to a crisp. The temperature must be sufficient to get the old life soup bubbling, seething, wiggling, and writhing but not so great as to kill it. The boiling and seething of life, the coagulating of blood, the eruption of suppurating sores, the teeming of maggots – disgust itself – operate in what we call the comfort zone.

We do not need to swallow things to be contaminated by them. A taste-based conception of disgust cannot account for the fact that most contamination takes place simply by contact rather than by ingestion and not just contact with the skin but with the extended covering that includes our clothing (even clothing we are not wearing but intend to put on) as well as the space we claim as our immediate bodily preserve. The approach of disgusting things causes us to cringe, shudder, or recoil in anticipation of offensive touchings. We have seen that some areas of our surface are more at risk, more sacred than other areas, and that all the orifices, although in different degrees, are points of serious vulnerability. Those places that are likely to cause disgust by being touched are also likely to cause disgust when they are used to touch another. Touching with or being touched by a shoulder or elbow is far less problematic than touchings involving hands, tongues, or genitalia.

Being touched by another under certain predictable circumstances elicits disgust. Take first the case of the person whom our sentinel senses of sight and smell, or our moral sense, already reveal as disgusting. Touchings from this person will disgust if they are attempts at greater intimacy, and will both disgust (because of what he is) and raise indignation (for what he did) if the touching is not a request for intimacy but takes the form of non-sexualized aggression. Disgustingly ugly people are given very little leeway. We tend to impute intentionality to their disgustingness, and thus we are unlikely to excuse their accidental touchings as accidents. They are blamed for not attending to the special duties to avoid contact that their pariah status imposes on them.

Even people who are not perceived as initially disgusting can quickly become so by getting too close without our permission. When they touch us impermissibly we treat them to a mix of disgust and indignation similar to that we direct toward the pariah. The difference is that these people are allowed the opportunity to plead their lack of intention. A ritually apt 'sorry' will prevent offense being taken, or remedy any offense already taken if the excuse is reasonably plausible and sincere. Plausibility regarding such 'accidents' usually depends on not having to raise the plea of accident more than once and on the relative triviality of the offense being excused. These not unattractive people are also given another benefit: they are often granted the privilege of having their unpermitted touchings processed as if they were proper requests for permission for the touching taking place. Such a touching is the first escalation in the ritual of courtship, and it directly involves disgust. For the touching is a request to consider the prospect of the ultimate sexual touching and whether that touching from the person in question would be disgusting. That first touching, that first gesture in the course of conversation when one lightly touches the other's arm, is thus raising only one serious question: do I disgust you?

Smell

In the diffuseness of the location of its sensors touch differs radically from sight, taste, smell, and hearing, all of which are centered at orifices and localized organs devoted to receiving those inputs. But though touch is diffuse in the location of its receptors the contaminating toucher is usually quite identifiable and localizable. Smell works just the other way, with a highly localized receptor, the nose, but often emanating from unlocalizable and diffuse sources. Smells are pervasive and invisible, capable of threatening like poison; smells are the very vehicles of contagion. Odors are thus especially contaminating and much more dangerous than localized substances one may or may not put in the mouth. Before germ theory existed nauseating smells bore the burden of carrying disease, while good smells were curative. Germ theory did little to undo this belief, as makers of home cleaning products well know. The aseptic must have a smell that accords with our beliefs about the smell of asepsis. And detergents must produce suds and be perfumed or they won't sell even though the suds and odorants pollute rivers and have no cleansing action whatsoever.

Smell combines with taste to give us the rich array of flavors we love and loathe. But smell gets there long before taste and we might wonder why, if our sense of smell were attuned, we should ever put nauseating foods in our mouth. The problem seems to be that even though smell is a powerful component of flavor the smell of things outside the mouth is very different from the olfactory effect they have once in the mouth (see Rozin 1982). Smell is thus not constructed to give a perfect indication of what might taste good. Any lover of strong cheeses and fishy fish knows this to be true. If smell alone were to control access to the mouth we would not only miss cheeses but repent of drinking perfume and eating flowers. Even a coffee lover has to feel that twinge of vexation in the falling off between its alluring aroma and its taste.

Whatever defensive role disgust plays for the biological organism would seem to be of little value if it had to wait until the sense of taste was engaged. Taste operates as a defense of last resort; it is meant to catch only those things that get by the outer sensory defenses. The eyes can be fooled by pleasant exteriors, as the nose can be by hypocritical aromas. But taste is no more foolproof a defense than touch or vision, for there is no guarantee that harmful things will taste bad. Taste can be tricked too. Poison may not be identifiable by taste, and otherwise unharmful things can taste too good, giving rise to the harms of addiction and surfeit. The bulk of the ingestive defense work is accomplished by smell not taste. We follow an easy rule regarding ingestion to which we admit a few carefully delineated exceptions: do not stick foul-smelling things in the mouth unless they are members of the limited class of items culture and experience identify as smelling bad but as being nonetheless nutritional and good tasting: thus cheese, fish, or cooked cabbage-family vegetables (there is also an exception for sex, which will be dealt with in a general and abstract fashion later).

We saw that touch provides a rich lexicon of terms to describe revolting tactile sensations and that the gradations in sensation are measured along qualitative axes of temperature, viscosity, texture, movement, adhesion, and so on. The lexicon of smell is very limited and usually must work by making an adjective of the thing that smells. Excrement smells like excrement, roses like a rose, rotting flesh like rotting flesh. Sometimes we attempt description by saying that rotting flesh smells like feces, or that a perfume smells like a rose (see Engen 1982, 1987, 1991; Rindisbacher 1992). What is missing is a specially dedicated qualitative diction of odor that matches the richness of distinctions we make with the tactile as with squishy, oozy, gooey, gummy, mucky, dank, and damp. Odor qualifiers, if not the names of things emitting the odor, are usually simple adjectives and nouns expressing either the pleasantness or unpleasantness of the smell, most of which merely mean bad or good smell: fetid, foul, stink, stench, rancid, vile, revolting, nauseating, sickening. Routine tactile sensation spurs language to inventiveness, while the olfactory and gustatory reduce us to saying little more than yum or yuck. One qualification: if perception of pain is considered a subset of tactile experiences and not the separate system of sensation it is, then to the extent that the tactile produces pain it abandons lexical richness for screams, moans, groans, sighs, grunts, and little more (on the language-destroying capacity of pain see Scarry 1985).

Our inability to describe smell other than by naming the thing that gives off the odor does not make smell any less central than touch to the way we conceptualize disgust. Without the odors of feces, urine, decay, and sweat, neither they nor life itself would be so disgusting. It is precisely the odor of these things that strikes the moralist of the ascetic stripe so deeply. Even in the bloom of youth our bodies produce reeking substances daily. Swift in his typically self-destructive way catalogues the sights and smells that greet the lover reconnoitering in his lady's dressing room and to his horror discovering her close stool. The poet is moved to a culinary simile in the mock heroic style (Swift 1967: 479):

> As Mutton Cutlets, Prime of Meat,
> Which tho' with Art you salt and beat,
> As laws of Cookery require,
> And roast them at the clearest Fire:
> If from adown the hopeful Chops
> The Fat upon a Cinder drops,
> To stinking Smoak it turns the Flame
> Pois'ning the Flesh from whence it came;
> So Things, which must not be exprest,
> When plumpt into the reeking Chest;
> Send up an excremental Smell
> To taint the Parts from whence they fell.
> The Pettycoats and Gown perfume,
> And waft a Stink round every Room.
> Thus finishing his grand Survey,
> The'Swain disgusted slunk away.

Swift makes clear that odors have the power to contaminate; for him they irrevocably destroy all desire and poison his overly sensitive consciousness. The simile of the stench of burning fat (notice this seems to be an odor barbecuists have long since reevaluated) suggests that the stuff we eat begins to mimic the process of its transformation into foul-smelling excrement even as it is being prepared for consumption. Everything man (and especially woman) touches turns to shit and then that same excrement comes back to stew us in our own juices. Or, more precisely, the vision is of us cured in our own smoke house, in which we provide both the smoke and the meat to be cured. The smells of excrement rise up to taint the parts from whence it fell, which in a paranoiac vision of contagion then fill all the room and all thought with stench.

The primordial scene for Swift was not coitus but defecation, and the horror of the latter was a function of the stench. The thought of defecation and its smell was the one thought whose power no other thoughts could resist. It made beauty a fraud and sexual desire a function of sustained and insistent self-deception. For Swift desire could not survive the close stool. If Swift's obsessions end in misogyny, the thought that men must defecate too could lead to the heresies of doubting Christ's divine nature. Freud's Wolf Man, tormented by the thought of Jesus defecating, solved the problem with the subtlety of a schoolman: 'Since Christ had made wine *out* of nothing, he could have made food *into* nothing and in this way have avoided defecating' (Freud 1953c: 63; see also Kundera 1984: 245–6). We get an inverse miracle of the loaves. Swift was not as resourceful as Wolf Man or, more likely, was unwilling to allow himself such facile self-deceptions. For him, the loss is not just the snuffing of desire but the loss of the sublimity that attends it, the loss of an illusion, which loss brings not wistfulness but the feeling of having been rendered a fool, hoodwinked by one's own desire and woman's mysterious abilities to aid one's self-deception. Thus the well-known lines: 'Nor wonder how I lost my Wits; / Oh! Caelia, Caelia, Caelia shits.' (Swift 1967: 531). The comic despair masks real bitterness that is not suppressed in other places: 'Should I the Queen of Love refuse, / Because she rose from stinking Ooze?' (Swift 1967: 480).

Desire requires that we suppress entirely thoughts of beginnings and endings. Gestation and decay are all condensed into the primal odor of feces. Its stench expands to capture the odors of sex, desire, generation, and decay. It poisons us by smoking our flesh on the outside and recorrupts the inside by being inhaled as vapors. Lear, soon to make an appearance, could imagine that an ounce of civet might sweeten his imagination befouled by the odors of copulation. Swift's imagination, however, gives him no possibility of relief. The daily recollection of the smells of the close stool banish sweet thoughts and fix themselves permanently to guard against the return of desire-creating illusion. 'For fine Ideas vanish fast, / While all the gross and filthy last' (Swift 1967: 525). The smell of feces, its vapors, produces thoughts that follow Gresham's law no less enthusiastically than money does. And thus it is on a suffusion of nasty excremental odor that Swift anticipates Freud's formulation of the anal character type with its linking of money, excrement, and cultural production itself (see Brown 1959: 192–3).

The linking of olfaction to the sexual has a long history to which we will return later. The ascetic monkly literature meditated on bad odors in an attempt to kill desire; Swift and Freud can be seen in some respects as continuing the tradition. The unrelenting misogyny is still there; it is always the odors emitted by women that kill male desire. (It seems men are much more likely to confuse anuses and vaginas than women are likely to confuse anuses and penises.) We never hear much about female abhorrence for male odors, which is little wonder given that with rare exception men were doing the writing. Even then, these crabbed men, in their hagiographies of female virgin saints, did not fail to indicate female revulsion for male bodies. The difference between the monks and Swift and Freud, however, is not their misogyny, but that the monks never came close to killing desire, while Swift and Freud were much better at rendering it vile by wishing it not to be.

Freud, like Swift, is not quite able to wrest the nose away from the excremental. In a long and famous footnote in *Civilization and Its Discontents* he supposes great consequences for the sense of smell that attended man's arising from all fours to walk erect. Standing up changed the placement of the nose relative to the genitals of others, but more precisely the relation of men's noses to women's crotches. He expounds at some length on the theme:

> The organic periodicity of the sexual process has persisted, it is true, but its effect on psychical sexual excitation has rather been reversed. This change seems most likely to be connected with the diminution of the olfactory stimuli by means of which the menstrual process produced an effect on the male psyche. Their role was taken over by visual excitations, which, in contrast to the intermittent olfactory stimuli, were able to maintain a permanent effect. The taboo on menstruation is derived from this 'organic repression,' as a defense against a phase of development that has been surmounted... This process is repeated on another level when the gods of a superseded period of civilization turn into demons. The diminution of the olfactory stimuli seems itself to be a consequence of a man's raising himself from the ground, of his assumption of an upright gait; this made his genitals, which were previously concealed, visible and in need of protection, and so provoked feelings of shame in him.
>
> The fateful process of civilization would thus have set in with man's adoption of an erect posture. From that point the chain of events would have proceeded through the devaluation of olfactory stimuli and the isolation of the menstrual period to the time when visual stimuli were paramount and the genitals became visible, and thence to the continuity of sexual excitation, the founding of the family and so to the threshold of human civilization. (Freud 1953d: 99–100 n.1)

The footnote continues by discussing the increasing cultural concern with cleanliness, which originates not in hygienic considerations but 'in an urge to get rid of the excreta, which have become disagreeable to the sense perceptions.' Nonetheless children have to be socialized into being disgusted by excreta:

> Upbringing insists with special energy on hastening the course of development which lies ahead, and which should make the excreta worthless, disgusting, abhorrent and abominable. Such a reversal of values would scarcely be possible if the substances that are expelled from the body were not doomed by their strong smells to share the fate which overtook olfactory stimuli after man adopted the erect posture.

The story is of the transformation of the sense of smell from the sense that excited periodic sexuality in times of rutting or with humans in times of menses to a diminished and devalued sense once man stood up. As the nose moves up, the olfactory stimuli diminish in their powers to excite, less it seems by diminishment of the sensitivity of the sense of smell than by a reversal in the valence of the stimuli it receives from below. What once attracted now repels; hence the broad acceptance of menstrual taboos. Man (and man means man in the restricted sense) is compensated for the betrayal of the nose by being given the power to stare and get excited all the time, not just once a month. Vision on high from a distance replaces closely sniffing around down below. Now man wants a woman around all the time; hence family organization begins and then civilization built upon the family model takes off from there. And what of woman? She had better stay with the man if she wants to protect herself and her children from other men who are now looking for sexual objects to control continuously, rather than sniffing around once in a while for periodic violent contacts.

Standing up does more than reverse the value of menstrual odor; it paves the way for the devaluation of everything in the genital region. The first stage in this process is one of 'organic repression.' This repression owes nothing to culture or society, being solely, according to Freud, the consequence of standing up, and it is directed toward the odors of menstruation. The second stage of devaluation of the olfactory is social, and it is directed toward feces. The 'merely' social impetus behind the second stage means that we remain more ambivalent about excrement than about menses, the aversion to which Freud supposes to be part of our biological make up. Very young children find their excrement 'valuable to them as being part of their own body which has come away from it,' and we consequently never quite learn to loathe our own excrement with much intensity: 'The existence of the social factor which is responsible for the further transformation of anal erotism is attested by the circumstance that, in spite of all man's developmental advances, he scarcely finds the smell of *his own* excreta repulsive, but only that of other people's' (emphasis in the original).

The *social* inculcation of disgust for feces recapitulates in the life of the individual male the progress of the entire male half of the species' *organic* development of disgust for the odors of menstruation. Yet in each case – the organic disgust with menses and the socially originating disgust with feces – more primitive aspects of the erotic are repressed and olfaction, formerly the engine of desire, now founds the very capacity to be disgusted by those things once desired. So it comes to be that disgust keeps us on our feet and out of bed. But it is more than just a tale of feces and menstruation. In yet another footnote following fast on the one we have been dealing with Freud notes that man's assumption of erect posture and the depreciation of the sense of smell threatened not only anal erotism 'but the whole of his sexuality... The genitals, too, give rise to strong sensations of smell which many people cannot tolerate and which spoil sexual intercourse for them' (Freud 1953d: 105–7 n. 3).

Freud`s story ultimately depends for its intelligibility on whether we accept his account of repression and sublimation, which in turn depends on our devaluation of down as opposed to up. Like most of Freud's accounts, this one provokes, engages, and seduces in its confident reductionism and suggestive possibilities. It has its problems, however. One wonders, first, about the distinction between disgust with menstruation and that with excrement, the one wired in organically, the other barely holding on by the socially constructed thread that tells us we must find it disgusting. To the extent that Freud's argument plays with the notion of ontogeny recapitulating phylogeny it is horror of feces that should precede horror with menstrual blood in the development of the species. Consider that we are hardly born with a loathing of menstruation, nor does the infant acquire it when he stands up and learns to walk. Unlike excrement, most of us don't even learn what menses is, let alone confront it, until years after we have confronted feces and learned to be disgusted by it. The two disgusts, it turns out, are not distinguishable by virtue of their putative organic or social origins.

The varying intensity and difference in treatment of the two may well lie in the fact that only half of us menstruate but all of us defecate. And the half that menstruate are not men. Freud stacks the deck unfairly here. He compares the weaker disgust of a man with 'his own' excrement with the implacable disgust of man for another's (woman's) menstruation. The appropriate comparison would be if a man is as disgusted with another's feces as with another's menstrual blood. Which disgust is stronger would be a nice empirical matter that I imagine would be subject to wide variation across individuals and cultures. But assuming with Freud for the moment that disgust for excrement is not as firmly in place as disgust for menstrual blood, could this difference not more satisfactorily be accounted for by the fact that among us the socialization regarding menstruation takes place at a later stage of development, long after the disgust mechanism has been primed, prepped, and fashioned by its interactions with excrement? Toilet training precedes sex education even today. Freud's account again depends on its purporting to describe only male disgusts and desires (for a feminist perspective see Kahane 1992).

The account seems to war with itself in another way. Just what happens to the sense of smell in this account? Does it grow weaker? Or does it simply change functions? Freud is clear that olfaction loses its capacity to impel sexual desire and suggests that the sense of smell is generally weakened, losing strength and function to vision. Yet perversely smell, because now associated with the vile and revolting, seems to be much stronger than when it was unambivalently a sense of desire. Freud abandons his usually non-adjectival style to pile up adjectives in an effort to capture our (and his?) panic in the face of excrement; feces is not only 'worthless' but 'disgusting, abhorrent, and abominable. Smell may no longer occupy the glorious role that vision assumed, but when it comes to the power to disgust it is no contemptible weakling. One wonders whether the attractive is ever quite as moving as an equal quantity of the loathsome (the teaspoon of sewage versus the teaspoon of wine again). Or is it more appropriate to ask whether culture reinforces many more aversions than it does attractions? It may not be the case that desire must merely overmatch the specific aversion opposing it before achieving fulfillment, but rather that once it overmatches the disgust opposing it, it still must confront other scruples before it can lead to action.

To gloss Freud's footnote adequately would lead us too far astray, but I want to make a few quick observations regarding it. Freud (1953d) draws an analogy between the displacement of the olfactory by the visual and the process by which new deities replace the old: 'This process is repeated on another level when the gods of a superseded period of civilization turn into demons.' The old do not disappear; they simply change their valence. Once gods, they are now devils and demons. Vision, the sky god, banishes smell to Hell where it becomes the god of the underworld. This conforms rather nicely to the conventional Christian cosmology in which light is associated with salvation, the proper end of desire, and Hell is a place of darkness visible, where fire gives no light but only loathsome evil stenches, a mixture of sulphur and excrement whose source is the bowels of Satan, who in his incarnation as Mephistopheles takes his name from the Latin word for pestilential odor.

Smell ranks low in the hierarchy of senses. That there are bad sights and bad sounds does nothing to undermine the glory of the 'higher senses' of vision and hearing; and that there are delightful fragrances does nothing to raise smell from the ditch. So low is smell that the best smell is not a good smell but no smell at all. And this sentiment predates the twentieth century American obsession with not smelling. Montaigne in the sixteenth century cites classical authors to the same effect: 'The sweetness even of the purest breath has nothing more excellent about it than to be without any odor that offends us' (Montaigne 1958: 228). Whenever a devil or the damned appear in medieval hagiography they give proof of their condition by stinking. Vision and hearing belong on high. They are the proper entrances to intellectual and contemplative pleasures; smell (and taste) and surely touch in the form of pain sensation are the senses of Hell, perhaps because they get closer to our core and are the senses of our bodily vulnerability.

The high/low opposition invariably makes disgust the domain of the low, whether that be genitals and anus or the dark and primitive. That the nose is on the face gives it no claim to credit. Its position, in fact, makes it dangerous in the extreme because the sense located there risks bringing us low on all fours with our eyes cast down on the ground. In the Western tradition smell ends up associated with the dark, the dank, the primitive and bestial, with blind and subterranean bestiality that moves in ooze. We are back with Freud and the association of smell with the (primarily female) genitalia. The imagery of *King Lear* plays on this theme insistently. Moral blindness and real blindness are understood to be consequences of vaginas. Says Edgar to the bastard Edmund regarding the blinding of their father: 'The dark and vicious place where thee he got / Cost him his eyes' (5.3. 173–4). And without eyes one can only smell things out: 'Go thrust him out at the gates, and let him smell his way to Dover' (3.7. 93). The blind world of *Lear* is a world of hopelessness, randomness, moral chaos, and despair. Only smell thrives, and that is why the atmosphere is so poisoned and depressingly frightening and filled with utter disgust with life. Smell thus exists in a kind of moral war with vision, with vision representing the forces of light and smell the forces of darkness.[3]

In its war with smell, vision depends for its virtue on its looking up or out or metaphorically in or within but manifestly not down. When Lear starts to hallucinate visions of copulation everywhere – "The wren goes to 't, and the small gilded fly / Does lecher in my sight" – images of sight are soon transformed into ones of olfaction. Disgust, for Lear, means bad smells, bad visions being bad to the extent that they suggest bad smells. For him disgust is primarily a matter of procreation, of life itself – the production of filial ingratitude and father-killing children – and that means we end up in that dark and vicious place that cost Gloucester his eyes. Strange, but no woman in the play is fertile; all procreation either has taken place prior to the play by women now dead or is enacted in the imagination. But that is more than enough, for the mere thought of it poisons imagination. Lear not only anticipates Freud in this matter, he pushes further (*King Lear* 4.6. 125–30):

> But to the girdle do the gods inherit
> Beneath is all the fiend's.
> There's hell there's darkness, there is the sulphurous pit, burning, scalding, stench, consumption; fie, fie, fie! pah! pah! Give me an ounce of civet; good apothecary, sweeten my imagination.

The interjections tell us this is no weak disgust. Lear is retching at the mere thought of the dark place. Memory produces disgust. The memory of smells (and tastes and touches) differs from memories involving the so-called higher senses of hearing and sight. When we remember a sight we resee it; when we remember sounds we rehear them; we also can will such memories, conjure them up on purpose; or they can come unbidden triggered by nothing special. What does it mean, however, to remember a smell, taste, or touch? We cannot conjure up the memory of a smell like the memory of a face (Engen 1991: 79–80). Nor do the tastes or smells of previously experienced things simply occur to us unbidden without molecules of that thing actually being perceived by our senses. If I desire to recall an odor that made me retch five years ago, or the taste of that bad meat that gave me food poisoning, I cannot do so. What I can remember is how I felt; I can recall the disgust, even reproduce it. I can remember gagging, retching, and a generalized sense of unpleasantness, strong enough to make sure I never will knowingly eat that food or put myself in a place to smell that smell again. But I am not doing this by imaginatively resmelling the smell, or retasting the taste in the way we can imaginatively reconstruct sounds and sights. Memories of taste and smell can only be triggered by a real experience of the same smell or taste. That present sensation seems to give memories triggered by olfaction and taste their peculiar generative power: would a visual memory of Swann and Odette have had the evocative power that actually smelling and eating a madeleine pastry had for Proust?

As a parting observation on smell note that the word 'stink' has a force-fulness that makes it not quite proper in polite conversation. One usually avoids it by using softer formulations such as 'smells bad.' Or one uses 'stink' while suffering a small anxiety regarding its likelihood of breaching decorum or of typing oneself as vulgar in a way that any number of words we would describe as 'swear words' would not. No word dedicated to the disgustful sensations of the other senses has this power. It is hard to date exactly when stink gets so powerful as to become somewhat improper. It is frequently used in the public language of moral condemnation in the sixteenth and seventeenth centuries, evidencing its power but not its vulgarity. The *Oxford English Dictionary* shows it to have become not quite proper at least by the late nineteenth century.

To what might we attribute the change? Its impropriety is clearly another step in the march of the 'civilizing process.' But perhaps it is something more concrete. One of the great accomplishments of the nineteenth century was ridding cities of the ubiquitous stench of feces and decaying animal matter by massive public construction of underground sewers. When man began walking upright he did not rise all that far above the stenches he emitted below. It just might be that Freud's theory of the final devaluation of smell depended on putting sewers underground as much as on raising man's nose above it.[4] It might even be claimed that the placement of sewers underground is a necessary precondition for and enabler of Freudian theory. Underground sewers were not an emblem of the repressed but the repressed itself, a burying of dangerousness. The sewers become the new Hell, the lower gastrointestinal base for the civilization resting upon it.

Notes

1. The viscous, Douglas (1966: 38) would argue, is anomalous because neither solid nor liquid. Douglas's account, it should be said, remains strangely unmotivated.

Disgust barely appears. It is all cold structure and its consequences. Inner states of individual actors are not her concern and so committed is she to her anti-psychological account that she does not simply ignore the emotions but seems to suggest they have no role at all in maintaining the structures of purity and pollution. See her discussion on p. 124.

2. I have indicated elsewhere (Miller 1997: ch. 3) a dissatisfaction with the Douglasian account that makes the impure a matter of anomaly, disorder, and failure to fit. The disgusting usually fits quite well; it just fits at the bottom end of the grid, from which vantage point it threatens all above it. The deconstructive point could be made against Douglas, which is that the anomaly holds the key to ordering the structure opposed to it. What she calls the structure is in fact a lesser structure included in a wider one, which opposes the anomalous to that which fits.

3. Vision (and hearing) are usually understood in aesthetic philosophy as higher senses, smell (and taste) as lower. The problem with smell is it is too immediate, not allowing for reflection, only sensation. Touch is ambivalent. Kant puts it high, Hegel low. See discussion and citations in Rindisbacher (1992: 17–18).

4. Elias links the devaluation of smell as against vision to the civilizing process, not as Freud does to the organic development of upright posture. See Elias (1978: 203).

Bibliography

Brown, N.O. (1959), *Life Against Death: The Psychoanalytical Meaning of History*, Middletown CT: Wesleyan University Press.

Darwin, C. ([1872] 1965), *The Expression of the Emotions in Man and Animals*, Chicago: University of Chicago Press.

De Sousa, R. (1987), *The Rationality of Emotion*, Cambridge MA: MIT Press.

Douglas, M. (1966), *Purity and Danger: An Analysis of the Concepts of Pollution and Taboo*, London: Routledge and Kegan Paul.

Elias, N. ([1939] 1978), *The Civilizing Process, vol. I: The History of Manners*, trans. E. Jephcott, New York: Urizen.

Engen, T. (1991), *Odor Sensation and Memory*, New York: Praeger.

—— (1982), *The Perception of Odors*, New York: Academic Press.

—— (1987), 'Remembering Odors and Their Names,' *American Scientist*, 75: 497–503.

Freud, S. ([1905] 1953a), *Three Essays on the Theory of Sexuality*, in *The Standard Edition of the Complete Psychological Works of Sigmund Freud*, ed. and trans. J. Strachey, vol. 7, London: Hogarth Press, pp. 125–245.

—— ([1911] 1953b), 'The Antithetical Meaning of Primal Words,' in *Standard Edition*, ed. and trans. J. Strachey, vol. 11, London: Hogarth Press, pp. 155–61.

—— ([1918] 1953c), 'History of an Infantile Neurosis,' in *Standard Edition*, ed. and trans. J. Strachey, vol. 17, London: Hogarth Press, pp. 3–123.

—— ([1930] 1953d), 'Civilization and Its Discontents,' in *Standard Edition*, ed. and trans. J. Strachey, vol. 21, London: Hogarth Press, pp. 59–145.

—— (1985), *The Complete Letters of Sigmund Freud to Wilhelm Fliess, 1887–1904*, ed. J.M. Masson, Cambridge MA: Harvard University Press.

Gerald of Wales (Geraldus Cambrensis) (1979), *Gemma Ecclesiastica*, trans. J.J. Hagen, Leiden: Brill.

Gross, J.J. and Levenson, R.W. (1993), 'Emotional Suppression: Physiology, Self-Report, and Expressive Behavior,' *Journal of Personality and Social Psychology*, 64: 970–86.

Haidt, J., McCauley, C. and Rozin, P. (1994), 'Individual Differences in Sensitivity to Disgust: A Scale Sampling Seven Domains of Disgust Elicitors,' *Personality and Individual Differences*, 16: 701–13.

Haidt, J., Rozin, P., McCauley, C. and Imada, S. (1998), 'Body, Psyche, and Culture: The Relationship between Disgust and Morality,' in G. Misra (ed.), *The Cultural Construction of Social Cognition*, New York: Sage.

Horkheimer, M. and Adorno, T.W. ([1944] 1994), *Dialectic of Enlightenment*, trans. J. Cumming, New York: Continuum.

Izard, C.E. (1984), 'Emotion-Cognition Relationships and Human Development,' in C.E. Izard, J. Kagan and R.B. Zajonc (eds), *Emotions, Cognition, and Behavior*, Cambridge: Cambridge University Press, pp. 17–37.

—— (1977), *Human Emotions*, New York: Plenum.

Kahane, C. (1992), 'Freud's Sublimation: Disgust, Desire and the Female Body,' *American Imago*, 49: 411–25.

Kristeva, J. (1982), *Powers of Horror: An Essay on Abjection*, trans. L.S. Roudiez, New York: Columbia University Press.

Kundera, M. (1984), *The Unbearable Lightness of Being*, New York: Harper and Row.

Levenson, R.W., Ekman, P. and Friesen, W.V. (1990), 'Voluntary Facial Action Generates Emotion-specific Autonomic Nervous System Activity,' *Psychophysiology*, 27: 363–84.

Miller, S.B. (1986), 'Disgust: Conceptualization, Development and Dynamics,' *International Review of Psychoanalysis*, 13: 295–307.

Miller, W.I. (1997), *The Anatomy of Disgust*, Cambridge MA: Harvard University Press.

Montaigne, Michel de (1958), *The Complete Essays of Montaigne*, trans. D.M. Frame, Stanford: Stanford University Press.

Newman, F.W. (1874), *Hebrew Theism*, second edition, London: n.p.

Ovid (1929), *The Art of Love and other Poems*, trans. J.H. Mozley, Loeb Classical Library, vol. 232, Cambridge MA: Harvard University Press.

Pope, A. (1715), *The Iliad of Homer*, London: n.p.

Rindisbacher, H.J. (1992), *The Smell of Books: A Cultural-Historical Study of Olfactory Perception in Literature*, Ann Arbor: University of Michigan Press.

Rozin, P. (1982), '"Taste-Smell Confusions" and the Duality of the Olfactory Sense,' *Perception and Psychophysics*, 31: 397–401.

—— and Fallon, A.E. (1987), 'A Perspective on Disgust,' *Psychological Review*, 94: 23–41.

Sartre, J.-P. ([1943] 1992), *Being and Nothingness*, trans. H.E. Barnes, New York: Washington Square.

Scarry, E. (1985), *The Body in Pain: The Making and Unmaking of the World*, New York: Oxford University Press.

Shweder, R.A. (1991), 'Menstrual Pollution, Soul Loss, and the Comparative Study of Emotions,' in *Thinking through Cultures: Expeditions in Cultural Psychology*, Cambridge MA: Harvard University Press, pp. 241–65.

Strack, F., Martin, L.L. and Stepper, S. (1988), 'Inhibiting and Facilitating Conditions of the Human Smile,' *Journal of Personality and Social Psychology*, 54: 768–77.

Swift, J. (1967), *Swift: Poetical Works*, ed. H. Davis, London: Oxford University Press.

Tomkins, S.S. (1963), *Affect, Imagery, Consciousness, vol. 2: The Negative Affects*, New York: Springer.

—— (1984), 'Affect Theory,' in P. Ekman (ed.), *Emotion in the Human Face*, second edition, Cambridge: Cambridge University Press, pp. 353–81.

Wierzbicka, A. (1986), 'Human Emotions: Universal or Culture-Specific,' *American Anthropologist*, 88: 584–94.

Part V

The Derangement of the Senses

The Senses Disordered

Throughout this book we have explored how the senses have been collected and ordered by different people at different times to form culturally coherent patterns of meaning. Now, in this last section, the senses are disordered, dispersed and fractured. The three chapters here all deal with experiences of the senses gone awry. In the first Hans-Göran Ekman describes the sensory disorientation experienced by the immensely influential Swedish writer August Strindberg (1849–1912) during a critical stage of his life. In the second Bob Desjarlais explores the chaotic sensory world of the homeless in Boston. In the third Chris Fletcher examines the conflicted perceptions of sufferers from environmental sensitivities. As noted in the introduction to the previous section, Steven Connor found that a relative inattention to sensory suffering left a hiatus in Serres' philosophy of the senses. Here this hiatus is richly filled with accounts of such suffering. The suffering discussed here, however, is of a particular kind for not only is it physically and mentally painful, but it is also displaced from the social paradigms that 'make sense' of suffering: it is both metaphorically and literally homeless. The only way it can be situated within conventional paradigms is through the model of madness, of mental derangement. A sane person would not think that buildings recede as he walks towards them, would not imagine she was being poisoned by perfumes, would not be living in the street.

Curiously, there are a number of striking parallels between Serres' sensory philosophy and Strindberg's sensory experiences. In a way, just as Thoreau can be seen as living Serres' fantasy of the ideal sensory life, Strindberg can be seen as living Serres' philosophy of everyday sensoriality. Without Serres' philosophical detachment, however, 'everyday' sensations can become unbearably intense and distressing. Serres describes the sensible world as continuously leaning, pulling in one direction or another. Strindberg finds himself clinging to a lamp post or swaying on a terrace due to his sensation of being thrown off balance by the material world. Sitting in a ruined amphitheater, Serres imagines it to have the shape of a giant ear, funnelling sound to its center. Strindberg finds the Marble Garden at Versailles similar to 'the auditory canal of a giant ear': 'I listen pressed against the wall... I can hear a rumbling sea, the wailing of crowds... ' Serres denounces the objectifying, distancing characteristics of sight. For Strindberg, sight's worst defect is its deceptiveness: it provides only an illusion of objective reality and personal detachment.

In *Les cinq sens* Serres speaks of the 'ceaseless unravelling and rekinitting of the body.' Strindberg experiences this ceaseless unravelling and reknitting in the way he understands the world through his body. At first he tries to accomplish the necessary reknitting through reason, even to the point of (apparent) irrationality. His experience of the buildings of Versailles receding as he walks towards them is due to an optical illusion. His need to cling to a lamppost is produced by the 'psychomagnetic' force of the post. His sensation of hearing a grasshopper in his pillow is caused by the flaxen fibers of the pillowcase having once registered the sounds of grasshoppers as they sang in fields of flax. However in this case rational interpretation seems inadequate, for Strindberg abruptly adds: 'But this is where "natural explanations" fall short, and I immediately put them aside!' (cited in Ekman 2000: 31).

Immersion in nature offers Strindberg a temporary respite from his sensory derangement. In the woods he feels he can 'let [his] rebellious thoughts roam freely' and 'listen and sniff the air like a redskin!' However, Strindberg cannot ultimately be at home with nature. His experience of disorientation is only resolved when he able to find his bearings within a mystical Christian cosmos (a resolution also hinted at by Serres). Significantly, Christianity also provided the saving grace for J.-K. Huysmans, author of the quintessential nineteenth century novel of sensory derangement – *Against Nature* (see Classen 1998: 116).[1]

Like Thoreau, but in a different manner, Strindberg is a 'genius of the senses.' To some extent one can only stand back, amazed, as he directs his surreal imagination into cavern after cavern of sensuous inquiry. If he in some ways appears a 'mad genius,' this is due in part to our modern understanding of the nature of the world. His attempt to make a science out of sensibility would not have been out of place in the eighteenth century, as is indicated by Roberts' essay on the sensuous chemistry of the Enlightenment (see also Riskin 2002). Even what appears to be Strindberg's 'maddest' notion, that he can taste the souls of the dead, would have seemed reasonable in a earlier era when souls were believed to emit odors of sanctity and sin.

Perhaps, in our own age, Strindberg's derangement would have taken the form of environmental sensitivities (ES). For the sufferers from ES, as for Strindberg, the visual world is dangerously deceptive. Through the eye-catching facades of modern life – furniture, paint, rugs, cosmetics – seep invisible toxic fumes, turning the dream worlds of consumer capitalism into corporeal nightmares.[2] Also like Strindberg, ES sufferers have no evident reason for their deranged sensations, for the world they perceive as threatening is judged by others to be safe. Fletcher notes that ES is medically unrecognized and often dismissed as a 'garden variety mental disorder.' In order to retain a sense of sanity, ES sufferers must 'work out a bodily logic of what remains illogical.' In the process of describing how ES suffers interpret and cope with their ailment, Fletcher's essay raises the disturbing question of who is more 'deranged': those who carelessly absorb the chemical effluvia of a synthetic world or those who reject it?

Fletcher coins the word 'dystoposthesia' to describe 'the incompatibility of bodies to the space they inhabit' produced by environmental sensitivities. The same term might also be applied to the homeless persons studied by Desjarlais in Boston.[3] Whether on the street or in a shelter they are incompatible with their sensory environment. Both sites offer a continual series of sensory assaults; brutal in the case of the street, distracting in the case of the shelter, with its constant hum of activity. Desjarlais describes how the homeless develop strategies to cope with their situation. Key among them is the reduction of intrusive sensory stimuli. When a 'quiet place' cannot be found, the body itself becomes 'silent,' numb to the world outside and the feelings inside.

Often silent, the homeless seem to live on the borders of language, as they live on the borders of society. Certainly they seem diametrically opposed to Serres' language-bound philosopher, sitting at his desk, trying to understand the world by looking through his window. The homeless have no desks, no writing, no windows, yet they are far from 'the paradisiacal times in which the body was free and could run and enjoy sensations at leisure.' Their sensory world is one of cold, hunger, violence and transience. Perhaps, from Serres' perspective, the homeless, while seemingly the ultimate outsiders, are still trying to pick their way through the frozen structures and jagged debris of the linguistic regime.

It should be noted, however, that sensory disorder is not only a matter of suffering. There is also an element of freedom and creativity in thinking, and living, 'outside the box.' Not all the homeless studied by Desjarlais want to be 'integrated' into society. As for Strindberg, he thought all systematizations of knowledge were too restrictive: 'disorder reigns in my universe, and that is feedom' (cited in Brandell 1974: 182).

Notes

1. In his nervous sensibility Strindberg seems to fit the nineteenth century model of the hypersensitive aesthete, for whom illness is 'the appropriate response to bustling, materialist modern life' (Classen 1998: 119). Ekman points out, however, that Strindberg's experience of derangement was no fashionable pretense, but a genuine

ailment. Nonetheless, Strindberg's perceptual disturbances still occurred within and were mediated by a particular aesthetic climate which emphasized alternative modes of sensory engagement. This ensured that his literary accounts of his deranged senses would find a cultural fit with many other literary endeavors of this period.

2. There is no more potent testimony to the materiality of the signifier than the experience of the ES sufferer. Reality is not disappearing into representation for them. The question of the materiality of media needs further study. For two very promising openings in this direction see Edwards (2001) and Simon and Barker (2002).

3. Desjarlais' 'Movement, Stillness' was originally presented as a plenary address at the Uncommon Senses conference, Montreal, April 2000.

Bibliography

Brandell, G. (1974), *Strindberg in Inferno*, trans. B. Jacobs, Cambridge MA: Harvard University Press.

Classen, C. (1998), *The Color of Angels: Cosmology, Gender and the Aesthetic Imagination*, London: Routledge.

Edwards, E. (2001), *Raw Histories: Photographs, Anthropology and Museums*, Oxford: Berg.

Ekman, H.-G. (2000), *Strindberg and the Five Senses: Studies in Strindberg's Chamber Plays*, London: Athlone.

Riskin, J. (2002), *Science in the Age of Sensibility: The Sentimental Empiricists of the French Enlightenment*, Chicago: University of Chicago Press.

Simon, B. and Barker, J. (2002), 'Imagining the New Order Nation: Materiality and Hyperreality in Indonesia,' *Culture, Theory and Critique*, 43(2): 139–53.

20

Strindberg's 'Deranged Sensations'

Hans-Göran Ekman

Antibarbarus

Immediately preceding and during his crucial Inferno crisis of the 1890s, August Strindberg struggled to distinguish reality from illusion through the use of his five senses (Ekman 1998). The first step in this process for Strindberg was to exchange his desk for the laboratory, which is perhaps not so very strange a step for so dedicated a naturalist. However, in Strindberg's case the reason prompting this change was not in order to achieve greater objectivity in his observations but rather to see through such quasi objectivity. During these experiments he would expose his delicate senses to a bombardment of sensations.

In *Antibarbarus* – which Strindberg wrote in Brünn in Mähren during October and November 1893 – he describes a number of chemical experiments that are intended to cast doubt on the established division of the elements in favor of his own monistic theory inspired by the German biologist and philosopher Ernst Haeckel (Brandell 1974: 280). Here he uses mainly the sense of smell in order to identify chemical substances. Never before had Strindberg lived in a world so filled with intrusive smells as during these chemical experiments, often performed in cramped hotel rooms.

An outside observer – the Finnish writer Adolf Paul – describes the interior of Strindberg's hotel room on Rügen during the summer of 1893: 'Then he spent the entire day standing over his crucibles, even during the worst July heat, usually clad only in his night shirt and slippers, a girdle round his waist and a straw hat on his head. It was hot as hell up there, and it smelled of pitch and sulphur!' (Paul 1930: 129). In Paul's account of Strindberg's savagely misanthropic moods that summer he remarks interestingly that Strindberg expressed a dislike of food – not primarily because it tasted bad but rather because he found it falsified and his sense of taste perverted:

> If he raised a glass of beer to his mouth, the response was immediately: 'horrible, falsified, not fit to drink!' What the German cuisine offered was simply: 'over-cooked swine fodder!' If he tasted fresh fish, then it was only 'sludge fish,' fried in 'false butter. The fishermen had trampled on it with their tarred boots, before it landed in the frying pan!' (Paul 1930: 130ff.)

In the novella *The Cloister* from 1898 Strindberg lets the male protagonist experience 'falsified' food at an inn on Rügen:

> To this was served a type of over-cooked swine fodder, so that you left the table hungry and remained hungry all day long. Everything was falsified, even the beer, and the innkeeper's family had first cooked the meat for themselves; the guests found only gristle and bones – precisely as one feeds dogs. (Strindberg 1994: 65)

Antibarbarus also contains instances of the way in which Strindberg shifts the focus from the object under scrutiny to the sensory perception itself. Such is the case, for example, during one of his countless experiments with sulphur:

> I place the crucible over the fire and allow the sulphur to melt. It becomes a golden amber fluid at 115° and only now does it smell, not of sulphur but of turpentine and resin, almost like floor-polish (= wax and turpentine). The temperature rises, the colour moves towards the red end of the spectrum, and orange overtakes the red, so rapidly that the orange fuses with the red and creates the mixed colour of reddish brown at 160°. A condensation, whether chemical or physical, or both, has occurred and now the smell of camphor appears. When I observed this for the first time, I did not trust my perhaps oldest and therefore most developed sense; instead I called my laboratory teacher. (Strindberg 1917: 119)

On another occasion Strindberg is prepared to admit that air contains combustible gas but doubts that this is nitrogen: 'What is nitrogen? How does it make itself known? How does it taste? How does it smell? How does it appear to the eye?' (Strindberg 1917: 168). The answer is that nitrogen can only be defined in the negative: 'It has no smell, no taste, no colour' (Strindberg 1917: 168). This irritates Strindberg who is now vacillating between doubting what lies beyond his sensory borders and doubting the senses themselves.

During this period Strindberg particularly questions the sense of sight. This can be seen in the so-called 'Fifth Letter' – a kind of sequel to *Antibarbarus* which was, however, never published. According to a title page, the 'Letter' discusses 'The Form of the Earth, and Astronomy,' and approaches these subjects via optics. The presentation as a whole apparently sets out to question the eye's ability to 'see correctly.' A second title page contains the following subheadings: 'Thoughts about the Sun, the Moon and the Stars in the World of Illusions.' The expression 'the world of illusions' refers at this stage to an illusory world in a literal sense. According to Strindberg, the phenomena he studied were intended to cast doubt on certain inadequate proofs that the earth is round. He also claimed that the same observations could prove that both the rings of Saturn and Jupiter's moons were illusory.

Strindberg now approaches total scepticism with regard to the reliability of sight: 'Optical phenomena! Where do these begin, and where do they end?' On the first page of the manuscript the eye is called 'defective' and on the last page 'deceptive.' At the expense of the sense of sight, Strindberg launches the idea of 'reflection' or 'an inner sense': 'the inner sense is more reliable than any organ and this organ does not reach the level of deductive power (= Fantasy)' (Strindberg n.d.: 4). Here Strindberg has taken yet another step in his long leave-taking of naturalistic attitudes and ways of thinking.

What is striking, however, is the speculative attitude that characterizes the published portions of *Antibarbarus*. Descriptions of individual experiments are often formulated as questions, with which Strindberg induces the reader to believe that the whole of contemporary chemistry was in fact full of question marks: 'Why does impure carbon bisulphate smell of selenium or rotten black radish and why does selenium, at 700°, smell of "unclean" carbon bisulphate?' (Strindberg 1917: 154). He himself offers no answer.

Again and again Strindberg is puzzled by the smells he perceives around him. Probably at no other period of his life did he employ his sense of smell as much, or on such unusual errands. It confirms an interest in olfaction, which remains an abiding part of his life, whether he wishes it to or not.

'Sensations détraquées' ('Deranged Sensations')

Strindberg's essay 'Deranged Sensations' from the end of 1894 (Strindberg 1894–5), is of great interest in terms of his wrestling with the complex problem of the reliability of the senses. The symptoms of his impending Inferno crisis, which are anticipated in those elements of paranoia already apparent during the time he spent on Rügen, do not improve but are merely translated to a new geographic and cultural context.

Gunnar Brandell (1974: 189ff) has pointed out that it was a Parisian fashion at the time to be 'crazy in an ingenious and sensitive manner.' 'Deranged Sensations,' however, is clearly far more beholden to authentic experience than literary fashion; least of all is there any indication in the text that Strindberg is seeking to follow in the footsteps of his French contemporary, Rimbaud, who in a famous letter of 13 May 1871 recommended a 'derangement of all the senses' as a means of reaching the unknown. Despite the fact that his essay is classified as a 'Vivisection,' Strindberg does not seek out situations that cause him stress; he simply finds himself in such predicaments and must choose between finding rational explanations for what he has experienced or taking to his heels. A good deal of the confusion conveyed by the text is due to this fact: the author is both vivisector and guinea pig. In addition, a solution to the crisis that has just begun is suggested in passing by Strindberg – a solution that he became interested in, in earnest, two years later.

When one first encounters the 'traveller' *Strindberg* (italic from here on to suggest an authorial persona) in 'Sensations détraquées,' he is exhausted after traveling for two days by train. His fatigue is accorded a kind of naturalistic explanation: he has been 'forced to breathe in the carbon dioxide and nitrogen fumes' (Strindberg 1917: 596) of his fellow travellers as well as coal dust and sulphur from the engine (Strindberg 1917: 597).

Rested after the trip *Strindberg* convinces himself in a rational manner that his exhaustion is responsible for certain curious reactions. Diverse optical illusions are explained 'scientifically' as the result of his brain having been shaken up by 'the jolting of the railway carriage' (Strindberg 1917: 597). When *Strindberg* is about to approach Louis XIII's pavilion at Versailles he has a strange experience. After walking for what he estimates is three-quarters of an hour, he feels he should have reached the pavilion or, at least, that it should at least appear larger than it had done before. Now, however, it seems that the building recedes as fast as he approaches it. Again he seeks a rational explanation, and once again the cause of his deranged vision is said to be the exhausting trip: 'This disturbance to my sense of vision is a natural result of the strenuous trip' (Strindberg 1917: 598).

After a night's sleep *Strindberg* is prepared for a new attempt. It starts out much like the first time, in that he does not feel as if he is getting any nearer to the pavilion. But this time he takes a more rational approach; he not only takes along a watch but also a map, and calculates that after walking for 10 minutes he should have only 500 meters left to the pavilion. He concludes that the day before he had evidently been the victim of an optical illusion: 'the perspective changes as I stride along; at the same time, my angle of vision increases, and this infernal play of invisible lines confuses my mind, where the irradiating rays of the enchanted palace imprint themselves. Once the solution to the problem has been found, I am at ease again' (Strindberg 1917: 599). Elsewhere in 'Sensations détraquées,' Strindberg writes: 'What a calming effect to be able to explain everything! It takes away the fear of the unknown' (Strindberg 1917: 599). The statement hardly supports Brandell's conclusion that Strindberg's text is an exhibition in a modish form of craziness.

Strindberg's attempt to cross the great open space of the Place d'Armes is likewise complicated by physical laws: 'The great building attracts me the way large bodies attract small ones' (Strindberg 1917: 600). When he suddenly discovers that he is drawn towards the palace, he searches among past experiences for something similar. However, he is forced to ask himself whether some unknown force might not be the cause: 'The learned deny this and maintain that energy is constant' (Strindberg 1917: 601). Then he employs a strategy which, on a larger scale, will help him through the full-blown Inferno crisis two years later: he gives the unknown phenomenon a name and is thereby able to establish a relationship to it and create a kind of meaning in chaos: 'I rebel against this blind, brutal power, and in order to be able to fight it more successfully, I personify it, I turn it into a god' (Strindberg 1917: 601).

In a fit of agoraphobia *Strindberg* clings to a lamp post,[1] but still seeks a 'scientific' explanation for his reaction. He adopts mesmerist models of explanation and imagines that the post acts as a 'fortifying medium of touch,' a 'psycho-magnet' that exerts a calming effect on his nerves. But alongside this pseudo-scientific explanation *Strindberg* gropes for a supernatural explanation – again anticipating the way in which he resolves the later crisis: 'an old habit of mine prompts me to raise my eyes towards this blue formation of gas, through which rays of warmth and light are filtered and which the faithful have rightly called heaven, for there live primeval forces' (Strindberg 1917: 602).

What then happens is that the author gives free reign to superstition and fantasy. Fantasy becomes a 'vessel' that helps him from the 'cliff' in the square where he finds himself. With its help Strindberg raises himself from the sphere of material reality, which he experiences as a tremendous release: 'What does it matter that, when all is said and done, they are merely shadows, like everything else! Now I am a poet and magician. I choose for myself the sturdiest of these steam ships, I carefully climb aboard... Onward... Wonderful, the crossing is completed!' (Strindberg 1917: 602).

In the park at Versailles *Strindberg* does not only experience visual phenomena. He is also intoxicated by the scent of flowers, and the breeze over the fields which carries waves of perfume (Strindberg 1917: 603). When *Strindberg* strolls on the terrace, he finds the ground swaying beneath his feet as if he were on a suspension bridge. Once again it is time for a 'reassuring conclusion.' Below the terrace lies the arched ceiling of the orangerie: 'in exerting a counter-pressure outwards, the arches ought to offer a superabundance of strength, against which the soles of my feet react, so that the impression is transmitted to my nervous system, whose sensitivity is heightened by my physical and mental suffering' (Strindberg 1917: 603–4).

Strindberg's peculiar perceptions also apply to hearing. He feels that the Marble Garden at Versailles is similar to 'the auditory canal of a giant ear, the auricle of which is formed by the wings of the building' (Strindberg 1917: 604; see Brandell 1974: 191). What follows seems to show that *Strindberg* is himself aware that his ideas so far oscillate between playfulness and seriousness:

> Captivated by this new fantasy and happy to have come upon this bizarre idea that I am like a flea in a giant's ear, I listen pressed against the wall... What a surprise!... I can hear! I can hear a rumbling sea, the wailing of crowds, abandoned hearts whose beats pump up an exhausted blood, nerves that break with a tiny dull thud, sobs, laughter and sighs! I ask myself if these are not subjective sensory impressions, if it is not myself I hear. No, I know every vagary of my senses by heart. (Strindberg 1917: 604–5)

The author refuses to believe that his hearing would trick him. He recalls having heard a sailor tell how, after three days at sea, he could still hear the ringing of bells through the concave side of the sails, which acted like a 'burning mirror.' Here Strindberg offers an imaginary blend of optics and acoustics.

The first section of 'Deranged Sensations' is dated October 1894. In the manuscript, the second part of the essay is dated December 1894 and contains, among other things, certain speculations regarding the function of the eye. One day upon waking, *Strindberg* 'sees' a net of bloody, red threads on the marble stove in his room and tells himself that it must be his own retina that has been projected there, enlarged. He believes that he can see projected in the same manner the blood vessels of his cornea and the red and white blood cells. The observation leads him naturally to the conclusion that the eye, the sense of sight, is not to be trusted. Just as he had wondered at Versailles if it was not himself he heard, he now asks if it is not himself that he sees. If so, the senses would be dead-ends rather than channels of information.

After a series of sensations of this type, it is a relief for *Strindberg* to leave the city where his senses are continuously exposed to stress. Out in nature he says he can both think clearly and experience his senses functioning sensitively but correctly – that is, not as an over-cultivated modern city dweller but more in the manner of a primitive savage. His description offers a Utopian image of the unadulterated senses at play:

> One beautiful morning before sunrise I enter that wood. Influenced by my surroundings, which I do not want to resist, I feel stripped of my civilised attire. I discard the mask of the citizen who has never acknowledged the so-called social contract; I let my rebellious thoughts roam freely, and I think, think !... without fear, with no reservations. Then I see with the penetrating vision of the savage, I listen and sniff the air like a redskin! (Strindberg 1917: 613)

'Études funèbres' ('In the Cemetery')

One year later, in autumn 1895, Strindberg finds himself in the middle of his Inferno crisis and writes the essay 'Études funèbres' or 'In the Cemetery' (1896). Only a few months later, in February 1896, he will move into the Hôtel Orfila on the rue d'Assas where the crisis peaks in June, provoking a series of sudden departures and flights from place to place.

Strindberg's portrayal of the cemetery of Montparnasse does not fit naturally into an elegiac literary tradition. Rather than depict a funereal mood, the author observes his sensory impressions. Strindberg is in search of a new world view, but philosophical thoughts and a literary approach still do not blend comfortably together. This gives the essay two principal aspects, part experimental data and scientific report, part literary description.

Strindberg achieves an autumnal mood by describing yellowing linden trees and withering roses. A thrush that no longer sings but utters sneering laughs adds an auditory dimension. The air of the cemetery is said to be unhealthy because of unwholesome vapors and *Strindberg* gets a taste of verdigris on his tongue, which he concludes is caused by the souls of dematerialized bodies floating in the air. As if this were not enough, the author collects a sample of this air in a bottle and takes it back with him to his hotel room where he pours a drop of acid on it: 'It swells up, this dead matter, it quivers, begins to come alive, exudes a rotten smell, grows still once more, and dies' (Strindberg 1917: 662).

The text of 'In the Cemetery' is dominated by feelings of discomfort: 'the dead exuded sulphurous odours and these unwholesome vapours created a taste of verdigris in my mouth' (Strindberg 1917: 664). Flowers too are associated with decay, when the author comes across roses and jasmine on the grave of the poet Théodore de Banville: 'If this was the dead man's wish surely he must have known that a cadaver smells of roses, jasmine and musk?' (Strindberg 1917: 666). Even more interesting is the author's reaction to a portrait of a six-year-old child on a small mausoleum. The description of this relief becomes a picture of innocence precisely because the child's sensory organs have not yet had to engage with a repulsive reality. In its purity the child seems related to the savage with which Strindberg had previously identified: 'a tiny nose, slightly flattened at the tip from habitually pressing against a mother's breast; placed there like a pretty ornament, with shell-shaped nostrils above a heart-shaped mouth, not meant for scenting prey or for catching perfumes or bad odours, not yet a real organ' (Strindberg 1917: 669).

In the essays from the 1890s in which elements of fiction never dominate – even if spontaneous ideas and a certain reverence for the imagination do appear – Strindberg can be observed making his way to a new way of thinking.[2] The first stage in this development becomes a study of his own senses and a stubborn clinging to the idea that he is not experiencing anything unreal. On the other hand, Strindberg admits – not without pride – that his sensibilities are abnormally heightened. From 1896 onwards, this attitude is documented above all in his diary. At the same time, another development is taking place: in his published essays Strindberg argues the opposite, namely that our senses are inadequate. This is a form of double bookkeeping that, in the long run, becomes extremely taxing on his psyche.

In the essays 'On the Action of Light in Photography' and 'A Glimpse into Space,' which were published in the journal *L'Initiation* in 1896, Strindberg reveals his doubts as to the reliability of the senses – referring now, as in the 'Fifth Letter,' to man's senses in general and not to his own alone. Strindberg's studies in chemistry, optics, and the other sciences led him increasingly to the point of view that no objective knowledge exists; rather, everything is subjective perception: 'Is the sun round because we see it as round? And what is light? Something outside of me or within me, subjective perceptions?' (Strindberg 1917: 353). Or differently phrased: 'Where does the self begin and where does it end? Has the eye adapted itself to the sun? Or does the eye create the phenomenon called the sun?' (Strindberg 1917: 354).

This freely subjective and anxiety-creating point of view accelerated the early course of Strindberg's crisis and makes him fumble for an outlook that can create meaning from chaos. During the Inferno period he reaches a point where the explanations to some of his experiences tend to become all too fantastic. Strindberg is on the verge of madness. What saves him is his acknowledgement of a world view where the notion that the senses are insufficient is almost an a priori assumption. According to this view an organizing divine power lies behind the ambiguous appearances of the material world. With his Inferno crisis resolved by spiritual revelation, Strindberg can transmute his 'deranged sensations' into the dramatic quintessence of the chamber plays he writes in the first decade of the twentieth century.

Notes

1. Regarding Strindberg's agoraphobia, see Brandell 1974: 190 ff. Brandell admits that 'agoraphobia's character of factual experience cannot be disputed.'
2. Brandell (1982: 139, 143) points out that in 'Études funèbres' Strindberg is on his way to finding his new style. Brandell sees the text as a sign that Strindberg wanted to be free of his obsession with chemistry and return to literature.

Bibliography

Brandell, G. (1974), *Strindberg in Inferno*, trans. B. Jacobs, Cambridge MA: Harvard University Press.

Ekman, H.-G. (1998), 'Strindberg's Senses, Symbols and Synaesthesia,' in M. Robinson (ed.), *Strindberg: The Moscow Papers*, Stockholm: Strindbergssällskapet, pp. 22–35.

Paul, A. (1930), *Min Strindbergsbok*, Stockholm: Norstedts.

Strindberg, A. (n.d.), 'The Fifth Letter,' Stockholm: Royal Library.

Strindberg, A. (1894–1895), 'Sensations détraquées,' *Le Figaro littéraire (Paris)* 17 November, 16 January, 9 February.

—— (1896), 'Études funèbres,' *La Revue des Revues* XVII.

—— (1917), *Prosabitar från 1890-talet*, Stockholm: Bonniers.

—— (1994), *Klostret Fagervik och Skamsund*, ed. B. Ståhle Sjönell, Stockholm: Nostedts.

21

Movement, Stillness

On the Sensory World of a Shelter for the 'Homeless Mentally Ill'

Robert Desjarlais

To offer some thoughts on the sensorial aspects of homelessness in North America, I would like to draw upon ethnographic research that I conducted in a homeless shelter in downtown Boston, the main findings of which are noted in a book entitled *Shelter Blues: Sanity and Selfhood among the Homeless* (Desjarlais 1997). Much of my research and writing has been oriented toward developing what I have come to call a 'critical phenomenology' of life in the shelter – a phenomenologically inclined account, that is, which attends at once to the concerns and lifeworlds of those living in the shelter and to the interrelated social, discursive, and political forces that underpinned those concerns and lifeworlds.

I wish to draw from one small and necessarily detached sliver of this research in order to detail a few of the ways in which people who stayed in the shelter adapted to – and lived out – the sensorial contours of that place. What concerns me in particular are certain subjective orientations to time, space, sound, otherness, meaning, and distress that were commonly adopted by many during their stays in the shelter. My aims are quite modest and somewhat unorthodox. I offer no solutions or specific prescriptions but rather a handful of observations and a tentative caution or two about how those committed to mental health policy might heed the needs of many now living on the streets or in shelters in North American cities. I am not going to discuss any of the large-scale economic or political dynamics that have come to shape the plight of impoverished or disabled Americans in the closing decades of the twentieth century, though, as noted in *Shelter Blues*, such dynamics were powerfully at work among the lives of shelter residents.

369

Nor will I refer at length to any of the psychiatric problems that presumably plagued those lives, even though a diverse range of cognitive and emotional difficulties clearly hindered the worlds of many. In fact, my thoughts will quietly work against the grain of such understandings, for I want to offer a 'redescription' of certain aspects of shelter life from a sensory-centered perspective – one that offers an analytic take on homelessness that is distinct from the medical and purely political-economic models that have tended to dominate the literature on the subject.

I take the word 'redescription' from Richard Rorty, who, in *Contingency, Irony, and Solidarity*, argues that any search for godlike, ahistorical 'truths' is futile, and that intellectual and moral progress is 'a history of increasingly useful metaphors rather than of increasing understanding of how things really are' (Rorty 1989: 9). Given this understanding, Rorty advocates a philosophical method that works to establish alternative vocabularies, to invent new tools to take the place of old ones, and, in general, to suggest new ways to think about the world and the place of humans in it. As he notes (Rorty 1989: 9)

> This sort of philosophy does not work piece by piece, analysing concept after concept, or testing thesis after thesis. Rather, it works holistically and pragmatically. It says things like 'try thinking of it this way' – or more specifically, 'try to ignore the apparently futile traditional questions by substituting the following new and possibly interesting questions.'

The point is not that psychiatric or political-economic approaches to the question of homelessness are necessarily misguided or incorrect. Rather, it is that by developing new ways to think about certain realities and social problems, we might establish new ways to configure the relation between cultural and subjective processes, and so hit upon new, intellectually generative ways of conceptualizing what it means to be human. All told, then, this chapter entails a plea for experimentation and difference in future research into the subjective worlds of those suffering from distress.

The Street

The shelter was set up by the Massachusetts Department of Mental Health, or DMH, in early 1981 to provide temporary housing for persons troubled by mental illness. To gain a bed in the shelter one had to be both homeless and mentally ill, which meant carrying a diagnosis of 'schizophrenia,' 'bipolar disorder,' or the like. A 'guest' would arrive from a local hospital, another shelter, or the streets to sleep on one of fifty-two cots set up in the gym of a mental health center that occupied one-third of a vast State Service Center. Those staying in the shelter were predominantly white (roughly a third were African-American, Asian American, or Latino), from the Boston area, and from lower class or lower middle-class families. Some stayed in the shelter for a few weeks, while a handful had been there for over 5 years. People typically left when they found a more permanent place to live, returned to the hospital, hit the street, looked for a better life outside of Boston, or were kicked out because of infractions of the shelter's rules concerning drugs or theft. I conducted fieldwork in this shelter for a 15-month stretch in 1991 and 1992, spending much of my time talking informally with shelter residents and staff members, observing everyday life while immersed in the 'deep hanging out' that is intrinsic to most forms of ethnographic research.

Many shelter residents had spent a significant time on 'the street,' which most spoke of as if it was a single location with a singularly forced sensorium of fear, cold weather, isolation, and transience. The weather, cold and inhospitable, could shock the senses. Street dwellers were cheated, accosted, and robbed by vague, impersonal others. The street's distractions and potential violence amplified fears and anxieties. The order of conduct there was largely one of fear, isolation, polarity, and reactions that constantly forced awareness of threats and otherness.

Roy Lerner, like others who came to bed down in the shelter, said the street was a 'pretty tough place.' He said he used to panhandle in front of Dunkin' Donuts and kept mostly to himself for 'safety reasons.'

Ralph Powell said he had lived on the streets 'from time to time' and had even eaten out of trash cans when he was desperate: 'I ain't proud of some of the things I did,' he said.

Tommy Frank and Greg Bagel said they slept in subways when on the streets. The former spoke of eating at McDonald and Burger King; the latter, of people stealing money from his pockets.

Logan Persian was sleeping in a warehouse by the Cambridge River before he came to the shelter. 'I had all my utensils there – a shelf, a bed – but it was getting cold.' When the warehouse burned down he slept in one of the trains in the train yard behind North Station. 'You try not to think about the cold too much,' he said, 'even if your thoughts wander. Then you go to sleep, wake up, and get the hell out of there.'

'Because you're afraid?' I asked.

'No. Because it's cold!' he said.

Women in particular spoke of the fear and isolation of the streets. Sylvia Covert, who lived there and in different shelters before coming to the Station Street shelter, said that the streets were 'terrible.' She spent many nights just walking around, unable to sleep, 'so frightened, terrified, afraid of being accosted.' 'The street makes you feel lonely, afraid. It makes you feel like crying,' said Yvonne Vince, who recalled 'wandering' around the streets and occasionally sleeping outside until she discovered the shelters. For Rose Crecco, life on the streets was 'pretty lousy.' Women more than men had to contend with the threat of rape and physical assault. They also had to deal with private matters such as menstruation in an inhospitable, semi-public arena.

Julie Mason told me that 'On the street, you can get robbed, beat up, knifed. It's dangerous. I would have lived on the street, but I never found a place that seemed safe... The street is tough. Homeless people are dying out on the streets. You lose everything but a sense of survival.'

Peter Vaughn, who said he felt 'alone' on the streets, similarly found that the streets were 'tough' and 'hard to take.' He slept under bridges and 'hid' for a week in a hole that he camouflaged with leaves and cardboard. 'There's no one to talk to. It's scary,' he said. 'If you're on the street,' he said on another occasion, 'you get beat up, disrespected, cheated, and robbed... Street people are very uncouth. The mentality is, "Nobody gives a damn about me, so I don't give a damn about nobody."'

Street living could involve police-enforced displacements from storefronts, parks, and other public areas. It could also entail a surreal social existence wherein people slept, ate, and bathed on the spatial and temporal fringes of the public sphere. People could be negated and reduced by prolonged exposure to the street. The end result was typically the stripping of sociality, a raw state of anxiety, and the redundancies of walking, hiding, eating, and bumming for change or cigarettes. You maintained the few words, possessions, acquaintances, and memories that you could, moving around 'like a ping-pong ball,' as one man described his plight.

The characteristic features of the street tied into how residents remembered time spent there. In speaking of what happened to them or how they ended up there in the first place, many spoke in impressionistic hues, as if recalling a vague dream whose sensorial or psychological features took prominence over any detailed plot or integrative schema. Often absent from their recollections was a sense of purpose, or any reason for their actions or the actions of others. Louise Colbate, for instance, spoke of being on the streets once: 'I didn't know where I was going,' she said. Peter, in turn, said that a person hit him once: 'I don't know why he did that,' he said. And when asked how he came to live nearby the building, Roger, a man blinded by cataracts who for seven years slept 'where he could' on the streets, he said: 'I don't know. I can't answer that.' The common absence of purpose and reason in these recollected actions suggests that the world's engagements with these individuals were, from their perspective, often bereft of intelligibility, reason, and meaning.

For many, the sensorium of the street involved a corporeal existence in which a person's senses and ability to make sense soon became dulled in response to excessive and brutal demands on those senses. Bodies sometimes became the most prominent instruments of engagement and awareness. As one shelter resident put it, 'When you're homeless, you end up with just your body because you don't own anything else.'

Life in the Shelter

Life in and around the shelter was neither as brutal nor as discombobulating as it could be on the streets. This was one of the main reasons that people sought refuge in a place appropriately known as a 'shelter.' 'I'm okay. I feel safe as long as I'm in the building,' said Joey, a long-term resident of the shelter, when asked how he was doing one day. Greg said that the place as a whole was good for 'detuning,' which I understood to be the process of dampening the shrill pitch of everyday life: 'There's not much pressure here,' he said. In turn, Sylvia Covert, who said she was 'desperate to find an answer to the rambling' of her mind, was looking for a place 'to recover from the shock of the elements outside.' She said she would stay in the shelter until it was safe for her to move out. In general, people oriented themselves on a sensory range between 'nervousness' and 'staying calm,' with many bedding down in the shelter in hopes of finding more of the latter.

Nevertheless, residents found that they still had to contend with too much otherness, too many interruptions, and too many brute facts. Distracting sights and sounds often entered from the fringes of awareness. The building itself was understood to be a bustling, 'distracting,' discombobulating place, in which noises, voices, interruptions, and the traffic of bodies were everpresent. 'It's hard to get a decent sleep here. Someone is always singing a song,' Helen Kessler once told me. There was also the constant threat of being 'kicked out' of the shelter for an hour, a night, or permanently.

Some of the otherness faced by residents involved commands and instructions asserted by staff. Some of it involved the pains people felt or the distractions they suffered. In general, schizophrenia has often been known to involve states of mind that attend in exceptional and wearisome ways to any and all perceptions, sensations, and environmental cues, with little ability to screen out distractions or unnecessary stimuli. People staying in the shelter had to contend with similarly discombobulating movements and noises. Their ailments increased the intensity of social engagements in their lives, and everyday fears and distractions heightened their distress.

Many heard voices distinct from those common to everyday social interactions. 'I hear voices,' Larry noted in a group meeting one day. 'Young men telling me that they're easy to sleep with. That scares me, it scares me.' Wendy said that she got headaches when the voices were bad. She tried to get rid of the voices by yelling and telling people how she felt. 'But I can't do that here,' she said. The voices provoked laughter or torment. On any given day there would be a few people in the lobby or shelter who were laughing or talking to themselves, looking pensive, or talking less to themselves than to the voices they heard.

People spoke of being 'emotionally tired' and of being unable to deal with 'distractions' when they arrived in the building. 'We're sensitive,' Carla Bataille explained to an acquaintance in the shelter one day. 'We can't deal with things. Every little thing bothers us, and we can't take shit. That's why we're here. We're not like the people outside [who lived apparently normal lives].' By living 'inside' she and others could remain one step removed. On another occasion Carla told me that she needed to be 'familiar' with an area before she was comfortable. She didn't want to be in a place where she always had to be 'on the look-out.' 'It's the adjustment that's the problem,' she said. 'It's okay when you're well. But when you're sick, it's hard to start off fresh each day.'

Psychotropic drugs helped many to make the kind of 'adjustments' that Carla spoke of. They helped residents to get rid of the 'voices' they heard and, for some, reduced levels of anxiety. At their best, the pharmaceuticals worked to integrate, rebalance, clarify, and calm a person's innards or faculties. 'I just took my medication – to smooth out the joints,' Joey told me one afternoon. At their worst, however, the medication excited, stiffened, immobilized, and clouded. Many got 'hopped up' or felt 'hyper' on medication. 'I think it's this medicine that's making me anxious,' Stuart told me. 'I really do. Whenever I take this medicine, I get anxious. I get the shakes and I feel hyper.' Henry's medications made him feel 'excited': 'I can't sit down for five seconds,' he said. 'I can't concentrate.' 'You might have noticed that I'm shuffling around a bit,' Roy said one day as we stood by the railings along the entrance to the lobby. He was shifting from foot to foot from the akathesia caused by Haldol, a neuroleptic pharmaceutical. 'It's the Haldol shakes. It's okay. I'm less nervous today.' 'I'm sorry about going on about New Orleans,' William Harding said one evening after raving on about life in his home town. 'But I get kinda hopped up after taking my meds. For about two minutes, you get hopped up after the meds, you see, and then it's all right about thirty minutes after. Then everything's okay.' When William walked away, another resident came over and said with a wry smile: 'We get to hear about New Orleans all the time, seven days a week.' His comment underscored the ways in which medications not only altered people's minds or bodies, but colored their relations with others.

In short, considerable effort was required at times to act, think, and move about in life. Many of the struggles suggested fundamental and often problematic engagements between a consciousness and a world at odds with that consciousness. Yet while these engagements could sometimes seem like affairs of blind force, people tried to set up routines in order to mediate the distractions or skirt any impinging fears or afflictions. Carla, for instance, spoke of her need to get 'settled in' to the world of the shelter, and, in general, to be 'familiar' with any area in which she lived. One man, in turn, said that he was trying to maintain a 'routine' in the shelter. Others spoke of similar orientations. 'This is my favorite spot,' said Roy Lerner, a man who lived for over two years in the shelter, when I approached him one day as he sat resting against the back of the elevator cavity, facing the shelter. 'I try to find a favorite spot and sit there every day, likes roots to earth.'

In effect, the routines could instill a sense of habit, regularity, or order. 'It's all right, it's better than nothing,' Joey Austen said when I complemented him on a new coat that he bought at a discount market. 'I'm trying to hang in there, you know. Hanging in is good. I'm all right as long as I'm busy. My father says an idle mind is an ill mind.'

Hanging in – good enough for many – helped people to attend to everyday life. People stayed busy by pacing, smoking cigarettes, talking with others, and carrying out chores and errands. They engaged in these activities not only to get things done or to pass the time but to instill a sense of safety and stability. When I asked Rose Crecco one evening what she had done that day, she said: 'Oh, you know, the usual boring stuff: smoking and eating and talking.' When I asked where she had been, she said: 'In and out, in and out, and I paced a bit today.' I later asked Roy Lerner how he spent his days. 'I go up to the social club,' he said, 'smoke cigarettes, drink coffee, listen to music, talk with people, you know.' For Roy, Rose, and others, workaday actions such as eating, talking, and walking became full-blown activities in their own right.

Another way that people dealt with things was to pace. Some found that pacing helped them to think or concentrate, others found it to be calming, and yet others used it as a means to burn off restless energy or to find some sense of equilibrium. Rose said she liked to pace because it 'relaxed' her. For Kevin, 'pacing up and down' was the way to change his 'luck.' It also helped to use up energy, 'so much energy from the meds.' For him, 'worries' were the main problem in the shelter; they threw off the equilibrium, the balance. 'If you have to get copies for something, or records at the hospital, it can get compressed in here, because of the close quarters and tight spaces.' He got to feeling 'tight inside,' 'constricted.' On top of this his medications made him feel 'excited': 'I can't sit down for five seconds. I can't concentrate.' One day he showed me one of his poems, which consisted of four lines jotted in a notebook:

> Pacing the floor
> pacing my mind
> walking the floor
> walking my thoughts

The Search for Stillness

Along with establishing habitual routines, those staying in the shelter sought refuge from the world in various ways. Many tried to find quiet places in the building's nooks and crannies where they could be alone for a spell, while some wore headphones to block out noise or the voices they heard.

Thelonious, a self-professed 'poet' who slept on the concrete benches outside the Center, found the discomforts of the street better than the hassles of shelter life. 'Sometimes it's just too distracting outside,' he told me, in reference to the busy area around the building. 'That's why I come here [inside the building], to get away from that. But sometimes people here are just as bothersome. Some of them act much younger than me, and so I feel I can't go anywhere.' The last line of one of Thelonious's poems went 'Hypersensory residualness wants to be within equatorial lines.' Given the hypersensory climate of the Center, in which sights and sounds lingered like unshakable residue, he and others tried, often unsuccessfully, to maintain some balance between comfort and distraction.

Some tried to find their own private, solitary domains in attempting to achieve a state of monadic being that might permit refuge from the presence of others in and around the shelter. Rose Crecco sought out the end of a long and winding corridor close to the shelter because, she said, it was 'quiet' and 'private' there. Irving Jackson said he liked to go to a quieter part of the building to 'get away' from the tiresome noises and conversations of the shelter. 'I've been up here since 9:30,' he told me one afternoon. 'I got here at 9:30 and slept until 12. Then I had lunch. I come up here. Too much noise, conversations downstairs. Same old conversations. Cigarettes, coffee. Coffee, cigarettes. I've been living here a long time and I'm getting tired of it.'

Alice Weldman found that reading the Bible helped her to reduce the worries and distractions that were an inescapable part of life in the building. 'If I can just read the Bible for fifteen, sixteen hours a day,' she told me one day, 'and just block out all the rest, then I'm okay.' One man, who he said he was easily 'distracted' and caught up in the doings of others, told me that he 'used to pick up a newspaper, you know, and hold onto a word, and that would calm me down,' and yet another said he worked on puzzles because they helped to 'calm' him.

Each of these efforts involved the focused contemplation of a single quality, task, or domain of meaning. In effect, sleeping, finding a private spot in which to dwell, holding onto a single word, or reading the Bible for hours on end were effective ways to step outside the flow of time.

Richard Groton once told me that 'The building keeps you out of your own little world. It's kind of distracting.'

'What do you do when the building distracts you?' I asked.

'Play dead.

To play dead was to stop existing, to stop living among others. Given the lack of calm in the building and people's anxieties, such efforts were not easy to pull off. Others tried to engage in ritualized, steady-state routines of 'pacing' as ways of moving energetically through space without engaging with or brushing up against others. For many, medication was a way to become desensitized. Richard told me that medications made him go into his 'own little world,' while Martin took Haldol to help him sleep at night: 'After taking it,' he explained, 'I'm out like a light. If I didn't take it, I would be up paranoid all night.' (More rarely, and depending on cash flow, some tried to find a smooth plane of joy or numbness through dope, crack, or alcohol.)

One danger for those who built their lives around a search for quiescence or timelessness was that they could lose the knack for feeling alive – or for feeling anything at all. Since shelter life, despite its many distractions, could be too mundane, it was sometimes difficult to keep active or maintain a sense of autonomy. 'I'm dissolving into the building up there,' Joey Austen said of his forced stay in the locked psychiatric ward on the fifth floor of the building. He then added, 'When I was homeless [staying in the shelter], well, geez, I could get out, smoke a cigarette in the lobby, take a shower. But upstairs, we're locked in.'

His comment recalled one woman's claim that she had lived in the shelter for so long that it was like she was 'part of the building now.' Both perspectives suggested that people could meld into their surroundings if they stayed in one place for days or weeks on end.

Others referred to similar affinities between institutional setting and personal constitution. 'Sometimes I go to my bed area,' one woman said, 'and it seems so kinda gloomy, dark. It looks moldy, though it isn't really moldy, you know?' Another woman told me that the shelter was 'like death row,' and said she sometimes saw the same faces in different shelters.

'How does that make you feel?' I asked.

'I don't feel anything,' she said.

The idea of not feeling recurred. 'I lost my mind,' Nancy Ange said in introducing herself one day.

'What does that feel like?' I asked in the course of the conversation.

'I don't feel. I don't feel. I feel numb,' she replied.

One day Martin Aaron showed me a poem he wrote called 'Sheol,' which is the word for the Hebrew netherworld. The poem told of the Los Angeles street scene, where 'people are hanging out, with no thoughts, no feelings.'

Some tried to get out of insensible funks by making themselves feel more of the world. 'I don't know what I was thinking about then,' said Henry Williamson of a razor he put to his wrist a few years back. 'I guess I did it because I was really depressed. When I cut myself, I felt alive, more alive than I felt before. Anyway, I wasn't depressed any more after that.'

A similar concern for 'feeling alive' was evident in something that Richard Groton, a sensory misfit of sorts who liked to touch objects and people, once told me when talking about the 'ruts' he sometimes fell into. 'It's like the shelter blues,' he said. 'I feel this sometimes, when I get depressed. Others too, I think. People begin to feel worthless as if they're not doing anything in their lives. I try to make people feel more alive by touching them, talking to them.'

For many, the sensory range involved a continuum between 'feeling nervous' and 'staying calm.' Nervousness implied an act of feeling; calmness implied a static state or a moment of quiescence or unfeeling. The former belonged to the passage of time; the latter, ideally, was bereft of it. Given this antipodal lot, it often made sense to try to get out of an insensible funk by making oneself 'feel more alive' – as when Henry cut himself, or when Richard 'mixed things up' with his neighbors to rid them and himself of 'the shelter blues.' At times, people found that sensation-rich engagements with the world around them were a good way to cut away from periods of stasis and numbness. Then again, many found that there was too much feeling in their lives, and few appreciated Richard's engagements. Those staying in the shelter wavered between wanting to feel more, or less, of the world.

Conclusion

For the people I worked with, then, sensory dynamics underpinned substantial features of their lives. To be homeless or to bed down in the shelter was to live out a specific kind of sensory existence. Day in, day out, life in the shelter entailed themes of distraction and routine, sensation and numbness, movement and stillness, timeliness and timelessness. For many, everyday life often implied strenuous efforts against opposition, of hitting up against a world filled with noises, bodies, pains, distractions, displacements, and bureaucratic powers. Life was double-edged, for whereas it involved the idea of carrying on with difficulty, it also entailed efforts to do away with hassles or constraints – to the point, at times, of trying to block out everything in seeking a 'degree-zero' way of being. To get away from constant tensions and fleeting distractions, some suspended the minutes of a day. Too much calm could get to a person after a while, however, and many tried to find ways to keep busy without getting bored. Often the trick was to find a balance between sensory overflow and walking around in a stupor. Many residents tried to work toward points of equilibrium, which often came down to a sense of stasis. The stasis, which made a good deal of sense, given how much was impermanent and unmanageable in people's lives, tended to grow more fundamental the longer a person stayed in the shelter.

In fact, people sometimes spoke of the dangers of getting 'settled in.' 'I was doing good at first,' Julie said of her stay in the shelter, 'but then I got settled in. Everybody's so used to doing nothing here. There's nothing to get you going.' While the process of getting 'settled in' could help some adapt to a sane and quiet existence, it could also make 'doing nothing' the general state of things. The shelter staff often found that the residents' 'routines' were 'self-defeating' because they negated opportunities for active engagements in life. For residents, however, the routines promised many the best chance for a relatively sane existence outside of hospitals. One man put it well when asked what advice he would have to a newcomer in the shelter: 'Live one day at a time,' he said, 'don't get ahead of yourself, and don't get too worried.'

In general, those staying for a time in the shelter rooted themselves in everyday routines, came to live within a repetitive temporal cycle, and usually resisted in ways that in the long run fueled their dependency. More than a few grew quite fond of their lives in the shelter and were afraid or reluctant to move on to other, more 'permanent' living arrangements, such as apartments of their own. The shelter was a no-man's limbo for the displaced, with residents trying to root themselves to a certain way of life and staff members trying to move people along. Staff and other service providers thus faced an uphill battle in trying to get people to take the steps necessary to move out, to find jobs, and to live supposedly healthier and more meaningful lives.

The catch here, however, is that the goals many would wish onto those considered mentally ill – from productive, full-time jobs to strong friendships and richly experienced lives – are not necessarily possible for, or wanted by, those under consideration. There were very good reasons for many shelter residents to look for 'smooth days' or to not get ahead of themselves. These efforts often enabled them to live in the best terms possible, given their concerns and circumstances. More durable labors or more intensive involvement in the lives of others could have invited additional distress and worries and thus destroyed the intricate, homeostatic balance that many took great pains to establish. Unfortunately, there are such strong positive moral connotations assigned to action, productivity, sociability, and deep and lasting intimacy in mainstream American society that it can be difficult to fathom that these ideals are not the best medicine for some. It is all too easy, in turn, to condemn those who do not live up to these proposed ideals, or to devise therapeutic agendas that work to mold people into sociable and productive members of an actively shared world. But because these agendas can be at odds with what helps people to 'hang in there,' engineers of mental healthcare and public policy would be wise to bracket their values and assumptions and try to understand, in good phenomenological fashion, the time-tested sensibilities and precepts of those they are authorized to care for. Simply put, we need to try to shirk some of the cultural models that haunt our work and try to think otherwise about the worlds of those plagued by pain and distress. We need fine-grained, anthropologically informed accounts of the phenomenal worlds of those suffering from distress, uncommon 'redescriptions' that might help us to map the cultural, political, and sensorial makings of human subjectivities as they take form in particular times and places.

Bibliography

Desjarlais, R. (1997), *Shelter Blues: Sanity and Selfhood among the Homeless*, Philadelphia: University of Pennsylvania Press.

Rorty, R. (1989), *Contingency, Irony, and Solidarity*, Cambridge: Cambridge University Press.

22
Dystoposthesia
Emplacing Environmental Sensitivities

Christopher Fletcher

What's in a Name?

Dystoposthesia, abnormal place experience, does not exist. There is no disease with this name in the diagnostic manuals of mainstream medicine nor do practitioners use the term colloquially. It is an invention of mine intended to cast the condition of environmental sensitivities (ES), which I will describe below, as a quasi-legitimate medical condition.

A name is a good point to begin a discussion of an illness that cannot be accommodated within conventional medical rationality and yet is eminently present in the bodies of those who suffer from the condition. Irony aside, dystoposthesia is a reasonably good descriptor of the sensory experience of those who suffer the effects of ES. In essence, ES is an incompatibility of bodies with the spaces they inhabit. It is a sickness that is characterized by highly divergent physical, affective, and behavioral 'reactions' to an equally broad list of environmental triggers. The quantities of substances that engage reactions are those of everyday exposures, much lower than required to provoke a response among those without ES. The majority of these reactions appear to be due to olfactory encounters but many are responses to foods consumed and to physical contact with synthetics of all sorts. Most public attention has been directed toward the voluntary use of fragrances and scented products but to people with ES almost everything encountered in daily life has a perceptible chemical component: rugs, linoleum, plastics, wallpaper, and so on. Likewise the ubiquitous combustion furnace and motorized vehicles of all sorts fill ambient space with chemical fumes of varying density. Environmental sensitivites is profoundly dystoposthetic illness, it is about being out of place in ways that most people aren't. It is a disease of place experience.

The name dystoposthesia is also a good beginning point for thinking through the social and spatial course of the illness. When sufferers come to the realization that their bodily states are linked to a sensory incompatibility to the places they inhabit a literal and metaphorical 'voyage' begins. People with ES search for new places of bodily coordination and reshape locations to the requirements of their conditions. They attempt to mitigate the effects of the qualities of space on the body by reforming place. Likewise, moving from a state of raw and formless illness experience to a socially sanctioned trajectory of sickness is fundamental to sharing and socializing experiences of bodily disease. Making collective sense out of individual sensory experiences also allows multiple readings of the body's state to occur while providing a narrative and practice structure on which to organize the self and social action.

As ES is a medically *un*recognized illness the adoption of a common trajectory among the afflicted contributes a great deal to establishing the social validity of individual bodily experience. The importance of biomedical legitimization in the social production of sickness and the social contextualization of suffering is well known to people with ES, who have organized effective political and social information campaigns aimed at enlightening the non-sufferer and orienting resources toward the relief of their condition. For people with ES to pin down the condition in medical phrase, if not the gaze, is an important venture of legitimizing bodily experiences with place.

Over time the terminology around ES has shifted repeatedly. The current use of 'ES' in Canada – specifically, the Maritime Provinces of Canada – follows the terminology used at the Nova Scotia Environmental Health Centre (NSEHC), a clinic just outside of Halifax where I conducted fieldwork on the illness, and is commonly accepted in the patient population, although the latter group tends to use a series of additional terms when speaking together to indicate variations of the illness recognized within patient and advocacy groups. A number of other terms that are roughly analogous to ES have come into use since the early 1980s. Among them chemical AIDS, twentieth century disease, total allergy syndrome, environmental hypersensitivity syndrome, environmental illness, ecological illness, chemical hypersensitivity syndrome, multiple chemical sensitivities (MCS), allergic to everything disease, chemical induced immune dysfunction, and environmentally induced illness. A UNEP-WHO-ILO- sponsored experts workshop of the International Programme on Chemical Safety (ICPS) recommended the term idiopathic environmental intolerance (IEI) be adopted in professional discourse in place of the various colloquial terms (IPCS 1996). A common feature of these is the relationship of bodily states to environmental conditions.

Other illnesses, such as sick building syndrome (SBS), fybromyalgia and chronic fatigue syndrome (CFS) share considerable symptom overlap with ES (Buchwald and Garrity 1994; Ziem and Donnay 1995; Kipen et al. 1999) and affect many patients who also claim ES. Sick building syndrome in particular is seen by many as an origin point for generalized ES and it plays an important role in the development of public awareness of ES in Halifax, Nova Scotia. Indeed, the condition first became widely known to the public through an outbreak at a local hospital (Camp Hill) that, at one point, afflicted one-third of the staff or about a thousand people. A characteristic of illnesses like ES is that the explanatory models engaged in popular and professional discourses shift, change and merge rapidly and unpredictably in ways that demonstrate the intellectual effort that goes into trying to find coherence in inchoate experience (see Kirmayer 1992). Thus ES, like dystoposthesia and the other terms that have been used to pin down various states of bodily dis-ease, emerges from a social imperative found in the discordance of experiential and authoritative renderings of the meanings of sensation.

The putative vectors of the illness, and the 'reactions' that people experience, engage the dominant and taken-for-granted modes of Being in the contemporary world in a tension-filled juxtaposition. The fixed, discrete and bounded individual body and experience of mainstream North American subjectivity (c.f. Martin 1994) is pitted against a porous, permeable and dynamic corporeality that I characterize as an ecological subjectivity. Through sensation and its discourses ES challenges the cultural logic of contemporary consumer society and the project of modernity generally in a way that is different from the resource rationality underpinning the mainstream environmental movement. Sensation, like the things sensed, has a social life in this instance unlike that of most, if not all, illnesses of the West. In particular it is the odors of consumption that move from the unconsciousness of users into the sensory awareness of sufferers. A vapor trail of meaning follows the path to the afflicted. The immediacy of the illness experience, and its undeniable realism for the sufferer, challenge the everyday presumptions of a rational world – suggesting that new conjunctions of people, objects and the spaces between them must exist for this mode of experience to Be. In this light sufferers present an emergent form of subjectivity grounded in the particularities of their experiences of the landscape they move through and brought to them by a particular sensory capacity. In effect, they present a subjectivity that is embedded in the environmental and social interactions particular to locale (Basso 1988; Appadurai 1995; Lovell 1998) and emerges in defiance of a universal and fixed biology. Environmental sensitivities generates cultural tension by materializing the 'pre-cultural' (Csordas 1990, 1994 viz. Merleau-Ponty 1962) and voiceless conjunction between feeling and knowing. What's more it grounds them in locality – that is, in the immediate perceptual realm – and in the broader configurations of physical and social geographies. 'Environmental sensitivities' is an emplaced phenomenon and, for its sufferers, their bodily states are interwoven with the places they inhabit.

Regional Contexts of Bodily Experience

A perplexing feature of ES for sufferers, scientists, politicians and others drawn up in its wake in Nova Scotia is the seeming regional prominence of the illness. What is it about this place that is different from others? Or, what is it about these people that is different from others?

Mary Lou's assessment of why ES is widespread in Nova Scotia locates the persistence of the illness in the structure of the medical system, the industrial history of the province, and the actions of individuals with ES:

> I think it's growing. I think people are being educated. I think it took the Camp Hill disaster here to open people's eyes to it and become aware of it... I *know*...
>
> Now, I think you'll find a lot of it [ES] is in this province because we have a lot of toxins in this province. We have the Sydney tar ponds. We have Minus Basin pulp and paper who poured stuff out into our water supply for years. I think they *might* be getting a little bit more environmentally conscious – over time. You know, we have the saw mills that were doing the same thing. We have the salt mines. We had the tin mines – Michelin plants polluting air and the water. So we've had a lot of toxins in a small province, as well.
>
> We're close to the water, which keeps us moist and moldy, you know. I can remember my father, when his brother got TB they went out west because it was so dry. And I've heard a lot of patients have gone to Arizona, here when we were on IV, improve come back here and get sick again. So, I think a lot of it is what we harbor in our air as well from around the globe. And there's a lot of the Valley, Annapolis Valley, sick and we've got a big apple industry in Nova Scotia. A lot of sprays. A lot of farm... other areas don't have [that concentration]...
>
> This province you could drive it, if you wanted to, in two days you could get from one end to the other...

The physical size of the province is an element of Mary Lou's understanding of the prevalence of ES in Nova Scotia. It is tempting to read an underlying discourse about different facets of smallness into this account. Mary Lou is making a comparative statement about Nova Scotia and other provinces which are physically larger and hence can diffuse a toxic burden more widely. Of course toxins don't recognize political boundaries and the statement points to the meanings Mary Lou attributes to her cognitive mapping of the province. In effect it is the waste and by-product pollutants remaining from the now obsolete history of industrialization in the province that contributes to the overall 'load' of toxins in the area and in the bodies of people with ES. In making these statements Mary Lou is forming an analogy between terrestrial environmental toxins and the bodily that is one facet of an emplaced discourse of illness. Her discourse of bodily states and causality is mirrored in academic histories of the region that generally emphasize a slow decline in economic and political significance that began when the

Province joined the Canadian confederation (Forbes 1980; Ross 1987; Reid 1990; McKay 1993, 1994; Fingard 1993).

Environmental sensitivities is of course a relatively recent phenomenon. The earliest anyone I spoke with placed their first reactions was in the 1970s, although some now reflect on earlier exposures to chemicals as having 'primed' their bodies to react the way they do. While sufferers generally claim an experiential high ground for the validity of the condition there are many critics who feel that ES is a groundless mass effort to shirk responsibility. For example a hotly discussed report in the *Halifax Chronicle Herald* (26 December, 1990: A12) quotes the author of a *Journal of the American Medical Association* study on chemical sensitivity saying that it is a 'garden variety mental disorder.' Similarly, conservative pundit David Frum, writing in the *Financial Post* (6/8 April 1996: 22), berated government for agreeing to fund treatments for a 74-pound, 17-year-old girl at an environmental clinic in Dallas. Her family was convinced she had environmental hypersensitivity disorder. Likewise, the province and city of Halifax received a great deal of press when a high-school student was investigated by police for assault on a teacher. His offence was reportedly wearing cologne to school. The student was never charged but the mere possibility attracted hostile attention to the legitimacy of the condition and focused scrutiny on the government.

In a social context ES exists quite defiantly as a physical illness made sensible by the collective bodily experience of its sufferers. It has a vibrant social life that is given structure by a limited number of activist/sufferers but is adhered to by thousands of people in Maritime provinces, especially Nova Scotia, and beyond. Suffering in the context of medical invisibility and experiential realism lends the fact of pain social ambiguity. Unlike sufferers of other kinds of illnesses, where medicine and experience can find common purchase, ES sufferers fashion their own authority over illness in isolation, and occasionally even hostility, from mainstream medicine. They derive a collective sensibility out of the experiential quagmire of ES by working out a bodily logic of what remains illogical. They develop a 'frame of body' (see James 2002) that displaces a frame-of-mind orientation to causality in biomedicine. That framing is explicitly about reconfiguring the relation of body to place.

Places of Healing and Illness

I had never been smelled by a scientist before. Standing in the vestibule of the staff entrance to the Nova Scotia Environmental Health Centre. I was subjected to an olfactory vetting before being granted access to the inner sanctum of this clinic. In this liminal portion of the building, neither in nor out, a man I had never met, yet knew to be a respected member of the scientific community, stuck his nose in my hair and inhaled, sniffed around my clothes, and told me to take off my shoes and socks before entering (I was provided with paper slippers).

Although I had heeded the forewarning to stop using commercial shampoos and laundry detergents several days before visiting, and was provided with odor-free, scent-sensitive, and natural alternatives at the organic food store around the corner from where I lived, I was only permitted access to the least secure portion (there are three levels) of the building. It takes months for a body's load of chemicals to be excreted, I was told. Consequently I was a potential danger to the clientele of the clinic and it would be best not to come into contact with them. Microbe-like, I breached the exterior wall of the clinic.

Many of the staff at the clinic, like almost all the patient population they try to help, have heightened olfactory capacities that are reflected in a medical history marked by medically unexplained illness experiences seemingly in association with completely mundane exposures to the chemical veil of everyday life: glues, formaldehydes, fabric softeners, photocopy fluids, paints, dyes... all of which are passed through unremarkably to those who do not have this capacity or history. My doorman colleague was not a sufferer of any particular condition. He simply worked day in day out with those who did. He served as an olfactory sentinel for those who metaphorized their own experience with airborne chemicals and odors as that of the canary in the coal mine. His nose had become attuned to the experiential realms of the afflicted; he had undergone a sensory enculturation of sorts. This subjectivity is contagious.

Calling the clinic a sanctum is not figurative. The building is a physical refuge for people with ES. The microbe-like analogy is a good rendering of the difference between sufferers of ES and those of us who do not live in the sensory realm of the clinic clientele and the many hundreds, indeed thousands, of people who link their bodily states of disease to the popular nosology of ES.[1] The non-afflicted, through our mundane uses of consumer products – from deodorizing pine tree silhouettes hanging from automobile mirrors, to the fabric softener in the clothes washer, to the $300-an-ounce perfume worn to the symphony fundraiser – are in many instances the unwitting sources of a variety of physical traumas suffered by the population of people who can no longer co-exist with this sensory onslaught. We penetrate *them* producing illness in ways that are only possible in this particular technological-consumer moment/environment.

The clinic was built with the highest degree of concern for the chemical properties of the materials that went into it and is operated as a cybernetic edifice that links healing arts, hypermodern mechanical and computer equipment, rigorous science, sick people, and an ongoing debate about the nature of sensation in the post-industrial present. Like the people who worked and suffered within it, the building had moods, good days and bad, was monitored directly and remotely, and was engaged in an intense and constant bodily introspection. The furniture was unvarnished, the materials unbleached cottons, the fax and photocopier vented away. While building the clinic many of the materials were minutely examined for their likelihood to provoke reactions and when a decision could not be reached to include or reject something, a particularly sensitive staff member would take it home and sleep with it under her pillow. Canary indeed.

The presence of symbolically potent medical technologies – the IV bag, the stethoscope, the syringe, the mask – administered by properly qualified nurses, doctors and therapists gave the clinic an air of medical normalcy. Nonetheless, the people who work in the clinic, those who suffer from ES, and even the building itself embody and engage a dialogue on the nature of experiential legitimacy. As noted previously, ES does not exist in standard medical nosology, it has no known etiology, and none is likely to appear soon given the number of variables involved and the range of symptoms attributed to the condition. Within mainstream medicine it is much easier to situate ES as a mental illness than as a bodily process. It has correspondence to broadly cast syndromes of collective delusion, occupational mass hysteria, somatoform disorders and the like (Stewart and Raskin 1985; Terr 1986, 1987; Brodsky 1987; Stewart 1987; Black 2000). It has no single cause and effect mechanism, nor a clear course to follow, making a bodily process difficult to imagine and locate. Of course, marginalizing medically undefined symptoms and illnesses to the mental realm is a, by now, well known trope of Western medical history, and one with which sufferers of ES are all too familiar. In interviews they repeatedly pointed to the histories of other diseases that have migrated from the mind to the body in medical nosology including multiple sclerosis, autism, AIDS, and asthma. The point of these stories is to demonstrate a degree of professional arrogance among medical professionals when their own knowledge base is insufficient to comprehend physical reality, and more pragmatically to link the suffering of people with ES to a trajectory of enlightenment that is personal, professional and social.

The power of the enlightenment trope is very real in that it supports an ongoing social movement around the disease, allows some practitioners the purchase to continue with their work despite professional marginalization and, at times, ridicule, and finally it permits the potential of new forms of illness to exist in social spaces regardless of whether people believe in their validity or not.

One feature of the sensory and social life of this illness is the extrapolation of scientific method – hard rationality – to create knowledge of individual states of bodily disorder by sufferers. All sufferers are tested continuously by the ecology they inhabit. Being afflicted with ES engages a remapping of all space into heightened sensory and personalized *places* with qualities, textures, temporalities and potentials that non-sufferers never imagine. In the same way that disease introduces the sufferer to their body anew, ES brings place into the consciousness of the body – recrafting the universal and implicit into the immediate and specific. It undermines the rationalist assumption that space is a constant field for human action (Casey 1986;

Rodman 1992), and thus transforms emplacement into an important variable in comprehending the human condition of suffering. Clearly a mechanistic view of disease process would not situate place as a realm of difference in the sufferer's world; it would simply look for causes and effects within the ecology. Working with the sufferers of ES has brought the importance of emplacement in illness experience to light.

The very successful efforts of the afflicted and their compatriots to dissuade the use of perfumes, colognes and other fragrant hygiene/beauty products in public space in Halifax indicates a remarkable reshaping of behaviour with strongly gendered orientations. Thus, interpersonal encounters – accidental, unavoidable, and wanted – are also occasions for experiments to occur and reactions to take hold. ES sufferers clearly share in the dominant ontology of the West – there are causes and effects, and these are located in an external, knowable, constant and rational world – and build what we could call a cognized experiential data set of bodily events in association with evident and assumed chemical products as they are encountered in space. From interviews with sufferers it seems that knowing space is accomplished through a distanced self-awareness and objectification of the body as an experiment in progress. Through witnessing the body's response to particular locales a sensory geography of reactions is developed. From these, people construct new ecologies for themselves reshaping their immediate worlds accordingly and creating new spatial itineraries that allow for the relatively comfortable movement through space. One person I spoke with, who had been largely free from the debilitating effects of ES after several years of searching for causes and cures, lived in a remarkable dwelling made of found pieces of wood, bent roots, hay, concrete, glass bottles. Her house was like that of a hobbit – organic, almost living, no angles only curves. She fashioned her dwelling out of what her body told her was debilitating about other dwellings she had lived in. Sitting in her kitchen was like being inside her stomach. While this dwelling was extraordinary everyone with ES undertakes a sensory inventory of the material goods in their lives and remodels accordingly. Houses are done over from the inside out, carpets, floors, furnaces, drapes, removed and replaced with chemically neutral new ones. People with few means move frequently and may become homeless in the process of finding a place to which their bodies can concur. In Halifax you can legally break your lease, without penalty, if you have demonstrable ES.

The reshaping of domestic space to reflect the trajectory of suffering and healing from ES is repeated on a larger scale in the reshaping of public space. Over time personal ecologies have begun to displace those that dominate the public realm. Indeed, one of the most prominent features of the social life of ES is the effect its sufferers have had on reshaping social norms in public places. A well coordinated, loosely affiliated network of organizations[2] has targeted the owners and managers of public buildings with information encouraging them to implement policies around the scented products used by employees, change the kinds of chemical cleaners used, change ventilation systems, and so on. Through public education, subtle coercion and effective advocacy work, public spaces are being transformed into idealized realms without odor. The now ubiquitous 'Scent Free Zone' signs at the library, school, office, and elevator signal the arrival of new moral configurations and sensory etiquette in the city. This represents a sensory reordering at a vast scale, imagine – as ES sufferers would like to – a city that is invisible to the nose, a space with no chemical content, a place of olfactory purity.

The investment of energy into this new urban ecology has clearly moral overtones that impact on established social conditions. The wife of a prominent local university administrator told me she got rid of her smelly old friends when they wouldn't conform to her sensory needs. Olfaction trumps class. Despite the success of the afflicted and their advocates in reorganizing the olfactory landscape of Halifax and beyond, the illness continues to consolidate its grasp within the population of the region. There is a counter trend at play here that again emplaces illness experience in the historical and economic particularities of the region – that is, the decay of public and private infrastructure that accompanies economic decline and political marginalization. Through dystoposthetic sensory experiences and the spatial reorganizations they provoke public space and social behavior are not only reformed they are re-imbued with a moral dimension. This is an important discourse of illness and space in the context of rapid, and until recently, politically unthinkable rationalization of the public sector workforce and the reorganization of the role of government in daily lives of many, if not most, people of the region.

June's illness narrative evokes these contradictory and unsettling changes in public and moral space. She is widely travelled and has very definite feelings about the negative effects of tourism on the traditions of people who come under the tourist gaze. Her feelings are superficially those of the political right – small government creates dynamic and flexible individuals, neo-liberalism creates dependant, rigid citizens –present in the local political discourse on the (under)development of the region. They are also about the impact of outsiders on values and desires as genuine features of locale. The Maritimes too are in the midst of re-imagining themselves through the optics of the Other. Tourism is a form of social penetration into the regional social and geographic entity, much like olfaction is to the individual body. In a context where tourism is celebrated as the only available economic adaptation, the links between bodily and territorial integrity are readily drawn. June's message about the effects of tourism is that it cheapens the quality of social and cultural integrity resulting in an inevitable downward spiral for those who are caught up in it.

The economic and class considerations of the interaction of the tourist and the local lead me to ask her about the effect of changing social programs and the end of traditional industries on regional social organization. Her response is to make an analogy to a father who has spoiled his children by giving them everything and then financially abandoning them when he retires. The metaphor of the State in senescence is very resonant in this region where government largesse anchored communities in difficult times until very recently. The result, for June, is that initiative has been lost and there may be no means left to recover:

> June: When I was growing up, and people before me, what did we have as toys? We had the little soldiers, we had building blocks, we had all kinds of things and we made things... I mean, there'd be games you could buy, and we had those too, but we were creative and we did things. And now, all of a sudden, you go to the toy stores and all those games come in boxes? There's no creativity anymore... People don't have the resources and initiative anymore. They don't have pride in what they do... They don't want to think... There's just no thinking, there's no... There's just not any depth,
>
> C.F.: Why is that happening? Why are people like that?
>
> June: Because we've taken away their sense of pride, their sense of working for things, their sense of accomplishment. There isn't that anymore.

The end result is a lack of community cohesion that translates into an incapacity for spontaneous, productive action in the absence of some form of official involvement:

> Two or three summers ago, there was a playground over in Dartmouth [sister city to Halifax across the harbour], in the North End, and it needed some repair. There was a few nails sticking out of one of the climbing things, and there was a board that was missing. And they had it on TV because the people were angry, okay, everybody's got to get angry. And why doesn't government come in here and fix this? And I thought, there's somebody in that neighbourhood with a hammer and a board in their basement.
>
> But, we've become so government dependent, why do that? Why spend 20 minutes of our time for our children to be safe, just because, why bother? The government should do it. And if a kid cuts himself on the nail, well we're up in arms.

It is interesting how this discourse on Maritime society emanates outward from the production of ES as a bodily experience to encompass much broader realms. June's interpretation of the decay of individual autonomy builds from an understanding of an inextricable relationship between moral and environmental landscapes. This perspective transcends what is otherwise, and usually discussed as, an economic and geographic history particular to the Maritimes:

> June: I mean, we're poisoning ourselves. I think with the additives to the food, the additives to the air, there's so much stuff. Like, lately I've been looking at

different animal testings and stuff, and they didn't do that years ago. I mean, for cleaning products and make-up and... they're torturing all these animals so that we can have better skin care, I mean... you know, that's ridiculous. And, they didn't do that years ago, and it's because they know it's toxic, and if we're putting on, we're absorbing that toxicity, you know, we're breathing it, we're eating it, it's in our total environment.

C.F.: All right. And that leapt to you as part of our culture, the fact that we consume those things...

June: We've become a very greedy society, and we're becoming a godless society. And that's all working together to make everything really awful.

For June the apparent greed of contemporary consumer society, and the abandonment of Christian values are emblematic of a single process. Her understanding, afforded by the view of the world fashioned in suffering, draws new configurations of meaning into a landscape of change. Despite the apparent reassurance that idealized notions of tradition and locality provide for June, in the end she too draws on global process and events to situate the local significance of ES. A problematic of suffering in local contexts that are not broadly acknowledged is analogous to the predicament of local cultures in the face of global forces of meaning and action.

Voyages and Trajectories

Dystoposthesia is also evident in the illness trajectories that many people described to me. They are in a near constant flight from uninhabitable places of work, faith, family, and consumerism towards often unattainable refuges of the chemical and odor free. In this relentless movement away from normative social spaces ES sufferers are afforded new views of the social practices they can no longer support. Bill, a retired salesman living in a condominium in a mid-size Nova Scotia town, talked about how he was obliged, at the funeral of an old friend, to shun his daughter because of her use of talcum powder. This experience reversed the normal flow of sympathy in the social encounter of bereavement reorienting attention toward the ES sufferer with physical symptoms and away from the emotional distress of loss. Privileging of physical states over emotional or mental states is a strong theme in the narratives of ES sufferers. Bill's narrative of the funeral expands to encompass a general observation on the nature of odor in social space.

If I meet a woman or someone on the street, I have to make sure that I know which way the wind's turning, blowing, so that I can get to windward rather than to leeward of them. Yeah. Every little thing you have to watch... Even in the stores, I go down to Sobeys [a large grocery store chain], that's a good place to shop, it's well ventilated. But when you come up, coming close to those freezers, there's another thing that bothers me. Freezers. Jesus. And if I talk to a woman down there, if she's got perfume on, I can smell... I have to walk away. Sometimes I feel stupid you know, and look, feel like I'm out of place, but it's not, it's just the way you have to live.

For Bill the normal social courtesies of speech and manner have become secondary to that of odor. A sensory shift that is unprecedented.

Darleen's experience with the use of personal fragrances by members of her church is another example of how illness experience, odor and social practice intertwine in the ES experience and produce new social constellations for the afflicted. She too had to leave her church because of her illness. In her case, the process transformed her understanding of the meaning of religious practice and fellowship in her community:

Darleen: I had a real struggle in the church that I was in and I didn't get anywhere with changing attitudes and I would sit at the back of the church and I brought in my air filter and you would think that people would understand that. ... but I would get things like people turning around during the sermon and motioning for me to turn the air filter off because they though it somehow hampered with the sermon. Not once did anybody realize that I felt isolated and lonely at the back of the church and if they wanted to be very Christian to me, they could come sit beside me. So it was a hard deal and in the end I just left. I did a little shopping around, and I haven't found a church that's scent-free so...

C.F. It's hard to do, I guess. A number of people have mentioned having problems with their churches. And it's sort of the last bastion of people wearing their Sunday dress...

Darleen: They just have to, when they get dressed up on Sunday, they just have to. And to even educate them [to] the fact that if they're not wearing perfume, their hair shampoo is [still] loaded with scent, their underarm deodorant, you know. And men on Sunday put on their aftershave and I mean I love aftershave. I just love it, but it doesn't love me. I don't know if we're getting off track. We'll have to use our time efficiently here.

Churches are prominent features of the physical and social landscapes of most communities in Nova Scotia. More than any other institution they embody the ideals of faith, community solidarity and historical continuity. For Darleen, the tenacious rituals of dress and odor in religious practice engendered a profound shift in her understanding of the ethos of the Christian community. Instead of offering her respite in her state of illness the religious service replicated the practices that have caused people like her to become ill and demonstrated how entrenched they can be. The contradiction between the professed values of the Church and the intransigence of churchgoers as regards her illness demonstrates how ES re-configures the social positioning of the sufferer through the mediation of the actions and meanings embedded in social spaces. The dislocation of the individual from religious practice was a common element in the narratives of people I interviewed. In many cases the disengagement from social practices like churchgoing was portrayed as a 'step' or 'stage' in the progressive disability brought on by ES.

Experiences with illness and the Church are indicative of the profound and generalized reshaping of the social world that sufferers experience – most typically the social disengagement that having the illness provokes, and the profound disturbance this poses to people who are ill. People spoke of searching for churches that were progressive in regard to scent-free policies (there are a couple that hold services designated as scent free) and actively working with Clergy to produce a supportable environment within the church, with some limited success. Reshaping the practices of chemical use inside churches, and the use of perfumes and other products by parishioners, is part of a larger effort to reshape odor in public space generally, as described earlier. Similarly to the way that curtailing Church attendance is a signifier of declining health to people with ES, many spoke of returning to church as evidence of progressive healing, a re-emplacement of the social being in the heart of the community. Obviously not everyone I spoke with had reached that 'stage' nor will they; many people have opted to remake their practice in light of their inability to participate in church services. Some have adopted private reflection, prayer and reading; others formed bible study groups with other afflicted people, and still others abandoned their former practices altogether and yet are moving towards a renewed sense of health.

As the narratives of ES sufferers show odor and its uses lead to an embodied social critique in which the double standards and hypocrisies of everyday community life are realized. In attempting to reshape the individual scent realms of the non-afflicted, new renderings of society are imagined and the entrenched nature of practices become evident. While Darleen's experience could be dismissed as a common interpretation of the small town as stifling and limited, her experience is not that of someone who becomes enlightened by the breadth of big-city ideas and social expansiveness. Rather, her experience of ES dis-emplaces her from the routine of the community and crafts a new understanding of people and place through the sensorial ecology of ES. The re-visioning that accompanies sensorial change is not distinguished by an epidemiology of rural dwelling or class.

Like Darleen, Bernice, the wife of a wealthy and respected businessman in Halifax, talks openly at a dinner party about the inability of her son to co-exist with the city environment, or to work, or to share in the social circles in which she is telling his story. She also blames the illness on global and local ecological features. In the first instance, the quality of the environment is diminished by industrialization and in the second her son is not treated because of the inertia of government to recognize and 'deal with' (cure, in other words) ES. She is positing a double marginality of the region that begins with the industrial success of other places – most notably, the east coast of the United States – that can and do pollute, and the relative poverty of the province to fund health care to resolve the problem of the riches of others. The irony of her location, social and for dinner, in making this discourse is not evident to her nor it seems to the others listening. They too know people with ES.

Concluding Spaces

The narratives of people who suffer from ES suggest that the condition radiates as potential experience from a conjunction of sensorial-, social-, and eco-logics. These become apparent in peoples' relations to each other and the places they share. As such ES reflects a manifestation of 'local biology' (Lock 1993, 2001) that is neither fully constructed, nor fully materialized. In a social context it is a problematic sickness that requires an engagement in the bodily truths of the sufferers by those who do not suffer. As a result the experiential reality of the illness and the afflicted is open to critique and ambiguity that return to shape the contexts of the sufferer. Sickness in this instance is not clearly localizable in the body nor the mind but moves between these and a third dimension, that of space. A theory of body alone cannot capture this process. Indeed, my argument is that an appreciation of the interactions of sensation and experience with place – a theory of illness emplacement – needs to emerge before ES can be rendered fully sensible in social and bodily contexts.

While it may be argued that ES is simply a projection of disenchantment – personal and regional – into the body and outward into the world, this adds nothing to understanding why this form of illness, in this place, and at this time, is the chosen path. Likewise, the bodies of the sufferers appear much more involved in their sensory realms than a social constructionist account would allow. From the perspective of emplacement, ES is the manifestation of something more significant than the embodiment of discontent with life in a marginal province, a place that *was*. The case of ES suggests an emergent subjectivity that exists despite, or simply in defiance of, its own impossibility. Environmental sensitivities would appear to be a frame of body that is emplaced in the particulars of a regional ethos and localized within, and in contrast with, universal bio-subjectivities. It is experienced and interpreted in resolutely local frames, but it co-exists with broader cultural framings of people and place. Through sensory experience of place, those afflicted with ES are enacting a major ecological trope in which we all participate but without the same kind of bodily attention – namely, the growing realization of the finite nature of 'nature' and our inexorable emplacement within an ecosystem of our own making that may not, in the end, support us. This is a cultural trope and, perhaps, an ecological fact with broad repercussions. Like a pebble in water, the underlying angst of the idea of the world as human habitat that is slipping away from us has ripples that are felt broadly and very loosely connect disparate shores to a barely visible centre. In this sense the idea of dystopsthesia can be seen as one with a broad purchase in contemporary culture.

Acknowledgments

I am grateful to all those who told me of their experiences with ES, to the staff of the NSEHC for allowing me to undertake my research there, and to Gilles Bibeau and Laurence Kirmayer for intellectual guidance. Despite my debt to all I am solely responsible for the content and interpretation presented here.

Notes

1. The true number of people who are self-diagnosed sufferers of ES and a range of symptomatically and similarly identified syndromes in Maritime Canada is unknown. They are considerable. While I was conducting fieldwork (1997–9) the waiting list at the NSEHC was roughly 1200 people long. This can only represent a small portion of those afflicted given the geographic breadth of the region, the newness of the clinic, and the widespread knowledge among the afflicted that actually getting into the clinic was next to impossible. There is no accepted medical definition for the condition (Cullen 1987), making even a general epidemiological profile impossible.

2. Among these organizations were nurses and public employee unions, advocacy groups for NSEHC patients and people on waiting lists for treatment, an organization devoted to the sensory quality of schools and an organization for people with 'invisible disabilities.'

Bibliography

Appadurai, A. (1995), 'The Production of Locality,' in R. Fardon (ed.), *Counterworks: Managing the Diversity of Knowledge*, London: Routledge, pp. 204–25.

Basso, K. (1988), '"Speaking with Names": Language and Landscape Among the Western Apache,' *Cultural Anthropology*, 3(2): 99–130.

Black, D.W. (2000), 'The Relationship of Mental Disorders and Idiopathic Environmental Intolerance,' *Occupational Medicine*, 15(3): 557–70.

Brodsky, C.M. (1988), 'The Psychiatric Epidemic in the American Workplace,' *Occupational Medicine: State of the Art Reviews*, 3(4): 653–62.

Buchwald, D., and Garrity, D. (1994), 'Comparison of Patients with Chronic Fatigue Syndrome, Fibromyalgia, and Chemical Sensitivities,' *Archives of Internal Medicine*, 154(18): 2049–53.

Casey, E.S. (1986), 'How to Get from Space to Place in a Fairly Short Stretch of Time,' in S. Feld and K.H. Basso (eds), *Senses of Place*, Sante Fe: School of American Research, pp. 3–52.

Csordas, T. (1990), 'Embodiment as a Paradigm for Anthropology,' *Ethos*, 18(1): 5–47.

—— (1994), *The Sacred Self: A Cultural Phenomenology of Charismatic Healing*, Berkeley: University of California Press.

Fingard, J. (1993), 'The 1880s: Paradoxes of Progress,' in E.R. Forbes and D.A. Muise (eds), *The Atlantic Provinces in Confederation*, Toronto: University of Toronto Press, pp. 82–116.

Forbes, E. (1980), *The Maritime Rights Movement 1919–1927: A Study in Canadian Regionalism*, Montreal: McGill-Queen's University Press.

IPCS (1996), 'Conclusions and Recommendation of a Workshop on Multiple Chemical Sensitivities (MCS),' *Regulatory Toxicology and Pharmacology*, 24(S): 188–9.

James, S.P. (2002), 'Heidegger and the Role of the Body in Environmental Virtue,' *The Trumpeter*, 18(1) http://trumpeter.athabascau.ca/content/v18.1/james.html, accessed 2 March, 2004.

Kipen, H.M., Kang, H., Hallman, W., Fiedler, N. and Natelson, B.H. (1999), 'Prevalence of Chronic Fatigue and Chemical Sensitivities in Gulf Registry Veterans,' *Archives of Environmental Health*, 54(5): 313–8.

Kirmayer, L.J. (1992), 'The Body's Insistence on Meaning: Metaphor as Presentation and Representation in Illness Experience,' *Medical Anthropology Quarterly*, 6(4): 323–46.

Lock, M. (1993), 'Cultivating the Body: Anthropology and Epistemologies of Bodily Practice and Knowledge,' *Annual Review of Anthropology*, 22: 133–55.

—— (2001), 'Menopause, Local Biologies, and Cultures of Aging,' *American Journal of Human Biology*, 13(4): 494–504.

Lovell, N. (ed.) (1998), *Locality and Belonging*, London: Routledge.

Martin, E. (1994), *Flexible Bodies: Tracking Immunity in American Culture from the Days of Polio to the Edge of AIDS*, Boston: Beacon Press.

McKay, I. (1993), 'The 1910s: The Stillborn Triumph of Progressive Reform,' in E.R. Forbes and D.A. Muise (eds), *The Atlantic Provinces in Confederation*, Toronto: University of Toronto Press, pp. 192–229.

—— (1994). *The Quest of the Folk*, Montreal: McGill-Queen's University Press.

Merleau-Ponty, M. (1962), *The Phenomenology of Perception*, trans. C. Smith, London: Compton Printing Works.

Reid, J. (1990), 'An International Region in the Northeast: Rise and Decline, 1635–1762,' in P.A. Buckner and D. Frank (eds), *Atlantic Canada Before Confederation*, second edition, Fredricton NB: Acadiensis, pp. 31–46.

Rodman, M.C. (1992), 'Empowering Place: Multilocality and Multivocality,' *American Anthropologist*, 94(1): 640–55.

Ross, E. (1987), 'The Rise and Fall of Pictou Island,' in L. McCann (ed.), *People and Places: Studies of Small Town Life in the Maritimes*, Fredericton NB: Acadiensis Press, pp. 161–88.

Stewart, D.E. (1987), 'Environmental Hypersensitivity Disorder, Total Allergy and Twentieth Centruy Disease: A Critical Review,' *Canadian Family Physician*, 33 (February): 405–10.

—— and Raskin, J. (1985), 'Psychiatric Assessment of Patients with "20th century disease" ("total allergy syndrome"),' *Canadian Medical Association Journal*, 133(November 15): 1001–6.

Terr, A.I. (1986), 'Environmental Illness: A Clinical Review of Fifty Cases,' *Archives of Internal Medicine*, 146(January): 145–9.

—— (1987), '"Multiple Chemical Sensitivities:" Immunological Critique of Clinical Ecology Theories and Practice,' *Occupational Medicine*, 2(4): 683–94.

Ziem, G. and Donnay, A. (1995), 'Chronic Fatigue, Fibromyalgia, and Chemical Sensitivity: Overlapping Disorders,' *Archives of Internal Medicine*, 155(17): 1913.

Sensory Bibliography

Forming Perceptions

The sensual revolution in cultural studies has precipitated an intense new focus on the senses as mediators of experience, eclipsing the role formerly played by 'discourse,' 'text' and 'picture.' The senses are constructed and lived differently in different periods and societies, and this fact has profound implications for how cultural subjects apprehend the environment, as well as other persons and things in their environment. The life of the senses is intimately linked to the life of the emotions, a subject which has also begun to receive increased attention, belying the old notion that the 'examined life' is an exclusive affair of the intellect.

One of the signs of this sensual-intellectual ferment is the publication of the *Sensory Formations* series.[1] This series brings together (in seven volumes) stimulating work belonging to the cross-disciplinary counter-tradition that has crystalized in recent years, partly as a reaction to the excesses of 'textualism' and 'ocularcentrism' in the academy, and more fundamentally as the successor to all the semiotic approaches, which are now in process of collapsing. The ruin of the Saussurean dream of a 'science of signs' (modeled on linguistics) is due to the growing recognition that neither the unconscious nor culture is, strictly speaking, 'structured like a language.'

The present book takes as its focus the interplay of the senses in cultural experience and expression. It is left to the other volumes in the *Sensory Formations* series to treat the senses individually. One of the rationales for such treatment, incidentally, comes from a review of Italo Calvino's *Under the Jaguar Sun*: 'The knowledge specific to each sense is apparent only when we are deprived of the others, and a new world is then revealed by the single sense that is not quite the same one we know with all five' (Wade 1989: 19).[2] Dominated as we are by visual models, we need to be reminded that the *voir-savoir-pouvoir* nexus, so brilliantly exposed by Foucault, is but one of many sensory infrastructures, another one being *sapore sapere* ('taste is knowledge'), the original title of the Calvino story included here. (See also 'Words of Sense,' Classen 1993a: Chapter 3.)

Considerations of space prevent a comprehensive review of the effects of the sensuous revolution in scholarship. In what follows, I offer instead a brief and partial survey, followed by a list of fifty sensational books that exemplify the research being undertaken in this dynamic new field of inquiry.[3] The latter works are distinguished by their sensitivity to the cultural and historical context of sensation. Imperfect and cursory as the following sketch may be, it is hoped that it will nevertheless help scholars interested in extending the bounds of sense within their respective disciplines from feeling like they are working in isolation, or that they need to invent the study of the senses from scratch. It will also, ideally, encourage more 'cross-talk' between the disciplines, for geographers of the senses have much to learn from historians, as do anthropologists and literary scholars, and vice versa.

The Senses across Disciplines

The sensual revolution is not only remaking scholarship. It is making news. 'History You Can See, Hear, Smell, Touch and Taste' proclaimed a recent *New York Times* article (Eakin 2003) about sensuous historiography. Certainly employing sensuous description has a particular charm for those wishing to enliven the dry bones of history and put readers 'in touch' with the past. The history of the senses, however, in its fullest development, is not only evocative – it is also interpretative: it makes sense of the past – through the analysis of sensory practices and ideologies. Constance Classen has explored a particularly impressive variety of topics in this area, ranging from the clash of Native American and European sensibilities which occurred after the Spanish Conquest (Classen 1993b) to the sensory underpinnings of Western religious, aesthetic and gender ideologies (Classen 1998). The subject of the senses in historiography has been reviewed by Carp (1997), Classen (2001), Godfrey (2002), Mark C. Smith (2003), Rath (2003) and Hoffer (2003).

More than any other discipline, anthropology confirms the importance of attending to the cultural life of the senses. For the striking variation in sensory practices and ontologies one finds across cultures clearly demonstrates that the senses are not just neutral data gatherers and perception is not confined to 'some grotto in the head.' The sensorium is dynamic, relational and political (not the private world psychologists posit), and our senses extend as far as our culture's technologies of sensing (corporeal and extracorporeal) permit them, and then some. This field is rich in sensuous ethnographies, a selection of which is included in the list of fifty books below. The subject of the senses in anthropology has been surveyed by Stoller (1989), Carp (1997), Classen (1997), Ingold (2000), and myself (Howes 2003).

The sensual revolution in geography is discussed in Pocock (1993), Rodaway (1994), and Zui (2000). Rodaway traces it to the 'cultural turn,' while Porteous (1990) grounds it in a reaction against 'remote sensing' and other excesses of the cartographic imagination. He proclaims that geographers should 'get their feet dirty' and lays out a methodology for 'intimate sensing.'

The most comprehensive source on the senses in sociology is Synnott's *The Body Social* (1993). Equally indicative of the new attention to the sociality of sensations are two books that elevate 'the second sense': Erlmann's *Hearing Culture* (2004) and Bull and Back's *The Auditory Culture Reader* (2003) – the first volume in the *Sensory Formations* series. These books are distinguished by their focus on the subject as a listener to and maker of sounds. In place of the model of 'look, but don't touch' (the socio-logic of the *flâneur*, sociology as *flânerie*), sociology becomes an exercise in 'deep listening' (Bull and Back 2003: 3).

The status of the senses in philosophy is touched on by Stewart (this volume) and has otherwise been reviewed in magisterial ('synoptic') fashion by Jay in *Downcast Eyes*. The latter work contains many penetrating insights concerning 'the denigration of vision in contemporary French thought.' However, it is limited by its focus on 'discourse' at the expense of practice and experience; its categorization of all of the philosophical positions it treats in terms of a single overarching (ocularcentric/antiocularcentric) binary when there are clearly other sensory currents coursing through the literature; and, its preoccupation with splitting or multiplying the gaze rather than acknowledging and tracking the intercourse of the senses. Carolyn Korsmeyer provides a savory antidote to Jay's verboscopophilism in *Making Sense of Taste* (1999), and there is a growing body of philosophical works that seek to fathom the multiple surfaces and intricacies of sense experience, as indicated by the list of books in the next section.

Studies of sensory imagery in literary works have long been undertaken (notably Vinge 1975). However, they were marginalized by the late twentieth century's fascination with 'vision and textuality' (for example, Melville and Readings 1995). This fascination is now shading into a new focus on senses and sensibilities, as exemplified by a number of recent publications, including *Poetry and the Fate of the Senses* (Stewart 2002) and *Sensual Reading* (Syrotinski and MacLachlan 2001). In his 'hors d'oeuvre' to the latter volume, Syrotinski observes that 'much contemporary theory and critical practice has coalesced into increasingly homogenized discourses of "the body" and "the subject"' (Syrotinski 2001: 7). *Sensual Reading* seeks to 'move beyond this homogenization' by rethinking and re-articulating 'the relationship between reading and the different senses' and serves up 'a critical fare of second sights, and double takes, a listening that is attentive to echoes and stuttering, a savoring of foretastes and aftertastes' (Syrotinski 2001: 7, 9).

Notes

1. The *Sensory Formations* series is complemented by the *Senses and Sensibilities* series (also published by Berg). The aim of the latter is to foreground the multiple

respects in which the perceptual is political by highlighting the clash of sensibilities along class, race and gender lines within each culture as well as between cultures in historic situations of 'culture contact' as well as today's 'multicultural' societies.

2. This suggestion must be tempered by the observation that Calvino nevertheless (re)incorporates the senses that are 'othered' in each of the short stories on smell, hearing and taste that make up *Under the Jaguar Sun*; that is, he admits them back into his narratives, but on different terms than those to which we are accustomed, on account of his experimentation with diverse alternative scenarios to the conventional Western hierarchy of sensing. This relational approach to the exploration of the sensorium is also characteristic of each of the volumes in the *Sensory Formations* series dedicated to the study of a specific sense modality, be it hearing or touch, or smell.

3. The impact of the sensual revolution on the humanities and social sciences is not only evidenced by the growing number of books on the senses, but also by the proliferation of conferences dedicated to exploring the varieties of sensory experience in history and across cultures. These include, for example:

'Sensual Reading,' University of Aberdeen (Aberdeen 1996).
'Material Memories: Design and Evocation,' Victoria and Albert Museum (London 1998).
'Coming to Our Senses,' Amsterdam School for Cultural Analysis (Amsterdam 1998).
'History of Sensation: 1400 to the Present,' Warburg Institute (London 1999).
'Religion and the Senses,' Princeton University (Princeton 1999).
'Uncommon Senses: The Senses in Art and Culture,' Concordia University (Montreal 2000).
'Hearing Culture,' Wenner Gren Foundation (Oàxàcà 2002).
'Engaging All the Senses: Colonialism, Processes of Perception and the Status of Artifacts,' Wenner-Gren Foundation (Sintra 2003).
'Geschichte des Sinne und (Sinnes) Erfahrung,' University of Vienna (Vienna 2003).
'The Senses Conference,' Thames Valley University (London 2004).
'Sensation and Organization,' SCOS (Halifax 2004).

Bibliography

Bull, M. and Back, L. (eds) (2003), *The Auditory Culture Reader*, Oxford: Berg.
Carp, R.M. (1997), 'Perception and Material Culture: Historical and Cross-Cultural Perspectives,' *Historical Reflections/Reflexions historiques*, 23(3): 269–300.
Classen, C. (1993a), *Worlds of Sense: Exploring the Senses in History and Across Cultures*, London: Routledge.
—— (1993b), *Inca Cosmology and the Human Body*, Salt Lake City: University of Utah Press.
—— (1997), 'Foundations for an Anthropology of the Senses,' *International Social Science Journal*, 153: 401–12.
—— (1998), *The Color of Angels: Cosmology, Gender and the Aesthetic Imagination*, London and New York: Routledge.
—— (2001), 'The Senses,' in P. Stearns (ed.), *Encyclopopedia of European Social History from 1350 to 2000*, vol. 4, New York: Charles Scribner's Sons, pp. 355–64.

Eakin, E. (2002), 'History You Can See, Hear, Smell, Touch and Taste,' *New York Times*, 20 December, A21.

Erlmann, V. (ed.) (2004), *Hearing Cultures*, Oxford: Berg.

Godfrey, S. (2002), 'Alain Corbin: Making Sense of French History,' *French Historical Studies*, 25(2): 381–98.

Hoffer, P.C. (2003), *Sensory Worlds in Early America*, Baltimore MD: Johns Hopkins University Press.

Howes, D. (2003), *Sensual Relations: Engaging the Senses in Culture and Social Theory*, Ann Arbor: University of Michigan Press.

Ingold, T. (2000), *The Perception of the Environment*, London: Routledge.

Melville, S. and Readings, B. (eds) (1995), *Vision and Textuality*, Durham NC: Duke University Press.

Pocock, D. (1993), 'The Senses in Focus,' *Area*, 25(1): 11–16.

Porteous, J.D. (1990), *Landscapes of the Mind: Worlds of Sense and Metaphor*, Toronto: University of Toronto Press.

Rath, R.C. (2003), *How Early America Sounded*, Ithaca: Cornell University Press.

Rodaway, P. (1994), *Sensuous Geographies*, London: Routledge.

Smith, M.C. (2003), 'Making Sense of Social History,' *Journal of Social History*, 37(1): 165–87.

Stewart, S. (2002), *Poetry and the Fate of the Senses*, Chicago: University of Chicago Press.

Stoller, P. (1989), *The Taste of Ethnographic Things: The Senses in Anthropology*, Philadelphia: University of Pennsylvania Press.

Syrotinski, M. and MacLachlan, I. (eds) (2001), *Sensual Reading: New Approaches to Reading in Its Relations to the Senses*, London: Associated University Presses.

Vinge, L. (1975), *The Five Senses: Studies in a Literary Tradition*, Lund, Sweden: Royal Society of Letters at Lund.

Wade, A. (1989), 'An Epistemology of the Senses,' *The New Leader*, 72(1): 19–20.

Zui, D.Z. (2000), 'Visuality, Aurality, and Shifting Metaphors of Geographical Thought in the Late Twentieth Century,' *Annals of the Association of American Geographers*, 90(2): 322–43.

Fifty Ways to Come to your Senses

The following list of fifty sensational books presents a cross-section of current sensory research in the humanities, social sciences and the arts.

Barker-Benfield, G.J. (1992), *The Culture of Sensibility: Sex and Society in Eighteenth century Britain*, Chicago: University of Chicago Press.

Bently, L. and Flynn, L. (eds) (1996), *Law and the Senses: Sensational Jurisprudence*, London: Pluto Press.

Bynum, W.F. and Porter, R. (eds) (1993), *Medicine and the Five Senses*, Cambridge: Cambridge University Press.

Camporesi, P. (1994), *The Anatomy of the Senses: Natural Symbols in Early Modern Italy*, trans. A. Cameron, Cambridge: Polity Press.

Cavell, R. (2002), *McLuhan in Space: A Cultural Geography*, Toronto: University of Toronto Press.

Chipps Smith, J. (2002), *Sensuous Worship: Jesuits and the Art of Early Catholic Reformation in Germany*, Princeton: Princeton University Press.

Classen, C. (1993), *Worlds of Sense: Exploring the Senses in History and Across Cultures*, London and New York: Routledge.

—— (1998), *The Color of Angels: Cosmology, Gender and the Aesthetic Imagination*, London and New York: Routledge.

Classen, C., Howes, D. and Synnott, A. (1994), *Aroma: The Cultural History of Smell*, London and New York: Routledge.

Connor, S. (2003), *The Book of Skin*, Ithaca NY: Cornell University Press.

Corbin, A. (1986), *The Foul and the Fragrant: Odor and the French Social Imagination*, trans. M. Kochan, R. Porter and C. Prendergast, Leamington Spa: Berg.

—— (1994), *Village Bells: Sound and Meaning in the Nineteenth Century French Countryside*, trans. M. Thom, New York: Columbia University Press

Danius, S. (2002), *The Senses of Modernism: Technology, Perception and Aesthetics*, Ithaca NY: Cornell University Press.

Desjarlais, R. (2003), *Sensory Biographies: Lives and Deaths among Nepal's Yolmo Buddhists*, Berkeley: University of California Press.

Drobnick, J. (ed.) (2004), *Aural Cultures*, Toronto: YYZ Books.

Eves, R. (1998), *The Magical Body: Power, Fame and Meaning in a Melanesian Society*, Sydney: Harwood Academic.

Feld, S. (1990), *Sound and Sentiment: Birds, Weeping, Poetics and Song in Kaluli Expression*, second edition, Philadelphia: University of Pennsylvania Press.

Finnegan, R. (2002), *Communicating: The Multiple Modes of Human Interconnection*, London: Routledge.

Frank, G. (2000), *The Memory of the Eyes: Pilgrims to Living Saints in Christian Late Antiquity*, Berkeley: University of California Press.

Geurts, K.L. (2002), *Culture and the Senses: Bodily Ways of Knowing in an African Community*, Berkeley: University of California Press.

Gilman, S.L. (1988), *Goethe's Touch: Touching, Seeing and Sexuality*, New Orleans LA: Graduate School of Tulane University.

Harvey, E. (ed.) (2003), *Sensible Flesh: On Touch in Early Modern Culture*, Philadelphia: University of Pennsylvania Press.

Higgins, H. (2002), *Fluxus Experience*, Berkeley: University of California Press.

Howes, D. (ed.) (1991), *The Varieties of Sensory Experience: A Sourcebook in the Anthropology of the Senses*, Toronto: University of Toronto Press.

—— (2003), *Sensual Relations: Engaging the Senses in Culture and Social Theory*, Ann Arbor: University of Michigan Press.

Jay, M. (1993), *Downcast Eyes: The Denigration of Vision in Twentieth century French Thought*, Berkeley: University of California Press.

Jordanova, L. (1989), *Sexual Visions*, Madison: University of Wisconsin Press.

Kahn, D. (1999), *Noise, Water, Meat: A History of Voice, Sound and Aurality in the Arts*, Cambridge MA: MIT Press.

Korsmeyer, C. (1999), *Making Sense of Taste: Food and Philosophy*, Ithaca NY: Cornell University Press.

Malnar, J.M. and Vodvarka, F. (2004), *Sensory Design*, Minneapolis: University of Minnesota Press.

Marks, L. (2000), *The Skin of the Film: Intercultural Cinema, Embodiment and the Senses*, Durham: Duke University Press.

Margulies, A. (1989), *The Empathic Imagination*, New York: W.W. Norton.

Mintz, S. (1995), *Sweetness and Power: The Place of Sugar in Modern History*, New York: Viking Press.

Neidhart, C. (2003), *Russia's Carnival: The Smells, Sights and Sounds of Transition*, Oxford: Rowman and Littlefield.

Pallasmaa, J. (1996), *The Eyes of the Skin: Architecture and the Senses*. London: Academy Editions

Rée, J. (1999), *I See A Voice: A Philosophical History of Language, Deafness and the Senses*, New York: HarperCollins.

Rindisbacher, H. (1992), *The Smell of Books: A Cultural-Historical Study of Olfaction in Literature*, Ann Arbor: The University of Michigan Press.

Riskin, J. (2002), *Science in the Age of Sensibility: The Sentimental Empiricists of the French Enlightenment*, Chicago: University of Chicago Press.

Rodaway, P. (1994), *Sensuous Geographies*, London: Routledge.

Schivelbusch, W. (1992), *Tastes of Paradise: A Social History of Spices, Stimulants and Intoxicants*, trans. D. Jacobson, New York: Pantheon.

Seremetakis, C.N. (ed.) (1994), *The Senses Still: Memory and Perception as Material Culture in Modernity*, Boulder CO: Westview Press.

Stewart, S. (2002), *Poetry and the Fate of the Senses*, Chicago: University of Chicago Press.

Stoller, P. (1997), *Sensuous Scholarship*, Philadelphia: University of Pennsylvania Press.

Sutton, D. (2001), *Remembrance of Repasts: An Anthropology of Food and Memory*, Oxford: Berg.

Synnott, A. (1993), *The Body Social: Symbolism, Self and Society*, London and New York: Routledge.

Syrotinski, M. and Maclachlan, I. (eds) (2001), *Sensual Reading: New Approaches to Reading in Its Relations to the Senses*, London: Associated University Presses.

Taussig, M. (1993), *Mimesis and Alterity: A Particular History of the Senses*. New York: Routledge.

Thompson, E.A. (2002), *The Soundscape of Modernity: Architectural Acoustics and the Culture of Listening in America, 1900–1933*, Cambridge MA: MIT Press.

Tilley, C. (2004), *The Materiality of Stone: Explorations in Landscape Phenomenology*, Oxford: Berg.

Tuan, Y.-F. (1995), *Passing Strange and Wonderful: Aesthetics, Nature and Culture*, Tokyo and New York: Kodansha International.

Contributors

Italo Calvino (1923–85) authored such marvelous works as *The Castle of Crossed Destinies* and *If on a Winter's Night a Traveller...*

Constance Classen teaches in the Department of Sociology and Anthropology, Concordia University, Montreal.

Alain Corbin is attached to the Centre de Recherches en Histoire du XIXe Siècle, Universités de Paris I–IV, and a member of the Académie Française.

Steven Connor is Academic Director of the London Consortium and Professor of Modern Literature and Theory at Birkbeck College.

Robert Desjarlais teaches anthropology at Sarah Lawrence College, New York.

Jim Drobnick is Senior Editor at *Parachute* art magazine, Montreal and a member of the Displaycult curatorial collective.

Hans-Göran Ekman recently retired from teaching literature at the University of Uppsala.

Steven Feld now teaches at the University of New Mexico in Santa Fe, where he also plays jazz and produces documentary sound art on the VoxLox label.

Chris Fletcher teaches in the Department of Anthropology at the University of Alberta, Edmonton.

Victor Carl Friesen is an independent scholar who lives in Rosthern, Saskatchewan. His abiding interest in Thoreau has issued in two books.

Kathryn Linn Geurts teaches in the Anthropology and African Studies Departments at Hamline University in St. Paul, Minnesota.

David Howes teaches in the Department of Sociology and Anthropology, Concordia University, Montreal and in the Faculty of Law, McGill University.

Dorinne Kondo is Professor of Anthropology and American Studies and Ethnicity at the University of Southern California.

Lisa Law recently moved from the National University of Singapore to the University of St. Andrews, Scotland where she teaches geography.

Marshall McLuhan (1911–80) was the Director of the Centre for Culture and Technology at the University of Toronto, and a prominent 1960s guru.

Carla Mazzio teaches English at the University of Chicago.

William Ian Miller is Professor of Law at the University of Michigan Law School, Ann Arbor.

Lissa Roberts teaches in the History of Science and Technology program at the University of Twente, Netherlands.

Marina Roseman is Lecturer in the School of Anthropological Studies, Queen's University, Belfast, and is also attached to the Department of Folklore and Ethnomusicology, Indiana University

Oliver Sacks M.D. is the widely acclaimed author of *The Man Who Mistook His Wife for a Hat*, *Seeing Voices*, and *Awakenings*.

Susan Stewart recently left her post as the Regan Professor of English at the University of Pennsylvania to become Professor of English at Princeton University.

Copyright
Acknowledgments

Index

SENSORY FORMATIONS

Series Editor: David Howes

- What is the world like to cultures that privilege touch or smell over sight or hearing?
- Do men's and women's sensory experiences differ?
- What lies beyond the aesthetic gaze?
- Who says money has no smell?
- How has the proliferation of 'taste cultures' resulted in new forms of social discrimination?
- How is the sixth sense to be defined?
- What is the future of the senses in cyberspace?

From the Ancient Greeks to medieval mystics and eighteenth century empiricists, Karl Marx to Marshall McLuhan, the senses have been the subject of dramatic proclamations. Senses are sources of pleasure and pain, knowledge and power. Sites of intense personal experience, they are also fields of extensive cultural elaboration. Yet surprisingly, it is only recently that scholars in the humanities and social sciences have turned their full attention to sensory experience and expression as a subject for enquiry.

This path-breaking series aims to show how the 'sensual revolution' has supplanted both the linguistic and the pictorial turns in the human sciences to generate a new field – *sensual culture*, where all manner of disciplines converge. Its objective is to enhance our understanding of the role of the senses in history, culture and aesthetics, by redressing an imbalance: the hegemony of vision and privileging of discourse in contemporary theory and cultural studies must be overthrown in order to reveal the role all senses play in mediating cultural experience. The extraordinary richness and diversity of the social and material worlds, as constituted through touch, taste, smell, hearing, sight and, provocatively, the sixth sense, are addressed in the volumes of this series as follows:*

Empire of the Senses: The Sensual Culture Reader (ed. David Howes) documents the sensual revolution in the humanities and social sciences, and reclaims sensation as a domain for cultural inquiry.

The Auditory Culture Reader (eds Michael Bull and Les Back) articulates a strategy of 'deep listening' – a powerful new methodology for making sense of the social.

The Book of Touch (ed. Constance Classen) maps the tactile contours of culture, exploring the powerful and often inarticulate world of touch, the most basic of our senses.

The Taste Culture Reader: Experiencing Food and Drink (ed. Carolyn Korsmeyer) serves up a savoury stew of cultural analysis, blending together the multiple senses of the term 'taste.'

The Smell Culture Reader (ed. Jim Drobnick) foregrounds the most marginalized, and potentially subversive, sense of modernity, in addition to sampling how diverse cultures scent the universe.

Cultures of Vision: The Alternative Visual Culture Reader (eds Elizabeth Edwards and Kaushik Bhaumik) explores and interrogates the multiplicity of stoic regimes within and outwith the Western tradition.

The Sixth Sense Reader (ed. David Howes) asks: What lies beyond the bounds of sense? Is the sixth sense ESP, electromagnetic sensitivity, intuition, revelation, gut instinct or simply unfathomable?

*Full publication details are available from the publishers, Berg, 1st Floor, Angel Court, 81 St Clements Street, Oxford OX4 1AW, UK; or consult http://www.bergpublishers.com